INCLUDING LAKE GEORGE, LAKE PLACID & WESTERN LAKE CHAMPLAIN

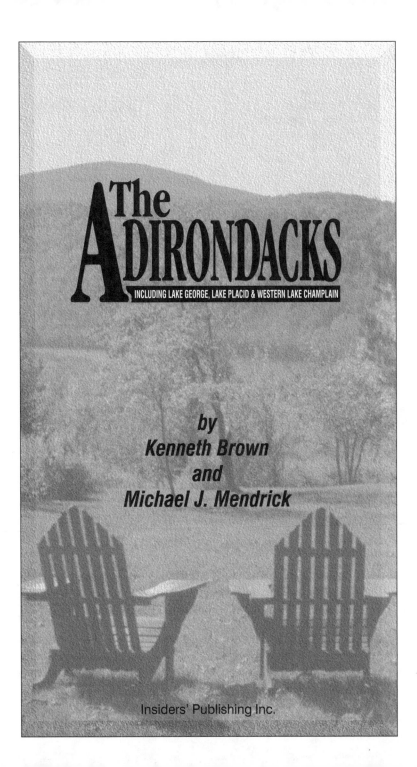

The ADIRONDACKS

INCLUDING LAKE GEORGE, LAKE PLACID & WESTERN LAKE CHAMPLAIN

by
Kenneth Brown
and
Michael J. Mendrick

Insiders' Publishing Inc.

Co-published and marketed by:
Press Republican
170 Margaret St.
Plattsburgh, NY 12901
(518) 561-2300

Co-published and distributed by:
Insiders' Publishing Inc.
105 Budleigh St.
P.O. Box 2057
Manteo, NC 27954
(919) 473-6100
www.insiders.com

•

FIRST EDITION
1st printing

•

Publications from The Insiders' Guide®
series are available at special discounts
for bulk purchases for sales promotions,
premiums or fundraisings. Special
editions, including personalized covers,
can be created in large quantities for
special needs. For more information,
please write to Insiders' Publishing Inc.,
P.O. Box 2057, Manteo, NC 27954 or
call (919) 473-6100 ext. 233.

ISBN 1-57380-041-4

Press Republican

President & Publisher
Brenda Tallman

General Manager
Dan Swift

Project Manager
Sean McNamara

Sales Executives
Scott Wilson
Steve Goss

Graphic Artist
Amy Putnam

Photography/Writing Coordinator
Roger Black

Insiders' Publishing Inc.

Publisher/Editor-in-Chief
Beth P. Storie

President/General Manager
Michael McOwen

Director of Advertising
Rosanne Cheeseman

Creative Services Director
Giles MacMillan

Sales and Marketing Director
Jennifer Risko

Director of New Product
Development
David Haynes

Managing Editor
Dave McCarter

Fulfillment Director
Gina Twiford

Project Editor
Dan DeGregory

Project Artist
Elaine Fogarty

Preface

In spring 1869 a small book entitled *Adventures in the Wilderness or Camp-Life in the Adirondacks*, written by William H.H. Murray, was published by Fields, Osgood and Company of Boston. The book was the first guide book on a wilderness region known as the Adirondacks.

Murray was a city man who had ventured to the vast wilderness of northern New York, and the book told of his adventures — his wilderness experience in the deep woods where the fishing and hunting were outstanding and "No voice of conversation, no sound of hurrying feet, no clangor of bells, no roll of wheels, disturb your meditation."

Adventures in the Wilderness was, however, unlike other guide books of the era in that it not only detailed Murray's adventures, but also told its readers how they too could venture into this unspoiled wilderness for a mere $125 for an entire month's stay. Even in the late 1800s the cost represented a bargain. (Believe it or not, one still might manage that $125 per month feat today, if one relied completely on a backpacking excursion.) The book set into motion "Murray's Rush" into the Adirondacks, as thousands of people set off to discover the rejuvenating qualities of a summer in the wild mountain and lake country of upstate New York.

There was, however, a slight problem. William Henry Harrison Murray put a little too much of his former preaching ways into the book and exaggerated a little too much in the process. Visitors who journeyed here under the advice of "Adirondack" Murray found too few guides to take them into the wilderness, too few hotels and restaurants to service their needs, too unreliable transportation and, worst of all, too little adventure. During summer 1869, the weather also proved uncooperative, and visitors struggled with an unusually cold and wet season, making what little adventures were available even worse. Those who entered Murray's Rush to the region became known as "Murray's Fools," as they discovered just how intolerable the Adirondack wilderness could be.

Visitors were outraged at Rev. Murray's "lies," and he ultimately resigned his ministry partly because of the resulting public outcry. While he may have exaggerated a wee bit, perhaps even lied, it's unlikely he did so out of malice, but rather because he was in complete awe of the unspoiled beauty of Adirondacks. He apparently wanted every American to explore this vast wilderness before they journeyed to faraway lands.

In many respects Murray accomplished his mission (although it bankrupted him). Americans read his book and began to pour into the region. Soon, visitors even found that they had suitable places to stay and the makings of a vacation that rejuvenated the mind, soul and body.

We tell you this tale of Adirondack Murray because, as the author of the region's first real tour guide, he is a part of the heritage of the Adirondacks. Murray's story also reminds us about the dangers of tall tales and why we need to keep our superlatives about this region of the country to a minimum and as close to the facts as possible. We certainly don't want to revisit the idea of Murray's Fools.

To his credit, though, Murray had a way with words and in many instances captured the essence of the Adirondack region. While this place — the largest wilderness area in the continental United States — can be described in facts, its physical attributes beg for esoteric inspection. What we wish to do is to describe some of these distinct features — the vast stretches of mountains; the hundreds upon hundreds of pristine lakes and ponds, some teeming with fish of record size; the forests within forests; all the things that characterize the Adirondacks — in an objective manner without losing the magic of this region.

The 6 million-acre Adirondack Park represents one of the greatest wilderness tracts in the United States, yet it is within a day's drive of some 30 percent of the nation's population. Wilderness — and we mean rugged, unspoiled, dangerous, awe-inspiring wilderness — is less than a five-hour drive from Boston or New York City. Atop a few of the high peaks in the region, you might even see the skyline of the city of Montreal, Quebec. But here in the Adirondacks, you won't find any metros or the hum of cars stuck in a rush-hour traffic jam. One won't even find many traffic lights. (Only three exist in Lake Placid, the region's most famous town.) While close to the modern world in a physical "travel" sense, the Adirondack wilderness remains far away from the civilized world in other ways.

The term "Adirondack Park" is almost a misnomer, thus misleading. Sure, it has official boundaries, but the Park is far from park-like. There are no picnic tables around every bend in the path, no signs directing you to the next scenic vista, no manicured play areas and no uniformed trail guides explaining why the bears are not kept in cages. This park is wilderness (officially "forever wild" wilderness in some sections) where you can walk or paddle for hundreds of miles without seeing any signs of civilization. In fact, civilization has even been officially banned in "forever wild" tracts, some of which cover more than 100,000 acres. A walk or canoe excursion into these howling wilds may be the just the thing to rejuvenate the heart, soul or mind — assuming it is all planned. Then again, if you get lost, you might quickly discover just how loud and frightening the silence of the Adirondack wilderness can be.

In most respects the wilderness experience remains the heart of the adventure in the Adirondacks, but then the tourist trade has evolved a bit since Adirondack Murray suggested that a good night's sleep meant resting on a bed of soft evergreen needles. Within the Park and along its boundaries — hence our repeated references to the Adirondack region — there are also adventures in fine and unrefined dining and lodging; adventures on paddleboats, ski jumps and sleds that slide down mountainsides; and adventures on mountain bikes, in-line skates and larger sleds, which zoom down the sides of mountains at 90 mph. You can hang off the ledge of a precipice — a deadly plunge awaiting a wrong move — or hang off a rock-climbing wall with a soft mat below to cushion your fall. You can ski, ride, roll, crawl, glide, slide, sail, soar, run, walk, skip, jump or dive to get from one spot to the next. The options are endless, and the choice of how you wish to move from here to there is yours.

Adirondack Murray once said that the most impressive thing about the Adirondacks was its silence. We agree. The wilderness doesn't scream at you up here. The loudest screech is often that of an owl; the loudest cry, the mournful and haunting wail of a loon. And then the sound is followed by a silence — a silence very different than the quiet we know in civilization.

You also can do absolutely, positively nothing in the Adirondacks. Imagine that. Imagine a vacation in which you do nothing, except perhaps contemplate the silence of the wilderness. This is about the only thing that you won't find in this guide. (What a concept — an Insiders' Guide on how to do nothing!) In this book, we give you information about things you may want to know, even need to know, but we have nothing to say about the sound of silence and how to just kick back, relax and enjoy this beautiful part of the world. We hope you will discover this by yourself in the Adirondacks, a place some say is named for those who eat the bark of trees.

About the Authors

Kenneth Brown

Twists and turns in Ken Brown's career have given him a unique background on both the human and natural histories of the Adirondacks.

For six years, Ken directed public-education efforts on environmental subjects for the state-run education and orientation facility for the 6 million-acre Adirondack Park. Many of his innovative educational programs, such as his design for a butterfly-house exhibit and interactive projects via the Internet, have been duplicated on a national basis and have earned him recognition as a "master teacher" in science education.

Working with North Country Public Radio, the region's public radio station, Ken also created the award-winning "Natural Selections" (formally called "Field Notes") radio program, now entering its seventh year of international syndication. The preparation and recording of this weekly science and nature program have given Ken a degree of expertise in a curious array of topics, including the secret life of dust balls and slimy things, killer plants and the strange behavior of insects and animals, many of which are found in the Adirondacks.

In 1995 Ken returned to freelance writing and began working on a corporate history, the second such history of his career. After nearly a decade of work with an environmental and natural history slant, his new project focused on the human element — the industrial history of logging, forestry and pulp and paper industries in the Adirondacks.

Ken lives with his wife and two children in Lake Placid where he tries to find a balance between the pleasures found in the natural wonders of the region and the economics of making a living.

Michael J. Mendrick

Michael Mendrick has been a resident of upstate New York since age 3, when his family moved to suburban Rochester. His first encounter with the Adirondack region was a traumatic one. At age 12, in front of dozens of laughing, finger-pointing fellow Boy Scout campers, he fell off a dock into 3 feet of cold Massawepie Lake water. It was more than a decade before he could summon the courage to return.

In 1985, at age 26, Michael moved to one of the Adirondack region's gateway communities, Saratoga Springs. He served as the first Executive Director of the Saratoga Convention & Tourism Bureau for 10 years. During his tenure at the Bureau, Michael learned a great deal about the neighboring Adirondacks and learned to love their beauty and diversity. He also fell in love with a woman whose family owned a camp on Peck's Lake in the southern Adirondacks. While he swears this had nothing to do with proposing marriage to Rebecca, under pressure he will admit that it didn't hurt.

Michael began his freelance writing career in 1991, as the author of the monthly humor column "A View From Askew" for *Poor Richard's Saratoga Journal*, an alternative newspaper serving Saratoga County, New York. He became a frequent contributor to *Laughing Matters*, a humor quarterly published by The Humor Project in 1992, and has since gone on to write humor for the nationally syndicated comic *Close to Home* as well as Russian-born comedian Yakov Smirnoff. His writing has appeared in numerous national trade and consumer magazines and newspapers, including *Live!*, *Convene*, *Association Management* and *American City Business Journals*. In addition to this work, Michael is the author/compiler of *New York State Trivia*.

Michael lives "three houses outside" Saratoga Springs with his wife, Becky, her son, Daniel, and most recent addition, Jeremy. They spend lots of time (and dollars) enjoying the Adirondacks throughout the year, with the possible exception of blackfly season.

Acknowledgments

Ken Brown

Many people contributed to this book and deserve recognition and thanks, including project editor Dan DeGregory at Insiders' Publishing, and Sean McNamara and Roger Black from the *Press Republican*. A thank you also is in order to staffers at the Adirondack Nature Conservancy, Department of Environmental Conservation, Lake Placid Public Library, Saranac Lake Public Library and the many chambers of commerce as well as individuals who contributed ideas, materials and expertise. A special thanks goes to all those nameless people who write all those free-for-the-taking brochures and pamphlets found in the information centers.

A job well done goes out to whoever invented e-mail. Without this digital wonder, I would have never felt a kinship with co-author Michael Mendrick (a.k.a. MJM). His almost daily messages served as not only a wake-up call, but also proof that bits and bytes can be humorous.

Lynn, my wife, and Ian and Katrina, my children, continue to survive these projects. With each new adventure, we discover a little more about each other, other ways to be patient and some new clue as to what makes our family our family. Thanks for the love.

Michael Mendrick

First and foremost, I want to thank my wife Becky for simply hanging in there and being as patient as humanly possible during this challenging project. Next summer, I promise we'll take the boys out and enjoy all the things I wrote about last summer.

My thanks and appreciation to co-author Ken Brown for his patience with my endless e-mails and his cooperation in trying to find common ground in how we could present so much information to you in an entertaining way.

Thanks to project editor Dan DeGregory for his professionalism, kindness and sense of perspective in trying to balance the many challenging aspects of this book. Also, thanks to project manager Sean McNamara for his enthusiasm and compassion throughout the many months of pulling this together. Roger Black of the *Press Republican* also deserves thanks for his role as "Unsung Hero of Additional Research" for this project.

Finally, thanks to the many staff professionals at area chambers of commerce, tourism offices, attractions, museums and other tourism-related businesses for their cooperation, assistance and enthusiasm about the project. I certainly hope you enjoy the book and see hundreds of visitors walking through your front door with a copy!

New York State Governor George E. Pataki's Foreword to
The Insiders' Guide® to the Adirondacks

Dear Friend of the Adirondacks:

As Governor of New York State, I am extremely pleased to welcome readers of this guide to the magnificent diversity of cultural and recreational opportunities that the Adirondacks offer in every season of the year.

The six million-acre Adirondack Park -- the largest American Park outside of Alaska -- is a unique blend of public and private lands. Created in 1892, the Park encompasses 2.6 million acres of public land and 3.4 million acres of private land, home to 130,000 year-round residents.

This unique patchwork of ownership enables visitors to enjoy the largest, most pristine wilderness east of the Rockies, as well as the outstanding cultural opportunities available in the Park's small towns. Drive through the Adirondacks and enjoy some of the most scenic roads in America. Whether you're interested in history, hiking, canoeing or painting, the Adirondacks offer it all.

While you're here, take a minute to learn about the Adirondacks' rich history. Public lands within the Park are protected by the "forever wild" clause in the State Constitution, a visionary step taken by our forefathers. Come to the Adirondacks and see America's only Constitutionally protected wilderness.

Teddy Roosevelt, hiking on Mt. Marcy on September 13, 1901, was told that President McKinley, wounded by an assassin's bullet a week earlier, was dying. His midnight ride from the heart of the High Peaks to the nearest train station, in North Creek, is commemorated by Adirondackers today.

The Winter Olympic Games have been held in Lake Placid twice, in 1932 and 1980. Today, visitors can enjoy the facilities built for those games, such as the bobsled run, as well as superb downhill skiing at Gore Mountain and Whiteface. If cross-country skiing is more your speed, the Adirondacks offer a lifetime of opportunities.

In the summertime, visitors enjoy thousands of miles of foot trails, some of the finest hiking in the country. From Lake George to the source of the Hudson River at Lake Tear of the Clouds, the Adirondacks boast unparalleled aquatic resources. Opportunities for fishing, hunting, canoeing and birdwatching are equally superb.

Visit the Adirondacks and see what New York State's great northern forest offers. You'll be glad you came.

Very truly yours,

George E. Pataki
Governor of New York State

Table of Contents

Directory of Maps

Adirondacks
& Surrounding Area

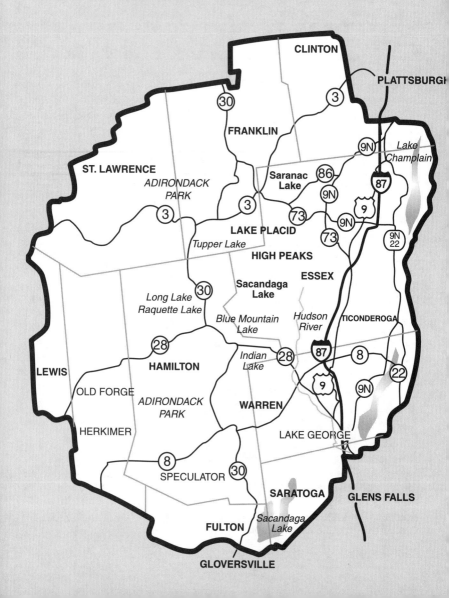

Lake Placid/Tri-Lakes Region

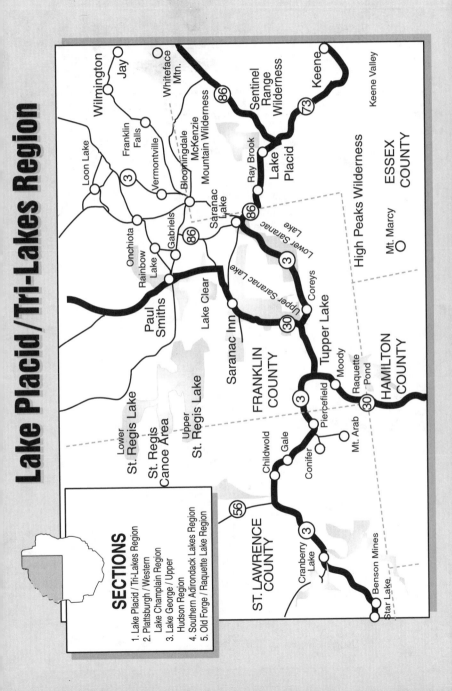

SECTIONS
1. Lake Placid / Tri-Lakes Region
2. Plattsburgh / Western
   Lake Champlain Region
3. Lake George / Upper
   Hudson Region
4. Southern Adirondack Lakes Region
5. Old Forge / Raquette Lake Region

Wilmington
Jay
Whiteface Mtn.
Loon Lake
Franklin Falls
Vermontville
Bloomingdale
McKenzie Mountain Wilderness
Sentinel Range Wilderness
Keene
Ray Brook
Lake Placid
Keene Valley
Onchiota
Rainbow Lake
Gabriels
Saranac Lake
Lower Saranac Lake
ESSEX COUNTY
Paul Smiths
Lake Clear
Upper Saranac Lake
High Peaks Wilderness
Mt. Marcy
Lower St. Regis Lake
St. Regis Canoe Area
Saranac Inn
Upper St. Regis Lake
Coreys
Tupper Lake
Moody
Raquette Pond
FRANKLIN COUNTY
HAMILTON COUNTY
Pierrefield
Childwold
Gale
Conifer
Mt. Arab
ST. LAWRENCE COUNTY
Cranberry Lake
Benson Mines
Star Lake

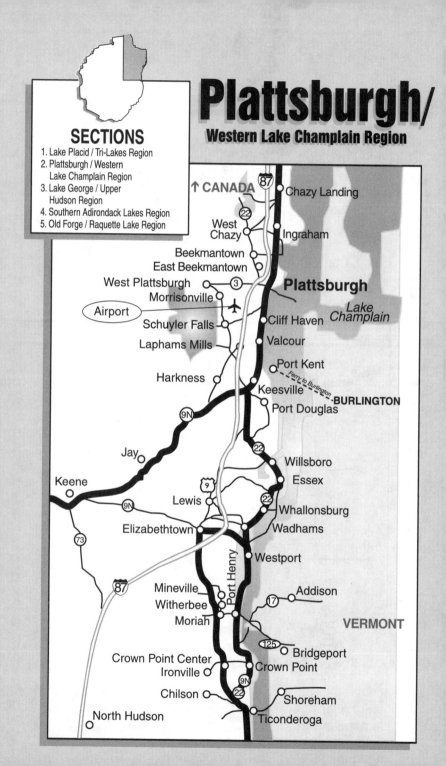

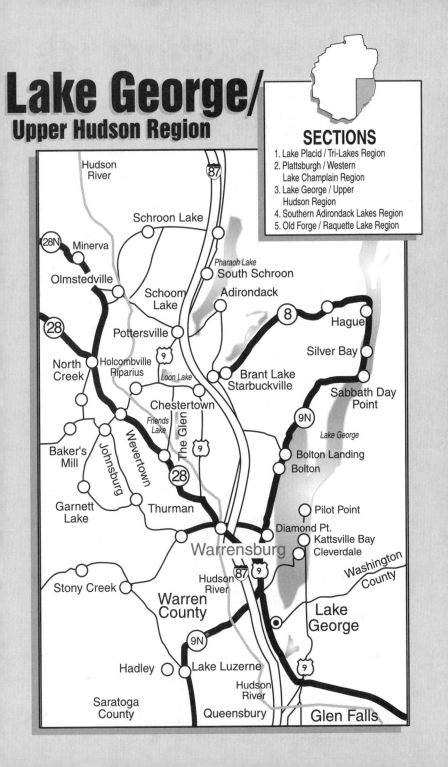

Southern Adirondack Lakes Region

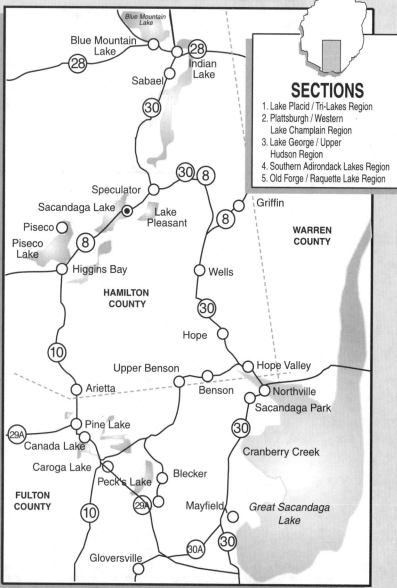

SECTIONS

1. Lake Placid / Tri-Lakes Region
2. Plattsburgh / Western Lake Champlain Region
3. Lake George / Upper Hudson Region
4. Southern Adirondack Lakes Region
5. Old Forge / Raquette Lake Region

Blue Mountain Lake

Blue Mountain Lake

28

28 Indian Lake

Sabael

30

30 8

Speculator

Sacandaga Lake

Lake Pleasant

Griffin

8

Piseco

WARREN COUNTY

Piseco Lake

8

Higgins Bay

Wells

HAMILTON COUNTY

30

Hope

10

Upper Benson

Hope Valley

Arietta

Benson

Northville

Sacandaga Park

Pine Lake

29A

30

Canada Lake

Cranberry Creek

Caroga Lake

Peck's Lake

Blecker

FULTON COUNTY

10

29A

Mayfield

Great Sacandaga Lake

30A 30

Gloversville

Old Forge/Raquette Lake Region

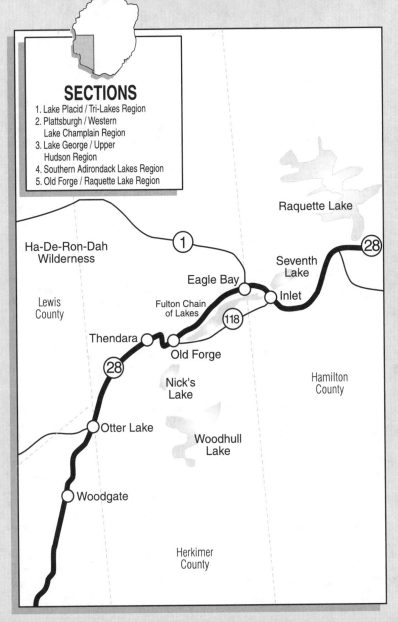

SECTIONS
1. Lake Placid / Tri-Lakes Region
2. Plattsburgh / Western
   Lake Champlain Region
3. Lake George / Upper
   Hudson Region
4. Southern Adirondack Lakes Region
5. Old Forge / Raquette Lake Region

Raquette Lake

Ha-De-Ron-Dah
Wilderness

Seventh
Lake

1

28

Eagle Bay

Inlet

Lewis
County

Fulton Chain
of Lakes

118

Thendara

Old Forge

28

Nick's
Lake

Hamilton
County

Otter Lake

Woodhull
Lake

Woodgate

Herkimer
County

How to Use This Book

At first glance, you might think it's silly for us to have a chapter called How to Use This Book. You *read* it, genius, right?! Well, kind of.

You see, an Insiders' Guide is different from most books that you've read. It's really more like a collection of separate booklets on a variety of topics all bound together by the same philosophy and style, and between the same covers. You can read this thing straight through (but you'd better have one long free weekend to do it), or you can read it chapter by chapter, here and there, whichever way your interest and intrigue takes you.

This chapter is simply to help you map out the voyage so you can learn what you need and read what you want — all so you can enjoy the magnificent Adirondacks with the most possible fun and relaxation and the least hassle and confusion. That's our goal: to help you enjoy and understand the Adirondacks, whether you ever visit here or not.

So here's how this thing works. Essentially, each chapter is set up to be self-contained, so you can read each one without being dependent on the last chapter for it to make sense. You'll want to make sure to read the introductions to each chapter carefully. Like the small print on an extended warranty, they include lots of important information on general conditions, assumptions, what's included and what's not, how the chapter is arranged, and where to go for more detailed information about the topic.

We have divided the Adirondacks into five regions, looking at the map clockwise from the top: Lake Placid/Tri-Lakes Region, Plattsburgh/Western Lake Champlain Region, Lake George/Upper Hudson Region, Southern Adirondack Lakes Region and Old Forge/Raquette Lake Region. There are no generally accepted "official" regions of the Adirondacks, so we tried to come up with the most practical assortment from a geographic and economic standpoint. That is, the regions include destinations and communities that are somehow linked economically or geographically, whether or not they are in the same counties. The county borders here are pretty erratic, and using them to identify regions likely would have caused more confusion than either you as readers or us as writers could have handled. Please note that we do occasionally take liberties with the geographic placement of towns bordering adjacent regions — for instance, in different chapter sections, we include Keene and Keene Valley in either the Lake Placid/Tri-Lakes or Plattsburgh/Western Lake Champlain region — depending on how each town logically is aligned with respect to its relative subject matter.

The book is written primarily as a travel guide, recognizing that the great majority of you reading this book are planning to visit (not live in) the Adirondacks — whether as a daytrip from Albany, New York, or a summer heat escape from Albany, Georgia. One thing that sets Insiders' Guides apart, though, from other travel guide books is that we include useful information for current or potential residents as well, such as chap-

> **FYI**
>
> Unless otherwise noted, the area code for all phone numbers listed in this guide is 518.

Photo: Mark Kurtz

Skiers will find no shortage of challenging terrain to traverse in the Adirondacks.

ters on education, media, healthcare and real estate.

While you don't have to read this book from beginning to end to have it be useful, we do have a suggested route for you to take that will provide you with all the stuff you absolutely *should* know, along with some flexibility on the stuff you might *want* to know.

We suggest you read straight through from the Preface (which gives a good feel for the lure of this place) to and including Climate and Outdoor Safety (which provides vital information on how to *safely* enjoy the Adirondacks). In between is History, which will help you understand how and why the Adirondacks came to be the unique wilderness park that it is today. Following History, we take you on a tour of all the regions in Area Overviews, which will give you a good snapshot of the geography, lifestyle and economics in the collection of places and communities that make up the Adirondacks. Then, you'll learn how to get here and how to get around here in (ironically) Getting Here, Getting Around.

Once you complete your Adirondack "basic training," you can skip around to your heart's content. If you've got kids, both the Kidstuff and Attractions chapters are a must to help you survive and thrive while bringing them along for a visit. You'll be happy to know that our recreation-oriented chapters — Ski-

ing, Golf, Other Winter Recreation (e.g. snowmobiling, skating), Other Summer Recreation (e.g. whitewater rafting, horseback riding), Hiking, Fishing and Hunting — all provide comprehensive overviews and detailed listings on how and where to enjoy these activities. Annual Events and Festivals as well as Arts and Culture will help you decide *when* to visit (if you want your stay to coincide with a specific festival or event) or what to do on a rainy day (attend a concert, learn a craft, or see an art exhibit). Even if you think you'll be too tired from all the recreation and culture to even consider anything resembling nightlife, check out the Nightlife chapter. We think you'll be pleasantly surprised by some of our "non-traditional, non-mirrored balls hanging from the ceiling" suggestions that won't require a late-afternoon nap to enjoy.

After you've read about the myriad things you can do here, you'll probably want to go back and review our Accommodations chapter (or the Camping chapter) to help you decide where to stay during your visit (because if you've gotten *this* far, you're definitely going to visit!) Then, on your way here, you can tease your taste buds by reading the Restaurant chapter and mapping out your culinary strategy for your stay.

If, from all you've read, you are convinced you just have to live here (well, at least for a summer), the Real Estate, Healthcare, Education, Media, Retirement and Worship chapters all should be of use and interest to you.

Whatever you do, don't read Beginning Thoughts first! Hey, where do you think you're turning the page to?! Get back here.

Finally, a disclaimer and a request. . . . First, the disclaimer: This is a huge place, filled with hundreds of interesting places to explore and dozens of communities to visit. While we have done our best to represent the collection of places that are the Adirondacks as fairly, comprehensively and accurately as possible, we likely have excluded some that deserve your consideration. Now, the request: If you have enjoyed an experience somewhere in the Adirondacks that we didn't include — whether a beautiful spot for a sunset, the perfect piece of apple pie, the ultimate hike for families, or the most romantic cottage in the universe — let us know. We'll check it out and make sure to include it for others to enjoy in the next edition of *The Insiders' Guide® to the Adirondacks*.

Contact us care of Insiders' Publishing Inc., P.O. Box 2057, Manteo, N.C. (another beautiful place!) 27954, or check out our web site (which includes a comment form) at www.insiders.com.

And now . . . the Adirondacks.

Legend has it that the word "Adirondacks" is a corruption of the Iroquois word "Ratirontacks," meaning "those who eat bark."

History

For some people, the entire history of the Adirondacks reveals itself in a single moment. That moment may occur during a hike when one pauses to finally notice the absolute silence of the backwoods, or in a canoe when the perfectly placid waters of the lake stop time. Others find it atop a high peak when they realize that in whatever direction they look, they see the same thing — a dense, forbidding and vast wilderness. Great cities — New York, Boston, Montreal — of the civilized world may be only hours away via interstate highways, but during this moment all traces of civilization cease to exist. The great Adirondack forest in all its raw beauty becomes the entire universe.

"If we could only bottle this view (pick one), this serenity, this moment, this beauty, this peace," one might say, "we would be millionaires."

It is in this sentiment, expressed in many different ways by visitors, that the history of the region becomes fully appreciated. When the first European explorers — most likely a party led Samuel de Champlain in 1609 — saw the vast natural resources of the region, they too wondered how to exploit the area's natural wealth.

The task would prove daunting. But it is in the pursuit of this goal that the region's history (and future) reveals itself. The essential conflict then as today is the same: How does one balance the needs of people with those of the environment? The debate surrounding the answer to this question began early in the region's history, yet the answer remains elusive.

The Rat-i-ron-tacks

Legend has it that the word "Adirondacks" is a corruption of the Iroquois word "Ratirontacks," meaning "those who eat bark." The Iroquois used the word to describe their arch enemies, the Algonquins, who according to the Iroquois were lousy farmers and forced to eat the bark of trees to survive the region's harsh winters. Some scholars dismiss this explanation as nothing more than a good tall tale and suggest that the Iroquois jumbled a word from the language of an unknown tribe that lived in the Saint Lawrence Valley in the early 1500s. The word originally meant "they of the great rocks" but, when passed on to the Iroquois, grew to mean "they who eat trees," or bark-eaters.

Professor Ebenezer Emmons only added to the confusion when he introduced the word "Adirondack" in print in 1837 with the first geological survey of the region. Emmons proposed to commemorate the Algonquin or "Adirondack" Indians who lived in the region by calling the mountains "the Adirondack group." Actually, Emmons wasn't even sure whether it was "literally true or not" that the Algonquin were ever called Adirondack, thus the name remains clouded in mystery.

What is known is that Native Americans avoided permanent settlement in the forests of the Adirondacks. For the most part, the Iroquois in the southern part of the region and the Algonquin and Huron tribes in the north were farmers, and the forests, with short growing seasons, poor soil and dense tree growth, offered few benefits to their agricultural societies.

At best, the forests of the Adirondacks served as a buffer zone to keep the warring tribes from each other's throats.

Throughout the 1600 and 1700s, European settlers would claim and conquer the wilds of New England and the mid-Atlantic colonies, but the Adirondacks remained essentially unchanged. The great "howling wild" or "dismal wilderness," as cartographer Thomas Pownall labeled the region in 1784, was largely bypassed by pioneers moving westward.

The reason for ignoring the region was

simple. Early settlers could find no easy way to capitalize on the region's vast resources, especially its wealth of trees.

The Indian Wars

Daniel Boorstein, the Pulitzer Prize-winning historian, describes history in terms of "verges," where one event needs to happen before the next event can occur.

The first significant verge with respect to Adirondack history occurred in 1609, when explorer Samuel de Champlain traveled with some Algonquin Indians through Lake Champlain, a name he himself gave the lake. When Champlain's party encountered a band of Iroquois, the French and Algonquin attacked. Although the Algonquin and Iroquois never got along, the attack marked the beginning of a French and Iroquois feud — a feud that would last until the French were driven out of the area in 1763.

Champlain discovered that the easiest route through the region was the Lake George to Lake Champlain water route. The English and French would battle over this corridor for many years, as both sides realized control of the land to the east and west rested with control over the waters. As early as 1690, the British Army established its first trading center in the region at Crown Point, but soon abandoned it. Some 40 years passed before the French seized the site in 1730 and constructed Fort St. Frederic.

As a counter move, the British built Fort William Henry on the south end of Lake George in 1755. The French reciprocated by building a fort on the north end of Lake George in Ticonderoga, originally called Fort Carillon, but known today as Fort Ticonderoga. During the French and Indian War, Gen. Louis Joseph Montcalm captured Fort William Henry in 1757 for the French. But while Montcalm won the initial battle, the French lost the war. When the war ended in 1763, the English ruled all of eastern North America.

Today, sites at Crown Point, Fort Ticonderoga and Fort William Henry help visitors relive this portion of the region's history.

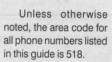

FYI

Unless otherwise noted, the area code for all phone numbers listed in this guide is 518.

The King's Trees

The next verge, which occurred in the mid- to late 1760s, further defined the chapter in Adirondack history that continues to evolve today.

Strategically, the British had little choice but to force the French from the region, as a key resource grew here which would allow the British to maintain their presence as a world leader. Majestic white pine, which grew straight, strong and more than 100 feet high, dotted the shores of Lake Champlain and Lake George. This white pine, the "King's Trees," would serve as the masts for Britain's naval and commercial ships. With the white pine, Britain could continue her dominance of the high seas — at least, that was the idea.

The British, however, soon found slight glitches in their plans for continued world domination. Although the trees were plentiful, the route to market was difficult. The easiest route to Britain from Lake Champlain was to the north, an area controlled by the ousted French. The other alternative — south via Lake Champlain to Lake George and then into the Hudson River — had its share of difficulties, mainly transporting logs overland from the lakes into navigable portions of the Hudson.

In addition to the physical challenges of transporting the white pine masts south to ports, the British encountered another problem: Colonists grew resentful of the redcoats removing these prime trees for their own use. The settlers wanted the king's trees for themselves, and their ire helped fuel a rebellion called the American Revolution (a.k.a. Revolutionary War).

Ethan Allen was the first colonist to contest British rule of the waters of Lake Champlain (and British control over the King's Trees), when his Green Mountain Boys demanded the surrender of Fort Ticonderoga in May 1775. A little more than a year later, on October 11, 1776, Benedict Arnold led America's first naval battle in the waters near Valcour, 50 miles north of Fort Ticonderoga. After a seven-hour battle, Arnold's ship went down, but he achieved his objective in delaying a British in-

Aside from the fortress itself, Ticonderoga draws visitors to view thousands of historical artifacts and live demonstrations of Revolutionary War life.

vasion from the north. In the next year the Americans lost control of the lakes, but in 1778 the English were driven from the area.

After the war, settlers began moving into the Champlain Valley, but as they looked westward to the mountains, they realized the same problem as prior settlers. The vast resources in the mountains remained trapped, as no means existed to get them to market.

As you sit atop an Adirondack mountain, or even survey the high peaks of the region from one of the many vistas, look for the highest mountain, Mount Marcy. At 5,114 feet Mount Marcy is New York's highest peak. On the southerly side of the peak, the Hudson River begins its 250-mile (as the crow flies) journey from Lake Tear in the Cloud to New York City. (The headwaters of the Nile River were discovered long before anyone knew the Hudson River originated in this tiny lake.)

The challenge at Mount Marcy was figur-

ing out a way to cut trees within 2,000 feet of the summit. Lumbermen did (see the subsequent "Growth of the Lumber Industry" section for a explanation of the process), then moved the spruce to market in New York City. They had no motorized vehicles or equipment, had to make their own roads and still had to realize a profit. A single tree weighed a few hundred pounds, and thousands were needed to support this lumbering venture. As an added woe, consider the plight of the lumber barons in the later part of the 19th century, who tried to realize a profit in an era of declining prices. Prices for lumber, like many other materials and goods at that time, ultimately plummeted by more than 50 percent due to improved production methods derived during the Industrial Revolution. (Ironically, the more efficient lumbermen became in their production methods, the more lumber prices declined.)

After the Revolutionary War, the American government, which was short on cash, paid its soldiers with unappropriated land, figuring the soldiers would settle on it. The new government, just like the British before them, hoped that the vast forest resources of the Adirondacks would attract these new settlers who, in turn, would provide the lumber necessary to build a new and prosperous nation.

At first, settlements grew quickly along the shores of Lake George, Lake Champlain and Schroon Lake, and settlers floated felled trees across the lakes in great rafts. Once the easily accessible trees near the shore became scarce, however, the settlements began to flounder, as there were no known means of transporting logs from the distant mountains to the lakes and then to the markets beyond.

The Growth of the Lumber Industry

Only a select few people are ever recorded in history books. And some people who made great contributions are simply lost, for whatever reason.

As you drive up the Northway (I-87) over Schroon River and past Schroon Lake, exit at the scenic rest stop and consider how the simple idea of two lumberjacks, Alanson and Normon Fox, from Brant Lake, influenced the history of New York State. The year was 1813. Marketable timber along the shores of Brant and Schroon Lake was diminishing rapidly, and the brothers knew they had to figure out a way to get logs from the distant mountains to the mill. If they or someone else couldn't solve

the problem, the emerging lumber industry soon would die.

During spring 1813, the region's streams and rivers flowed fast and high with waters from the melting snow. The brothers decided to use the sheer force of these freshets to float or drive logs one at a time down mountain streams into the Schroon River and on to a mill site. Although it is likely that the first log drive had its share of technical problems, the idea worked — and marked the beginning of the era of the great river drives. Within the next 50 years, the Fox bothers and others like them would devise ingenious methods of using spring freshets to move millions of logs downriver — an idea that made New York State the dominant lumber-producing state in the country.

River drives also set into motion a series of events that eventually led to the creation of the largest park in the continental United States — the Adirondack Park.

Although the Fox bothers are credited with the idea of river drives, Abraham Wing, son of the founding father of Glens Falls, apparently perfected the idea. Although Wing immediately realized the potential of river drives, he also realized the one drawback that plagued his father and every other would-be lumber baron of the early 1800s. It was one thing moving logs from the mountains to Glens Falls but quite another getting them past the falls and downriver to markets where the finished lumber could be sold.

Wing initiated plans to solve the problem by petitioning state leaders for an 8-mile-long "feeder canal" to connect Glens Falls with Fort Edward. The Glens Falls Feeder Canal, which began as little more than a 4-foot ditch, eventually served as the vital link to bring the natural resources of the Adirondack region to markets along the state's 524-mile-long canal system and along the navigable sections of the Hudson River. (The historic canal system in New York State is now part of a 220-mile-long, recreational Canalway Trail System. For information, call (800) 4CANAL4.)

So, single logs were driven from the high peaks of Mount Marcy down rivers to Glens Falls, where they were milled by companies such as Morgan Lumber Company, which eventually became International Paper, and Finch, Pruyn & Company, which now manufactures fine paper. From Glens Falls, the lumber, along with lime, potash, charcoal and iron, was shipped via canal boats to Albany and New York City. (While this paints the big picture, the fine details of how a tree finds its way from atop a mountain down through the great dismal forests and to the river still need to be explained.)

The Adirondack Museum in Blue Mountain Lake (see our Attractions chapter) captures for visitors the era of logging camps and the great Hudson River log drives in memorable fashion, but the lumberjacks' ingenuity and efforts can be appreciated by all who hike the region's trails. No matter where you look, no matter how impossible it seems, lumbermen figured out ways to move logs, primarily spruce, from the mountains to sawmills downriver. Initially, trees were cut by ax, then hand saws. First oxen and then horses skidded the logs from where they fell to sites where the lumber could be loaded by hand onto sleds. Without ever taking a college course in physics, loggers soon realized that even with a team of oxen, 4 or 5 tons of logs couldn't be moved on a wagon across the usually soft terrain of the forest. But if the terrain was frozen, a single horse could pull a load using the same principal skaters use to glide across the ice. Unlike those sledding for fun, who seek the fastest way down a hill, sledders sought the safest routes to bring tons of wood on a single load down mountains to a "banking" ground, where logs were dumped on the frozen surface of a lake or pond.

All winter the logs would pile higher on the lake. A man-made dam prevented the logs

from flowing from the banking ground until spring. Once the spring waters peaked, the dam would be opened to release the logs, one at a time, into the stream or river. The force of the water flushed the 13-foot logs downstream. On some streams, additional dams were constructed to catch the logs, allowing a build up of sufficient water to flush the logs even farther downstream.

During high-flow times, a log could float 70 to 90 miles in a few weeks. During drier times, two years might pass before the log reached the mill. And during the most difficult times, thousands of logs would form a jam in the river. Often a single log would cause the jam, and once the river driver freed the culprit log, thousands quickly would follow. Many a river driver discovered the logs moved faster than they could — and many tragically lost their lives in the process.

In 1872 logging in the Hudson River watershed reached its peak — 213,800,000 board feet of lumber was milled.

Adventures in the Wilderness

By the late 1800s, New York State reigned supreme as the nation's most prolific lumber producer, with most of the supply coming from the Adirondack region. Just as the timber industry was reaching its peak, a minister from Boston, William Murray, published *Adirondacks in the Wilderness*, an account of his hunting, fishing and boating experiences in the region. The book soon became a hit and changed the region forever.

Soon after publication of Murray's book, the Adirondacks entered into what has been heralded as the Gilded Years, between 1870 and 1910. Backwoods homes, such as the one constructed by Paul Smith on the shores of Lower St. Regis Lake grew into a majestic hotel, attracting the rich and famous from all over the world. P.T. Barnum, of Barnum & Bailey Circus fame, slept there and had a brook and pond named after him; Teddy Roosevelt also visited. It's been said that, at one time, legendary hotelier, guide and teller of tall tales, Paul Smith, saw his name in print more than the President of the United States.

Marked trails enable hikers to enjoy the best of each
season the Adirondacks region has to offer.

Backwoods inns along Lake George, Lake Placid, the Saranac Lakes, Blue Mountain Lake and elsewhere grew in opulence and soon rivaled the best hotels in the world. Along with the world's first industrial use of electricity, the Adirondacks featured the first hotel with electricity throughout — the Prospect House in Blue Mountain Lake. By the late 1800s, more than 50 hotels, each with a capacity of more than 100 guests, dotted the region, with the Prospect House accommodating nearly 500 guests.

Families came for the entire summer, bringing along chests full of their finest china, linens and silk dresses. The fashionably dressed guests, being treated like royalty (a few of them were), served in marked contrast to the harsh life of the lumbermen in the region.

As the Adirondacks began to top the fashionable-place-to-be list, wealthy summer residents including J.P. Morgan, the Vanderbilts and the Rockefellers began building what came to be known as the Adirondack Great Camps. (More than just a single building or summer home, Great Camps are something akin to a small village.) Great Camps of the era often included main residences, guest cabins, dining halls and game rooms. The primary facilities required the support of a large

staff who were housed in separate quarters and worked in the Camp's blacksmith and carpentry shops, stables and gardens.

The architectural style of the camps was a combination of rustic materials from the wilderness, such as log beams and fieldstone fireplaces and elegant items imported to the area.

Unfortunately, only a few of these rustic wonders have survived, with the majority succumbing to fire, as did most of the major hotels in the region. Only a few Great Camps remain, and only two — Camp Sagamore in Raquette Lake and White Pine Camp in Paul Smiths — are open to the public on a regular basis (see Attractions). Others have been converted to restaurants and country inns (see Restaurants as well as Bed & Breakfasts and Country Inns).

Another significant, although highly localized, event occurred during the Gilded Years. In 1876, Dr. Edward Livingston Trudeau came to Saranac Lake to live out what he believed would be the last years of his life. Trudeau, an outdoor enthusiast and friend of Paul Smith, was suffering from tuberculosis. To his astonishment, his health was restored during his stay in the village, a turn of events that formed the basis for establishing Saranac Lake as a pioneering health resort. The village grew into the world-renowned home of the Trudeau Sanitorium, another fashionable destination resort of the late 1800s.

A Conflict Emerges

At the same time the East's greatest wilderness became a fashionable playground, especially for the wealthy, the timber industry prospered by producing first lumber then paper to meet the needs of a growing nation. Therein lay a conflict: The growth of the lumber and other industries in the region depended upon cutting trees and using the very natural resources that made the region increasingly attractive to the emerging tourist industry.

In 1885 the first step was taken in creating the Adirondack Park when the state Legislature enacted the Forest Preserve Act, protecting all state land "forever" as wild forest. In 1892 the Adirondack Park was created by law, and in essence, battle lines were drawn pitting industry against an emerging conservation movement that would grow increasingly powerful.

Verplanck Colvin, who first surveyed the region for New York State, wrote eloquently about the Adirondacks as "the wonder and glory of New York" and led the crusade to protect the region on behalf of the citizens. Yet the decision to preserve this vast tract of wilderness "for the people" was neither as enlightened nor as clear-cut as often is suggested.

One of the most cited reasons for the need to create the Park was the destructive practices of the lumber industry, which was accused of clear-cutting, denuding vast sections of forest and continually abusing the region's natural resources. While many lumber operators could be taken to task for their "cut and run" tactics, various records from the late 1800s suggests that some operators actually were practicing what could be considered early rudiments of scientific forestry by selectively cutting trees (cutting only usable trees), not clear-cutting them (cutting every tree in sight). Soon after the turn of the century, Finch, Pruyn & Company of Glens Falls, one of the largest owners of Adirondack forest lands, became one the first companies in the country to practice forest management using the principles behind the emerging idea of scientific forestry — managing or farming a forest to increase its yield. (Many of today's modern forestry practices evolved from the pioneering work of early industrial foresters in the Adirondack region who worked cooperatively with government and university foresters.)

While the destructive practices of the logging interests served as the focal point in the public discussion to create the Adirondack Park, a number of other items also fueled the debate. Primary among them was the fact that the state began acquiring vast tracts of land in the region. Initially these acquisitions had nothing to do with protecting or conserving the wilderness. The fact is the state repossesed the land because the property owners failed to pay taxes on it. Thus, taxes had as much to do with creating the Adirondack Park as did the concepts of conservation and preservation.

The rich history of the lumber and other industries in the region is featured at the Adirondack Museum (see our Attractions chapter) in Blue Mountain Lake, considered one of the best museums of regional history in the country. The Adirondack Park Visitor Interpretive Centers in Paul Smiths and Newcomb offer interpretive programs on the creation of the Adirondack Park and the rise of the conservation movement in the region in the 1800s.

INSIDERS' TIP

The name Benedict Arnold connotes one word from an elementary school history lesson — traitor. Arnold, in his attempt to sell plans of West Point to the British, became one, but until that point was arguably America's greatest war hero. Arnold was involved in America's first naval battle, on Lake Champlain, in the seizing of Fort Ticonderoga and in the defeat of Gen. Burgoyne in the Battle of Saratoga.

Another course of history began to unfold following the creation of the Adirondack Park Forest Preserve. This history, however, was — and is — as much about the future as the past — a history that makes the Adirondacks a truly unique Park and place to live.

The Adirondack Park

The concept of the Adirondack Park is distinct in the history of conservation and preservation not only in this country, but also in the world.

When the Legislature enacted the Adirondack Park Act, it created an unusual situation by placing both public and private lands within the boundaries, or the "blue line," of the Park. Thus, public lands in the Forest Preserve belong to "all the people of the state," and any business or individual can own his or her piece of the Park.

When the Park was created, the citizens of New York State owned 681,374 acres of the approximately 2.8 million acres within the original "blue line." Within the next 100 years, the State would increase its holdings from the original 25 percent to the 43 percent (or 2.6 million acres) owned today and expand the size of the Park to encompass nearly 6 million acres. Thus, ownership of the Adirondack Park, the largest park in the continental United States, today rests more in the hands of private concerns than public. This fact not only creates a management nightmare, but also raises some fundamental questions regarding the rights of individuals and society at large.

Citizens living within and beyond the Park's boundaries debated land-use issues 100 years ago, and they continue to do so today.

By the early part of the 20th century, the Adirondack region began fading out of the limelight. While it still remained a popular sum-

mer resort area, tourism waned from its heyday of the 1880s and '90s. The man who created the catalog system found in almost every library throughout the world soon would change that. Melvil Dewey, the originator of the Dewey Decimal System, launched a new idea for tourists in what would become the world-famous Lake Placid Club. Dewey introduced the idea of a winter tourist season, with a full range of winter activities from skating to sleigh rides to skiing.

As more individuals began to take up winter sports, more competitions among athletes appeared, which helped refocus attention on the region in general and Lake Placid in particular. The 1932 Olympic Winter Games reminded the world of the region's beauty.

In the depths of the Great Depression, New York Gov. Franklin D. Roosevelt officially opened the III Olympic Games on February 4, 1932, in the tiny village of Lake Placid. By the end of the day's events, Jack Shea, a local speed skater from Lake Placid, became the first athlete to win two gold medals at the same Olympics.

Sonja Henie also won a gold medal — in figure skating — the second for the "Norwegian Doll." (Henie eventually won a third consecutive Olympic gold medal in figure skating — a feat that has never been equaled.) American bobsledder Billy Fiske led his team to gold in the four-man competition. There was, however, a curious footnote to his victory. Fiske actually won the medal after the Olympics were officially over. It seems the 1932 Winter Games were held in conditions more suitable for the Summer Games, as the region experienced its warmest seasonal conditions in more than 100 years. Because of the balmy temperatures, the bobsled races were postponed until after the closing ceremony.

Throughout the middle part of the 20th cen-

Prior to the late 1800s, paper was made from rags, straw and other materials. In 1869, a paper maker by the name of A. Pagenstecher figured out how to grind wood into a pulp to make paper. After he ran out of suitable wood at his first mill site in Massachusetts, he moved his operations in 1869 to Lazerne, near Lake George. Eventually this mill was the basis for the formation of International Paper.

tury, more and more people visited the region. This increase in visitation created an interesting series of dilemmas.

The problem was essentially the same as in the past: How could the region's natural resources be protected while allowing the residents of the region to reap the economic benefits of a burgeoning tourism market? The scale of the problem was magnified not only by the increase in population, but also by the steady increase in leisure time. By the 1960s, the recreational opportunities available in the Adirondack region were well known, and residents and non-residents alike sought ways to capitalize on the tourist trade.

The construction of Interstate 87 (a.k.a. the Adirondack Northway) in the 1960s exemplified the ongoing challenge in the region. Prior to the Northway's existence, visitors traveled country roads into the region. These back roads had a limiting effect on tourism, as travel was both slow and inconvenient. The Northway and the Interstate highway system changed that by fostering economic growth in the North Country.

While economic prosperity sounds good, it often rubs against the environmental grain. The Northway raised this conflict to a screaming pitch. The Northway improved the economy, but raised a couple of significant questions: 1) How could a major interstate highway be constructed on land designated "forever wild" by the state's constitution? and, 2) How should the Adirondack Park be managed in these changing times?

In 1971, the Adirondack Park Agency (APA) was created to establish management policies for public land in the Park and to draft land-use and development plans for private lands. Thus, the APA establishes policy for protecting both the parklike atmosphere and the economic well-being of the people in the Park.

To accomplish this dual goal, the APA enacted policies that placed restrictions on the development and use of *all* Park land — public and private — in order to protect its ecol-

ogy. This action prompted even more heated debate.

Private landowners grew outraged. While more than 50 percent of the land in the Park was owned privately, the State nonetheless began imposing restrictions on how individual landowners could use their land. Landowners argued that this infringed on their Constitutional rights.

Zoning laws that soon appeared regulated: 1) the distance buildings need to be set back from water; 2) how many buildings could be constructed on a given tract of land; and 3) which economic activities could take place and where. Landowners who purchased property for speculation found that in some areas designated as "resource management," 42 acres were required to construct a single building.

It then was argued that if private landowners could use their land as they saw fit, public lands also needed regulation. Motorized vehicles would soon be banned from wilderness areas. Bicycles would also be banned from other sections. And if an Adirondack lean-to existed on "forever wild" land, it would have to be removed since man-made structures were not wild.

Everyone had an opinion — and everyone voiced it, especially as the Adirondack region planned to host the 1980 Winter Olympic Games in Lake Placid. These games became a staple of sporting lore for the brash Team U.S.A.'s stunning ice hockey upset of the heavily favored Soviet Union team as well as American Eric Heiden's five gold medals in speed skating.

The 1980 Winter Olympics also may be remembered, perhaps, as the world's first "environmental" Olympic Games. Planners had to not only devise ways to stage the games for the world to enjoy, but also plan the events to minimize the impact on the environment.

Today the debate continues at every monthly meeting of the APA, at every town planning board meeting and at every environmental review session as individuals from all walks of life try to manage the balancing act between economic benefits and environmental impact with respect to the Adirondack Park.

[Many Adirondack] towns . . . cater to summer tourists only. Once summer ends and the hardwoods don their early October colors, many visitor-oriented businesses hibernate for the next six months.

Area Overview

The Adirondacks isn't a place, really. It's a collection of places — of towns, mountains, lakes and rivers — each with its own character and appearance, yet all sharing the bond of a common environment, along with a common concern for the environment. In this chapter, we want to give you a feel for the individual character of the many places that make up the Adirondacks. Admittedly, the written page is a poor substitute for the experience of wandering into a town for the first time, hiking on a trail someone said you had to try, or canoeing into the coves of a lake you've never seen before like some great explorer of the 1500s.

Here, we whet your appetite. In the pages that follow throughout this book, we show you how, where and when to discover this magnificent world for yourself. So get in your car and start exploring. Around every turn is another scenic view, another lake to canoe, another trail to hike, another shop to browse. The Getting Here, Getting Around chapter will give you some good guidelines for how and where, but *when* is up to you. We also suggest you call or visit the local chambers of commerce and historical societies to find out more about the communities of the Adirondacks. We list the complete addresses (both street and mailing) plus phone numbers for the chambers and (or) tourism organizations responsible for each area at the conclusion of each section in this chapter. So, if while reading this book you're ever unsure where to go next for more information, this chapter is probably your best solution.

We consider two factors in this overview — the towns themselves and the general natural setting. What follows is a description of what you can expect in the "major" towns and villages and a brief overview of wilderness areas within the Adirondack Park.

Because the geographic area is so vast — remember, this area is larger than all of Vermont (and many other states, for that matter) — the overview follows what could be a driving tour of the region. The tour begins in Lake Placid, and along the way, many small towns and villages are mentioned, but not described. Places like Vermontville, Bloomingdale and Mineville appear on some maps, but they are not towns in the sense that stores and shops exist there. In some cases, "downtown" and "uptown" may be a single convenience store with the downtown area consisting of the beer and soda coolers and the uptown section housing a small collection of video rentals and junk-food favorites.

It is also important to realize that many of the towns in the region cater to summer tourists only. Once summer ends and the hardwoods don their early October colors, many visitor-oriented businesses hibernate for the next six months.

Lake Placid/ Tri-Lake Region

The three largest villages in the Adirondack Park — Lake Placid, Saranac Lake and Tupper Lake — form what marketing people call the Tri-Lakes region. But hundreds of lakes dot the area, thus the term Tri-Lakes is a misnomer. Because the term is so widely used, however, we'll stick with it in describing the region and the villages of Lake Placid, nearby Wilmington, Saranac Lake, Tupper Lake and areas west of these towns.

The Tri-Lakes region is often called the "High Peaks" — also inaccurate since most of the High Peaks are near Lake Placid and east of the village in towns such as Wilmington (home of Whiteface Mountain), Keene, Keene Valley and Elizabethtown, not west in towns such as Saranac Lake and Tupper Lake.

The 46 highest mountains in the Adirondacks clearly dominate the region's scenery, with the Tri-Lakes villages among the towns with the highest elevations in New York State. No matter where you travel from the Tri-Lakes, you travel downward in elevation. Even this becomes slightly confusing to the uninitiated as one travels, for example, "down to Plattsburgh" even though the drive from here is north — typically "up to Plattsburgh."

While Lake Placid is the best known village in the region, all the villages in the Tri-Lakes region offer some of the finest all-season recreational opportunities in the Northeast — and arguably in the country. Each of the Tri-Lakes towns has a ski slope. Whiteface, in Wilmington, is the most recognizable mountain, but Big Tupper in Tupper Lake is becoming increasingly popular. Saranac Lake even has a small ski mountain, Mount Pisgah, that's perfect for novices. Cross-country skiing, skating, sledding, winter festivals and events of every kind can also be found in these villages during the cold-weather months.

Spring, summer and fall also are filled with recreational opportunities that take full advantage of the region's mountains, forests, lakes and wilderness setting. While Lake Placid in particular may bill itself as a winter sports capital, visitors are more plentiful there — and throughout the entire region, in fact — during the summer months, especially July and August. In many towns the local population doubles, even triples, in number as summer residents visit their second homes.

Although we describe the Adirondack villages, remember that these towns are amid the wilds of the Adirondacks. You can drive for hours in the middle of night without finding any sign of the civilized world, let alone anything open for business. You can walk in many areas for days without seeing another person. What you will see is trees and more trees for miles upon miles. Towns — in some cases only a store in the front of a home — suddenly appear, and before you know it, there's nothing but trees, lakes and wilderness. Other towns may appear as a dot on the map, but that dot may be only a cluster of homes, perhaps a convenience store that may or may not have gas pumps. And that convenience

store may only be open when it is convenient for the owner! Understanding this dynamic will help you plan your travels accordingly.

For additional information on the region, contact the Lake Placid/Essex County Visitors Bureau, Olympic Center, Lake Placid, N.Y. 12946, 523-2445 or (800) 44-PLACID, or the Adirondack Regional Tourism Council, P.O. Box 2149, Plattsburgh, N.Y. 12992, 846-8016 or (800) ITS-MTNS.

Communities of the Region

Lake Placid

In 1980 the world watched as the small village of Lake Placid, with a year-round population of only 2,000 or so residents, put on a show known as the Olympic Games. Today, these games seem defined by a single event — the U.S. Hockey Team stunning their mighty Soviet counterparts 4-3 to win the Olympic gold medal. To many, the victory is generally considered one of the greatest moments in sports history. It is also one that helped define Lake Placid in the minds of many.

Visitors and residents alike have long been enchanted with the natural beauty of the High Peaks region of the Adirondacks, yet nature alone was not always enough to attract a year-round stream of tourist to an area that has depended heavily upon the tourism dollar for its survival.

The U.S. Hockey Team's victory, along with Eric Heiden's record-setting five gold medals in speed skating and the overall quality of the 1980 games, changed that. Lake Placid became recognized as the self-proclaimed or unofficial capital of winter sports in America. This boded well for the village, as the secret that Melvil Dewey, founder of the famed Lake Placid Club, discovered at the turn-of-the-century was finally recognized worldwide: The Adirondack region was not just a summer resort area, but a four-season vacation destination, and every season offered something special.

Today, Lake Placid relies upon its worldwide fame as an Olympic training facility and

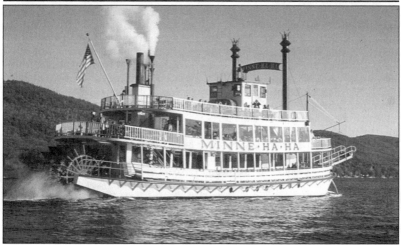

Photo: Warren County Tourism Department

Passengers aboard the *Minne-Ha-Ha* get a beautiful
view of Lake George and its unique shoreline.

sports center and the natural beauty of the High Peaks region of the Adirondacks to promote itself as a resort town. The range of visitor services in the village rank among the finest and most diverse in the world: highly acclaimed resorts and mom-and-pop motels; renowned and run-of-the-mill restaurants; great gift boutiques and tourist traps; and an array of recreational facilities.

The focal point of the village for athletes of all ages is the Olympic Regional Development Authority (ORDA), which operates all the former Olympic venues, including the Olympic Arena, with its three (sometimes four) ice skating rinks, Mount Van Hoevenberg, with its luge and bobsled tracks and cross-country ski center, the Ski Jumping Complex and Whiteface Mountain. ORDA provides plenty of activities for athletes and visitors alike throughout the entire year (see Attractions).

The village, however, also has a more easygoing nature centered upon the lakes, streams and mountains in the area. There are activities for every age, ability and taste. Visitors can take a carriage ride around the lake, play golf on one of many courses, canoe on the calm waters of Mirror Lake or water ski on Lake Placid itself. The public beach, although small, is delightful with its

sandy shores and clean, cool waters. There's plenty of shopping in the many fine and a few tacky stores along Main Street, and after a round of retail reconnaissance, slump in a lazy chair in the shade-covered park overlooking the lake (right next to the public library in the center of the village.)

If you are visiting the region and looking for a one-stop shopping mecca with something a bit different than a mall, Lake Placid offers the largest and most varied choices in the region. The shopping district consists primarily of Main Street, a .75-mile stretch between the Olympic Arena and the famed Mirror Lake Inn (see Accommodations). Along the way, shoppers will find everything from high fashion to T-shirts with stupid slogans, embroidered shirts advertising Lake Placid, craft stores and antique shops, ice cream and pastry parlors, minimalls and specialty stores stocking just hats or imagination games, for instance. The street is short enough to visit all the shops of interest while the kids comparison shop for their souvenir.

Although hotels and motels can be found throughout the village, the main drag of small mom-and-pop establishments can be found on Sentinel Avenue, which intersects Main Street at the Lake Placid Hilton. Dozens of motels (and one hotel) fill the avenue, and most are walking distance to the Main Street district. A number of hotels and lodges also can be found at the entrance to the village along N.Y. Route 73, but these are a mile-long walk to downtown.

The High Peaks surround the village and serve as a constant invitation to hike, ski or snowshoe one of the many trails that traverse the greatest wilderness east of the Mississippi River. You don't need to hike the tallest mountain to enjoy the wilderness in this region, as you'll find hikes for every ability and desire (see Hiking).

The two primary lakes in the village, Mirror Lake and Lake Placid, provide water recreation of all sorts during the summer months. No motor boats are allowed on Mirror Lake, making it a lazy spot to enjoy a quiet canoe, paddleboat or sailboat ride. A public beach and the toboggan slide can be found behind the U.S. Post Office on Main Street. Motor boats are allowed on Lake Placid itself, and water skiers and wake boarders take full advantage of the sport. Both lakes also provide exceptional fishing opportunities.

A small shopping center with a large supermarket and drug store is on the outskirts of the village on Sentinel Avenue (N.Y. 73).

Eight miles west of Lake Placid is Saranac Lake, but before we travel to Saranac, let's have a look at the town of Wilmington (see next section).

For additional information, contact the Lake Placid/Essex County Visitors Bureau, Olympic Center, Lake Placid, N.Y. 12946, 523-2445 or (800) 44-PLACID.

Wilmington

The famed Whiteface Mountain, site of the 1980 Winter Olympic Alpine ski events, is a few miles east of Lake Placid on N.Y. Route 86. Contrary to popular perception, Wilmington, not Lake Placid, is the home of Whiteface Mountain. (See our Skiing chapter for details.)

Although its "downtown" is only a loosely knit collection of service stores with one or two gift shops, Wilmington offers plenty of recreational opportunities, including skiing and mountain biking on Whiteface, fishing in the Ausable River and plenty of hiking and cross-country skiing trails. Although there are a few ponds and lakes in the area, this is more mountain and river country. Old logging and mining roads provide great backcountry and Telemark skiing opportunities.

Santa's Village (see Kidstuff), the first theme park in the United States, is here, as is the Whiteface Veterans' Memorial Highway, which allows car travelers to ride to the top of Whiteface. The Whiteface Memorial Highway was constructed as a result of some influential visitors who didn't want to climb to the summit, but wanted to go by car. Then-governor of New York and future U.S. President Franklin D. Roosevelt initiated the construction, which was completed in 1935 and named in honor of the veterans of World War I.

A number of small hotels dot the area, and a few close during the winter months.

For additional information, contact the Whiteface/Wilmington Regional Visitor Bureau, P.O. Box 277, Wilmington, N.Y. 12997, 946-2255, or the Lake Placid/Essex County Visitors Bureau (see the previous section for contact information).

Saranac Lake

Saranac Lake is a 10-minute drive west of Lake Placid on N.Y. Route 73. Between it and Lake Placid is Ray Brook, home of a New York State police barracks, the Department of Environmental Conservation and the Adirondack Park Agency offices.

Norman Crampton's *The 100 Best Small Towns in America* named Saranac Lake the No. 1 small town in New York State and No.

INSIDERS' TIP

One of the best views of Schroon Lake is from the parking lot of a funeral home along U.S. Highway 9, just south of the village. You'll think it's a rest area parking lot from the looks of it (in a "permanent" sense of the word, it is!), but it's a private lot, so soak in the view quickly and move along.

Profile: The Adirondack Park

The Adirondack Park is the largest park in the continental United States, encompassing nearly 6 million acres. It is nearly three times larger than Yellowstone National Park and is larger than every other national park in the lower 48 states. It is approximately the same size as the entire state of New Hampshire. About 130,000 people live year round in the 105 towns and villages within its boundaries. Also within the Park are 2,800 lakes and ponds and more than 1,200 miles of rivers fed by an estimated 30,000 miles of brooks and streams. These waters form the headwaters for most or part of five major watershed basins: Lake Champlain and the Hudson, Black, St. Lawrence and Mohawk rivers.

Animal life includes some 55 species of mammals, including whitetail deer, black bear and an occasional moose, 218 species of birds including the bald eagle and 193 nesting bird species, 35 species of reptiles and amphibians and 86 species of fish. And more than 30 tree species grow within the region.

The Park boasts more than 2,000 miles of hiking trails, more than half of which are maintained by the state. One trail runs 130 miles north to south from Lake Placid to Northville, New York, through sections of the greatest wilderness east of the Mississippi River. A canoe route from Old Forge in the southwest portion of the Park follows a string of lakes, ponds, rivers and portages to end nearly 100 miles away at Saranac Lake in

— continued on next page

Photo: Plattsburgh/North Country Chamber of Commerce

Enjoying the Adirondacks doesn't have to involve physical exercise; a summer picnic is its own reward.

the High Peaks section of the Park. Another canoe route, in the St. Regis canoe area, offers travel through 57 interconnecting lakes and ponds.

The western and southern Adirondack regions offers gentle landscapes of hills, lakes, ponds and streams. In the northeast, 46 "high peaks" — 42 are more than 4,000 feet high — spread across 1,200 square miles. This High Peaks section of the Park — specifically Lake Placid — was the host site of the 1932 and 1980 Olympic Winter Games.

The Adirondack Park is, by all ecological and aesthetic standards, a gem. Sixty-million people reside within a day's drive of the Adirondacks and its vast tracts of pristine wilderness, making it the world's most accessible wilderness area to the greatest number of people.

The range of sports and outdoor recreation opportunities is also unparalleled. The Park offers boating of all kinds, horseback riding, camping, picnicking, hiking/ mountaineering, hunting, fishing, swimming, water skiing, scuba diving, downhill and cross-country skiing, ice skating, ice boating, snowmobiling and snowshoeing. The U.S. Olympic Committee has designated the Lake Placid/Wilmington area as a major winter sports training center. In addition to the 1932 and 1980 Olympic Winter Games, the Lake Placid area also has hosted numerous national and international sporting events and continues to do so every year.

Land Regulation

The large size and the rugged and varied topography makes it difficult to define the Adirondack Park as a single unit. The Adirondack Forest Preserve is comprised of both public and private lands within the configuration of the "blue line," which bisects 10 of the region's 12 counties and many of its 105 towns and villages.

Within the Blue Line, New York State policies establish land management categories for both public and private lands. The *New York State Land Master Plan* sets policy for the management of the nearly 2.5 million acres of state-owned land, which is protected by the State Constitution as "forever wild." Developed by the Adirondack Park Agency (APA) in cooperation with the Department of Environmental Conservation (DEC) and approved by the Governor, the *Master Plan* was first adopted in 1972 and is revised as needed. The actual management of state land is carried out by DEC forest rangers, foresters, environmental conservation officers and other state personnel.

Public lands are categorized as follows:

•Wilderness: Sixteen tracts of the Adirondack Forest Preserve, comprising almost 1 million acres, are designated "Wilderness." These areas are reserved for such uses as camping, hiking, canoeing, fishing, hunting, trapping, snowshoeing and ski touring. Buildings and access by motorized equipment and bicycles are prohibited.

•Wild Forest: This comprises the largest category of land (totaling 1.3 million acres). A variety of outdoor recreational activities are allowed, including the use of motorized vehicles in designated places.

•Other Designations: Primitive and Canoe areas are managed similarly to Wilderness areas; Intensive Use areas (public camp grounds, developed beaches, boat launch sites) and State Historic Sites are managed similarly to Wild Forest.

Private land is governed as follows:

The Adirondack Park Land Use and Development Plan applies to the approximately 3.5 million acres of private land in the Park. The plan is designed to conserve the Park's natural resources and open-space character by directing and clustering development so as to minimize its impact on the Park. It also preserves ecologically sensitive land for agriculture, forestry and scenic vistas.

Under the plan, all private land is mapped into six land-use classifications: hamlet,

— continued on next page

moderate-intensity use, low-intensity use, rural use, resource management and industrial use. Specific guidelines govern the intensity of development within each category, based on number of buildings per square mile. New regional projects require permits.

Public and private lands also fall under special regulations that govern 1,200 miles of Adirondack river corridors designated as part of the State Wild, Scenic and Recreational Rivers system. These rules are designed to protect the waters from siltation due to erosion, pollution by sewage and other wastes, and construction of dams and inappropriately placed bridges. They regulate development within a quarter-mile of each bank so as to preserve these rivers in their natural, free-flowing states. The APA administers the river system on private land within the Park, and the DEC has dominion over the sections that flow through public land.

More than 14 percent of the Adirondack landscape is wetland. These areas serve a valuable environmental function by retaining flood waters, acting to purify surface runoff water and generally providing excellent habitat for fish and wildlife. Many unique forms of vegetation, such as pitcher plants, sundew and bog rosemary, also are associated with wetlands. The New York State Freshwater Wetlands Act, designed to protect these valuable resources, is administered by the Adirondack Park Agency within the Park.

---

11 in the nation. It is not only the largest village within the Adirondack Park, but also one of the most active, with events scheduled at a frantic pace throughout the year, including the oldest winter carnival in the United States (held in February; see Annual Events) and boat races and evening concerts of all sorts during the summer. The winter carnival and the many "cure cottages" in the village serve a direct link to its historic past and a doctor named Livingston Trudeau.

In 1873 Dr. Trudeau was diagnosed with tuberculosis (a.k.a TB). As his health deteriorated, he decided to return to the Adirondacks to die in a place he loved. Soon after arriving at Paul Smith's Hotel in Paul Smiths, his health unexpectedly improved. Curiously, every time he tried to leave the Adirondacks, his fever returned.

By 1884 Trudeau, then in his mid-30s, had established the first successful TB sanitarium in the United States on a 16-acre fox run purchased by local guides for Trudeau in Saranac Lake. Trudeau's combination of rest, fresh air and nourishing meals would serve as the foundation of his "cure" for TB, a disease then considered deadly and incurable.

By the turn of the century, the once tiny village of Saranac Lake became the leading TB treatment center in the country, with a population of 8,000 during its peak cure days. (Trudeau's original laboratory is next to the Paul Smith's College dormitory, behind the Hotel Saranac. The building remains closed and unoccupied.)

"Cure" cottages, houses with large sleeping porches and other accommodations for TB patients, still dominate the architectural style of the village, making it a wonderful place to stroll the streets looking at the unique structures. Patients would rest on these porches,

---

INSIDERS' TIP

The Warrensburg Chamber of Commerce operates a Visitor Information Booth from May until October along U.S. Highway 9 just as you enter the village. There is a designated parking lane adjacent to the booth, but it is very close to the traffic lane of what is a continually busy road, so we advise caution in parking and getting out of your car.

even during the coldest days of winter, breathing in their cure. (The Saranac Lake Winter Carnival began more than 100 years ago as a way to entertain patients during the dreary days of winter.)

The village of Saranac Lake, like its nearby neighbor Lake Placid, does not flank the lake for which it is named. Lake Flower borders the downtown area, with the Saranac Lakes a few miles away on N.Y. Route 3. (Lake Placid sits on Mirror Lake.)

Although there are a number of unique gift shops in the village, shopping in Saranac Lake caters more to a local than tourist trade. Three major supermarkets, a number of large drug stores and a large department store can be found in the village.

Recreation in the Saranac Lake area is dominated by the three Saranac Lakes — Upper, Middle and Lower. Each lake has a personality of its own, and one could argue forever about which is more beautiful.

Lake Colby, with a town beach and great fishing, is on N.Y. Route 86 on the outskirts of the village. The Adirondack Medical Center (see our Healthcare chapter) is opposite Lake Colby. Paul Smiths, which consists of Paul Smith's College (see Education), the Adirondack Park Visitor Interpretive Center and White Pine Camp, is approximately 15 minutes west. The villlage of Malone is 30 minutes north of Paul Smiths.

Travelers heading to Plattsburgh drive east on N.Y. Route 3 from Saranac Lake. Plattsburgh is approximately 45 miles away, and along the way you'll pass through some small — *very* small — towns such as Bloomingdale, Vermontville, Black Brook and Saranac.

For additional information, contact the Saranac Lake Chamber of Commerce, 30 Main Street, Saranac Lake, N.Y. 12983, 891-1900 or (800) 347-1992.

Tupper Lake

If the three villages comprising the Tri-Lakes were named after the lakes upon which the village sat, Tupper Lake would be Raquette Lake. Tupper Lake (the lake, not the village) is outside of the village proper.

Tupper remains very much tied to its historic past as a logging town, with its annual Field Days serving as the focal point of the summer.

Tupper offers visitors a laid-back setting, especially when compared to its neighbors, Saranac Lake and Lake Placid. There aren't as many tourist-related facilities such as hotels and restaurants to choose from, but in terms of outdoor activities, Tupper plays second fiddle to no village.

Big Tupper Ski Center offers challenging trails for downhill skiing and snowboarding without the high sticker price and crowds found at Whiteface. The rivers and lakes in the region, including Tupper Lake itself, provide for plenty of fishing, canoeing, windsurfing and swimming activities. Mountain biking and bike touring opportunities abound.

A large supermarket and a department store are on N.Y. Route 3 in Tupper Lake. These facilities are the closest to the Cranberry Lake area (see next section), west of Tupper on N.Y. 3 and one of the largest wilderness areas in the Park.

For additional information, contact the Tupper Lake Chamber of Commerce, 60 Park Street, Tupper Lake, N.Y. 12986, 359-3328.

Cranberry Lake

Cranberry Lake Wild Forest and the Five Ponds Wilderness area surrounds the small town of Cranberry Lake. Although the town boasts a few restaurants, marinas and inns, this area is among the wildest in the Park, and wilderness is its prime attraction, especially for hikers and canoeists in search of remote,

INSIDERS' TIP

These days you can pick up a bag of ice at any convenience store, but in the early 1900s, Old Forge and Raquette Lake were the place to get ice — lots of it. In fact, the New York Central Railroad used to get more than 50,000 tons of ice from the ice-cutting operations in this region for use in its icehouses of the day.

rarely traveled routes. The lake, the third-largest in the Adirondacks, meets civilization only near the village. If you plan on getting lost on a hike, this is the place to do it; you can wander the longest distances here without seeing signs of civilization. A few convenience stores can be found, but the closest major supermarket is in Tupper Lake.

Continue west on N.Y. 3 and you will eventually end up in Watertown, near the St. Lawrence River and the Canadian border. The drive along N.Y. 3 between Tupper and Watertown will make you appreciate the extent of the hardwood forests in the Adirondacks.

Plattsburgh/Western Lake Champlain Region

Compared to the highest peaks in New York, Split Rock, along the shores of Lake Champlain and the lowest point (about 400 below sea level) in the lower 48 states, seems worlds apart. The distance is approximately 50 miles from Lake Placid to the city of Plattsburgh, but the difference is dramatic. Wherever you travel in the Plattsburgh and Lake Champlain Valley, the Adirondack Mountains serve as the backdrop. You can drive along a country road dotted with farms and apple orchards in the valley and within minutes get lost along a backwoods road in a wilderness of mountains, forests and lakes.

The Lake Champlain Valley was settled long before pioneers ventured into the mountains to form permanent settlements, thus many of the towns and villages have greater historical roots, dating back to the middle 1700s. (For the most part, the towns in the mountains formed in the middle and late 1800s.) Important military battles were fought in towns such as Crown Point and Plattsburgh, and a number of fine museums retell the tales of these colonial wars. The early life of settlers in the valley also is captured in museums such as the Penfield Museum, where the electric age was born, the Kent Delord House and the 1812 Homestead. While historic re-creations such as Colonial Williamsburg, Virginia, may be more famous, the small town of Essex, New York, on the shores of Lake Champlain, boasts one of the most intact ensembles of pre-Civil War village architecture in the nation.

Early settlers, like today's tourists, took full advantage of the valley's prime attraction and resource, Lake Champlain, often called the "sixth Great Lake." The 155-mile-long lake, which begins near the Canadian border and ends near Lake George, sits between the Green Mountains of Vermont to the east and the Adirondack Mountains to the west. With these mountains as backdrops, the lake's setting, deep dark blue waters and varied shoreline are truly spectacular. Lake Champlain is a four-season recreational mecca, with sailing, fishing, boating and swimming featured during the warmer months and ice fishing during colder months.

Plattsburgh, the main city on the New York side of the lake, sits almost directly opposite Burlington, Vermont. All the other towns and villages in the valley are much smaller.

For additional information on the region, contact the Plattsburgh-North Country Chamber of Commerce, 101 West Bay Plaza, P.O. Box 310, Plattsburgh, N.Y. 12901, 563-1000, or the Adirondack Regional Tourism Council, P.O. Box 2149, Plattsburgh, N.Y. 12992, 846-8016 or (800) ITS-MTNS.

Communities of the Region

Plattsburgh

The city of Plattsburgh, with a population of 21,000, is the largest city in the northern Adirondack Region. The city is named for pioneer Zephaniah Platt, who first settled the area shortly after the American Revolution. Due to its strategic location on the shores of Lake Champlain, the settlement became home to military installations — and remained such for more than 200 years. Only recently did the city's last military installation, the Plattsburgh Air Force Base, close.

The city's most famous battle occurred in 1814, when 1,500 American regulars, supported by a few thousand militia, crippled the advance of British troops during the War of 1812. British statesman/prime minister Winston Churchill once declared this battle "the most decisive engagement of the war."

Today the city is known for its year-round

recreation, its many historical sites, the State University of New York (SUNY) at Plattsburgh (see Education), and its emerging industrial facilities. For locals in the northern tier of New York State and for its Canadian neighbors 15 minutes (driving) to the north, Plattsburgh also is known as a regional shopping destination.

Plattsburgh is, in many ways, two cities. The shopping area on N.Y. 3, just off Interstate 87, is a dense cluster of malls, including two major enclosed malls, large supermarkets and several strip malls dotting both sides of N.Y. 3. Visitors, however, rarely travel to the "other Plattsburgh" — the downtown section of the city. Here you will find a number of quaint shops and restaurants, along with a beautiful river and lakeside park — perfect for a pleasant walk or bike ride.

The Heritage Trail, a walking tour of the city, begins in the downtown area near the historic City Hall. The self-guided tour continues along a stretch of lakefront and passes a number of historic homes, including the Kent Delord House Museum, a landmark colonial farmhouse constructed in 1797.

The city also boasts one of the finest beaches in the region, just north of the downtown area in Cumberland Bay, which also includes camping facilities in the state park. Because of its location on Lake Champlain, water activities dominate the summer activities, with the annual Mayor's Cup sailing race and Landlubber Festival the highlight of the season (see Annual Events).

Plattsburgh is approximately 20 miles from the Canadian border, and Montreal is less than an hour's drive away. The city is conveniently located off I-87 exits 35, 36 and 37. While I-87 or the Northway is the fast and sure route to the city, back roads such as N.Y. 9 often provide wonderful views of the lake and farm country and are a worthwhile diversion.

For additional information on the region, contact the Plattsburgh-North Country Chamber of Commerce, 101 West Bay Plaza, P.O. Box 310, Plattsburgh, N.Y. 12901, 563-1000.

Keeseville

Keeseville is the home to the oldest tourist attraction in the country, the Ausable Chasm (see Attractions), and offers one of the region's largest selection of the architectural styles of a 19th-century industrial community. The historic section of the village includes 147 buildings and bridges on the National Register of Historic Buildings. Three bridges in the community have been cited as historic civil engineering landmarks. The Keeseville Riverside Park, the site of the Prescott Mill, provides a spectacular view of the Ausable River falls and the historic district.

While Keeseville offers plenty of history and the Ausable Chasm, it offers relatively few tourist traps. In terms of services, a number of small supermarkets and convenience stores can be found downtown.

Port Henry and Moriah

Port Henry rose to prosperity in the late 1800s because of the rich deposits of iron ore found in the area. Since then the town has had its ups and downs, but its beautiful setting on Lake Champlain makes it hard to overlook for too long. The town of Moriah, which includes the village of Port Henry, boasts some 28 miles of shoreline and some 70 miles of fishing streams. (Port Henry appears on many maps, but the town of Moriah doesn't.)

The legendary Champ, Lake Champlain's own version of the Loch Ness Monster, has been sighted most frequently in Bulwagga Bay off Port Henry. A large billboard on N.Y. Route 22 provides a running account of Champ sightings. Bulwagga offers a quiet haven for

---

FYI

Unless otherwise noted, the area code for all phone numbers listed in this guide is 518.

Photo: Warren County Tourism Department

Prospect Mountain provides a popular view of
Lake George and the surrounding countryside.

boaters and attractive winds for windsurfers during the summer months. During the winter, a village of ice-fishing shanties rises on the frozen bay.

A number of historic buildings, along with small supermarkets, convenience and service stores and gifts shops can be found in the downtown area of Port Henry.

For more information, contact the Moriah Chamber of Commerce, P.O. Box 34, Port Henry, N.Y. 12936, 546-7261.

Essex and Westport

Essex is on the National Register of Historic Places because it is one of the nation's most intact pre-Civil War villages. The village's unique architecture and location on the shores of Lake Champlain have attracted many artists, making it the closest thing to an artist's haven in the region. A number of artists and craftspeople offer their wares in small shops in many of the town's historic homes. The main street section of Essex is small — less than a half-mile — but the shops, lovingly restored historic houses and restaurants are distinctive.

Nearby Westport, a quaint 19th-century village, also provides plenty of charm for a perfect getaway weekend at a country inn or historic hotel. Westport offers a 18-hole championship golf course at Westport Country Club, professional summer theater, a country fair and plenty of activities on the lake. (See Annual Events and Other Summer Recreation for related information.)

Both Essex and Westport vie for the title of "The Best Kept Secret of the Adirondacks."

A ferry to Vermont leaves from Essex regularly during the summer months, so if you are planning a trip to the Green Mountain State, leave a few hours early to stroll through these scenic little towns on the shores of Lake Champlain. If you plan to boat on Lake Champlain, either town will be a prime choice for a prolonged stay on land.

For information, contact the Westport Chamber of Commerce, P.O. Box 394, Westport, N.Y. 12993, 962-8383.

Elizabethtown/Keene/ Keene Valley Area

Elizabethtown, or E-Town, is the government seat of Essex County, but that doesn't mean it's a big village. Downtown consists of a few stores, restaurants and small inns and motels. Like many other small villages in the region, the prime tourist attraction is the natural beauty of the area.

The Adirondack Center Museum, nine-hole Cobble Hill Golf Course, Lincoln Pond Campground and a large supermarket can be found in E-Town. During the summer months, there is a beautiful colonial garden hidden behind the Adirondack Center Museum, just off N.Y. Route 9.

The valley towns of Keene Valley and Keene are on the other side of Giant Mountain Wilderness Area from Elizabethtown. The Keene towns are known for spectacular valley views of the High Peaks. Hikers, rock climbers and cross-country skiers are likely to dream of these towns as the network of trails from the area, many leading to the High Peaks, including Mount Marcy, present many excellent choices. While the towns themselves never feel crowded, the trails often are, especially during the summer months. If we had to pick a picturesque mountain town in the region, Keene Valley would likely top our list. For well more than 100 years, artists have been attracted to this valley because of the views. Both Keene and Keene Valley have no real "downtown" sections, but rather offer a few craft and convenience stores that sort of ramble down N.Y. 73. These valley towns offer a number of charming country inns and bed and breakfasts, and both are only a 15- to 30-minute drive to Whiteface Mountain and Lake Placid.

N.Y. Route 73 makes its bid as one of the most beautiful roads in America from Exit 30 on the Northway (I-87), down through Keene and Keene Valley and up through the Cascades into Lake Placid. The route covers some 28 miles, but along the way you'll pass a number of mountain lakes, the famed Ausable River, a dramatic waterfall, numerous high cliffs and some views no artist ever could capture completely.

North Hudson/Newcomb

North Hudson is more a state of mind than a village proper. It is the home to Frontier Town

(see Attractions), off Exit 29, and little else, but it deserves mention because Boreas Road (County Route 2) may be the most beautiful road in America. Sure, the superlatives come from the locals, but the "most beautiful road" title may be an understatement. The road winds its way past Blue Ridge Falls, the Boreas River (famous for its trout and many historical log drives) and Elk Lake, which *National Geographic* once called "the jewel of the Adirondacks." (We wonder how one jewel of a lake is selected in an area that could be considered a fine jewelry store of lakes.)

If you have little time to spend in the Adirondacks and are just passing through, take an hour or so detour on the Boreas Road and add your vote to the pageant of beautiful roads.

N.Y. Route 73 and Northway Exit 30 are only some 10 miles away from the Boreas Road and Exit 29, so if you are conducting a survey as to the world's most beautiful roads, this is an area to check out. Be sure to gas up, however, as the fuel supply is very limited on these routes.

Northway Exit 29 is also one of the routes to take to Newcomb, home of the smaller of the two Adirondack Park Visitor Interpretive Centers, the Santanoni Great Camp and access to Adirondac, the ghost town of the Adirondacks. While it may not be the place for souvenir or any other type of shopping, Newcomb is opposite the Keene Valley side of the High Peaks and, therefore, offers access to the High Peaks themselves as well as other wild country.

Ticonderoga

This town is best known as the site of historic Fort Ticonderoga, which houses the largest collection of cannon in North America. While the fort is the focus of much attention, locals may suggest that the real reason why the French constructed the fort was to keep all the great fishing in the area for themselves. (They're just kidding.) Ti (for all those too lazy to pronounce the name) is an angler's paradise, as it is bordered by Lake Champlain, Lake George and LaChute River.

The small village bordered by farmlands and Lake Champlain has a number of fine shops and restaurants.

For additional information, contact the Ticonderoga Chamber of Commerce, 425 Montcalm Street, Ticonderoga, N.Y. 12883, 585-6619.

Lake George/Upper Hudson Region

The Lake George/Upper Hudson region is perhaps the most diverse of all Adirondack regions. The environment ranges from the civilized conveniences of the quasi-metropolitan Glens Falls at the southern tip of the region, to the wild and not-to-be-tamed upper Hudson River in the region's northern reaches; from the commercial and tourist-driven southern shore of Lake George to its peaceful, mountain framed northeastern arm nearly 30 miles distant; from the unhurried pace of a Schroon Lake boat ride to the frantic pace of a Lake Luzerne area rodeo.

It's a region where you can find just about any form of recreation you could possibly have the energy to pursue. And tens of thousands of visitors do just that every year — look for fun here each summer. Most find more than they have time for, and thus make an annual pilgrimage. Some, dissuaded by a rainy week and bracing lake water, don't return. Their loss. Others make this their winter-fun destination, with the slopes of Gore Mountain and miles of cross-country trails beckoning them.

In 1646, Lac du Saint Sacrement ("The Lake of the Blessed Sacrement") was the name given by the French Jesuit missionary Isaac Jogues to the body of water we now know as Lake George. The lake was given its present name in 1755 by Sir William Johnson to honor King George II of England. The 32-mile-long lake is fed by underground springs, has more than 100 miles of shoreline and more than 200 islands. It boasts some of the cleanest and clearest water of any major lake in the United States.

Few lakes played a bigger role in the birth of America than did Lake George. James Fenimore Cooper's classic The Last of the Mohicans was based on the battles in this region during the French and Indian Wars in the 1750s. In 1775, the north end of the lake at Fort Ticonderoga was the sight of the colonists' first victory in the American Revolution, as Ethan Allen and the Green Mountain Boys seized the fort from the British, along with Benedict Arnold (still a "good guy" at the time). These days, the biggest battles on the lake are between parasailing outfits trying to lure business.

Yes, much has changed in the Lake George area, but the natural beauty remains as awe-inspiring as the day when Thomas Jefferson wrote, "Lake George is without comparison, the most beautiful water I ever saw."

For general tourism information about the region, contact the Warren County Tourism Department, Municipal Center, U.S. Highway 9, Lake George, N.Y. 12845, 761-6366, (800) 95-VISIT.

Communities of the Region

Bolton Landing

Bolton Landing is about 10 miles north of Lake George village along the western shore of Lake George. It is home to about 2,000 people year round who enjoy one of the most scenic settings in all of the Adirondacks. From the town, the view of Lake George takes in the two tallest mountains that rise from the eastern shore, Black Mountain and Buck Mountain (see our Hiking chapter), along with Tongue Mountain to the north and farther along the western shore. The shoreline here is broken up by a series of little coves and dozens of islands, including the largest island, which serves as the home of The Sagamore Resort, one of the most famous resorts in the Adirondacks (see our Accommodations chapter).

Bolton Landing evolved from an Indian campground along a wilderness trail to an enclave for America's rich and famous who built their summer estates along the shore here. The mansions, stables and boathouses that lined the shoreline in the late 1800s gave this area the nickname "Millionaire's Row." While some of those exclusive estates still exist, Bolton Landing is now very much a community that welcomes visitors of all means. The village is quaint and less "touristy-looking" than Lake George village, and offers a small but pleasing variety of shops and restaurants, with occasional glimpses of the nearby lakefront a visual "bonus round" for your strolling.

You can find out more about Bolton Landing by contacting the Bolton Landing Chamber of Commerce, N.Y. Route 9N, P.O. Box 368, Bolton Landing, N.Y. 12814, 644-3831.

Chestertown

Chestertown is the primary town serving the area that includes Friends Lake, Loon Lake and Brant Lake. All three lakes are relatively small, with Brant Lake the longest at about 5 miles in length. The population of the town is approximately 3,500, which makes it one of the larger communities within the Adirondack Park. Seriously.

The Town of Chester was established in 1799, and originally was made up of about 500 farmers, blacksmiths, millers and lumbermen. The lumber industry was the big ticket here, as logs were transported via the Hudson and Schroon rivers to the Glens Falls area, where they were milled.

Now, Chestertown is centrally located within a recreational paradise, with Schroon Lake just 10 miles to the north, Lake George a little farther to the southeast, and Gore Mountain about the same distance to the west. Its location at the intersection of U.S. Highway 9, N.Y. Route 8 and Interstate 87 make Chestertown convenient to all of the southern and central Adirondacks. The area boasts some fine restaurants and country inns as well as a good collection of antique and craft shops. Main Street (U.S. 9) is attractive and quaint for its couple of blocks, and the Grand Union supermarket makes up for its lack of quaintness by serving its purpose as the "stock-up" center for the area.

The area is served by the North Warren Chamber of Commerce, N.Y. Route 8, P.O. Box 490, Chestertown, N.Y. 12817, 494-2722.

Glens Falls and Queensbury

The "metropolis" of the southeastern Adirondacks, Glens Falls actually sets about 10 miles south and east of the "blue line," the nickname given to the Adirondack Park boundary. In feel and lifestyle, though, it is very much an Adirondack community.

With a population of more than 15,000 in the city proper, and another 25,000 or so in the surrounding communities of Queensbury and Hudson Falls, this is the closest thing to an urban area that you'll find in these parts. Even so, its nickname of "Hometown U.S.A.," which was tagged back in a 1944 article in *Look* magazine about typical small towns, still seems to fit. This is an intimate, comfortable community that is very much family-oriented. In fact, a 1996 issue of *Reader's Digest* named Glens Falls as the "16th best place to raise a family in America."

This area was first settled in 1763 by Abraham Wing, who built a sawmill and named the community Wing's Falls. It would still be called that if Abe was any good at cards, but he lost the name in a card game to Col. Johannes Glen, who promptly changed it to Glen's Falls. The apostrophe eventually was dropped.

Glens Falls and neighboring Queensbury, collectively, are now known as one of the primary cultural centers of the Adirondacks, and home to such artistic groups as the Lake George Opera Festival, Glens Falls Symphony Orchestra, The Hyde Collection art museum and The Chapman Museum (see our Arts and Culture chapter). Glens Falls is also the home of the only real professional sports team in the entire Adirondack region, the Adirondack Red Wings of the American Hockey League, who play their home games at the Glens Falls Civic Center.

Queensbury is probably the most suburban of all Adirondack communities, bridging the geographic gap between Glens Falls and Lake George. You'll find a big variety of attractive home developments in Queensbury, and just about any major franchise store or restaurant you can think of. Hey, every now and then, even canoeists and hikers need an Olive Garden-fix.

For more information on Glens Falls, contact the Adirondack Regional Chamber of Commerce at 136 Warren Street, Glens Falls, N.Y. 12801, 798-1761.

Hague/Silver Bay

At the northern end of Lake George along the western shore, far from the bright lights and miniature golf courses of Lake George village, are the decidedly noncommercial communities of Hague and Silver Bay. Hague is home to only about 700 residents, but they enjoy what many consider to be the most beautiful and peaceful part of Lake George. They also enjoy some of the best bass fishing in New York State, according to locals (see our Fishing and Hunting chapter).

While somewhat isolated geographically, Hague does benefit from serving as the eastern terminus of N.Y. Route 8, one of only three east-to-west highways that traverse the Adirondack Park. So, for what it's worth, you can travel from Hague all the way to Utica without ever changing routes. Frankly, our suggestion would be to stay in Hague — it's too beautiful to leave.

Just a few miles south of Hague along the western shoreline is Silver Bay. This tiny dot on the map is best known as the home of the Silver Bay Association, founded by the YMCA as a summer camp in 1904 (see the Arts and Culture chapter).

To find out more about the northern end of Lake George and the Hague/Silver Bay area, contact the Hague/Silver Bay Chamber of Commerce, N.Y. Route 9N, Hague, 12836, 543-6353.

Lake George Village

Without a doubt, this is the commercial tourist hub of the southern Adirondacks. Here you'll find more than 100 places to stay, just as many places to eat, and nearly as many places to play minigolf. It is decidedly geared towards vacationing families and the partying youth of America, at least in the summer months. As bustling as Lake George is in the summer, it is nearly as quiet the rest of the year. Although some efforts have been made to change all that — every so often someone comes up with another idea like a convention center or a festival site to strengthen the economy during the rest of the year — Lake George finds a way to stay virtually the same, year after year. For many folks, from the 2,000 or so residents to the tens of thousands of summer visitors, that's just fine. They like Lake George just the way it is.

While the village is now the home of cruise boats, parasailing, Jet Ski rentals, minigolf, wax museums and more T-shirt shops than churches; it began its history as an important outpost in American history, as the site of the Fort William Henry (see the Attractions chapter). Fort William Henry was the sight of the battles in the 1750s during the French and Indian Wars that became the basis for the classic book *The Last of the Mohicans*. The original site of the fort was reconstructed in 1953, and now serves as (you guessed it) one of the primary tourist attractions in the village.

Lake George is now also the home of such major attractions as The Great Escape theme park, Lake George Steamboat Company, Prospect Mountain Veteran's Memorial Highway, The Factory Outlets of Lake George, and dozens of other smaller diversions that will gladly accept your money. It is also the sight of one of the prettiest waterfront strolls in America. The nicely landscaped promenade from the Steel Pier to Canada Street along the waterfront faces north, straight up the length of the mountain-framed lake. If you catch it just right, late in the day or at the crack of dawn before the boats and Jet Skis take over, it is a sight of sheer natural beauty that will stay with you for a long time.

To find out more about Lake George, contact the Lake George Regional Chamber of Commerce, U.S. Highway 9, P.O. Box 272, Lake George, N.Y. 12845, 668-5755.

INSIDERS' TIP

Have your cameras (and your vehicle's brakes) ready when driving around the Old Forge area. It's a protected area for deer, and they are as common a sight as dogs and cats. It can make for a beautiful scene, but you should drive with extra care as the entire area is, in effect, a "deer crossing."

Lake George (East Shore)

The eastern shore of Lake George along N.Y. Route 9L is far less commercial than the southern and western shore, and serves as the hub of boating activity for the lake. There are several large marinas in the bays along this shore, at Dunham's Bay and Cleverdale. The east shore also serves as the starting point for some of the best hiking in the region, particularly at Buck Mountain and Black Mountain (see the Hiking chapter). From small camps to sprawling estates, hundreds of lucky folks call this their summer home. About halfway up the eastern shore, development and roads yield entirely to the lake and its mountains, presenting her as the "Queen of American Lakes."

Lake Luzerne

The Lake Luzerne area is home to about 4,000 people, seven spring-fed lakes, the merging of the Sacandaga and Hudson rivers, and an entirely different atmosphere than nearby Lake George. Part of what's called the "Dude Ranch Trail" by tourism promoters (for its prevalence of riding stables and ranch resorts), Lake Luzerne is more rustic, less hurried and more peaceful than its commercial neighbor 10 miles to the northeast. Its location within a 15-minute drive of either Lake George or Saratoga Springs to the south makes it an ideal hub for a wide variety of cultural and recreational pursuits. The village of Lake Luzerne is just across the Hudson River from the neighboring small town of Hadley. The Rockwell Street bridge that connects the two offers a scenic view of the Rockwell Falls of the Hudson River. The Hudson serves as the border between Warren and Saratoga counties.

The Town of Lake Luzerne was founded on April 10, 1792, and was originally called Fairfield. In the early 1800s, the water power of the Hudson provided most people in the area with work in the sawmills, gristmills and tanneries of the day.

These days, tourism is the reason most come to the area, in search of an old-fashioned Adirondack experience without the bright lights and thrill rides. This area is not without culture, though. The Lake Luzerne Music Center and the Chamber Music Festival (see the Arts and Culture chapter) provide summer visitors with sophisticated entertainment amid the Adirondack woods. For those in search of a little more kinetic activity, the whitewater rafting and tubing on the Sacandaga River offers a heart-pumping alternative. For hikers, nearby Hadley Mountain provides one of the best views in all the southern Adirondacks, and is a relatively easy climb (see the Hiking chapter). In the wintertime, the Lake Luzerne Winter Carnival helps to keep the blood pumping after the lakes freeze.

For more information on the Lake Luzerne area, contact or visit the Lake Luzerne Chamber of Commerce at N.Y. Route 9N, P.O. Box 222, Lake Luzerne, N.Y. 12846, 696-3500.

North Creek

North Creek has evolved from a center for the logging industry in the early 1800s into one of the biggest hubs for year-round recreation in the Adirondacks today. In many re-

---

INSIDERS' TIP

Lake Champlain Fun Facts:
•**The lake holds an estimated 6.8 trillion gallons of water.**
•**The deepest part of the lake is 400 feet.**
•**The lake holds one of the best collections of historic shipwrecks in the United States.**
•**Fossil outcrops from one of the oldest coral reefs (500 million years old) are found on Isle La Motte, northeast of Plattsburgh.**
•**A total of 318 species of birds breed or live in the Lake Champlain basin.**
•**In 1989 the United Nations designated the Champlain-Adirondack region as an international biosphere reserve, the fourth-largest in the world.**

spects, both roles are due to its location along the banks of the upper Hudson River. While the river used to carry thousands of logs downstream in the springtime river drives of the last century, it now carries thousands of whitewater rafting enthusiasts from early spring right through mid-October. The river also carries thousands of gallons of water via pipeline to the snowmaking guns of nearby Gore Mountain Ski Center, a state-owned major ski mountain on the verge of a huge expansion that will make it a player among eastern ski resorts (see the Skiing chapter).

North Creek was actually one of the first hubs for winter recreation in the Adirondacks (along with Lake Placid). In the 1930s, trains from New York City would pull in with skiers anxious to try out the new rope tow at the North Creek Ski Bowl, one of the first ski centers in the country.

The town received national attention as early as 1901. North Creek served as the terminus for "Teddy's Wild Ride," so named for then-Vice President Teddy Roosevelt's dangerous, middle-of-the-night carriage ride along a dark and twisty trail en route to the North Creek train station, following his hike on Mount Marcy. Roosevelt then traveled to Buffalo to be sworn in as President after the assassination of William McKinley.

The North Creek area is home to the world's largest garnet mine, the Barton Mines (see Kidstuff), a planned scenic excursion train at the restored North Creek Station, and five cross-country ski centers, several of which offer terrific mountain biking in the summer. Speaking of mountain biking, the list of summer recreational options in the North Creek area grew by one in 1997, as Gore Mountain introduced lift-served mountain biking that's as tough on your "guts" as it is on your legs.

The village of North Creek seems on the verge of making the transition from just a small town in the mountains to a legitimate resort destination. Leading the charge is The Copperfield Inn, an elegant resort hotel built in the early 1990s and recently expanded (see our Accommodations chapter). The Copperfield Inn is a symbol of the faith that locals have in this community, and their enthusiasm for its future. Elsewhere on Main Street, quaint shops and cafes are beginning to join the hardware stores and insurance agencies to offer a more attractive mix of services to the visitor. Remember the name North Creek. We think you're going to hear a lot about it in the coming years.

If you want to find out about North Creek now, and not wait until Christie Brinkley or some other celebrity builds a home there before checking it out, contact the Gore Mountain Region Chamber of Commerce, Main Street, North Creek, N.Y. 12853, 251-2612.

Schroon Lake

Schroon Lake reminds us of that old beer commercial that says, "All the taste, half the calories." In this case, it's "all the beauty, half the commercialism" (of Lake George, that is). One visit and you'll see what we mean. The lake itself — about 9 miles long and up to 1.5 miles wide — was formed when glacial debris dammed up what was then a valley. The lake is actually just a wide section of the Schroon River, which flows into the lake from the north and empties out in the south on its way to meet the Hudson River near Warrensburg.

The area around Schroon Lake and the Schroon River were first popular with settlers as logging country in the early 1800s, and the Town of Schroon was established in 1804. The first river drive took place here in 1813, and lumbering continued as the primary industry until the 1870s. Then, as The Adirondack Railroad began operating from Saratoga Springs to nearby North Creek, tourism started to emerge as the predominant money maker.

By the early 1900s, steamboats would carry wealthy travelers who lived in big eastern cities like New York and Philadelphia from Pottersville at the south end of the lake to the large resort hotels of the day near the village of Schroon Lake. The summer season continues to be the primary focus of the economy here today, as this has become a very popular area for campers and boaters. It is perhaps better known these days as a summer residential area than as a vacation destination, as Lake George continues to offer the majority of lodging and entertainment options in the region.

The village of Schroon Lake seems to be straddling the fence between quaint and attractive resort community and plain old struggling small town. Main Street offers an eclectic mix of the trendy, the basic — and the closed. Our visit found such sites as an attractive gift shop followed by an empty restaurant followed by a bustling general store. No doubt the challenges of maintaining a healthy year-round economy in a predominantly summer resort area are in evidence here. There's no question about the setting, though — it's magnificent. The town offers a very nice free public beach within a short walk of Main Street as well as a public pier and waterfront park with the prerequisite bandstand. Schroon Lake also offers a brand-new (in 1997) and very attractive Grand Union grocery store with such big-city features as a salad bar and service deli. It'll seem like a bigger deal once you're here — trust us.

Schroon Lake boasts an active cultural calendar as well, with the Boathouse Theatre and Seagle Music Colony (see Arts and Culture) offering a wide variety of entertainment throughout the summer. Perhaps the most visible influence in Schroon Lake is that of the Word of Life ministry. Word of Life owns a great deal of land on and around the lake, including the lake's largest island, a ranch, family campground and large inn.

For more information about the Schroon Lake area, contact the Schroon Lake Chamber of Commerce, P.O. Box 726, Schroon Lake, N.Y. 12870, 532-7675 or (800) 9-ADK-MTS. The chamber operates a visitor information center in the summer, just off Main Street adjacent to the town park and overlooking the lake.

Warrensburg

This southern Adirondack "metropolis" of about 4,000 residents benefits from its location immediately off Interstate 87 ("the Northway") Exit 23. We'd give it the co-title of "Most Accessible Adirondack Community by Car," along with its neighbor Lake George one exit to the south. Even a hundred years before the Northway was opened in 1966, Warrensburg benefited from its location near the confluence of the Hudson and Schroon rivers. In the early and mid-1800s, Warrensburg

was a hub of logging operations due to its river proximity.

Most locals agree that the village is named for James Warren, who arrived in 1804 and set up shop in both a tavern and a general store. Unfortunately, Warren only lived here for seven years, as he drowned in 1811 when his skiff overturned on what was then called the West River (now Hudson). His son Nelson Warren went on to be a prominent mill owner here.

The Warrensburg of today is an interesting mix of folks and the places they shop and hang out. You'll find pseudo-suburbanites here, with one toe in the Adirondacks and the other in the fast lane of the Northway south to Glens Falls and the working world. You'll also find genuine backwoods and North Country kind of folks, with a checked flannel on their backs and a pickup in their gravel driveway. In town, you'll find everything from elegant bed and breakfast inns and restaurants to honky-tonk taverns, and from quaint shops to your basic building supply depot. It's a town that perhaps best represents the "cosmopolitan divide" between civilization and the woods.

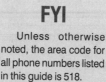

FYI

Unless otherwise noted, the area code for all phone numbers listed in this guide is 518.

On winter weekends, busy Main Street (U.S. Highway 9) gets clogged with ski-rack-laden vehicles on the way to or from Gore Mountain, about a half-hour distant. In the spring, it's whitewater rafting enthusiasts on their way to North Creek and Indian Lake for their adventure down the Hudson River Gorge. In the summer and fall, vehicles carrying anything from campers to hikers to antique hunters crawl along the 2-mile-long commercial vein that is Main Street. In fact, the number of antique dealers in the area has helped Warrensburg to become known as the "Antique Capital of the Adirondacks."

Warrensburg keeps the calendar full of big events as well, hosting the Smoke-eaters Jamboree in July, the Warren County Country Fair in August and the "World's Largest Garage Sale" in October (see Annual Events chapter).

To learn more about Warrensburg, contact the Warrensburg Chamber of Commerce, 136 Main Street, Warrensburg, N.Y. 12885, 623-2161.

Southern Adirondack Lakes Region

This is perhaps the least commercial and populous of all our Adirondack regions. And that, visitors and residents alike will tell you, is a great part of its appeal. What we refer to as the Southern Adirondack Lakes Region for our purposes is a roughly triangular-shaped area with Blue Mountain Lake at the top, Great Sacandaga Lake at the lower right corner, and the Caroga/Canada Lake area at the lower left corner. It is a region best known for its outdoor recreational opportunities among the numerous lakes, mountains, rivers and wilderness areas. Fishing, hiking, boating, cross-country skiing, snowmobiling and biking are all very popular pursuits, and recreation enthusiasts love the unspoiled beauty and lack of human competition for space here. Even in midsummer, you are unlikely to have a problem with crowds of other visitors for just about any activity you're interested in. You won't find that to be the case in the more commercial areas of Lake George, Lake Placid and Old Forge.

While many of the places in this region don't have the name recognition of other areas in the Adirondacks — and they may have less to offer in terms of sheer numbers of attractions, restaurants and other services — that certainly doesn't mean you can't have a perfectly enjoyable experience here. In fact, this region probably has the most "local finds" of those we cover. Riding the Ferris Wheel at Sherman's Park overlooking Caroga Lake, relaxing on the beach at Pine Lake, renting a canoe at Peck's Lake or Canada Lake, camping on an island on Indian Lake, learning a new craft at the Adirondack Lakes Center for the Arts in Blue Mountain Lake — these are all things you probably never have heard of, but are well worth your time discovering. The good news is, we cover all of them in detail throughout this book.

The region's only real commercial area actually lies just outside the southern border of the Adirondack Park; the small cities of Gloversville and Johnstown, with a combined population of about 25,000. Known as the "Glove Cities" for their history as one of the nation's leading leather-industry centers, Gloversville and Johnstown at one time had more than 400 glove manufacturers and produced 95 percent of all American-made gloves.

Together, they now serve as the "stock-up" center for the Southern Adirondack Lakes Region as well as the center for media and service businesses such as law and accounting firms and real estate agencies. It is here that you will find the only real supermarkets in the region, and it is here that you will find the only real industrial activity as well. Spalding makes Top-Flite golf balls at a local plant; Wal-Mart receives returned merchandise from all over the northeast at their huge return center; and a collection of leather and glove manufacturers still ply their trade (and sell their goods at outlet stores).

In many ways, Gloversville and Johnstown play the same support role for the Southern Adirondack Lakes Region as does Glens Falls for the Lake George/Upper Hudson Region and Plattsburgh for the Plattsburgh/Western Lake Champlain Region — they are not Adirondack communities in the pure geographical sense, but in an economic sense they are all very much interdependent.

Since "Lakes" is part of the region's name, we better mention them. There's a bunch, the primary ones (roughly from south to north) being Great Sacandaga Lake, Peck's Lake, Caroga Lake, Canada Lake, Piseco Lake, Lake Pleasant, Indian Lake, Sacandaga Lake (a different one) and Blue Mountain Lake.

The Great Sacandaga Lake is the second-largest lake within the Adirondack Park. Actually, it's a reservoir resulting from the damming of the Sacandaga River in 1930, a move made to help tame the Hudson River from its occasional springtime tantrums that could cause havoc in Glens Falls and as far downriver as Troy and Albany. At 29 miles long by a maximum of 6 miles wide, it is a close runner-up to Lake George in size, but lags behind significantly in most other physical characteristics. The mountains that surround the lake are smaller, the cottages that ring the lake are less luxurious, and the restaurants and lodges that front the lake are fewer than in Lake George. It is, in effect, a simpler lake — one that has not evolved a great deal in appearance for many decades. One thing for which it does rival Lake

The Adirondack Forty-Sixers and the High Peaks

In 1937 a group of hikers formed a club called the Adirondack Forty-Sixers, which consisted of individuals who climbed each of the 46 highest peaks in the Adirondacks.

Membership in the Forty-Sixers club was based on a 1920 survey of the 46 highest peaks in the region. These 46 High Peaks became commonly known as the High Peaks.

But the High Peaks designated in the initial survey were not the 46 highest peaks in the Adirondacks. A 1985 survey revealed a more accurate list. So, what were the original 46 highest peaks and what are the correct 46 highest peaks?

The original 1920 survey had the 46 highest peaks (elevation in feet above sea level) as: Marcy (5,344 feet), Algonquin (5,114), Haystack (4,960), Skylight (4,926), Whiteface (4,867), Dix (4,857), Gray Peak (4,840), Iroquois (4,840), Basin (4,827), Gothics (4,736), Colden (4,714), Giant (4,627), Nippletop (4,620), Santanoni (4,607), Redfield (4,606), Wright (4,580), Saddleback (4,515), Panther (4,442), Tabletop (4,427), Rocky Peak Ridge (4,420), Macomb (4,405), Armstrong (4,400), Hough (4,400), Seward (4,361), Marshall (4,360), Allen (4,340), Big Slide (4,240), Ester (4,240), Upper Wolf Jaw (4,185), Lower Wolf Jaw (4,175), Street (4,166), Phelps (4,161), Donaldson (4,140), Seymour (4,120), Sawteeth (4,100), Cascade (4,098), South Dix (4,060), Porter (4,059), Colvin (4,059), Emmons (4,040), Dial (4,020), East Dix (4,012), Blake Peak (3,960), Cliff (3,960), Nye (3,895), and Couchsachraga (3,820).

The revised 1985 survey added MacNaughton (4,000), Green (3,980), Lost Pond (3,900), Moose (3,899), Snowy (3,899) and Kilburn (3,892).

So, which ones do you climb to become a Forty-Sixer? Contact the organization to find out the criteria. For information write Adirondack Forty-Sixers, RFD 1, Box 390, Morrisonville, N.Y. 12962.

Winter in the Adirondacks is stunning in its stark beauty.

George is boat traffic, as the wide open expanses of water attract a big display of power boats, sailboats and personal watercraft (i.e. Jet Skis) on any given summer Saturday.

Caroga Lake, Indian Lake, Lake Pleasant and Blue Mountain Lake are both communities and their namesake lakes, so we'll cover them altogether in the following "Communities of the Region" section.

Peck's Lake is actually a private lake, owned by (you guessed it) the Peck family, who operate a marina and campground and own much of the property surrounding the lake. About half of the 4-mile-long lake is developed, with good-sized summer and year-round homes the standard along the north and south shores. Peck's Lake is known as a good fishing lake (see the Fishing and Hunting chapter) as well as a fine place to canoe the interesting shoreline and its many coves.

Canada Lake, a few miles farther north along N.Y. Route 29A, is also about 4 miles long, running predominantly from east to west. About half the lake's shoreline is developed, although more so with seasonal cottages than the larger homes of Peck's Lake. It is also home to the Canada Lake Store & Marina, one of the nicest general stores we've seen (see the Shopping chapter's "Milk and Light Bulbs" section).

As you venture north on N.Y. Route 10, you'll come to the small but picturesque Pine Lake, home of one of our favorite Adirondack beaches (see Other Summer Recreation). Next up, some 18 miles beyond, is Piseco Lake in the central portion of this region. Piseco is a good-sized lake, about 8 miles long and 2 miles across. It is known primarily for the three popular state campgrounds that string along the northern shore — Poplar Point, Little Sand Point and Point Comfort. We cover all three in the Camping chapter. Piseco is also known for the popular hike that begins at Little Sand Point and climbs to a scenic view from the top of Echo Cliffs on Panther Mountain. Again, we've got that covered, in the Hiking chapter (see what you've got to look forward to!?). Piseco offers two other noteworthy amenities: the Piseco Airport, for general aviation planes (see Getting Here, Getting Around); and the Irondequoit Inn, with its lodge, campsites, boat rentals and fabulous breakfasts (see Bed & Breakfasts and Country Inns).

About 10 miles to the northeast of Piseco is Sacandaga Lake, home of the popular Moffitt Beach State Campground (which, naturally we have covered for you in the Camping chapter). Sacandaga Lake feeds into Lake Pleasant, which in turn feeds into the Sacandaga River on its way to the Great Sacandaga Lake; hence the connection in names.

The mountains in the region range in elevation from around 2,000 to just less than 4,000 feet in elevation, with some of the biggest including 3,749-foot Lewey Mountain (near the southern end of Indian Lake), 3,759-foot Blue Mountain (overlooking Blue Mountain Lake and village) and 3,900-foot Snowy Mountain, which stands sentinel over Indian Lake and is a popular (and challenging) hike.

For general information on the Southern Adirondack Lakes Region, we suggest you contact the two county tourism organizations that serve the area: Fulton County Regional Chamber of Commerce & Industry, 2 N. Main Street, Gloversville, N.Y. 12078, 725-0641, (800) 676-3858; and the Hamilton County Tourism office, County Office Building, White Birch Lane, P.O. Box 771, Indian Lake, N.Y. 12842, 648-5239.

Communities of the Region

Blue Mountain Lake

Blue Mountain Lake is a tiny hamlet that overlooks the beautiful island-studded lake of the same name, and is itself overlooked by Blue Mountain. Geographically, it serves as the unofficial "heart" of the Adirondacks, with its location at the confluence of N.Y. routes 28 and 30 and within a two-hour drive of virtually all reaches of the Adirondack Park.

The hamlet forms somewhat of a crescent around the eastern end of the lake, with the dark wooden facade of Potter's Restaurant greeting you where N.Y. 28, N.Y. 30 and the lake all come together. It seems hard to believe that more than a century ago one of the biggest and most modern hotels in the world stood nearby. The Prospect House, built in 1881, entertained the rich and famous in its six-story frame with 300 rooms and state-of-the-art conveniences such as an elevator and electric lights in every room. In fact, the Prospect House was the first hotel in the world to feature such amenities. As with almost all of the grand hotels of the day, the Prospect House eventually met its end by fire, and today casual visitors aren't even aware it ever existed. Of course, a visit to the nearby Adirondack Museum will take care of that in a hurry, as they have an extensive exhibit on the grand resort hotels of the day.

For as small as the community of Blue Mountain Lake is, it is certainly one of the biggest cultural centers in the entire Adirondacks due to the presence here of the Adirondack Museum and the Adirondack Lakes Center for the Arts. The Adirondack Museum is internationally acclaimed and recognized as one of the finest regional museums in the world. It is, quite simply, a "must see" while in the Adirondacks. The museum also is the sight of many major events during its May-to-October season. You can learn more about the museum in the Attractions chapter. The Adirondack Lakes Center for the Arts (ALCA) offers concerts, theater, films, coffeehouses, workshops and exhibits throughout the year (see the Arts and Culture chapter).

The beauty and cultural offerings of Blue Mountain Lake has drawn many artisans and craftspeople to the area, most of whom have galleries or shops that display their work. Check out the Shopping chapter for some suggested places to explore.

For more information specifically on Blue Mountain Lake, contact the Blue Mountain Lake Association at 352-7659 or Hamilton County Tourism (see information at the end of the previous section).

Caroga Lake

Caroga Lake is a small community of 1,500 or so folks flanked by the two Caroga lakes — West Caroga Lake and East Caroga Lake. Both branches of the lake are small, with a mile in any direction about as far as you can go before hitting one shore or the other. The most prominent landmark on West Caroga Lake is Sherman's Park (see our Kidstuff and Nightlife chapters) with its lush landscaping, turn-of-the-century restored carousel, Ferris wheel and large restaurant/dance hall fronting the lake.

East Caroga Lake is the site of the Caroga Lake State Campground (see Camping).

This is the first town you come to within the Adirondack Park as you travel north on N.Y. Route 29A. The town itself comes and goes pretty quickly outside your window, with just a few general stores and roadside eateries to let you know you're "in town." Within the town borders you also will find some of this region's big recreational assets, including Royal Mountain Ski Area and the Nick Stoner Golf Course. You can pick your own blueberries (but you can't pick your relatives — is that how the saying goes?) at the Timberlane Blueberry Farm (see Kidstuff) in July and August. For history buffs, a visit to the Caroga Historical Society & Museum (see Arts and Culture) is worthwhile.

More information on the Caroga Lake area can be found by contacting the Fulton County Chamber of Commerce (see the previous section for contact information).

Indian Lake

Indian Lake is a lake, a town and a hamlet at just about the center of this region. The lake is distinguished by its long (nearly 14 miles) and slender (about 1 mile at its widest) profile. It is a popular lake with canoeists, as its narrowness and many islands scattered about make it an interesting and safe place to explore. Some of the islands have state-owned campsites as well (see our Camping chapter). The largest mountains in the central Adirondacks overlook the northwestern shore of Indian Lake, including 3,900-foot-high Snowy Mountain.

The town is indirectly named for one of its first settlers, Sabael Benedict, a member of the Abanakee Indian tribe who came here with his family in 1762. Records show that old Sabael (and we do mean *old*) lived to be 108 — pretty good in these rugged climes even these days. Indian Lake remained largely undiscovered until the Adirondack Railroad, linking Saratoga Springs to North Creek, was built in 1871. This brought wealthy vacationers within 20 miles of Indian Lake, and many began to venture to Indian Lake via horse-drawn buckboard wagons, then farther into the beauty of its surrounding wilderness with guides.

Today, Indian Lake's location about half-way between the cultural offerings of Blue Mountain Lake and the recreational opportunities of the North Creek area (and within a 20-minute drive of each) makes it a desirable hub for both vacationers and outdoor enthusiasts. Indian Lake is known as the starting point for whitewater rafting through the Hudson River Gorge, recognized as some of the best rapids in the East. Hunting, fishing, hiking, camping, snowmobiling and cross-country skiing are all popular recreational pursuits in the Indian Lake area.

To find out more about how you can enjoy the Indian Lake area, contact the Indian Lake Chamber of Commerce, Main Street, P.O. Box 18, Indian Lake, N.Y. 12842, 648-5112 or (800) 328-LAKE.

Lake Pleasant/Speculator

These two communities, the hamlet of Lake Pleasant and the village of Speculator, combine to serve as home to about 1,500 year-round residents on either end of picturesque Lake Pleasant. Those numbers swell about sixfold during the summer months, when the area's six state campgrounds and hundreds of seasonal homes fill up with folks. The area prides itself on what it *doesn't* have — traffic lights (not one!), malls, hustle-bustle. What is does have is a bigger deer population than human, three huge wilderness areas (Siamese Ponds, West Canada Lakes and Silver Lakes) that surround it and hundreds of miles of trails for bikers, hikers and snowmobilers to enjoy. In fact, the 130-mile-long Northville-Lake Placid trail for hikers runs right through the heart of this area.

In the central area of Hamilton County, the lake is about 3 miles long by 1 mile wide, and is popular with everyone from fishing enthusiasts to canoeists to seaplane pilots, who hold a fly-in "seminar" here in June each year.

The hamlet of Lake Pleasant sets along both sides of N.Y. Route 8 at the western end of the lake. It serves as the county seat for Hamilton County. While there isn't a "Main Street" as such, "downtown" is probably best defined by the area around the county courthouse sitting up on the hill on one side of N.Y. 8 and the scenic nine-hole Lake Pleasant Golf Club sitting on the other. On the other hand, Speculator does offer at least a collection of shops, restaurants and a few motels clustered around the "Four Corners," which is what locals call the intersection of N.Y. routes 30 and 8. Speculator is the home of the Camp-of-the-Woods, a religious camp and conference center established in the 1930s. Just outside of town is Oak Mountain Ski Center, which first opened in 1948 and has been closed in recent years due to financial difficulties, but hopes to reopen in 1998.

For more information on this recreational paradise, contact the Adirondack Speculator Region Chamber of Commerce, N.Y. routes 30 and 8, P.O. Box 184, Speculator, N.Y. 12164, 458-4521.

Northville

Northville is a small village of about 1,200 residents at the north end of the Great Sacandaga Lake near the entry of the Sacandaga River. It is the biggest village directly on the lake, and features a good old-fashioned Main Street that still shows some pretty good signs of life. The location of the village just off N.Y. Route 30, the primary north-south route through the central Adirondacks, gives this community true gateway status to the wilderness and recreational areas beyond to the north.

The Adirondack Country Store, Lapland Lake Nordic Vacation Center, Northampton Marine and the Inn at the Bridge are all noteworthy nearby attractions and businesses that we cover elsewhere in this book. For boating and fishing enthusiasts, Northville's location

INSIDERS' TIP

When the U.S. military built Fort Montgomery at the northern tip of Lake Champlain, they mistakenly built it on Canadian soil. Fort Montgomery (a.k.a. Fort Blunder) proved to be a unique way for the country to obtain more land as the site — it's now privately owned — was subsequently deeded to the United States.

on one of the biggest lakes in the Adirondacks makes it a desirable destination. Campers enjoy the nearby Northampton State Campground directly on the lake. For residents, the combination of an attractive community that's within a 20-minute drive of both the conveniences of Gloversville and the wilderness of the central Adirondacks provides for an enjoyable lifestyle.

Northville is an active community as well, with a number of special events throughout the year, such as the Old Fashioned Christmas celebration (see Annual Events).

You can find more information about Northville through the Fulton County Chamber of Commerce & Industry (see the prior section for contact information) or the Northville Merchants Association at P.O. Box 1055, Northville, N.Y. 12134, 863-8902.

Old Forge/ Raquette Lake Region

The Old Forge/Raquette Lake Region stretches from one end of the famous Fulton Chain of Lakes to the other and beyond to Raquette Lake. The "chain" begins at Old Forge pond, travels through a mile-long channel to First Lake and then continues unbroken for 14 miles to Fifth Lake. After a half-mile break, or "carry," Sixth and Seventh Lake are linked together, followed by a carry to stand-alone Eighth Lake. Besides the eight lakes in the chain, the region is held together geographically by N.Y. Route 28, which runs along the shoreline of the lakes. N.Y. 28 also serves as the lifeline to the relatively metropolitan amenities of Utica, just about an hour's drive southwest of here.

A century ago, it was the railroad that served as this region's lifeline, bringing thousands of wealthy travelers to Old Forge, where they would embark on steamships to the many resort hotels, such as The Forge House, and "Great Camps" of the day. In fact, the "Fulton" in Fulton Chain of Lakes is named for Robert Fulton of steamship fame. President Benjamin Harrison built a camp on Second Lake in 1895 named Berkeley Lodge.

Farther east, Raquette Lake is the fourth-largest lake in the Adirondacks and home to many of the storied Adirondack Great Camps. The lake is deceptively small in appearance, but it's many bays and peninsulas give it almost 100 miles of shoreline. Among the Great Camps built on Raquette Lake were Bluff Point, built in 1877 for magazine mogul Robert Collier; Echo Camp, built in 1883 and once owned by Gov. Phineas Lounsbury of Connecticut (which likely ruffled some feathers in Hartford); Camp Pine Knot, built in 1876 by entrepreneur William West Durant for railroad executive Collis Huntington; and the most famous of all, the Great Camp Sagamore (which is actually a few miles south on Sagamore Lake; see Attractions). Raquette Lake can best be seen from the deck of the cruise boat *W.W. Durant*, which offers scenic lake tours and dinner cruises in an atmosphere reminiscent of the Gilded Age of the late 1800s (see Attractions).

The Old Forge/Raquette Lake Region is one of the most popular in the Adirondacks for three distinctly different activities: canoeing, whitewater rafting and snowmobiling. In the summer and fall, canoeists can enjoy routes throughout the Fulton Chain and beyond that can take them as far as Saranac Lake village with all but 8 miles of carry out of the 90-mile distance achieved on the water. In the wintertime, the Fulton Chain is but a small part of the more than 500 miles of snowmobile trails that can be explored in the region. Many of the trail systems around Old Forge are regularly patrolled and meticulously groomed, and draw thousands of "sledders" from throughout the east. Whitewater enthusiasts can test their skills and courage in the springtime on some of the wildest rapids in the eastern United States on the Lower Moose River southwest of Old Forge.

The area is also known for its hiking and camping, with popular state campgrounds such as Nick's Lake, Limekiln Lake and Brown's Tract Pond filling up from May into October. The easy and scenic hike up to the top of Bald (a.k.a. Rondaxe) Mountain's 2,350-foot summit, which seemingly overhangs the shores of First Lake, is a very popular way to get a grand view of the Fulton Chain and the surrounding wilderness. We cover all of this for you in more detail within the Camping and Hiking chapters, respectively.

Your best bet for obtaining information on this region, including Old Forge, Inlet and Raquette Lake, is to contact or visit the Central Adirondack Association, Tourist Information Center, N.Y. Route 28, Old Forge, N.Y. 13420, (315) 369-6983. The Hamilton County Tourism office (see Southern Adirondack Lakes Region section for contact information) also covers Raquette Lake and Inlet.

Communities of the Region

Inlet

As a town of only 400 or so folks, you might think Inlet is hardly worth mentioning, but that's hardly the case. Inlet's picturesque location at the eastern end of Fourth Lake, the largest of the Fulton Chain of Lakes, makes it one of the most popular vacation spots in the region. Being halfway between the other popular destinations of Old Forge to the west and Blue Mountain Lake to the east help its case as well.

As N.Y. Route 28 winds through town, you'll find an attractive selection of gift shops and restaurants as well as a variety of housekeeping cottages and motels. In addition to the usual variety of Adirondack recreational activities such as hiking, biking, boating and such, you can enjoy scenic seaplane rides out of Inlet (see Attractions). Inlet is also the home of one of the best golf courses in the Adirondacks, the Inlet Golf Club. The town's two parks, Arrowhead Park and Fern Park, offer a wide variety of activities and special events, along with amenities such as the free public beach at Arrowhead and the ice skating pavilion at Fern Park.

For specific information on Inlet, you can contact the Inlet Area Chamber of Commerce, N.Y. Route 28, Inlet, N.Y. 13360, (315) 357-5501.

Old Forge/Thendara

Named after an iron mine that failed way back in 1819, Old Forge is a village within the sprawling Town of Webb that serves as the year-round home to about 1,500 hardy folks. With more than 200 inches of snow in a typical winter season, and wintertime temperatures that can easily dip below minus-30 (without windchill!), hardy folks are about the only species that can survive and thrive up here.

There are a lot of good reasons to try to survive up here, for it is an area of year-round natural beauty (with the possible exception of November, when the leaves are gone but the snow hasn't arrived yet; or April, when the snow is gone, replaced by mud). With both a vibrant summer season and winter season, Old Forge has become one of the most popular and commercial tourism centers in the entire Adirondacks, joining Lake George and Lake Placid as one of the "big three" visitor destinations.

While separated as communities by the Moose River, Old Forge and Thendara are linked visually and economically by the string of gift shops, motels and restaurants that line N.Y. Route 28 for a couple of miles. "Downtown" Old Forge (downtown is a relative term in these parts) is reflected in the waters of Old Forge Pond that it partially encircles. Overlooking the picturesque setting are the chutes and slides of Enchanted Forest/Water Safari, which has grown over the years into one of the biggest attractions in the Adirondacks, drawing around a quarter-million visitors in its short summer season.

There's a big selection of gift shops in and around town, but none as huge and imposing (or as pricey, according to locals) as Old Forge Hardware, a great place to browse on a rainy day. You'll find plenty of variety in both lodging and dining choices here as well, from the basic to the elegant.

In addition to the canoeing, snowmobiling and whitewater activities mentioned earlier, Old Forge has its own ski center, McCauley Mountain. With a reputation for demanding terrain, McCauley is popular with serious skiers in the region as well as cross-country skiers who can enjoy the surrounding trail network here.

Those who prefer indoor activities with a cultural flavor can enjoy the many programs at the Old Forge Arts Center, or first-run movies at the Strand Theatre (see Nightlife).

Perhaps the simplest and most beautiful attractions around Old Forge are the deer, whose protection from hunters here make this "the place to be" for Bambi and friends. A half-dozen or more deer at a time are a common sight, and many will come right into residential yards where kindly folks have set up troths of food for them.

Thendara, whose name means "Rim of the Forest," has been transformed from a center for the logging and railroad industry (its station was the terminus for the railways from the south) to an integral part of the area's tourism industry. Two of it's most popular attractions are the Adirondack Scenic Railroad excursion train, and the Donald Ross-designed Thendara Golf Club, both of which we cover in the Attractions and Golf chapter, respectively.

Wilderness Areas

Initially, we wondered how we could accurately describe the vast wilderness areas of the Adirondacks. Fortunately, the Department of Environmental Conservation and the Adirondack Park Agency provide a framework, as the state had to develop a plan to manage the public lands of the Park. This comprehensive master plan is detailed in (what else?) the *New York State Land Master Plan*, a 68-page guide first published in 1972 by the Adirondack Park Agency. While it's rather dry reading — it provides list after list of recommendations — it is, however, an important document inasmuch as it defines how the citizens of New York State are to manage the great natural treasure that is the Adirondack Park. (The *Master Plan* is filled with technical descriptions and terms regarding land management, which makes for dry recreational reading, but if land-management plans are your thing, consider that the Adirondack Park — the primary subject of the *Master Plan* — often is cited as a model for effective management of public and private lands.)

What follows are brief descriptions of the designated Wilderness Areas in the Park. For a profile of the Park, including a digest of the *Master Plan*, see this chapter's "Profile: The Adirondack Park" Close-up. (For more information on recreational opportunities on these lands, see the Fishing and Hunting chapter.)

In the 1970s, New York State legislation defined 15 "Wilderness Areas" of more than 10,000 acres and one area of fewer than 10,000 acres (a canoe area managed as a wilderness area) within the Adirondack Park as requiring special protection. In addition to the following Wilderness Areas, New York State also has protected many of the rivers in the region with special classifications. Some 155 miles of rivers have been designated as Wild Rivers, with restrictions similar to those of Wilderness Areas. Another 511 miles have been designated as Scenic Rivers, and 540 miles as Recreational Rivers.

Lake Placid/ Tri-Lake Region

High Peaks, the largest Adirondack wilderness area, covers 193,000 acres including almost all the mountainous region between Lake Placid and Newcomb. There are 112 bodies of water, and elevations range from 1,040 feet to 5,344 feet. The topography includes some small areas of low-lying swampland, especially along the rivers, but is predominantly high mountain country. Lake Tear of the Cloud, the source of the Hudson River and adjacent to Mount Marcy, is at 4,300 feet. The tops of Mount Marcy and Algonquin include two rare and endangered alpine summit habitats.

Jay Mountain, the smallest wilderness site, encompasses 7,100 acres east of Jay. Although covering less than the 10,000 acres necessary for technical designation as a wilderness area, Jay was included because of its unique ecology and the fact that no trails exist in the area. A plan to include additional land in the Jay Wilderness area has not been realized yet.

McKenzie Mountain, sometimes referred to as Saddleback, north of Ray Brook, covers 38,000 acres and includes portions of the Saranac River. It includes eight bodies of water altogether, and elevations range from 1,463 feet to 4,869 feet. Although the area is close to the villages of Saranac Lake and Lake Placid, it retains a rugged wilderness atmosphere of dense softwood forests at higher elevations and mixed hardwoods on the lower terrain. The terrain is steep and rugged in many sections.

Sentinel Range, at 23,000 acres, is between Lake Placid and Wilmington. Although the area is near one of the most popular villages in the region, it plays second fiddle to

Photo: Mark Meschinelli

Experiencing the Adirondacks first-hand is like stepping into a picture postcard.

the High Peaks wilderness area in terms of its popularity with hikers. It includes five small ponds, and elevations range from 1,375 feet to 2,893 feet.

St. Regis Canoe Area encompasses 20,000 acres west of Paul Smiths and includes 58 lakes and ponds. This area, along with Five Ponds, may be heaven on earth as far as canoeists and anglers are concerned. In some sections, canoeists can travel for some 30 to 40 miles among dozens of lakes with only short carries of the canoe overland. The lake fishing in this area is among the finest anywhere. (Technically, St. Regis Canoe Area is not an official wilderness area. Though designated a "Canoe Area," it is managed as a wilderness area, so we include here, albeit not in the official Wilderness Area count. Officially there are 16 Wilderness Areas plus St. Regis Canoe Area.)

Five Ponds, near Cranberry Lake and Stillwater Reservoir, may be the most remote and least used of all the Adirondack wilderness areas. It is 101,000 acres, includes 95 bodies of water, and ranges in elevation from 1,486 feet to 2,460 feet. This is one of the few locations in the eastern United States were stands of virgin timber can be found. It's also an area where anglers, hunters and experienced campers can travel for miles into the deep backwoods to rid themselves of any scent of the civilized world. Although not as rugged as the High Peaks area, Five Ponds is as remote and wild as wilderness gets. Don't even think about exploring this region without a good map and practiced orienteering skills!

Plattsburgh/Western Lake Champlain Region

Dix Mountain, southeast of Keene Valley, consists of 45,000 acres adjacent to the High Peaks. It includes 12 bodies of water, and elevations range from 940 feet to 4,857 feet. Four trailless peaks — South Dix, East Dix, Hough and McComb — exist in the area. Hikers and campers find this area very attractive.

Giant Mountain, between Elizabethtown and Keene, is a 23,000-acre area. There are only two bodies of water within the area, and elevations range from 700 feet to 4,627 feet. The topography is steep and rocky. Because of the range of elevation, the range of temperature and soil conditions makes for great differences in forest types.

(Note: Although we place Dix and Giant Mountain in the Plattsburgh/Western Lake Champlain Region, most hiking guides and hiking maps include them in the High Peaks region.)

Lake George/ Upper Hudson Region

Hoffman Notch, near Minerva, is popular with anglers and hunters. It covers 36,000 rugged and mountainous acres, includes eight bodies of water, and ranges in elevation from 960 feet to 3,693 feet.

Pharaoh Lake, east of Schroon Lake, comprises 46,000 acres and more than 35 lakes and ponds. Pharaoh Lake is one of the largest lakes in the Adirondacks totally surrounded by forest preserve land. Elevations in this area range from 860 feet to 2,551 feet.

Siamese Ponds, between North River and Speculator, includes parts of the Sacandaga River. Its 112,000 acres include 67 bodies of water, and elevations range from 1,280 feet to 3,472 feet. Although much of the area was logged in the early 1900s or burned in fires, the forest has reestablished itself over most of the area, with excellent stands of both hardwoods and softwoods.

Southern Adirondack Lakes Region

Blue Ridge, south of Blue Mountain Lake, is a 46,000-acre site. It includes 19 bodies of water, and elevations range from 1,700 feet to 3,744 feet. The forest in this area remains greatly affected by a massive blowdown of old-growth spruce and hemlock in the 1950s.

Silver Lake covers 105,000 acres near Piseco. Included in the area are 48 bodies of water, and elevations range from 820 feet to 3,250 feet. Silver Lake, Mud Lake, Rock Lake and Loomis Pond are popular trout fishing spots.

West Canada Lake, west of Speculator, includes more than 160 lakes and ponds in its 157,000 acres. Elevations range from 1,390 feet to 3,899 feet. Because of the number of streams in this area, it is considered prime trout fishing country.

Old Forge/ Raquette Lake Region

Ha De Ron Dah, west of Old Forge, has the most unique name among the Adirondack wilderness areas. It includes 27,000 acres and 59 bodies of water. Elevations range from 1,440 feet to 2,340 feet. The terrain is primarily low rolling hills, with many beaver meadows and wetlands. Extensive forest-fire damage has resulted in many areas being covered with brush and small trees.

Pigeon Lake, north of Big Moose, is 50,000 acres. There are 64 bodies of water, plenty of wetlands and miles of streams, making this prime trout fishing territory. The elevations range from 1,700 feet to 2,900 feet, thus the terrain is more rolling than mountainous.

Pepperbox, north of Stillwater Reservoir, includes 15,000 acres of relatively flat land (for the Adirondack Mountains, that is) with a few rolling hills. It is the least accessible of all the Adirondack wilderness areas as it is predominantly wetlands. If you can get there, you'll find 40 bodies of water and elevations from 1,360 feet to 2,168 feet.

Auto travel into the Adirondack Park has improved dramatically since the expansion and completion of the interstate highway system, which includes three divided superhighways that either skirt or traverse parts of the Adirondacks.

Getting Here, Getting Around

While the railroad was the first effective means of bringing visitors into the Adirondacks late in the 19th century, it should come as no surprise that the automobile is now the leading mode of travel to and within the Adirondack Park. Travel by rail, while still available, has diminished from more than a dozen rail companies at the turn of the century to the present-day limited service by Amtrak along the region's eastern corridor.

Although it is perhaps not as "romantic" to think of driving your cup-holder-laden minivan along a superhighway deep into the Adirondacks, it certainly is a lot more convenient and flexible than relying on the rail service of a century ago. As rugged and remote as the Adirondacks can still feel, it's a lucky break for us that it really isn't very difficult to get either to or around this beautiful wilderness. That's assuming, of course, that your fuel tank is full, your oil light is off, your tires have plenty of tread, and there's no antifreeze puddled under your car. The Adirondacks may be much easier to travel about than in the "old days," but you still wouldn't want to break down along some stretches of its lonely roads.

Auto travel into the Adirondack Park has improved dramatically since the expansion and completion of the interstate highway system, which includes three divided superhighways that either skirt or traverse parts of the Adirondacks. Once within the Park, auto travel is relatively simple, mainly because there aren't many options for getting from here to there. For the most part, that isn't a disadvantage. The primary highways for north/south and east/west travel are both scenic and (usually) in good shape.

Depending on the tightness of your schedule and your sense of adventure (think John Candy and Steve Martin in *Planes, Trains and Automobiles*), air travel is either an interesting and scenic or a frustrating and impractical means of travel to the Adirondack region. There are no major airports within the Adirondack Park, and the size and convenience of the commercial airports near the perimeter depend entirely on your frame of reference.

What follows is a look at the suggested auto travel routes for entering and traversing the Adirondack Park as well as other transportation options. The bottom line: Relax, enjoy the scenery and stop looking at your watch! These ancient mountains aren't going anywhere.

Getting Here by Car

Since the great majority of visitors to the Adirondack Park travel from the either the north or south, we will dedicate the greatest detail to those journeys.

From Points South into the . . .

. . . Eastern Adirondacks

Depending on where you are starting out and where in the Adirondacks you want to end up, you have at least a few choices for entering the Adirondack Park from the south, all involving superhighways for at least part of your journey. The most direct and fastest (speed limit and otherwise) route into the eastern Adirondacks from points south is Interstate 87. From New York City to Albany, this is known as the "Thruway" (officially the Governor Thomas E. Dewey Thruway, but New Yorkers will likely greet you with a blank stare if you call it that). From Albany north to the Canadian border (approximately 175 miles), I-87 is called the Adirondack Northway.

At Exit 24 of the Thruway, to stay on I-87 northbound, you have to leave the Thruway, make your way through the toll booths (it can take some time on a Friday afternoon) and then enter the Adirondack Northway portion of I-87. Keep in mind that from the entrance to the "Northway" (as locals abbreviate it) to at least Exit 11, this six-lane superhighway also serves as a major commuter route for Albany-area workers who live in the northern suburbs of Latham, Clifton Park and Malta. Traffic is fairly heavy most of the time, and during rush hour — generally 4 to 6 PM — it can crawl along at 35 mph. For an added bonus, factor in heavy tourist traffic on weekends, toss in some bad weather, and you'll find the first 20 miles or so of your Adirondack Northway experience can be considerably less serene than you would expect of something with the name "Adirondack" attached. The good news is that once you clear Saratoga Springs (exits 13 through 15), the Adirondack Northway lives up to its name. It is a well-maintained, beautiful stretch of interstate highway that will lead you directly into and through the easternmost section of the Park.

I-87 is the only interstate highway that runs through a portion of the Adirondack Park — for just less than 100 miles from approximately Exit 20 at Queensbury to Exit 35 at Ausable Chasm. So picturesque is the journey, it was named "America's Most Scenic Highway" by the Federal Highway Administration when it opened in 1966. Many of the Adirondack's primary visitor destinations are accessible off I-87, including Lake George, Gore Mountain, Schroon Lake and the Lake Placid/Whiteface Mountain area. You will find rest areas as you head north near Exit 27 (Schroon Lake) and approximately 5 miles north of Exit 30 (Keene Valley).

. . . Central Adirondacks

If the south-central Adirondack region is your destination, then you'll want to enter the Park from one of a few exits along Interstate 90, the New York State Thruway. If you are traveling north on I-87 from New York City or beyond, you are already on the Thruway. You just need to make sure that at Albany you stay on the Thruway heading west as it becomes I-90 (remember, I-87 becomes "the Northway" beyond Albany). You then have several options for northbound entry into the Adirondack Park, beginning with Exit 27 at Amsterdam. This will take you up N.Y. Route 30 along the Great Sacandaga Lake and (eventually) to Blue Mountain Lake, the geographic heart of the Adirondacks.

If your destination is one of the small lakes that string along the southern boundary of the Park, including Peck's Lake, Caroga Lake, Canada Lake and Pine Lake, then you'll want to leave the Thruway at either Exit 28 (Johnstown) or Exit 29 (Canajoharie). From Exit 28, you'll take N.Y. Route 30A north past Johnstown to its neighbor (and rival) Gloversville, then head northwest on N.Y. Route 29A through Gloversville, past Peck's Lake and into the town of Caroga Lake. Here you will pick up N.Y. Route 10, which will take you into the southern Adirondack interior. Get-

FYI

Unless otherwise noted, the area code for all phone numbers listed in this guide is 518.

INSIDERS' TIP

Be prepared to slow down as you drive around the Adirondacks during the summer months, for two reasons: 1) to enjoy the view; and 2) the road construction and repair doesn't give you much choice. "Road-repair season" is pretty short around here due to the short summer, so don't be surprised to be inconvenienced during your travels.

Photo: ORDA

This aerial view encompasses the village of Lake Placid,
Mirror Lake, Lake Placid and Whiteface Mountain.

ting off the Thruway at Exit 29 will put you directly onto N.Y. 10, about a half-hour south of the Adirondack Park boundary. It zigs and zags a few times along the way, so pay attention to the highway signs as you make your way through the metroplex of Stone Arabia and Ephratah.

In some cases, if you are approaching the Adirondacks from the southwest, such as eastern Pennsylvania, it might make sense to take Interstate 88 from Binghamton northeast to Schenectady, where it intersects with the Thruway. From there, simply follow the previous directions. This is your best bet if your destination is the southern or eastern Adirondacks.

. . . Western Adirondacks

If your destination is the western portion of the Park, then you have three primary options, depending on where your journey begins. From the southeast, your best bet is to take the New York State Thruway (I-87 and I-90) north to Albany and then west to Utica. At Exit 31, take N.Y. Route 12 north to either N.Y. Route 8 (if you are heading east towards Speculator) or N.Y. Route 28, which will lead

you into the Park toward the Old Forge area. From the southwest, head north on I-81 from Binghamton through Syracuse. From there, you'll either head east on the Thruway to Exit 31 at Utica (see previous directions), or, if your destination is the northwestern Adirondacks, continue north on I-81 to Watertown. At Watertown, exit the Interstate for N.Y. Route 3, which is the primary west-to-east highway for the northern Adirondacks.

. . . Northern Adirondacks

If your point of origin is south and east of the Adirondacks, the best bet is to take I-87 north from Albany along the eastern section of the Park, then exit anywhere from Exit 30 to Exit 38. If you are starting out south and west of the Adirondacks, take I-81 north from Syracuse to Watertown and then exit for N.Y. 3 eastbound toward Cranberry Lake.

From Points North into the Adirondack Park

Your suggested routes into the Adirondack Park from the north come down to three choices, depending on your starting point. First, let's assume you are starting out somewhere in Canada, because that's the only place directly north of the Adirondacks and New York State. If you are coming from the Montreal area, you have a relatively simple trip with about 35 freeway miles, beginning with Can. Highway 15 southbound to the U.S. (New York State) border. From that point south, the road becomes Interstate 87 (Adirondack Northway). You can exit at several points along its 100-mile journey through the region. If you are crossing over the border farther west, at Cornwall, Ontario, then your choices are either N.Y. Route 37 east to Malone, or west to Massena. At Malone, pick up N.Y. 30 south for about 20 miles into the Park. From Massena, look for N.Y. Route 56 south, travel through the college town of Potsdam and then 15 miles to the Park border. If you need to reach the southern portion of the Park, your choice is either to take the Adirondack Northway (I-87) south to exits 27 through 21, or take N.Y. 30 south straight down the "spine" of the Adirondacks. N.Y. 30 may look more direct, but in most cases the Northway is the faster option.

From Points West into the Adirondack Park

Frankly, most folks do not arrive out of the western horizon into the Adirondack Park, unless they are boating, kayaking or otherwise propelling themselves across the 193-mile length of Lake Ontario. While this smallest of the Great Lakes sets some 60 miles to the

west of the Park boundary, most of the square miles between the two are dominated by the sparsely populated Tug Hill Plateau. Therefore, most visitors' points of origin are to the north and south. You'll want to follow the directions in the "From Points South . . ." or "From Points North . . ." sections as they pertain to the western Adirondacks.

From Points East into the Adirondack Park

For most east-to-west travel into the Adirondacks, you'll have to "drive" your car across water. Now hang on — it's easier to do than you might think. And no, it doesn't involve any ramps, high speed or the need to change your name to Knievel. It involves a ferry ride across Lake Champlain.

The entire eastern border of the Adirondack Park is guarded by the clear, cold waters of Lake Champlain and, farther south, Lake George. To enter the Park, you can (from north to south) either traverse Lake Champlain via four ferries (see the section on ferry service later in this chapter), cross bridges at Rouses Point (on the Canadian border) and Crown Point, or drive around the southern tip of Lake George via U.S. Highway 4 from Vermont to N.Y. Route 149. This route will unload you on U.S. Highway 9 smack-dab in the middle of the "Million Dollar Half-Mile" outlet shopping area, near the village of Lake George at Exit 20 of the Northway. From there, if you have any money left, you can head north on I-87 (Adirondack Northway) up the eastern flank of the Park.

Mileage Chart for Primary Adirondack Destinations

Distance From:	Old Forge	Lake George	Lake Placid
Albany	136	53	142
Boston	302	222	308
Buffalo	248	311	346
Montreal	215	173	117
New York City	295	214	300

Getting Around by Car

Once you are within the Park boundaries, auto-travel options become limited to a small collection of north/south and east/west highways. This is good because it is simple to master the routes and their destinations. This is bad because you may find yourself 20 miles by air, yet 60 miles by car from some of your intended destinations. Enjoy the scenery (there's plenty of it!) — it's all you can do.

North and South

There are five primary north/south routes through the Adirondack Park, all of which run from the central part of the Park east to the Vermont/Lake Champlain border. From the center working your way east, your options include the following.

N.Y. Route 30

This is the longest north/south route in the Adirondacks, covering about 170 miles from Mayfield in the south (Great Sacandaga Lake) to the northern Park border just south of Malone. Along the way, you will travel through (or past) Speculator, Indian Lake, Blue Mountain Lake, Long Lake, Tupper Lake and Paul Smiths.

Interstate 87 (Adirondack Northway)

Certainly the quickest of all Adirondack routes, this superhighway enters the Park near the village of Lake George (Exit 21) and rolls north for nearly 100 miles within the Park, exiting near Ausable Chasm (Exit 34). You will pass by Warrensburg, Chestertown, Schroon Lake and exits for Lake Placid (Exit 30) and Elizabethtown (Exit 31) as you head north.

U.S. Highway 9

This used to be the primary north/south route for travelers making the trip between New York City and Canada, but the opening of the "Northway" (which runs basically parallel) relegated U.S. 9 to secondary status. While it is less traveled by those trying to get from Point A to Point B, it is still a busy highway in sections, with many lodging properties, restaurants and attractions either on or near this route. Within the Park, U.S. 9 mostly shadows the Northway, running from Lake George past Schroon Lake and then north through Elizabethtown and on to Ausable Chasm. This is "Main Street" for the Plattsburgh/Western Lake Champlain region.

N.Y. Route 9N

N.Y. 9N rambles and rolls from Corinth in the far southeast corner of the Park northeast through Lake Lazerne, then along the entire length of Lake George. From Ticonderoga at the northern tip of the lake, it joins forces with N.Y. Route 22 north along Lake Champlain to Westport. Then, in an act of cartographic defiance, it veers off from N.Y. 22, heading back west through Elizabethtown to Keene, where it turns north yet again for the journey along the East Branch of the Ausable River. As you can probably guess, this is a much more scenic than practical route.

N.Y. Route 22

N.Y. 22 skirts the length of Lake Champlain from Whitehall in the south to Ticonderoga, then north through Crown Point and Westport to Plattsburgh and beyond. N.Y. 9N joins N.Y. 22 for part of the journey. With lake views to the east and mountains to the west, it is one of the most scenic of all Adirondack thoroughfares.

East and West

If you thought the five north/south routes were too many to get a handle on, you're in luck. There are only three real options for trans-Adirondack auto travel, and none of them come close to a straight line. From the north, working your way south, the options include the following.

N.Y. Route 3

N.Y. 3 traverses the northern third of the Adirondacks in a northeast to southwesterly direction. Beginning at Plattsburgh on the western shore of Lake Champlain, it runs a fairly straight course southwest to Saranac Lake, then on to Tupper Lake, where it begins a 50-plus-mile stretch of lonely road through the northwest lakes area, including Cranberry Lake. Approximately 40 miles beyond the Park boundary is the city of Watertown, where you can link up with I-81 north or south. By that time, you may very well be thrilled by the sight of 18-wheelers and four fast-moving super-highway lanes.

N.Y. Route 28

Look on any map of the region and you will see the graceful arch of N.Y. 28 as it rises and falls across the lower third of the Adirondacks. From west to east, it takes in many of the most popular recreational areas in the Park, including Old Forge, Raquette Lake, Blue Mountain Lake, Indian Lake, North Creek (home to Gore Mountain), proceeding through Warrensburg and down to the Village of Lake George.

N.Y. Route 8

N.Y. 8 enters the Adirondack Park approximately 25 miles northeast of Utica and zig-zags in a generally northeasterly direction across the lower third of the Park. Along the way, it passes Piseco Lake, Lake Pleasant and Speculator, where it hooks up with N.Y. 30 for a stretch. Beyond to the east is Wevertown (where it crosses with N.Y. 28), Chestertown (where it crosses the Adirondack Northway) and finally the Lake George community of Hague, where N.Y. 8 finishes its journey.

Other Notable Routes

In addition to the aforementioned major thoroughfares, chances are good that you'll encounter one or more of the following routes during your travels through the Adirondacks.

N.Y. Route 86

This route connects some of the Adirondack region's most popular areas in a (mostly) west to east direction, from Paul Smiths to Saranac Lake to Lake Placid and on past Whiteface Mountain to Jay.

N.Y. Route 73

The approximately 40-minute drive along N.Y. 73 from Exit 30 of the Northway west to Lake Placid is one of the most spectacular in the Adirondacks, passing through both Keene and Keene Valley (the "home" of the High Peaks region).

N.Y. Route 374

From Plattsburgh northwest to Chateaugay, N.Y. 374 cuts across the north-east corner of the Adirondack Park. It runs through Dannemora, past Chazy Lake and both Upper and Lower Chateaugay lakes.

N.Y. Route 28N

Forming a "baby arch" atop the big arch of N.Y. 28 (see the previous "East and West" section), this route breaks off the "mother route" at North Creek and wanders through some of the most isolated and beautiful landscapes in the Adirondacks on its way to Long Lake. At about the midpoint is Newcomb, site of one of two Visitor Interpretive Centers in the Park.

N.Y. Route 10

This north/south route serves the lakes of the south-central Adirondacks, including Caroga Lake, Canada Lake and Pine Lake. It ends up at Piseco Lake where it yields to N.Y. 8 (see the previous "East and West" section).

Adirondack Air Travel

As mentioned in the introduction, your opinion of air travel into and around the Adirondacks will depend a lot on your frame of reference. Let's put it this way: You can travel by air into the Adirondacks. Just don't expect in-flight movies, and be thankful you aren't handed a pair of goggles as you embark. There is one airport within the Park that offers commercial air service, and a few more around the perimeter. In addition, there are several private and general aviation airports and airfields

---

INSIDERS' TIP

Remember that I-87 and "the Northway" are one and the same north of Albany. Also, until you get past Exit 10, the Northway is a commuter freeway for the Capital District, so expect heavy traffic during early morning and late afternoon.

that you can fly your own airplane into. (If that's the case, somebody on your staff might be reading this book *for* you.)

We'll look at all the options here. Please note the three-letter abbreviation for each airport in parentheses.

Commercial Air Service

Within the Park

Adirondack Regional Airport (SLK)
N.Y. Rt. 186, Lake Clear • 891-4600

About 4 miles northwest of town, near Lake Clear, Adirondack Regional is the one airport within the Adirondack Park that offers regularly scheduled commercial air service. Commutair, operating as USAirways Express, (800) 428-4322, provides five flights in and out of Saranac Lake on Sunday through Friday. There is no air service on Saturdays. Commutair uses 19-seat turboprops and offers service to Albany, New York, and Burlington, Vermont (see subsequent entry). A small restaurant is available, and you'll find a few newspaper vending machines but no shop. Upon arrival, taxis are available by calling the following services: Adirondack Express, 523-2335; Fletchers Limousine, 359-2339; Gene's, 523-3161; Jan's, 523-1891; La Vignes, 891-2444; Lucky 8, 359-3849; and Northway Limousine, 891-0338. Rental cars are available from the following: Avis, 523-3506; Hertz, 891-4075; and Mason, 891-6686. For those of you piloting your own equipment, the airport sits at an elevation of 1,663 feet and operates from 8 AM until 8:30 PM. There are two runways: one is 6,573-by-150 feet of grooved asphalt; the other, 3,998-by-100 feet of asphalt. Aviation services such as fueling and maintenance are provided by North Country Aviation Inc., which operates from 8 AM until 9 PM, and can be reached by phone at 891-1262.

Near the Perimeter of the Park

The following airports offer regularly scheduled commercial air service and are within a short drive of the Adirondack Park border. The good news is that, from almost any major city in the United States, you are only one air connection and an hour by car from the beauty of the Adirondacks. We will assume that, in this case, you are going to fly one of the commercial airlines into these airports, and therefore we have not included specifics on the airport specs and services for private aircraft. If you are piloting your own equipment, you can fly directly into the Adirondack Regional Airport at Lake Clear (see previous section) or any of the several options listed later in the chapter.

We include the commercial airports as they appear on a map, working clockwise from the northern Adirondack Park border. In particular, the airports at Burlington, Vermont, and

Photo: Plattsburgh/North Country Chamber of Commerce

Beautiful Adirondack landscapes abound along most rural highways.

Albany, New York, offer a healthy schedule of flights on several airlines as well as numerous car rental options. Even though they are outside the Park, these may prove to be the easiest and most convenient "Adirondack" airports to use for long-distance travel.

Clinton County Airport (PLB)
198 Airport Rd., Plattsburgh • 565-4795

Near the western shore of Lake Champlain, this airport is within a half-hour drive of the Adirondack Park boundary. You can get to Lake Placid within an hour's drive. Only one commercial carrier serves the airport — Commutair, operating as USAirways Express, (800) 428-4322. Of its approximately 15 arrivals and departures, most make an eight-minute hop across the lake to Burlington, where connections elsewhere are available. There is some limited service to Albany as well.

The Airport Cafe offers basic coffee shop eats as well as newspapers, magazines and some sundries.

Taxis are available from AAA, 562-1010, and City Taxi, 561-7777. You can obtain rental cars from Avis, 563-4120, and Hertz, 563-2051.

Burlington International Airport (BTV)
Airport Dr., South Burlington, Vt.
• (802) 863-2874

Across Lake Champlain from the Adirondack Park, this airport may not be just a hop and a skip from the Adirondacks, but it is just a car rental and a ferry ride away. You can expect to be in Lake Placid approximately two hours after leaving the airport, including the ferry crossing to Port Kent, New York (see ferry service information later in this chapter). This airport is a convenient option if your destination is the Lake Placid/Tri-Lakes region or the Plattsburgh/Western Lake Champlain region. Burlington International Airport offers approximately 130 daily arrivals and departures and is served by Continental Express, (800) 525-0280, Business Express (Delta), (800) 345-

---

INSIDERS' TIP

Most of the length of the Northway has been increased to a 65 mph speed limit. But from south of Exit 8A (Clifton Park) all the way to the Thruway entrance (about 11 miles), the speed limit is reduced to 55 mph, so be careful!

3400, USAirways and USAirways Express, (800) 428-4322, United and United Express, (800) 241-6522. USAirways offers the most jet service, with six daily flights inbound and outbound to its Pittsburgh hub. United offers two jets inbound and outbound each day, both serving its Chicago hub. The Delta Connection, operating as Business Express, has 11 daily flights to and from Boston.

For food and refreshments, you can choose from either One Flight Up, the full-service restaurant and lounge on the upper level, or a small snack bar on the lower level. Fenton Hills operates two gift shop/newsstands in the terminal as well.

Upon arrival, taxis are available through Commencers, (802) 863-1889. You can rent a car from Avis, (802) 864-0411, Budget, (802) 658-1211, Hertz, (802) 864-7409, or National, (802) 864-7441.

Albany County Airport (ALB)
Dallesandro Blvd., off Albany-Shaker Rd., Albany • 869-5481

Serving the Capital Region of New York State, the Albany County Airport is about an hour's drive from the southern border of the Adirondack Park at Lake George. It is the most convenient option for commercial air travel if your Adirondack destination is either the Lake George/Upper Hudson region or the Southern Adirondack Lakes region. The airport offers nearly 150 inbound and outbound flights daily on 12 airlines. These include the following carriers: Airtran, (800) 247-8726 (offering nonstop flights to and from Orlando); American Airlines, (800) 433-7300 (nonstop jet service to its Chicago hub); American Eagle, (800) 433-7300 (commuter service to JFK International Airport in New York City); Business Express, (800) 345-3400 (Delta's commuter service with flights to JFK and LaGuardia in New York City and Logan Airport in Boston); Continental Express, (800) 525-0280 (commuter service to metro New York City via Newark Airport); Delta Airlines, (800) 221-1212 (nonstop jet service to its hubs in Atlanta and Cincinnati); Downeast Express, (800) 983-3247 (commuter service to Hartford and Portland, Maine); Northwest Airlines, (800) 225-2525 (nonstop jet service to its hub in Detroit); United Airlines, (800) 241-6522 (nonstop jet service to its hub at Chicago O'Hare); United Express, (800) 241-6522

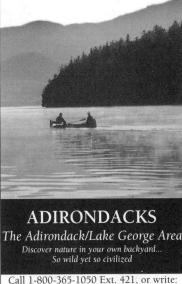

(commuter service to Washington Dulles Airport); USAirways, (800) 428-4322 (by far the biggest carrier in Albany, with more than 90 inbound and outbound flights including nonstop jet service to Baltimore, Charlotte, Philadelphia, Pittsburgh and Washington National Airport); and USAirways Express, (800) 428-4322 (commuter service to several Northeast cities, including New York State communities of Buffalo, Islip at Long Island, Rochester, Syracuse, Plattsburgh and Saranac Lake/Lake Clear).

The Albany County Airport offers a full-service restaurants and lounge on the upper concourse as well as two snack bars. You'll find newspapers and gift items at two locations in the terminal. (Be forewarned, the Albany Airport is in the midst of a massive expansion project that will replace the circa 1959 terminal with a new facility almost double its size. Although much needed, you can expect the usual noise, dust and logistical inconveniences of a major construction project in the months leading up to completion of the new terminal.)

Upon arrival, taxis are available by contacting Airport Taxi, 869-2255, or Carey Limousine Service, 869-8230. Car rental companies serving the airport include Alamo, 786-3967, Avis, 869-8404, Budget, 456-8563, Hertz, 869-6925, and National, 785-3247.

Oneida County Airport (UCA)
Airport Rd., Oriskany • (315) 736-9404

This airport is about midway between the cities of Utica and Rome. Flights arriving here bring you within a 45-minute drive of the southwestern Adirondacks and the Old Forge/Raquette Lake region. Airlines serving the Oneida County airport include USAirways Express, (800)

428-4322, which offers 10 inbound and 10 outbound flights Monday through Friday to cities such as Philadelphia, Boston and New York City. On Saturday that number drops to four, and on Sunday you have five flights to choose from.

You'll find a small coffee shop as well as vending machines with snacks and newspapers in the terminal.

Rental cars are available from Avis, 763-3140, Hertz, 736-5201, National, 736-7625, and Thrifty, 736-4544. You can get a taxi or limo from Frank Brognano Limo, 736-9601.

Watertown International Airport (ART)
Airport Dr., Dexter
• (315) 639-3809

If your destination is the northwest corner of the Adirondacks, you might want to consider flying into Watertown International. However, since it's at least an hour's drive from the Park's border, you might be better off flying directly into the Adirondack Regional Airport (see previous entry) at Lake Clear/Saranac Lake. There are only a couple of flights in and out of Watertown Monday through Friday, provided by Mesa Airlines (operating as USAirways Express), (800) 428-4322.

Your options for renting a car include ADR Leasing, (315) 788-1216, Avis, (315) 788-4141, Dollar, (315) 639-6006, and Thrifty, (315) 788-8364.

Private and General-aviation Airports

For those of you in the enviable position of piloting your own aircraft into the Adirondacks, you have at least five destinations to choose

FYI

Unless otherwise noted, the area code for all phone numbers listed in this guide is 518.

INSIDERS' TIP

If you plan frequent northbound travel along the New York State Thruway (I-87) from metro New York City to Albany, and then beyond to the Adirondacks, keep in mind that Exit 24 at Albany (the entrance to the Northway) can be very busy on weekends. You may want to invest in an E-ZPass electronic tag, which allows you to slip through the traffic in a specially designated lane virtually without delay at toll booths on the Thruway system. Call (800) 222-8655 for details.

from that will land you either in or near the Park. We have listed these airfields as they appear on a map, working clockwise from the north.

Lake Placid Airport (LKP)
Cascade Rd., Lake Placid • 523-2473

Just a mile outside town, across N.Y. 73 from the Olympic ski-jumping complex, the Lake Placid Airport is the most convenient option for landing you smack in the middle of the activity hub for the Adirondacks. The airport operates from 9 AM until 5 PM daily from September through June, then extends its hours to 8 AM until 8 PM during July and August. The airport sits at an elevation of 1,744 feet and has a 4,200-by-50-foot asphalt runway.

Taxis are available from Gene's, 523-3161, and you can rent a car from Hertz, 523-3158, Ken's, 523-4396, and Mason, 891-6686.

General-aviation services, including fueling and maintenance, are available from Adirondack Flying Service, 523-2473. There is no landing fee at Lake Placid Airport; tie-down costs $5 per night.

Ticonderoga Municipal Airport (4B6)
Shanahan Rd., Ticonderoga • 585-9779

Near the northern tip of Lake George, this airport is convenient if your destination is the southern section of Lake Champlain, the northern section of Lake George or the Schroon Lake area. This airport is not attended and has no set operating hours. It sits at an elevation of 250 feet and has one asphalt runway that is 4,000-by-60 feet.

For a rental car, call Wicker Ford at 588-2888.

Keep in mind that there are no general-aviation service companies operating at Ticonderoga, thus there are no landing or tie-down fees or services.

Warren County Airport (GFL)
County Line Rd., Glens Falls • 792-5995

Approximately 12 miles southeast of the village of Lake George, the Warren County Airport is a good option for anyone whose final destination is the Lake George/Upper Hudson region of the Adirondacks. This airport's claim to fame is the Adirondack Balloon Festival, which it hosts in late September (see our Annual Events chapter). Each year, nearly 100 hot-air balloons of all shapes and sizes take off here and soar above the surrounding countryside, to the delight of thousands who gather to watch.

The airport sits at an elevation of 328 feet, and is open for operations 24 hours a day. It offers two runways: a primary runway of grooved asphalt that is 5,000-by-150 feet, and a secondary runway that is 4,000-by-100 feet and paved with asphalt.

General-aviation services are available from Glens Falls Flight Center, 793-5605. For single-engine aircraft and multi-engine aircraft weighing less than 6,000 pounds, there is no landing fee. Multi-engine aircraft weighing more than 6,000 pounds are charged between $15 and $50, depending on the weight. Aircraft tie-downs and parking cost from $5 to $12, again depending on the size of the aircraft.

Half-hour- and hour-long scenic plane rides provide a beautiful aerial introduction to the Lake George region (see our Attractions chapter for details).

Taxi service is available from Adirondack Taxi, 793-4646, City Cab, 793-6666, and the Lake George Taxi Co., 668-9600. If you need to rent a vehicle, your options are A Xpress, 743-1055, Enterprise, 745-5020, Hertz, 792-8525, and Thrifty, 792-2221.

Saratoga County Airport (5B2)
Geyser Rd. (Saratoga County Hwy. 43), Milton • 885-5354

If you are flying your own aircraft and need to get into the Great Sacandaga Lake area of the southern Adirondacks, this is a good option. Although about 20 miles from the nearest Park border, the Saratoga County Airport is convenient to N.Y. 29, which will take you to the southern tip of the Park within 30 minutes driving time. The airport operates from 7:30 AM until sunset, except in the summer months when the rich and famous descend upon Saratoga in their private jets right up until 10 PM. The elevation of the field is 433 feet, and it offers two concrete runways. The primary runway is 4,700-by-100 feet, and a secondary runway is 4,000-by-100 feet.

General-aviation services, including maintenance and fueling, are available from

Richmor Aviation Inc., 885-5354. Landing fees at the Saratoga County Airport only apply during the thoroughbred racing season (late July through Labor Day) and only if no fueling service is required. Otherwise, the fee for twin-engine planes is $12, and $17.50 for jets. Aircraft parking is $5 per night year round.

Taxi service is available from Saratoga Taxi, 584-2700. Your car rental options include Enterprise, 587-0687, and Hertz, 792-8525.

Fulton County Airport (NY27)
off N.Y. Rt. 67, Johnstown • 762-0220

This is another good option if your destination is the Southern Adirondack Lakes region, including the Great Sacandaga Lake. The airport is only about 20 minutes by car from the southern boundary of the Adirondack Park at Mayfield. It also provides easy access to the chain of lakes that runs along N.Y. 29A and N.Y. 10, including Peck Lake, Caroga Lake, Canada Lake and Pine Lake. Airport operating hours are 8 AM until 6 PM. The field sits at an elevation of 881 feet and offers one 4,000-by-75-foot asphalt runway.

Response Aviation, 762-0220, is available to provide aviation services until 8 PM. There is no landing fee at Fulton County Airport, and tie-down costs $4 per night.

For taxi service, call Glove City Taxi at 725-8294. If you need to rent a car, your options include Belvedere Limo, 762-0231, Chrysler, 762-4636, and Penguin, 762-3183.

Piseco Airport (NY43)
off N.Y. Rt. 8, Piseco • 548-8794

This is the one airfield in the interior of the south-central Adirondacks that offers a paved runway. The asphalt runway is 3,015-by-50 feet and sits at an elevation of 1,703 feet. The airport operates from 8 AM until 4:30 PM daily.

Services for aircraft are provided by Piseco Airport Services, 548-8794. It won't cost you anything to land at Piseco Airport, but it will set you back $2.14 per night to park your aircraft.

You're pretty much on your own once you leave the airfield, so don't expect a lineup of cabs. Your best bet is to make sure someone, or someone's car, is there waiting for you.

Malone-Dufort Airport (MAL)
N. Bangor Rd., Malone • 481-5521

If your destination is the far northern reaches of the Adirondack Park, this airport may be a good option for you. It is about 10 miles north of the Park via N.Y. 30. At Malone, you can learn how to parachute, but you can't get fuel for your plane, so you're going to have to pick your priorities. On approach you will find two runways at Malone: a primary, asphalt-paved runway that is 4,000-by-100 feet, and a secondary runway, also asphalt-paved, that measures 3,245-by-75 feet. The airport is open for operation from 8:30 AM until 9 PM.

Malone Aviation, 481-5521 is available for flight instruction and parachute lessons. For aircraft maintenance, contact North Franklin Aviation Services at 483-1063.

If you need a rental car, you can contact Northern Air at 483-7442.

Seaplane Service

In the Old Forge/Raquette Lake area, which features dozens of lakes and ponds strung along one after the other, seaplane travel is a viable and attractive option. Though no regularly scheduled service exists, you can set up charter trips by contacting one of the following companies: Bird's Seaplane Service, Sixth Lake, (315) 357-3631; Helms Aero Service, Long Lake, 624-3931; or Payne's Air Service, Seventh Lake, (315) 357-3971.

Adirondack Train Travel

While train travel to the Adirondacks is not the primary means of getting to the mountains as it was at the turn of the last century, it can still be a scenic, relaxing and enjoyable alternative to fighting the weekend traffic on

INSIDERS' TIP

If you are planning to take a bus into the Adirondacks, don't be surprised if your "station" in these small communities is in the back of a diner, convenience store, sub shop or the like.

Pristine scenes abound throughout the Adirondack region.

the Northway (I-87). That is, provided you're not in a big hurry, and you have arranged transportation once you arrive at the station of choice. The truth is, train service to the Adirondacks will get you close to where you want to go, but probably not as close as you would like.

Amtrak's Adirondack
Penn Station, Seventh Ave. and 32nd St., New York City • (800) USA-RAIL

Your option for train service (notice there was no "s" at the end of "option") is Amtrak's *Adirondack*. This train runs northbound from Penn Station in New York City up along the Hudson River to Albany, takes a quick jaunt west to Schenectady, then veers to the northeast through Saratoga Springs and Glens Falls. From there, it heads pretty much straight up the Champlain Valley along the western shore of Lake Champlain, making stops in Ticonderoga, Port Henry, Westport,

Port Kent, Plattsburgh and Rouses Point before crossing over into Canada on the way to Montreal. As you might expect, the southbound trip repeats the stops beginning with Montreal.

Westport is probably your best bet for hopping off (please, wait for the train to stop!) en route into the interior of the Park. A shuttle service called the CHAMP Express meets the train with its 18-passenger minibuses for the 40-minute transfer to Lake Placid (see the subsequent section on bus travel for more details). You only have one train to choose from each day (Monday through Saturday) in either direction, with the northbound service (currently Train 69) leaving New York City at 8:25 AM, arriving in Westport at 2 PM and scheduled for arrival in Montreal at 5:50 PM. On Sunday, the departure out of New York City (Train 71) is pushed back a couple of hours until 10:35 AM, arriving in Westport at 4:10 PM and scheduled for arrival in Montreal at 8:05

PM. Southbound, the *Adirondack* departs Montreal (Train 68) Monday through Saturday at 10:30 AM, stops at Westport at 2:17 PM and is scheduled for arrival in New York City at 8:10 PM. On Sunday, it (Train 70) leaves Montreal at 12:40 PM, stops in Westport at 4:27 PM and travels on to a scheduled arrival in New York City at 10:10 PM (just in time to get some sleep before the Monday morning "rat race" begins!).

Amtrak is doing an admirable job of customizing this service, adding such features as: equipping the cars to carry skis in the winter; offering regional Champlain Valley food and beverage specialties such as Saranac beer and cheesecake baked by the nuns of New Skete; and printing the menus in both English and French for the convenience of both American and French-Canadian travelers. Be aware, however, that services and the accuracy of travel timetables tend to vary.

Amtrak prints an attractive *Adirondack Travel Guide* that specifically describes this service, and we suggest you check it out first before making any arrangements. For both the guide and more specific information, call the listed number.

Adirondack Bus Travel

For a considerably less elegant yet still serviceable means of getting to the Adirondacks, you can opt for bus travel. You just can't opt for it very often, though, because there is only one bus by one company each day that makes the trip from New York City northbound into the Adirondacks.

Adirondack Trailways
Port Authority Terminal, Eighth Ave. and 41st St., New York City • (800) 858-8555

Adirondack Trailways is the one bus company that serves communities within the eastern third of the Adirondack Park. It has service that departs the Port Authority Terminal in New York City at 10 AM and makes stops in several Adirondack communities, including: Lake George (2:30 PM); Warrensburg (3:05 PM); Chestertown (3:15 PM); Pottersville (3:25 PM); Schroon Lake (3:40 PM); North Hudson (3:55 PM); Keene (4:47 PM); Lake Placid (5:10 PM); and Saranac Lake (5:25

PM). Southbound, Adirondack Trailways stops in Saranac Lake (coming from Canton) at 10:45 AM, continuing on through the same communities on the long journey back to New York City with a scheduled arrival at 6:15 PM. With all the variables involved in bus travel, these schedules are subject to change often, so make sure to call ahead to get specifics. The fare from New York City to Lake Placid, for instance, costs $50 one way and $83.73 round trip.

CHAMP
Main St., at the Hilton Hotel, Lake Placid • 523-4431

Within the Adirondacks, you can use the CHAMP Express for minibus service between Saranac Lake, Lake Placid and the Westport train station (one shuttle each day for drop-off and pickup) as well as two daily shuttles between Ticonderoga and Elizabethtown. The morning shuttle leaves Ticonderoga at 7:25 AM en route to Elizabethtown; it leaves Elizabethtown at 5 PM to return to Ticonderoga. The shuttle to and from the Westport train station costs $15 each way.

Oh Yeah, the Ferries

Last but not least (certainly not in the scenery department!) are the four different ferry crossings you can choose from to get into the Adirondack Park from Vermont, across Lake Champlain. If you drove from parts of New England, or flew into the Burlington International Airport, a ferry ride is going to be tough to avoid. Most times of the year, you won't want to! It's a beautiful trip regardless of where you cross Lake Champlain, with the Adirondack "High Peaks" off on the western horizon and the Green Mountains of Vermont back over your shoulder to the east. Your options are:

Lake Champlain Transportation Company
King Street Dock, King St., Burlington, Vt. • (802) 864-9804

This company operates three of the ferry crossings, and only one operates year around — the commuter service between Grand Isle, Vermont (just north of Burlington), and

Plattsburgh, New York. From Vermont, take Interstate 89 to Exit 17, then follow the signs (about 12 miles) to the ferry. Don't worry about winter crossings; the ferries are enclosed, and the trip takes just 12 minutes across the narrow passage. In fact, your kids will have a great time watching the ice float by on the way across. The Grand Isle ferry costs $6.75 for the car and driver one way, and $12.25 round trip. There are nominal additional charges for extra passengers, and children younger than 6 travel free. This ferry runs from 5 AM until 1 AM — every 20 minutes from 8:40 AM until 9 PM and every 40 minutes the rest of the day.

About 16 miles south of the Grand Isle ferry is the Burlington to Port Kent, New York, ferry. It operates from mid-May through mid-October and makes the crossing at one of the widest points on Lake Champlain. To get here on the Vermont side, take Interstate 89 to Exit 14W, then follow the signs 2 miles to the ferry. The crossing takes just longer than an hour, but you'll be too busy taking in the views to notice. This ferry will land you close to Ausable Chasm, one of the natural wonders of the Adirondack region (see our Attractions chapter). The cost is $12.75 for the car and driver for a one-way trip. The Port Kent ferry service operates from 8 AM until 6:35 PM in the spring and fall, with most departures from Burlington every hour or so. Summer ferry service is more frequent, with departures from Burlington running from 7:45 AM until 7:30 PM.

Travel 10 miles or so farther south and you will come to the Charlotte, Vermont, to Essex, New York, ferry. From the Vermont side, take U.S. Highway 7 to Vt. Highway F-5, then proceed 3 miles to the ferry. Basically, if the lake's not ice-covered, the ferry is running — generally early April to early January. The crossing time is only 20 minutes, and the cost for a one-way passage is $6.75 for you and your car. You get a bit of a break on the round trip, which costs $12.25. The Charlotte ferry operates from 6 AM until 10:30 PM during the summer months, with departures generally every half-hour. That service cuts back to hourly departures from 6 AM until 7 PM in the early spring and late fall/early winter. As always, we suggest you check ahead of time for the most recent fares and schedules.

Shorewell Ferry Co.
Vt. Hwy. 73, Larrabee's Point
• (802) 897-7999

The shortest of all ferry crossings on Lake Champlain (only six minutes), this ferry operates from early May until late October. It departs from the far southern end of the lake, where it is no wider than a river. The ferry operates continuously from 8 AM until 6 PM, except in July and August when it runs until 8 PM. The cost is $6 one way, $10 for a round trip. Although you may not think a six-minute ferry crossing is worth the trouble, it will save you a good hour over driving around the narrow (but still too deep to cross in a car!) southern end of Lake Champlain.

A temperature swing of 75 degrees — from a high of 60 at midday to a low of minus 15 at night — is possible during the winter.

Climate and Outdoor Safety

Climate

If you don't like the weather, just wait a few minutes. If you don't like the weather, just cross to the other side of the street. If you think it's cold out now, just . . .

No matter what you say about the weather in our region, there probably is a degree of truth to the statement. If you say it often enough, it may even become the season's favorite cliché. The weather in the Adirondacks can be bizarre on a good day!

A temperature swing of 75 degrees — from a high of 60 at midday to a low of minus 15 at night — is possible during the winter. A balmy summer day, where you can't wait for a swim in a cool lake, can be followed with an evening where the vegetable garden needs protection against frost. During the peak summer tourist season, the average temperature in the region does not break the 70-degree barrier, topping off at 69 degrees in July and 67 degrees in August. That's cool, and in the evening, it gets even cooler.

While the forecasts for cities such as Boston or New York City indicate sweltering heat waves, 250 miles away in the Adirondacks, humidity disappears and temperatures drop. Our conditions become what everyone else desires. And it is these beautiful warm (but not excessively hot) summer days and comfortable evening temperatures — ideal for sleeping — that earn the region its reputation for being the "cool" summer destination. Cool temperatures also reign from December through March, when the average temperature does not break the freezing mark. During one stretch a few years ago, the daily high didn't even break zero for weeks. When these conditions prevail, the word "cold" barely describes the frigid air. So, the general rule: During the summer, pack a sweater for your travels. During every other season, pack a sweater and a parka. But add to the rule this warning: When you hike, canoe or travel into the Adirondack wilderness, be prepared for the worst. The unpredictable nature of the weather in "this here neck of the woods" can be downright dangerous, while being incredibly beautiful at the same time. The beauty of the region can lull you into a false sense of security — something you definitely should avoid.

Call Me Unpredictable

Exactly why is the North Country's weather so variable? Within a three-hour drive from the St. Lawrence Valley on the western side of the

---

INSIDERS' TIP

Lightning is made up of two stages. The first stage is a leader that advances towards earth in 150-foot stages at 93 miles per second. Once the leader strikes the ground, it is followed by a second return stroke that travels upwards at 31,000 miles per second. The human eye can't distinguish between the two stages, thus we see the entire bolt as being one.

Adirondack Park, through the Adirondack Mountains and into the Champlain Valley on the eastern side, you travel through three very distinct regional climate zones, and within these zones are numerous microclimate zones. If you look at the region from outer space, the Adirondack Mountains rise like a mile-high pimple about 120 miles long by 80 miles wide between the relatively flat Champlain and St. Lawrence valleys. When compared to the great mountain ranges of the world, such as the Alps or Rockies, the Adirondacks are not so tall. They do not cover a large geographic area, are not particularly high and appear only as a minor blemish between two lowland regions. On a global scale of things, the Adirondacks are a mere blip, but as you travel from the valley up the mountains, the temperature drops 3.5 degrees (on average) for every 1,000-foot rise in elevation. So, while it may be balmy in the Champlain Valley, the conditions atop the mountains could kill unprepared trekkers. Great differences also can be experienced from town to town. Lake Placid and Keene Valley, for example, are only 15 minutes apart by car, but when the first crocuses of the season are flowering in Keene, the snow still may cover the gardens in Lake Placid.

The greatest danger of getting trapped in unseasonable conditions occurs during the first signs of spring and fall. During the first warm day of spring, for example, many a hiker dusts off the boots and heads for the trails in every valley beyond the High Peaks. At base camp, spots of snow may be found, along with good old muck and mud. But 1,000 feet up the trail on the shady side of the mountain, the muck remains frozen under literally feet of snow. The possible rain shower in the valley below becomes a snow squall on the mountain, and for the unprepared, it may be too late to run back to the car for warmer clothing. Every year there are new stories to tell about the lost hiker trapped in unseasonable weather conditions. Some of the hikers are amateurs; others, seasoned veterans who have climbed the Himalayas and such. All survivors tell the same story: "It was so nice in the valley, in Albany, in New York City . . . that I never believed it could be so different in the mountains."

It can be, and is, different. Aside from the rise in elevation, another factor can play havoc on the region's weather — the Great Lakes. During the winter months in particular, winds move across the lakes, collecting moisture. The moisture then is deposited, usually as snow, on the western portions of the Adirondacks. Although a snow squall could be dumping a foot of "lake effect" snow in the St. Lawrence Valley, it could be clear and sunny "down the road apiece." In some instances these local snow storms can deposit feet of snow in one town and leave another town a few miles away unscathed. (During winter 1997, some towns were hit with some 7 to 10 feet of snow within a few weeks, while the ground remained barren less than an hour's drive away.)

Although many weather forecasts may predict possible lake effect snow, the range of these storms is highly unpredictable. Generally, lake effect storms are most severe in localized areas near the shores of Lake Erie and Lake Ontario, but sometimes the range of these storms extends into the High Peaks region of the Adirondacks. Three areas in the Adirondacks seem to be affected more than others: Old Forge, Newcomb and Paul Smiths. At times the entire Adirondack region may be barren of snow, but people will be snowmobiling in the snowmobile capital of the region, Old Forge, or cross-country skiing in

www.insiders.com

See this and many other **Insiders' Guide®** destinations online — in their entirety.

Visit us today!

INSIDERS' TIP

The total energy in a thunderstorm exceeds that of an atomic bomb. Although lightning is incredibly powerful, it is of such short duration that its energy cannot be harnessed for practical use.

Paul Smiths. Paul Smiths, the site of one of the two Adirondack Park Visitor Interpretive Centers (VICs), is a real curiosity. In past winters, when the ski trails in Lake Placid — only 25 miles away — were devoid of snow, conditions at the VIC were ideal. Newcomb, the site of the other VIC, is another known snow pocket. Unfortunately, the unusual conditions appear as footnotes in weather forecasts only after they happen, so it is best to prepare for the worst. On the flip side, the weather may be fine during your visit — warm sunny days followed by cool mountain breezes for a good night of summer sleeping, or crisp days of winter with the sun glistening off fresh snow.

What to Wear, What to Bring

What you should bring depends a lot on what you plan to do. Obviously, if you plan to snowshoe up Mount Marcy in the middle of January, you will need to take some serious mountaineering equipment and clothing — and we highly recommend that you consult a knowledgeable guide and do some serious homework on the subject. For those with a slightly less ambitious itinerary, the following serves as a guide.

Shoes

Yes, you should bring shoes — and they should not be new! Break in your hiking boots, jogging or walking sneakers and casual shoes in advance, as no matter what you do, you will do some walking. Those new shoes may make only a small blister, but how that rubbing against a sore can ruin a vacation. For any type of hiking, hiking boots, not sneakers, are recommended. The terrain can be rugged, with exposed tree roots and rocks on the trail. Sneakers provide little cushion when you bang your toe against a root and provide little support for the ankles when a rock slips from underfoot. Treat your hiking boots with a good

water sealant. Even during the dry months of summer, trails still can have wet stretches. Remember that cotton socks can be miserable when wet, so treat yourself to a few pair of woolen or specially designed hiking socks. Wash these before you hike in them to take out the roughness. Insulated, waterproof boots are a necessity during the winter months.

Clothing

No matter what any fashion designer might say, we Adirondackers have a sense of fashion. After all, we have perfected the layered look and the art of the public striptease. We know that the weather can change in a time shorter than a coffee break, so we carry all possible clothing accessories along with us and add or remove them according to our tolerance for warmth or cold. While you may not be caught dead with the sweater over the untucked shirt over the T-shirt elsewhere (not to mention the rain jacket tied by the arms around your waist), it works here because it is practicable. The goal is to be comfortable under all conditions. And being comfortable does distinguish a good vacation from a bad one.

Avoid cottons, which absorb water and do not retain body heat. Wear synthetics in summer and wool in winter.

No matter how short a hike you plan, dressing in layers is a necessity, especially if you chill easily. Changes from sunny sections of a trail to shaded ones can be dramatic, even during the summer. Under some circumstances, the change may be much as 10 degrees, as the crowns of trees not only block out sunlight but also trap cool temperatures near the ground. Children and seniors often have less tolerance for such changes in temperature and thus should carry an extra layer of clothing for both comfort and safety.

During the winter months, layering helps control body temperature and prevent you from overheating. For skiers this layered approach is particularly important, especially as

INSIDERS' TIP

Maine is the only state on the eastern seaboard with more black bears than New York. An estimated 4,000 black bears live in New York, with the vast majority residing in the Adirondacks.

physical activity prompts a sweat. Remove and add layers as necessary to stay comfortable.

And don't forget the rain jacket and pants. Rain shouldn't stop you from enjoying the outdoors; there is still plenty to do in the rain, as long as you are prepared with the proper gear.

Preparations for the Secret Seasons

Every season in the Adirondack region is dramatic in its own special way, but some seasons deserve special mention.

Nature's Light Show — Fall Colors

Beginning in mid-September and continuing through October, the hardwoods begin their spectacular show of color that will dazzle the eye with every shade of red, orange and yellow. What makes the show in the Adirondacks as brilliant as anywhere else? There are an estimated 200,000 leaves on a single, mature birch or beech tree. Within the Adirondack Park's 6 million acres, more than half the trees are hardwoods. With a few hundred hardwoods growing on an acre, and each tree with an average of 50,000 leaves . . . you get the picture — a zillion leaves changing color. But also add a warm fall rain to the picture, followed by sunny breaks — it's magic as the sunlight turns the rain drops into prisms reflecting colors everywhere.

Remember Christopher Columbus? He has nothing to do with the Adirondacks, except that he serves as a reminder that the peak leaf-peeping season occurs around the same time as his holiday in mid-October. The High Peaks region peaks first, with surrounding regions following suit days, possibly weeks, later.

Peak season depends on the weather, but not as is commonly thought. Cold temperatures of fall actually have little to do with the leaves changing color. The shorter days of fall or the decreasing amount of light triggers a response in the tree to shut down the production of food for winter. The tree does this by turning off the flow of chlorophyll, the green stuff in its leaves. As the chlorophyll exits the leaf, the green color also exits to reveal other colors, many of which were always in the leaf but hidden by the green. The cold temperatures don't contribute to this response in any marked way.

Just as the trees prepare for winter, leaf peepers should also be prepared for winter conditions when visiting.

Frigid Days of Winter

We don't boast about it to tourists too much, but a number of record lows in the country often are recorded in the Adirondacks. Sub-zero conditions for extended periods of time are possible, so if you plan on skiing, snowmobiling or doing some other activity outside, you will need Arctic-type clothing that leaves no skin unprotected. We're not kidding about sub-zero conditions, and the temperature is not just a few degrees below zero! When an Arctic air mass settles on the region, nighttime temperatures have been known to hover around 30 degrees below zero. Daytime conditions often are not much better. Add a slight wind, and you will wonder how Santa Claus ever survives at the North Pole because people can't survive these conditions for long. At times, conditions get so cold that the major recreational areas close because of the danger of frostbite. So, heed our warning if you plan on

The rolling rugged Adirondack landscape lures adventurous
outdoor enthusiasts from far and wide.

enjoying the outdoors during the winter. As you prepare to make your winter fashion statement, you also need to remember to prepare your car accordingly. Check your antifreeze and battery, and change your oil to a cold-weather grade. Also check the air in your tires regularly during cold spells, as the tires tend to deflate. Strange as it may seem, don't forget your sunglasses. The sun reflects brilliantly off white snow — a potential hazard to your eyes.

Mud Season

When the winter snow melts, mud grows long before the flowers do. Conditions can be rather yucky, so bring along boots. April is the yuckiest month, and at times, the cruelest. Those April showers that bring May flowers sometimes dump as much as a foot of snow!

Blackfly Season

There are some 26 species of blackflies found in the Adirondacks, but you need be aware of only two. There is the mid-May to early June fly, *Prosimulium mixtum*, and the one that appears from May to early July, *Simulium venustum*. These flies, a mere one-sixth-inch long, seek out humans to bite. Fortunately, only female flies bite — about half the population. Unfortunately, the bite is nasty and draws blood.

There are some secrets to diminish the attacks by these vampire-like flies. Since they are attracted to carbon dioxide, you can try not breathing. If that is inappropriate, some studies suggest that they are particularly attracted to people wearing shades of blue, purple and purple-red but avoid citrus orange, yellow and bright green. Bug hats with netting covering the head, face and neck are commonly used and can be purchased for approximately $15 in sporting good stores. Don't be embarrassed wearing one on the golf course — or anywhere else. Blackflies will find exposed skin of any kind, so if they are particularly attracted to you, don't wear shorts and short-sleeve shirts. Many bug sprays work and will limit the bites. Try various sprays, as some work better than others. If one doesn't work, try another. Pay close attention to bites on children.

The dreaded fly is short-lived; the season lasts only a few weeks. Strangely enough, not all people are bothered by the flies.

Outdoor Safety

Within the Adirondack region there are thousands of miles of hiking trails. The vast majority are clearly marked and, with the aid of a trail guide or map and a compass, relatively easy to follow. They are not necessarily easy to hike, however, especially if the couch has been your best friend lately.

How do you select the best hike for you and your family? Promotional brochures describe the Adirondacks as the greatest wilderness area east of the Mississippi. And we do mean wilderness. No human settlements — and perhaps no humans — will be seen for 20, 40 or 60 mile stretches, such as along the famed Lake Placid to Northville trail. On other less traveled trails, you might not see any hikers, so while the solitude may be just what the doctor ordered, you also need to realize that no doctor will magically appear if you suddenly twist your ankle. You and your party will have no choice but to deal with whatever problem occurs.

As you consider a backcountry experience, you must answer one basic question: How confident are you to deal with a crisis on the trail? There are many details to consider: Do you know what to do if you get lost? Are your first-aid skills sufficient to handle a twisted ankle or a severe cut? Can you set up camp in an emergency? Are you physically capable of the challenge? Don't kid yourself about how good of shape you are in. A trail guide may indicate a hike of only a mile, but a steep grade uphill can turn the trek into a mile-long nightmare if your body is not accustomed to the exercise. For long, extended hikes deep into the backwoods, you must be able to answer the previous (and similar) questions affirmatively and with total confidence in your abilities. Confidence comes with experience, and while we may have been boy or girl scouts in the distant past, the Adirondack backwoods is not the place to relive what we thought we once knew. It could be very dangerous.

Safe Hiking

To better ensure a safe and enjoyable hike, remember the following basic rules of thumb:

• **Don't Overdo It!** You don't have to hike the tallest mountain, the toughest trail, the greatest distance to have a meaningful back-woods experience. There are some great sites and trails that will meet all your require-ments, so don't immediately jump on the recommendations of others. A trail may be a great hike, but it may not be right for you. That "oh, it's not that bad of a hike" actually may be a truly bad hike if it is too difficult for your situation. Plan your hikes carefully. If you can, ask specific questions about the trail in advance and consider your physical abilities realistically.

•**Never Hike Alone.** Companions are for safety as well as for sharing the experience. In an emergency, there is safety in numbers. This raises a perplexing issue. During peak hiking season (in summer and early fall), many of the most popular trails are crowded with people. And as overuse is causing severe dam-age to certain trails in the region, various agen-cies are recommending alternative trails. So which trail do you select — the popular and crowded one, or the less traveled path? De-pending on your experience and abilities, per-haps the alternative trail is not your best choice. Perhaps you would feel more comfortable hik-ing the crowded trail, secure in the notion that, in case of an emergency, someone will soon be by to help you. Consider this dilemma care-fully.

•**Never Keep Secrets.** Always sign in and out at trail registers and provide accurate in-formation. Rangers take these registers seri-ously and will make inquiries about those who fail to check out, so give them the courtesy of a good-bye note. Also let others know about your plans: What is your route, your destina-tion and your anticipated arrival time back home? Let the front desk at your hotel know about your plans. Those sitting home are your best safety net and will be the ones to send in the troops if you fail to return on time. Keep them informed.

•**Don't Drink the Water.** Bring plenty of high-energy food — trail mix, candy bars and fruit — and water. Each person should carry a minimum of two quarts of water in an un-breakable container for an average day-long hike. Bring more water on strenuous hikes. Although the water may look crystal clear and drinkable, all water sources are considered contaminated by giardia protozoan, which causes "beaver fever," an intestinal disorder characterized by nausea, vomiting and diar-rhea. Although the disease is not deadly, its effects are extremely uncomfortable. Use wa-ter purifiers, iodine tablets or bring water to a rolling boil for a full five minutes to kill pos-sible contaminants. Don't underestimate the hunger and thirst of kids. Consider doubling their usual intake of food and drink, as they will quickly burn off the nourishment and ask for more.

•**Be Prepared.** What's the worst that could happen? Prepare for it. Generally, this means you should carry a map and compass (as-suming that you know how to read a trail map), a flashlight, waterproof matches or some other illumination, a first-aid kit and gear appropri-ate for the hike and potential emergencies. Also consider sunscreen, insect repellent and rain gear. Naturally you will make choices as to what is appropriate for your particular hike and leave certain items behind. The choice shouldn't be a casual one, especially if you are unfamiliar with the trail or it's off the beaten path. It remains a cliché, but it is better to be safe than sorry, especially if you are traveling with kids.

•**Whistles, Whistles, Whistles.** If you de-cide to carry only one item, carry a whistle. It is far easier to blow a whistle than to yell for help hours on end if you get lost or hurt. Chil-dren need to be taught that the whistle is not a toy and is to be used in an emergency only.

Trail Etiquette

Carry it in, carry it out. That means *every-thing*. Just because an item is biodegradable doesn't mean you should toss it aside or bury it. Carry a plastic garbage bag into the backcountry with you, and bring your trash out with you. (For smokers, this also means cigarette butts.)

How to Poop in the Woods

With thousands of people potentially hik-ing a trail every year, human waste can cause serious ecological problems. On many popu-lar trails, privies or outhouses are provided, especially near campsites. Use them, as they will minimize the human impact on an area. When privies are not an option, human waste

In late fall, Adirondack hardwoods shed their many colored and shaped leafy garb.

should be buried under 4 inches of soil — not just beneath fallen leaves or forest duff — and be at least 150 feet from any source of water. While many point to beavers as the cause of beaver fever, humans continue to contribute to the problem. Remember to pack the one item most people forget to bring on a hike — your own toilet paper.

Respect Trail Signs

Always pay attention to and abide by posted trail signs, especially those on Alpine summits. Trail signs are posted for your safety, so stay on marked trails. On various alpine summits, trail signs also urge you to walk on rocks and avoid stepping in areas with even the smallest bits of soil. Amazing as it seems, a little patch of soil may be the result of hundreds of years of work by nature, and a single misplaced foot can trample away this handiwork in an instant. The summits of a number of Adirondack mountains are home to a variety of endangered Alpine plants. Join the effort to protect them by respecting trail signs.

If You Get Lost . . .

What to do if you get lost? First and foremost, don't panic. Stay dry, keep warm and stay put. Such rules are easier said than done, but they will save your life. If you can, build a fire for your own heat and comfort as well as for a beacon to help searchers locate you. In addition to searching for lost hikers on foot, rescue teams use motorized vehicles when possible, including aircraft. A fire is invaluable because it easily can be spotted from the air. If the weather is particularly cold, and you have to spend a night in the woods, build a shelter using dead wood, boughs from evergreens and dead leaves. Keep the shelter small — just big enough to fit you snugly and comfortably. Shelters are particularly important if the conditions are wet, as one trick in staying warm is staying dry. Consider your options before nightfall, and set up your shelter in the daylight hours if possible.

Remember, water flows downhill. If you are physically capable and feel that you can find your way out, follow streams; they nearly always lead to some sign of civilization. You need to consider your physical state carefully. Do you have the energy and skills to find your way, or is it better to stay put?

In case of an accident, one person should stay with the injured person, if possible. When a party leaves the injured person, don't overestimate your skills in locating the person again. Half the battle is getting help, but the other half is returning to the injured person. Look for and remember details! Your best safety net is letting someone know your schedule and your plans before you venture out on the trail. Contact forest rangers about your friends in the backcountry who are late and long overdue.

Fun Outdoor Facts

A Blanket of Clouds

Why is it colder on nights without clouds? The sun emits many different kinds of radiation. Some of it is light, some is felt as heat and some is not sensed at all. On cloudy days, short-wave radiation passes through the clouds and helps heat soil and water, especially the ocean. This heat then is radiated back into the atmosphere in the form of long-wave radiation. This long-wave radiation cannot penetrate cloud layers and remains trapped between the clouds and the ground. Thus, clouds act as a blanket, holding in heat. On cloudless nights, without this heat-trapping blanket, this radiation escapes into the atmosphere.

Big Black Bears

Black bears are one of the largest yet least often sighted mammals in the Adirondacks. Males are generally much larger than females. How large do black bears get? Males grow to about 60 to 70 inches tall and weigh 300 pounds on average. Some, however, can reach 600 pounds. Females range from 50 to 60 inches in height and weigh 150 to 200 pounds. Bears tend to be secretive, nocturnal animals and have a limited range of habitat, making them difficult to spot in the wild. Sightings usually occur around sites with "people food," such as dumps and campgrounds. An observant hiker can find signs of bear activity. Look for broken limbs on fruit trees, beehives or bee-inhabited trees that have been torn apart, dug up stumps and overturned rocks.

There is a huge variety of independently owned motels, cabin complexes and cottage resorts scattered throughout the Adirondacks.

Accommodations

OK, so here's a sobering statistic for all of you who love to endlessly browse through brochures in search of the perfect place to stay on your vacation. You potentially could look through a stack of more than 750 of them in planning your Adirondack trip — that's how many hotels, motels, resorts, cabins, cottage complexes, country inns and bed and breakfast inns there are listed in the Adirondack Tourism Council's *Accommodations Guide*. Granted, not every place prints a brochure, but the choices are overwhelming. For example, in the Lake George area alone, more than 150 lodging choices are available.

We'll come clean right up front and admit that we only include a small selection of all that's out there for you to choose from. Our goal is to give you a representative sample of what to expect in the Adirondacks in terms of lodging, so that you can pick and choose your location and your priorities. If you want a quiet, rustic cabin on a peaceful lake — we have that. If you want a bustling, highly acclaimed resort with its own island, golf course and cruise boat — we have that too. If you want a quaint country inn with its own network of cross-country ski trails, guess what? We have that too. You simply need to decide what type of adventure you want, or commit to coming back every year so you can try out every type of adventure that's here.

With a few exceptions, the lodging properties we list here are open on a year-round basis. We include only seasonal properties in cases where there are very few or no year-round lodging options available in that area, or if their reputations and facilities are particularly outstanding. In any event, we let you know in each listing.

We divide our accommodations into two categories: "Resort Hotels and National Chains"; and "Motels, Cabins and Cottage Resorts." For bed and breakfast inns and country inns, see the separate chapter that follows this one. For campgrounds, see the Camping chapter. Makes a lot of sense so far, doesn't it?

Within "Resort Hotels and National Chains," we include lodging properties that offer a wide variety of amenities and activities — golf, tennis, spas, horseback riding, etc. — and properties that fly a "flag" (that is, they're affiliated with a national chain such as Holiday Inn or Ramada). We know some folks prefer the known commodity a chain provides, not to mention the frequent-traveler bonus points.

There is a huge variety of independently owned motels, cabin complexes and cottage resorts scattered throughout the Adirondacks. We include them here under "Motels, Cabins and Cottage Resorts." In many cases, these places have been owned and operated by the same families for generations — and visited by the same families year after year for generations as well. Although they don't have name recognition or sprawling grounds, these can be real finds that serve up a perfect getaway for two, or a fun-filled family vacation. After all, the real attraction in most cases is what's outside the front door, so don't overlook such establishments in your search.

Now, some assumptions. Unless we state otherwise, lodging properties listed here accept major credit cards, offer heat and air conditioning, color/cable TV, housekeeping service, ice and vending machines. Also, as much as these properties would love to have you visit, unless we mention otherwise, you'll need to leave your pets at home.

If special considerations such as handicapped accessibility and nonsmoking rooms are a priority to you, we suggest you call and confirm availability with the accommodation of your choice before making a reservation. As a rule, the larger the accommodation, the better the chance that it offers such a specific type of rooms. Another issue you'll want to address, particularly if you're planning to visit in July or August (by far the two busiest months) is if there are any minimum-stay requirements. Many of the cottage resorts require a one-week stay during those months, so be sure to ask about it.

One last thing to help you find what you're looking for in this chapter: We arrange our listings for both lodging categories within each region, recognizing that you will probably choose an area to visit first, then look for accommodations within that region. Lodging choices in each category are presented in alphabetical order within each town, and each town is listed in alphabetical order as well. For example, within the Lake Placid/Tri-Lakes Region, all accommodations for each category will be listed for Lake Placid (in alphabetical order) prior to any listings for Saranac Lake. It sounds more confusing than it is.

For a good "one-stop" accommodations listing for the Adirondacks, it's tough to beat the *Accommodations & Camping Guide* published by the Adirondack Regional Tourism Council. To get a copy, write them at P.O. Box 51, West Chazy, N.Y. 12992 or call (518) 846-8016.

FYI

Unless otherwise noted, the area code for all phone numbers listed in this guide is 518.

Price Code

We include a price code for your reference that will give you an idea of what to expect in lodging costs during your Adirondack visit. The code is based on an average double occupancy rate during peak season. In other words, this is the range you can expect to pay for one night, two people, on a summer weekend.

Price-code Key

$	Less than $60
$$	$60 to $80
$$$	$80 to $120
$$$$	More than $120

Lake Placid/ Tri-Lakes Region

Resort Hotels and National Chains

Best Western Golden Arrow Hotel
$$$ • 150 Main St., Lake Placid • 523-3353

The Golden Arrow is one of the few hotels directly on Mirror Lake, and the view from this place is breathtaking. All the 130 rooms in this full-service hotel are large, with two doubles or a king-size bed and accompaniments typical of such national chains.

A private, white sandy beach is available for sun and fun during the summer months, and guests also have free use of canoes and boats. The heated indoor pool and a small but well-equipped gym are open year round. Suites and condos with fireplaces and Jacuzzis are also available. Goldberries family-style restaurant, Tiffany Lounge and Roomers Night Club are part of the complex, as is a well-appointed conference center.

As with most full-service facilities in the region, package deals often are available, so be sure to ask.

Howard Johnson Resort Lodge
$$$ • Saranac Ave., Lake Placid • 523-9555, (800) 654-2000

This full-service resort offers conference and banquet facilities, an indoor swimming pool with Jacuzzi, free boating and tennis, access to its own hiking, biking and cross-country ski trails and its award-winning Ho-Jo's restaurant.

The complex has received Howard Johnson's Five Star Quality Assurance Award for the past six years, so it is obviously doing everything right. There are 92 guest rooms, including suites. The lodge can accommodate as many as 425 guests in its largest reception area. A tropical atrium with a sun room, bar and pool makes for a relaxing setting.

LAKE PLACID RESORT

Hotel and Golf Club

" In the center of the village, overlooking the lake."

199 Room full service Resort Hotel. All rooms have a coffee maker, microwave, and refrig.freezer. Rooms & suites with fireplaces & jacuzzis also available. Chalets and condos. Amenities include two 18-hole championship golf courses, 9-hole short course, 11 tennis courts, private beach, health club, indoor pool, four unique restaurants, narrated boat tours, and 26,000 square feet of event & meeting space. Vacation packages including golf and skiing from $49 to $89 per person.

To make reservations call 1-800-874-1980

Resort Golf House

1 Olympic Dr., Lake Placid, NY 12946 (518)523-2556   http://lpresort.com • info@lpresort.com

Lake Placid Hilton
$$$ • One Mirror Lake Dr., Lake Placid • 523-1120

The Hilton, a three-building complex on Main Street, is one of the larger conference facilities in the village with more than 10,000 square feet of meeting and banquet space, suitable for every size group.

The main building features the Terrace Room Restaurant and the Dancing Bear Lounge, an indoor pool and Jacuzzi, outdoor pool, game room and conference rooms. An indoor pool, Jacuzzi, exercise room and game room also are available in the Lakeside building. The smallest of the three buildings overlooks Mirror Lake. All rooms are large and are appointed with either double and queen-size beds. And the Hilton's famed Sunday brunch, at approximately $12 per person, remains one of the best deals around.

Lake Placid Hilton offers various discount packages throughout the year, including a family plan where kids younger than 18 stay free.

Lake Placid Resort
$$$ • One Olympic Dr., Lake Placid • 523-2556, (800) 874-1980

In the early part of the 1900s, Lake Placid began building its reputation as the winter sports capital of the world through the efforts of Melvin Dewey, at the Lake Placid Club, who introduced to visitors the pleasures of winter activities such as sledding and skiing. The main lodging facility of the original club (the building closed long ago) was recently destroyed by fire, but the spirit of the Lake Placid Club lives on in what is now known as Lake Placid Resort.

Lake Placid Resort is comprised of the former Lake Placid Club, with its historic golf course, boathouse and buildings, and facilities known as the Grandview Sunspree Resort, or as the locals know it, the Holiday Inn. The combined facilities make Lake Placid Resort one of the largest full-service resorts in the entire region, with a private beach club on Mirror Lake, a championship golf course and a host of other recreational activities available on site, including cross-country skiing, boating, tennis and fishing.

The main lodging facility provides 209 rooms, 13 suites and six rooms with fireplaces and Jacuzzis. A few chalets with fireplaces also are available. There are some 14 meeting rooms in the main complex, ranging from small spaces for up to 30 people to large reception rooms accommodating 1,000 that are among the largest in the entire Adirondack region. The complex also houses a health club with a pool, sauna, whirlpool and computerized exercise equipment.

Artiro's serves as the dining and entertainment facility in the main lodge, and three additional facilities are offered at other sites. The elegant Veranda Restaurant, across the street from the lodge, offers an international bill of fare in a casual Adirondack setting with terrace views of Mirror Lake. The Boat House restaurant, above the resort's beach facilities on Mirror Lake, provides casual dining with spectacular views rivalled only by those at the Golf House Restaurant. The Golf House, which overlooks the golf course, serves continental cuisine, as does the Boat House.

Lake Placid Resort has planned a great many renovations over the next few years for all Lake Placid Club properties.

Mirror Lake Inn

$$$$ • 5 Mirror Lake Dr., Lake Placid • 523-2544

"Exceptional." "Exquisite." "A Classic." "Memorable." Pick a compliment from any review. For 11 consecutive years, Mirror Lake Inn has earned kudos from reputable publications. It seems likely that the 124-room inn will continue to earn its rating for excellence because it consistently pays attention to its guests, offering an array of services you might expect of a first-class facility plus a few extras, such as a spa and a skin- and hair-care salon.

The inn offers a range of rooms, from doubles with private balconies overlooking Mirror Lake to split-level "Placid Suites," each with a private whirlpool and balcony. All rooms are tastefully decorated.

A private beach, two indoor swimming pools, conference facilities, tennis courts and, during the winter, a ice rink on the lake are available to guests. The on-site restaurant is known throughout the area for its fine dining and view.

Ramada Inn

$$$ • 8-12 Saranac Ave., Lake Placid • 523-2587

The Ramada overlooks Mirror Lake, and many of its 90 rooms afford views of the lake and the mountains. All rooms feature coffee makers and data-port phone jacks and include either a queen-size bed or two double beds.

This hotel, like all other full-service facilities in the area, offers an indoor swimming pool, whirlpools, exercise equipment (treadmill, stepper, cycle and Cross Trainer), game rooms and business meeting and banquet rooms for as many as 200 guests. It also features a good family restaurant (Nik's Place) in a beautiful greenhouse setting overlooking Mirror Lake.

The Ramada is walking distance to all of the shops on Main Street. Be sure to ask about local discount coupons to area attractions and lift tickets to Whiteface Mountain.

Adirondack Comfort Inn

$$ • 148 Lake Flower Ave., Saranac Lake • 891-1970

This 69-room full-service hotel offers everything that you'd expect of a Comfort Inn — cable TV, complimentary coffee and newspapers, and coin-operated washers and dryers — plus a touch of the Adirondacks. There's an indoor pool, meeting rooms and a family-style restaurant on the premise plus an outdoor pond and Lake Flower across the street for your boating and fishing pleasure.

Hotel Saranac

$$ • 101 Main St., Saranac Lake • 891-2200

The Hotel Saranac was acquired by Paul Smith's College in 1961 and has been operated as a full-service hotel and educational facility. As many of the staff are students — yes, they're graded on their performance — the quality of service is always exceptional.

The hotel has long served as the focal point of downtown Saranac Lake. The 92 rooms, including five minisuites, are tastefully appointed.

Dining is available in one of three restaurants, and all benefit from the culinary expertise of the award-winning chef/instructors of the college. Every Thursday evening a team of students prepare a special feast for the "Thursday Night Buffet." The buffet serves as a big part of the students' final grade, so they try to outdo the previous team's effort, resulting in a meal to write home about for less than $15 per person. The menu varies every week, and we suggest you make reservations early, especially during the summer. No question in our minds (or stomachs) — the Thursday Night Buffet represents the best deal in the entire region.

The Hotel Saranac also offers five banquet rooms with a maximum capacity of 400 guests, a gift shop, bakery and travel agency. Although there are no recreational facilities, the hotel makes up for it in ambiance and service.

Motels, Cabins and Cottage Resorts

Lakeshore Motel
$$ • 54 Saranac Ave., Lake Placid • 523-3113

The 23-room Lakeshore Motel sits on the shore of Lake Placid. The accommodations are comfortable, with many rooms offering lakefront views. Patrons can enjoy free use of rowboats, canoes or paddleboats (or bring your own boat), a barbecue area and private sandy beach for swimming or fishing. The motel is easy walking distance to Main Street.

Mountain View
$$$ • Main St., Lake Placid • 523-2439, (800) 499-2668

Mountain View is a small motel that overlooks Main Street, making it convenient to all facilities in the village. All 20 rooms, which offer double or king-size beds, recently have been completely refurbished, and most come equipped with microwaves and small refrig-

erators. A private beach on Mirror Lake is available to guests.

Placid Bay Motor Inn
$$$ • 70 Saranac Ave., Lake Placid • 523-2001

This motor inn, situated on the shore of Lake Placid and conveniently located in the Main Street area, offers 21 rooms, some with kitchenettes, suites and cottages. The cottages can accommodate a family of eight.

Swiss Acres Inn
$$ • 189 Saranac Ave., Lake Placid • 523-3040, (800) 464-4690

The Swiss Acres Inn and Restaurant is a family-owned and operated establishment just minutes from Main Street in Lake Placid. The 40-room inn offers an outdoor pool, hot tub and sauna as well as a comfortable lounge. Family units with kitchenettes and group packages are available.

The restaurant serves international and American fare at very reasonable prices. The breakfast special in particular is a real bargain at $2.50.

Four Seasons Motor Lodge
$$ • N.Y. Rt. 86, Wilmington • 946-2247

If you can't wait to get to the slopes, or need a midday nap after a morning of skiing, this 25-room hotel at the base of Whiteface

Mountain fills the bill. All rooms have two double beds. It's just a 10-minute drive to Lake Placid from here.

Hungry Trout Motor Inn
$$ • N.Y. Rt. 86, Wilmington • 946-2217, (800) 766-9137

Whiteface Mountain is a good snowball's heave away as is the famed Ausable River, making this inn a good base camp for skiing or fishing. This quality-rated motor inn offers spacious rooms with picture-window views of the nearby mountains. Each room has an in-room coffee maker, cable TV, private bath and telephone. Two-room suites with kitchenettes are available — perfect for families.

Pioneer Village
$$ • N.Y. Rt. 86, Ray Brook • 891-4572, (800) 625-4572

Pioneer Village provides housekeeping cottages and campsites. Each of the 14 cottages sleeps five and provides just the basics — towels and linens. A small playground and barbecue grills are available. If you have a family, want to cook out a bit, don't want to spend the big bucks and intend to hike and fish the Tri-Lakes area, this place is a good deal.

Gauthier's Saranac Lake Motor Inn
$$ • 143 Lake Flower Ave., Saranac Lake • 891-1950

This 31-unit motel on Lake Flower is one of the larger ones in the area. Most rooms at this basic lodging have two double beds, others have one king bed. Canoes and boats are free to guests.

Sara-Placid Motor Inn
$$ • 120 Lake Flower Ave., Saranac Lake • 891-2729, (800) 794-2729

This 17-room motor inn across the street from Lake Flower offers motel rooms, suites and housekeeping units by the day or week. All the motel units, which have been recently remodeled, offer king-size beds, and some include kitchenettes. The one- and two-bedroom housekeeping units offer full kitchenettes with dinnerware and appliances.

Paddleboats and barbecue grills are avail-

able to all guests. An added bonus for guests is the public park directly across the street with lighted tennis and basketball courts.

Shaheen's Motel
$$ • N.Y. Rt. 30, Tupper Lake • 359-3384

This 33-unit motel is one of the larger ones in the Tupper Lake area. The basic rooms are large, clean and comfortable. An outdoor heated pool is open during warm months.

Adirondack Hotel
$$ • N.Y. Rt. 30, Long Lake • 624-4700, (800) 877-9247

This small, 19-room hotel, built in 1853, is one of the few historic hotels remaining in the Adirondacks. The unique blend of Victorian and Adirondack rustic design stands out, as does the view of Long Lake from here. Rooms with private baths are available at a slightly higher rate than those with shared baths.

The hotel features two restaurants, one for light fare, the other for fine dining in a classic Adirondack rustic setting.

Plattsburgh/Western Lake Champlain Region

Resort Hotels and National Chains

Budgetel Inn
$$ • 16 Plaza Blvd., Plattsburgh • 562-4000

With 107 rooms, this is one of the larger budget hotels in the region. The inn offers various room options with twin doubles, one queen- or one king-size bed per room. A number of rooms for the budget-minded business person include data ports for portable computer or fax equipment. An indoor swimming pool and spa also are available.

The inn offers a few nice touches, such as free local calls, in-room coffee makers and a free continental breakfast served in the room. It is conveniently near the shopping area along N.Y. Route 3.

Comfort Inn
$$ • 411 N.Y. Rt. 3, Plattsburgh • 562-2730

This motel bills itself as an "affordable resort." Your kids will surely agree, as the facility includes an indoor pool with a 70-foot slide, a family fun center with arcade games, a laser-tag room, racquetball courts, weight rooms and an on-site brewpub serving 10 of its own different beers. The inn continues to expand its offerings in the recreational area; plans for a disco and miniature golf course are in the works. Meeting facilities for up to 160 people are available.

Standard rooms include two double beds and a refrigerator. You'll also find suites, handicapped-accessible units and rooms with a whirlpool.

Days Inn of Plattsburgh
$$ • 8 Everleth Dr., Plattsburgh • 561-0403

This member of the national chain offers 112 rooms with a choice between a queen or two double beds per room. An indoor and outdoor pool are available for guests, along with a Jacuzzi, game room and small fitness room. A free continental breakfast of toast, muffins, bagels, doughnuts and beverages is served daily in a small coffee lounge. Like most other accommodations along the shopping district on N.Y. Route 3, this inn offers comfortable accommodations at a reasonable price — just don't expect a lot of great scenery right outside your door. A few mountains can be seen in the distance, but I-87 Exit 37 is amid the best view that this highly commercial shopping district has to offer.

Econo Lodge
$$ • N.Y. Rt. 3, Plattsburgh • 561-1500

The Econo Lodge is a bargain for traveling families. You'll find an indoor and outdoor swimming pool, and the rooms are clean and comfortable. This 125-room lodging, the largest in the Plattsburgh area, provides an indoor and outdoor pool. It is near the N.Y. 3 shopping malls and access to I-87.

Howard Johnson
$$ • 446 N.Y. Rt. 3, Plattsburgh • 561-7750

With 120 guest rooms, HoJo's is one of the largest full-service facilities in the Plattsburgh region. Queen, king and twin double beds are available. Guests can enjoy the indoor pool, game room and exercise room with rowing machines and an eight-station workout. An in-house restaurant and lounge also are available.

Meeting rooms can be arranged to serve small business groups of as many as 475 guests. Like other full-service facilities, arrangements can be made to meet all business and catering needs.

The hotel is adjacent to the Champlain Center North mall complex and surrounded by small strip malls, so while shopping opportunities are great, the scenery isn't.

Ramada Inn
$$ • N.Y. Rt. 3, Plattsburgh • 561-5000

This 102-room Ramada Inn is one of the larger hotels in the Plattsburgh region. Most rooms are spacious, with 12 king-size rooms available. Three on-site banquet rooms can accommodate parties of 50 to 275 people. The standard amenities include a large heated indoor pool, a health spa and a comfortable restaurant and lounge. The Ramada is conveniently located near the major malls (see Shopping), just off I-87 Exit 37.

Super 8 Motel
$$ • N.Y. Rt. 9N, Plattsburgh • 562-8888

On the north end of town, a few miles from the major shopping malls, this 61-room Super 8 offers what the chain is known for — basic, economical lodging. An indoor pool and conference rooms are available.

INSIDERS' TIP

The New York State Hospitality & Tourism Association prints a good map of New York State that also serves as a travel guide and accommodation listing. While limited to its membership, the guide still offers a good variety of options and is a useful resource. NYSHTA also has a free room-reservation service for anywhere in New York State; call (800) ENJOY NY. For a copy of the NYSHTA map, call (518) 465-2300.

Charming accommodations are springing up throughout the Adirondacks.

Photo: Plattsburgh/North Country Chamber of Commerce

Motels, Cabins and Cottage Resorts

Marine Village Cottages
$$ • 82 Dickson Point Rd., Plattsburgh • 563-5698

On Lake Champlain, 9 miles from downtown Plattsburgh, Marine Village has 25 three-bedroom housekeeping cottages six two- and three-bedroom mobile homes and trailer sites. Facilities easily accommodate a family of six to eight. During summer, guests can bring their own towels and linens or rent them for $12 per week. Kitchens in all units include a small stove, refrigerator and basic utensils. Units generally rent on a weekly basis. Although there are no organized recreational activities, a beach, playground, sports fields and boat docks are available.

Villa Motel
$$ • 1875 U.S. Hwy. 9, Keeseville • 834-7579

A mile south of Ausable Chasm (see Attractions), this 60-unit motel offers just the ba-

sics. It's not fancy, but it is a clean and comfortable place to lay your head. An outdoor pool is available. The motel also offers good deals on housekeeping units.

Cedars On the Lake
$$ • 3666 U.S. Hwy. 9, Peru • 562-1552

The nine cabins here offer basic sleeping accommodations (single, twin or double beds) for two to eight people, a TV and private bathroom facilities. Although the one- and two-bedroom cabins are sparsely decorated, you'll hardly notice since the view from the cabin door overlooks Lake Champlain. The facility offers a private beach, boats for guests and docking space for folks who bring their own watercraft. The cabins are available May through October.

Davis Motel and Housekeeping Cottages
$$ • U.S. Hwy. 9, Schroon Lake • 532-7583

This complex is situated on 10 acres and provides an unusual array of services for such a small facility, including playgrounds, shuffleboard and basketball courts, lawn games and a beach. Various types and sizes of motel rooms are available, including some efficiencies. Each of the cottages — most flank the lake — has a comfortably furnished living room, two or three bedrooms, an electric kitchen and a complete bath. Boat rentals and dockage also are available.

Dun Roamin' Cabins
$$ • U.S. Hwy. 9, Schroon Lake
• 532-7277

Before the Northway (I-87) existed, U.S. 9 was the primary road into the heart of the Adirondacks. Nowadays, drivers zip past towns like Schroon Lake at 65 mph and never realize what they are missing. When you are Dun Roamin', or done speeding as the case may be, check into one of these little cabins in Schroon Lake. People relaxed in them long before superhighways existed — and they still relax in them today.

This nine-cabin complex offers daily and weekly rates and makes for great place to kick back with the kids. Towels and linens are included. Six units offer kitchens stocked with cooking and eating utensils.

Yellow Coach Motel
$$ • U.S. Hwy. 9, Schroon Lake
• 532-7570

This small motel provides eight pleasant rooms and a two-bedroom apartment at great rates, so if you just want a standard home base, it just may do. Two motel units include a small refrigerator. The beach and boat dock are just a short walk away.

Lake George/ Upper Hudson Region

Resort Hotels and National Chains

The Sagamore
$$$$ • off N.Y. Rt. 9N, Bolton Landing
• 644-9400, (800) 358-3535

We try to avoid unnecessary superlatives in this book, but when it comes to The Sagamore, superlatives are absolutely unavoidable. Without question, this is one of the finest resorts and one of the most beautiful settings in North America, and we dare anyone to prove us wrong! Seriously, this is quite a special place, with a long history of gracious hospitality dating back to 1883. That's when hotel executive Myron Brown pulled together some of his Philadelphia millionaire buddies with the goal of building an exclusive resort community on Lake George. Together they bought Green Island and built the original hotel on the site. The island is just off Bolton Landing and is connected by a small, almost unnoticeable bridge.

The Sagamore has not been without its challenges throughout its history. It was twice damaged by fire and rebuilt, once in 1893 and again in 1914. The main hotel was fully reconstructed in 1930 and today looks much as it did then (which is to say, magnificent). One of the highlights in the resort's history is its 1954 hosting of the prestigious National Governor's

---

INSIDERS' TIP

OK, this isn't a perfect science, so don't get mad at us if we're wrong here, but if you're traveling midweek, you generally don't need a reservation for a room at most hotels and motels in the Adirondacks — even in summer. Granted, there are exceptions — horse-show and rugby weeks in Lake Placid are examples — but far and away, the Adirondacks remain busiest on the weekends. So if you're not sure of your itinerary, you can probably leave at least Monday through Wednesday nights undecided and safely find a suitable room. After Wednesday, it gets iffy; weekends, you're taking a chance of sleeping in your car without a reservation.

Conference, presided over by Vice President Richard Nixon. Unfortunately, later years became difficult for the sprawling resort, and it eventually closed for a couple of years in 1981.

The "modern history" of The Sagamore dates since 1983 when it reopened at the hand of developer Norman Wolgin (also of Philadelphia). A partnership under the name of Green Island Associates was formed to restore the hotel to its former grandeur and to develop new facilities and amenities that would make it into a truly world-class resort once again. They succeeded, and the years since have seen The Sagamore grow more and more popular. In fact, according to Managing Director Robert McIntosh, 1995 and 1996 were two consecutive record years for business at The Sagamore.

One visit here and you will see why The Sagamore is so popular with families, honeymooners, conferences and virtually anyone interested in an unforgettable experience. It starts with the setting. The roughly wedge-shaped island that serves as the home of the hotel and its facilities sets just off the beautiful village of Bolton Landing like a huge earthen cruise ship moored for a permanent visit. The island is about 10 miles "up lake" from Lake George village, near the "Narrows" with its dozens of islands and looked over by some of the biggest mountains along the lake. In a word, it's spectacular.

The facilities and amenities here include just about anything you could dream up in a vacation fantasy (well, except for choice of companions — we'll leave that part to you). You can enjoy the seven tennis courts, the beach and cabana, the indoor pool and fitness center, miniature golf, racquetball and a multitude of planned recreational activities without ever leaving the island. If you want a good reason to get off the island for a while, we can't think of anything better than a round of golf at their famous Donald Ross-designed par 70 championship course (see our Golf chapter), which is just a couple of miles away by hotel shuttle.

Another fun way to leave the island is via *The Morgan*, The Sagamore's own 19th-century replica touring vessel. An afternoon or evening aboard this intimate two-level cruise boat, with its rich wood decor and wonderful meals (lunch or dinner), is an experience you'll want to include during your stay. The food service on land is special as well, and includes The Sagamore Dining Room, the casual Mr. Brown's Pub, The Club Grill at the golf course, and Trillium, the resort's fine-dining restaurant (see our Restaurant chapter).

Accommodations include 100 rooms in the main hotel building, another 240 (including 120 suites) in the townhouse-style Lakeside Lodges, and 10 bi-level suites in the Hermitage Executive Retreat. All accommodations are beautifully decorated and generously appointed.

As you can tell, we're pretty impressed by The Sagamore. While it is one of the most expensive accommodations in the Adirondacks, we think every dollar you spend here will be matched by an equal number of smiles on the faces of you and your family.

FYI

Unless otherwise noted, the area code for all phone numbers listed in this guide is 518.

The Queensbury Hotel
$$$ • 88 Ridge St., Glens Falls
• 792-1121, (800) 554-4526

This small, European-style hotel in the heart of Glens Falls prides itself on providing "affordable luxury at the gateway to the Adirondacks." While a few miles outside of the Park boundaries, The Queensbury is certainly convenient to all the attractions, culture and recreational opportunities in the southeastern Adirondacks. Lake George is only a 10-minute drive away, and Saratoga Springs is only 20 minutes to the south. Plus there's plenty to do and see right here in Glens Falls and neighboring Queensbury (see Area Overviews as well as Arts and Culture).

The hotel is a handsome brick building, with colorful awnings lining its streetscape and adding to its European flavor. Inside, the surroundings are elegant and refined, but still comfortable and unpretentious. A business executive would feel comfortable bringing clients here for an important lunch, just as a mom and dad would bringing their kids for a little weekend escape.

Guests can enjoy the fitness center, indoor pool and Jacuzzi. You can leave the kids in the room with an in-room movie and slip down to Fenimore's Lounge for a quiet drink, or enjoy a fine meal in the hotel restaurant. The Queensbury has 127 guest rooms, including six that are handicapped-accessible. All rooms are tastefully decorated with a European feel. If you want casual elegance and a good value as well as a convenient base for southern Adirondack exploring, The Queensbury is worth a look.

Best Western of Lake George
$$$ • N.Y. Rt. 9N at I-87 Exit 21, Lake George • 668-5701, (800) 234-0265

This attractive motor inn commands a prime piece of real estate just off the Northway (I-87), up on a rise overlooking the lake and just far enough from the center of the village to be peaceful without being inconvenient. Facilities here include both a small indoor pool with whirlpool and an outdoor pool with patio. A continental breakfast and coffee station are set up in the lobby for guests' convenience.

Included in the 87 guest rooms are some "ultra suites" and bi-level deluxe suites with two bedrooms, fireplace and full kitchen. The suites also have the best views of the lake and are perfect for the week-long family vacation. You can bring the family pet along too, as long as you keep him on a leash.

The Best Western is owned and operated by the Flacke family, who also operate the Fort William Henry Motor Inn (see subsequent listing) and the seasonal Travelodge of Lake George.

Days Inn
$$ • U.S. Hwy. 9, Lake George • 793-3196, (800) 274-7111

If shopping is a priority while you're on vacation, you might want to make this your lodging hub. This Days Inn is set right in the heart of what's called the Million Dollar Half-Mile of Factory Outlets (see Shopping), about 3 miles south of Lake George village. Not only is the location attractive to shoppers, but the rates also are more attractive than many "on the lake" lodging properties. You'll find more than 75 factory outlets within a few blocks of your room, and The Great Escape theme park (see Attractions) is just a mile or so away. On site, you can enjoy the convenience of the attached full-service restaurant and the comfort of the indoor pool and Jacuzzi. There is a total of 110 guest rooms here, and nonsmoking rooms are available upon request.

Fort William Henry Motor Inn
$$$ • 50 Canada St. (U.S. Hwy. 9), Lake George • 668-3081, (800) 234-0267

The Fort William Henry Motor Inn is a clean, comfortable and well-appointed lodging option. Set on an 18-acre bluff overlooking (and virtually overhanging) the south shore of Lake George, this motor inn benefits from one of the best locations in the area. From here, you can walk to dozens of attractions, shops and restaurants in the village of Lake George. Fort William Henry Museum is adjacent, and the cruise boats of Lake George Steamboat Company and Shoreline Cruises are just a few steps down the hill, as is the beautiful lakefront promenade that's perfect for strolling. For the kids (and the kid in you), you'll find the two courses of Fort William Henry Miniature Golf just outside your door.

At the inn, you'll find both indoor and outdoor pools, a sauna and Jacuzzi plus three restaurants and a lounge. Accommodations include 99 guest rooms, and suites are available. Leashed pets are allowed here, adding to the family-friendly atmosphere.

Holiday Inn – Turf at Lake George
$$$ • U.S. Hwy. 9, Lake George • 668-5781, (800) HOLIDAY

Owned by the Hoffman family, who for many years has operated the very successful Holiday Inn – Turf in Albany, this hotel has much to offer above and beyond the typical chain-type property. First of all, its setting atop a rise high above the southern shore of Lake George gives this place some of the most panoramic lake views of any lodging facility. Secondly, as home of the Lake George Dinner Theater (see Nightlife) from June into October, the Holiday Inn – Turf gives its guests more than four months of professional equity theater.

Recreational facilities and activities are extensive here and include an outdoor Olympic-size pool, children's pool plus an indoor pool with whirlpool and sauna. Your kids can also enjoy the playground and game room while you burn off some dinner-theater calories in the exercise room. The property also has an attractive restaurant and lounge with lake views.

Accommodations include 105 lake- and mountain-view rooms, some of which are suites and handicapped-accessible rooms. This is definitely a step above the typical Holiday Inn, and it's a great place to vacation, get away or do business year round.

Roaring Brook Ranch & Tennis Resort
$$$ • N.Y. Rt. 9N, Lake George • 668-5767

Celebrating its 50th season in 1995, Roaring Brook is a hybrid between a dude ranch and a tennis resort. It is set on a large wooded compound just off N.Y. 9N, only a few miles from Lake George village yet in a totally different environment. The buildings and grounds here are comfortable and rustic — certainly not luxurious, but it wouldn't be a ranch if it was, right? The emphasis here is on outdoor recreation, including horseback riding on their own trail system, tennis on one of five available courts (two lighted), archery, volleyball, horseshoes, badminton, table tennis — you get the picture. It's kind of like the summer camp you attended as a kid, only now you can bring along your own kids.

There are three pools to choose from, including one indoors, plus saunas and an exercise facility. Your kids will enjoy the large playground as well. In the summertime, Roaring Brook offers special Children's Programs at no extra charge, with trained counselors leading a variety of fun and educational activities for the 4- to 7-year-old set.

Roaring Brook operates as a MAP (Modified American Plan) facility, meaning your breakfast and dinner are included in your lodging package. There is a big variety of accommodations here, with a total of 136 guest rooms spread out among several lodges and buildings. All rooms have wall-to-wall carpeting, color TV, in-room phones and two double beds. Some rooms are larger and more modern than others, so you should ask or take a look first if you get a chance before making a commitment. From family reunions to family getaways, Roaring Brook is a fun and casual alternative near lots of additional fun and excitement.

The Copperfield Inn
$$$$ • 224 Main St., North Creek • 251-2500, (800) 424-9910

What began in the early 1990s as a small, luxurious brand-new country inn has continued to evolve into a full-scale all-season resort. It is still small, intimate and luxurious, but now The Copperfield Inn has added such amenities as a full-service health club, new conference facilities and a ballroom, a new configuration for their dining and lounge facilities and a series of new suites to their already

---

INSIDERS' TIP

If you're staying at The Sagamore, be sure to check out the little flyer called "Environmental Awareness at The Sagamore." This storied accommodation takes an active role in trying to protect the fragile environment of the Adirondacks by using biodegradable laundry products, limiting the use of fertilizers and pesticides on the grounds, and giving you the option to not change towels and linens each day in order to reduce waste water and chemical consumption.

The Adirondack region is a paddlers' paradise rivalling canoeing meccas such as Minnesota.

impressive lineup. Clearly one of the rising stars in Adirondack hospitality, The Copperfield Inn has enjoyed great success in its young life. With the ongoing major expansion at nearby Gore Mountain ski center, and the revitalization of the North Creek Train Depot to operate an excursion train underway, the inn seems poised to ride the wave of excitement that is carrying North Creek along to a new era of popularity not seen since the "ski trains" of the 1930s used to pull into town.

You'll find 25 large and luxurious guest rooms here, complete with terry cloth robes, evening turndown service, marble oversize baths, bedside CD-stereo players, even in-room ski racks. A series of eight new suites that feature fireplaces, whirlpool tubs and balconies has been added.

You'll enjoy fine dining here as well, as the Gardens restaurant serves up such delights as steak au poivre, rack of lamb, seafood stuffed shrimp and pesto chicken in an atmosphere of casual elegance. Trapper's Tavern is the new "rustic Adirondack" lounge for checking out the ball game or dancing to live entertainment, and if you'd rather just sit and listen, you can enjoy the sophisticated piano lounge.

The motto at The Copperfield Inn: "Rough it by day, and let us pamper you by night," in reference to all the nearby outdoor recreation. We think they have the right idea.

1000 Acres Ranch Resort

$$$ • 465 Warrensburg Rd., Stony Creek • 696-2444, (800) 458-7311

The 1000 Acres Ranch Resort calls itself ". . . the prettiest, most relaxin', most excitin' ranch this side of Montana!" After visiting this sprawling resort along the banks of the Hudson River in the Adirondack foothills about 13 miles west of Lake George, we have to agree. This is quite a place, with not just "something" for everyone, but "lots" for everyone.

First of all, its secluded setting in a narrow river valley along the Hudson and nestled between two mountain ridges is striking. The extensive variety of facilities and activities here is not just striking, it's practically overwhelming. Some of what's available to see and do: guided horseback riding; golf on the resort's own par 35, 2829-yard riverside golf course; tennis; volleyball; canoeing; fishing; hiking; softball — in fact, just fill in the activity of your choice, and you'll probably find it here. Plus, you can enjoy unique activities you won't find elsewhere such as the weekly professional rodeo at the resort's own stadium with barrel racing, calf roping and all the other stuff that makes us bruise just thinking about it.

The grounds are nicely landscaped, with river views from just about anywhere. You can enjoy both the outdoor pools (adult and kiddie) and the indoor pool with its adjacent hot tub. Throughout the week, there are plenty of planned activities and entertainment for both kids and adults if you run out of your own ideas. They can be as simple as a game of Wiffleball for the kids to a "guest vs. staff" softball game for the adults.

1000 Acres operates as a FAP (Full American Plan) facility, and breakfast, lunch and dinner are served family style daily in the big main lodge. Meals are of the "good eats" variety, with such things as Italian Buffet night, Texas Barbecue night and big daily breakfast buffets to keep you fully fueled.

There's a big variety of accommodations spread out in motel-style buildings, small lodges and cabins. Altogether, there are more than 80 guest rooms and 20 cabins to choose from. It seems like almost every week 1000 Acres is featuring some kind of special promotion or package, so call and ask the staff to send you the whole shebang.

Rydin'-Hy Ranch Resort
$$$ • Sherman Lake, off I-87 Exit 24, Warrensburg • 494-2742

Along with 1000 Acres (see previous entry), this is one of the few remaining "dude ranch" resorts left over from the days when lumbermen hung their hats here rather than vacationing families. Similar in respects to 1000 Acres, Rydin'-Hy stands apart by its setting directly on Sherman Lake, a private spring-fed lake known for its good fishin'. Although there's no golf course here (as at 1000 Acres), the lake setting allows for other activities such as water skiing, lake cruises on the resort's pontoon boat, speedboat rides and swimming on the sandy beach. Rydin'-Hy also offers downhill (granted, down a *small* hill) skiing on the resort's own slope with T-bar lift as well as snowmobiling, sledding and ice skating. All the usual camp-type activities are available, such as tennis, shuffleboard, horseshoes and the like plus horseback riding on the extensive trail system here.

The centerpiece of the sprawling 800-acre complex is the huge log main ranch house, with its massive stone fireplaces, lobby living room, game room, indoor pool, cocktail lounge and the Lakeside Dining Room where all meals are served. Speaking of good grub, there's plenty of it here for you and yours, served up family style. All three meals are included each day in your lodging package (FAP) as are recreational activities.

For accommodations, you'll find a selection of 65 guest rooms in the lakeside main lodge, motel units and an additional 10 chalet cabins. Each of the main lodge rooms overlooks the lake, has both indoor and outdoor entrances, and is furnished with two double beds and a full bath. The chalet cabins include a living room, two bedrooms (double bed in one, a double and two single beds in the other) plus 1½ baths. All rooms are within an easy walk of the beach, pool and main lodge.

You and your family can have fun year round at the Rydin'-Hy Ranch, but keep in mind that the best dates (and rooms) get booked first, so reserve early.

Motels, Cabins and Cottage Resorts

You will find more than 100 such accommodations in the Lake George/Upper Hudson region. We have provided a modest sample of what's available here, but certainly not with the intention of excluding lodging properties that are of equal quality or value. If you've had a particularly wonderful experience at a facility we haven't mentioned, we welcome your suggested additions for future editions of this book.

Bonnie View on Lake George
$$$ • 6694 Lake Shore Dr. (N.Y. Rt. 9N), Bolton Landing • 644-5591

This 9-acre landscaped lakefront resort is one of dozens along Lake George that provides a combination of motel units, efficiencies (rooms with kitchens) and housekeeping cottages along with a variety of recreational activities. Bolton Landing is regarded as one of the prettiest spots on the lake, and the views from this resort's waterfront certainly support that. You'll find a private sand beach, fishing piers, rowboats, a sun deck, heated swimming pool, tennis and basketball courts, barbecue grills and a children's playground among the many amenities here.

The accommodations include 50 motel units, 28 housekeeping cottages and five efficiency units to choose from. All accommodations come with color cable TV and private baths. Three of the cottages also come with fireplaces. Bonnie View is open to enjoy from early May until mid-September.

Panther Mountain Inn
$$ • Main St. (U.S. Hwy. 9), Chestertown • 494-2401

If you are looking for a pleasant, clean inn that's a good value and home base for your craft shopping, river running or ski bumping, this could be your solution. The Panther Mountain Inn is in the heart of attractive Chestertown and is walking distance to a variety of shops and the local movie house. Upstairs is a large front porch and a comfortable lobby where you can sit and map out your vacation plan of attack. Downstairs, you'll find a lounge with assorted games, a pool table and a selection of homemade deluxe sandwiches for a quick lunch before heading out (or a relaxing lunch after returning).

Accommodations include 14 rooms, all with private bath, color cable TV, refrigerators and individual-control heat and air. Panther Mountain Inn provides for a comfortable stay in any season.

Treasure Cove Resort Motel and Cottages
$$$, no credit cards • Lake Shore Dr. (N.Y. Rt. 9N), Diamond Point • 668-5334

About 5 miles "up lake" from Lake George village, the Treasure Cove Resort is just one of more than two dozen motel and cottage resorts strung along Lake Shore Drive in the area known as Diamond Point. This is an attractive area to stay on the lake because it is only five minutes by car from the excitement (and noise) of Lake George village, but in a little more peaceful, less commercial setting. Amenities at the Treasure Cove include two outdoor pools (one heated) and a big playground for kids. You also will find a kid-friendly level sandy beach and a boat dock — you can rent motorboats and rowboats here — with a sun deck at its end where you get a great view down the lake. One other special feature at the Treasure Cove is Ted's Charter Fishing Service, with its two 26-foot fully-equipped boats departing twice daily during the season in search of salmon, lake trout and bass.

Accommodations include a total of 50 guest rooms divided up by lakeview efficiencies, lakeside two- and three-bedroom cottages (some with fireplaces), and two-room efficiencies with full kitchens. All guest rooms have color cable TV and air conditioning. The Treasure Cove is open from mid-April until mid-October.

Trout House Village Resort
$$$ • Lake Shore Dr. (N.Y. Rt. 9N), Hague • 543-6088

If you think there's nothing worth traveling north of The Sagamore for, think again. Far at the north end of Lake George, where the T-shirt shops and minigolf are but a distant memory (and drive — about 20 miles), you'll find this four-season resort of lodges, log cabins and cottages. Many locals feel the "real" Lake George is up here, where it remains much as it was (albeit friendlier) during the Revolutionary War times. The views of the lake from here are magnificent, and if you previously had spent time down in Lake George village you'll hardly believe that it's the same lake.

Trout House has been owned and oper-

Photo: Mark Meschinelli

This snow-spotted, early winter Adirondack landscape depicts
a sampling of what's to come as the season progresses.

ated by the Patchett family since 1971, and their pride in the place shows everywhere you look. The main lodge, built in 1925, offers country inn lodging in nine elegant yet homespun bedrooms. Each is individually decorated to display its own charm. Three of the rooms have kitchen facilities as well. Few simple pleasures are as relaxing as sitting on the front porch here and rocking your troubles away.

In addition to the lodge, you'll find a collection of 12 very nice log cabins ranging in size from a studio to three bedrooms. All of the cabins face the lake and have a deluxe kitchen, fireplace, full bath and private porch. Some of the cabins have whirlpool tubs and queen beds as well. You also can choose from about a half-dozen less expensive cot-

tage and motel units — smaller but still nicely furnished.

It's hard to imagine when a visit here wouldn't be fun and relaxing. In the winter, there's ice skating, ice fishing and cross-country skiing (not to mention just sitting in front of the fire with a book). The warm weather means swimming along the 400-foot sandy beach, taking out a bike, canoe, kayak or paddleboat, fishing or working on your putting on the beautifully conditioned Grace-Nelson Memorial putting green. If you get them rolling pretty well, you can take your game up to the nearby Ticonderoga Golf Course (see our Golf chapter) and see if your stroke works under pressure.

Whether for a family reunion, staff retreat or romantic getaway, you won't find much better or friendlier than the Trout House Village Resort.

Colonel Williams Motor Inn

$$$ • U.S. Hwy. 9, Lake George
• 668-5727, (800) 334-5727

This well-kept motor lodge is just a couple of miles down U.S. 9 from Lake George village. The first thing you'll notice is the distinctive yellow clock tower rising above the inn — a nice touch. Upon further exploration, you'll appreciate the variety of amenities here, including both an outdoor and indoor heated pool with sauna, Jacuzzi and exercise area. Another special touch here is the children's play area — not just a standard-issue playground, but a colorful and imaginative fantasy land with an oversize wooden train, rocket ship and castle to explore. You'll also appreciate the on-site Laundromat and the daily "breakfast wagon" set up in the lobby.

Accommodations include 45 guest rooms and recently added two-bedroom units and a suite. All rooms have a refrigerator as well — another good feature for long-staying families. This is certainly a good option to consider if being within walking distance to the village is not a priority. Colonel Williams Motor Inn is open from May until October.

Dunham's Bay Lodge

$$$ • 2999 N.Y. Rt. 9L, Lake George
• 656-9242, (800) 79-LODGE

This distinctive resort complex with its imposing stone lodge is along the less commercial east shore of Lake George a few miles north of the village. From this lodge at the base of Dunham's Bay, hence the name, the perspective of Lake George is much smaller and intimate than it is from the village.

The resort has a total of 54 guest rooms within the main lodge and surrounding motel units plus 10 housekeeping cottages with one or two bedrooms. The emphasis here is definitely on watersports, with its private beach, boat docks and large indoor/outdoor pool complex with Jacuzzi. You can water-ski, learn to sail, rent a boat or just hang out in the attractive restaurant and lounge that overlook the water and watch everyone else get wet. If you've been to Lake George before and think you've got the area memorized, try Dunham's Bay Lodge for a whole new set of memories. Dunham's Bay Lodge is open from late May until mid-October.

The Georgian

$$$ • 384 Canada St., Lake George
• 668-5401, (800) 525-3436

If a Catskill resort and a Pocono honeymoon resort had a baby resort, this would be it. The Georgian is big, busy, colorful and ornate. It's also right in the heart of the village, with 400 feet of its own lakefront. If you like crowds and excitement (particularly during the summer months) you'll like it here.

Amenities here include a heated pool with Jacuzzi, cocktail lounge with entertainment, large dining room, boat dock and private beach. You can choose from 167 guest rooms, including the Penthouse suites and Honeymoon Jacuzzi suites (complete with heart-shaped tub). While there's a lot of rooms here, many of them face the parking lot, not the lake, so make sure to ask to get the location you want. The Georgian is open year round.

Mohican Resort Motel

$$$ • U.S. Hwy. 9, Lake George
• 792-0474

This year-round family resort motel is 3 miles south of Lake George village and just a mile or so from the factory outlet area and The Great Escape theme park (see the Attractions and Kidstuff chapters). There are lots of family-friendly features here, including an indoor heated pool, outdoor pool, kiddie pool, two Jacuzzi tubs and a sauna. Non-water–related fun includes a big wooden playground for kids, basketball court, game room with pool table and a nice picnic area. All 43 rooms are equipped with full baths and color cable TV, including HBO. Unlike many area motels, the Mohican has an on-site coffee shop for breakfast and snacks. All in all, it's a good value and a good location to base the clan for a week or weekend in Lake George.

Southern Adirondack Lakes Region

Resort Hotels and National Chains

Holiday Inn Johnstown-Gloversville
$$ • 308 N. Comrie Ave. (N.Y. Rt. 30A), Johnstown • 762-4686

If you're a fan of national chains, this is about your only choice within this region, and it's actually set about 10 miles south of the Adirondack Park border along a busy commercial highway. It is the first major lodging property you come to if you're heading north toward the Adirondacks from N.Y. State Thruway Exit 28, and probably a better place to spend a first night "on the way" than to make a whole vacation out of it.

You'll find the dependable type of lodging, service and amenities you expect from a national chain like Holiday Inn, but nothing really to set it apart. There are 100 rooms, all tastefully decorated, along with a restaurant, lounge and outdoor heated pool. If you happen to be staying for business, you'll appreciate the breakfast service that begins at 6:30 AM, the data-port jacks on all guest room phones for those laptops with modems, and free local calling.

Motels, Cabins and Cottage Resorts

The Hedges
$$$$, no credit cards • off N.Y. Rt. 28, Blue Mountain Lake • 352-7325

Although only open from mid-June until early-October, The Hedges deserves a mention due to its setting, collection of beautiful and rustic accommodations and facilities, and long history of excellent service. Set on a secluded and scenic spot along the shore of Blue Mountain Lake, The Hedges offers a variety of attractive accommodations. The Main House is wonderfully decorated and offers four guest rooms, all with private baths. The Stone Lodge has six rooms upstairs, all with private baths, and a three-bedroom suite with fireplace on the first floor. In addition to the two lodge buildings, you can also choose from a collection of one- to four-bedroom cottages strung along the lakeshore.

The Hedges only offers a Modified American Plan (MAP) to guests, which includes breakfast and dinner with your lodging. While visiting, you can explore the shoreline of Blue Mountain Lake in one of the canoes or rowboats, swim or sunbathe on the private sandy beach, play tennis on the clay court (easy on the knees!), read in the well-stocked library, or get some indoor recreation in the game room.

Hemlock Hall Lodge & Cottages
$$$, no credit cards • Maple Lodge Rd., Blue Mountain Lake • 352-7706

This is another fine seasonal lodging choice on Blue Mountain Lake, set along the north shore about a mile off N.Y. 28 and 30. Besides the magnificent setting, you'll find an impressively restored main lodge with ornate woodwork and a two-sided stone fireplace. Accommodations range from lodge rooms with shared bath to cottages with two or three bedrooms to a four-room motel. All guests participate in the Modified American Plan in July and August, with optional European Plan (no meal) rates available at other times. There is a private beach and rowboats available for guests to use. Hemlock Hall is open from mid-

May until mid-October (sound familiar?) and is popular with both family vacationers and reunions.

Potter's Resort
$$$ • N.Y. Rts. 28 and 30, Blue Mountain Lake • 352-7331

Potter's is strategically located in the "can't miss it" intersection of N.Y. 28, N.Y. 30 and the lake itself. You simply can't come to or through Blue Mountain Lake without running right past it. The main lodge, with its restaurant and lounge, has a classic dark wood Adirondack lodge look and is open daily during the summer months and on weekends in the spring and fall. The motel has 10 guest rooms, four of which feature fireplaces. In addition, you can choose from about a dozen housekeeping cottages of various size, most of which have porches and some that have fireplaces. The accommodations are open from Memorial Day until late September. Potter's has its own private beach for guests, a tennis court and a dock for visitors' boats.

Camp Driftwood
$$$, no credit cards • 199 Sabael Rd., Indian Lake • 648-5111

About 3 miles south of the hamlet of Indian Lake along 700 feet of beautiful lakefront property, Camp Driftwood offers 10 housekeeping cottages both along the shore and set back into the woods. The biggest has three bedrooms, a screened porch, fireplace and deck. All cottages have full kitchens and wood stoves. The use of boats, canoes and firewood are all included in the rates here, as is the peace and quiet.

Timberlock Camp
$$$$, no credit cards • off N.Y. Rt. 30, Sabael • 648-5494

Toward the southern end of Indian Lake, Timberlock is a seasonal resort with nearly a century of hospitality history behind it. It is nearly as rustic now as it was then, with the emphasis here on the natural setting, good hearty food and plenty of activities for young and old.

Timberlock offers a collection of a dozen or so lodges and cabins with wood stoves, full baths and screened porches. It operates as a Full American Plan facility, so all your meals are included in the lodging price. Activities include horseback riding, canoeing, sailing, fishing, water skiing and tennis on the four Hartru courts available here. Timberlock celebrated its 96th season in 1997 and is open from late June until late September.

Wilderness Lodge
$$$ • off N.Y. Rt. 28, Indian Lake • 648-5995

Aptly named, the Wilderness Lodge is set far from anywhere — and adjacent to the 112,000-acre Siamese Ponds Wilderness Area. Even so, you'll find comfortable lodging here with some conveniences and amenities not available in some other more accessible locations plus food that is worth the adventure to get here. There are a half-dozen lodge rooms with color TV, private baths and air conditioning plus a collection of fully equipped two- and three-bedroom vacation homes to choose from.

The restaurant is highly regarded, featuring "all you can wish" hearty breakfasts and nightly dinner selections such as prime rib, seafood, veal and pasta prepared in both traditional and imaginative ways.

The Wilderness Lodge is open year round. It draws hikers in the summer and fall and cross-country skiers and snowmobilers in the winter.

Burke's Cottages
$$$, no credit cards • Lake Shore Dr., Sabael • 648-5258, (516) 281-4983 in winter

Set along the north shore of Indian Lake, Burke's offers five recently renovated housekeeping cottages on a year-round basis. Four of the cottages have fireplaces, and all are tastefully decorated with carpeting, full baths and kitchens. Some cottages also feature large decks or screened porches, so make a specific request if you're interested. You can enjoy Burke's private beach for swimming, or simply stroll the 3 acres of manicured lawns and perennial gardens. This is a quiet, scenic spot from which you can enjoy the multitude of recreational opportunities nearby such as whitewater rafting or hiking to the top of Snowy Mountain, or simply give in to watching the boats go by between cat naps.

Bearhurst

$$$, no credit cards • South Shore Rd., Speculator • 548-6427, 842-6609 in winter

Occupying a large piece of attractive lakefront property along the shore of Lake Pleasant, Bearhurst is actually a miniature Great Camp setting. The estate was built in 1894, and visitors now stay in what originally were functional buildings on the grounds such as the pump house and the boathouse. Each of the five buildings has been converted to comfortable, nicely appointed guest quarters with living rooms, fireplaces and full kitchens in addition to the bedrooms. The grounds are beautiful, and there is a private sandy beach and lakeside gazebo from which guests can enjoy the surroundings. Bearhurst is only open from June through September, and it's convenient to several interesting shops and good restaurants in and around Speculator.

Old Forge/ Raquette Lake Region

Resort Hotels and National Chains

Holl's Inn

$$$$, no credit cards • South Shore Rd., Inlet • (315) 357-2941, (315) 733-2748 off-season

While only open in the months of July and August, the long history and great reputation of Holl's Inn make it worth inclusion here. Set on the shore of Fourth Lake, the largest of the Fulton Chain of Lakes, Holl's Inn has been operated by the Holl family as a full-scale summer resort since 1935. Holl's operates as a Full American Plan facility, meaning your rate includes breakfast, lunch and dinner daily in their lakefront dining room. At some properties, this can be an inconvenience for guest (if the food isn't so good, but you're "locked in" to eating at the hotel). Here, we can assure you it's part of the pleasure, as the food service is excellent, and the view changes every evening even though the setting does not.

Don't be surprised to see deer walking the grounds as they head down to the water for a drink. As mentioned in the Area Overviews chapter, this is a protected area for deer, so sightings are common and part of the area's unique charm.

There are plenty of activities and facilities here to enjoy for every member of your family, from swimming at the private beach to canoeing to tennis to lounging in the library. A total of 48 guest rooms are available between the original hotel building, the lakefront motel units and two new cottage units. All rooms have private baths.

For an old-fashioned Adirondack summer retreat, you can't do much better than Holl's Inn. We suggest you start setting up that next (or first) family reunion for next July now.

Best Western Sunset Inn

$$$ • N.Y. Rt. 28, Old Forge • (315) 369-6836

The one "national flag" lodging property in the area, this modern well-appointed inn was totally renovated in 1996. The inn is along a busy stretch of N.Y. 28, just a couple of minutes from the Thendara Golf Club (see Golf) and amid a big collection of gift shops and restaurants.

Best Western Sunset Inn offers 52 guest rooms, ranging from economy to deluxe to Jacuzzi suite rooms. Some of the special features here include an indoor heated pool (which can come in handy almost anytime of the year in Old Forge!), an outdoor sun deck, a Jacuzzi hot tub and sauna, a picnic gazebo with gas grill and a tennis court. While there is no on-site restaurant, a free continental breakfast is provide for guests.

You can enjoy a stay at the Best Western Sunset Inn any time of the year. If you're interested in snowmobiling, you'll be happy to know you can hop on the Town of Webb trail network directly from the inn. However, it is B.Y.O.S. (Bring Your Own Snowmobile).

Water's Edge Inn & Conference Center

$$$ • N.Y. Rt. 28, Old Forge • (315) 369-2484

With Enchanted Forest/Water Safari (see the Attractions and Kidstuff chapters) out the

Photo: Plattsburgh/North Country Chamber of Commerce

This Adirondack landscape provides a pastoral palette for a country road.

front door, and Old Forge Pond and Fulton Chain of Lakes outside the back door, this 62-room facility is perfectly positioned for both business and pleasure. All rooms have a private balcony overlooking the water, the Old Forge Lake Cruises dock, the municipal beach and the town beyond. The public space is clean and attractively appointed. The library with stone-fireplace overlooking the water is particularly impressive. Also attractive is Riley's, the on-site restaurant and lounge, which also overlooks Old Forge Pond. Above and beyond just being a serviceable "hotel restaurant," Riley's has a good reputation for service and food that matches its setting. The Water's Edge Inn also caters to business groups with its 150-person Lakeside Conference Room and 20-person Board Room, both set up with audiovisual equipment.

Whether visiting for business or vacation, all guests here can enjoy the indoor pool and sauna, spacious lawns and decks that line the waterfront. In the summertime, the Water's Edge is also the home of the Mountain View Theater Company (see Arts and Culture), offering live dinner theater several nights a week.

The Water's Edge Inn & Conference Center is open year round.

Motels, Cabins and Cottage Resorts

The Waldheim

$$$$, no credit cards • Big Moose Rd., Big Moose Lake • (315) 357-2353

If you're such a big fan of seclusion that even the Fulton Chain of Lakes seems too cosmopolitan for you, check out The Waldheim. This complex of 15 housekeeping cabins was established in 1904 on 300 secluded acres that border state wilderness land. Each of the cabins was built from the logs of trees right here on the property, and all come equipped with fireplaces and plenty of rustic Adirondack atmosphere. The Waldheim is a Full American Plan property, so all meals are included in your lodging package and are served in the quaint, antique-filled dining room. For activities, there's relaxing, canoeing, relaxing, hiking, reading and relaxing — and taking a nap if all that relaxing gets too strenuous! If you want to get away from it all — and that includes TV, phones and clocks — The Waldheim could be the perfect place for your summer of fall retreat. You can enjoy a stay here from mid-June until Columbus Day. One last thing — you *can* leave home without it (credit cards, that is) because they won't do you any good here anyway. This place is old-fashioned right down to the payment method.

The Kenmore

$$$, no credit cards • off N.Y. Rt. 28, Fourth Lake • (315) 357-5285

About 8 miles northeast of Old Forge, this is another old cottage resort that dates all the way back to 1901. It is set along the north shore of Fourth Lake and features 14 heated housekeeping cottages ranging from one to four bedrooms in size. With the exception of linens, the cottages come completely equipped and furnished. Five of the cottages feature fireplaces.

Guests can enjoy the gradual sand beach with its gentle slope into shallow water (perfect for little bathers), free canoe use, horseshoe pits, volleyball and basketball courts, a campfire area and a playground for kids. Generations of families have been returning year after year to The Kenmore to enjoy their "favorite cabin" and the peaceful setting.

The Kenmore is open all year with the exception of April.

Clayton's Cottages

$$$, no credit cards • Sixth Lake, off N.Y. Rt. 28, Inlet • (315) 357-3394

Set on small, uncrowded Sixth Lake just east of Inlet, Clayton's offers 11 nicely equipped lakeside housekeeping cottages on a year-round basis. Each cottage features an enclosed porch, fireplace, newly decorated kitchens, color TV, wall-to-wall carpeting and private bath with showers. Guests can enjoy the private sandy beach, lakefront sun decks near the two docks, canoes, a picnic and play area. In the wintertime, snowmobile enthusiasts can directly access the region's vast trail network from here. If you're looking for modern conveniences in a secluded setting, Clayton's is a good alternative to consider.

Deer Meadows Motel & Cottages

$$ • N.Y. Rt. 28, Inlet • (315) 357-3274

Open almost year round (with the exception of yucky, mucky, muddy April), Deer Meadows offers an attractive 10-unit motel and six housekeeping cottages, all set along scenic Seventh Lake in the Fulton Chain of Lakes. There's no lack of modern conveniences or comfortable touches here. The motel units are fully carpeted with queen beds, color cable TV and in-room coffee makers. The cottages have the same appointments plus fireplaces, complete kitchen facilities, grills and picnic tables.

You can enjoy the sandy beach, free rowboats, the game room, or even tinkering with your snowmobile in the heated garage. Since Deer Meadows is directly on Snowmobile Trail A, the garage becomes a busy place in the wintertime.

Clark's Beach Motel

$$$ • N.Y. Rt. 28, Old Forge • (315) 369-3026

This is certainly one of the best locations in the area, right on Old Forge Pond in the center of town and adjacent to the municipal beach. Just about everything in Old Forge is within walking distance, making this a good hub for visits to the Enchanted Forest/Water Safari theme park (see the Attractions and Kidstuff chapters), Old Forge Lake Cruises or browsing at Old Forge Hardware (see Shopping).

You'll find 42 guest rooms here, some with private screened porches facing the lake. All rooms have color/cable TV, and there are a few two-bedroom efficiency units with kitchens and private balconies overlooking Old Forge Pond. Kids will enjoy the indoor heated pool, and you can save some dollars on the kennel back home because this is one of the rare lodging properties to welcome pets. There's also a complimentary coffee lounge with magazines and games. Clark's Beach Motel is open year round.

Country Club Motel
$$ • N.Y. Rt. 28, Old Forge
• (315) 369-6340

If you're a golfer, this is the place to check Thendara Golf Club (see Golf) is literally just beyond the back yard here. Country Club Motel is also convenient to the Adirondack Scenic Railroad (just a mile down the road) and all of the attractions in and around Old Forge (see Attractions). The motel has spacious, nicely landscaped grounds and is set back far enough from busy N.Y. 28 that road noise is not a problem.

You'll find 27 nicely maintained guest rooms here, each with a shower/tub combination, small refrigerator and microwave, color/cable TV and in-room coffee. Some rooms come with queen-size beds; others are furnished with double beds. All guests can enjoy the outdoor heated pool.

The Country Club Motel is open year round.

Policies at small
independently owned
inns are as variable
as the Adirondack
weather, so it's
always best to ask.

Bed & Breakfasts and Country Inns

Twenty years ago, your choices of bed and breakfasts and country inns throughout the Adirondacks would have been somewhat limited. These days, virtually every corner of the region and every town boasts at least a couple of quaint, beautifully restored and presented inns that you can enjoy. Altogether, you have more than 100 bed and breakfast inns throughout the region to choose from. The Adirondacks are truly blessed with great riches when is comes to wonderful bed and breakfast and country inns, and you'll feel blessed as well when you visit.

We define bed and breakfast inns as generally smaller places (fewer than 10 rooms) that strictly serve some form of a morning meal (whether continental-style or a full-frontal omelette attack) to overnight guests only. Country inns are generally larger, say 10 or more rooms, and have a restaurant that is open to the dining public for dinner as well. Since owners and operators of these types of lodging are a proud sort (and rightly so) and can be kind of sensitive about how they're categorized, we do the prudent (and cowardly) thing and lump the two together in this chapter.

Three things you should be conscious of before making a reservation with a bed and breakfast or country inn are the deposit, minimum-stay and cancellation policies. In many cases, these can be quite strict, so if you want to avoid a dispute when you change your plans at the last minute, make sure you understand your obligations up front. Other things that can vary widely and you should double-check include handicap accessibility and the availability of nonsmoking rooms. Also, some of the inns that feature full-service restaurants offer (or sometimes require) guests be on a Modified American Plan, with breakfast and dinner each day included in the room rate. Policies at small independently owned inns are as variable as the Adirondack weather, so it's always best to ask.

Now, some assumptions. Unless we state otherwise, all lodging properties listed here accept major credit cards, offer heat and air conditioning, color/cable TV (at least in the common area), housekeeping service and private baths. As the name implies, we will assume each inn offers you a full breakfast when you finally roll out from under that snugly quilt. Also, as much as these properties would love to have you visit, unless we mention otherwise, you'll need to leave your pets at home.

One last thing to help you find what you're looking for in this chapter: Lodging choices are presented in alphabetical order within each town, and each town is listed in alphabetical order as well. For example, within the Lake Placid/Tri-Lakes Region, all accommodations will be listed for Lake Placid (in alphabetical order) prior to any listings for Saranac Lake. It sounds more confusing than it is.

Price Code

We have included a price code for your reference that will give you an idea of what to expect in lodging costs during your Adirondack visit. The code is based on an average double-occupancy rate during peak season. This rate includes a full breakfast each morning. In other words, this is the range you can expect

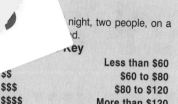

... night, two people, on a ...d.

...key

	Less than $60
$	$60 to $80
$$	$80 to $120
$$$$	More than $120

Lake Placid/ Tri-Lakes Region

Bark Eater Inn
$$$ • Alstead Hill Rd., Keene • 576-2221

The Bark Eater is much more than just a country inn, as it also offers its own horseback-riding and cross-country–ski trails, even a polo field. The inn, a 150-year-old farmhouse with two fireplaces and three spacious common rooms, is filled with antiques. There are seven bedrooms with shared baths in the main lodge and four bedrooms with private baths in the renovated carriage house. A hand-hewn log cottage deep in the woods is ideal for groups.

Joe-Pete Wilson, former U.S. Olympic Nordic team member and U.S. national team competitor in bobsledding and biathlon, serves as host and resident teller of tall tales. A hearty, old-fashioned country breakfast is included in the room rate. Family-style dinners are served by candlelight in the main house. The dinners here are legendary, as Wilson likes not only a hearty meal, but also a gourmet one.

Adirondack Rock and River Lodge
$$ • Alstead Hill, Keene • 576-2041

Rock and River combines its guide service (see Other Summer Recreation) with lodging in either its Climbers Lodge or Guides Lodge. Accommodations range from a lean-to to a bunk bed to a private room with shared bath. This place caters to climbers; amenities include only the basics.

For recreation, climb the indoor stone

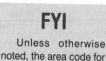

FYI

Unless otherwise noted, the area code for all phone numbers listed in this guide is 518.

climbing wall in the main lodge. The spacious lodges offer views of the mountains and open fields, and are adjacent to biking, hiking and skiing trails. A hearty breakfast is included in the room rate.

This guide service specializes in mountain- and ice-climbing instruction, wilderness medicine and kayak tours. Check out the courses and package deals at the lodge.

Trails End Inn
$$$ • N.Y. Rt. 73, Keene Valley • 576-9860

This 1902 Adirondack lodge is a rustic, romantic and secluded bed and breakfast inn in one of the most beautiful valleys in the region. This Adirondack-style camp features wide-board pine floors, brick fireplaces and plenty of common areas for guest comfort.

The main lodge houses seven spacious guest rooms and two suites decorated with antiques and reproductions. Guest rooms are all different and accommodate two to five people. Some rooms have a fireplace, claw-foot tub or sleeping porch. A two-bedroom cottage complete with a kitchen and Jacuzzi garden tub for two also is available.

Delicious all-you-can-eat country breakfasts are served family-style and include fruit, homemade bread and assorted sweets.

The Lodge at Lake Clear Junction
$$$ • N.Y. Rts. 186 and 30, Lake Clear • 891-1489

The Lodge at Lake Clear Junction has a long history (100 years) in the region as an lodging for stagecoach and railroad visitors. The rustic accommodations (all facilities were hand-constructed by the original owner using found and imported materials) are situated on 25 acres of waterfront on Lake Clear, which is appropriately named.

The lodge itself offers four comfortable rooms filled with antiques. Two old-fashioned chalets and two guest houses — some with kitchens, all hand-crafted with a pioneer spirit — make for a home away from home. Some accommodations include Jacuzzis and fire-

Marinas dot the numerous coves and bays of Lake Champlain.

places and cost more than a basic one-room cabin.

The breakfast offerings vary daily. Fresh-baked bread and muffins and fresh fruit — expect something in-season in your pancakes — always are available. (See our Restaurants chapter for related information.)

The Lodge at Lake Clear Junction has been recommended by *National Geographic Traveler* and *SKI* magazine.

Adirondack Mountain Club Lodges and Facilities

$ • Adirondack Loj Rd., Lake Placid
• 523-3441

The Adirondack Mountain Club (ADK) is a nonprofit organization dedicated to providing opportunities for environmentally responsible outdoor recreation in the Adirondack Park. ADK also offers mountain cabins, guest rooms and campground facilities at its Adirondack Loj site at the base of Mount Marcy, just a few minutes outside of Lake Placid, and at Johns Brook Lodge, in Keene Valley, a 30-minute drive from Lake Placid.

Adirondack Loj, originally built by Henry Van Hovenberg, opened in 1890 on the shores of Heart Lake. The Loj has space for up to 46 guests in a combination of private and family rooms or in a coed bunk room. Although the rooms are comfortable and clean, it is likely that you will not be spending much time in yours, as the Loj is situated amid some of the best hiking trails in the Adirondacks. You can pick a short, but challenging hike, for example, up Mount Jo for a good view of Heart Lake and the High Peaks, or the Loj can serve as you base camp for exploring Mount Marcy, New York's highest peak.

You can drive you car to the Loj, but a 3.5-mile hike is necessary to get you to Johns Brook Lodge. Don't be misled by the relatively easy hike to Johns Brook because the trails surrounding the lodge offer some of the most challenging hikes in the region. Johns Brook Lodge can accommodate 28 guests in two family rooms and two coed bunk rooms.

ADK also offers a variety of workshops, seminars and activities throughout the year. A few words of advice: Make reservations early for any accommodations. During the summer and fall months in particular, the Loj is a haven for the thousands of hikers climbing many of the High Peaks. You won't be alone, and your greatest challenge will be discovering a wilderness without people.

Lake Placid Lodge Restaurant and Hotel
$$$$ • Whiteface Inn Rd., Lake Placid • 523-2700

In 1882 a German family built an Adirondack camp on edge of Lake Placid with a perfect view of Whiteface Mountain. The camp, like many built during the era, grew to grand proportions, with tall stone fireplaces and long twig-framed porches. In 1946 the camp became the Lake Placid Lodge, and it continues the tradition of the luxurious camp hidden in the quiet woods.

www.insiders.com

See this and many other **Insiders' Guide®** destinations online — in their entirety.

Visit us today!

The Lake Placid Lodge captures the wonderful history and spirit of the Adirondacks, while offering many modern pastimes like an 18-hole golf course and tennis courts. The 22 guest rooms, named for the region's high peaks and lakes, are filled with rustic twig and birch-bark furniture, Adirondack antiques, Oriental rugs and art work by local artisans, creating a luxurious but comfortable setting. Most rooms have large stone fireplaces, and all have private baths, some with deep soaking tubs and views of Lake Placid and Whiteface Mountain.

Many of the cabins on the shore of Lake Placid have been recently renovated. All have stone fireplaces, private baths and gorgeous lake and mountain views. The one-room, one-bedroom and two-bedroom cabins sleep four comfortably and include either double or queen beds, color TV, phone and small refrigerator.

A full breakfast menu is served daily in the on-site restaurant (see our Restaurants chapter).

Mount Van Hoevenberg Bed & Breakfast
$$$ • N.Y. Rt. 73, Lake Placid • 523-9572

This small bed and breakfast, situated next to the Olympic cross-country skiing facility a few miles from downtown Lake Placid, offers three private rooms in a country farmhouse or four cozy cottages. The facility serves as a great base camp for loafing around, chasing the elusive trout in nearby streams, hiking, cross-country skiing or mountain biking at the Mount Van Hoevenberg complex (see Attractions, Kidstuff and Skiing). An outdoor sauna makes for a relaxing experience, especially after skiing the nearby trails.

South Meadow Farm Lodge
$$$ • Cascade Rd., Lake Placid • 523-9369

You don't have to help with the farm chores to earn your keep at this small farm, but you still can enjoy the farm animals lingering about. There are five rooms here, two with shared baths, in the main lodge with large fireplace and piano, and "posh" camping in four log cabins. The cabins have no electricity, but rather candlelight and wood-stove heat; comfy beds are a pampering alternative to sleeping mats and sleeping bags. Ski trails are just outside the door.

A hearty home-style breakfast is included in your room rate, and lunch and dinner are optional.

Spruce Lodge Bed & Breakfast
$$$ • 31 Sentinel Rd., Lake Placid • 523-9350

All eight comfortable rooms in this lodge offer private baths and accommodate one to

INSIDERS' TIP

The Adirondack Bed & Breakfast Reservation Service can set you up in dozens of properties around the region. Keep in mind that you are paying for the convenience through a commission they receive from the inn, so you may be paying a few more dollars for your room, but the expertise and guidance often is worth it. You can contact them at 10 Park Place, Saranac Lake, N.Y. 12983, 891-1632 or (800) 552-2726.

four guests. The lodge itself exudes a home-like feel with its large common room and country-style furnishings, and it's only a few minutes from Lake Placid village. A two-bedroom cottage, which accommodates up to eight people, also is available.

The daily continental breakfast consists of hot and cold cereals, breads and beverages.

Stagecoach Inn
$$$ • 370 Old Military Rd., Lake Placid • 523-9474

This historic inn, one of the oldest in the region, served as a stagecoach stop beginning in 1833. As you enter, a unique yellow birch staircase immediately sets the tone: This inn posseses a distinctive 19th-century Adirondack rustic character. *Vogue* and *Gourmet* magazines have sung its praises.

There are nine guest rooms here, and each has its own distinct personality. None of the rooms are big, as each originally was designed to accommodate the overnight traveler without a carload of luggage. All, however, are comfortable and filled with antiques, including brass and white-iron beds, handmade quilts and some unusual antiques. (A few of these antiques — among them, foot warmers and contraptions to remove boots from tired feet — may require explanation, as they are rather unusual.) A few rooms have fireplaces and private baths.

The inn serves a memorable breakfast to its guests. Items include fresh bread, pastries, fruit and, perhaps, cheese souffle and French toast.

Northbrook Lodge
$$$$ • White Pine Rd., Paul Smiths • 327-3379

This former Adirondack Great Camp is situated on 10 acres of the unspoiled Osgood Pond (see Area Overviews). While other great camps may offer grander facilities, Northbrook seems to capture the very essence of what camping was about in the early 1900s.

Northbrook offers 16 rooms, all with different personalities and private entrances. All cottages face the water. The atmosphere here is peaceful, relaxing and friendly. If the mood strikes, great fishing, hiking, canoeing and swimming are just a few steps from your room.

Guests are served breakfast and dinner in a rustic lounge filled with antiques. Menu se-lections vary, and the chef will cater to guests with special dietary needs. After dinner, you may retreat to the boathouse lounge and listen to the cry of loons in the night.

Northbrook is open from mid-June to mid-September and welcomes families.

The Point
$$$$ • off N.Y. Rt. 3, Saranac Lake • 891-5674, (800) 255-3530

The Point is in a class by itself, having consistently achieved the highest ratings as one of the world's great country inns. (It's the only country house in the world to be awarded the Best Country House Hotel award four times by Andrew Harper's "Hideaway Report.")

The Point, originally Camp Wonundra, the home of William Avery Rockefeller, reflects the Great Camp tradition for gracious style in a rustic, picturesque setting on Upper Saranac Lake. It offers guests all their meals (in Great Camp tradition, black tie is suggested for the men on Wednesday and Saturday) in the Great Hall, an elegant and comfortable hall with giant fireplaces at each end.

Eleven distinctive guest quarters are spread among four buildings, all with views of the lake. The guest rooms include an eclectic mixture of antiques, custom-made beds and furnishings and stone fireplaces in a suite-type setting.

After enjoying a gourmet breakfast in your room, you can wander miles of wooded hiking trails, relax in the library, enjoy a drink on a stone patio overlooking the lake or partake in a variety of self-directed activites. In addition to swimming at the private beach, guests have access to canoes, rowboats, speedboats, sailboards and a classic 30-foot mahogany Hackercraft. During the winter months, hiking pathways become quiet trails for cross-country skiing.

The Point has few or no equals in the Adirondack region — or perhaps in the country. The price of an all-inclusive (three meals, unlimited liquor, access to all facilities and equipment and lodging) stay for two begins at $825 per night, and the cost reflects the high quality of accommodations here.

Cold River Ranch
$$$ • N.Y. Rt. 3, Tupper Lake • 359-7559

This small turn-of-the century lodge in a wilderness setting is the closest thing to a "dude ranch" in the area. The ranch offers horseback riding (see Other Summer Recreation), cross-country skiing, hiking and biking trails and easy access to the Saranac Lake canoe routes. It also offers six comfortable rooms — three with double beds, three with twin beds. All guests use a shared bath. Guests have access to some 150 miles of hiking and horseback-riding trails from the ranch.

This secluded lodge provides a breakfast of fruit, muffins and fresh breads and will generally cater a country breakfast to your tastes.

The Wawbeek on Upper Saranac Lake

$$$$ • 553 Panther Mountain Rd., Tupper Lake • 359-2475, (800) 953-2656

The Wawbeek is a turn-of-the-century Great Camp set on a 40-acre site amid dense stands of giant hemlock on the shores of Upper Saranac Lake. The camp has separate structures for dining and sleeping, as was the tradition in the era of the Great Camps built in the late 19th and early 20th centuries.

The dark-shingled main lodge has five bedrooms, each with its own bath, and an inviting Great Room dominated by a massive stone fireplace. The walls and ceilings throughout the two-story lodge are original knotty pine. Porches upstairs and down, furnished with rockers and wicker, offer a stunning view of Upper Saranac Lake. Nine cabins and a cottage are also available, with some overlooking the lake.

This year-round resort offers snowshoeing, cross-country ski and walking trails, a sandy beach, canoes, sailboats, bikes and tennis courts. The Wawbeek consistently receives the highest recommendations from national magazines, including *Travel and Leisure* and *National Geographic*. Guests can choose breakfast items from a varied menu.

Plattsburgh/Western Lake Champlain Region

Crown Point Bed & Breakfast

$$$ • Main St. (N.Y. Rt. 9N), Crown Point • 597-3651

This venerable Victorian mansion — it's more than a century old — is set on 5½ acres of woodland and meadows. The elegant Crown Point offers five antique-filled rooms, all with private baths. Its Victorian style in an area known for Adirondack rustic makes this inn architecturally distinctive.

Looking for water-related activities? Lake Champlain is just outside the door. The inn also provides a hot tub, game room and gourmet breakfast. Ask about the two-night–stay special (champagne, dinner, lake cruise and more) for couples — offered Sunday to Thursday.

Stony Water Bed & Breakfast

$$$ • Roscoe Rd., Elizabethtown • 873-9125, (800) 995-7295

Elizabethtown doesn't qualify as a tourist trap. Consequently, accommodations are few and far between. If you discover E-Town in your travels, you'll find Stony Water one of few lodging choices in this tranquil and beautiful mountain village. Fortunately, it's a good choice.

The sound of two mountain streams help lull you to sleep in this small, fully restored historic Adirondack farmhouse furnished with antiques. Four spacious rooms, all with private baths, are available for nightly stays. A room with a kitchenette and a two-bedroom cottage are available by the week. A well-

---

INSIDERS' TIP

If you've made a reservation at a lovely inn for this weekend and the weather forecast doesn't look good, our advice is: Go anyway! The charm of a bed and breakfast or country inn is its ambiance, its ability to take you to a different era, its sumptuous food. In many cases, they are near quaint shops and interesting museums. So let it rain — you can still have a great time (and not lose your deposit!)

stocked library with fireplace is available for all guests.

Essex Inn
$$$ • 16 Main St., Essex • 963-8821

Built in 1810, this historic inn offers six spacious rooms, four with private baths. The rooms are tastefully decorated in period furnishings. The inn's full-service restaurant offers a range of continental choices for breakfast, lunch and dinner in its two dining rooms and on the veranda. A small in-house bookstore, which specializes in regional titles, adds yet another element of charm to this inn.

Aunt Polly's Bed and Breakfast
$$ • N.Y. Rt. 28N, Newcomb • 582-2260

During the era of the stagecoach, Aunt Polly ran this inn — hence its name. This 1845 inn has been completely restored since, and guests find solace as well as good snowmobiling and cross-country ski trails during the winter on the 70-acre site with beaver pond and nesting loons. The three bedrooms — all share a bath — are tastefully decorated with antiques.

Expect a hearty, country-stlye breakfast to start your day. Newcomb is a rather quiet place, so Aunt Polly's well-stocked library of books and videos keeps guests entertained in the evenings (assuming other plans are not in order).

Murdies Bed and Breakfast
$$, no credit cards • N.Y. Rt. 28N, Newcomb • 582-3531

The town of Newcomb is in the heart of the Adirondacks, surrounded by miles upon miles of wilderness. If you are looking for a base camp to explore the southern side of the High Peaks, Murdies is one of two lodging choices (also see previous entry) in the area.

This small farmhouse includes three guest rooms with shared bath. You can expect a clean room with double or single beds, reasonable rates and a home-cooked breakfast each morning. Murdies is not fancy, but after a full day hiking, skiing or fishing, it is a comfortable place to rest your weary bones and ready yourself for tomorrow's adventures.

Point Au Roche Lodge
$$$ • 463 Point Au Roche Rd., Plattsburgh • 563-8714

This modern lodge, adjacent to the Point Au Roche State Park (see Attractions), overlooks Lake Champlain. Spectacular views of the Green Mountains can be had from the decks of many of the eight guest rooms. All rooms have private baths, and some feature Jacuzzis and fireplaces. A full breakfast is served daily.

Schroon Lake Bed & Breakfast

$$$ • U.S. Hwy. 9, Schroon Lake
• 532-7042

Rumor has it that infamous gangster Dutch Schultz once slept here. If he did, he surely left relaxed. The six large rooms are tastefully decorated with antique king- or queen-size brass or four-poster beds and other elegant things from the past. From the large porch, guests are treated to a beautiful view of the Pharaoh Wilderness area (see Area Overviews).

An outstanding breakfast is prepared daily for guests by proprietor and former food writer Rita Skojec, so expect a real treat. Scrumptious gourmet delights include apple-walnut French toast with fruit sauce, Adirondack eggs Benedict or orange Belgian waffles.

Silver Spruce Inn

$$$ • U.S. Hwy. 9, Schroon Lake
• 532-7031

Although Dutch Schultz may have slept down the street (see the previous Schroon Lake Bed & Breakfast entry), it's likely the gangster enjoyed the speakeasy in this inn's cellar during Prohibition. The Silver Spruce's long and colorful history, however, is only part of its stately charm. Although the inn boasts 28 rooms, only two suites and two spacious bedrooms are reserved for guests. The rooms are decorated with antiques and quilts, and each has a private bath with oversize porcelain tub. If you are looking for a quiet, relaxing getaway, this inn, just across from the Schroon River Falls, may be a good hideout.

A country-style breakfast is served daily in the large, antique-adorned dining room.

Stone Wells Bed and Breakfast

$$$ • 331 Montcalm St., Ticonderoga
• 585-6324

Stone Wells is in a historic cobblestone house, constructed by the Clark brothers in 1921 in the center of Ticonderoga, that's listed on state and national registers of historic places. The house features five guest rooms (one with private bath), three shared baths, a spacious dining room and living room with fireplace. The guest rooms are decorated simply but comfortably with some antiques and many Adirondack furnishings made by Stone

Wells's owner. Each day begins with a full breakfast that includes juice, coffee, sweetbreads and fresh fruit.

All Tucked Inn

$$ • 53 S. Main St., Westport • 962-4400, (888) ALL-TUCK

On the serene shores of Lake Champlain and just a short drive from the pristine High Peaks, All Tucked Inn is a magical, whimsical place where troubles flee and peace presides. Situated in the historic village of Westport, this inn offers nine lovely rooms, each with a private sparkling bath. Many rooms feature views of Lake Champlain and Vermont's Green Mountain range.

A bountiful breakfast is included in the room rate, and four-course dinners also are available.

The Inn on the Library Lawn

$$$ • One Washington St., Westport
• 962-8666

Since 1875 this inn has been the architectural and social centerpiece of Westport, and it continues to maintain the charm and features of a bygone era. The 10 rooms here, all with private baths, vary in terms of their antique furnishings and sleeping arrangements. One suite with a queen bed and sitting room also is available. Other rooms include either single, double or queen beds. A well-stocked library, lounges and deck areas add to the cozy atmosphere. A hearty, four-course homemade breakfast is included in the room rate.

Westport Hotel

$$ • N.Y. Rt. 9N, Westport • 962-4501

Next door to the Depot Theater, which in turn is near the Westport train station, this quaint hotel is the perfect retreat for a quiet dinner, an evening of quality entertainment at the Depot (see Arts and Culture) and breakfast on the porch before you begin another day of adventures. The historic hotel, established in 1876, the same year that railroad service began operating in the Lake Champlain valley, offers 12 charming rooms with antique furnishings in a relaxed, homey setting.

If you are passing through during the off-season (November through May) and wish to stay at the Westport, be sure to ask about special packages.

Lake George/ Upper Hudson Region

Friends Lake Inn
$$$$ • Friends Lake Rd., Chestertown • 494-4751

Without dispute, this is one of the premier lodging and dining experiences in the entire Adirondack region. Formerly known as Murphy's Friends Lake Inn, it was originally built in the 1860s as a boarding house for transplanted tannery workers. Later in the century, it became a summer retreat for many looking to escape the heat and crowds of New York City. They would take the Adirondack Railroad to its stop at the "Glen" (where N.Y. Route 28 now crosses the Hudson River), then continue in horse-drawn buggies for the few remaining miles to the inn.

These days, guests enjoy the combination of decor and elegance that honors those glory days of the "Gilded Age" with modern conveniences and comforts such as whirlpool tubs and cable TV. What really sets today's Friends Lake Inn apart from much of its competition are its recreational opportunities, fine dining and creative events.

Within the grounds of the inn are 32 kilometers of groomed cross-country ski trails in the winter (see Skiing), mountain biking in the summer, and a private beach on Friends Lake. You can also enjoy hiking, nearby golf and whitewater rafting on the Hudson.

The restaurant, featuring "new American" cuisine, and its wine selection are regarded as among the best in the Adirondacks. On the menu you might find such temptations as rack of lamb, breast of duckling and Hunter's Pie (a stew of beef, venison and sausage covered with a pastry crust). In August 1997, the inn received *Wine Spectator* magazine's "Grand Award" for its wine collection — one of only five places worldwide to receive the annual honor — which includes more than 15,000 bottles. A testament to just how good the restaurant here is: Many people drive a long way just for dinner — without staying in the mar-

velous lodging. For those interested in something a little lighter, the Friends Lake Inn has introduced a new "Bistro Menu" that features such items as Black Angus cheeseburgers, Caribbean-style fish cakes, grilled chicken sandwiches, microbrews and the like. Naturally, the country breakfasts here are magnificent as well.

Throughout the year, you can enjoy a number of special events here, from murder mystery weekends to cross-country ski and fondue parties to chocolate lovers festivals. As far as we're concerned, any weekend here is a special event.

As you can imagine, the accommodations here are quite special as well. You can choose from a total of 16 rooms and suites, all with period furniture, antiques, quilts and private baths; some have fireplaces and whirlpool tubs. The two most recent additions are Adirondack Great Camp-style rooms, named Fieldstone and River Rock for the large stone fireplaces built into the rooms. These suites feature rustic furniture, maple floors, a private entrance, feather beds and large luxury bathrooms with whirlpool tubs.

You've probably figured out by now that this is not exactly the least expensive lodging in the Adirondacks. However, for a special occasion of just a whimsical splurge any time of the year, the Friends Lake Inn is tough to beat and certainly an experience to create lasting memories.

Landon Hill Bed & Breakfast
$$$ • Landon Hill Rd., off N.Y. Rt. 8, Chestertown • 494-2599

Only open since 1995, this handsome inn on a hill just north of Chestertown already has established a reputation as one of the nicest lodging choices and best values in the region. It's location just off N.Y. 8 (for east/west travel) and very near I-87 Exit 25 (for north/south travel) make it convenient to a number of recreational, shopping and cultural activities. The attractive village of Chestertown is within a short walk for your browsing pleasure, as is Dynamite Hill Park, where you can skate, sled and ski under the lights during the wintertime.

The extra touches are what makes the difference here — from the boot warmers the owners happily supply guests to the plentiful area maps and trail guides to the free companionship provided by Gus and Brenna, the resident Labrador retrievers. Coffee and muffins are served by the wood stove before breakfast, and you need to fight the temptation to have a second muffin because you don't want to ruin your appetite for the omelettes and the quiche.

The signature feature of the inn is the large oak spiral staircase that winds its way to the second-floor accommodations. There, you will find two large rooms with private baths and two additional rooms that share an adjoining bath. In addition, downstairs you will find one bright and spacious room with a large private bath, recommended by the owners for those in need of handicap accessibility.

Landon Hill may be a relatively new bed and breakfast inn, but we think it will be here for a long time. It's open year round.

The Lamplight Inn Bed & Breakfast
$$$ • 2129 Lake Ave., Lake Luzerne • 696-5294, (800) 262-4668

Just 10 miles from Lake George and 18 miles from Saratoga Springs, The Lamplight Inn has evolved into quite an impressive country inn complex in recent years. Included on the grounds are the original huge 1890 Victorian Main House, the Brookside Cottage and the Carriage House.

The Main House features 10 second-floor bedrooms (five of which feature gas fireplaces) with private baths, central air and in-room phones. It is an imposing yet intimate structure, set up on a small rise with a handsome gated entrance and large covered porch beckoning travelers to stop and stay. Inside, the public areas are beautifully furnished without being too cluttered or ornate. The beamed ceiling, Oriental rugs and two fireplaces add warmth (figuratively and literally) to the atmosphere.

Next door sets the Brookside Cottage — once the caretaker's cottage for the inn and recently renovated into two bedrooms each with queen bed, gas-burning fireplace, private bath, TV, phone and air conditioning.

The newest accommodation available at The Lamplight Inn is the Carriage House. There you will find five bedrooms — each features queen bed, fireplace, whirlpool tub, private porch, TV, phone and central air — one of which is handicapped-accessible.

The Lamplight Inn recently obtained a liquor license, so now you can enjoy wine or beer here without bringing it along. The proprietors claim a memorable enough breakfast that you "won't need lunch," and we're not about to argue with them. It is a highly regarded and much written about inn, featured in the December 1993 issue of *Country Inns* magazine. Whether for a holiday, summer vacation, or getaway for your own special occasion, we're sure you will enjoy the hospitality and accommodations here.

FYI

Unless otherwise noted, the area code for all phone numbers listed in this guide is 518.

Goose Pond Inn
$$$ • Main St., North Creek • 251-3434

For something on not such a grand scale as the Friends Lake Inn or Garnet Hill Lodge, but without missing a beat in comfort, convenience or gourmet breakfasts, this charming Victorian bed and breakfast inn fills the bill.

In the more-and-more charming village of North Creek along the Hudson River, and just a mile from the slopes of Gore Mountain, the Goose Pond Inn can make great headquarters for a weekend of outdoor adventure or indoor reading. Accommodations include four guest rooms, each with private bath and filled with antiques and collectibles. Breakfast is the main attraction here, and owner Jim Englert makes sure you won't soon forget his specialties — brandied French toast with sauteed apples and Belgian waffles with flambéed bananas. (Yum — we picked the wrong time of day to write about this stuff!)

As for the inn's name — well there is a pond, and there are a couple of resident geese anxious to have you pass along whatever muffins you can't finish. The Goose Pond Inn is starting to get the attention it deserves, and was recently written up in the *Yankee Magazine Travel Guide*.

Garnet Hill Lodge
$$$ • 13th Lake Rd., North River
• 251-2444

Depending on what you want out your visit, the Garnet Hill Lodge can be anything from an upscale Adirondack lodge just perfect for relaxing and taking in massive amounts of calories to a full-scale recreational resort just as good at burning them back off again.

Garnet Hill is probably best known as one of the premier cross-country ski resorts in the United States. Says who? Says the readers of Snow Country magazine, who recently named it as one of the top 10 Nordic centers in the country. Besides all it has to offer winter enthusiasts (see Skiing), Garnet Hill has so much more to enjoy throughout the year. Its setting on a hilltop high above Thirteenth Lake and adjacent to the Siamese Ponds Wilderness opens up such seasonal activities as fishing, canoeing, swimming, hiking, mountain biking (on the ski trails), even tennis on one of two courts. Nearby Gore Mountain offers terrific downhill skiing in the winter, and the rushing waters of the Hudson River offer "downhill" rafting and tubing as well in the spring and summer. There's so much to choose from here, you may just have to take a yearlong sabbatical and move up here to experience it all!

If you decide to do just that (or even a long-weekend sabbatical — a little easier to swing with the boss) you're not likely to tire of the hospitality, lodging or food service available here. Accommodations include the Log House, which is the main lodge building and includes the restaurant and lounge on the first floor, and 16 nicely appointed rooms upstairs. Nine of those rooms have balconies that offer a sweeping view of Thirteenth Lake and the mountains beyond, and all rooms have private baths. The Log House has a striking interior, with massive log pillars, an imposing granite fireplace and a commanding view from the restaurant.

In addition to the Log House, guests can choose from the Tea House, the Birches and the Big Shanty. The Birches is a separate building just a short walk from the Log House with five spacious bedrooms and a common room. The Tea House provides real luxury, with two large guest rooms with whirlpool tubs plus a sauna and hot tub on the lower level. Finally, there is Big Shanty, a real Adirondack lodge dominated by its huge stone fireplace and including seven guest rooms.

The restaurant itself is a destination, and many folks make a lengthy trip just to enjoy its setting and fine food. The generous portions seem designed to keep carbo-burning skiers happy and fully fueled, and you'll find a good selection of beef, pasta and seafood dishes to choose from. Resist the temptation to fill up on the wonderful homemade bread here because you'll want to leave room for the equally wonderful homemade desserts at the end of the evening.

Garnet Hill Lodge is a wonderful destination any time of the year.

House on the Hill Bed & Breakfast
$$$$ • N.Y. Rt. 28, Warrensburg
• 623-9390, (800) 221-9390

You can tell a lot about a place by browsing through the guest book. When all you find is nothing but names and addresses, and the last date signed was four months ago, you have to wonder. Here, it's page after page of genuine testimonials like these: "Rarely are elegance and simplicity married so handsomely" and "You exceeded all standards in charming and exquisite decor, cleanliness, delicious breakfast, attention to detail and most important — gracious hospitality." Yes, guests here sure seem to go home satisfied, and it's easy to see why.

This 14-room Federalist-style homestead, built more than a century ago, offers a total of five beautifully decorated guest rooms, each with a queen bed, along with its own style and personality. Four of the five rooms offer private baths, and three of those baths come with Ultra Thermo-Masseur Baths, which sound relaxing enough that you'll just have to try them out for yourself.

In the mornings, coffee and fresh-baked muffins are served in your room (you have to get out from under the comforters on your own, however) as a prelude to the full and custom-made breakfast available at your request in the sun room. You can take your time to soak up both the last morsels of muffin and the view of the surrounding 176 acres from either the sun room or the large wraparound porch.

In addition to the features and hospitality you'd expect in a first-class lodging property, the House on the Hill has on display an interesting collection of original art and prints from noted artists such as Renoir, Salvador Dali and even pop-art's Peter Max. They also pride themselves on keeping a spotless, dust and smoke-free environment, and it makes a difference that guests can appreciate. The House on the Hill has been featured in *Country Victorian* magazine.

You can enjoy a visit here on a year-round basis. House on the Hill is near the antique shopping of Warrensburg, the downhill skiing at Gore Mountain, the whitewater rafting on the Hudson River and the man-made attractions of Lake George.

Merrill Magee House
$$$$ • 2 Hudson St., Warrensburg • 623-2449

This well-known and highly regarded country inn and restaurant is set in a Greek Revival-style house that dates back to the early 1800s. As old as it is, the Carrington family that owns it has successfully found a balance between retaining its 19th-century charm and providing popular 20th-century conveniences (like a spa room with a hot tub, for example).

The inn is set in the heart of Warrensburg and allows for easy strolling to the town's many shops and restaurants. Save one of your evening meals for right here, though, as the proprietors offer fine candlelight dining seven nights a week throughout the year and a fabulous Sunday brunch from mid-May until mid-October.

You'll find two different lodging settings here. The Family Suite, upstairs in the main house, offers two bedrooms, a sitting room with TV, and a refrigerator. The two rooms are furnished with double beds and country quilts and share a bath with one of those big, deep claw-foot tubs you can practically scuba dive in. The Peletiah Richards Guest House, set behind the main inn, offers 10 guest rooms loaded with lots of charm and cozy features such as king or queen beds, fireplaces in every room, handmade quilts and private baths.

The combination of its convenient setting, lovely landscaped grounds, fine dining and beautiful accommodations makes the Merrill Magee House a winner on all fronts. If you don't have a special occasion coming up to celebrate here, we suggest you make one up.

Southern Adirondack Lakes Region

Trailhead Lodge
$$ • Washburn Rd., Benson • 863-2198

A few miles south of N.Y. Route 30, this old farmhouse is situated at the southern end of the famous Northville-Lake Placid hiking trail (which winds its way north along streams and rivers for 130 miles!). More outdoorsman-lodge than antique-hunter bed and breakfast, it was originally built as a two-room, fireplace-heated cabin in the 1850s. Since then, the lodge has undergone several additions to attain its current configuration. Its greatest attraction is its setting, literally where the road ends and the trail and wilderness beyond begin. A visit here is not unlike the experience you would have enjoyed a century ago.

In the wintertime, guest can enjoy some of the best cross-country ski trails in the East at the "next door neighbor's place," namely Lapland Lake Cross-Country Ski & Vacation Center (see Skiing). During the warm months, hiking is the main attraction — from day hikes to nearby mountain tops such as Cathead (see Hiking) to multi-day adventures on the Northville-Lake Placid trail.

For accommodations, the Trailhead Lodge offers four rooms with double beds and one room with a twin bed. All bedrooms have been restored in recent years, all have shared baths, and none have TVs. However, this is not a place to come and catch up on the latest soaps. The living area downstairs will warm you with hearty country breakfasts in the dining room, a fireplace and a game room.

To get the most enjoyment out of a stay at this special place, sign up for a guided trip with owner John Washburn (great-grandson of the original owner) or John's son Michael. Both are licensed Adirondack guides and extremely knowledgeable about backpacking, canoeing, hiking and backcountry ski trips.

1870 Bed & Breakfast
$$ • 36 W. Main St., Indian Lake • 648-5377

This inn takes its name from the year it was built and is set on what was once a working farm. You can stroll the 40-acre grounds and enjoy the aromas from the flower garden and the tastes from the raspberry patch. The decor is comfortable but not overly elegant — more like a nice old neighbor's house than a fancy inn. That's just fine with us, and it should be with you too, because the reasonable rates here will save you some money to spend on lots of fun stuff nearby, including whitewater rafting on the Hudson or a day at the Adirondack Museum.

The common living area for guests has all the comforts of home, including a fireplace, cable TV and board games and puzzles if you've forsaken "the tube" while on vacation. Overnight accommodations include four rooms on the upper level that share a bath, and one room with its own private bath downstairs. The 1870 Bed & Breakfast is open year round.

Inn at the Bridge
$$$ • 641 Bridge St., Northville • 863-2240

Built in 1903, this country inn is certainly in a "can't miss it" location. It is literally the first thing you see when crossing the bridge from N.Y. Route 30 into the village of Northville. Set up on a hill to the left as you cross over the bridge, the stately white Queen Anne Victorian is a striking presence. The view *from* the inn is even nicer than the view approaching the inn. From the large wraparound porch or gazebo on the lawn, you can see where the Sacandaga River widens to join the Great Sacandaga Lake, the second-largest body of water within the Adirondack Park. To your right and left are the foothills of the southern Adirondacks.

The Inn at the Bridge is as conveniently located as it is scenic. Just across the bridge is a public beach and the Sacandaga Park. Walk a couple of blocks in the opposite direction and you're on Main Street in the attractive village of Northville, and within easy walking distance of the Adirondack Country Store (see Shopping).

The inn's decor keeps its Victorian flavor throughout, including in the 32-foot parlor room with its fireplace, couches, television and games. All six guest rooms have private baths and comfortably refined furnishings. A full breakfast is served each day, and dinners are available on weekends to the general public as well as guests. The Inn at the Bridge is truly a great place to relax and enjoy the southern Adirondacks all year.

The Irondequoit Inn
$$$ • Old Piseco Lake Rd., off N.Y. Rt. 8, Piseco • 548-5500, (800) 497-0350

What a pleasant find this is! Popular with the western New York crowd from Rochester and Syracuse, The Irondequoit Inn is really more than just a country inn. The first two impressions you get are of the unique sign framed by white birch logs along the road that signals your arrival, and the view of unspoiled Piseco Lake from the hilltop location of the main lodge. You feel instantly welcomed and relaxed, and that feeling won't likely go away until you sadly check out. The day we visited, a large family was spending the weekend for a reunion. From the looks on their faces as they sat and chatted on the large wraparound porch overlooking the lake, they might *still* be there (call ahead to find out if they've left yet!).

That's pretty much how this place started out too. In the late 1800s, a group of businessmen and friends, after enjoying many a visit, bought the buildings and land here so they would have a permanent place to hold their own family gatherings. From the surroundings to the varied reasons people come here, much is the same now as it was then.

The Irondequoit Inn is actually a complete vacation complex, offering a main lodge with nine guest rooms (with three shared baths), a two-bedroom housekeeping cottage, a one-bedroom efficiency cottage and even a number of lakeside and wooded tent sites for camping. In fact, even though Piseco Lake boasts three large state campgrounds along it shores, the Irondequoit Inn is the only place on the lake where you can camp and also take a shower (score one for the Irondequoit, as far as we're concerned).

A couple of tennis courts are available to guests (although we think it would be hard to keep your eye on the ball with Piseco Lake as the backdrop to your opponent's serve), as is a private beach. You can even rent a canoe and paddle out to an undeveloped private island a little way offshore to enjoy a picnic. To fuel all of this activity, you can count on one of the heartiest of all Adirondack breakfasts, served in the dining room and featuring seven kinds of pancakes plus omelettes and other baked goodies. The public is welcome to join in for breakfast, and at only $6 a tummy, who could blame them?

So what's the bonus round? Well, you can enjoy all of this almost all year, with the exception of April and from mid-November until Christmas.

Old Forge/ Raquette Lake Region

Big Moose Inn
$$$ • Big Moose Rd., off N.Y. Rt. 28, Big Moose Lake • (315) 357-2042

This country inn is about 5 miles west of Eagle Bay on Big Moose Lake. The real treats here are the unspoiled scenery (you'll think you are the only folks in the world!) and, somehow amid all this wilderness, an incredible restaurant. So well regarded is the restaurant, it recently was voted "Best Individual Restaurant in the Snowbelt" by *Snow Goer* magazine for the third consecutive year. The inn is chef-owned, so you know the food is going to be an important facet of the experience here. You can enjoy continental cuisine and homemade just-about-everything from breads to desserts. We expect this is the kind of place where a lot of people go for a nice dinner, then the dinner becomes so nice and the evening so special — they just have to stay for the night. Not a bad idea.

If you choose to do the same, you'll have your pick 16 rooms, all with private bath and most with a nice view of Big Moose Lake. If you've got plenty of room on the plastic, you can top off your fine dining experience by renting the one suite with king-size bed, fireplace and Jacuzzi. If and when you finally get up the next morning, you can enjoy a hike on one of many nearby trails (see Hiking), a peaceful

canoe ride on the lake, or an invigorating snowmobile ride — although likely not all on the same day.

The Big Moose Inn is open almost year round, with the exception of April (when you probably wouldn't want to visit anyway because of the weather) and part of November.

Cinnamon Bear Bed & Breakfast
$$$ • N.Y. Rt. 28, Inlet • (315) 357-6013

Offering four large guest rooms and what the proprietors call a "mountain breakfast," the Cinnamon Bear is as cozy and cute as its name. All rooms are furnished in a comfortable country style, and all beds are draped with those big fluffy comforters that inspire sleeping in. You can enjoy this fine inn any time of the year, but you'll have to choose whether to come here in the summer for canoeing on the Fulton Chain of Lakes or in winter for cross-country skiing and snowmobiling. Since it's right on Trail A, you have direct access to the vast network of snowmobile trails this region is known for. If you want to enjoy the culture of Blue Mountain Lake and the attractions of Old Forge from one spot, this place is convenient to both.

Moose River House Bed & Breakfast
$$$ • 12 Birch St., Thendara • (315) 369-3104

This elegant Victorian home, built in 1884, is adjacent to the popular Adirondack Scenic Railroad and flanks the banks of the Big Moose River. It is one of the few bed and breakfasts in the world, we suspect, where you can launch a canoe from its grounds, paddle along a scenic and peaceful river route, then be picked up and returned to your starting point via excursion train. Sounds to us like the perfect way to burn off some of those big breakfast calories. Afterward, you can lounge on the lovely covered porch and start to strategize about what you'll have for dinner at the neighbor's house, which in this case happens to be the fine dining of the Van Auken's Inne (see next listing).

For your overnight accommodations, you can choose from five rooms — two with private baths and queen beds, two rooms with a shared bath, and a suite with its own kitchen, living area and bath. Moose River House is open all year.

Van Auken's Inne
$$$ • off N.Y. 28, Thendara
• (315) 369-3033

Van Auken's Inne has two distinct advantages: its location opposite the historic Thendara Train Station and the Adirondack Scenic Railroad; and a first-class upscale restaurant. As plans in 1998 call for the rail service to be extended south all the way to Utica (about 50 miles), things could get a lot busier around here when visitors by the carload are dropped off at the Inne's front door. In fact, this is how things used to work at the turn of last century before the automobile took over as the primary means of transportation to and around the Adirondacks.

Whether by car, train or seaplane (that's also a possibility at the nearby Fulton Chain lakes), visitors who spend some time here will surely enjoy the inn and its surroundings. Besides the excursion train, Van Auken's Inne is adjacent to the Big Moose River and convenient to the highly regarded Thendara Golf Club (see Golf) and the many shops and attractions of Old Forge, just a mile or so down N.Y. 28.

The chef and owner of Van Auken's Inne is a CIA graduate (fortunately for you, in this case we are referring to the Culinary Institute of America) and specializes in creating innovative new American cuisine. Make sure to enjoy a beverage on the large pillar-adorned porch before or after your dinner. In addition to breakfast for guests, Van Auken's is open year round for lunch and dinner. Overnight guests can choose from 12 rooms, all with private bath.

**From North To South
Fine Restaruants In The Adirondacks
Run By White Management**

Mangia
WOOD-FIRED PIZZA & PASTA

1562 New Scotland Ave.
Slingerlands, NY 12159
439-5555

418 Route 3
Plattsburgh, NY 12901
562-5555

Stuyvesant Plaza
Albany, NY 12203
482-800

**Log Jam
Restaurant**

Rtes. 9 & 149
Lake George, NY 12845
(518) 798-1155

MANGIA CAFE

Shopper's World Plaza
15 Park Avenue
Clifton Park, NY
(518) 383-6666

BUTCHER BLOCK
STEAK & SEAFOOD

Rt. 3 & I-87, Exit 37
Plattsburgh, NY 12901
(518) 563-0920

1632A Central Ave.
Albany, NY 12212
(518) 456-1653

Restaurants

First of all, dining out in the Adirondacks is a lot more sophisticated than you might think. Oh sure, there are plenty of places where you can sit in your red-and-black–checked flannel ensemble and order a steak and a beer without ever taking off your baseball cap. What's local dining without "local flavor?" The surprise is that, even in this remote and vast wilderness, you also will find candle-lit dining rooms where such delicacies as venison-stuffed red-pepper ravioli with blackberries are being served. In the mood for sliced chilled duck breast with mango chutney? You can find it on the menu of a table here that is almost an area code away from the nearest metroplex. Want a big old slab of prime rib? You won't have any problem tracking that down either around here (*without* the services of a Adirondack guide). Nor should you come across any shortages of pasta, seafood, Italian, Mexican or Chinese cuisine, or anything else your heart desires (or is clogged by).

As one restaurant owner we visited said, the key is "good groceries." Good groceries equals good eats, whether pan-seared, oven-roasted or grilled over an open flame. You can go as fancy or as basic as you want around here, and in some cases you'll be surprised at how "fancy" the food is in some of the most "basic" settings. The good news: Virtually anywhere you go in the Adirondacks, you'll be close to good food and friendly folks anxious for you to enjoy it.

As you can imagine, in a region this big and this popular, there are hundreds of potential places to pull up a chair and have a good

meal. Some have been around for generations, some have quickly established themselves within a few short years, and some will open and close between the time these words are written and the time you read them. The restaurant business is tough and volatile, with lots of change-over even in big cities populated by millions of hungry residents. So, we have tried to limit our listings here to places that have either been around for a good length of time, or show great promise for doing so.

For the most part, we include independent, stand-alone restaurants here — those that are not a part of a hotel or inn. However, you'll find several mentions of worthy dining experiences in Bed & Breakfasts and Country Inns as well as in Accommodations, as many of the inns listed there also offer fine restaurants and dining rooms that are open to the public.

With one exception, we do not include franchises and chains in our listings for a couple of reasons. First, there are only a few places within the Park where they even exist, and that's pretty much limited to a smattering of fast-food franchises in the high-traffic areas such as Lake George, Lake Placid and Old Forge. The only full-service chain restaurants, such as The Olive Garden or Ponderosa, are in perimeter cities such as Plattsburgh, Glens Falls and Gloversville. In any event, we assume you are pretty familiar with the species, thus we dedicate our limited space to the local and the noteworthy.

You also won't see roadside burger joints listed here, with the exception of our "Five Great Burger & Soft Serve Spots" feature at

INSIDERS' TIP

If you've got restless kids during dinner and you're lucky enough to be at such lakefront restaurants as The Algonquin on Lake George or Lanzi's on the Great Sacandaga Lake, take them down to the docks to check out the boats and the view and keep them diverted between their hamburger and ice cream.

the end of the chapter. For the most part, every decent-size town has one, and you can tell when you're within 200 yards whether or not they're any good. Are there cars in front and a line at the window? Then it's probably just what you're looking for if you have a hankering for a hamburger.

As a rule, it's always a good idea to at least call ahead and ask if a restaurant you're interested in takes reservations (particularly if you are visiting on a summer weekend). Not all will, but for those that do, it will be tough for you to get in without a long wait if you don't get your name on the list.

Now, for some all-important, always entertaining assumptions. Most of the restaurants listed here are open year round, but we indicate for you in each case what their situation is. You can assume that all restaurants in this chapter accept major credit cards; we indicate in the header when that isn't the case. You also can assume that you will find children's menus at our selected restaurants; we indicate if that's not the case. All restaurants in New York State are required to provide both smoking and non-smoking sections, and virtually all restaurants included here are accessible to handicapped patrons. Most have bars and serve beer, wine and liquor unless we note otherwise.

FYI

Unless otherwise noted, the area code for all phone numbers listed in this guide is 518.

arrange restaurants within each geographic region alphabetically by town, then alphabetically by the name of the restaurant. For example, all of the restaurants we cover in Lake Placid are listed alphabetically in the "Lake Placid/Tri-Lakes Region" section prior to any restaurants in Saranac Lake. If you were able to figure it out in the Accommodations and Bed & Breakfasts chapters, you should have no problem with it here. We don't break down restaurants into different categories such as American, Continental, Seafood, etc., because there are so many places here that are versatile enough to span several categories. So, you'll just have to read about them and trust that our descriptions are lucid and enlightening enough to guide you in the right direction.

Our intent with this chapter is to provide you with a "buffet" of dining options in the Adirondacks. By no means is it intended to be an all-inclusive list, and we welcome your suggested additions for the next edition should you have a terrific experience at a restaurant we don't mention.

Now, on with the "chow." Sorry.

Lake Placid/
Tri-Lakes Region

Dumas Restaurant
$ • N.Y. Rt. 3, Childwold • 359-2540

N.Y. Route 3 between Tupper Lake and Watertown is a lonely road with few diversions. The vast stretches of forests don't need much in the way of roadside services, and you'll find few — especially gas stations — provided. While you can get a snack at many of the service stations, a full-course, sit-down restaurant that's open all week all year is as rare as winning the New York State lottery. Thank goodness for Dumas Restaurant.

If you get hungry during your Route 3 journey, Dumas in Childwold is your best (and only!) choice for miles. Dumas serves basic fare for breakfast, lunch and dinner. The menu won't make any food critic's hit list, but any

Price Code

To help you plan out your culinary costs, we include a simple price code based on an average dinner cost for two people, not including alcoholic drinks, dessert, tax or tip. In other words, here's what a couple of entrees and maybe a split appetizer will cost you.

Price-code Key

$	Less than $20
$$	$21 to $40
$$$	$40 to $60
$$$$	$60 and more

Finally, here's how to find the perfect spot for your Adirondack dining experience. We

trucker, local or starving traveler will certainly remember the satisfying meal here the next time they're passing through. Every night there's a different home cooking-type (meat and potatoes with gravy plus a vegetable, that is) dinner special.

Cranberry Lake Inn
$$ • N.Y. Rt. 3, Cranberry Lake
• (315) 848-3301

There's not many choices for lunch and dinner out this way in one of the wildest region's of the Adirondack Park. Fortunately, this family-style restaurant, serving American fare, is not only a good choice as a gathering spot (especially the lounge area), but also a good choice for food. The prime rib on weekends is a house specialty.

A Piece of Cake
$ • N.Y. Rt. 73, Keene • 576-9943

A deli and pastry shop must be something special to deserve mention in this Restaurants chapter, and A Piece of Cake earns its inclusion — and not just because owner Vickie is, according to local lore, "a piece of work." Whether you're coming into or leaving the region, or just planning to take a hike with the family, the sandwiches here make a meal for your entire trip. They are as tall as some of the tales you will likely hear told by the locals passing the time on the porch. Hikers, take note: We highly recommend the box lunch. Any of the pastries are good bets as well.

The deli opens around 7 AM and closes mid- to late afternoon, usually between 3 and 4 PM.

Monty's Elm Tree Inn
$$ • N.Y. Rt. 73, Keene • 576-9769

Monty's reputation ranges far and wide. A few stories about this place are even legendary, but you'll have to dig them up for yourself. *The New York Times* once heralded Monty's thick and juicy hamburgers — not your "normal" fast-food burgers — as the finest in the

INSIDERS' TIP

If you want to maximize your enjoyment of a restaurant with a scenic view, pay attention to when "sundown" will be, so you can make your reservation for a half-hour or so ahead of time. That way, you can enjoy your wine, take in the sunset and be a hero with your companion — all by checking the local paper's weather page.

world. If you disagree, a lively debate may take place in the bar or on the porch. This is a good place for a family meal of typical American fare. Lunch and dinner are served during summer, but it's dinner-only the rest of the year.

Alpine Cellar Restaurant
$$ • N.Y. Rt. 86, Lake Placid • 523-2180

For German-food lovers, the authentic menu of the Alpine Cellar has long been a favorite of the locals and tourists. It's all here — rouladen, sauerbraten, bratwurst, bauernwurst, schnitzel and 75 varieties of German beer. The servings are hearty, so bring along an appetite. The House Platter is a consistent favorite.

You'll find the Alpine Cellar just before the Lake Placid Club golf course on N.Y. 86. Dinner is served nightly.

Arturo's
Holiday Inn, 1 Olympic Dr., Lake Placid • 523-2556

Literally in the center of the village on a hill overlooking the famed Olympic Arena, Arturo's is off the Holiday Inn's main lobby. It offers an Italian/American menu with something to please virtually any taste. The pasta buffet is particularly popular with the regulars.

Arturo's serves breakfast, lunch and dinner daily, and if your staying at the hotel, room service is available.

Averil Conwell Dining Room
$$$ • Mirror Lake Inn, 5 Mirror Lake Dr., Lake Placid • 523-2544

Many paintings of old Lake Placid by Averil Conwell decorate Mirror Lake Inn (see Accommodations), hence the name of its dining room. The cuisine served in this elegant setting has a slight Adirondack influence with venison and trout always on the menu, along with a variety of other adventurous meals, including chicken, beef, pork and seafood dishes prepared with flair. What about pork tenderloin saddleback, pan-seared scallops or warm pear streusel? Yum.

The dining room overlooks Mirror Lake. The inn certainly makes any list of special places for a special night out. The dress code is "neat casual," meaning no T-shirts, but you might wish to dress up a bit more as restaurant reviewers consistently give the Averil Conwell Dining Room highest ratings for atmosphere, service and food. Let's call it a casual but sophisticated place for breakfast or dinner.

Black Bear Restaurant
$$ • 157 Main St., Lake Placid • 523-9886

You can't miss this place on Main, unless of course you can't see the big black bear guarding the door. During the summer, the bear presides over the line for the soft ice cream near the outside window. The restaurant offers some tables with nice views of Mirror Lake, but without the high sticker price of other spots on the lake. This place is a good choice for a family meal. The food is not fancy, but the traditional American menu offers a good selection of burger and sandwich platters plus chicken, fish and beef entrees and salads. This family restaurant serves breakfast, lunch and dinner daily.

www.insiders.com

See this and many other **Insiders' Guide®** destinations online — in their entirety.

Visit us today!

Charcoal Pit Restaurant
$$ • Saranac Ave., Lake Placid • 523-3050

Ask some locals where they like to eat, and the Charcoal Pit consistently makes the list. The restaurant serves Greek-American cuisine for dinner in an Adirondack-casual atmosphere. Although the Greek food is the specialty, the menu has choices for everyone, including charbroiled steaks and chops, prime rib (the house specialty), seafood and a good children's menu. The Charcoal Pit is on the outskirts of the Main Street section of town by the plaza with the Grand Union supermarket.

Cottage Café
$$ • 5 Mirror Lake Dr., Lake Placid • 523-9845

The Cottage Café offers a pub-style menu (sandwiches, nachos, chili) for lunch and dinner, but the quality of the food is only part of the reason why this place is always packed.

The primary reason may be the fact that it sits on the shore of Mirror Lake and has a spectacular view of the High Peaks. During the summer, dining and drinks are available on an outside deck. A few brave hearts sit on the deck in the winter near an outdoor wood stove. Its location on the lake also makes this place popular for an after-dinner drink.

Ere's Pizza and Ristorante
$$ • 37 Main St., Lake Placid • 523-2980

This little restaurant overlooking Mirror Lake is nothing fancy, but that hardly matters if you want some real homemade Italian cooking at a very reasonable price. Everything is made fresh in-house, even the pasta. Most pasta dishes weigh in on a full plate. The view makes this a great spot for a relaxing lunch of grinders, pizza, calzones or salad or a hearty dinner. Ere's is down the hill in the band-shell park in the middle of town.

Goldberries Restaurant
$$ • 137 Main St., Lake Placid
• 523-1799

When you need to please everyone in your crowd, Goldberries, which overlooks Main Street, meets the challenge. Serving breakfast, lunch and dinner, this family restaurant with a large soup and salad bar offers American, Italian and international menu choices of pasta, chicken, beef and seafood, delicious cakes and desserts and a good selection of microbrews and imported beers. During the summer, Goldberries is often crowded, so it must be doing something right.

Great Adirondack Steak & Seafood Co.
$$ • 34 Main St., Lake Placid • 523-1629

This is exactly what the name implies — a steak and seafood restaurant featuring prime rib, live Maine lobster, hand-cut steaks and fresh seafood. An odd collection of antiques accents the dark, wood-paneled interior. The food and service are consistently good, which probably is why the place is consistently packed for lunch and dinner, especially on busy weekends. Since most restaurants in these mountains are not generally known for seafood, seafood lovers should note that this place exists. Although many restaurants offer

seafood dishes, there is generally greater variety here.

Hungry Moose
$$ • 219 Main St., Lake Placid
• 523-3222

The Moose, opposite the Olympic arena, offers a breakfast, lunch and dinner menu with something for the entire family. The restaurant is a good choice if the troupe can't agree on what to eat. Order a full meal (the Friday and Saturday night prime rib special is a great deal) or try something off the rather substantial "Lite Menu," with its smaller portions and low-fat items. Even the kids will find something that they like on the traditional American menu.

Interlaken Inn
$$$ • Interlaken Rd., Lake Placid
• 523-3180

If there is a hidden gem in the village of Lake Placid, this is it. Although the Interlaken is well known by locals, it is down a side street (the first past the Mirror Lake Inn) and, therefore, often overlooked by visitors. Everything about this small, award-winning restaurant is special — the elegant Victorian atmosphere, the service and the food. The menu is limited, but for a good reason — it changes regularly because the chef likes to make special dishes, such as duck au poivre, rack of lamb with a wild mushroom appetizer, or something equally delicious (and time-consuming to prepare). Because this is a small inn, it is one of the few places in town where it is absolutely necessary to make your dinner reservations early, especially during busy weekends.

Jimmy's 21
$$ • 21 Main St., Lake Placid • 523-2353

Jimmy has long disappeared from the scene, but every new owner keeps the name because everyone knows Jimmy's 21 as the little Italian-American restaurant that overlooks Mirror Lake. Jimmy's has a long-standing reputation for fine food and service. All the pasta dishes are made in-house, and the veal and seafood dishes are longtime favorites. The lunch menu of soups and sandwiches is reasonably priced and a good value, even without the view of Mirror Lake.

Lake Placid Lodge
$$$ • Whiteface Inn Rd., Lake Placid
• 523-2700

Some places have an Adirondack camp look but are not the real thing. Lake Placid Lodge (see Accommodations), part of a former Great Camp, is the real McCoy with rustic furnishings and a camp-like feel. Of course, we're not talking about roughing it, but rather an "Adirondack-sophisticated" camp where one can dine on the porch or get an indoor table with candles, fine china and service fit for royalty — not to mention a view of Lake Placid and the High Peaks. The New American cuisine is the extreme opposite of the camp cooking you might remember as a youngster. (Then again, the camps we went to as kids served roast Muscovy duck with braised red cabbage and local wild mushrooms, or lobster ragout with a truffle pasta and ginger butter sauce.) The dinner menu here is innovative, the setting rustic and classical, and the evening will be one to remember. Breakfast and lunch also are served.

Mister Mike's Pizza
$ • 332 Main St., Lake Placid • 523-9770

While large national pizza chains have come and gone in Lake Placid, Mr. Mike's remains. The reason may be because a family of four can still dine on home-style pasta dishes with a salad or pizza for less than $25. Or maybe it's because Mr. Mike's is not an anonymous corporation, but rather Mr. Mike and family, known by everyone in the village and a few tourists as well. There's nothing fancy about this place, but that's exactly why dinner here is so comfortable.

Mr. Mike also operates Pizza Express, opposite the Hilton, on the other end of Main Street. Pizza Express is open for both lunch and dinner.

Nicola's Over Main
$$ • 90 Main St., Lake Placid • 523-4430

The family that operates Mr. Mike's Pizza (see previous entry) also runs this decidedly upscale dinner-only restaurant. A wood-fired oven adds a unique element to the Greek and Italian cuisine — and especially to the taste of the pizza. If your kids are picky about their pizza, and don't like something different, you might be better off at Mr. Mike's. If, however, you crave a more ambitious meal, Nicola's comes highly recommended. It has received a number of rave reviews in national publications such as *Bon Appetit*.

Mykonos Restaurant
$$ • 38 Saranac Ave., Lake Placid
• 523-1164

If you don't believe that everything in this authentic Greek restaurant is homemade, you can watch the chef make it. The two-levels in the restaurant give the place a very spacious and comfortable feel. If you have never tried Greek food, like something a little different or want a touch of spice, this *taverna* would get our nod. Gyros, souvlaki and kebabs are on the lunch menu, with moussaka, lamb, veal stew, seafood and Mediterranean pasta on the dinner menu.

No. 1 Chinese
$ • 211 Main St., Lake Placid • 523-4800

No. 1 is the No. 1 Chinese restaurant in town. So what if it's the only Chinese restaurant? The food is consistently good, as is the variety. The items marked "spicy" are as good as they are spicy. Many of the taller tourists in the world eventually notice that stretching space is in short supply in many resort restaurants, but No. 1 provides patrons plenty of room to unravel their legs after a filling lunch or dinner. Take-out is available.

Three Guys & I Deli
$ • 89 Saranac Ave., Lake Placid
• 523-GUYS

If you're tired of fast food but don't want to do the "restaurant" thing, this New York-style deli offers breakfast, lunch and dinner menus

---

INSIDERS' TIP

We can't stress it enough: If you're going out to dinner, call ahead. See if the restaurant is open, see if they take reservations, etc. The restaurant business is full of variables, so "better safe than hungry."

of light fare at reasonable prices. Instead of just one "designer" coffee flavor of the day, this place offers at least a half-dozen. The best deals are the daily specials (a vegetarian offering is usually among them), but the homemade soup (a meal by itself) and the thick sandwiches have a loyal following among the locals. Catering is also available.

Woodshed
$$ • 237 Main St., Lake Placid • 523-9470

Woodshed has long been a popular gathering place for locals as the American-style dinner menu, with a touch of Italian, offers good choices to satisfy all at a reasonable price. There is generally a good selection of fresh seafood on the menu, along with charbroiled ribs, steaks and chops. The atmosphere is casual, and there is a good kid's menu.

The Woodshed is directly opposite the Speed Skating Oval on Main Street. A small bar section makes it a good place to recuperate after a skate on a crisp winter night.

The Hungry Trout Restaurant
$$$ • N.Y. Rt. 86, Wilmington • 946-2217

This upscale restaurant has a couple of things going for it — a spectacular view overlooking the lighted waterfalls of the Ausable River and an adventurous menu that offers fresh rainbow trout, venison, salmon and distinctly seasoned steaks. The restaurant is about 15 minutes from Lake Placid, but only a few minutes from the slopes at Whiteface Mountain. If you want a warm-me-up and a fine dinner to follow up a day of skiing, this place will fill the bill.

Lily Rose's
$$ • N.Y. Rt. 86, Ray Brook • 891-3514

This restaurant between Lake Placid and Saranac Lake opens early (at 6 AM) and closes late (at midnight), and the early-hour angler and night owl in particular should note these unusual opening and closing times. The menu offers plenty of the basics for every meal — from a big plate of pancakes for breakfast, to sandwich and burger platters for lunch, to Italian-style meals for diner. The restaurant has been known to feature a country music or jazz band on busy weekends.

The Belvedere Restaurant
$$ • 57 Bloomingdale Ave., Saranac Lake • 891-9873

The "Bel" is one of those places where the facade may cause you to hesitate about entering; it looks as if it has seen better days. But the Bel's reign as a favorite local watering hole and Italian restaurant is far from over. The gossip in the separate bar is sometimes even better than the home made pasta dishes, served in a spacious but sparsely decorated dining room. The Bel serves dinner daily.

Casa Del Sol
$$ • 154 Flower Ave., Saranac Lake • 891-0977

Casa is the place for Mexican food, even if it is the only place serving Mexican food in the area. It remains one of the few restaurants in the entire region where you can expect to wait for a table for lunch or dinner, so be warned, especially if the kids are restless. If you like Mexican food, however, the wait simply adds more spice to Casa's reputation. Don't bother trying to beat the line with reservations; they don't take any. Directly across the way is a Casa's retail store, where you can check out the hottest spices, new Mexican cookbooks and other south-of-the-border items while you wait for a table.

Corvo Italian Restaurant
$$ • 94 Main St., Saranac Lake • 891-0510

Directly opposite the Hotel Saranac (see next entry), Corvo's is a popular spot for Italian-style chicken, veal, seafood and pasta for lunch or dinner. The menu here is rather extensive, with plenty of choices (there are some eight to 10 different veal dishes and more than a dozen pasta dishes, all made fresh daily). You can expect two different dining experiences here, depending upon whether you sit in the sun room or the dark paneled lounge.

Corvo's is a favorite spot of many locals, who often dine early so that they can make the movie in the small theater below the restaurant.

Hotel Saranac
$$ • 101 Main St., Saranac Lake • 891-2200

The Apollos Smith Dining Room, formerly Lydia's, in the Hotel Saranac (see Accommodations) has long been the centerpiece of downtown Saranac Lake for breakfast, lunch and dinner. Culinary students from Paul Smith's College work with the hotel's chef to serve up daily specials to go along with what may be called a traditional but progressive menu of beef, pork, fish and poultry dishes. The Hotel Saranac also offers food service — primarily soups, salads and sandwiches — in its Boathouse Lounge. Both the dining room and the lounge have long been popular business meeting and dining spots. The famed Thursday Night Buffet is dollar for dollar one of the best bargains in the entire region. A team of generally four students from the college spend weeks planning a gourmet meal and serve it to guests in the hotel's beautifully restored ballroom. Each week the menu theme changes, but one can expect at least three different entree choices. While the students are graded by their professors on the meal, the smiles of the guests and requests for second helpings serve as the best possible grade. When people refer to "Adirondack hospitality," Paul Smith set the trend more than 100 years ago, and the students of the college maintain those high standards today.

Red Fox Restaurant

$$ • N.Y. Rt. 3, Saranac Lake • 891-2127

A mile outside the village of Saranac Lake on the road to Tupper Lake, this cozy and popular dinner-only restaurant with fireplaces roaring in the winter specializes in steaks, prime rib, fresh seafood and Italian entrees. The restaurant often features live music on Saturday nights. The Red Fox may not look like much from the outside, but locals will attest to their memorable meals here.

St. Regis Restaurant

$$ • N.Y. Rt. 86, Paul Smiths • 327-3574

The St. Regis suddenly appears in the middle of what seems like nowhere, between Gabriels and Paul Smiths. If you have been traveling about for a bit and haven't seen any place to eat for a while (a likely scenario in these parts), this is a friendly place for a home-cooked lunch or dinner of pretty much standard fare. The large, spacious dining room offers some nice views, and a small area with a counter and stools is a good place to hunker down to take in some gossip and a quick bite.

Charlie's Inn

$ • Junction Rd., Lake Clear Junction
• 891-9858

If you are snowmobiling or cross-country skiing in the Lake Clear and Paul Smiths area, or fishing in the St. Regis chain of lakes, you might want to mark Charlie's Inn on your map. It serves lunch and dinner basics like chicken and shrimp in a basket, hamburgers, sandwiches, fish platters and homemade pizza. The bar, which is separate from the dining room, has been known to get rather lively.

The Lodge at Lake Clear Junction

$$$ • N.Y. Rts. 186 and 30, Lake Clear
• 891-1489

This is a classic Old World restaurant where every dinner is made fresh and from scratch. Dining here is as much about the experience as it is about the food. The 100-year-old lodge was constructed in the pioneer spirit of the Adirondacks and as such maintains a distinctive rustic look. The food has a German/European flair, and the roasts, poultry, special pasta and fish dishes and hearty soups all seem to taste even better served with the family heirloom silver and antique glasses.

The Lodge at Lake Clear's restaurant is truly in a class by itself. It not only makes everyone's "must visit" list, but also generally occupies the top spot. It is doubtful that even St. Peter would be seated without reservations as seating is limited to 40 guests. (See our Accommodations chapter for lodging information.)

Park Restaurant

$$ • 320 Park St., Tupper Lake
• 359-7556

This plain and simple family restaurant long has been a landmark in Tupper. The lunch and dinner menu has something for everyone, but leans toward Italian. The red sauce and the breads are homemade. There is plenty of space in the Park, making it a good spot for a large gathering.

Wawbeek on Upper Saranac Lake

$$$$ • 553 Panther Mt. Rd., Tupper Lake
• 359-2475, (800) 953-2656

The Wawbeek restaurant is part of a historic nine-building Great Camp built at the turn of the century (see Accommodations). Among the unique features of this restaurant paneled in dark rope-trimmed wood is the fireplace with a recessed hearth and built-in seats. An enormous moose head, rumored to be the one Teddy Roosevelt shot not long before he was rushed back to Washington to assume the presidency upon William McKinley's assassination, presides over the Moose & Bear Lounge. (This makes for better fiction than fact.) The restaurant is considered an Adirondack classic in both its atmosphere — it is, after all, part of a Great Camp — and its progressive menu. There are daily luncheon specials and a specially priced Monday night buffet.

Plattsburgh/Western Lake Champlain Region

The Deer's Head Inn
$$ • Court St., Elizabethtown • 873-9903
Founded in 1808, this is the oldest inn in the Adirondack Park. Over the years, the owners have perfected a pleasant dining experience in all three attractively decorated dining rooms. The fireplace and book-lined shelves in the lounge set the tone for the overall casual, relaxed atmosphere. The standard lunch menu includes soups, salads and sandwiches, while the dinner menu features similarly standard chicken, beef and pasta dishes as well as some fancier daily specials.

Old Dock Restaurant
$$ • Lake Shore Rd., Essex • 962-4232
Near the Essex ferry, the Old Dock is a popular place during all hours of the day and evening as people linger over their meal watching the comings and goings of the boat traffic on Lake Champlain. (During the winter, patrons ponder when the ice will melt.) The menu is traditional American all year, but it seems even more so during the summer when the burgers and ribs are served up from an outdoor barbecue.

Anthony's Restaurant & Bistro
$$$ • 538 N.Y. Rt. 3, Plattsburgh
• 561-6420
Anthony's casual but stylish country elegance heightens the experience of dining on the progressive continental cuisine and traditional steakhouse fare. The fine wine selection has

earned *Wine Spectator's* "Award of Excellence." Just up N.Y. 3 from Plattsburgh's shopping-center district, Anthony's is a good spot for a casual lunch or fine dinner. A moderately priced bistro menu also is available, and a piano bar offers musical entertainment most evenings. Anthony's is deservedly popular, so call for reservations.

Arnie's Restaurant
$$ • 22 Margaret St., Plattsburgh
• 563-3003
Arnie's seems like it has been around forever. (In the restaurant business, more than 40 years *is* forever.) This casual family restaurant remains a popular spot for everything Italian (pizza, pasta, veal, antipasto) plus a selection of chops, steaks and chicken.

Bootleggers Pub and Brewery
$ • 411 N.Y. Rt. 3, Plattsburgh
• 561-6222
In the Comfort Inn (see Accommodations), near the major malls, Bootleggers is as much about entertainment as it is about food. This is the place that entertains with video games, laser-tag rooms, a large-screen TV, pool tables and more. The lunch and dinner menu includes wings, grilled chicken, ribs and other foods designed for the casual diner on the go.

The Butcher Block
$$ • 15 Booth Dr., Plattsburgh
• 563-0920
If you are mall-hopping and don't want a fast-food place, The Butcher Block long has been a favorite spot to meet friends for drinks, lunch or dinner. The airy solarium gives this place a very comfortable feel. The service and classic American fare makes for a pleasant experience.
The restaurant is just off N.Y. Route 3, near the traffic light at the exit to the Northway (I-87). Look for the sign or you may miss it. (If you do miss it, any local can tell you where it is; a meal here often is included on their shopping list for a mall visit.)

Golden Buffet
$$ • 770 N.Y. Rt. 3, Plattsburgh
• 562-2233
This Oriental (Chinese, actually) and continental restaurant is known for its all-you-can-

eat buffet. You'll find Cantonese, Szechuan and Hunan recipes as well as American favorites, including ribs. While not fancy, the sheer size of the buffet ensures that you'll find something you will like.

Golden Buffet is in the Airport Plaza, about a mile west of the Champlain Mall. Lunch and dinner are served daily.

Howard Johnson Restaurant
$ • N.Y. Rt. 3, off I-87 Exit 37, Plattsburgh • 561-7750

If you are in Plattsburgh for the day, in particular to shop at any of the numerous malls flanking N.Y. Route 3, Howard Johnson offers a great central location and prices that allow you to feed the entire family without putting a major dent in your shopping budget. Large, comfortable and accomodating for busy diners, this restaurant features a menu replete with basic breakfast, lunch and dinner fare. This place is an especially good choice if your party includes youngsters.

Mangia Pizza and Pasta
$ • 496 Cornelia St., Plattsburgh • 562-5555

Near all the major malls in Plattsburgh, the fast service in this small restaurant makes it ideal for people on the go who want a decent but quick sit-down meal in a quiet setting away from the malls. A menu board posted near the entrance describes the various sandwiches, soups and salads for lunch, while dinner selections focus on pasta dishes. The pizza menu is sure to satisfy the kids.

Red Lobster
$$ • Champlain Center South, N.Y. Rt. 3, Plattsburgh • 566-7083

OK, we break from our "no national chains" rule here, but Red Lobster gets a mention because it's one of the few restaurants in the region that really specializes in seafood, and it consistently serves quality food — and, in some cases, considerable quantity — at reasonable prices for lunch and dinner. The place is generally crowded and noisy, but no one seems to notice as they claw that last bit of juicy lobster or Alaskan king crab out of the shell.

Royal Savage
$$ • U.S. Hwy. 9, Plattsburgh • 561-5140

The Royal Savage is one of those classic restaurants where your parents took you as a kid — and now you take your parents for lunch or dinner. The service and food was good years ago, and the attentive staff and traditional fare including steak, fish and chicken are still good today. Senior citizens get a great dinner deal on Tuesdays.

The Royal Savage is a few miles south of Plattsburgh, on the shores of Lake Champlain. It closes in winter.

Windows on the Bay
$$ • 444 Margaret St., Plattsburgh • 563-1111

Few ever tire of visiting this restaurant for lunch, a full-course dinner or an after-work tall cool one. Aside from the friendly service and great menu, the view of Lake Champlain is stunning. During the warm-weather months, there is outside dining; during the winter, you can enjoy the view through plenty of windows. Check out the Friday and Saturday buffets and the Sunday brunch. The buffets are not only a bargain ($9.95 for adults and $6.95 for children), but also a treat with leg of lamb, roast turkey and pork and Virginia ham. There's always a good special on the progressive American menu.

Chesapeake's
$$$ • U.S. Hwy. 9, Schroon Lake • 532-0367

This fine restaurant in a beautiful Victorian setting is named after a couple of Chesapeake

Bay retrievers (yes, dogs). Now, that's a risky choice, and there are a few jokes to be had here (the owners have heard them all), but we'll pass on the obvious opportunity because Chesapeake's comes highly recommended for its Adirondack-size portions and ambitious home cookin' that is a cut finer than most home-cooked meals. If you haven't eaten in a week — you'll need the extra tummy space to clean your plate — stop here. While the prime rib special on Monday night and Surf and Turf on Tuesday are great deals, every night seems to have a choice special.

Now about those dogs and the name . . . Chesapeake Bay retrievers are a hearty breed, developed to withstand harsh winter conditions. Since this dinner-only restaurant is open year round, the owners figured they'd best name the place after a breed that thrives in Adirondack winters.

Terrio's Carriage House
$$$ • U.S. Hwy. 9, Schroon Lake • 532-7700

In the late 1800s, this place was a carriage house. While it still has the feel of an old building, especially in the upstairs lounge with its floor-to-ceiling antique look, this dinner restaurant is now a bit more elegant. The menu is progressive, with a wide selection of seafood (expect nightly specials, including lobster Tuesdays), beef (Thursday is $13.95 steak night), poultry, wild game and pasta dishes prepared in range of styles. How does Cajun chicken, fresh Italian fettuccine or charbroiled filet mignon with bourbon butter or pepper jelly sound? The upstairs lounge offers a light menu of wings, burgers, clams and salads.

Le Bistro
$$$ • Westport Yacht Club, Old Arsenal Rd., Westport • 963-8111

Every table in this upscale dockside restaurant overlooks Lake Champlain, but even with this beautiful ambiance, the food remains the highlight, especially the dinner specials. As the name implies, the focus here is on continental French fare, and Le Bistro's reputation ranks it among the region's best dinner restaurants, even among highly discriminating diners.

Lake George/ Upper Hudson Region

The Algonquin
$$$ • N.Y. Rt. 9N, Bolton Landing • 644-9442

The Algonquin enjoys one of the most picturesque settings in the entire Adirondacks: a wooded cove on Lake George facing the mountains that line the eastern shore. This is one of those places that can be ideal for anything from a quick bite on the outside patio after a day of sailing to a special-occasion, fine-dining experience upstairs in the Topside Dining Room. The decor is somewhere between rustic and nautical — the effect being one of cozy comfort for patrons as they gaze out on the boats bobbing gently at the adjacent docks. There's dock space for patrons too, so sail on in. You can enjoy everything from burgers and sandwiches to continental cuisine such as Greek shrimp (sauteed shrimp with feta cheese, tomatoes, scallions, garlic and spices) and pasta Athena (spinach, mushrooms, roasted garlic, feta cheese and marinara sauce over penne pasta) as well as more traditional fare such as veal Marsala and chicken Monterey. The Algonquin serves lunch and light fare from noon on, and dinner entrees beginning at 5 PM daily during its season from early May until mid-October.

House of Scotts
$$$ • N.Y. Rt. 9N, Bolton Landing • 644-9955

Celebrating 25 years of serving what they call "bountiful country dining" to happy patrons along the west shore of Lake George, the House of Scotts is an attractive restaurant conveniently set in the heart of picturesque Bolton Landing. You can pick your atmosphere — from bright and colorful with hanging baskets of flowers and floral print tablecloths on the large covered outside deck to more dark and intimate inside the dining room. The House of Scotts is chef-owned and operated, and pride in the food's preparation and presentation is evident here. The menu includes a wide variety of items, from the simply good (prime rib, sirloin steaks and broiled seafood) to the classic and upscale (poached salmon, roast duckling). Complimentary with all entrees is the big and bountiful soup and salad bar, a new feature in 1997. You can enjoy lunch and dinner seven nights a week at the House of Scotts from mid-April until the end of October, and the breakfast buffet Sundays (along with Saturday mornings in the summertime).

Trillium

$$$$ • The Sagamore, off N.Y. Rt. 9N, Bolton Landing • 644-9400

The highly acclaimed, award-winning Trillium at the Sagamore Resort Hotel is simply one of the premier gourmet dining experiences in all of upstate New York, much less the Adirondacks. While the view of Lake George from the dining room is beautiful, the view *around* the dining room is equally impressive. Everything here oozes elegance, from the carpeting to the table settings and window treatments. It's like sitting in the palace dining room of some benevolent dictator. How do we know he's benevolent? Well, you're in his dining room and not his dungeon, right? Anyway, this is a special place for celebrating special occasions (as is everything associated with the Sagamore; see the Accommodations and Golf chapters). Unlike most restaurants in the Adirondacks, however, the atmosphere here is decidedly (and proudly) formal; jackets for men are required. You won't mind, though — this is the kind of dining room you'll *want* to dress up for.

The food is gourmet "New American" cuisine, which basically means you'll find a lot of fancy combinations of foods you recognize and eat regularly, just not ever before prepared quite like this. Some examples to tempt you include: char-grilled jerk duck breast (a Caribbean-inspired concoction, not revenge on a duck with a "fowl" attitude); roasted sliced pork tenderloin; and the "signature" entree, pan-seared striped bass (served with zucchini and jumbo lump crab cake). As you would expect, the presentation is creative and attractive (here, it is taken very seriously as part of the total package), and the service is outstanding. The wine list has won an award from *Wine*

Spectator magazine, and the desserts are (you guessed it) "to die for."

You might also expect that the tariff will be quite impressive as well, and you won't likely be disappointed if you're shooting for a personal record bill for a dinner for two. Frankly, this isn't the kind of place to go if you're worried about that sort of thing. It's a place to splurge, relax and indulge, so pamper yourself and your special one. If you want to change clothing sizes within 24 hours, go to Trillium for dinner on a Saturday night, then follow it up the next morning for what is arguably the biggest Sunday brunch in the Adirondacks. You can enjoy a special evening at Trillium any night of the year.

Rene's

$$$ • White Schoolhouse Rd., off N.Y. Rt. 8, Chestertown • 494-2904

Who said you couldn't find Swiss and French cuisine in the Adirondacks? You certainly can here, where chef and owner Rene

FYI

Unless otherwise noted, the area code for all phone numbers listed in this guide is 518.

Plattner has been combining old-world traditions with "new American" cuisine for 15 years now. Combined with a beautiful setting on a hilltop with spectacular views, there is much to recommend about a visit to this highly regarded local favorite. While the setting here is peaceful and scenic, Rene's is easy to get to from just about anywhere in the eastern Adirondacks (being within a few short miles of I-87 Exit 25), making the term "locals" apply to just about anyone from Glens Falls to Elizabethtown.

Chef Rene and his wife and partner, Barbara, began their culinary careers in native Switzerland, and at one time worked in the kitchens of television's Chef Tell before leaving big-city life for a life in the mountains. One visit here and you'll be glad they made the change — and you made the trip. You can enjoy such specialties as Swiss potato soup, lobster ravioli in basil cream or braised salmon au fruit confit (trust us, it works!), but make sure to save room for Barbara's dessert creations. You won't want to miss such temptations as a lacy almond fruit basket (a cookie basket brimming with fresh berries over homemade ice cream, covered with raspberry coulis and whipped cream). Or how about Key lime white cheesecake? Ready to pick up the phone yet?

The news gets better — you can enjoy Rene's anytime of the year, with dinner served daily.

The Barnsider Smoke House Restaurant
$$ • U.S. Hwy. 9, Lake George • 668-5268

If you love barbecue (and you know who you are), look no further. The atmosphere is casual and friendly — it's the kind of place where they don't seem to mind if you make a big mess. There's a small dining room inside, a large outside covered deck off the back, and a new (in 1997) upper deck that overlooks busy U.S. 9 and catches a lot of sun late in the day.

The Barnsider offers finger-lickin', lip-smackin', darn-pleasin' Memphis-style barbecue at its yummiest and messiest. What's "Memphis-style," you ask? Well, we're no experts on this particular topic, but it's got to do with using a closed-pit barbecue oven and wood smoking with hardwoods from right here in the Adirondacks. Look, you don't have to cook it, you just have to order it and enjoy it! And you will — we guarantee it. From half-chickens to full racks of pork ribs plus lots of combination plates, sandwiches and munchies such as Cajun chicken wings and "just-right" onion rings, this is a place where you can get downright hedonistic and primal in celebrating your carnivorism. For those not so inclined, you can also find non-barbecue stuff like grilled swordfish, pasta with shrimp and chicken kebabs.

Your kids will like it here too, even if they don't like barbecue. The children's menu has simple staples such as peanut butter and jelly and grilled cheese sandwiches as well as miniature portions of ribs and chicken for the more adventuresome tots. Don't wait around to enjoy this — the Barnsider is open for lunch and dinner only from early May until Columbus Day weekend.

The Boathouse
$$$ • N.Y. Rt. 9N, Lake George • 668-2389

You can't get any closer to lakefront dining than this — a converted boathouse that actually sits out into the lake. Its location just a mile or so north of Lake George village provides convenience to all the action there, but a welcome respite as well. The decor and atmosphere is decidedly nautical, and you'll want to try to get a table out near the lake end of the restaurant for the best views. You can also enjoy outside dining under umbrella tables along the dock, or semi-outside dining under the octagonal roof that covers the second-floor portico. One note of caution: The Boathouse is not air-conditioned (and the vast majority of evenings doesn't need to be), so it can be uncomfortable on a humid July evening. Fortunately, casual attire is the rule here, so leave the sport coat at home and come in your shorts (nice shorts, that is, along with a shirt and shoes). If you're out on the lake for a day of boating or sailing, you can pull your vessel right in to the dock here for the perfect end to a summer's day.

You'll find a good selection of beef, chicken and seafood here, along with daily Chef's Specials. They proudly serve Black Angus beef, with two cuts of prime rib and a 16-ounce Porterhouse as the main attractions. You can also choose from such items as Seal Island shrimp, seafood Alfredo and a variety of fresh fish. The Boathouse is open from May until October and serves breakfast, lunch and dinner daily.

The Coachman
$$$ • U.S. Hwy. 9, Lake George • 793-4455

If you'd like to know what it feels like to dine in an Adirondack Great Camp without having to come up with the cool million or so to buy one, a visit to The Coachman is a much better bargain. It's imposing presence along U.S. 9 (and easily visible from I-87 that runs parallel) is even more impressive when you walk up to the huge front doors and enter this vast yet somehow cozy restaurant. Originally called The Red Coach when it opened nearly 50 years ago, you can still see such reminders as the wood-carved red stagecoach that separates the lobby area (yes, this place is big enough to have it's own lobby) from the lounge. More recent history has shown The Coachman owned by the DeSantis family for more than 25 years now.

The atmosphere inside is "Adirondack lodge" all the way, with large exposed log beams and posts, stone fireplaces and dark wood throughout. The space is broken up nicely, giving the sprawling square footage a much more intimate feel than you might expect. In addition to the main dining room is the Governors Room, which serves as a separate banquet area for as many as 125 people.

The Coachman is a versatile place — a good spot for anything from a business lunch to a post-skiing light supper to a special night out. It is almost directly across U.S. 9 from The Great Escape theme park (see Attractions and Kidstuff), and just a mile or so down the road from the Lake George factory outlet area known as the "Million Dollar Half-Mile" (see Shopping). As such, it is popular with families and shoppers and serves a healthy number of motorcoach tour groups visiting the area (particularly during "leaf season" in September and October).

While you'll find a good selection of entrees here, including lots of seafood, poultry and veal, the big attraction is beef — and the main attraction is the prime rib, which comes in three different cuts. Duck, chicken, turkey, pork, lamb, lobster, shrimp and salmon all make appearances on the diverse menu, so there's plenty for everyone to choose from. Whatever you choose, you'll also be treated to what has been voted year after year by *The Chronicle* newspaper as the "Best Salad Bar" in this area. This eight-sided pavilion features dozens of hot and cold items, homemade soup and fresh-baked breads. (We find it ironic that the octagonal salad bar is the same shape as a "stop" sign when you'll be tempted to do anything but.) The promise of their own on-site baker should be enough to have you at least *attempt* to save room for dessert, which includes lots of homemade pies, pastries and cakes.

You can enjoy lunch and dinner daily at The Coachman any day of the year except Christmas.

East Cove

$$$ • N.Y. Rt. 9L, Lake George • 668-5265

A longtime local favorite that is just enough off the beaten path to be easily (and unfortunately for unsuspecting diners) overlooked, the East Cove is definitely worth the short diversion out of Lake George village. It is just beyond the Million Dollar Beach and up the hill a bit along Beach Road to N.Y. Route 9L, where it sits right at the intersection. The decor is (you guessed it) another Adirondack-style log cabin, with exposed posts and beams along with nautical hints and photos reflecting Lake George's past. This is not a particularly big place, so expect to wait for a while if you show up on a summer weekend at 7 PM. Even if you do have to wait, we expect it will be well worth it.

The casual surroundings don't lead on to the fancy food you can find here, with nightly specials offering such creative items as lemon pepper penne Sonora (with bay scallops, shrimp, tomatoes and scallions tossed in a spicy southern cheese sauce) and sea scallops Nantucket (with Dijon-crumb topping and lemon garlic butter). The menu offers a big selection of beef, veal and pork, including prime rib (three cuts), center-cut pork chops, wiener schnitzel and veal and artichokes. You'll also find a variety of chicken dishes, such as chicken Victoria (a crabmeat-stuffed boneless breast, baked and served with mushroom supreme sauce) and chicken Santa Fe (a boneless breast sauteed in olive oil with broccoli, sun-dried tomatoes, feta cheese and fresh herbs). The house specialty is the fresh fish, with items like grilled salmon (served with chardonnay dill sauce) and fillet of sole East Cove (egg-dipped and sauteed with white wine and lemon butter) making regular appearances on the specials list. If you're looking for a lighter meal or at least something a that hits the wallet a little easier, you can choose from a half-dozen or so items on the "Light Meals" menu such as chicken teriyaki and fish 'n chips.

East Cove is one of those much appreciated places that not only serves great food for the adult crowd, but also tries to please its littlest patrons. The children's menu is reasonably priced ($3.95 to $4.95 is typical), and as one of the staff told us, "If they don't see anything on it they like, we'll make them something they do." Pretty accommodating attitude for a "fine dining" restaurant, if you ask us.

The East Cove is open year round, seven

Lakeside dining is prevalent throughout the Adirondack Region.

days a week during the summer and Wednesday through Sunday the rest of the year. You can also enjoy their Champagne Buffet Brunch every Sunday from 11 AM until 2:30 PM.

Log Jam Restaurant
$$$ • U.S. Hwy. 9, Lake George • 798-1155

The Log Jam celebrated its 20th anniversary in 1996, and it has evolved during its existence to become one of the most popular and well-regarded restaurants in the Adirondacks. By far, it is the most attractive restaurant we have ever visited that sits at the back of a shopping center parking lot (the good news — there's lots of parking; the bad news — there's lots of pavement). Even this less-than-ideal setting is overcome by a sea of wildflowers that line the wooden fence surrounding the small "front yard" they have created here.

Once inside, the impression gets even better. Built from Adirondack native pines to resemble a logging camp, the walls here are adorned with snowshoes, skis and other Adirondack-related items. It's hard to imagine that the guys working the Hudson ever had it *this* good. Every one of the series of rooms is warm, attractive and inviting — from the bright and cheerful greenhouse to the main lodge room to the beautiful lounge with its massive stone fireplace and huge wooden bar (made from the wood of an former estate at Diamond Point on Lake George). For small group functions of up to 50 or so people, there's even a dedicated banquet room here, complete with antler chandeliers and stone fireplace.

Much of the attractiveness of the Log Jam is in the attention to Adirondack details: old camp utensils on display around the 40-item salad bar; dessert menus displayed on parchment tied between the fork of a birch twig; wood-burning stove in the lobby. None of these things is necessary, yet having them adds a memorable ambiance to the setting. Of course, all of this wouldn't matter if the food wasn't any good, and fortunately that's not a problem here.

It's hard to imagine you couldn't find something on the menu to get excited about. Feel like beef? How about three cuts of prime rib, and two cuts each of New York sirloin, filet mignon and steak au poivre. Feeling more creative? You can choose from such "never-have-time-to-fix-this-at-home" items as blackened chicken Oscar, veal and tortellini Portobello, barbecued Cajun seafood platter and crabmeat stuffed shrimp. Of course, you can always just keep it simple and pick out your own live Maine lobster from the Log Jam tank. The 40-item salad bar, featuring homemade dressings, soups and specialty breads, is included in the price of all entrees. Try to pace yourself!

If you're in the mood for just a warm fire and some munchies after skiing, the lounge is the perfect place to enjoy the bar menu with such tummy-warmers as French onion soup au gratin, Cajun barbecued wings, fried whole clams, and Adirondack fries (potato wedges fried and served with a creamy garlic and horseradish dip — don't worry, didn't you just burn a bunch of calories on the slopes?).

The Log Jam is one of those versatile restaurants that is enjoyable for anything from a family night out (a kid's menu with items from $5.95 to $8.95 is available) to a special night out for two. You can enjoy lunch and dinner here 363 days a year, but you'll have to make other plans for Thanksgiving and Christmas.

Mario's

$$ • 429 Canada St. (U.S. Hwy. 9), Lake George • 668-2665

In an area well-stocked with log cabin and lodge-style restaurants, Mario's will remind you more of the city you came from than the wilderness you are visiting. The restaurant has been family-owned and operated since 1954, and has become an "institution" for vacationing families in Lake George (particularly the large contingent from metro New York City that make it here each summer). It is a large white house toward the north end of Lake George village, and you won't find a single exposed wooden beam or Adirondack chair in the whole place. Instead, you'll find a more

sophisticated decor that reflects the upscale Italian dining here.

The extensive menu offers a variety of Italian seafood entrees such as shrimp and eggplant parmigiana, seafood pasta alla Mario (fresh scallops, shrimp, crabmeat and mushrooms in a fine cream sauce with a touch of sherry) and seafood fra diavolo. You'll also find a big selection of chicken and veal Italian dishes (piccata, parmigiana, Marsala), along with traditional pasta dishes such as manicotti, lasagna and ziti. If you just want prime rib or sirloin steak, you'll find these items on the menu too. All entrees come with hot Italian bread, tossed green salad, garden fresh vegetable and potato du jour or a side of pasta.

Mario's is open year round for lunch and dinner and also serves breakfast daily during July and August.

Montcalm

$$$-$$$$ • U.S. Hwy. 9, Lake George • 793-6601

The Montcalm is just off I-87 Exit 20 at the beginning of the shopping stretch of factory outlet centers on the "Million Dollar Half-Mile." It combines elements of an Adirondack lodge (exposed log beams crisscrossing the length of the high ceiling) with French and Indian Wars-related decor and themes. The restaurant is named for the French Gen. Marquis de Montcalm, who presided over the capture of Fort William Henry and its British troops in 1757 (the inspiration for the book and film *Last of the Mohicans*). The "lodge" is divided into two large sections on either end, with a somewhat dark and dated lounge toward the back.

Critically speaking, the Montcalm has been regarded as one of the area's best places for fine dining for many years, winning several awards such as "Best Nice Dinner Out" and "Best Service" from *The Chronicle* newspaper. While it is one of the more expensive restaurants we have visited, and therefore may not be your ideal choice for a "quick bite with the kids," the menu does tempt one to arrange for a babysitter and indulge for an evening. You'll find such items as rack of lamb, prime rib (two cuts) and a New England Shore Dinner (a copper kettle filled with lobster, steamed clams, shrimp and corn on the cob), among other chicken and veal dishes. There's lots of fresh fish here as well, including salmon, fillet of sole, swordfish and scrod. A Cafe Menu with lighter fare such as pasta dishes is also available.

This is one place where you'll want to save room for dessert, as their own on-site baker whips up tempting treats like pecan pie, cheesecake, carrot cake and even chocolate chip cookies that are so good the restaurant sell them out of a cooler near the register to take home with you. The Montcalm serves lunch and dinner daily throughout the year.

Tamarack Inn

$$ • 440 Canada St. (U.S. Hwy. 9), Lake George • 668-5400

If you love the Adirondacks and just can't get enough Adirondack decor, memorabilia and architecture, you'll feel very much at home here. Built to resemble (we'll give you three guesses) a log cabin lodge, the Tamarack Inn is an attractive and warm setting for anything from fine dining to a couple of drinks and a snack. At the north end of Lake George village (just across from Mario's; see previous listing), the Tamarack offers just about anything you might be in the mood for. Veal, poultry and fish are all well-represented here in items such as grilled honey chicken (chicken breast marinated and grilled with honey, garlic and mozzarella), veal Capriccio (sauteed veal scallopines with mushrooms, prosciutto, Marsala sauce and mozzarella) and mixed grill of seafood (scallops, shrimp and swordfish). You'll also find some slightly different type of beef dishes, such as Yankee pot roast and beef burgundy au poivre, along with the sirloins and filets mignon. If you're a combo-lover, check out the veal and shrimp Dijon, or the ribs and shrimp (half-rack of barbecue baby back ribs with grilled shrimp over pasta).

The Tamarack is a great place to get a hearty breakfast too, with Flapjack Pete's Colossal Breakfast (two pancakes, two eggs, bacon or sausage and home fries) one of the favorites, along with stuffed French toast (filled with raspberry jam).

With the exception of December, the Tamarack Inn is open daily for breakfast, lunch and dinner.

Smith's Restaurant

$$ • Main St., North Creek • 251-9965

This Main Street fixture since 1924 serves up a variety of "good eats" in an unpretentious, non-touristy atmosphere that depends heavily on local trade. All the more reason to visit, particularly if you're in the mood for such basics as roast pork or roast turkey dinners (served with stuffing, mashed potatoes and a generous ladling of gravy) and homemade pies. In fact, the raspberry pie was recently acknowledged by *Yankee Traveler* magazine as the best in the Adirondacks. You'll also find some German-style dishes here such as knockwurst and sauerbraten. If you're skiing at nearby Gore Mountain, or rafting the Hudson, this is a great place to fuel up on the hearty breakfasts or relax after a day of adventure.

Smith's Restaurant is open year round for breakfast, lunch and dinner.

Highwinds Inn

$$$ • Barton Mines Rd., off N.Y. Rt. 28, North River • 251-3760

Remember the venison ravioli and the chilled sliced duck breast we mentioned in the chapter introduction? Remember how we said you could find it at a remote little place in the middle of the wilderness? Well, this is the place we were talking about. There — the secret is out. Highwinds Inn is a small, intimate country inn set high up on the back side of Gore Mountain. Along with creative cuisine, it offers some of the most panoramic views of any restaurant in the Adirondacks. The restaurant overlooks the pristine, unbroken nature of the Siamese Ponds Wilderness Area (see Area Overviews). This is one of those places you are highly unlikely to just "happen upon," and if you do, you may well not be seated for a long time without reservations, as the dining room only has 10 or so tables. They fill up in a hurry on summer weekends, as diners from throughout the region enjoy such tempting dishes as seafood en croute (shrimp, scallops and cod baked with a cream sauce in puff pastry), pan-seared loin of lamb and filet of beef (served with a roasted garlic demiglace) and sauteed Idaho rainbow trout. If you get too stuffed to drive, there are four guest rooms upstairs where you can recover for the night, if you haven't been beaten to them by others with the same idea.

Highwinds Inn is open for dinner nightly in the summer and weekends in the fall and winter (not including November, December and March through May when they are closed). The restaurant and inn is open in January and February to serve the hungry cross-country and downhill skiers that populate the region at centers such as Gore and Garnet Hill Lodge (see Skiing). One other thing: If you want to enjoy a bottle of wine with dinner, make sure to bring your favorite along with you — there's no bar or liquor license here.

The Grist Mill
$$$ • River St., Warrensburg • 623-3949

At one time a working mill along the Schroon River, The Grist Mill enjoys a well-earned reputation as one of the best restaurants (and nicest settings) in the southern Adirondacks. The dining room in the circa 1824 building literally overhangs the often boisterous Schroon, which is flood-lit at night. As good as the food is here, the setting and building itself are a big part of the attraction that draws diners from as far away as Saratoga Springs (about 40 miles to the south). The mill has been meticulously restored, and the many interesting artifacts and items that reflect its past are displayed throughout the two levels. If by chance you have to wait for that perfect riverside table, you'll be sure to enjoy the Fieldstone Tavern, a beautifully rustic lounge downstairs that opens to a riverside deck.

Once back upstairs, you can choose from some of the most creative and nicely presented dishes in the region, including such items as

pan-seared loin of lamb (with spicy mustard and rosemary brown sauce), poached salmon fillet (with a port tarragon cream sauce) or twin tenderloins of beef (charbroiled and served with barley malt compound butter).

The Grist Mill is open year round, daily in the summertime and Wednesday through Sunday the rest of the year. You are sure to enjoy a memorable evening of what they call "American Heritage Cooking" at The Grist Mill, so take your time and savor the experience.

Southern Adirondack Lakes Region

Avery's Inn
$$$ • N.Y. Rt. 10, Arietta • 835-4014

Overlooking the marshes of the West Branch of the Sacandaga River, the Avery Inn is a big old lodge that suddenly appears as you wind your way along remote N.Y. Route 10 between Caroga Lake and Piseco Lake. The first time you see it, you'll swear it's a mirage. It just seems too big to be sitting out here, not just in the middle of nowhere, but rather more on the outskirts of nowhere. Nevertheless, it's real — in fact it has been sitting here greeting and serving visitors for more than 100 years. Inside you'll find a vast dining room with high ceiling, wooden floor and tables for as many as 150 diners. So how does anybody know about this place? They know, evidenced by the fact that when we pulled in to visit at 5:30 PM on a September Saturday, there were already 15 cars in the parking lot.

Folks make the trip here for the casual,

INSIDERS' TIP

If you really want the inside scoop on what to do and see in the Adirondacks, check out a community barbecue fund-raiser sponsored by a local church, fire department or civic group. Some barbecues, like the annual ones put on by fire departments in North Creek, Newcomb, Saranac Lake, Paul Smiths and Blue Mountain Lake, are decades old, so you know that they have perfected the sauce. In addition to helping some worthwhile causes, a family of four can eat for $25 or so and, while chatting with the locals, get the best Insider insights. Check the local newspapers or ask at the local chamber of commerce for possibilities.

family-style atmosphere and the good "All-American" food. On the menu, you'll find Black Angus prime rib, pork tenderloin, shrimp scampi, filet mignon, sole stuffed with crabmeat and other basic staples of a good meal out. They also offer a couple of "Lite Entrees," such as a petite filet mignon, and vegetarian selections like stuffed peppers and pasta primavera.

The restaurant is normally open weekends January through March, closed in April, open weekends again in May and June, Wednesday through Sunday in July and August, and then weekends again in September and October. At press time there was a possibility Avery's would be closed in 1998 for extensive renovations, so call ahead before venturing out.

The Italian Scallion

$$ • N.Y. Rts. 28 and 30, Blue Mountain Lake • 352-7776

OK, so you're deep in this Adirondack wilderness, 100 or more miles from the nearest authentic Italian neighborhood, and you've got this craving for chicken Parmesan. Now what?! Luckily, The Italian Scallion arrived on the restaurant scene recently to make that type of diner's nightmare a thing of the past. Anything but "lodgy" in appearance, this bright little spot is the place to go to get your "sauce fix." You'll find good sauce on lots of traditional favorites here — from lasagna to linguine to our favorite you-just-can't-go-wrong dish, chicken Parmesan. In addition, you'll find an interesting selection of nightly specials to choose from, and you'll want to make sure to wrap up your evening with a specialty coffee or cappuccino from the coffee bar.

During the summer months, The Italian Scallion is open daily for both lunch and dinner. If you're visiting for lunch, you might want to try the yummy pizza or hot Italian grinders (basically a warm sub on a crusty Italian roll). The rest of the year, you can satisfy your old-world cravings weekends only.

The Outlet

$$ • N.Y. Rt. 10, Caroga Lake • 835-3911

Near the southern fringe of the Adirondack Park, The Outlet is adjacent to the marshlands of the Caroga Lake outlet. The setting is more peaceful than spectacular, but certainly provides a pleasant view to divert your eyes to when the conversation wanes. The recent addition of an outside deck makes this an even more attractive dining spot on a warm summer evening (pending mosquito and blackfly count). The decor here is relatively simple, with just enough atmosphere so it doesn't seem like you're in a banquet room. The food is pretty straightforward too, including a big selection of steaks (filet mignon, Porterhouse, Delmonico, New York strip — they're all here), some poultry, veal and pork dishes, and a good assortment of fish and shellfish items. You certainly shouldn't have any problem finding something here that you're in the mood for.

While The Outlet is not necessarily a "destination" restaurant, or a place we'd recommend for a special evening for two, it's a good value in a nice setting that's just right for a casual dinner out when the camp fridge is empty. The Outlet is open throughout the year for dinner.

Dick and Peg's Northward Inn Restaurant

$$$ • N.Y. Rt. 29A, 4 miles west of Gloversville • 725-6440

Just a mile or so south of Peck's Lake and just within the Adirondack Park boundary, Dick and Peg's has been a family-owned and operated "institution" in this area for more than 20 years. Unlike some Adirondack restaurants that offer sweeping views of lakes and mountains, walking in to Dick and Peg's is like walking into a neighbor's cozy den. The dark wood walls are adorned with decorative white lights, giving the place a ski lodge-on-Christmas feel, even in the middle of summer. The bar and lounge area is as big as the dining room, so if you have to wait for a table (a good possibility on a summer weekend), relax and enjoy the atmosphere. The warmth carries over to the service and hospitality as well, with Dick behind the bar, Peg stepping out from her kitchen duties to check on your dinners, and son Bob making sure your table service is without compromise. Steak and seafood are the specialties here, along with the generous salad bar. Dick and Peg's serves dinner only from Tuesday through Saturday and is open year round.

Oak Barrel Restaurant
$$ • N.Y. Rts. 28 and 30, Indian Lake
• 648-5115

The Oak Barrel's claim to fame is the historic Old Nassau Bar that dates back to the early 1900s, originally came from Princeton, New Jersey, and still displays the image of the Princeton Tiger. The restaurant is attractively decorated without overdoing it by covering every square inch of wall space with Adirondack knickknacks. For 20 years now, the Oak Barrel has been serving central Adirondackers a big selection of steaks, seafood, veal, chicken and pasta at value-conscious prices. For folks more interested in a quick bite, they also serve pizza, burgers and chicken wings, along with other munchies. Homemade desserts include cheesecake and toll house pie (we're there!), along with an assortment of specialty coffee. You can visit the Oak Barrel for lunch and dinner from April until mid-November.

The Firetower Restaurant
$$ • N.Y. Rt. 8, Lake Pleasant • 548-3513

This is the only restaurant we've ever been to that had a chalkboard on the front porch for people to write down their moose sightings in the area. The Speculator/Lake Pleasant area considers itself the "Moose Capital of the Adirondacks" since the big mammals were reintroduced into the region during the early 1970s, and seeing one (while a pretty rare experience) makes for a fun pastime around these parts. Inside this casual family-style restaurant, most of your sightings will be of Italian-American food such as pizza and pasta dishes. Pizza is the star attraction here, with three sizes, three crusts (plain, garlic or sesame), 20 different available toppings and a variety of "House Specialty" pizzas giving you plenty to choose from. To wash down your pie, you can choose from more than 40 different kinds of beer from around the world — a pretty good selection for the Adirondacks. For those looking for the American side of the "Italian-American" equation, you can also choose from a selection of steak, seafood and chicken dishes. There's no better follow-up to a yummy homemade pizza than some yummy homemade desserts, and you can give in to Peter's deep-fried ice cream, chocolate cream pie, Key lime pie and

even some excellent chocolate chip cookies baked right here.

You can enjoy breakfast, lunch and dinner at The Firetower. While it had been a year-round operation for many years, they have opted to go to a May-through-October schedule in 1998.

Lanzi's on the Lake
$$$ • N.Y. Rt. 30, Mayfield • 661-7711

Everything about Lanzi's is big: big place, big servings, big deck, on a big lake, big reputation, big crowds on summer weekends. As one of the very few places actually on the water at the Great Sacandaga Lake, Lanzi's is a very popular summer spot for hungry boaters, vacationers, camp owners and area residents from nearby Gloversville and Johnstown. It's a very impressive place too — very contemporary in style, with lots of glass, oak and brass throughout, along with high ceilings, a huge stone fireplace and floor-to-ceiling windows facing the lake. The deck alone can seat 135 people.

Lanzi's on the Lake isn't just a restaurant, it's almost become the "unofficial festival site" for the area. In the summertime, they schedule everything from reggae festivals to chili cook-offs to beach parties that have been known to draw 4,000 people to their sprawling grounds along the lake. Even on non-event weekends, Lanzi's can serve more than 600 dinners on a Saturday night. In the wintertime, Lanzi's keeps business hot by arranging snowmobile races, winter volleyball tournaments and what they call "frozen lake bakes" (clambakes, that is).

The five Lanzi brothers (Lou, Chris, Tony, Joe and Larry — and you didn't think we'd know their names!) all are vitally involved with every facet of the restaurant, and they provide patrons with a big selection of upscale Italian as well as contemporary American fare. Everything is homemade here, from the pasta to the salad dressing (a family recipe since 1957) to the marinara sauce. Traditional Italian favorites, seafood and pasta combinations, along with steaks, veal and chicken dishes are available. While at first glance you may think the menu is a little expensive, in reality you are buying both dinner tonight and lunch tomorrow, so don't sweat it.

Lanzi's on the Lake is open daily from May until October for lunch and dinner, and Thursday through Monday during the rest of the year. If you can't get in to Lanzi's or don't feel like waiting for a table on a summer eve, you may want to try their new sister restaurant, the Sport Island Restaurant, 108 Riverside Boulevard, Northville, 863-2003. It is just "up the lake" a few short miles, and is set right on the beach at the Sacandaga Park.

Zak's Waterfront
$$ • 306 Woods Hollow Rd., Mayfield • 883-8351

While Zak's is technically *on* the Great Sacandaga Lake, it's really set along an inlet that leads about a half-mile out into the lake. No matter — it's still a nice setting for a restaurant, and the boats streaming past and docking at the adjacent Wood's Hollow Marina make for visual entertainment. And while not nearly as big, fancy or obvious as Lanzi's on the Lake (see previous entry), Zak's holds some special charms of its own that make it worth considering for dinner. The restaurant is a couple of miles off N.Y. Route 30, and it doesn't reveal itself until you are almost convinced that you missed it somewhere along the way. Once there, you'll be pleasantly surprised by how quaint and attractive the inside of the restaurant is. The small dining room and adjacent bar have a nautical (but not *too* nautical) decor, and there's a small back deck that overlooks the marina and inlet. One nice feature that comes in handy but doesn't impose on the dining room is an adjacent game room, which can keep the kids busy while you wait for your entrees or enjoy some post-dinner coffee.

Another pleasant surprise here is the creative dishes on the menu, with influences that range from Italian to Mexican to Cajun. Items include stuffed prime rib (thinly sliced prime rib bracciole, stuffed with black wild rice, fresh herbs and mozzarella cheese, then sauteed in port wine and shallots), chicken Palermo (boneless breast strips sauteed, tossed with oregano, marinara sauce and heavy cream, then served over linguine) and Sonny's paella (boneless chicken, sausage, shrimp, scallops, clams and mussels simmered in garlic, onion and fresh herbs and served over rice). As tempting as this all sounds, save room for dessert because it's something special. We were "forced" to sample both the apple blueberry crisp (with vanilla ice cream, of course) and the chocolate peanut butter pie, and we can proudly report the plates were sent back to the kitchen *very* clean. You can enjoy Zak's year round.

Rockwood Tavern
$$, N.Y. Rts. 10 and 29, Rockwood • 762-9602

Good groceries, friendly folks, a casual setting, big variety and good value all combine to make the Rockwood Tavern a real find that you wouldn't normally come across in the Adirondack travels (without us cluing you in, that is). Its location a few miles south of Caroga Lake, with the southern boundary of the Adirondack "blue line" literally running through the back yard, makes the Rockwood a good place to stop on the way in or out of the Park. If you are staying anywhere in the Great Sacandaga Lake, Peck's Lake or Caroga Lake areas, this is a great neighborhood tavern to visit whenever the cupboard is bare or you just don't feel like cooking. It doesn't matter what mood your taste buds are in, for here you'll find a surprisingly big variety of menu items and specials available that venture far beyond typical tavern fare. The night we visited, choices ranged from shrimp scampi to calf's liver to veal Parmesan to New York strip. The folks at the Rockwood like to experiment with new combinations as well. One result of such an experiment — chicken Sylvia (boneless breast grilled, served with broccoli, roasted peppers, mushrooms and pasta) — was so popular, it became a regular menu item. Most places don't consider their salad creations to be house specialties, but here you simply must try the broccoli salad, which is kind of a luxurious cousin to cole slaw with broccoli as the main attraction and a "secret" dressing that makes it all work. If you're looking for something lighter than a full dinner or you are stopping for lunch, consider the pizza (another local favorite here).

Whichever way your taste buds take you, we're sure you'll make some new friends and discover a new favorite at the Rockwood Tavern. Stop by any time of the year for lunch or dinner, and say hello to Russ for us.

The Inn at Speculator
$$-$$$ • N.Y. Rt. 8, Speculator • 548-3811

This large country inn-style restaurant, set along the northern shore of Lake Pleasant (one of the lesser known yet beautiful lakes in the Adirondacks) is about as far as you can get from the crowded streets and restaurants of Lake George, Lake Placid and Old Forge. There's nothing pretentious about this place; it's attractive yet not fancy — the kind of place that locals and summer camp renters alike can feel comfortable in and enjoy. You can choose from several settings here, ranging from a collection of dining rooms to a large bar and lounge area to a good-size outside deck. You can also choose from several menus: the "light supper" menu with its smaller portions and lower prices; the "junior menu" for kids; the "seniors menu" for those who qualify, and the regular "full freight" menu for the rest of us. The food selections here are surprisingly upscale for the casual surroundings and include such items as veal, steaks, chicken and seafood in solo appearances and a variety of combinations. Breakfast is available here on weekends, and the inn is open for lunch and dinner year round (with the exception of Wednesdays).

Melody Lodge
$$ • N.Y. Rt. 30, Speculator • 548-6562

Melody Lodge offers one of the prettiest dining views in the Adirondacks, looking south toward Lake Pleasant (just a mile or so distant) and the Silver Lake Wilderness Area beyond. When the weather cooperates, you can dine on the covered front porch and take in the crisp air to help get your appetite into overdrive in a hurry. Inside, the lodge feels like a log cabin you'd retreat to for the weekend. If it's a little (or a lot) too brisk outside, you can enjoy fireside dining in one of two dining rooms, or cozy up to the attractive bar in the lounge area. If you like spicy foods to keep you warm, try to steak by George with its generous seasonings. You'll find a variety of other offerings including chicken and seafood dishes plus a tempting collection of homemade desserts.

The Melody Lodge has been serving guest since the late 1930s, and we're guessing it will be here for a long time to come. You can enjoy lunch and dinner here daily in summer and on a reduced schedule during the winter months (call ahead).

Old Forge/ Raquette Lake Region

Eckerson's
$$ • N.Y. Rt. 28, Eagle Bay • (315) 357-4641

Eckerson's location along the Eagle Bay Snowmobile Trail between Old Forge and Big Moose Lake keeps it as busy on winter weekends as summer weekends. The big selection of steaks, chops, veal, poultry, Italian and fresh seafood dishes keeps locals coming back for more throughout the year as well. Daily specials include a fish fry on Fridays, prime rib on Saturdays and roast turkey dinners on Sundays. Owner and chef John Wright takes great pride in his preparation — stop by and enjoy the results of his labor of love. Eckerson's is open year round for dinner.

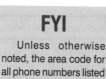

FYI

Unless otherwise noted, the area code for all phone numbers listed in this guide is 518.

Seventh Lake House
$$$ • N.Y. Rt. 28, Inlet • (315) 357-6028

The Seventh Lake House has the reputation as one of the very best restaurants in the entire Adirondack Park, serving creative contemporary American cuisine. In fact, *Upstate New York* magazine recently honored it with the Excelsior Award, ranking the Seventh Lake House as one of the "Top 40 Restaurants in Upstate." It is set along the eastern end of the Fulton Chain of Lakes between Inlet and Raquette Lake, and it overlooks Seventh Lake with picture windows along the back and an outside covered deck. Inside, the upscale decor reflects the quality of the entire dining experience here.

Using ingredients from regional and specialty suppliers whenever possible, the Seventh Lake House presents a variety of creative dishes featuring pasta, lamb, chicken, fresh fish and steaks. Specials you may happen upon include such dishes as salmon with maple sauce, pork rib roast or shrimp and scallop stew (served with vegetables in an acorn squash). As you can imagine, the appetizers and desserts here are excellent as well, so try to pace yourself. This is definitely one of the "special occasion" restaurants in the central Adirondacks. The Seventh Lake House is open daily from June through September, with a reduced schedule the remainder of the year that you should call to confirm.

Daiker's Inn
$-$$ • N.Y. Rt. 28, Old Forge • (315) 369-6954

Daiker's is a casual restaurant and bar on Fourth Lake that calls itself "The Fun Place to Be." Nothing too complicated about that, and it's hard to argue with them. Open year round, Daiker's in the summertime offers boat docking and a large outdoor deck overlooking the lake. In the winter, Daiker's is accessible by Snowmobile Trail #5, and sledders enjoy the large fireplace inside to warm them from the combination of frigid temps and fast sleds. The food here is as casual as the surroundings, with an emphasis on pizza, burgers, sandwiches and wings. The fish fry is very popular on Friday evenings. This is also one of the few places around to offer live musical entertainment on weekends year round (see the Nightlife chapter).

Keyes Pancake House & Restaurant
$ • Main St., Old Forge • (315) 369-6752

As you know from reading about the Old Forge area, this is a popular family vacation destination. As such, a place like Keyes is definitely "key" to include in your plans. This is a place where you can get pancakes or omelettes at three in the afternoon if you feel like it (and sometimes kids do!), along with a big variety of sandwiches (Reubens and hot beef sandwiches are particularly popular). You'll also find the family-friendly burger baskets, chicken baskets, spaghetti (with homemade sauce) and house favorite chicken and biscuits. You won't be able to order beer or wine,

as alcohol is not served here. Keyes is open for breakfast, lunch and dinner in the summertime; breakfast and lunch only during the winter.

The Muffin Patch
$ • Main St., Old Forge • (315) 369-6376

Another great breakfast or lunch option in Old Forge is The Muffin Patch. Combining a restaurant, bakery and ice cream shop, there's lots here to tempt every member of the family. They pride themselves on their over-stuffed omelettes, Belgian waffles, homemade soups and club sandwiches, which combined with a specialty sundae could help you hit your calorie quota for the week in one sitting. The Muffin Patch is open daily for breakfast, lunch and supper (until 8 PM) during July and August, then daily (except Wednesdays) for breakfast and lunch only throughout the rest of the year. There's no bar here, but rather the ice cream window is open in the summer, and it stays open until 10 PM.

The Old Mill
$$$ • N.Y. Rt. 28, Old Forge • (315) 369-3662

This is certainly one of the "you can't miss it" restaurants in the Adirondacks — right on the main drag between Old Forge and Thendara, its huge working water wheel spinning slowly out front. The inside is equally impressive, with the post and beam lounge area and its windows facing the adjacent Moose River giving you a beautiful setting to enjoy a beverage before dinner or linger afterward.

All dinners here kick off with a family-style serving of the daily homemade soup (a welcome tummy-warmer on a crisp day) and are supplemented with generous salads and fresh-baked bread. The menu is varied, with beef and seafood the most prevalent items. Some house favorites include New York tenderloin, stuffed chicken breast, Alaskan king crab legs, steamed shrimp, rack of lamb and stuffed pork chops.

The Old Mill is a little on the expensive side for a family dinner, but for a special night out is worth the occasional splurge to enjoy the quality surroundings, service and food. You can enjoy dinner at The Old Mill year round.

Riley's

$$ • N.Y. Rt. 28, Old Forge
• **(315) 369-2484**

In the Water's Edge Inn & Conference Center, Riley's goes beyond just being a serviceable hotel restaurant to a place worth a visit in its own right. Its setting overlooking Old Forge Pond (the beginning or end of the Fulton Chain of Lakes, depending on how you look at it) provides patrons with a view of boaters in the summer and sledders (snowmobilers, that is) in the winter. The theme at Riley's is "casual lakeside dining at reasonable prices." With breakfast and lunch buffets six days a week at $6.95, and a huge Sunday brunch (featuring hand-carved meats, omelettes made to order, waffles, seafood Newburg, chicken a la king and more) for only $9.95, we think they've succeeded. The salad bar at Riley's is an attraction, with a 12-foot-long display of fresh vegetables, homemade breads and soups to get your meal off to an enjoyable start. Dinner selections include a variety of steak, seafood, chicken, veal and Italian dishes. For a lighter meal, consider relaxing in the attractive lounge and selecting from the variety of sandwiches and munchies. Save room for a cup of cappuccino and (or) a homemade dessert, then walk off at least a little of it by strolling along the pond. Riley's is open year round and serves as the home of the Mountain Theatre Co. dinner theater in July and August (see Nightlife).

Trails End Restaurant

$$ • North St., Old Forge
• **(315) 369-2632**

This may very well be the most attractive restaurant in America that's attached to a bowling center. The traditional smoky-snack-bar-next-to-the-lanes description doesn't apply

here at all. In fact, this is really just a good old-fashioned family restaurant that happens to be joined (via the bar and lounge) to a small six-lane bowling center. So what's good about that? Think about it. You just finished up a long day at the Enchanted Forest/Water Safari (see Attractions) across the street, you'd love to just relax and enjoy a nice meal of home cooking, but the kids are still wound up from their numerous plunges down the Killermanjaro water slide. What better way to keep them entertained (and within supervision-distance) while you relax and eat than letting them bowl a few games? Now it's all starting to make sense, isn't it? The only problem is, once the kids see the yummy stuff on your plates, they may want to suddenly stay close to mom and dad.

Trails End is named for its proximity to the vast snowmobile trail network in and around Old Forge, one trail of which begins right outside the door here. On summer and winter weekends both, this place is bustling with fun-loving folks with a "need for speed" (whether sliding down the tubes at Water Safari, skiing down the slopes at McCauley Mountain, or flying down the trails on snowmobiles). All that action kicks up a pretty good appetite, which you'll need to handle the generous portions served here.

The decor is "country quaint" with lots of attention to detail you might not expect (but certainly appreciate). You can go as light or heavy as you want on food, from the simple (pizza, half-pound burgers, hot turkey sandwiches) to the hearty (fettuccine Alfredo with shrimp, chicken cacciatore over pasta, 24-ounce grilled sirloin steak). Friday nights the fish dinner special offers three options (deep-fried, broiled or beer-battered); on Saturday nights, come in a "prime rib" mood for the Queen or King cuts. You can enjoy a visit to

INSIDERS' TIP

During busy days in popular tourist towns like Lake Placid and Lake George, restaurants along the main drags get rather crowded. Sometimes the quality of the food and service suffers, as the staff can barely keep up. If the restaurant looks overly crowded, or the wait appears intolerable, consider driving to a restaurant on the outskirts of town (where the locals most likely are dining). Without much effort, you should find a restaurant without the wait and crowds.

the Trails End for dinner anytime of the year and for lunch on weekends.

The Farm Restaurant
$, no credit cards • N.Y. Rt. 28, Thendara • (315) 369-6199

There's no lack of great spots to take the gang out for a big breakfast or hearty lunch in these parts, and this place is certainly at the top of the list. With more than 1,000 farm tools and wooden items on display throughout this big eatery, The Farm lives up to its name in the decor department. You can tell the folks who work here are used to serving up good food in a hurry here, and the prompt service keeps the crowds flowing quicker than the gallons of maple syrup. If you love a big breakfast, you'll love it here (once you can make a decision between the collection of omelettes, flapjacks, waffles and mountain-style hash on the menu). Lunches include homemade soups, hot and cold sandwiches and a variety of salads. If the kids get restless, you can send them outside to the children's play area and take your time with an extra cup of always fresh-brewed coffee.

The Farm Restaurant is open for breakfast and lunch only, and is closed from late October until early December and from March until early May. While you'll find lots to fill your tummy here, you won't find a bar and lounge (but we're guessing you weren't looking for one here anyway).

The Knotty Pine
$$-$$$ • N.Y. Rt. 28, Thendara • (315) 369-6859

The Knotty Pine has a reputation as one of the nicest and most popular area restaurants for those evenings when you want to "go out and dine" as opposed to just "getting something to eat." It's the kind of place where you'll want to spend the entire evening relaxing and enjoying the surroundings and the fine food.

Formerly a big old house, The Knotty Pine has been converted into an attractive setting for dinner, with a cozy bar for pre-dinner cocktails just off the entrance. The dinner menu includes such favorites as chicken, veal, pasta, seafood and choice beef entrees. On Fridays, the fish dinner (served fried, broiled or beer batter-dipped) is very popular. You can also choose from the selection of nightly dinner specials, featuring items such as lemon dill salmon and the always popular prime rib. Make sure to enjoy (but not overindulge on) the terrific homemade soups, breads and desserts throughout the evening. You can enjoy dinner year round at The Knotty Pine.

Five Great Burger & Soft-serve Spots

As promised in the chapter introduction, here is our collection of great hamburger and ice cream hits from throughout our five regions of the Adirondacks. This is not say these are the five "best," just five drive-ins that are deservedly popular and good ambassadors of good eats that you can look for in your travels.

Lake Placid/ Tri-Lakes Region

Tail o' the Pup
$ • N.Y. Rt. 86, Ray Brook • 891-5092

If there is a classic roadside diner in the region, this is it. Smoked chicken and ribs are always cooking on the outdoor grill during the summer. Kids can dine for less than $4. A lobster/clambake takes place Thursday through Sunday, while the lobster lasts. Seats are available inside, but most patrons select a picnic table under the tent so they can eat and watch the world drive by. To get a frozen after-dinner cone, however, you must cross the street to the summer-only stand that offers soft yogurt.

Plattsburgh/Western Lake Champlain Region

Butcher Block
$$ • N.Y. Rt. 3, just off I-87, Plattsburgh • 563-0920

The Butcher Burger, with a half-pound of charbroiled lean ground beef served on a hard roll, stands on its own tasty reputation but shares its local fame with the accompanying

Unspoiled views, such as this one in Garnet Hill, summon visitors
and residents alike to stop and savor the moment.

Photo: Warren County Tourism Department

all-you-can-eat soup and salad bar. Soups are homemade, breads are baked locally, and salads include an amazing assortment of toppings — all for around $6.

The ice cream isn't soft but comes from local (well almost, just across Lake Champlain) legends Ben & Jerry. Vanilla and chocolate are always available, along with one of their world-famous uniquely named and concocted flavors.

Lake George/
Upper Hudson Region

Martha's
$ • U.S. Hwy. 9, Lake George • 793-0372

Lots of places serve soft vanilla, chocolate and a twist thereof, but Martha's is one of the few spots you'll also find such soft serve delights as raspberry creme twist, maple walnut and Creamsicle. You can also order Martha's DandeeCreme (their trade name) in pints and quarts, in Cool Cookies (huge ice cream sandwiches) and as ice cream cakes, along with the regular assortment of shakes and sundaes. Separated from the ice cream stand by a dozen red-and-white–umbrella tables in a picnic area

is The Grill at Martha's, which serves up a good variety of burgers, fried fish, chicken sandwiches, fried clams and hot dogs. Add the view across the street of the rides at The Great Escape (see Attractions), and you've got just about the perfect summer family fun-food experience. Martha's is open from April until the end of September.

Southern Adirondack
Lakes Region

King of the Frosties
$ • N.Y. Rt. 8, Speculator • 548-3881

Another "you can't miss it" location in the heart of beautiful downtown Speculator, King of the Frosties offers both inside dining and a sidewalk cafe for enjoying their big selection of casual and fun food. You'll find breakfast, lunch and light dinner items on the menu as well as plenty of burgers and ice cream and fries (oh my!). (Sorry, but that sentence reminded us of *The Wizard of Oz* for some reason.) On summer eves, the line forms early for soft and hard ice cream, and King of the Frosties is a good place to be and be seen in Speculator.

Old Forge/
Raquette Lake Region

Pied Piper Drive In
$ • N.Y. Rt. 28, Old Forge
• (315) 369-3115

The Pied Piper shares one big thing in common with Martha's in Lake George: Both are set right across the street from a major theme park (in this case, Enchanted Forest/Water Safari; see Attractions). You can't get much more convenient than that. For more than 30 years, the Greene family has been serving visitors and residents, alike, their tasty combos of broasted chicken and homemade chili, along with the usual drive-in food staples — burgers and hot dogs. For those chilly days (which can be just about any day in Old Forge), you'll find their enclosed addition for sit-down dining a blessing. You'll also find some items here that you don't get at a typical drive-in stand, like a salad bar, beer and wine list. Oh yeah, you'll find a good variety of hard and soft ice cream too. The Pied Piper Drive In is open year round.

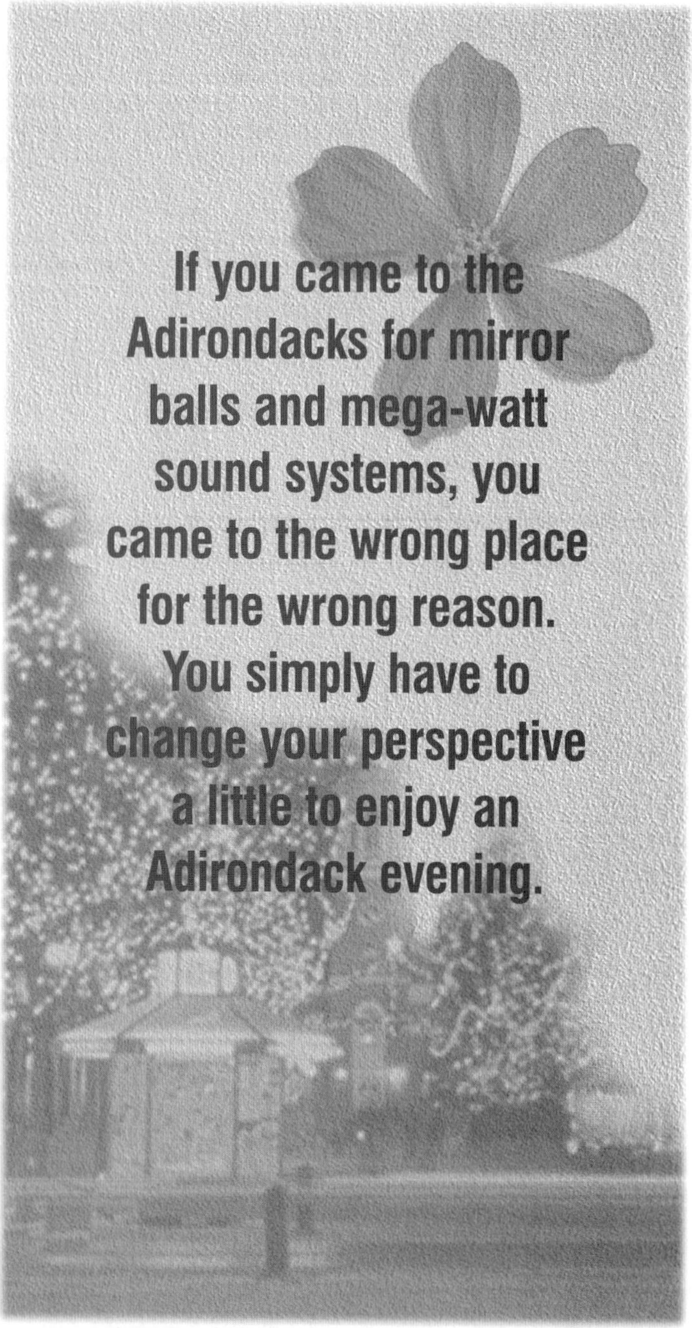

If you came to the
Adirondacks for mirror
balls and mega-watt
sound systems, you
came to the wrong place
for the wrong reason.
You simply have to
change your perspective
a little to enjoy an
Adirondack evening.

Nightlife

To be honest, we weren't sure whether to call this chapter Nightlife or Nocturnal Life because the animal nighttime activity in the Adirondacks rivals or exceeds their human co-inhabitants' throughout most of the year. So, we include a little of both here.

That's not to say there is nothing to do at night in the Adirondacks. Let's just say you've got to pick your spots, both on the calendar and geographically. On a weekend in Lake George or Lake Placid in midsummer, you'll have more options than time to enjoy them all. On a February Tuesday evening in Indian Lake, your list of nightlife options will be considerably shorter (or maybe even nonexistent if you don't have a satellite dish and you just finished your most recent paperback). The cold, hard truth: If you came to the Adirondacks for mirror balls and mega-watt sound systems, you came to the wrong place for the wrong reason. You simply have to change your perspective a little to enjoy an Adirondack evening.

Rather than looking up at a dazzling mirror ball suspended from the blackened ceiling of a smoky disco, you can look up at an even more dazzling moon suspended in the blackness of the Adirondack night sky. We guarantee the impression it leaves will be much longer lasting than the eight-minute dance mix of some Madonna tune!

Need another example of the unconventional? Consider the ritual of an invigorating walk around Mirror Lake with revelers to ring in the New Year. There's no falling ball, no instant replay of the last year's party in the new year and no one shouting loud noises. Generally, the walk begins at the town hall about 30 minutes before the witching hour of midnight on the eve of the New Year.

Naturally, you don't need a holiday to take a walk during the evening hours. Night walks are part of the way of life here. Generally, after the sun sets, the mosquitoes also disappear, so there is little chance of a mass mugging for your blood.

With this "Adirondack" perspective in mind, we include a sampling of evening and nighttime activities, both conventional ("When the Sun Goes Down . . .") and not so ("Nature's Nighttime Spectacle"). For example, listening to a live band at a club is conventional; hunting for the mythical Adirondack "snipe" is not.

Since concert and performance information changes so frequently, we suggest you consult the newspapers listed in the Media chapter to give you the most current and localized updates for wherever you are staying. They should also give you an indication of cover charges when they apply (they're variable and inconsistent — it's best to just call ahead). As a rule, you're likely to find small cover charges of two or three bucks for live bands on summer weekends.

Another good option for evening activities would be to consult the Arts and Culture chapter for listings of organizations and venues that offer musical and theatrical performances.

When the Sun Goes Down . . .

Lake Placid/ Tri-Lakes Region

Lake Placid Center for the Arts
91 Saranac Ave., Lake Placid • 523-2512

The largest art center in the region offers a variety of activities, including classic films, community theater and even special performances by notable artists such as modern dancer Rebecca Kelly. The schedule tends to be busiest during the summer months, but generally there is always something going on here to either amuse or enlighten. Classic flicks cost $5 per person, while admission to artist performances cost around $20.

Casey's
444 Main St., Lake Placid • 523-2357

Casey's, housed in an old opera house, offers anything but opera. There are three big-screen TVs, a bar menu including hot wings, a pool table and an occasional band. Similarly occasional cover charges are nominal — around $2 a head. There is a dining room with daily lunch and dinner specials. During the summer, guests sit outside on a small deck overlooking Mill Pond waterfalls.

Dancing Bear Lounge
Lake Placid Hilton, Main St., Lake Placid • 523-4411

The Dancing Bear is the only sure place for live entertainment every weekend year round in Lake Placid. The music may be country, rock, jazz or a combination of all genres on a given night. The lounge is in the Hilton. There's never a cover.

Mud Puddles
3 School St., Lake Placid • 523-4446

Mud Puddles bills itself as a sport's bar, but it is much more. It's a party bar, with dancing, pool tables and crowds of fans screaming at the antics of some sports team — or just crowds screaming at the antics of some special event, like the Mud Puddles version of MTV's popular program *Singled Out*. Mud Puddles hosts an occasional band on busy weekends and on evenings during the summer months. Cover charges are rare.

Cascade Ski Touring Center
Cascade Rd., Lake Placid • 523-9605

When the moon is full, a special breed of creatures come out of hiding in the Lake Placid area — no, not vampires, but rather cross-country skiers at the full moon ski party at Cascade Ski Touring Center, a mile or so east of the ski-jumping complex in Lake Placid. Naturally, the party dates vary from month to month and depend upon the snow conditions, but generally fall on the Saturday night clos-

est to the full moon. Skiers glide along the groomed trails toward a bonfire where food and some liquid warm-me-ups are served. The $7 fee includes the trail access, hot dogs, beer and live music. Dress in layers because if the skiing doesn't warm you up, the band will.

Roomers
137 Main St., Lake Placid • 523-3611

If you look in any of the Yellow Pages directories for nightclubs in the Tri-Lakes, Roomers is it. A DJ gets the young-ish crowd rocking, while the non-dancers shoot pool or play darts. For food, everyone runs across the street to Bazzi's Pizza. Roomers is near all the major hotels on Main Street. You'll almost never pay a cover here.

FYI

Unless otherwise noted, the area code for all phone numbers listed in this guide is 518.

Waterhole #3
Main St., Saranac Lake • 891-9502

The Waterhole may be the best choice for being the region's classic rock 'n' roll bar (the atmosphere is clearly more "bar" than "nightclub"). The music is always loud, gets the feet moving and, at times, features some famed '60s acts such as Leon Russell or Commander Cody (who lost his Airmen). The atmosphere is dark, generally crowded and rocking friendly.

Live music can be heard most every Friday and Saturday nights from 10 to 2 AM. The cover charges range from $3 to $5 — expect to pay more for big-name performers.

Don't hesitate to drop by the Waterhole. The people have no choice but to be friendly; the police station is directly opposite this favorite, er . . . watering hole.

Plattsburgh/Western Lake Champlain Region

Airborne International Raceways
Broderick Rd., Plattsburgh • 561-3208

Saturday night is race night at this small but popular stock-car track. There are regular and modified races, along with demolition derbies and other bang 'em-ups. Races begin at 7:30 PM, and admission is $6 to $12 for adults, depending on the stature of the race, and $3 for children.

M/V Juniper Tour Boat
Dock St., Plattsburgh • 561-8970, (800) 388-8970

On a warm, clear Adirondack night, the sky is ablaze with stars. A four-hour dinner cruise (6 to 10 PM) on Lake Champlain on the *M/V Juniper* is one way to appreciate sunsets, the night sky and perhaps things romantic. The dinner cruise with dancing under the stars costs approximately $30 per person, and reservations are required. The dinner menu is limited to a single choice of steak, fish or chicken.

JC's Jazz Club
Bridge St., Plattsburgh • 561-5117

This is a small club, featuring jazz and a little bit of the blues on weekends. The kitchen is open until midnight, and the menu includes a good selection of light fare and sandwiches, making JC's a popular spot after the movies or an evening shopping. If you're downtown during the day, check out their luncheon specials.

Long Branch Saloon
9 Bridge St., Plattsburgh • 566-8126

There's no pretense here; befitting its name, this place features a saloon-type atmosphere. It's either new country music or old, classic dance rock on Friday and Saturday, beginning at 9:30 PM. The crowd is a mix of young and young-at-heart who love to dance in every form except the line. On Thursday and Sunday evenings, a DJ serves up tunes for dancing. There's never a cover.

Monopole
7 Protection Alley, Plattsburgh • 563-2222

With three separate bars in three separate parts of a historic building, you have some choices regarding your entertainment. On weekends, one bar generally rocks with some form of live musical entertainment. The mix is eclectic and might include blues, reggae, rock or jazz. A pool table is featured in another of the bars. Food service consists of wings and pizza. Depending upon the music, a minimal cover charge may be imposed.

Douglas on Silver Lake
18 Douglas Ln., Ausable Forks • 647-8061, (800) 201-8061

If you are out this way, you are either lost or visiting the Douglas on Silver Lake campground; but if you like country music, you might want to get directions — and pay close attention because one wrong turn will leave you miles from anywhere in the middle of nowhere. Douglas on Silver Lake is a campground — and more. The restaurant offers basic meals, with specials on weekends (most entrees are less than $10), and doubles as a dance hall on weekends during the summer, with country and classic oldies rock. (See our Attractions chapter for more details about happenings at Douglas.)

Galley Restaurant
Washington St., Westport • 962-4899

In the full-service Westport Marina, The Gallery turns from a restaurant during the day and evening hours into a hot spot with live music every Friday and Saturday night during the summer. The music varies from soft rock, to jazz, to whatever. There's never a cover, and light food is available.

General's Gate
136 N. Champlain Ave., Ticonderoga • 585-2730

This sports bar and Italian-American restaurant overlooks LaChute River, which connects Lake Champlain to Lake George. The

INSIDERS' TIP

If you're really dying to find some decent dancing and live music in the middle of the Adirondack winter, and you're staying in the Lake George area, then make the 30-minute drive down the Northway to Saratoga Springs (see the Daytrips chapter). The town has a legitimately lively downtown restaurant and club scene year round.

bar offers a horseshoe pit, Foosball, darts, air hockey games and a mix of musical entertainment — soft rock, country and pop — on the weekends.

Lake George/ Upper Hudson Region

Adirondack Red Wings
Glens Falls Civic Center, Glen St., Glens Falls • 798-0202

This is probably the only place in the Adirondacks where 3,500 people regularly gather on a Wednesday night in January. So if you're looking for a combination of exciting professional hockey action and the warmth of your fellow humans on a cold Adirondack night, this is as good as it gets. The Red Wings have been entertaining fans in Glens Falls as a member of the American Hockey League since winter 1979-80. The team has had great success, winning the league's championship (The Calder Cup) four times since then. The top farm club of the 1997 Stanley Cup Champion Detroit Red Wings, you can always count on a fun and entertaining evening at an Adirondack Red Wings game (particularly when the arch-rival Albany River Rats are in town!). The Red Wings play 40 games from November through March, and tickets cost from $7 to $11.

The Boardwalk Restaurant & Bootleggers Pub
Lower Amherst St., Lake George • 668-5324

This longtime Lake George food-and-fun "landmark" is right on the lake in the heart of Lake George village, overlooking its own marina. It is open from May into October, and offers a wide variety of musical entertainment several nights a week. Oldies, acoustic, contemporary and progressive rock are some offerings you can enjoy here, along with a full dining menu (see the Restaurant chapter) and a beautiful view of the lake from the outdoor patio.

D.J's Night Club
Canada St., Lake George • 668-9803

If you really like to dance, and we mean dance all night, D.J's should be on your itinerary. Here you can dance seven nights a week from 8 PM until 4 AM to great tunes spun by some of the area's top disc jockeys. You'll also find a large dance floor with a light show, three cocktail bars and a game room with billiards and darts. D.J's is open from May until October.

Duffy's Tavern
10 Amherst St., Lake George • 668-5323

Another restaurant/club combo that overlooks the lake, Duffy's offers live entertainment and dancing seven nights a week during the summer months. The three bars offer a Happy Hour from 4 until 7 PM Monday through Friday, and the new cabana and raw bar offers alfresco dining and entertainment. If you're a fan of reggae (and in the summertime everyone should be!), stop by Duffy's any Sunday night to get your weekly fix. Duffy's is open year round for dining, but only offers entertainment during the summer months and during the Lake George Winter Carnival.

Funny Bone Comedy Club
Tiki Resort, N.Y. Rt. 9N, Lake George • 668-5744

Hosted by area comedian and impressionist Steve Van Zandt, this is the only comedy club in the region. From June through August, you can enjoy comics from the club scene in Atlantic City, Boston and New York City as well as national TV appearances on Letterman and Comedy Central. Showtimes are Thursday through Saturday at 8:30 and 10:30 PM. It'll cost you $12 to get in, then you have to be thirsty enough to buy at least two drinks.

Hoyt's Cinemas
Aviation Mall Cinemas 7, Aviation Rd., Queensbury • 793-3332
Route 9 Cinemas 5, N.Y. Rt. 9L, Queensbury • 793-5233

If you want to catch a first-run flick, these are your only year-round cinema options in

Loony Tunes

Loon sounds — wails, yodels, tremolos and hoots — are among Nature's most haunting and beautiful heard in nature. The extravagant, mournful wails at night are probably part of a territorial defense. (If you've never heard the sound, imagine a sad ghost playing clarinet in an empty concert hall.) Loons like to keep track of each other. During the day, they can see each other, but during the night their cries, termed night chorusing, are the only way to track one another. Night chorusing often begins with a single call followed by a succession of yodels, tremolos or tremolo duets, as loons from miles around "converse" with one another. Although the chorus can be heard throughout the summer, it peaks during early spring.

Close-up

Yodels, produced only by males, serve as a territorial warning for distant rivals to stay away. Scientists suggest that each male loon can be identified by its unique vocal signature. Then again, see if you can discern one from the other!

The laughing loon — it's a common restaurant name here in "Loon Country" — may be a bird feeling threatened. The tremolo's laugh, with its trembling quality, may be heard in duet, as two loons may be announcing to rivals that they are indeed a pair. (The Common loon, *Gavia immer*, the most familiar of the five loon species with its distinctive black and white plumage, is generally monogamous.)

Hoots occur between pairs or between a parent loon and its chicks. Often the hoot precedes some distinct visual action, such as a dive or a territorial display.

Loons are highly territorial and defend a 100- to 300-acre plot as their own from the time nest sites are secured until the one or two chicks are fledged. Pairs consistently return to the same place to nest year after year.

Many lakes and ponds in the Adirondacks only have one suitable nest per each entire body of water, even though the lake may be large enough to accommodate another pair. Loons require low, boggy shoreline as nest sites, with adjacent deep water for flight and feeding.

— continued on next page

Photo: Nancy Revoir Dezotell

The all-time loon "boomtown" may be Stillwater Reservoir in the western part of the Adirondack Park. The 8-mile-long man-made lake on the Beaver River has anywhere from eight to 15 nesting pairs. Yet, it is a most atypical loon habitat because of heavy boat traffic and fluctuating water levels, which makes many nesting sites risky. In addition, acid rain has eliminated fish in nearly every small pond and tributary in the area. The acid die-off in these smaller ponds may be the reason so many loons head to Stillwater.

Loon populations rise and fall in the Adirondacks, but average about 150 nesting pairs and 250 non-breeding adults. Winter habitats along the Atlantic and Gulf coasts are becoming more critical to the loon's survival than their summer habitat in the Adirondack Park.

the Lake George/Upper Hudson Region. Both are operated by the national chain Hoyt's, and the 12 screens offer a good mix of the latest film releases. In particular, the Aviation Mall Cinemas 7 are conveniently just off Adirondack Northway Exit 19 within a half-hour's drive of much of the region.

King Neptune's Pub & Night Club
Kurosaka Ln., Lake George • 668-2017

King Neptune's is a sprawling entertainment complex — right on the water in Lake George village — that includes the pub, two outside decks, three bars, a private party room and a grand banquet room. Neptune's (as locals call it) is open every month except November and March for dining, but entertainment is pretty much limited to the summer months (as is the case with most clubs in Lake George). On Friday and Saturday summer nights, it would be hard to find a better place for live blues and rock 'n' roll. Many regional favorites from Albany to Lake Placid play at Neptune's, and even though you probably haven't heard of groups like The Refrigerators (horn-based blues and rock) and the Out-of-Control Band (rhythm and blues), trust us — it's worth checking out.

Lake George Dinner Theatre
Holiday Inn-Turf, U.S. Hwy. 9, Lake George • 668-5781

Produced and performed by a professional equity company, Lake George Dinner Theatre offers one show per summer season that runs nightly except Sunday. In 1997, the show was the comedy *Don't Dress for Dinner*. The show and dinner costs $43 (including tax and gratu-

ity) — a pretty good deal for a good meal and professional theater.

Lake George Steamboat Company
Steel Pier, Lake George • 668-5777

If you find the four walls of a night club a little confining, the wide-open waters of Lake George might just fill the bill for you with this fun alternative form of nightlife. The *Minne-Ha-Ha* is an authentic paddlewheel steamboat that takes a Moonlight Dance Cruise with live entertainment Saturday nights from late June through Labor Day. The cruise departs at 10 PM and lasts two hours (but we're guessing it will seem a lot shorter than that to you serious dancers). If you get too hot from all that hoofing, escape to the cool breezes of the upper deck and enjoy the lights of the Lake George shoreline. You can enjoy the cruise for $14.75 for folks 12 and older, $7.50 for children ages 3 through 11. On the other hand, shouldn't the kids be in bed by now?!

Painted Pony Rodeo
N.Y. Rt. 9N, Lake Luzerne • 696-2421

If you'd rather watch horses and bulls dance than do it yourself, here's a fun alternative that everyone in your family can enjoy. In the heart of Dude Ranch Country between Lake George and Lake Luzerne, Painted Pony offers real championship-level rodeo from early June until Labor Day. Enjoy an evening of barbecue and bull riding (you eat, they'll ride) starting at 8 PM Saturday nights in June and then every Wednesday, Friday and Saturday night from July 4th through Labor Day. Admission to the rodeo is $10 for adults and teens ($8 in advance), $7 for children 12 and younger ($5 in advance). The barbecue dinner (we think it's a requisite part of the evening) costs $8 for adults and teens, $6 for children 12 and younger, and you can choose the $2.99 kid's plate for your littlest bronco busters.

Southern Adirondack Lakes Region

Adirondack Lakes Center for the Arts
N.Y. Rt. 28, Blue Mountain Lake • 352-7715

Check out the schedule here to find out which of the many music, art, crafts and theater offerings are being presented throughout the summer. The 1997 schedule included the Adirondack Ensemble (a chamber music group), acoustic folk music and Irish music, all presented in a coffeehouse setting.

Lanzi's Restaurant
N.Y. Rt. 30, Mayfield • 661-7711

If you don't have a waterfront deck of your own from which to enjoy the sunsets, try the 135-seater at Lanzi's, a popular restaurant on the southwestern shore of the Great Sacandaga Lake (see the Restaurants chapter). After finishing your meal, walk out to the docks and then retire to the deck, where you can enjoy an after-dinner drink or coffee while listening to live music on weekends. It is a simple pleasure that's not to be missed.

Royal Mountain
N.Y. Rt. 10, Caroga Lake • 835-6445

For evening excitement of the loud and fast variety, check out the motocross action at Royal Mountain. Every Wednesday evening at 7 PM in the summertime, racers run the course at the base of this ski area to the screaming delight of hundreds of fans. Admission is only $5, but doesn't include ear plugs (a worthwhile investment as far as we're concerned).

Sherman's Restaurant, Dance Hall and Park
N.Y. Rt. 10, Caroga Lake • 835-4110

Sherman's offers a great combination for Southern Adirondack evening fun in the summertime. You can start your evening by riding the carousel, Ferris wheel or mini-coaster. The nighttime view of adjacent Caroga Lake and the illuminated carousel pavilion from the top of the Ferris wheel is beautiful. Adjacent to the amusement rides is Sherman's Restaurant, a huge place that is so close to the lakefront that you can't see anything but water when you look out the windows. There's a big stage and generous dance floor that hosts live bands on Tuesdays, Saturdays and Sundays during summer. Sometimes it's Big Band, sometimes country, sometimes rock 'n' roll, but it's always lots of fun. Sherman's is open Saturday and Sunday from Memorial Day weekend until Fourth of July weekend, then Tuesday through Sunday until Labor Day. On nights when there is entertainment, the cover charge is normally $3 per person.

Old Forge/ Raquette Lake Region

Daiker's Inn
N.Y. Rt. 28, Old Forge • (315) 369-6954

Between Old Forge and Eagle Bay, Daiker's is a casual restaurant and bar with a large outdoor deck overlooking Fourth Lake

INSIDERS' TIP

For a night of star-filled entertainment "under the stars" and convenient to the southern Adirondacks, you can't beat the Saratoga Performing Arts Center (just a half-hour's drive south of Lake George). The 5,100-seat indoor/outdoor amphitheater is the summer home of the New York City Ballet and the Philadelphia Orchestra. You also can catch more than two-dozen pop, rock, blues and jazz concerts featuring national touring artists from June through August.

(great in the summer) and a big, cozy fireplace inside (essential in the winter). You can enjoy live musical entertainment Wednesdays and weekends during summer and on weekends during the busy snowmobile season in winter. There is usually a small cover charge, ranging from $2 to $4 depending on the performers.

The Tamarack Cafe & Movie House
N.Y. Rt. 28, Inlet • (315) 357-2001

Here's a place you can make a whole evening out of it: dinner at The Tamarack; a first-run movie at the adjoining Movie House; and, to top it off, a stop at the Make Your Own Sundae stand for a post-flick treat. The whole place has an authentic "Adirondack Camp" look to it, from the fishing gear inside to the cedar-log exterior. The cinema has one screen, but it often shows two or three different films at a time at separate screenings. You may not see the big releases on the same day they open in New York in LA, but you will within a month or so (and way ahead of the video release). Besides the regular 7 and 9 PM showings, there's a "rainy-day" matinee at 2 PM any day it rains. Admission to the movies is $5.50 for adults and teens and $4.50 for children 12 and younger. The Tamarack is open year round.

Mountain Theatre Co.
Main St., Old Forge • (315) 369-2484

To get your summer theater fix, head to The Water's Edge Inn & Conference Center, which serves as the home of this professional dinner-theater group. Now in its 10th year, the Mountain Theatre Co. presents performances two nights a week in July and August. Productions in 1997 included the Broadway-musical revue *Street of Dreams* and the comedy *A View From Here*. Tickets, including dinner and the show, cost $20 to $25 per person.

Raquette Lake Navigation Co.
off N.Y. Rt. 28, Raquette Lake
• (315) 354-5532

For a fun, scenic and relaxing evening, consider a moonlight cruise aboard the 60-foot *W.W. Durant*. The double-deck cruise boat has an open deck above, an enclosed windowed deck below and comfortably holds 125 people. The moonlight cruise departs at 10 PM and plies the waters of Raquette Lake for about 90 minutes while you enjoy live music, the elegant turn-of-the-century decor and the lights of the shoreline. The cruise costs only $5 per person, but doesn't include drinks or food. Still, it's a bargain and a beautiful way to spend a moonlit Adirondack night. See the Attractions chapter for more details on the *W.W. Durant*.

The Strand Theatre
Main St., Old Forge • (315) 369-6703

In the heart of Old Forge village, this historic art-deco movie house is open all year and shows the latest popular film releases. Each film usually shows for about a week — enough time to make the rounds of locals and visitors alike. Bargain matinees are shown at 1:10 and 3:50 PM and cost $4 for all ages. Additional screenings are at 7 and 9:40 PM and cost $5.50 for adults and teens and $4.50 for children (12 and younger) and seniors.

Nature's Nighttime Spectacle

Nature holds its own cache of after-hours activities that can be enjoyed virtually anywhere in the Adirondacks region. The following are a few possibilities we'd like to share.

Moth Hunting

Moths come out at night during the summer. No one knows exactly how many moth species exist in the Adirondacks, so if you went out on a moth hunt and kept accurate notes of the ones you witnessed, you would be contributing to our scientific knowledge.

What most folks don't know is that some 50 moth species are active during the winter months in North America. (Although this may sound like another snipe-hunting yarn, we're not kidding about winter moths. They do exist.) When the conditions are ideal, the moths come out of hiding and fly about looking for a quick meal, usually sap. As soon as the temperature drops — for some species the transitional temperature for activity is freezing (32 degrees) — the moths disappear and revert to a torpid state.

Many winter moths burrow under leaf litter in the forest. Although snow cover protects the moths from deadly temperatures, the snow also prevents them emerging from their burrows and flying about (which is why they are not often seen in climates such as the Adirondacks).

It is likely that a few winter moths exist in the Adirondacks, but specific species are not known. Discovering those that *do* exist is not a high priority for many moth fanciers, and such a study is rather challenging.

There is a distinct connection between the study of moths in winter (or summer) and nightlife — and if you read this far, you deserve to know what the connection is. One way that scientists lure winter and summer moths for study is by concocting a mixture of molasses, sugar, mashed (and rotten) fruit — and stale beer. The beer is an essential ingredient, as it gets the concoction fermenting. Curiously, beer is also an essential ingredient in nightlife and has been known to create a fermenting state of mind.

If you decide to make your moth lure from the remnants of your after-hours exploits (a.k.a. stale beer), simply brush it on a tree. With a little luck, the right temperatures and conditions, some moths (and plenty of other insects) might come around to enjoy their own version of nightlife, tasting the fermenting juices on the tree. We really aren't kidding about any of this. In fact making the moth lure is even fun to do with kids. Moths and a few butterflies love to dine on foul-smelling things, and the more gross the concoction, the more moths that likely will be attracted. Although there is no specific formula for the mixture, its viscosity should be close to that of paint. The paste is brushed onto a tree. Since the paste is gross, paste it on trees out of the way of people. Believe us, you don't want to lean against this stuff.

Stargazing with Edgar Allan Poe

We're not talking about movie stars, but heavenly ones. With no obstructions, no cities filling the night sky with artificial light and clear, pollution-free skies, the Adirondack region is prime stargazing territory. On a clear, moonless night, the number of stars you see is astounding, which raises a perplexing question: If there are so many stars, all of which produce light, the night sky should not be black, but rather ablaze with starlight. Why, then, is the sky still cast in darkness?

As you ponder the question, tell a favorite story of Edgar Allan Poe, who not only told a few good dark stories, but also provided a sound answer to the aforementioned question. Once upon a time, Poe posited, the universe began. It is not forever and doesn't go on forever — and there just aren't enough stars to make the night sky bright.

Some 100 years later, science seemingly confirmed Poe's idea when a Dr. Harrison from the University of Massachusetts suggested that only light from stars 15 billion light-years away reaches earth, and that galaxies can't live forever and burn out with age. Didn't Poe say that?

Snipe Hunting

The Adirondack snipe is a notorious and highly elusive creature. No one has seen one in more than 100 years, but we all know that snipes exist. Exactly what do they look like? No one knows, but it has been said that one will know a snipe when one sees it. Some say the snipe is harmless; others describe its behavior as being more like a trickster. In either case, no snipe has ever physically harmed anyone. Mental anguish, however, is a distinct possibility.

We would all sleep easier if a snipe was found. Although there is no financial reward for finding one, the finder will become a lifelong hero and a legend for all time.

Since we have no idea what snipes look like, where they live or how they live, your search can begin anywhere at any time. If you do find one, please report the sighting to anyone who will believe you or call the special telephone number found somewhere in the Yellow Pages of any telephone directory.

Sitting around a campfire is a good time to make up a yarn (yawn) about snipes or some other imagined creature of the night.

There are more than 100 craft shops, studios and galleries that offer some representation of regional products and craftsmanship.

Shopping

First, a confession. This was perhaps the most dangerous (financially speaking) chapter in the entire book to research. There are simply way too many fascinating, attractive places to shop and spend your money here in the Adirondacks. We survived the experience (although our credit cards are still on line-of-credit life support), but make no promises that you'll be able to do the same. So read on at your own discretionary-income risk!

For a geographic area this big and this dependent upon visitors, it would be pretty easy to do a whole *Insiders' Guide to Shopping in the Adirondacks*. There are more than 100 craft shops, studios and galleries that offer some representation of regional products and craftsmanship. There are nearly 100 outlet stores offering every conceivable variety of clothing and dry goods. There are dozens of general and country stores with their own variety of local specialties mixed with staples of existence. There are dozens more sports- and recreation-related stores and outfitters, offering equipment, supplies and even guide services for all forms of winter- and summer-recreation fun. Virtually every town has a general store, video store, T-shirt shop and a couple of antique shops, so we're not able to list every one in existence. Most towns of any size have at least a Grand Union (it may be circa 1960s, but it's still a supermarket for these parts), a Stewart's convenience store or, if you're in a real Adirondack metroplex, an Ames Discount Department store.

Next, a disclaimer: This chapter includes a sampling of shopping experiences that you can enjoy in the Adirondack region. It represents just a few "snapshots" out of the whole album, and many interesting and worthy shops are surely not included here. That is not intentional, just practical. Besides, half the fun of shopping is the exploring and discovering new places you happen upon, so we don't want to spoil the fun by telling you about every single nook and knickknack cranny.

Many craft stores, galleries and antique shops have seasonal hours or are only open for part of the year. It's always best to call ahead, particularly if you're taking a long, adventurous ride out to some remote little studio. (Unless otherwise noted, all establishments in this chapter are open year round.)

We have laid out this chapter first considering where you are, and then what you want and need. That is, we are first giving you the geographic regions, and then within each region, we have provided six shopping categories.

"Everything Adirondack" includes crafts, artwork, books, furniture and gift items that are Adirondack-inspired or related. "Malls and Outlets" is pretty self-explanatory, and you'll find considerably more of the latter than the former in the Adirondacks. "Milk and Light Bulbs" is just a fun way to say "general stores" — places where you can find everything from groceries to fishing poles to hardware. "Fun Stuff" is the place to look for recreational equipment and supplies. What home is complete without some "Antiques, Knicks & Knacks" (our category for antique shops and general gift shops)? Finally, we include a sampling of "Bookstores" for those of you who, like us, find it hard to resist good reading material — especially when on vacation.

Lake Placid/ Tri-Lakes Region

Everything Adirondack

The Birch Store
N.Y. Rt. 73, Keene Valley • 576-4561

Many folks (not us, of course!) seem to be cruising along too fast when this store pops up on N.Y. 73. If you find that to be the case, you're driving beyond the speed limit. Slow down and enjoy the charm of Keene Valley and this shop, with its unusual collection of Adirondack decorative furnishings (many are hand-crafted) and clothing for camp and cottage.

Evergreen Trading Company
N.Y. Rt. 73, Keene • 576-9141

A handmade quilt, a divorce (there's a lawyer's office here), a piece of pie, a vacation house and a crafted candle — all in the same store? It's Keene's version of a mall, and it's really quite friendly and charming. There's something of interest for everyone. If you're driving by between 1 and 3 PM on a Sunday afternoon during July and August, be sure to stop in; some of the region's finest craftspeople, musicians and artists hang out on the porch and demonstrate their skills.

North Country Taxidermy and Trading Company
N.Y. Rt. 73, Keene • 576-4318

That antler chandelier you've always wanted for your camp — here's where you can find it! You'll also find some mounted animals, bear rugs and items from local artisans, such as baskets and pottery. We're never quite sure what new discovery we'll make here, which is part of this store's fun.

Adirondack Craft Center
93 Saranac Ave., Lake Placid • 523-2062

This is the largest craft center in the region. It offers traditional, rustic and contemporary items from more than 300 local artisans and in every price range. You'll find a potpourri of goods including rustic furniture, glassware, pottery, jewelry, baskets and wood carvings. The center adheres to rigid standards, so only the best resident artisans are represented here.

Adirondack Decorative Arts and Crafts
104-106 Main St., Lake Placid • 523-4545

This is a good place to go if you have to decorate your camp from top to bottom in the Adirondack style or are just looking for "something Adirondack" as a reminder of your vacation. This large store, complete with its own waterfall, offers everything from rustic bed frames, bookshelves and cabinets to decorative items for the wall, shelf, bath, bedroom and even the outhouse. In case you are wondering where to get an outhouse, there's one for sale here.

Adirondack Store and Gallery
109 Saranac Ave., Lake Placid • 523-2646

Long before Adirondack crafts, designs and motifs became fashionable, there was the Adirondack Store and Gallery. On the outskirts of Lake Placid's main shopping district, just past the Cold Brook Plaza, this is one of the original stores with an Adirondack theme and products. It hasn't lost its touch over the years — just accumulated more Adirondack things, including antique table settings, Winslow Homer prints, antiques with a new look and new items with the antique look, bird feeders, rustic furniture, soaps for camp and soaps to smell good . . . the list goes on.

Adirondack Trading Company
91 Main St., Lake Placid • 523-3651

There's no trading allowed, but there's an Adirondack trinket, gift and accessory for every taste and budget. Items fill every possible niche in the store and range from one-

FYI

Unless otherwise noted, the area code for all phone numbers listed in this guide is 518.

of-a-kind pieces of rustic furniture to T-shirts, sweat shirts and sweaters with animal motifs, hand-crafted soaps, candles, jewelry and whatnots.

Caribou Trading Company
Hilton Plaza, Main St., Lake Placid • 523-1152

The non-shoppers in your group can sit and relax with a fresh-brewed cup of coffee on one side of the store, while the shoppers browse among the unusual assortment of handmade pottery, wood carvings, jewelry and metalwork on the other side. A good selection of New Age books and music can be found here too.

Darrah Cooper Jewelers
14 Main St., Lake Placid • 523-2774

This is one of the few full-service jewelry stores in the area. It carries many of the standards in jewelry and a good selection of unusual items — many relating to the Adirondacks, such as gold pendant pack baskets and pine cones.

Discoveries
76 Main St., Lake Placid • 523-1954

Kids and adults alike call this the "cool" store because of its unique and eclectic collection of gifts, games, books and locally made crafts, including pack baskets and rustic furniture. Take a good look at the quality and design of the bookshelves and tables; they are made by a couple of kids, calling themselves "Kid's Twigs." If you are in need of amusements for a long ride home or a rainy night at camp, you should find something to entertain you here. You'll also find a good and unusual selection of books for kids.

Flowering Tree
Hilton Plaza, Main St., Lake Placid • 523-4612

This is one of the few shops in the region catering to Native American arts and crafts, including furniture, jewelry and decorative arts. A small gallery section of the store offers a selection of original prints. A few products are made locally. If you're in need of something different in the way of books, you will find many good reads with a Native American theme here.

Moon Tree Design
22 Main St., Lake Placid • 523-1970

Moon Tree is one of the few shops on Main Street where one-of-a-kind, hand-crafted items can be found in abundant variety. A few items are locally made. Many items are rather unusual, especially the pottery, ceramics and metalwork.

HandYcraft Store
N.Y. Rt. 86, Wilmington • 946-2235

This store has a clear purpose: to offer an A-to-Z range of hand-crafted items by local artisans at A-to-Z prices. Somehow it manages to meet that goal every year with its unique crafts sold at reasonable rates. The artisans are as eclectic as the wares: A few years ago, the store stocked items from a 9-year-old rustic-furniture maker and a 95-year-old quilter. The store is open seven days a week from late May through Columbus Day.

North Country Wood Works
216 Saranac Ave., Lake Placid • 523-4531

This shop produces Adirondack, rustic and unfinished furniture. It also manufactures and sells the famed Adirondack chair at a reasonable price and will ship it anywhere.

Asplin Tree Farms
N.Y. Rt. 86, Saranac Lake • 891-5783, (800) 858-7336

This tree farm, about 8 miles from the village of Saranac Lake, is a great place to get your Christmas tree and holiday balsam wreaths. An on-site gift shop offers a collection of balsam pillows, soft sculptures, ceramic gifts, Adirondack crafts and bags of balsam fir needles to remind you of the refreshing scent of the Adirondack air. The store is open Memorial Day through Christmas.

Kate Mountain Pottery and Company
41 Broadway, Saranac Lake • 891-2726

This small studio offers antiques, fine collectibles, soaps, candles, dried flower arrangements and pottery. Items here have an Adirondack motif made by Kate.

Small Fortune Studio
71 Main St., Saranac Lake • 891-1139

Small Fortune refers not to this studio's prices, but rather to its size and its owner, Tim Fortune, a nationally recognized painter who can be seen at work here Tuesday through Saturday. Tim's work ranges from small landscapes to large, multi-paneled Adirondack scenes.

Casagrain Studio and Gallery
10287 N.Y. Rt. 3, Tupper Lake • 358-2595

This is one of those studios where you see the sign, but always seem to be driving too fast to stop. Slow down and consider stopping here, though, as the oils and prints in this small studio of wildlife artist Gary Casagrain capture the essence of the Adirondacks.

Leather Artisan
N.Y. Rt. 3, Childwold • 359-3102

Leather Artisan is in the middle of Childwold, which is in the middle of nowhere. Although you won't be able to buy gas for miles, you can buy a wide variety of handcrafted designer leather accessories (belts, hats, purses, etc.) here, most of which are made on the premises. The shop is open daily May through December.

Malls and Outlets

Ames Department Store
N.Y. Rt. 86, Saranac Lake • 891-2850
N.Y. Rt. 3, Tupper Lake • 359-3325
Cornelia St., Plattsburgh • 561-0050
N.Y. Rt. 9N, Ticonderoga • 585-6797

Residents living in Adirondack Park or within the Blue Line are accustomed to driving an hour or two to major malls for a day of shopping. What suburbanites might consider "normal" shopping options are limited within the Park. Folks in the Adirondacks either make due, use mail-order or pack up the kids for what is generally a day-long excursion. Sometimes, however, you just need a department store, and Ames is the only major chain actually within the "blue line" (the Park's boundary). It can be a vacation-saver if you forgot to pack something — clothing for you or the kids, sleeping bags, a battery-operated alarm clock to rouse you from your slumber on the inflatable mattress in your tent, or the latest heavy metal CD that your teenager just has to have the day it's released.

Milk and Light Bulbs (General Stores)

Norman's General Store
N.Y. Rt. 3, Bloomingdale • 891-1890

If you pass this way more than a dozen times, you qualify as a local; thus, you'll stop in to catch up on the comings and goings and purchase that loaf of bread that you forgot.

Hickok's
N.Y. Rt. 30, Fish Creek (Saranac Lake)
• 891-3328

If you visit Fish Creek, you will likely visit Hickok's for maps and camping supplies, fishing tackle, bait and accessories for your boat. Motor boat and canoe rentals are available if you want to explore the miles and miles of ponds and lakes in this region.

Hoss's Country Corner
Lake St., Long Lake • 624-2481
111 Park St., Tupper Lake • 359-2092,
(800) 952-HOSS

Hoss's combines everything expected from a classic country store (i.e. groceries and clothing) with items to meet the needs of the modern-day tourist (i.e. gifts, crafts, books and sporting goods) and somehow makes it all work. The store in Long Lake has long been a

---

INSIDERS' TIP

Shopping in the Adirondacks is more fun and less frustrating when you don't have a schedule, so give yourself plenty of time for exploring. It easy to underestimate how long it will take you to drive from one town to the next, and it's easy to get hung up in a shop you find just a little too fascinating to leave just yet.

focal point of community activity — the place to swap fishing tales and other gossip. The store in Tupper has a more modest inventory than the one in Long Lake and instead is geared more to the gift trade.

Fun Stuff
(Recreational Equipment)

All Season Sports
1 Wilmington Rd., Lake Placid • 523-3757

All Season can solve your problem if you forget your golf clubs, tennis racket, hockey helmet or other essential sporting goods and don't want to buy it new — it carries new and used sports equipment for both sale and rent. It's one of the few places where you can even rent fishing gear. If you don't need a top-of-the-line equipment or are a little tight on funds, this is a good place to check out for a deal on bicycle and golf club rentals.

Christmas Creations
31 Main St., Lake Placid • 523-8210

"It's beginning to look a lot like Christmas," and Christmas Creations is open year round with a thousand ornaments and holiday collectibles. The store also offers an selection of fudge and homemade candies.

Cobbler Shop
233 Main St., Lake Placid • 523-3679

This is the place to rent ice skates or have your skates or shoes repaired. The Cobbler Shop might even be able to fix your torn backpack. The store also carries a good selection of tourist-related gifts and items relating to both figure skating and ice hockey.

The Edge In Sports
220 Main St., Lake Placid • 523-1973

If you are into ice hockey, The Edge is everything a hockey store should be. In fact, according to the NHL (National Hockey League, for those unfamiliar with the league or the sport), The Edge is one of the "best little hockey" stores around. You can't rent skates here, but you can purchase some new or used skates, along with everything else to play the game or show off your favorite pro team's latest fashion. During the summer months, there's an influx of soccer-related items.

Eastern Mountain Sports (EMS)
51 Main St., Lake Placid • 523-2505

EMS is a chain of outdoor outfitters found mostly (but not exclusively) in the eastern United States. It carries everything related to camping, hiking, kayaking and mountaineering. Many items are the high-quality EMS brand. The book selection of hiking and nature guides and general outdoor-related books is excellent. Sometimes you'll even find a novel by the likes of Edward Abbey thrown into the mix. EMS sponsors a number of programs throughout the year on hiking, low-impact camping, kayaking and mountaineering. It also offers equipment rentals, including cross-country skis, snowshoes, recreational kayaks, tents and camping gear. It can outfit a family of four with tents, packs and sleeping bags for about $150 for a weekend. The staff is knowledgeable about its products, so if you have questions about the latest and greatest gear for adults or kids, these are the people to ask.

High Peaks Cyclery and Mountain Adventures
331 Main St., Lake Placid • 523-3764

High Peaks Cyclery has received a slew of awards for its retailing efforts — which counts for something. But even if you could care less about awards and simply are looking for great service, a huge selection and knowledgeable sales people, you should check out this place. High Peaks bills itself as a bike shop, but it is far more than that. During the winter, snowboards and cross-country skis are available. (During the summer, you'll find some great deals on winter sports equipment.) Along with bikes and skis, you'll find mountaineering equipment, hiking boots, clothing, backpacking equipment . . . in other words, if you need equipment to get from point A to point B, across whatever terrain, you will find it here.

But High Peaks is not just about selling you outdoor equipment; it provides service on all the items it sells and sponsors plenty of games, good times and events to let you test the gear — or just have a little fun. Throughout the summer months, High Peaks sponsors various bike races and programs — many geared for children and families — such as mountain bike excursions and rock climbing. (Be sure to check out the rock-climbing room.)

Bikes rent for about $20 per day. High

Peaks offers tent and backpack rentals at $15 per day; multi-day packages are available, You will also find a great selection of trail maps and guides here, along with hiking boots and equipment. (See our Kidstuff chapter for related information.)

Jones Outfitters Ltd.
34 Main St., Lake Placid • 523-3468

At the base of the band shell park in the middle of town, this shop carries Orvis fishing supplies, gifts and clothing. Almost all items relate to fishing. There's a good selection of clothing for the female angler here. Kayak and canoe sales and rentals are also available. Tuition to an Orvis-endorsed fly-fishing school is approximately $300 for a weekend of instruction.

Maui North
134 Main St., Lake Placid • 523-7245

This is primarily a full-service bike and board (snow, skate and wake) shop. Snowboard rentals cost about $20 per day, including boots. Boarders will find the latest designs here, including a range of "rad" clothing.

Mountain Run
359 Main St., Lake Placid • 523-9443

How do former U.S. Ski Team members make a living today? For five years, Sue Cagen skied with the best. Today, she and her husband, Dana, operate Mountain Run, a full-service sports shop, with downhill skiing and snowboarding emphasized during the winter, and skateboarding, cycling, water skiing and in-line skating the rest of the year. The expertise of the owners and staff — former and current employees include junior race coaches, a former World Cup racer and snowboard coaches — is part of the shopping experience. These folks know their stuff, and whether you are purchasing or renting, they welcome your questions. Their expertise has earned the store a national reputation for its custom tune-ups on skis and snowboards.

INSIDERS' TIP

If there is one thing as variable as the Adirondack weather, it's the operating times of shops. Always check ahead, or play "retail roulette" and hope you're lucky.

The shop rents bikes for $20 per day, in-line skates for $15 a day, skis with boots and poles for $18 a day and snowboards at $28 day. Skateboarders can access the only half-pipe in the area for $2 per session. Mountain Run sponsors a number of special events during the year, including water-skiing competitions and tournaments, bike rodeos and ski and snowboard competitions. Call for more information.

Placid Planet Bicycles
200 Saranac Ave., Lake Placid
• 523-4128

Placid Planet had everything to do with bikes — and bikes alone — including sales, rentals and service. It sells both new and used basic and higher-end bikes plus the latest new and used clothing, fancy helmets, basic biking supplies and plenty of parts for repairs. The stock of high-end mountain bikes, suitable for trail or road riding, rent for approximately $20 per day.

Placid Planet and friends sponsors Tuesday evening (6:30 PM) mountain bike rides and Saturday morning (9 AM) road bike rides in and around the area — free for folks with their own bikes. Besides taking an enjoyable excursion, you can get some free advice on mountain or road biking. Placid Planet sponsors many free clinics and rides throughout the year, so call or drop by to check out what's planned.

U.S. Olympic Spirit Store
Main St., Lake Placid • 523-7207

This shop, owned and operated by the U.S. Olympic Committee, offers officially licensed clothing (sweats, warm-ups, T-shirts), gifts and accessories related to the Olympic Games.

Adirondack Sport Shop
N.Y. Rt. 86, Wilmington • 946-2605

If fly-fishing is your sport, pay attention. The owner of this shop, Fran Betters, has a bit of a reputation in the fly-fishing world: He's written a few books on the subject, and his ties are so famous, a beer — AuSable Wulff — is even named after one. Fran will not only sell you the best fly for the moment, but also serve your other angling needs, including that custom fly rod you've always wanted. The shop also has a unique selection of gifts for your favorite angler. Fran offers a series of free clinics during the summer plus stream orientation, guide services and fishing instruction. The advice here is always free.

Hungry Trout Fly Shop
N.Y. Rt. 86, Wilmington • 946-2217

As the name implies, this small shop specializes in rods, reels, flies and other equipment you'll need to catch a hungry trout. Guide service also is available. Hungry Trout is open May through October.

Lake Placid's international acclaim as a winter sports center attracts thousands of visitors to its downtown shops.

The Mountaineer
N.Y. Rt. 73, Keene Valley • 576-2281

If you are going to "the 'Dacks" (the short and hip nickname for the Adirondacks) for serious rock or ice climbing, find your way to The Mountaineer. The people here know their stuff and can explain it to folks planning their first an alpine adventure as well as tech-weenies who crave the technical jargon and details about the latest equipment. You will find everything for mountaineering here plus a great selection of clothing, boots, camping and hiking gear for those without the foggiest idea what mountaineering is. The store has arguably one of the most complete collections of maps, trail guides and climbing books in the region. In January 1997, The Mountaineer joined Adirondack Rock and River Guides to sponsor the first Adirondack International Mountaineering Festival, a two-day series of clinics for novice and experienced mountaineers alike. Many sessions were limited to eight or fewer people, enabling all participants personalized attention. Call for information about similar upcoming events and clinics.

All Season Outfitters
168 Lake Flower Ave., Saranac Lake • 891-6159, (800) 236-5217

This canoe and camping store sells and rents canoes, kayaks and general camping equipment. A shuttle service is available to pick up canoeists at their take-out point. Trip planning and guide services are also available.

Barkeater Bicycles
48 Main St., Saranac Lake • 891-5207

Barkeater specializes in mountain bikes and equipment. This full-service bike shop also offers some of the best prices on rentals, with entry-level mountain bikes at $15 per day.

Blue Line Sport Shop
82 Main St., Saranac Lake • 891-4680

Sooner or later, you'll end up at Blue Line for your hunting, fishing and general outfitting needs. This store has everything: inexpensive lures, shotgun shells, hiking boots for kids, canoes, backpacks, sleeping bags . . . the works. This not a chain store, but rather a sport's shop with its own personality — and personalities. Every salesperson in the store seems to know the latest fishing hotspot, which may or may not be the same spot recommended by another salesperson. (Chances are both spots are good.) If you have questions about a fishing pole for the kids, where to go and what lure to use to catch the big one, just ask.

St. Regis Canoe Outfitters
Floodwood Rd., Lake Clear • 891-1838

This outfitter rents and sells a full line of camping gear, but because of its out-of-the-way location (4.1 miles off N.Y. 30 on Floodwood Road), it is used primarily by those canoeing in the St. Regis Wilderness area — the site of some of the best canoeing in the region. Trip planning and guide services are available. This outfitter offers one of the most informative brochures available on canoe excursions.

Adirondack Canoe & Kayaks
96 Old Piercefield Rd., Tupper Lake • 359-2174, (800) 499-2174

You can rent or buy all of your camping and canoeing equipment here. Shuttle transportation is available, as is planning for extended trips. If you are looking for off-the-beaten-path routes to explore, the staff here can turn you on to some good options in the Tupper Lake area. It's best to call for shop hours during the winter months.

Tip Top Sport Shop
40 Park Ave., Tupper Lake • 359-9222

This old-fashioned sporting goods store is replete with personality. You can obtain all of your basic fishing and hunting items here as well as other sports equipment, such as snowshoes, cross-country skis and hiking supplies.

World Cup Ski and Bike
58 Park St., Tupper Lake • 359-9481

This is the closest thing to a snowboarder's paradise in the region. Because the shop is a demo center for many small and large snowboard and contour-ski manufacturers, you will find some unusual items here for sale and rent. World Cup sponsors many demo days at nearby Big Tupper Ski area, so be sure to ask about dates, especially if you want to check out the very latest equipment. During the summer, the snowboards are replaced by bikes. The shop offers expert repairs at some of the best rates around, and rentals are in the $15 to $20 range.

Antiques, Knicks & Knacks

Antique Center
103 Main St., Lake Placid • 523-3913

This center is easy to find — just look for the antiques overflowing onto the sidewalk on Main Street in the center of Lake Placid. A number of dealers are housed here, and items range from hand-size collectibles to large pieces of furniture. There is generally a good selection of Adirondack items here, including pack baskets, twig items and furniture.

Grammy's Antiques and Dolls
8 Sentinel Rd., Lake Placid • 523-1783

Grammy's general offerings tend to be on the small scale. Her specialties are toys and dolls, including America's favorite, Barbie.

Lake Placid Antique and Craft Center
121 Cascade Rd., Lake Placid • 523-0055

For whom was the huge rustic chair outside of this antique complex constructed? Under no circumstances will it fit in your car. You can, however, find its maker inside — in one of the 25 antique and craft shops under one roof. This is a good place to find an unusual gift — baskets, tole paintings, photography, Russian folk art, rag rugs, rustic items, wood carvings, sheepskin hats and mittens. Each vendor rents a space, and given the variety of folks selling their wares, there's generally a better than average supply of items here.

Old Friends Mercantile
52 Saranac Ave., Lake Placid • 523-0125

To find this store, look for the whimsical (to us, at least) display of carved bears in various poses and other oddities on Saranac Avenue, just off the main drag in Lake Placid. The consignment shop offers a little of everything to suit everyone's taste, including folks who aren't enthralled by the outside display. You'll find some good "junque" here, including barely worn used clothing, glassware, trinkets and hand-crafted "Welcome" signs.

George Jaques Antiques
Main St., Keene Valley • 576-2214

Jaques specializes in Adirondack antiques, and what he can't find in the way of rustic furniture and things, he makes. His collection, as well as his own work, is well known in the region. The shop is generally closed during the winter months.

The Goldmine
Bloomingdale Rd., Saranac Lake • 891-0347

The Goldmine is a large, rambling building halfway between Saranac Lake and Bloomingdale. It's packed with large and small items. Many of the larger items, such as old horse-drawn buggies, won't fit in the shop. Someone once propped an old gasoline pump near a horse-drawn carriage, but no one is sure if the juxtaposition was an ironic commentary.

Forest Murmurs
N.Y. Rt. 3, Vermontville • 327-9373

In an old church, this small studio specializes in antique and handmade Adirondack furnishings as well as general antiques. It's best to call ahead for hours.

Red Barn Antiques
Onchiota Rd., Loon Lake • 891-5219

The barn building itself is an antique, and its five rooms and two lofts are filled with antiques, collectibles and gift items, including Depression glass, china and rustic and antique furniture. Hours are irregular, so call ahead.

Bookstores

Bashful Bear Book Store
Main St. (N.Y. Rt. 73), Keene Valley • 576-4736

Actually this is a "books and beans" store. The combination may sound slightly offbeat — and it is — but that's all part of the fun. There's some 10,000 titles of new and used books plus a fine selection of natural foods, beauty and healthcare items. The selection of books makes it obvious that the owners love good books of every kind. You'll find something new off the bestseller list, something that perhaps should be a bestseller but isn't, and a few used paperbacks to shove in your back pocket for your next hike. If in doubt about a selection, ask; the response will be friendly and enthusiastic, never bashful.

The Bookstore Plus
89 Main St., Lake Placid • 523-2950

This is the only place in town to find the latest hardcover bestseller. The paperback selection is extensive, and there's enough variety so the kids can find something of interest too. The "Plus" part consists of cards, basic office supplies and art supplies.

With Pipe and Book
91 Main St., Lake Placid • 523-9096

This store offers the region's largest selection of new and old Adirondack books, prints and maps. There's a great selection of used fiction in paperback and hard cover downstairs. As the name implies, a good selection of pipes and tobacco accompanies the books.

Fact & Fiction Bookshop
17 Broadway, Saranac Lake • 891-8067

This small bookstore is a newcomer to the scene. Although its selection is modest, it offers a good range of books including bestsellers, children's books and just plain interesting titles.

INSIDERS' TIP

Need a T-shirt? Canada Street in Lake George is a great place to look. You'll find dozens of shops featuring thousands of shirts in all colors, sizes and degrees of good taste.

Plattsburgh/Western Lake Champlain Region

Everything Adirondack

Adirondack Craft Loft
4426 N.Y. Rt. 22, Plattsburgh • 561-1037
Just off Exit 36 of I-87, the craft loft has a huge and diverse selection of hand-crafted items from some 60 of the area's artists and crafters. You'll find soaps, candles, dolls, folk art, stained glass, pottery, ceramics, wood crafts and more.

Silver Dragonfly
17 Bridge St., Plattsburgh • 563-9334
This small shop in downtown Plattsburgh offers a selection of hand-crafted items from around the region. There's a good variety of jewelry, especially beaded stuff, as well as a few oil paintings and plenty of fine pottery and glassware.

Stained Glass and Dollhouse Shoppe
104 Margaret St., Plattsburgh • 563-5912
This place is two shops in one, and if stained glass or doll houses are your thing, you will be delighted with the selection here.

Glassware, created on the premises, includes small reflectors for windows, large panels, lamps and other collectibles.

Yarborough Square
672 Bear Swamp Rd., Peru • 843-7057
This gallery is one of those places that has to be discovered. Everything is hand-crafted, including the building itself, with a waterfall emerging from a mantle. Unlike many galleries, this one exhibits elements of fun, with some whimsical displays and craft items. The inventory covers the range of "normal" crafts (jewelry, pottery, woodwork, etc.) and includes a few unusual items of the same type as well.

The Candy Man
N.Y. Rt. 9N, Jay • 946-7270
This place is heaven for chocolate lovers. The homemade chocolate is sooooo rich, soooo creamy and made on premise. When in need of a treat, this place is where the best diet plans come to a tasty end.

Jay Craft Center
N.Y. Rt. 9N, Jay • 946-7824
What a life! — to not only love your work, but also live where you work. And then to open up part of your home — a restored grange building— to the public, so they can enjoy and, hopefully, purchase some pottery (your

own handiwork) or crafts (made by others). In the Jay Craft Center, you will find artists Cheri Cross, Lee Kazanas, or perhaps someone else filling in, who can tell you about the artisans who made the jewelry, leather works, wooden ware, candles, toys or prints. Once (sometimes twice) a year, the center conducts a special sale on pottery seconds; be sure to ask when this will happen.

Young Studio & Gallery
N.Y. Rt. 86, Jay • 946-7301

Half the fun of visiting a studio is having the chance to watch an artisan at work. In this small studio, 1 mile from the Village Green in Jay, you can watch Sue Burdick Young at the pottery wheel or check out the etchings made by her husband or one of the 40 other artists represented in the studio. The items include fine prints, hand-painted silk, furniture, jewelry, woodcrafts and more. The studio is open year round. During the winter and off-season months, it is generally closed Sundays and Mondays.

Hand Made
Main St., Essex • 963-8589

On the corner of Main and School streets, this new shop features hand-crafted items. Everything is locally made, from the hammocks to the baskets, soaps and hand creams.

The Store in Essex
1 Main St., Essex • 963-7121

The Store and the American Bird and Craft Studio are housed in one historic stone building near the ferry dock in Essex. In The Store, you'll find a great mix of antiques and crafts. The studio features stained glass, jewelry, baskets, sculpture, prints and photographs.

Westport Trading Co.
Main St., Westport • 962-4801

The best thing about this gallery could be watching owner Kip Trienens making stained glass. Then again, there are some 150 artisans represented in the gallery, so its hard to pick a favorite among the African masks, Eskimo carvings, stone works, woodwork, met-

alwork and all that stained glass reflecting light every which way. The gallery is generally open during normal business hours, but it is best to call ahead if you want to visit, especially during the off-season.

Adirondacks Rustic Gallery
Charley Hill Rd., Schroon Lake
• 532-9384

The rustic furniture of Barry Gregson is distinctly his own. Barry uses gnarled wood, roots and burls to make imaginative pieces that are as comfortable to sit in (assuming it is a chair) as they are to look at. Gene Armstrong, who specializes in white birch mirrors, and Jerry and Jessica Farrell, who create painted clocks, also are represented in the studio.

FYI

Unless otherwise noted, the area code for all phone numbers listed in this guide is 518.

Malls and Outlets

Aside from the Champlain Centers (see this section's entry), you will find numerous strip malls and national franchises all along N.Y. Route 3, east and west of these major malls. Sam's Club, Wal-Mart, Staples, Ames Department Store . . . Wendy's, McDonald's, Burger King, Pizza Hut . . . Ford, Cadillac and Honda dealerships — if it has a national advertising campaign, if your kid's can sing the jingle, odds are you'll find it along N.Y. 3, also known as Cornelia Street.

Champlain Centers North and South
N.Y. Rt. 3, off I-87 Exit 37, Plattsburgh
• 561-8660

These two nearly adjacent malls are like thousands of other enclosed malls throughout America. The North mall, the larger of the two, houses Sears, JCPenney and approximately 30 other retailers, the majority of which belong to major chains, including Foot Locker, Bath and Body, Toys 'R Us and Gap. Price Chopper and Kmart serve as the focus of the South mall, which tends to have more discount retailers than its northern neighbor. (The South mall has plans for extensive renovations as of this writing.)

Plattsburgh malls draw shoppers from both the United States and Canada.

Milk and Light Bulbs (General Stores)

Richard's Grocery, Bait & Tackle
71 Johnson Ave., Plattsburgh • 563-1444

Both the early and late bird can find worms here because Richard's is open seven days a week from 7 AM to 9 PM. The store carries most all of the basic fishing and hunting needs, including archery supplies. You'll also find basic groceries, including bread, beer, soda and snacks.

Fun Stuff (Recreational Equipment)

Adirondack Rod and Reel
597 N.Y. Rt. 9N, Keeseville • 834-5306

This shop offers a complete line of hunting and fishing supplies. If you know little about fishing in these parts, this is a good place to get your questions answered. It's closed Tuesday, but you can call the store's fishing hotline (see listed number) for up-to-date information about hot spots.

Champlain Angler
N.Y. Rt. 22, Willsboro • 963-8266

The Angler offers everything needed for fishing and hunting, including licenses, bait, supplies, charter services and guide services. These folks even guarantee fish on their charter trips!

Maui North
18 Durkee St., Plattsburgh • 563-7245

This ski, bike and board (skate and wake) outfitter offers a full service department for everything it sells. (See the "Lake Placid/Tri-Lakes Region" entry for more information.)

Viking Ski and Bike Shop
453 Upper Cornelia St. (N.Y. Rt. 3), Plattsburgh • 561-5539

This is the regions largest ski shop, with a

complete line of cross-country, snowboard and alpine rentals. There's also a huge selection of clothing. Every time we drive past, there's another sign for the latest sale, so keep an eye out if you're thinking about new equipment. During the summer, Viking transforms into a full-service bike shop. Mountain bike rentals begin a $15 per day. Rollerblades are also available at $10 a day. This is the place for information on the best bike routes in the Plattsburgh and upper Lake Champlain region.

Antiques, Knicks & Knacks

The Bargaineer
39 Bridge St., Plattsburgh • 561-3525
This antique shop is in downtown Plattsburgh, near the Farmers' Market and Samuel de Champlain Park. As it name implies, The Bargaineer offers bargains for every budget, especially in the glassware and furniture departments.

Black Bear Antiques
5452 Peru St., Plattsburgh • 562-6658
The Black Bear specializes in art pottery and porcelain. There is also a good selection of art glass, jewelry and old toys and games. It's open all year by chance or appointment.

Trinity Park Antiques
36 Miller St., Plattsburgh • 561-1517
If costume jewelry is your thing, this is a place to check out. There is also gold and silver jewelry, depression glass, tins, prints and other collectibles.

The Old Red Barn
N.Y. Rt. 22, West Chazy • 493-2217
This is one of the few places where you can buy hand-crafted items and learn a craft. There's a little bit of everything for sale here, including hand-quilted items, baskets, paintings, dolls and wood items. Pottery and craft classes are also held. The Old Red Barn is open Friday through Sunday only, or by appointment.

Don's Antiques
N. Main St., Ausable Forks • 647-8422
Don's is heavy into glass, including depression, pattern and carnival glass, and collectibles. Furniture and a general line of antiques rounds out his collection. The store is open year round, but it is best to call for specific hours.

Bookstores

Cornerstone Bookshop
110 Margaret St., Plattsburgh • 561-0520
This bookstore is everything that you expect in a used bookstore — thousands of titles, stacked in every which way, in every nook and cranny, on every subject. While the books are everywhere, the collection is well organized, making things fairly easy to find. Cornerstone stocks about an equal number of fiction (housed in the basement) and nonfiction (on the first floor) titles — about 50,000 books in all. There's also a great selection for kids.

Friar Tuck Bookshop
Consumer Square, N.Y. Rt. 3,
Plattsburgh • 561-6819
Hardcovers and paperbacks are always discounted here. In addition to an average selection of books, the store offers maps, magazines, greeting cards and gifts.

Royal Discount Books
Champlain Center North, N.Y. Rt. 3,
Plattsburgh • 562-0343
This is the largest discount book seller in the northern section of the Adirondacks, making it a store always worth checking out. There's also a large selection of the latest paperbacks and hardcovers. The store is well organized, with plenty of categories making things easy to find. The service is rather good as is the kid's section.

Waldenbooks
Champlain Center North, N.Y. Rt. 3,
Plattsburgh • 561-5349
This is not a large Waldenbooks, relatively speaking, but it offers the same services as the larger stores in this chain. Expect the latest bestsellers, fiction and nonfiction hardbacks and paperbacks and a variety of specialty subject titles.

Farmer's Markets

Farmer's Market
Durke St., Plattsburgh • 563-7642

Farmers from all over the North Country bring out their homegrown produce and home-made jams, jellies and relishes for sale at this large farmer's market in Downtown Plattsburgh. The market is held rain or shine in the market pavilion every Wednesday and Saturday, June through October, from 9 AM to 3 PM.

Lake George/ Upper Hudson Region

Everything Adirondack

Harness Shop Artisans
Main St. (U.S. Hwy. 9), Chestertown • 494-3295

One of the oldest buildings in the area serves as home for the works of more than 160 regional artists, craftspeople, authors and composers. You'll find rustic Adirondack furniture, Adirondack-inspired books and music, paintings, photography, weavings, wooden ware and on and on. Occasionally you'll also happen upon an artist demonstration in progress. You can enjoy browsing here year round, and probably take care of all your Christmas shopping in one stop (along with gift wrapping, since it's offered free here).

Hearthside Artisans II
N.Y. Rt. 9N, Diamond Point • 668-2172

Just 4 miles north of Lake George village, this quaint little shop offers unique gifts and collectibles hand-crafted by local art-ists and craftspeople. You'll find decorative paintings, wood-carved items, jewelry and a Christmas section to tempt you. If you're exploring between Lake George and Bolton Landing, this is a terrific "stop-off-and-shop" spot.

Indian Tepee Gift Shop
Main St., Bolton Landing • 644-9672

While not *everything* here is Adirondack-related, there's certainly enough of it to qualify for inclusion here. There's lots to explore here under one roof, from the Yankee scented candles of the old-fashioned Country Store to the nautical wares of Captain's Cove to the nutcrackers and ornaments of the Christmas Spirit section. Specialties here include Adirondack and Lake George memorabilia, hand-crafted Indian artifacts, silver jewelry and pottery. You can browse one of the largest footwear departments in the Adirondacks, where you'll find a big selection of Minnetonka and Quoddy moccasins, Sperry Topsider boat shoes and Tru-Stitch sheepskin slippers. A fun feature here are the animated figures throughout that bring the shops to life. Visitors have been enjoying the Indian Tepee Gift Shop for nearly 40 years now.

Moose Creek Limited North
10 N.Y. Rt. 149, Lake George • 745-7340

Walking into this beautiful store is like walking into the ultimate fantasy Adirondack lodge. It is filled with the casual elegance of dark wood, forest greens and deep reds. And while it might be called Moose Creek Limited, it might better be called Moose Creek Income Unlimited, because that's the situation you'd better be in to shop here. The sales associate proudly announced that they would be doing upcoming interior-design work for the Adirondack Great Camp Sagamore. Pretty good credentials, if you ask us. The quality

INSIDERS' TIP

One of the favorite pastimes for visitors and locals alike is shopping or simply strolling along Main Street, Lake Placid. The street is packed with many fine shops, a few not-so-fine shops, plenty of restaurants and some small parks from which to enjoy the view of Mirror Lake.

of the furnishings and accessories here is superior, and the prices reflect that at every turn of the tag. Like that cushioned wicker chair over in the corner? You can take it home for $799. How about that neat paddle rack on the wall, complete with five paddles? Yours for only $589 (can't you buy a *canoe* for that?!). And if you really want something special to impress the neighbors, try the 6-foot-by–6-foot antler chandelier — yours for the price of a loaded Plymouth Neon ($11,399). Our advice: Make this a rainy-day stop, think of it as a museum — and don't turn over any tags.

The Ralph Kylloe Gallery
N.Y. Rt. 9N, Lake George • 698-4100

A couple of miles toward Lake Luzerne from Lake George village, this design gallery disguised as a 5,000-square-foot log cabin is filled with antique and rustic Adirondack furnishings. You'll find the prerequisite antler chandeliers, birch-bark cupboards and tables, lamps, baskets, Old Hickory chairs and a guide boat's worth of accessories. The gallery also offers complete design and decorating services. It's a fun place to browse even if you're not in the market for snowshoes to mount on your wall.

The Silo
537 Aviation Rd., Queensbury • 798-1900

Conveniently located just off Exit 19 of I-87 (the Northway), this is one of the most attractive shopping experiences in the entire region. Three levels of exploring await you, divided into dozens of nooks, crannies and rooms — all featuring a new and different selection of goods and goodies. The Silo has the look of an old-fashioned country store, but with an Adirondack flavor. Some of the sections you'll find here include: The Gift Shop, featuring pottery, Adirondack furniture, wooden ware, a holiday section, a gallery of works by Thomas Kinkade (the "Painter of Light" known for cre-

ating the illusion of backlit artistic landscapes) and a "Classic Pooh" corner; The Country Store, featuring gourmet chocolates, maple products, regionally-produced jams and sauces; The Bakery, tempting you with fresh-baked pies, muffins, cookies and other goodies; The Florist, with fresh-cut flowers, gift baskets and silk arrangements; The Garden Center, with a display of unusual bird houses, wind chimes and outdoor furniture; and last (but definitely not least to us!), The Eatery, which offers everything from hearty breakfasts to deli sandwiches to light dinners. There's so much to see, you theoretically could eat all three meals here! Oh yeah, and about that silo — the bottom serves as part of the restaurant, and the top level is filled with a display of stuffed animals.

Sutton's Marketplace
U.S. Hwy. 9, Queensbury • 798-1188

This is another attractively laid-out complex of shops that combines upscale elegance with casual country and Adirondack-style offerings. Sutton's offers a combination of different themed sections, including a Country Furniture Store, Clothing Boutique, Bakery & Gourmet Food Shop, Gift Shop, Garden Furniture Center and a pleasant Cafe for relaxing and refueling. You'll also find products from Crabtree & Evelyn, Godiva Chocolates, Brown Jordan and Caspari. Sutton's is particularly beautiful around the Christmas holidays and can be either a great family outing or an easy place to take care of family gift shopping.

Trees
Main St., Bolton Landing • 644-5756

This is a lovely shop along Bolton Landing's attractive and scenic Main Street that overlooks Lake George. It offers a large selection of Adirondack books and Adirondack-made craft items. Some of what you'll

---

INSIDERS' TIP

The Lake Placid Public Library offers one of the best deals in the village of Lake Placid — previously read paperbacks for a dime and hardcovers for a quarter. If you find something of interest, you might even up your ante since the money will be used to expand the library.

find here includes Adirondack chairs, birch frames, twig signs and pack baskets, along with a good assortment of guidebooks and maps to the region.

Malls and Outlets

Aviation Mall
Aviation Rd., Queensbury • 793-8818

In a region not known for its malls (and not interested in becoming known for its malls), Aviation Mall is the one option in the region for the "All-American" food-courted, movie-complexed, anchor-stored indoor shopping experience. It's just off Exit 19 of the Adirondack Northway (I-87) and is therefore within an hour's drive of just about anywhere in the southeastern or central Adirondacks. You'll find a recently expanded JCPenney, Sears, Caldor, T.J. Maxx and Klein's All-Sports as the primary stores, along with about 80 other specialty shops. You'll also find the aforementioned cinema with

seven screens, along with your basic fast-food court. You probably didn't come to the Adirondacks to shop at a mall, but every now and then you're bound to appreciate that it's here.

Basket Barn of Vermont
U.S. Hwy. 9, Lake George • 798-5504

Need a basket? How about 30,000 of them?! Well, if you need more than one or less than 30,000, you'll find what you need at this incredible emporium of all things wicker. Basket Barn is part of a three-store collection (the other two are in Freeport, Maine, and Manchester, Vermont) that grew out of the Wilson family basket-making business in 1957. Now, you'll find wicker furniture and accessories, along with thousands of silk and dried flowers, throw rugs, pillows and even wicker stuff for your pets.

Basket Barn is in the heart of the "Million Dollar Half-Mile" outlet shopping strip, which features the four major outlet centers listed subsequently.

The Factory Outlets of Lake George
**U.S. Hwy. 9, Lake George • 792-1483,
(800) 748-1288**

Banded together under the same marketing banner, this is actually a collection of four adjacent outlet complexes strung along a half-mile stretch of U.S. 9, just a couple miles south of Lake George village. Combined, they offer more than 70 national outlets and a great way to spend a rainy day — along with whatever available balance you have left on your credit cards.

The **French Mountain Commons Outlet Center** features American Tourister, Fieldcrest Cannon, Oneida Silver, OshKosh B'Gosh, Tommy Hilfiger and more. Just across the street is the **Lake George Plaza Outlet Center**, offering Anne Klein (the store, not the designer), Bass Shoes, Izod, Nautica, Polo/Ralph Lauren and Timberland, among others. Next door you'll find the **Adirondack Outlet Mall**, with Barbizon, Bugle Boy, Champion Athletic Wear, Corning/Revere and the Book Warehouse. The Adirondack Outlet Mall also offers a particularly nice feature for winter shopping: a hallway. You can enter your shop of choice either from outside or from the mall-like corridor inside. Finally, the last in the string is the **Log Jam Factory Stores**, with a Levi's Outlet, London Fog, L'eggs-Hanes-Bali and a Carter's Childrenswear.

Milk and Light Bulbs (General Stores)

Adirondack General Store
Adirondack Rd., Adirondack • 494-4408

Along the east shore of Schroon Lake in the town of Adirondack (yes, Virginia, there is a town named Adirondack), this in one of those general stores you can count on year after year. How do we know? Well, it's been around for more than 150 years so far, so the chances are pretty good it'll be there for your needs too! The Adirondack General Store offers the classic mix of groceries, a deli and souvenirs, along with camping and fishing supplies. It is open year round.

The Crossroads
N.Y. Rt. 8 at I-87 Exit 25, Chestertown • 494-3821

Convenient to Loon Lake, Brant Lake and Schroon Lake, The Crossroads offers a combination of groceries, sporting goods and outdoor wear. You can also obtain hunting and fishing licenses to go along with the bait, tackle, guns and ammo you bought. Some of the clothing lines in stock include Woolrich, Sorel and Dickie. You'll also find Gold Star gasoline, which the staff claim is the world's best regular 88-plus–octane gas. (Let us know if you notice a difference.)

Harris Grocery
N.Y. Rt. 9N, Lake Luzerne • 696-2058

If you're vacationing along what's referred to as the "Dude Ranch Trail" between Lake George and Lake Luzerne, this is your place for everything from cold cuts and cold beer to frozen food. Actually, Harris offers a good selection of "room-temperature" items as well, such as T-shirts and sweat shirts, toiletries, and fishing and camping supplies. Harris Grocery has served visitors and residents for more than 37 years.

Lake George Mini Chopper
Amherst St., Lake George • 668-2337

Open all year, this scaled-down version of a Price Chopper (the Albany-based grocery chain) offers the essentials in groceries, videos, deli items and some beach-related toys — perfect when you don't feel like driving 15 minutes down to Glens Falls for the larger full-service "superstores" such as Hannaford and Super Kmart Center. It is just one block off Canada Street, the main drag in the village.

Fun Stuff (Recreational Equipment)

Beaver Brook Outfitters
N.Y. Rts. 8 and 28, Wevertown • 251-3394, (888) 454-8433

In a historic church building, this all-season sports store offers hiking, camping and fishing equipment and supplies on a year-round basis. It is also an Orvis dealer, with both fly-fishing and spin-fishing equipment, and stocks a good selection of Adirondack maps, trail guides and books. If you've got everything you need except a canoe and some hiking boots, don't worry — you'll find them here too. When the weather turns cold, you can also pick up a pair of cross-country skis or snowshoes.

Cunningham's Ski Barn
Main St., North Creek • 251-3215

This is a busy place. It's a hub for downhill and cross-country skiing equipment and clothing in the winter, and an operator (as Hudson River Rafting Company) of whitewater rafting trips in the spring and summer (see our Other Summer Recreation chapter). Some brands of alpine equipment available here are Volkl skis, Salomon and Marker bindings, and Technica boots. For cross-country equipment, you can check out the Germina skis and Salomon boots. If you're all set for equipment, then make sure your equipment is "all set" by getting an expert preseason tune-up here.

Ellsworth Sport Shop
U.S. Hwy. 9, Lake George • 668-4624

If fishing is your sport, this is your shop. It has everything you need for every type of fishing — spinning, trolling and fly. You'll find rods, boots, bait, the whole works here. Plus there's a selection of hunting supplies, including guns, ammo and the area's largest selection of knives.

The Outdoorsman Sport Shop
Lake Shore Dr. (N.Y. Rt. 9N), Diamond Point • 668-3910

Just up the lake a few miles from Lake George village, The Outdoorsman offers both hunting and fishing equipment, supplies, bait and ammo. In addition to the big supply of rods and reels for sale, you can rent the same for just $10 a day. It is open year round, with limited hours in the winter.

Rick's Bike Shop
328 Quaker Rd., Queensbury • 793-8986

Biking is big in the Adirondacks, and this is the place to go for one of the biggest selection of bikes of all types — road bikes, mountain bikes and hybrids. You'll find Trek, Giant and Specialized bikes here, along with a full line of accesso-

ries and clothing. Dependable service, a friendly staff and good advice round out the offerings here.

Syd & Dusty's Outfitters
U.S. Hwy. 9 and N.Y. Rt. 149, Lake George • 792-0260

Walking up to the entrance of Syd & Dusty's, the first thing you notice are the huge log pillars that support the porch roof. The next thing you notice is the collection of kayaks and canoes displayed on that porch, tempting your sense of adventure. Once you enter the big, open, log cabin-on-steroids display area, there's so much fun stuff hanging from the walls, you don't quite know where to start. Fortunately, the friendly staff here is more than eager to guide you around. In fact, they'll not only guide you around the store, but also guide you in a raft down the Hudson and Sacandaga rivers (see the Other Summer Recreation chapter for more information). Once you get a feel for the place, you can choose from a wide variety of hiking, camping, backpacking, climbing, canoeing and kayaking equipment, supplies and clothing. Syd & Dusty's is also a dealer for Patagonia and The North Face outerwear. Oh yeah, did we mention trail food in foil packets? How about a packet of Chicken Rotelle or Black Bart Chili with Cheese? Thankfully, if you've got a craving for the stuff, you can find it here.

If you want to "try before you buy," rent a kayak for $25 a day and enjoy the waters of the nearby Hudson River or Lake George. In the winter months, the store stocks a selection of Burton and DNR snowboards plus Tua, Kartu and Black Diamond cross-country and backcountry skis and boots. Syd & Dusty's is open year round.

Antiques, Knicks & Knacks

Clen's Collectibles
N.Y. Rt. 8, Riparius • 251-2388

Between Chestertown and North Creek, Clen's offers a general line of antiques and collectibles, along with furniture, linens, glassware, jewelry and vintage clothing. It's worth a stop if you're exploring the shops in the Chestertown to Warrensburg region, known for its proliferation of antique shops. It is open daily in July and August, and the rest of the year by appointment.

Diamond Cove Antiques
N.Y. Rt. 9N, Diamond Point • 668-5787

Adjacent to the Diamond Cove Cottages, you can enjoy exploring here from early May until mid-September. You'll find a collection of antique post cards, Lladro depression glass, dolls, Hummels, Irish Belleek china and other assorted items that might just be what you're looking for.

Glenwood Manor Antiques
Glenwood Ave., Glens Falls • 798-4747

This is perhaps the region's largest antique shop, with four floors displaying items from 35 dealers, all set within the walls of a historic home. Glenwood Manor has been in business for 15 years and has become a regular stop for serious collectors and casual browsers alike. You can visit year round, with extended hours in July and August.

The Hour Glass Shoppe of Bolton Landing
Main St., Bolton Landing • 644-9706

In scenic Bolton Landing along the western shore of Lake George, this shop is a browsers paradise. You'll find a nice selection of crystal, antiques, furniture items, art work, Adirondack-related books and prints, dolls and holiday items.

Riverside Antiques Barn
River St., Warrensburg • 623-3949

In a town known for its antique shops, this new center for dealer offers more than 9,000 square feet of antiques, folk art, books and gifts in a restored 1830s shirt-factory building.

Bookstores

Book Warehouse
Adirondack Factory Outlet Mall, U.S. Hwy. 9, Lake George • 793-0231

In the one enclosed mall along the "Million Dollar Half-Mile" of factory outlets, the Book Warehouse discounts every one of its thousands of books in stock. You'll find savings of as much as 75 percent off the list price on some titles, although the bestsellers are discounted considerably less (but hey, they're still discounted!). In addition to all kinds of general-interest hardcover, paperback and trade books, they have a good selection of Adirondack-related titles.

Lauriat's
Aviation Mall, off I-87 Exit 19, Queensbury • 761-0139

This is a good-size all-purpose bookstore, part of a national chain and well-stocked with all the current hardcover and paperback titles. You'll also find a big selection of audio books here as well as a "Books of Local Interest" section that includes Adirondack-related titles. It's one of the few places in the Adirondacks where you can browse for books until 9:30 PM nightly.

Southern Adirondack Lakes Region

Everything Adirondack

Stuff-n-Such
N.Y. Rt. 29A, Caroga Lake • 835-2042

This small but attractive shop sits in a little cabin along the road and has evolved from a tiny gift shop to a miniature emporium of Adirondack-related items. You'll find Adirondack-theme note cards, art, photography, books, music and clothing here throughout the little rooms both downstairs and up. Also upstairs, on the balcony overlooking the road, is an informal tourist information center worth checking out.

Stuff-n-Such is a good stop to make on your way into the south-central Adirondacks. The hours vary, but to pull off the road and check the door will only cost you about 30 seconds, so give it a try.

Adirondack Country Store
252 N. Main St., Northville • 863-6056

Closing in on its 10th year in operation, this is one of the nicest and most extensive Adirondack-related stores we have visited. For those of you staying in the southern Adirondacks or entering the park via N.Y. Route 30, this serves as a convenient and enjoyable introduction to "all that is Adirondack." You can stroll among the seven different rooms filled with such items as bent Hickory furniture, Adirondack chairs, pottery, decoys, lamps, watercolors and more. Many of the items here are created by craftspeople from surrounding communities near the Great Sacandaga Lake and beyond. There's a good selection of Adirondack-related books, maps and music as well. Any time of the year is a good time to pick up a new ornament in the Christmas room. The Adirondack Country Store is worth a diversion off the highway, if not a trip of its own. It's open year round, and staff will ship any item you like via UPS (convenient since Adirondack chairs don't fit so well in the back of a sedan).

Adirondack Museum Shop
N.Y. Rts. 30 and 28, Blue Mountain Lake • 352-7311

You just know that the official shop in one of the finest regional museums in the country has got to be good — and it is. We're guessing some folks probably peek in at the shop on their way into the museum grounds and never make it to any of the exhibit buildings! That's how much there is to see and explore here. You'll find a big selection of Adirondack-related books, prints and music. There's also baskets, games, miniature rustic furniture and a selection of jewelry items. You can even buy plans to build your own canoe or Adirondack lean-to! The shop is open along with the museum from Memorial Day weekend through Columbus Day weekend.

Blue Mountain Lake Pottery
N.Y. Rts. 30 and 28, Blue Mountain Lake • 352-7611

This attractive shop features the work of regional artists and craftspeople. You'll find pottery, paintings, weavings and wooden ware among the items here. You can visit daily during July and August, and weekends in June. That's it, so don't wait around!

Cedarwood Gift Shop
Post Office Building, Main St., Blue Mountain Lake • 352-7675

As Blue Mountain Lake is the home of the Adirondack Museum and the Adirondack Lakes Center for the Arts, it is also popular as the home for some attractive craft shops such as this. Open from June until October, the Cedarwood offers a selection of "North Country" crafts and gifts, including baskets, books, jewelry and other items. It certainly makes a trip to the Post Office a little more interesting.

The Shop at ALCA
N.Y. Rt. 28, Blue Mountain Lake • 352-7715

Within the Adirondack Lakes Center for the Arts, this shop offers a wide selection of regional crafts, jewelry and wooden ware. You'll also find furnishings and accessories for the home or camp, such as picture frames and planters. The shop is open daily during the summer months and limited hours the remainder of the year.

Malls and Outlets

While there are no major malls or outlet shopping centers within this region, the Gloversville area at the southern gateway to the region is famous as a home to leather manufacturers and outlets. We have included a sampling here for your enjoyment and winter warmth.

The Glove
31 Union St., Gloversville • 725-8160

When they say this is a "genuine" factory outlet store, they're not kidding. This is a real leather "shop" for Pique Glove Ltd. where you can watch gloves being cut and sewn. You can then make a selection from the wide variety of men's and women's dress, casual, work, golf and ski gloves available. You can also choose from a variety of leather accessories. The Glove is open Monday through Friday throughout the year as well as Saturday's during November and December. With any luck, you'll be able to finish off your holiday shopping with this one stop.

SWANY Glove Outlet
Crossroads Industrial Park, N.Y. Rt. 29, Gloversville • 725-3333

From November to February, you'll find a

wide selection of gloves with such names as Pierre Cardin, Ralph Lauren Polo and Freezy Freakies (don't ask!). You'll also find alpine and cross-country ski gloves as well as the same style gloves worn by members of the U.S. Snowboard team (which may or may not be a big deal to you).

St. Thomas Inc.
35 W. Eighth Ave., Gloversville
• 725-3115

You'll find a variety of factory closeouts and samples here, including wallets, attache cases, handbags, portfolios and more. It is open Monday through Friday from February through December, with additional hours on Saturday from Thanksgiving to Christmas.

Milk and Light Bulbs (General Stores)

Canada Lake Store
N.Y. Rts. 29A and 10, Canada Lake
• 835-6069

From the outside looking in, this is an attractive log cabin-style general store, with fresh produce on the front porch and newspapers stacked up for purchase. From the inside looking out (the back), it's even more attractive, as it sits above and adjacent to the shore of Canada Lake. The store includes a gas pump out front, groceries, a deli, fishing, boating and water-skiing equipment, along with a nice section of camp clothing (i.e. sweat shirts and T-shirts) in the back. This is probably your best bet for essentials between Gloversville and Lake Pleasant.

Charles Johns Store
N.Y. Rts. 30 and 8, Speculator
• 548-7451

We stopped here during that calendar purgatory of late March, between winter and spring, and the rest of Speculator was, shall we say . . . quiet. Not Charles Johns, though. This place, either a small supermarket or a big general store (depending on your frame of reference), was hopping busy. People were buying groceries and hardware supplies, ordering take-out from the deli, browsing through the big book section, and chatting up the local news and gossip. We were impressed by both the level of activity and the variety of offerings here. So if you're bored or out of everything, stop by and spend some money and a chunk of the afternoon.

The Lake Store
N.Y. Rt. 30, Indian Lake
• 648-5222

This complete general store offers a good selection of meats and groceries, along with hunting, fishing and camping supplies. You'll also find clothing, moccasins, hiking boots (a specialty here, in good supply) and gift items. The Lake Store is open daily throughout the year.

The Station
junction of N.Y. Rts. 28 and 30, Blue Mountain Lake • 352-7318

This is your year-round place in the highly seasonal Blue Mountain Lake for groceries, deli goods, beer, gas and other basics of life.

Fun Stuff (Recreational Equipment)

Adirondack Mountain Sports
Main St., Indian Lake • 648-0215

This is the place to go within the region for Polaris snowmobiles and ATVs. You'll find sleds, parts and accessories as well as helmets and clothing. Snowmobile service and repairs are also available.

Blue Mountain Outfitters
Steamboat Landing Building, N.Y. Rt. 28, Blue Mountain Lake • 352-7675

If you are looking to buy your own canoe, check out this place. It stocks We-no-nah (the canoe, not the singer), Mad River and Old Town canoes. You'll also find a good selection of outdoor gear, Adirondack books, maps and trail guides, fishing bait and tackle. Blue

Shoppers in the North Country will find no shortage of retail options to satisfy their yen to spend.

Photo: Plattsburgh/North Country Chamber of Commerce

Mountain Outfitters is open May through October.

Havlick Snowshoe Co.
N.Y. Rt. 30, Mayfield • 661-6447

Did you even know that there are different shapes and styles of snowshoes?! It was a surprise to us, too, until we checked out this place. Snowshoeing is a great alternative form of winter recreation, and Havlick's will set you up with everything you need to enjoy the experience. You'll find a variety of pack bags and bindings as well as camp equipment and even canoes. In the summer, you'll also find inflatable floats and other water-related fun stuff here.

Gloversville Sport Shop
Bleeker St., Gloversville • 725-1322

This full-line, full-service sporting goods store is a few miles outside the Adirondack Park, but it might be your best bet to find a good variety of recreational equipment to use within the region. You'll find sportswear and team sports equipment plus downhill and cross-country skis and boots in the fall and winter.

Antiques, Knicks & Knacks

Newton's Corners Antiques
N.Y. Rt. 8, Speculator • 548-8972

While this shop is open throughout the year, you'll need to call ahead to make sure exactly when. Assuming you work that part of the equation out, you'll find a selection of pottery, glass, linens, jewelry and quilts to rummage through.

The Red Barn
202 S. Main St., Northville • 863-4828

After a stop at the nearby Adirondack Country Store (see the previous "Everything Adirondack" section), you may want to check out The Red Barn for its collection of baskets, furniture and other collectibles. While it's open from May into October, you'll want to call ahead before visiting, or simply take a chance by popping in.

Bookstores

Adirondack Museum Shop
N.Y. Rts. 30 and 28, Blue Mountain Lake
• 352-7311

This excellent museum shop carries an extensive collection of Adirondack-related books, including literary collections, guidebooks and art books. For more information on the shop, see its listing in the previous "Everything Adirondack" section.

Charles Johns Store
N.Y. Rts. 30 and 8, Speculator
• 548-7451

As mentioned in the previous "Milk and Light Bulbs" section, Charles Johns also has a large display of books, both general-interest and Adirondack-related, for your reading pleasure on those dreary November afternoons.

Mysteries on Main Street
43 N. Main St., Gloversville • 725-7373

About the only book-specific store we know of in the southern part of this region, Mysteries on Main Street offers a lot more than just mystery novels. Established in 1982, you'll find close to 10,000 titles ranging from the latest hardcover bestsellers to children's books to used paperbacks. There's a good selection related to local and Adirondack history and topics as well.

Old Forge/ Raquette Lake Region

Everything Adirondack

The Artworks
Main St., Old Forge • (315) 369-2007

This storefront artisan cooperative began in 1989 after two local craftspeople met over tea at a local restaurant and decided the time had come to band together and display their work. Out of that meeting evolved The Artworks, which now features the work of more than 20 regional artists and craftspeople. All

the work on display is original hand-crafted work, and often times you'll get to witness works in progress as well. You will find pottery, wreaths, watercolors, photography, woodwork, baskets, jewelry and more. Everything here reflects the spirit and style of the Adirondacks. It's definitely worth a visit, and fortunately you can visit year round.

Moose River Trading Company
N.Y. Rt. 28, Thendara • (315) 369-6091

Billing itself as a "classic store for folks who love the Adirondacks," it's easy to see why people who love the region would love this store. It seems as much a museum of Adirondack dry goods and art as a store. You'll find classic pack baskets, Filson woolens, Tubb's snowshoes, hiking boots, camp cookware, lamps and lanterns among the dry goods. For art, there's a variety of prints, photographs, books and note cards to choose from. For a great gift, try one of their "Guide's Choice" combination gift sets, including coffee (lots of flavors), jams, pancake mix and maple syrup.

You can enjoy a visit to the Moose River Trading Company any day of the week, any week of the year.

Malls and Outlets

The Factory Store
N.Y. Rt. 28, Old Forge • (315) 369-2006

In the Thendara Mini-Mall, this is the place where you can save big on famous manufacturer firsts, overruns and selected irregulars. You'll find more than 30 brand names represented here, including Arrow, Columbia, Duofold, Gap, White Sierra and others. Visit and save year round.

Milk and Light Bulbs (General Stores)

Adirondack Grocery
N.Y. Rt. 28, Otter Lake • (315) 369-3112

About 10 miles south of Old Forge, this is a good place to stop on your way into the region. Gas, groceries and videos, along with fishing, camping and snowmobile supplies, make this a valuable one-stop shop.

Old Forge Department Store
Main St., Old Forge • (315) 369-6609

Inlet Department Store
Main St., Inlet • (315) 357-3636

OK, so you can't buy groceries at these two cooperatively owned and operated stores, but there's so much other stuff here we had to include them. As a combination of a general store and an Ace Hardware store, you can find just about anything you need for the home, camp or camper. Fishing supplies, camping supplies, toys for water fun, clothing, kitchen ware, bug spray — all the Adirondack staples are here. You'll also find a variety of craft and art supplies for those rainy days in search of a hobby as well as paints and stains for those sunny days in search of a project.

Old Forge Hardware
Main St., Old Forge • (315) 369-6100

This is nearly as much an attraction as it is a practical shopping experience. In fact, you can easily spend a lot longer exploring this huge emporium of all things necessary and interesting than your original errand would have warranted. You'd best prepare a good excuse for being gone so long before you even get here. Along with the basics that you'd expect in a hardware store, the highlight here is the terrific bookstore section with a big selection of Adirondack-related books, guides and maps. You'll also find a gourmet food section, a fireplace room and a Bargain Basement (which, of course, is *upstairs*). While this is a great place to browse, locals might tell you it's a tough place to find a bargain. But who cares? You're on vacation!

DiOrio's Big M Supermarket
Main St., Old Forge • (315) 369-3131

It may not be the most quaint and rustic store in the Adirondacks, but this grocery certainly has the basics covered — and it is conveniently in the heart of Old Forge. You'll find fresh produce, a deli, health and beauty aids, camping supplies, film, ice and just about anything else you'd need to restock the fridge and pantry.

Fun Stuff
(Recreational Equipment)

Big Moose Yamaha
N.Y. Rt. 28, Eagle Bay • (315) 357-2998

Here's the place to buy what you need for winter or summer fun. For winter thrills, check out the big selection of Yamaha and Arctic Cat snowmobiles, parts and accessories. Want to try it out to see what all the noise (literally, engine noise) is about? As of last winter, you could "rent a sled" at Big Moose for (are you ready?) $200 a day. Sounds expensive, but considering the insurance costs the outfitter has to pay, not to mention the money that you would have to lay out to buy one of these things, it's a pretty reasonable deal. And you're guaranteed some major fun here in the "Snowmobile Capital of the East." You can also rent helmets (a practical and legal prerequisite) for $10, but you'll have to figure out your own combination of clothing to keep warm. Unless, of course you want to spring for a whole new snowmobile outfit, which the folks here are happy to help you with. How big is the snowmobile business here? They're open here seven days in the *winter* (a true rarity in these parts!), with limited hours in the summer. In the summer, Big Moose Yamaha is the place to check out Boston Whaler fishing boats, Dynasty pleasure boats, Aqua Patio (you've got to love that name) pontoon boats and Yamaha Waverunners.

Hodel's Pro Hardware
N.Y. Rt. 28, Inlet • (315) 357-2341

We include Hodel's here because, in addition to hardware, it offers one of the area's most extensive fishing and camping sections. You'll find a big selection of hiking boots, walking sticks, camping supplies, fishing tackle and live bait. One nice feature for adults is the game arcade — to keep the kids busy while you browse for the perfect rod.

Moose River Company
Main St., Old Forge • (315) 369-3682

Celebrating 10 years in business in 1997, this sporting goods store offers much more than just recreational equipment and supplies. First, the basics. You can find a big selection of fishing gear, camping equipment, canoes, boating accessories, guns and ammo, knives, maps and compasses for your outdoor-recreation needs. Now, the bonus round. Even if you're not a big outdoor enthusiast, you can enjoy browsing here through the collection of Adirondack books, prints, artwork, pack baskets, birch-bark gift items and rustic furniture. You don't have to "need" anything to enjoy a visit to the Moose River Company.

Mountainman Outdoor Supply Company
N.Y. Rt. 28, Inlet • (315) 357-6672

Like canoeing? Think you might like canoeing? Are you willing to even give it a try? If you can answer yes to any of these questions (or even if you can't) make a visit here and check out their more than 200 canoes and kayaks in stock. You can choose from more than a dozen brands, including Prijon, Old Town, Dagger and Walden Paddlers. Throughout July and August, this company also host a series of "demo days," when manufacturer reps are available to help answer questions and demonstrate their products. If you want to just get a feel for the whole paddling thing, you can rent one of three different classifications of canoe, with costs ranging from $21 a day to about $30 a day, depending on the craft's size and weight. You can try out kayaks the same way, with costs ranging from $16 for small solo kayaks to $36 per day for larger "touring" kayaks with room for gear.

Old Forge Outfitters
N.Y. Rt. 28, 4 miles south of Old Forge • (315) 369-6699

Yet another good option for outdoor equipment and clothing, you can find a big selection of fun stuff as well as stuff to help you have fun here. Check out the selection of kayaks, canoes and mountain bikes for fun transport options. When you're ready to settle in under the stars for the night, you'll find all your camping needs here, plus the maps and guidebooks to help you stay on course the next day. Old Forge Outfitters is open seven days a week.

Sporting Propositions Ltd.
Main St., Old Forge • (315) 369-6188

The motto here is "Sports For All Seasons," and this place lives up to it. This is the biggest ski shop between Utica to the south and Lake Placid to the north. You can choose from such brand names as Atomic skis, Nordica and Technica boots, Salomon bindings as well as a full line of ski clothing and accessories. For summertime fun, you'll find mountain biking, in-line skating, tennis, golf and watersports equipment and supplies.

Antiques, Knicks & Knacks

Fabric Hutch Gift Shop
Main St., Old Forge • (315) 369-6878

This folk art gift shop is based in Old Forge, with four other (non-Adirondack) locations throughout New York State. You'll find a wide variety of items here, from hand-woven baskets to pottery, country furniture to candles. There are no real surprises here, but it's pleasant browsing just the same.

Holly Woodworking Gift Shop
N.Y. Rt. 28, Old Forge • (315) 369-3757

Along with the usual assortment of gift items like pottery and candles, the real attraction here is the wooden gift items made right here in the workshop. We think it's a lot more rewarding to take home a locally made gift instead of a overseas-produced replica, don't you agree? In addition, you'll also find a good selection of moccasins and other decorative accessories for the home.

Twin Oaks Gifts
Main St., Old Forge • (315) 369-6439

If you're a big fan of Boyds Bears, Cat's Meow Villages and Mary Engelbreit Creations, you are in luck here, because they're all well-represented. You can also find a nice selection of candles, throw rugs, weather vanes (you can never run out of those), nostalgic tins and art work.

Village Peddler Gifts
N.Y. Rt. 28, Eagle Bay • (315) 357-6002

You guessed it — more candles, pottery, tins, blankets, bird houses and the like. In addition, you'll find some children's games and toys, along with a selection of T-shirts and sweat shirts.

Wildwood Enterprises
Main St., Old Forge • (315) 369-3397

If you want to visit a place that deals in buying and selling antiques (rather than just your average gift shop), this is worth a visit. The specialty here is the "best of the Adirondack past," and you'll find some interesting paintings, prints, new and old Adirondack books (see subsequent "Bookstores" section), stoneware, baskets and rustic furniture.

Bookstores

Old Forge Hardware
Main St., Old Forge • (315) 369-6100

As written about in the previous "Milk and Light Bulbs" section, Old Forge Hardware is a huge emporium of just about anything under the sun (or gray clouds, as is likely the case). The book "section" in the back of the store is bigger than most independent or even mall "chain" bookstores and has a big selection of both general-interest and Adirondack-related titles. This definitely a browser's paradise.

The Sagamore Institute
Sagamore Rd., off N.Y. Rt. 28, Raquette Lake • (315) 354-4303

Part of the Great Camp Sagamore complex, this small bookstore carries primarily titles related to Adirondack history and the Sagamore. It's not a place to go browse for books on a Sunday afternoon, but you should make it a part of your visit to the Sagamore camp.

Wildwood Enterprises
Main St., Old Forge • (315) 369-3397

Wildwood buys and sells antiques, including some interesting paintings, prints, stoneware, baskets and rustic furniture (see the previous "Antiques, Knicks & Knacks" section). But Wildwood is also a bookstore, and you'll find a large selection of regional and Adirondack-related titles plus older and used books of general interest.

Some attractions . . . are sprawling, modern and ever-evolving places that offer new additions to their menus of fun virtually every season. Some others . . . have barely changed in the last century, and that is much of their appeal.

Attractions

You'll find dozens, if not hundreds of fun, interesting and beautiful places you *can* visit in the Adirondacks. For our purposes here, we define "attraction" as something you *should* make the effort to visit if time and legal tender allow. The majority of attractions in the Adirondack region are either related to children and family vacation activities or historical and cultural organizations. As such, you'll find that with many of our listings in this chapter, we refer you to the Kidstuff chapter or the Arts and Culture chapter for more detailed information related to those interests.

The attractions we include here may appeal to kids or have cultural significance, but their appeal is broad enough that they transcend any one category and appeal to all ages and most budgets. Some attractions, such as The Great Escape and Enchanted Forest, are sprawling, modern and ever-evolving places that offer new additions to their menus of fun virtually every summer season. Some others, such as the Natural Stone Bridge and Caves or the Great Camp Sagamore, have barely changed in the last century, and that is much of their appeal. Everything covered here is worth a visit, and it's up to you to decide what you're in the mood to explore. In any event, you're not likely to be disappointed.

Lake Placid/ Tri-Lakes Region

[Ed. note: All Olympic Regional Development Authority (ORDA) venues are included in a separate subsection at the end of this geographic section.]

High Falls Gorge
N.Y. Rt. 86, Wilmington • 946-2278

A few minutes outside Lake Placid, the Ausable River plunges in dramatic fashion between high granite cliffs, resulting in a 700-foot waterfall. Although the waterfall is neither as dramatic nor as large as Ausable Chasm, it is nonetheless impressive. The self-guided walk here is an easy, relaxing way to enjoy a beautiful setting of forests and rugged river. Admission is $5 per adult, $1.50 per child. The gorge is open from late May through Columbus Day.

Lake Placid Marina Cruises
Lake Placid Marina, Mirror Lake Dr., Lake Placid • 523-9704

Each year thousands of visitors visit Lake Placid (the town) and never see Lake Placid (the lake). The town sits on Mirror Lake, which is often mistaken for Lake Placid. A 16-mile scenic cruise departs rain or shine during the summer months from the marina on Mirror Lake Drive. In addition to the beautiful scenery, the cruise is the best way to see many of the famous camps on the lake. During the summer, tours leave at 10:30 AM and 1, 2:30 and 4 PM. Admission is $6.75 for adults, $4.75 for children and $5.75 for seniors.

Uihlein Sugar Maple Field Station
Bear Cub Rd., Lake Placid • 523-9337

If you are curious about how the maple syrup on your pancakes is made, a short trip to the field exhibit of the Uihlein Sugar Maple Field Station will answer your questions. The small exhibit explains the simple process.

The field station is only a short drive from Main Street. (Attention cyclists: Bear Cub Road makes for a nice bike ride.) Although the exhibit it is generally open daily during summer from 1 to 5 PM, it is best to call since hours are rather flexible.

U.S. Luge Training Center
35 Church St., Lake Placid • 523-2071

Near the Adirondack Medical Center (see our Healthcare chapter), the Luge Center is the only indoor luge training facility of its kind in the nation. A free tour, which explains the training process and the practice starting run in the complex, with accompanying video is offered weekdays at 2 PM. The Luge Center also provides a special training program for children who were involved in winter sessions during the summer months in the facility. (See our Kidstuff chapter for more information.)

Adirondack Fish Cultural Station
off N.Y. Rt. 30, Saranac Lake • 891-3358

This state-operated fish hatchery raises landlocked Atlantic salmon from fry to yearlings in large display pools. Children will be amazed at the sheer number of fish being raised, and anglers will wonder how to catch such prized specimens in the wild. The station is open daily year round from 9 AM to 5 PM; hours may be extended during the summer.

Lorraine's Boat Rides
21 Duprey St., Saranac Lake • 891-2241

The lakes in the region are major attractions, but without a boat it's tough to appreciate the scenery. Lorraine's makes it easy with a relaxing cruise of the Saranac River with a guide who will give you a naturalist's view of the action. Cruises are at 11 AM, 2 and 5:30 PM. Admission costs $8 for adults and teens, $7 for children 12 and younger.

Adirondack Park Visitor Interpretive Centers (VICs)
N.Y. Rt. 30, Paul Smiths • 327-3000
N.Y. Rt. 28N, Newcomb • 582-2000

The VICs (no one besides officials ever uses the entire name) serve as the state's designated education and orientation centers for the entire Adirondack Park. Both centers offer regularly scheduled interpretive walks with naturalists, slide presentations on the history and the four seasons of the Park, displays and various educational programs including lectures and activities for kids.

The Paul Smiths VIC, the larger of the two, is 1 mile north of Paul Smith's College in Paul Smiths. More than 5 miles of hiking trails traverse virtually every Adirondack habitat, from bogs and marshes to old-growth and managed forests. The Barnum Brook Trail, the shortest of all the trail loops, is wheel-chair-accessible and provides an excellent overview of the ecology of the region. Other trails, all of which have interpretive signs, focus on forest ecology, wetlands and forest management practices. A boardwalk on the Forest Ecology Trail traverses a bog and wetlands, providing hikers a close-up view of a habitat normally not seen in everyday travels. During the winter months, the expanded trail system offers excellent cross-country skiing opportunities. During the summer months, the Paul Smith VIC opens a butterfly house exhibit, where visitors can see all stages of butterfly development. Special programs, including naturalist-led canoe paddles, evening star-watching and children's programs are held throughout the year (see our Kidstuff chapter).

The setting for the Newcomb VIC focuses on lake ecology with trails exploring Rich Lake. Where as the natural beauty of the landscape at the Paul Smiths VIC is subtle and diverse, the scenery at Newcomb is downright spectacular. During the winter months, the Newcomb VIC trails provide excellent snowshoeing opportunities; free snowshoes are available for visitors' use.

The VICS also offers exhibitions, classes, workshops and festivals that provide environmental education for all ages. Admission to both centers is free, and they are open year round, except on Christmas and Thanksgiving. The hours are generally 9 AM to 5 PM.

White Pine Camp
off N.Y. Rt. 86, Paul Smiths • 327-3030

In 1907, businessman Archibald White began construction of White Pine Camp, which would eventually contain 20 buildings, including an owners cabin, dining hall, guest cabins, boat houses, staff quarters and an indoor bowling alley. President Calvin Coolidge made the camp his summer White House for 10 weeks in 1926. In this quiet retreat, the nation's business was conducted. Eventually the camp was purchased by the Stern and Levy families, including the daughters of the president of Sears Roebuck. They donated the camp to

FYI

Unless otherwise noted, the area code for all phone numbers listed in this guide is 518.

Paul Smiths College, which used the camp for college housing until it was sold for its present use.

White Pine Camp is one of the few Adirondack "Great Camps" open to the public. It is situated on the secluded Osgood Pond and includes 20 architecturally unique buildings, antique furnishings, exhibits and walking trails. Ask about special games and activities for children.

The camp is open daily from 10 AM to 5 PM, June through mid-October; call for the schedule of limited hours during rest of year. Admission is $9 per adult and $4.50 per child.

XTC Guest Ranch
Forest Home Rd., Saranac Lake
• 891-5684

XTC (say it real fast and you'll get the drift of the name) is on a 150-acre estate, with access to a variety of trails. The ranch offers horse-drawn sleigh rides and snowmobile excursions during the winter months, and horse-

back riding, cattle drives and a children's riding camp during the summer. The ranch boasts the largest riding stable in the Tri-Lakes area, and it's home to two world-champion horses. A horse-drawn sleigh or covered wagon ride under the stars, followed by dinner (about $40 per person) in a log cabin, is offered in the fall and winter months.

Olympic Regional Development Authority

Olympic Arena
Main St., Lake Placid • 523-1655,
(800) 462-6236

This New York State agency operates the facilities built for the XIII Olympic Winter Games, held in Lake Placid in 1980. These include the Olympic Center, which houses three ice skating rinks and the Lake Placid Winter Olympic Museum with exhibits and displays recounting the 1932 and 1980 Olympic Games; the Olympic Sports Complex at Mount Van Hoevenberg, site of the biathlon range and the bobsled and luge runs, which offer bobsled rides both winter and summer; the Olympic Jumping Complex, home to the Kodak Sports Park Freestyle (skiing) Jumps and the 90- and 120-meter ski jumps (with an observation platform atop the 120-meter tower); and Whiteface Mountain with its skiing and sightseeing facilities. The sites are in and around the village of Lake Placid, and most are open year round.

There is always something going on at one of the sites throughout the entire year, so if you are in the Lake Placid region give ORDA a call for a listing of events. Some events will even surprise you: The annual ski jumping competition held on the 4th of July weekend. (Fortunately snow is not required for this international competition; a plastic surface replaces snow.) With three ice skating rinks, there's always hockey, speedskating (short track) or figure-skating practices, competitions and ice shows. People travel for miles to see the Saturday night ice shows held during the summer months. These shows feature many of the region's finest youngsters and some of the world's best figure skaters trying out their new routines.

All ORDA facilities are open to the public during normal business hours. With few exceptions, no admission fees apply to enter and look around. Many visitors, for example, take full advantage of the cool conditions at the ice rinks during a hot summer day to watch figure skaters practice. Sometimes you may even see one of the world's top skaters working out, or an Olympic champion skating on a session with a 10-year-old future champion. (Some of the young skaters are just as fascinating to watch as the seasoned pros.) When watching sessions, please remain quiet and respect the privacy of all athletes.

Additional activities and descriptions of events and facilities sponsored by ORDA can be found in the Kidstuff, Skiing and Annual Events chapters.

Olympic Center
Main St., Lake Placid • 523-1655

The Olympic Center, site of the skating and hockey events during the 1932 and 1980 Olympic Winter Games, is a state-of-the-art international training and competition facility. The center has three ice rinks; weight, dance and exercise rooms; a small museum; and offices. Tours of the facility are available during the summer. The fee is $4 for adults, $2 for kids and $3 for senior citizens. The tour includes admission to the Olympic Museum (see previous Olympic Arena entry for details). (Self-guided tours of the Olympic Center are free.)

Whiteface Mountain
Veterans' Memorial Hwy., off N.Y. Rt. 86, Wilmington • 523-1655

Veterans' Memorial Highway ascends 8 miles to the summit of Whiteface, the fifth-highest mountain in the Adirondacks. The last 5 miles are the most spectacular, as the road winds upward through a changing forest and an alpine summit environment. At the summit

Photo: ORDA

Visitors can take a turn around the Olympic Speed Skating Oval where Eric Heiden won a record five gold medals at the 1980 Winter Olympics.

parking area, there is a short hike or an elevator ride to the top of the mountain, where you'll have a 360-degree view of the surrounding wilderness. On a clear day, you can see Montreal and the Green Mountains of Vermont. It is always best to call for visibility conditions.

The highway is open mid-May to early September. The rates are $8 per car and driver, $4 per passenger, $5 per motorcycle and driver. (The maximum charge for a non-commercial vehicle is $25.)

Whiteface Mountain Chairlift Sky Ride
Whiteface Mountain Ski Center, N.Y. Rt. 86, Wilmington • 946-2223

A chairlift takes you from the base lodge to the summit of Little Whiteface Mountain (elevation 3,600 feet). The view is dramatic, though it's not a great vista like one afforded from Whiteface Mountain. You can walk down from the mid-mountain station along a nature trail with waterfalls and pools of Stag Brook. The chairlifts are open early June to mid-October. The cost is $7 for adults and teens and $4 for kids 12 and younger and seniors.

Olympic Ski Jump
N.Y. Rt. 73, Lake Placid • 523-2202

The site of the ski jumping events during the 1980 Olympic Winter Games is the most visible man-made landmark in the High Peaks region — it can be seen from miles away, jutting high above the tree line. You can take an elevator ride up the 120-meter hill with its 26-story jump tower all summer for a spectacular view of the surrounding wilderness. A aerial free-jumping complex, officially called the Kodak Sports Park, provides a ski jump where world-class freestylists twist, turn and flip in the air before landing in a 750,000-gallon pool of water.

Admission to complex, including chairlift and elevator rides, costs $7 for adults and $4 for kids and seniors; $4 is also the per-person rate for groups. The Olympic Ski Jump is open mid-May to mid-October.

Mount Van Hoevenberg
N.Y. Rt. 73, Lake Placid • 523-4436

Mount Van Hoevenberg was the site of the bobsled, luge, cross-country skiing and biathlon events during the 1980 Olympic Winter Games. You can try you luck rocketing down part of the run in the "Summer Storm" bobsled on wheels with a professional driver and brakemen. The rates are $20 per person. Bobsled and luge rides also are available during the winter months. A trolley tour of the facilities is offered for $4 per adult, $3 per senior and $2 per child.

Mountain biking is available on more than 60 kilometers of interconnected trails on site. There's no excuse for not trying mountain biking here, as you'll find trails suitable for riders of all abilities, bike rentals, even mountain biking lessons. The trail-access fee is $4 per day. Bike rentals, including helmets, cost $25 per day. Be sure to ask about specials and multi-day rates.

United States Olympic Training Center
421 Old Military Rd., Lake Placid
• 523-2600

Lake Placid is home to one of the two official Olympic Training Centers in the United States (the other is in Colorado Springs, Colorado). The complex provides housing for as many as 300 athletes at one time, a sports-medicine facility, a gym, weight rooms and a dining room. Visitors can tour the facility for free during normal business hours. A short video explains the center's operations.

Plattsburgh/Western Lake Champlain Region

Point au Roche State Park
19 Camp Red Cloud Rd., Plattsburgh
• 563-0369

Old-time residents know the area as Fantasy Kingdom, the name of a theme park that once operated here. Although the site has a long history, it is the newest state park in New York and therefore not as well known as its nearby neighbor, the popular Cumberland Bay Park (see our Camping chapter). Point au Roche provides no camping facilities, but includes a sandy beach, biking and walking trails (the bike trails, in particular, come highly recommended) and a nature center, which offers educational and recreational programs

throughout the summer. A public boat launch also is available.

Point au Roche State Park is open sunrise to sunset daily. A $5-per-carload entry fee is charged weekends from Memorial Day weekend through the third weekend in June, then every day through Labor Day weekend; entry is free the rest of the year. Visitors also may purchase a season pass ($39 per car), which grants access to any New York State park.

Tourboat M/V Juniper
Dock St., Plattsburgh • 561-8970

The *Juniper* offers a two-hour cruise, focusing on the historical aspects of Lake Champlain, for $7.95 per person, and an evening dinner cruise with a choice of steak and seafood entrees for $29.95 per person. A party cruise with a live band also leaves the docks every Tuesday evening at 11 PM; reservations are suggested (see Nightlife). The cruise line is open from May to September, but the schedule varies in the early and later part of the season, so it is best to call ahead.

Ausable Chasm
U.S. Hwy. 9, Ausable • 834-7454,
(800) 537-1211

Some 500 million years ago, the Ausable River sculpted massive stone formations, creating the breathtaking Ausable Chasm. In 1870 the chasm became the first tourist attraction in the United States. In January 1996, the first of two devastating floods wiped out the many man-made structures. The floods threatened closure of the site to visitors, but the chasm is back in operation and, as the marketing saying goes, is better than ever. Steel bridges allow you to cross and recross the mighty gorge with its massive stone formations, including the famed Elephant's Head, along the .75-mile self-guided walk. At the halfway point, called Table Rock, visitors can select either a 15-minute guided river-raft ride down the rapids or continue on foot for another .75-miles. The entire walk can take one to two hours at a leisurely pace, so bring along some drinks and snacks.

While there is plenty of great scenery in the region, the Ausable Chasm is a trip that should not be missed. The walk along the river

is spectacular — worthy of a few rolls of film. Admission to the chasm with river-raft ride is approximately $20 per person.

Douglas Camp on Silver Lake
Silver Lake, 18 Douglas Ln., Ausable Forks • 647-8061, (800) 201-8061

This is one of those places that could end up in every section of this book, so we made it an attraction — and, in many ways, it is. It offers $20-per-night lakeside campsites; housekeeping camps; canoe, party boat ($30 per 30 minutes) and Sea-Doo rentals ($1 per minute); horseback riding ($25 per hour), pony rides and hayrides. There's a video and game room, a room with pool tables, a room with live music on weekends during the summer and a restaurant. Oh, there is also Silver Lake, which offers good fishing and swimming (courtesy of Mother Nature) and recreational activities (courtesy of Douglas). (See Kidstuff for additional information about Douglas Camp on Silver Lake.)

Frontier Town
U.S. Hwy. 9, North Hudson • 532-7181

America's oldest western theme park, which opened in 1952, still delights visitors, taking them back in time to the days of the Old West and the nation's pioneer days. At the time Frontier Town was constructed, many historical artifacts were abundantly available

in the area, and the owners managed to collect many of them for display in the theme park, including the 1857 Concord Stage Coach, which served the Indian Lake-North Creek Stage Line through the turn of the century. Frontier Town also has the only remaining trip hammer forge in existence.

Frontier Town features six complexes in the 100-acre park that includes a stagecoach ride through the Bad Lands inhabited by desperate outlaws. In Pioneer Village, constructed entirely of log buildings, visitors get a glimpse of life of the early settlers, including what it was like in a pioneer home, school and church. There's also a number of commercial buildings of the period, such as a weaver's cottage, leather shop and general store. Dances and songs of native New York Indians are performed in a replicated Native American village.

Main Street is the site of live-action excitement with a Wild West Show, shoot-out, cavalry ride and the Speedy Gonzales Show. There's also a rodeo, stagecoach rides and other western-type adventures, as visitors travel through Roth's Forge Village, a replica of a Civil War town with working models of a forge, water-powered grist mill and saw and tannery mill.

Admission from June 27 through September 1 is $12.45 per adult and $10.45 per child. The park is open daily from 9:30 AM to 5 PM.

Photo: Warren County Tourism Department

Besides "thrill" rides, The Great Escape, in Lake George, also offers many tamer rides for young children.

Crown Point State Historic Site
N.Y. Rt. 17, Crown Point • 597-3666

One hundred years before the American Revolution, Great Britain and France struggles for control of Crown Point, a vital area in the region. In 1734 the French built Fort St. Frederic, the first fort to appear on Lake Champlain, on the peninsula known as Pointe a la Chevelure, translated as Crown Point. For the next 24 years, the site of the stone fort ensured France's control of Lake Champlain until French troops there succumbed to a British force of more than 12,000 men in 1759 (the fifth British campaign to oust the French; the previous four had failed). In 1775 colonial forces attacked the British garrison on the site and captured 114 pieces of cannon and other heavy equipment sorely needed by American troops. However, "His Majesty's Fort of Crown Point" reverted back to British control after the Americans evacuated the site and remained occupied by Gen. John Burgoyne until the end of the war.

Only the ruins of the fort remain, so visitors must imagine what transpired here. A small visitors center and interpretive trails amid the ruins helps explain the history of the site.

Admission is $4 per passenger vehicle. The center is open May through October, Wednesday through Saturday from 10 AM to 5 PM, and Sunday 1 to 5 PM.

Fort Ticonderoga
N.Y. Rt. 74, Ticonderoga • 585-2821

In the early history of North America, a stone fort overlooking Lake Champlain served as an important military base in the struggle between the British and French for control of the region. Fort Ticonderoga, originally named Fort Carillon by the French in 1755 when it was built, was the site of numerous famous battles. In 1759, Lord Jeffery Amherst captured the site from the Marquis de Montcalm. The fort remained under British control until Ethan Allen and his Green Mountain Boys from Vermont caught the British by surprise and captured the fort. In 1908 restoration on the fort began, making Fort Ticonderoga the nation's first restored historical museum.

Today the fort is a lively place, where every attempt is made to bring history to life. This little fact makes it particularly attractive to families with children, as the museum offers more than just static displays. Black-powder rifles and cannon-fire drills, fife-and-drum rolls, encampments and re-enactments of battles are all part of the schedule of events. Exhibits within the fort offer artifacts of the battles of the French and Indian Wars and the American Revolution.

Admission to the fort is $8 for adults and teens, $6 for children ages 6 to 12; kids 5 and younger get in free. A cruise on the M/V Carillon is available from the fort for $5 per adult and teen, $3 per child. You get a lake view of Fort Ticonderoga and Mount Defiance, from which the British took cannon aim at Fort and Mount Independence, a fort in Vermont where colonists in turn took aim at Fort Ticonderoga. The museum at "Fort Ti" is open early May through October. It is best to call for a schedule of events, especially encampments and reenactments.

Lake George/ Upper Hudson Region

Adirondack Balloon Flights
The Silo restaurant, just off I-87 Exit 19, Queensbury • 793-6342

This is a beautiful way to see the natural wonder of the Adirondack region. Anything that goes several hundred feet up in the air is going to trip off the "extreme-sensors" for some people. At the same time, anything as quiet and peaceful as floating above the scenic valley between the Adirondacks to the west and the Green Mountains to the east registers pretty high on the serenity scale as well.

Flights are available daily from April through November, and take off either at sunrise or sunset, when the winds are most calm. Call for exact times, and plan on a total of

about three hours from pickup to return. Now, before you hop in the car, keep in mind this is a good example of "you get what you pay for." That is, it's a special treat — and costs like it. The rates for a one-hour flight work on a sliding scale, from $175 for a single person to $120 per person in a group of six. Call for more specifics on special family, private and spring rates. For more kid-related information on this attraction, see the "Natural Selections" section of the Kidstuff chapter.

Fort William Henry
Canada St., Lake George • 668-5471

Take a trip back to the times of the colonial frontier at Fort William Henry, on one of America's most historically significant sites. A modern restoration of a log fortress originally built in 1755 during the French and Indian Wars, Fort William Henry is set at the southern end of Lake George. It provides an entertaining and educational look at a crucial period in American history as well as the region's role in giving birth to our nation. While visiting the fort today, you can see multimedia presentations on the history of the fort and the battles fought here. You can also sit back and watch the original 50-minute 1936 film classic *The Last of the Mohicans*, presented hourly in the Cooper Theater. The Cooper Theater is named for James Fenimore Cooper, the famous 19th-century writer and author of the classic *The Last of the Mohicans*, the setting of which was this fortress and its surroundings. You'll also see hundreds of colonial and Indian artifacts that have been recovered from the site during ongoing archeological digs.

During July and August, "Living History" tours are conducted by guides/historians who will not only tell you about the past, but also

---

INSIDERS' TIP

If you'd like to take a lake cruise, but think the kids will be bored before the boat clears the pier, try the one-hour Paddlewheel Cruise on the steamboat *Minne-Ha-Ha*, which is operated by the Lake George Steamboat Company out of Lake George village. From the glass-enclosed engine room to the bright red paddlewheel churning while the steam calliope plays happy tunes, kids won't have time to get bored — and you'll have just enough time to relax.

demonstrate skills that were needed then, such as musket loading and firing, cannon firing and musket-ball molding. You'll also see recreations of the officer's quarters, barracks, dungeon and cemetery. New in 1997: a "Storytelling Hour" every evening at 7 PM, during which actors in character tell tales of life during the French and Indian Wars. The combination of this magnificent physical setting at the southern end of Lake George with the deep sense of American history here make this a must-visit attraction.

You can visit Fort William Henry from May through mid-October seven days a week. Mid-June through Labor Day, the fort is open from 9 AM until 10 PM, and from 10 AM until 5 PM on other dates of operation. Admission is $8.50 for adults and youth 12 and older, $6.50 for children ages 3 to 11, and free for little history buffs younger than 3.

Glens Falls Flight Center
Warren County Airport, County Line Rd., Glens Falls • 792-5995

The Glens Falls Flight Center can actually take you where you *want* to go rather than wherever the wind takes you. It may be a little less romantic than a hot-air–balloon ride, but if you want to see a lot of the region from above in a short period of time, this is the way to do it. You can take either a half-hour or an hour-long ride, and either let the pilot give your a tour of the region or request your own route. In any event, seeing Lake George from the air is well worth the price of admission, which is $45 for the half-hour flight, and $80 for the full hour. For this rate, you can have a total of three people in your flying party. Seated in the "high-wing"–design Cessna 172, everyone has an unobstructed view of the beautiful landscape below. Scenic flights are offered daily year round, but you should call ahead to make a reservation.

The Great Escape/ Splashwater Kingdom
U.S. Hwy. 9, Lake George • 792-3500

With more than 125 rides, shows and attractions, The Great Escape/Splashwater Kingdom offer lots for everyone in the family. You'll find three roller coasters, a "giant wheel," plenty of other thrill rides, a big selection of kiddie rides, live entertainment and a huge water park all within it's boundaries. We include extensive write-ups on The Great Escape within both the "Non-serene & Extreme" and the "Big Fun for Little Ones" sections of the Kidstuff, so check out that chapter for more detailed information.

The Great Escape is open weekends in late May, then daily from early June through Labor Day. The park is also open one weekend in late September for its Octoberfest (see our Annual Events chapter).

Operating hours vary throughout the season, basically ranging from 9:30 AM to 6 PM midweek and until 10 PM on summer weekends. As you might expect with an attraction of this magnitude, it is pricier than many other entertainment options, but still a good value for all that if offered. For adults and children taller than 48 inches, admission costs $22.99 for one day and $29.99 for two consecutive days. The price for children shorter than 48 inches is $16.99 for one day and $23.99 for two consecutive days. (Pricing is related to height restrictions for various rides at the park.) Parking is free, as is admission for toddlers 2 and younger.

Lake George Steamboat Company
Steel Pier, Lake George • 668-5777, (800) 553-BOAT

For more than 180 years (since 1817!), the Lake George Steamboat Company has been plying the crystal clear waters here. Fortunately (for them and us) the vessels have changed a few times since they began, but the tradition of hospitality has not. You can choose from a variety of lake cruises on one of three vessels during the cruising season, from early May through late October.

The three-deck steamboat *Minne-Ha-Ha* (Indian for "Laughing Waters"), with its bright red paddlewheel and steam-driven calliope, offers one-hour cruises weekends from late May through late June and again from Labor Day through Columbus Day. In July and August, the departures are daily. You can also

---

FYI

Unless otherwise noted, the area code for all phone numbers listed in this guide is 518.

enjoy cruises Saturday evenings in summer: The 10 PM Moonlight Cruise features live entertainment and dancing.

The *Mohican* also features three decks (two enclosed), and its slender hull was designed to allow it passage through some of Lake George's most beautiful and tricky channels between its more than 200 islands. The *Mohican* offers a 2¼-hour Paradise Bay Cruise, negotiating "The Narrows" portion of the lake for a journey into one of its most beautiful and popular spots, and a 4½-hour Discovery Tour that cruises the entire 32-mile length of Lake George. The Paradise Bay Cruise is offered once daily from Memorial Day through Columbus Day. The Discovery Tour is available daily during the summer.

Last, but no where near least, the company's newest and biggest cruise boat is the *Lac Du Saint Sacrement*. At 190 feet long and with four decks, this is the biggest cruise boat in the Adirondacks — able to carry as many as 1,000 passengers. Its appointments are decidedly upscale, with lots of brass, glass and dark wood to take you back to the time of elegant 19th-century steamers. The *Sac* (as locals abbreviate it) offers brunch, lunch and dinner cruises, all of which last about 2½ hours. It's on the water from early May until late October, with cruises most days at 11:30 AM and 6:30 PM. The schedule varies and the cruises are very popular (particularly with the motor coach tour set), so call ahead for details and reservations.

All Lake George Steamboat Company cruises are narrated, pointing out the many mansions, islands and folklore that accompany the sites. Adults can spend anywhere from $7.75 for the one-hour *Minne-Ha-Ha* cruise to $29.75 for the *Sac* dinner cruise. Children ages 3 to 11 generally cost about half-price to tag along, and kids younger than 3 can cruise for free. Stowaways, when discovered, are made to sit and listen to a two-hour recording of Lake George Jet Ski traffic at full volume (just kidding).

Natural Stone Bridge & Caves
Stone Bridge Rd., off I-87 Exit 26, Pottersville • 494-2283

This is a beautiful, peaceful and somewhat old-fashioned 1950s-type tourist attraction.

From the series of signs that beckon you and guide you along as you approach to the big wooden caveman standing at the entrance, you know you're not in EPCOT anymore. And that's just fine with us, because this is one of those underrated spots that offers fun, education, a beautiful setting and warm smiles. It's been owned and managed by the same family since (gulp!) the Revolutionary War. How's that for the ultimate in "mom and pop" operations?!

The star attraction here is the 180-foot-long stone bridge on top of which sets the gift shop and main building, and under which runs a river. To see it, you take a self-guided tour that leads you along trails to caves, grottoes and other geological wonders courtesy of the glacial age 10,000 years ago. According to co-owner Jan Beckler, the Natural Stone Bridge is one of the oldest rock formations in the nation, containing marble rock that dates back nearly a billion years (give or take a hundred-million). One suggestion: The only restrooms are near the beginning of the trail, so stop there first before venturing out. The sound of rushing water won't do you any favors once you're underway.

A snack bar and coffee shop are available, as are pleasant shaded picnic areas. Save time for the extensive rock and gift shops. See our write-up in the "Natural Selections" section of the Kidstuff chapter for more kid-related information. The Natural Stone Bridge and Caves are open from late May through Labor Day, 9 AM to 7 PM; and Labor Day through Columbus Day, 10 AM until 6 PM. Admission is $8.50 for adults and teens, $4.25 for children ages 6 to 12, and free for children younger than 6. One nice feature here is that your admission fee will get you in all season, so you can come back and enjoy this peaceful setting again and again.

Shoreline Cruises
on Lake George, Kurosaka Ln., Lake George • 668-4644

Unfortunately (and undeservedly), Shoreline Cruises is sometimes thought of as the "other" cruise line serving Lake George. This is simply because their boats aren't as big, and their location not quite as obvious as Lake George Steamboat Company (see previous entry). However, if you like your cruises on the more "intimate" side with a few dozen other passengers instead of a few hundred, this may be your preferred choice. Hey, the lake looks pretty much the same regardless of the boat deck you're standing on!

Shoreline Cruises has a fleet of five boats, including three small single-level tour boats (the *De Champlain*, *Ethan Allen* and *Algonquin*), the two-level *Defiance*, and the three-level wooden yacht *Horicon*. The small tour boats offer one-hour shoreline cruises, departing every half-hour, plus special Fireworks Cruises on Thursday nights at 10 PM in July and August. (The village of Lake George makes every Thursday night like July 4 with its series of fireworks displays throughout the summer.)

The *Defiance* offers four one-hour cruises daily in summer, along with summertime Sunset Happy Hour Cruises departing Wednesday through Sunday at 7 PM. The *Horicon*, clearly the fleet's flagship and most luxurious vessel, offers a 2½-hour Paradise Bay Cruise daily at 1 PM (lunch is optional), along with a Moonlight Entertainment Cruise with live music and dancing every summer evening at 10 PM. While cruises are available from early May until late October, schedules vary with the seasons, and you should call ahead for details.

Adult cruising costs range from $7.50 for a one-hour tour boat ride to $19.95 for a luncheon cruise. The cost for children ages 3 to 11 is generally about half the adult fare, and kids younger than 3 can ride along for free.

Prospect Mountain
Veterans' Memorial Hwy., off U.S. Hwy. 9, Lake George • no phone

This is a bargain of a natural show, and one you shouldn't miss.

At the southern end of Lake George Village, you can drive 5 miles up and around and up some more to this 2,030-foot summit. Once you arrive at the parking area (just a

hundred feet or so below the summit) you can either stroll up a paved walkway, hike up or take one of the continuously running "viewmobile" shuttles to the top. There you'll find what's advertised as the "100-mile view." Well, sometimes . . . maybe. That fact is, the view is awesome from here, looking north up the length of 32-mile-long Lake George and the mountains that surround it. To the east you can see the Green Mountains of Vermont and, on rare humidity-free occasions, the White Mountains of New Hampshire; and to the northwest, the High Peaks area of the Adirondacks.

To witness this splendor will cost you $5 per carload, and you can embark on this "voyage to the top of the view" from late May through late October. You can access the mountain from 9 AM until 5 PM daily. We also include Prospect Mountain in the "Natural Selections" section of the Kidstuff chapter as a terrific family picnic spot (on calm days, anyway).

Southern Adirondack Lakes Region

Adirondack Animal Land
N.Y. Rt. 30, Mayfield • 883-5748

You're never too old for the zoo! As the only "wildlife park" in the region, Adirondack Animal Land is well worth a visit for animal lovers of all ages. The Adirondack region is known for its wildlife, but not the tigers, lions, zebras, monkeys and even the giraffe you'll find here. The park is set on 75 acres and provides natural settings for its hundreds of exotic birds and animals. Owners Dave and Patty Eglin say they created Adirondack Animal Land because, "We simply love animals, and we always have." Their commitment is evident in their effort to develop an attractive

INSIDERS' TIP

For a combination of man-made and natural attractions that can't be beat for scenery and serenity, take one of the many lake cruises available throughout the Adirondacks during the peak fall foliage season of early October. It's one of nature's "greatest shows on earth!"

Photo: ORDA

Visitors can ride with a professional driver down the Olympic bobsled run.

and educational attraction that puts the needs of the animals before the desires of humans. They have worked hard to provide healthy, comfortable and natural settings for all of their animals.

The park is open from late May through Labor Day, seven days a week. Hours are normally 10 AM until 5 PM. Admission is reasonable: just $6.75 for adults and teens and $4.75 for children ages 1 to 12. You may think $4.75 is steep for a 1-year-old, that is until you see their eyes light up throughout the day.

The Adirondack Museum
N.Y. Rt. 30, Blue Mountain Lake
• 352-7311

Without a doubt, this is one of the region's must-see attractions. There is simply no better place in the Adirondacks to be exposed to so much of what the region and its people represent. With 23 indoor and outdoor exhibit areas that showcase how people lived, worked

and played throughout the region's history, this constitutes an all-day visit. So extensive and well done is The Adirondack Museum that the *New York Times* called it "the best of its kind in the world." *National Geographic Traveler* referred to it as "the Smithsonian of the Adirondacks."

More than 100,000 people visit The Adirondack Museum each year during its season from Memorial Day weekend through mid-October. If that doesn't seem like a lot of visitors, consider that the vast majority come here during July and August only. Notable exhibits include "Boats and Boating in the Adirondacks, 1840-1940," with its collection of beautifully restored wooden boats; "The Age of Horse," in the Adirondacks building, with 50 or so horse-drawn vehicles; and "Logging the Adirondacks." You also can check out the original locomotive passenger car from the railroad that linked Raquette Lake and Blue Mountain Lake as well as many more exhibits and artifacts. In addition, an art exhibit called "These Glorious Mountains: Masterworks of the Adirondacks" displays many of the best paintings from the extensive museum collection. The museum has a collection of nearly 100,000 Adirondack-related artifacts, and selected samples are displayed in the exhibit called "Small Things Remembered: Four Decades of Collecting Adirondack History."

You may have a hard time venturing past the Museum Shop in The Gatehouse. With its tempting variety of Adirondack gifts, books, souvenirs and art work, you'd better save this for last or you're sure to be carrying a lot of stuff around the grounds with you all day.

If we haven't given you enough reasons to visit, throughout the museum's season — Memorial Day weekend through mid-October — dozens of activities, special events and festivals take place here, including the No-Octane Regatta and the Rustic Furniture Fair (see Annual Events chapter), that make every visit a new adventure celebrating a very old land.

The Adirondack Museum is open daily in-season from 9:30 AM until 5:30 PM. Admission costs $10 for adults, $6 for children ages 7 to 16; kids younger than 7 get in free. (See our Kidstuff, Arts and Culture and Annual Events chapters for related information about The Adirondack Museum.)

Old Forge/ Raquette Lake Region

Adirondack Scenic Railroad
Thendara Railroad Station, off N.Y. Rt. 28, Thendara • (315) 369-6290

You and your family can relive the golden age of railroading on the line that carried the rich and famous to their summer camps

and grand old resort hotels at the turn of the century. Departing from the Thendara Railroad Station, you can experience magnificent scenery as you ride in vintage open-window coaches through the forest and past lakes and rivers. This scenic adventure is available from early-May until late October; train rides are scheduled weekends only in May, Saturday through Wednesday from Memorial Day until the third week in June, and then daily except Friday until the end of October.

Train rides head northbound to Carter Station, featuring miles of unspoiled and rugged terrain along the way, or southbound along the beautiful Moose River to Minnehaha. Rides generally last about an hour altogether. For an extra theatrical thrill, you may want to take a ride on a Tuesday in July or August when the Loomis Gang seems to always "rob" the train. And, if you happen to be around on Thanksgiving weekend, you might want to bring the kids along for the Santa Claus Special, featuring an appearance by you-know-who for two days only until the train slips into railway hibernation until the following spring.

The fare for the Adirondack Scenic Railroad is $7 for adults and teens, $4 for children ages 2 to 12, and free for children younger than 2.

Enchanted Forest/Water Safari
N.Y. Rt. 28, Old Forge • (315) 369-6145

The man-made thrill headquarters of the western Adirondacks, this combination theme park and water park provides plenty of fun for everyone.

While the Enchanted Forest section of the park has about a dozen pretty standard amusement rides, most of the thrills here are of the wet variety, courtesy of what is billed as New

---

INSIDERS' TIP

For an even more rewarding and enjoyable day, tie in your visit to your chosen Adirondack attraction with one of the dozens of special events and activities that many places schedule throughout their operating seasons. Notable attractions such as The Adirondack Museum, Olympic Regional Development Authority facilities and the major theme parks usually print calendars of events that are available for the asking.

York State's largest water park. Water Safari may or may not still be the biggest, but with 23 water rides to choose from, it's plenty big enough. And, thanks to recent improvements, it is the warmest water park, now featuring heated water. In an area where nighttime temps can get pretty chilly, even in midsummer, that's a big benefit.

The heart-pumpers at Water Safari include Killermanjaro (that really is how it's spelled), billed as a 280-foot plunge of breathtaking thrills, and the Bombay Blasters where you get to shoot straight down a 160-foot water tube. You can also try body surfing in the new Tidal Wave Pool (if you can avoid the hundreds of other bodies!).

Themed areas specifically for your smallest thrill-seekers include Animal Lane, with it's kiddie rides and Mother Goose's menagerie; Storybook Lane; and the Wild West-themed Yukon Village.

At Water Safari, the Pygmy Pond includes a kid-size river tube ride, shipwreck slide and activity wading pool with fountains. Next door at Calypso's Cove, little racers can enjoy the miniature go-cart track.

The Enchanted Forest Railroad continuously runs a circuit around the park's perimeter throughout the day, with departures approximately every 15 minutes from the Train Station near the park entrance. For another view of the park, try out the Skyride (like a chairlift without the ski mountain). If you've had enough of water slides and wild rides for the moment, you may want to take a break to sit and watch one of the two daily circus shows, or the continuous performances of the "Country Jamboree" at Klondike Kate's restaurant.

Enchanted Forest/Water Safari is open daily 9:30 AM until 6 PM from mid-June until Labor Day. Admission is $16 for anyone 12 and older, $14.50 for children ages 2 to 11, and free for toddlers younger than 2.

Great Camp Sagamore
Sagamore Rd., off N.Y. Rt. 28, Raquette Lake • (315) 354-5311

Great Camp Sagamore is something everyone who visits this part of the Adirondacks should try to see. The creation of the great Adirondack entrepreneur William West Durant, this huge lodge was built in 1897 and became the home of the Alfred Vanderbilt family in 1901. The lodge was designed to look like a Swiss chalet, and it's the centerpiece of an elaborate complex that includes 27 buildings and (what else?) an open-air bowling alley. There is also a dining hall, guest cottages, an artisan's barn, blacksmith shop and boathouse.

Besides now serving as a museum and attraction for visitors to enjoy, the Great Camp Sagamore also hosts attendees of workshops and small conferences throughout the summer.

If you're within a tank of gas, we strongly recommend you save a day during your Adirondack visit to experience this gem of rustic elegance (it sounds like a contradiction, but it applies in this case). Guided tours of the com-

INSIDERS' TIP

According to legend, Native Americans were the first to have sighted a huge, long-necked underwater creature swimming in Lake Champlain. Records indicate that the creature, known as Champ, favors Bulwagga Bay, just south of Port Henry, as more sightings have been there than anywhere else. Speculation suggests that Champ is related to a plesiosaur — a long underwater reptile with flippers, a medium-length tail and a small flat head — that lived 65 to 195 million years ago. "Champ Sightings" are posted on a board on N.Y. Route 9N/22, just south of Port Henry. If you spot Champ during your travels, do not attempt to capture it or do it any harm, as the sea monster of Lake Champlain is protected by law in both New York and Vermont. To report a Champ sighting, contact Phenomena Investigations, P.O. Box 2134, Wilton, N.Y. 12886.

Photo: ORDA

Cross-country skiers take advantage of the 50 kilometers of trails at the Olympic Sports Complex, where Olympic World Cup and National Championship events are held.

pound last about two hours and begin each day at 10 AM and 1:30 PM from Fourth of July weekend to Labor Day, and then weekends only until Columbus Day. The cost is $7 for adults and $3 for children.

After the tour, the gift shop is worth a stop, and a coffee shop is available as well if you need to personally "refuel" before your departure (if you can convince yourself to leave!).

See our Arts and Culture chapter for more about Great Camp Sagamore.

Bird's Seaplane Service Inc.
N.Y. Rt. 28, Inlet • (315) 357-3631

Here's a way to combine the beauty of the Adirondack's natural setting with the exhilaration of an airplane ride. And not just an airplane — a seaplane! You and your kids are sure to love the scenic 15-minute rides offered by Bird's. In fact, just the takeoff and landing on the water make the trip worthwhile.

Bird's has 35 years of flying experience and operates seven days a week from mid-April through mid-November. The cost is $40 for one or two passengers 10 and older, then $20 per additional passenger (10 and older) up to a total of five passengers. It's $10 for children ages 5 to 10 and $5 for kids younger than 5. So, for as little as 50 bucks, your family of four can have an experience you'll all remember for years.

McCauley Mountain Chairlift Rides
McCauley Mountain Rd., off Bisby Rd., Old Forge • (315) 369-3225

We mention this attraction in the "Natural Selections" section of the Kidstuff chapter, but kids don't have any exclusive rights to beauti-

ful scenery and a breathtaking ride, so we include it here just for you and your special someone to enjoy.

Unlike the Lake George region, there are no hot-air balloon flights available in Old Forge/Raquette Lake region to soar you above the magnificent landscape, but this is the next best thing. For $4, you can take the ride up the 2,200-foot-long double chairlift that ascends more than 600 vertical feet up the side of McCauley Mountain. A beautiful view of the central Adirondacks and Fulton Chain of Lakes awaits you at the summit. Some whitetail deer also make their home here and are used to being photographed, so bring your camera. The free parking, picnic area and nature trails make McCauley a good spot to take your time and enjoy the surroundings.

The McCauley chairlift operates on weekends from Memorial Day until mid-June, from 10 AM until 5:30 PM. Weekdays, the lift operates from 9 AM until 4:45 PM. From mid-June through Labor Day, you can ride every day except Tuesday and Wednesday. Fall foliage rides operate on weekends from Labor Day through Columbus Day.

Old Forge Lake Cruises
Main St. Dock, N.Y. Rt. 28, Old Forge • (315) 369-6473

You can enjoy a relaxing and scenic narrated boat tour of the Fulton Chain of Lakes aboard the two steamship replicas: the *Clearwater* and the *Uncas*. Both boats are modern namesakes of their original counterparts, two of the most famous steamboats in the Adirondacks during the late 1800s. The original *Clearwater* and *Uncas* carried the

---

INSIDERS' TIP

In the early 1900s, the journey to the Adirondacks from New York City may have begun with a boat ride up the Hudson River on the Albany Night Boat, then a train ride the next morning from Albany to Riverside, where a stagecoach would take visitors to Wells House in Potterville (the house can still be seen from I-87). After lunch the coach would continue to Schroon Lake where passengers would board the steamboat *Evelyn*. After four stops, the boat would arrive at the Schroon Lake village landing where passengers would board a horse-drawn coach to their hotel. (Source: "Scaroon," a pamphlet produced by the Schroon Lake, North Hudson Historical Society.)

wealthy of the day to their summer "camps" and the many grand old resort hotels of the era. Now, you can enjoy the same route and see such landmarks as President Harrison's summer home and the largest log structure in the eastern United States, along with miles of pristine water and beautiful shoreline. Both vessels have two decks: one enclosed and heated, and the other (up top), an open deck for the best vantage points (and the coolest).

You can visit and cruise from early June until mid-October, with the biggest variety of cruises available from July 1 until Labor Day. Most scheduled cruises last 2 to 2½ hours. As schedules can vary, you should call ahead for exact times before visiting. If you're more interested in the romantic than the scenic, you may want to try the Moonlight Cruise on the *Uncas*, which departs daily during the summer months at 7:30 PM for two hours of live entertainment and dancing. Cruise fares are between $9 and $10 for adults and teens (depending on the cruise), and half-price for children 12 and younger.

Raquette Lake
Navigation Company
off N.Y. Rt. 28, Raquette Lake
• (315) 354-5532

For a fun, scenic and relaxing excursion, consider cruising the waters of Raquette Lake aboard the elegant *W.W. Durant*, named for the famed Adirondack entrepreneur and builder of the late 19th century. The 60-foot double-deck cruise boat comfortably holds 125 people, has an open deck above and an enclosed windowed deck below, and elegant turn-of-the-century decor throughout.

Raquette Lake is the largest natural lake in the Adirondacks, with more then 99 miles of zigzagging shoreline and dozens of coves and bays to explore. In fact, it can be a pretty confusing lake to navigate on your own, which is all the more reason to leave it to the captain of the *W.W. Durant*. It is also the site of many classic old "Great Camps." During your cruise you'll see and hear the stories of Camp Pine Knot, built in 1876 an owned at the time by Collis Huntington, builder of the Southern Pacific Railroad; Echo Camp, built in 1883 and owned at one time by Connecticut Gov. Phinneas Lounsbury (much to the chagrin of his fellow Connecticut statesmen, we suspect); and Bluff Point, built in 1877 and owned at one time by Robert Collier of *Collier's* magazine fame.

The cruise season begins in May with a limited weekend schedule, runs a full schedule of cruises daily from the end of June through the end of August, and then weekends again from the beginning of September through the end of October. You can choose from 1½-hour lunch cruises, 1½-hour scenic afternoon excursions, and three-hour dinner cruises. You can also enjoy a moonlight cruise that departs at 10 PM on Wednesday and Saturday evenings and plies the waters of Raquette Lake for about 90 minutes while you enjoy live music, dancing and the lights of the shoreline (well, some lights anyway — 80 percent of the shoreline is owned by the state and designated "forever wild"). The cruise costs only $5 per person, but doesn't include drinks or food.

Fares for other scheduled cruises range between $8.50 for the scenic excursion to $35 for the dinner cruise. For children younger than 10, the excursion cruise costs $6.50, and the lunch and dinner cruises are half-price (provided the boat is not sold out, according to management). You should call ahead for exact times and cruise schedules. Also keep in mind that weekend cruises are very popular, and the *W.W. Durant* is not nearly as large a vessel as those operated by the Lake George Steamboat Company (see previous entry). In other words, an advance phone call can save you the disappointment of being turned away.

Here you will find thrilling rides made of steel, water-spilling slides made of fiberglass and chilling rides pulled by dogs. You'll also find peaceful trails, scenic rides by rail and beaches for fun with pails.

Kidstuff

From the prehistoric to the prefab, from the pure and natural to the neon and plastic, the Adirondacks offer everything you and your kids could ever want (with the possible exception of a straight week of sunshine). Here you will find thrilling rides made of steel, water-spilling slides made of fiberglass and chilling rides pulled by dogs. You'll also find peaceful trails, scenic rides by rail and beaches for fun with pails. OK, so much for the rhyming copy.

The fact is, the vastness and diversity of the Adirondack region reflects its tremendous variety of activities and attractions geared toward families and kids. We've listed more than 50 such options for you here, and we're certain there are at least another 50 out there waiting to be discovered.

Generally, there are three big hubs for kid-related activities and attractions: Lake Placid, whose Olympic attractions and sports-orientation are geared more towards older kids and teens; Lake George, the family and kid "champ" of the Adirondacks; and Old Forge, the "western Adirondack" headquarters for family fun. In particular, Lake George and Old Forge have dozens of miniature golf tracks and arcades to choose from, ranging from elaborate and nearly beautiful to tacky and in need of a paint job. We haven't covered those types of activities individually, but trust us — you won't be able to miss them in these towns!

We divide our adventures into four categories with varying degrees of ease for parents and corresponding fun for kids (which usually work conversely). "Non-serene & Extreme" covers the high-energy, big-thrill activities that your older kids will beg to do. Sooner or later, you'll run out of excuses, so consider entries in this section your suggested solutions. "Natural Selections" is for those families who want to enjoy the environmental attractions and activities without boring the kids to death. We think we've found some good combinations here to keep everyone happy (well, *relatively*

happy). Next, we include a section called "Big Fun for Little Ones," because toddlers and pre-schoolers aren't about to just hang out in their stroller. Parents, you know that — and so do we. Finally, we throw in a fun little section called "A Baker's Dozen Great Hikes for Kids." These are all suitable for youngsters — without sacrificing the thrill of scenic vistas and the peace of the woods. For the most part, we've left recreational activities that are enjoyable for kids, such as biking, boating, rock climbing, horseback riding and watersports, to the chapter called Other Summer Recreation.

Unless otherwise noted, all operating hours and rates quoted are from 1997. Also, all attractions and activities that charge a fee for admission accept major credit cards unless noted.

As you'll soon see, family fun in the Adirondacks is about doing, not reading, so let's get at it!

Non-serene & Extreme

Lake Placid/ Tri-Lakes Region

Bobsledding and Luge for Kids
Olympic Center, Main St., Lake Placid
• 523-1655 Ext. 296

Did you ever wonder what it feels like to careen down an Olympic mountain on a bobsled or a luge? It's fast, it's wild and once a kid tries it, he or she won't stop talking about it — ever. In an effort to interest youngsters in the sport of bobsledding and luge, the U.S. federations of both sports teamed up with Olympic Regional Development Authority (ORDA) to provide kids ages 8 to 12 the opportunity to strap on helmets and pads and jump in a sled to race like demons down the site of the 1980 Olympic bob and luge world championships.

There are two ways to take a ride. Pay approximately $30 for a single ride during the day, or join the Junior Bob and Luge Club. The cost is $30, but the fee allows you to ride every Friday from 5:30 to 8 PM from late December through mid-March. During these sessions, which traditionally are held on Friday, kids should get to drive a two-person bobsled and the luge a few times, so it's a bargain for those even spending just the day in town. You'd better believe that on the second run, your kids will try to go even faster as they scream and laugh even louder!

By the way, many of the people helping out the kids are members of the junior or senior bobsled and luge teams who are returning a favor for all the help others have given them.

Climbing The Wall
High Peaks Cyclery, 331 Main St., Lake Placid • 523-3764

When all else fails, The Wall will silence your kids, even the 4-year-old. The Wall is 2,500 square feet of indoor climbing space where the kids (and you, mom or dad) can try climbing every imaginable cliff from vertical to inclined and overhanging. Cushions on the floor will break your fall, but that's not the idea. The idea is to challenge yourself, to climb that cliff that no one has ever climbed before, using your hands, feet, guts and determination. On The Wall there are no excuses, so don't take any from your kids. Show them that the old folks in the world can hang with the best of them. At only $5 for two hours or $10 a day, The Wall is radical entertainment for the entire family. (We're not kidding. If you can walk, you can climb The Wall.)

High Peaks Cyclery (see our Shopping chapter's entry for additional information) began offering family adventures in summer 1997. Each day of the week, a new challenge awaits, including mountain biking, hiking, rock climbing (the real thing, with bodies hanging in midair in a harness), sea kayaking and horseback riding. Everything about High Peaks is first-class, so if a member of the staff says

your youngster can handle it, cast your doubts aside. This crew has plenty of experience with kids — and hesitant adults. The family adventures range in price from $20 to $55, depending upon the experience, and all necessary equipment as well as professional instruction are included.

Gold Medal Adventures
**Olympic Center, Main St., Lake Placid
• 523-1655 Ext. 296**

If your child dreams of a gold medal in a future Olympics, these adventures will provide a thrill to last a lifetime. Beginning in late June and running through late August, kids can learn what it takes to be a champion in a series of different hands-on adventures, sponsored by the Olympic Regional Development Authority. The activities offered change daily. On Monday, for example, kids may try mountain biking on the Olympic Mountain, followed by rock climbing and a sky ride at Whiteface; on Tuesday, water polo may be the game at the Olympic Jumping Complex, along with clinics on bobsledding. The challenges run Monday through Thursday, 10 AM to 3 PM, and range from bobsledding and luging on wheels to freestyle skiing training on trampolines to indoor rock climbing.

Gold Medal Adventures include all transportation, equipment, lunch and souvenirs. The cost per child is approximately $65, with discounts for multiple-day programs. Space is limited, so if you wish to participate, book early. Many hotels in town can make the arrangements for you.

In-line Skating on the Oval
Speed Skating Oval, Main St., Lake Placid

When the ice melts on the 1980 Olympic speed-skating oval, a smooth cement surface is exposed. There are no cars, no trucks speeding past, no obstructions and no excuses. This is your chance to be a blade runner. While a few people sit and watch, most everybody puts on their in-line skates and cruises a few times around the track. Four revolutions equals a mile, so many a calorie can be lost and much "kid energy" dissipated.

Photo: Adirondack Nature Conservancy

A child gets a close-up view of plants at the Silver Lake Nature Preserve.

If you didn't bring your in-line skates, rentals are available at High Peaks Cyclery, a few hundred yards down the street. (See our Shopping chapter for details.)

Mountain Biking at Whiteface and Mt. Van Hoevenberg
Whiteface Mountain, N.Y. Rt. 86, Wilmington • 523-1655
Mount Van Hoevenberg, N.Y. Rt. 73, Lake Placid • 523-1655

The highest vertical drop in the East — that's how Whiteface Mountain is billed for skiing. Want to try your luck on a mountain bike? Take the chairlift to a variety of intermediate and advanced trails for a 2,100-foot drop to reality at the base. Other trails wind through the valley, along the Ausable River or even into the town of Wilmington, where you can tell your tales of daring over a soda.

The package of trail access and chairlift costs $15 per day for adults and $10 for children.

Mountain biking also can be enjoyed on more than 60 kilometers of interconnected trails traversing the site of the 1980 Winter Olympic Games at Mt. Van Hoevenberg. There's no excuse for not trying mountain biking here, as there are trails for all abilities, not to mention rentals, even lessons.

The trail fee is $4 per day. Bike rental, including helmet, is approximately $25 per day. Ask about specials and multiple-day rates.

Swimming in The Flume
Ausable River, N.Y. Rt. 9N, Jay

This qualifies as a radical sport because it is absolutely, positively the greatest extreme swimming hole in the entire region, if not the entire world. Best of all, it's absolutely, positively *free*. If your kids are the adventurous type, they will love swimming — well, it's not quite swimming — here.

The Flume is essentially a series of small waterfalls near the bridge in Jay. During the summer months, when the water in the Ausable River reaches its lowest level and weakest flow rate, huge boulders become exposed in this section of the river. Kids and adults sit between the cracks in the rocks and under ledges, letting the cool — perhaps cold — waters rush over them. Others try to sit in pools of water formed by the rocks, but despite its relatively low flow, the river still moves along at a fairly rapid rate. The effect is swimming as fast as one can to stay in the same place. (This shouldn't remind one of work.) Some will even attempt to ride down sections of slippery rocks on their bottoms.

There is no doubt about it, the flume is cool. But, there are no lifeguards — you swim at your own risk. Kids and adults occasionally get hurt as the rocks can be slippery and the force of the water can be more than smaller bodies can handle. So be forewarned: THERE IS AN ELEMENT OF RISK. But this swimming hole in Jay also makes for lasting childhood memories.

www.insiders.com

See this and many other **Insiders' Guide®** destinations online — in their entirety.

Visit us today!

Thousands of people swim here safely every year, so take a look and make your own judgment about how appropriate it is for you; just don't overestimate your ability to negotiate the falls.

Jay is approximately 20 minutes from Lake Placid. The Flume is behind the small park in the center of town, opposite the *Adirondack Life* magazine building.

Toboggan Rides
Parkside Dr., Lake Placid • 523-3209

In most towns tobogganing certainly doesn't cut it as a radical sport. A ride down the chute in Lake Placid and onto the ice of Mirror Lake, however, may fill the bill. Speed? Well, yeah, you go about 40 mph, which is plenty fast; but once you hit the sheet of ice, the fact is you are pretty much out of control. So, don't scream your head off on the ride down, but rather wait until you realize that you have no idea how the ride will end. (Don't worry too much — there's plenty of frozen lake on which to decelerate.)

The chute is near the municipal beach on Mirror Lake, behind the post office. Admission

is $3 per person plus a fee to rent a toboggan. Bring your own cushion because the kids will make you do it again and again, and your natural cushion (we're not talking ego) may not be enough for the bumps. Naturally, the chute is open only after the lake freezes.

Plattsburgh/Western Lake Champlain Region

Bootlegger's
Comfort Inn, 411 N.Y. Rt. 3, Plattsburgh • 562-2730

Bootlegger's bills itself as a family fun restaurant, and it lives up to its growing reputation among local kids as a good place to eat. Don't count on them sitting at the table with you — laser tag, the largest arcade in the region, a miniature golf course and other cool things to do await in the Comfort Inn complex. Naturally, all of these activities come with a pay-as-you-play price of 50¢ to around $5. Weekend hours are from noon to 10 PM.

You can enjoy the activities without going to the restaurant, but you may want to consider enjoying one of the eight beers brewed on the premises while the kids amuse themselves. Menu items are in the $5 to $10 range, so you don't have to go broke with the whole package.

Tubing on the Saranac River
Access from N.Y. Rt. 3, Clayburg

The Saranac River flows from Saranac Lake some 65 miles and empties into Lake Champlain in Plattsburgh. Saranac Lake is in the mountains, Plattsburgh is in the valley; obviously, the river flows downhill. Along the way there are a few waterfalls, some whitewater and a number of dams. You might point out a few of these waterfalls to your kids and explain in tall-tale fashion how you accidentally went over the greatest falls ever in a barrel when you were a kid and lived to tell about it. (Remember, you were lucky to have been in a barrel because you don't think you would have survived if you were on an inner tube.) Tell them about these exploits for two reasons: 1) in the Adirondacks we tell tall tales to amuse ourselves; and, 2) you want to keep the kids wondering if they'll come upon any waterfalls on the 5-rivermile inner-tube trip downriver. Although you won't encounter any waterfalls, the sheer anticipation makes the trip even more fun.

Bring your own inner tubes; there are no rentals anywhere. The trip will take an hour or so. Even though the journey is leisurely and relatively slow, life jackets are recommended for everyone.

The journey begins in Clayburg, a few miles west of Plattsburgh on N.Y. Route 3. Turn at the sign for Douglas Camp on Silver Lake Road. Almost immediately you will notice a pull-off. If you have two cars, park one here because this is your exit site. About 5 miles down the road, you'll find another river access point. Put in here and float downriver to your exit at the pull-off near N.Y. Route 3, which generally is visible.

Lake George/ Upper Hudson Region

Aqua Adventure Water Slides/ Skateland Family Fun Center
U.S. Hwy. 9, Queensbury • 792-8989

"Family fun center" is a good description for this place, as this multifaceted complex offers something for every one of your clan from little tyke to teen terror. The Aqua Adventure Water Slides offer two slides that curve and loop for 250 feet from the top of a 31-foot tower. Thirty-one feet may not seem very high until you are looking down *from* 31 feet! Parents, here's some good news — you can watch for free. Our guess is it's going to look like too much fun to just sit around though, so bring your swimsuit, just in case you get ambitious. A picnic area, snack bar and changing facilities are all available. You can either choose from an all-day rate of $9.50, or you can take 10 slides for $7. Plummet down and around from 11 AM until 6 PM Memorial Day through Labor Day. (See "Big Fun for Little Ones" for more information on kiddie water fun.)

Laser Storm is an indoor, high-tech game of tag, with low-power lasers providing the "ammunition" and special sensor vests providing the target. Moms and dads, what better way to get back at your kids for all the hassles they cause under the guise of "family fun?" Laser Storm is open daily year round from 10 AM until 11 PM during the summer months, with limited hours otherwise (call ahead). Admission is $3.50 for all the vests you can hit.

Also inside and air-conditioned is the decidedly less futuristic Skateland Roller Rink, where you can show your kids an activity that was fun (and still is) when you were a kid. Admission is $3.25, and rental skates are available. Skateland Roller Rink is open year round with the same hours as Laser Storm.

Rounding out the offerings here is the LeMans Go-Karts. Be forewarned, though. At $3.50 per five-minute ride, and with kids that will likely want to ride over and over, this could get expensive in a hurry. You might want to save it for late in your visit and leverage your departure with the promise of "one ride before we go." The go-carts run from 10 AM until (yikes!) midnight during the summer, so take a nap in the afternoon, folks. From April until Memorial Day, and again from Labor Day through October, you can still race the kids, just for fewer than 14 hours! Call for schedule to be sure. (See the "Big Fun for Little Ones" section for more information.)

The Great Escape/ Splashwater Kingdom
U.S. Hwy. 9, Lake George • 792-3500

With more than 125 rides, shows and attractions, The Great Escape and Splashwater Kingdom offer lots for everyone in the family. We've given an overview of the park in the Attractions chapter, and here we focus on the "Non-serene & Extreme" elements of the 140-acre theme park.

At The Great Escape, non-serene and extreme are defined by The Comet, a classic wooden roller coaster that is ranked among the top five in the world by *Inside Track*, the magazine for coaster enthusiasts. The Comet was constructed in 1946 and for decades generated thousands of Canadian screams at its home in the Crystal Beach Amusement Park along the northern shore of Lake Erie. You'll fly along the 4,200 feet of track at speeds of more than 50 mph, and the first drop of 95 feet will look and feel twice as high.

Two other coasters round out the rail thrills. The Boomerang Coast to Coaster was new in 1997 and stands as a scary sentinel right next to U.S. 9 for all to see and shiver at. It's a very unusual design compared to The Comet — looking somewhat like a huge version of one of those soft pretzels you get in the local mall food court. Basically, it loops around forward, then loops around backward! Look, you'll have to try it out, then you can try to describe it to *your* friends. The park's original roller coaster, the Steamin' Demon, seems mild by comparison to The Comet and The Boomerang. Oh sure, it does a couple of corkscrew loops, but that's pretty basic stuff these days for coaster enthusiasts. Still, the Steamin' Demon is a good place to "warm up" the kids and gauge their courage level for the day.

Other rides for "extreme" thrills are the Pirate Ship (you know, that huge boat that swings back and forth), Giant Wheel (a very big Ferris wheel with four-person gondolas instead of seats), the Condor (you don't want to know) and the Flying Trapeze (it looks a lot more mellow from the ground than from one of its seats that swing you out and around). The Desperado Plunge Flume Ride is pretty tame, except for the obligatory final plunge into the water.

Speaking of water, for wet and wild thrills, let your kids explore Splashwater Kingdom and its collection of water slides, pools and playgrounds. It's all included in the Great Escape admission price. The "extreme" experiences here include a raft ride down the Black Cobra, 430 feet of twisting black (as in dark) tubes. Other choices are the Banshee Plunge, with its straight drop from atop a 45-foot tower; inner-tubing down the 425-foot Twister Falls; or sliding in your bathing suit down the 425-foot Blue Typhoon. New in 1997 was the Lumberjack Splash, a 25,000-square-foot wave pool, and Paul Bunyan's Bucket Brigade, a

five-story tree-house tower that dumps 1,000 gallons of refreshing Adirondack water on those below every few minutes. For wet fun without changing into swimwear, try the Raging River Rapids Ride, which (kind of) replicates a whitewater raft ride.

For information on little-kid–friendly attractions and activities at The Great Escape, check out the separate listing in the "Big Fun for Little Ones" section. The Great Escape is open weekends in late May, then daily beginning in early June and continuing through Labor Day. The park is also open one weekend in late September for its Octoberfest (see our Annual Events chapter). Operating hours vary throughout the season, basically ranging from 9:30 AM until 6 PM midweek to a closing time of 10 PM on summer weekends.

As you might expect with an attraction of this magnitude, it is pricier than many other entertainment options, but it's still a good value for all that's offered. For adults and children taller than 48 inches, admission costs $22.99 for one day and $29.99 for two consecutive days. The price for children less than 48 inches tall is $16.99 for one day and $23.99 for two consecutive days. Pricing is related to height restrictions for various rides at the park. Parking is free, as is admission for toddlers 2 and younger.

House of Frankenstein Wax Museum

213 Canada St., Lake George • 668-3377

OK, how do we put this? This is perhaps the goriest, bloodiest, most politically incorrect "interactive" museum we've ever survived a visit to. In other words, your teenagers will love it! Frankly, we have mixed feelings about the "House of Frank." Some of what you will see here is cleverly done, and some of what you will see is totally overdone.

First, the good (or ghoul) stuff. Many of the featured players from classic horror films — *Frankenstein, Dracula, Dr. Jekyll and Mr. Hyde, The Wolfman* and *The Mummy* — are

---

INSIDERS' TIP

Even though you're "up North," the sun is still plenty strong during the summer. A day at the water park or theme park can turn into a miserable evening without the proper sunscreen.

featured here. Their displays are detailed and cleverly interactive. For example, you can push a button and see the transformation of Count Dracula into a bat (achieved with mirrors — ironic for a vampire), or you can see Dr. Jekyll become Mr. Hyde with one press of the green light beckoning to the side of the display.

Frankenstein's monster comes to life, and a woman gets a quick fry in the electric chair, all at your fingertips. You'll also find a couple of interesting replications of Edgar Allan Poe stories here — *The Raven* and *The Pit and the Pendulum*. As the pendulum swings back and forth, closer and closer to its intended victim, the story is recited over the speaker above.

Unfortunately, most of the remaining displays are ghastly, gross or both. Displays of such recreational staples as "The Ant Torture" and "Flayed Alive" need no further description. Moving at a steady pace, it took us a good 20 minutes to make our way through the museum, and another 10 minutes to recover with an ice cream cone out front. Parents, heed well — this is not for children younger than 10, and probably best left to your teenagers.

The House of Frankenstein is open from mid-April until the end of October; the rest of the year, it's dead. (Sorry.) Admission is $5 for adults and teens, $2.75 for children ages 6 through 12 and free for those 5 or younger (but we can't imagine taking them through here). If you have a family with three kids and two adults, you get the bargain-package rate of $15.50. Please note that credit cards are not accepted. You also have to pay for the post-visit therapy sessions on your own.

Lake George Action Park
U.S. Hwy. 9, Lake George • 668-5459

Another combo of go-carts, laser guns and a smattering of rides such as the Sea Dragon and a carousel await your family here at the site of the former Gaslight Village Amusement Park. It's the most convenient amusement park to the center of Lake George Village and the lakefront, so it's worth a stop if you're walking around town, the kids are getting restless and you don't feel like moving the car.

Lake George Action Park is open during the summer months only, daily from 2 PM until 10:30 PM. Adults can spend the whole day

here for $12.95, and children shorter than 58 inches can get in for $7.95. We're serious — that's how it works.

Lake George Batting Cages
U.S. Hwy. 9, Lake George • 668-2531

If you want to relive the golden days when you could take a mighty cut at a hard slider and send it over the wall, or if you've got kids that dream of the major leagues, this is a easy place to have fun. You can choose from five baseball and five softball pitching machines as well as five different speeds from "Little League" to what we consider "Don't Bother." The machines are coin-operated and cost $1 for a token that will serve up 14 pitches. (Note: You'll have to shell out cold, hard Washingtons — four silver or one paper — for the tokens; credit cards are not accepted.) The staff proudly points out that's two more pitches per token that other batting cages down near Albany. From our not-exactly-cat-like reflex perspective, that also means you have two more chances per buck to get clocked in the noggin! Our advice: Sit down with an ice cream cone in hand instead of a bat and watch your kids swing away.

Lake George Sports Outlet
179 Canada St., Lake George • 668-4791

Lake George Sports Outlet is primarily a sports-related retail store, but if your kids are into collecting sport cards, they could kill 20 minutes browsing here on a rainy day. If the weather is cooperating, you can rent in-line skates here and take your chances on the busy sidewalks of Lake George Village. It'll cost you either $15 (for eight hours) or $10 (for four hours), and that includes wrist, elbow and knee pads. It doesn't include transportation to the emergency room — that's up to you.

Mountain Biking at Gore Mountain
Peaceful Valley Rd., off N.Y. Rt. 28, North Creek • 251-2411

The Fourth of July 1997 marked a new era of independence at Gore Mountain, New York State's second-biggest ski center. That was the day that the 7,500-foot, high-speed triple lift starting carrying riders with their mountain bikes 1,500 vertical feet up the face of Gore's

Photo: Dave Paczak

It's Christmas year round at Santa's workshop in Wilmington.

lower mountain. That was also the day virtually all of them came screaming back down, whooping and hollering and celebrating the freedom of enjoying the mountain under the warm summer sun.

Now you can try to keep up with your kids or simply ride up with them and spread out a picnic while they try out the variety of terrain that spills down the mountain from the top of the triple lift. You have a bunch of options for enjoying Gore in summer, from one scenic ride up the lift ($8 for adults and teens, $5 for kids ages 7 through 12) to a half-day of lift and trail access ($10 for adults and teens, $8 for kids ages 7 through 12) to a full-day (9 AM to 4:30 PM) of lift and trail access ($15 adults and teens, $10 kids ages 7 through 12).

Bike and helmet rentals are available at Gore, from kid sizes to adult, and range from $3 for a helmet to $35 for a full-size, full-suspension mountain bike all day. You can bring the tiny ones along too, and leave them in the good care of the Bear Cub Den Nursery during operating hours for $5 per hour per child. The cafeteria is also open, and you're going to need it after working up a sweat as you bump and jump your way down the slopes.

In 1997, Gore was open Friday through Sunday, July 4 through September 1, then Saturday and Sunday from September 6 until Columbus Day weekend. Who said Gore was just for skiers and snowboarders?

Rock Sport Indoor Climbing Facility
138 Quaker Rd., Queensbury • 793-4626

Foul weather doesn't mean you have to cancel your mountain-climbing plans — you just have to change your goals a little. And while a climb at the Rock Sport Indoor Climbing Facility will top out at just under 35 vertical feet, it doesn't mean you won't be challenged. In fact, you will find 4,000 square feet of climbing walls with different routes that are fun for everyone from first-timers to experts. Rock Sport is open all year, 4 to 10 PM Monday through Friday and noon to 6 PM weekends. Your first visit will cost you $15 for a day pass, rental of shoes and safety harness, and instruction. Once you're hooked, it is $7 for a day pass and $6 for rental equipment. Full food service is not available, but beverages and snacks are. This place definitely gives a little more excitement to the phrase "hanging out," so give it a try.

Water Slide World
U.S. Hwy. 9, Lake George • 668-4407

The original water park in the Lake George area, Water Slide World continues to be a very popular spot for teens looking for fun, sun and each other. It offers a big selection of slides in various configurations, speed and intensity as well as some water playgrounds for little kids (see "Big Fun for Little Ones" section). In addition to the slides, there's also the Hurricane Wave Pool, which tosses 3-foot waves at swimmers every 15 seconds or so. Beware though — the combination of a crowded pool, breaking waves and a concrete bottom can result in some bangs and scrapes if you're not careful.

Water Slide World offers changing areas, a beach-themed gift shop and the usual summer concession food fare such as hamburgers and ice cream cones. The park is open daily mid-June until Labor Day from 9:30 AM until 6 PM. The admission price for adults and kids 11 and older is $19.95; for children 10 and younger (and taller than 39 inches), it is $17.95; for young children 35 to 39 inches tall, the admission is $9.95; and for toddlers shorter than 35 inches, admission is free. Admission prices are related to height because access to certain slides is height-restrictive (just like some amusement park rides). One deal to keep in mind if you are visiting the area for more than a week is the season pass for $65. You'll make that up in about three visits. Unfortunately, if you're just coming along to chaperone, you are still going to have to pay "full freight" to get in. Our suggestion is to drop off the older kids and spend the $19.95 on lunch somewhere overlooking the lake. The kids probably don't want you "overlooking them" anyway.

Southern Adirondack Lakes Region

Unlike the highly commercial and tourist-oriented Lake George and Old Forge regions, the Southern Adirondack Lakes Region does not have a selection of man-made amusement parks and attractions to provide your older kids with non-serene and extreme thrills. In-stead, this region offers tremendous natural resources and related challenging activities such as whitewater rafting, rock climbing and hiking. You can also choose from most any watersport, from water-skiing to Jet Skiing to parasailing. All of these activities and options are covered in the Hiking and Other Summer Recreation chapters, and we refer you there for lots of ideas on keeping the thrill-seeking kids happy.

Old Forge/ Raquette Lake Region

Calypso's Cove
N.Y. Rt. 28, Old Forge • (315) 369-6145
Next door to and operated by Enchanted Forest/Water Safari, this amusement center includes such high-energy fun as an 1,100-foot-long go-cart track, batting cages and an arcade for older kids. There are also some more sedate activities for little ones (see the separate listing under "Big Fun for Little Ones"). Admission is free; most activities are pay-as-you-play or coin-operated. Calypso's Cove is open daily 11 AM until 10 PM during the summer.

Enchanted Forest/Water Safari
N.Y. Rt. 28, Old Forge • (315) 369-6145
The man-made thrill headquarters of the western Adirondacks, this combination theme park and water park provides plenty of the "non-serene" scene. We provide an overview of the parks in the Attractions chapter, but here we focus on the wild stuff.

While the Enchanted Forest section of the park has about a dozen pretty standard amusement rides, most of the thrills are of the wet variety, courtesy of what is billed as New York State's largest water park. Water Safari may or may not still be the biggest, but with 23 water rides to choose from, it's plenty big enough. And, thanks to recent improvements,

INSIDERS' TIP

After a day at The Great Escape, head across the street to Martha's for a Creamsicle-flavored soft ice cream. Go ahead, spoil your supper!

it is the warmest water park — now featuring heated water. In an area where even in mid-summer the nighttime temps can get pretty chilly, that's a big benefit.

The heart-pumpers at Water Safari include Killermanjaro (that's really how it's spelled), billed as a 280-foot plunge of breathtaking thrills, and the Bombay Blasters where you get to shoot straight down a 160-foot water tube. You can also try body surfing in the new Tidal Wave Pool (if you can avoid the hundreds of other bodies!).

For specifics on hours, amenities and costs at Enchanted Forest/Water Safari, see the listing in the Attractions chapter. Also, we include a mention of some of the options for young children and toddlers in the "Big Fun for Little Ones" section later in this chapter.

Natural Selections

Lake Placid/ Tri-Lakes Region

Dog-sled Rides
Mirror Lake, Mirror Lake Dr., Lake Placid

Don't believe those movie folks who bark "mush" to get the dog-sled teams moving. "Hey, let's go" is more realistic. Once the lake is frozen, dog-sled rides are offered daily during daylight hours at Mirror Lake in Lake Placid. Teams run behind the Best Western Golden Arrow Hotel (hotel staff can tell you if tours are running; call 523-3353) and at the opposite end of town. The half-mile ride around the lake takes approximately 10 to 15 minutes and costs $5 per person.

Lake Placid Club Resort
Mirror Lake, Mirror Lake Dr., Lake Placid
• 523-2556

Want to tire out your kids? Put them in a paddleboat on Mirror Lake and let them pedal-paddle away. Paddleboats, canoes and Sunfish sailboat rentals are available at the Boathouse on Mirror Lake Drive at the Lake Placid Club Resort, or at the base of the small park at 1 Main Street. Rentals costs $15 per person and are available daily from 10 AM to 6 PM.

Bat-watching
Near lakes and streams throughout the Adirondacks

Bats have gotten a bad name over the years. Yet, they are one of nature's most gentle and beneficial creatures. A single bat eats some 2,000 to 3,000 insects a night (a most effective means of pest control) and is an essential seed-disperser and pollinator.

Rabid bats are rare, and there is absolutely no evidence of bats getting tangled in people's hair. (A bat's built-in "sonar" is even more sophisticated than the best human-engineered sonar.)

Around dusk during the summer months, bats emerge from their daytime roosting spots and begin their hunt for flying insects. It is an ideal time to watch the aerial acrobatics of these amazing animals.

Bats prefer to live relatively close to water — especially streams, marshes and lakes — so a dockside vantage point is generally a good spot for bat-watching.

The Butterfly House
Adirondack Park Visitor Interpretive Center, N.Y. Rt. 30, Paul Smiths
• 327-3000

If you are wondering how to get kissed by a butterfly, the secret is to perspire. Butterflies love sweat, as it is filled with salt, a necessary ingredient in a male butterfly's diet. Head inside The Butterfly House during the summer months at the Visitor Center in Paul Smiths, try standing still, and don't wipe that perspiration off your face or hands. The first of its kind in the country, The Butterfly House — designed by Ken Brown, co-author of this guide — allows visitors an up-close and personal look at the variety of butterflies found in the region and the special plants needed for their development.

A dedicated staff of knowledgeable volunteers is always present to explain and show you the butterfly's entire life cycle and the relationship these winged insects have to plants. It is best to visit during a sunny day — the butterflies will be most active. If you want to see a butterfly emerge from its chrysalis, it's most likely to occur near the 10 AM opening time. If The Butterfly House captures your imagination, ask for information on how to raise your own butterflies.

Games Kids Play

Kids know about the environment. They know about destruction in the rain forests, pollution issues and endangered species. Many elementary school-age kids can even explain the lifestyle of threatened animals, such as manatees and bald eagles. Their heads are filled with a staggering array of facts about the world around us.

Facts do not make up for experience, however. While kids might be able to recite neat items from an ecology lesson, they often have had little hands-on time with the real thing. Watching a television show on the backwoods is not the same as going there, and consequently the expectations of a child are often very different than reality.

On television, forests are filled with exotic creatures and plants. In the Adirondacks, kids will see plenty of plants, but the creatures will remain elusive. Unfortunately, most wild animals want nothing to do with human folk and avoid us as if we had a plague. Yet, as they walk through the woods, children often expect to see that moose, coyote or bear they learned about in school or on TV. When they don't encounter wild creatures — it is more likely that they won't — their hike or nature walk might become boring, and their questions might begin to focus upon: What do we do?

It often takes some careful nurturing to get children to appreciate the simpler pleasures of nature. Don't be surprised if your kids seem bored on your first hike in the woods. Many times they simply don't know what is expected.

What can you do on a hike? What behavior is acceptable, and what is not? What do you look for?

Perhaps, the most important thing you can do on your first hike is slow down. Give the kids plenty of time to explore what is going on about them and encourage them to move off the beaten path to investigate something of interest. Adults have had their entire lives to become conditioned to the world, and we often forget what it is like to see something for the first time. We may have seen a million babbling brooks, a zillion trees . . . but that brook babbles a different tune to children. (In fact, many young children believe rivers, streams and brooks are alive.) Give them all the time in the world to explore these potentially new sights, sounds and sensations. The goal of a hike with kids is not to get to your destination as fast as possible, but to make your destination every possible point of exploration along the way.

A few other suggestions include:

• **Explore with all your senses.** Sight is our dominant sense, but the forest is filled with subtleties challenging our other senses. Listen! What do you hear? As you walk along the trail, listen for sounds. When you hear something, pause and listen quietly. Does the sound repeat itself? If it does, an animal may be around. Noise may scare it away, so upon hearing a sound, pause or stop and remain quiet as you look for what caused the noise.

• **Take a walk blindfolded.** Have your child take you — or you lead your child — on a blindfolded walk. Stop to touch, smell and listen. When leading a child, don't answer his or her questions immediately. Let the child discover and consider the answers. Mosses and tree bark are rich in texture to the touch. What's that smell? It's easy to tell when you are in a forest filled with balsam firs; the smell will remind you of Christmas. But what about the smell of skunk when there are no skunks, or the sweet fragrance of wintergreen? Try to find out what is producing the odor, however pleasant or unpleasant that odor may be. (The skunk smell without a skunk in sight is skunk

— continued on next page

Photo: Ken Brown

Kids enjoy a hike along an Adirondack stream.

cabbage, a foul-smelling plant found near wetlands. Another foul-smelling plant — also one of the more beautiful plants in the region— is the red trillium, also known as stinking Benjamin.)

•**Shrink your world.** Within a single square foot of forest floor, there's more wildlife than in the greatest zoo in the world. Thousands of creatures exist under the leaves and in the soil. The creatures are small, some even microscopic; but with a hand lens or a pocket microscope, you can discover the world of the small.

Remember those old-fashioned, clunky microscopes way back when? Well, manufacturers have not only shrunk them to fit into the palm of your hand, but also improved the magnification and reduced the cost to the $10 range — and that includes the price of a few batteries for illumination. Look for a pocket microscope that can be placed directly on an object, as opposed to moving the object under the microscope.

For younger children the greatest problem with a microscope is the eyepiece and the focus, so look for a pocket model with an oversized eyepiece and a small focal range. A good science and nature store should have a demo model for your kids to check out.

Place the microscope on leaves, the bark of a tree, the soil, on rotting logs . . . and on mosses, lichens and molds (the latter three are personal favorites). You know that orange slimy stuff growing out of a really decayed log? (Wow, is it cool!) And in case you've always wondered what distinguishes a real Harris Tweed jacket from the competition . . . well, it's in the lichens used to dye the jacket. Lichens are rather unusual plants in that they are actually two plants in one (an algae and a fungus.) Lichens exist in an array of amazing colors and grow on trees as well as rocks.

How do lichens grow on rocks? That's an interesting question — one that raises another interesting point: It matters not if you don't always have the answer. Kids ask adults questions because they always seem to get an answer. It makes things easy for them. But, when adults admit they don't know something, a whole new scenario unfolds. Kids begin to speculate — and they begin to wonder. They make adults wonder, especially if their hypotheses make sense. Curiosity isn't killed with the cat. . . . It's killed when we stop wondering.

So, about that lichen atop a rock — is it eating the rock? No way. Then where does it get its food? There aren't many other choices. The pizza man delivers it? No way. Well, maybe it isn't a pizza man, but it must be delivered. Maybe by ants, mice or worms? Maybe. But where are the ants, mice or worms? If you find the biggest rock in the middle

— continued on next page

of nowhere, you might notice lichens atop the rock. Unless it is the pizza man, there's only one way for the food to arrive. It comes from above, from the air. Why don't lichens grow on rocks in the city? Even a lichen doesn't want polluted air.

• **Learn about animal behavior.** Wondering, "Where are the animals?" Wildlife isn't about to put on a show just because you have arrived. You will have to work to see some animals besides the noisy red squirrel. Generally, most animals are not very active during the day and prefer to move about during dawn and dusk. Adjusting your time schedule to those hours when animals tend to become more active will increase your odds, but it isn't enough.

Animals need to balance their safety with their ability to get food and water. The game of survival is simple — to get something to eat without becoming something to eat. Although animals have devised specific methods to increase their rate of survival, a general rule applies to most species: They seek food and water near places that offer good protection. The edges of forests or habitat transition zones — areas where one habitat changes into another — suit this need. Look for animals along these edges, such as where a forest meets a meadow or a forest meets a wetland area.

Edges or transition zones often are not blatant or even large areas, especially deep within a forest. A small edge where a few fallen trees opens up an area to sunlight can produce dramatic results. One of the best examples of how animals use edges is seen with deer. Look for an open field bordered by trees. Just before sunset, deer often can be seen feeding along the edges of the field. The slightest noise or motion, however, drives them back into the protection of the forest only a few leaps away.

The number and species of butterflies will vary throughout the summer months. Admission to The Butterfly House is free. Daily hours are 10 AM to 4 PM from mid-June through August.

Plattsburgh/Western Lake Champlain Region

Essex County Fish Hatchery
Creek Rd., Crown Point • 597-3844

If you can't catch any trout on your own to examine, stop by the Essex County Fish Hatchery to see what rainbow, brook and brown trout look like. Don't try counting them. There are 30,000 or so, and the kids will giggle with delight and amazement at what happens during feeding time. The frenzy is better than kids on the last day of school.

Admission costs 50¢ per person. The hatchery is open every day year round from 8 AM to 4 PM.

Ferry Excursions
Cumberland Head, Plattsburgh • 561-2055
N.Y. Rt. 22, Essex • 963-7010
Dock St., Port Kent • 834-7960

Three ferries travel between New York and Vermont during the summer — from Essex to Charlotte, Port Kent to Burlington and Plattsburgh to Grand Isle. Don't bring your car, even though you can; we suggest you just hop aboard and enjoy the inexpensive cruise. The round-trip cost is $2.25 per person from Essex or Plattsburgh, and slightly higher from Port Kent.

INSIDERS' TIP

Some of the kids attractions in the Adirondacks might seem tame compared to Disney World and Universal Studios. Our suggestion: Don't compare. They are entirely different worlds, and your kids will have just as much fun with the "low-tech and hokey" as they would anywhere else.

While there is plenty to do in Burlington (see our Daytrips chapter), there is not much near the other docks, so pack a picnic and plan on some simple explorations. The ferry returns every 30 minutes or so. (See our Attractions chapter for other boat excursions in the region. We decided to include this option here because it is priced right for a family with plenty of kids.)

Ledgetop Orchards
Lake Rd., Crown Point • 597-3420

The Champlain Valley produces some of the finest apples in the region. Only a few orchards, however, allow you to pick your own McIntosh apples. The cost varies from year to year but generally is less than $1 per pound. Apple-picking starts in September; cherries can be gathered at Ledgetop in July, and pumpkins in October.

Rulfs Orchard
Bear Swamp Rd., Peru • 643-8636

In early summer, there seems to be no stopping the proliferation of plump, juicy and sweet strawberries. Late June and throughout July are the best picking times, but it is best to call ahead to see how the harvest is faring. Rulfs Orchard also offers baked goods, jams, jellies and locally grown produce in-season during normal business hours as well as hay rides to the pumpkin patch in the fall.

Viewing Northern Lights
Any area devoid of artificial light

Generally, northern lights put on the best shows after midnight during clear nights in March. Northern lights (aurora borealis) are often a faint, fog-like glow in the northern sky. In fact, many people have seen northern lights without recognizing them. Auroras come in various shapes and intensities, ranging from fog-like glows, streamers and flashes to rayed arcs and gigantic multicolored (usually red and green) ribbons or flaming curtains. Auroras can change quickly from one form to another.

Unlike clouds, auroras do not block the view of stars. Auroras are caused by electrically charged particles emitted by wind storms on the sun. When the particles reach the earth, they interact with gases in the ionosphere. The resulting energy is seen as light.

Visitor Interpretive Center Programs
N.Y. Rt. 28N, Newcomb • 582-2000
N.Y. Rt. 30, Paul Smiths • 327-3000

Saturdays are for kids at the visitors centers (VICs) in Paul Smiths and Newcomb. A major focus in the VICs' programming is education, and kids play an important role. Every Saturday at 1 PM throughout the school year, staff and volunteers offer hands-on programs. Kids might build bird houses, create craft items from natural materials or make casts of animal tracks. During the summer months, a limited number of special programs and events for kids are offered, including trail walks and canoeing. Many of the programs are free; a few require a small materials fee.

Lake George/ Upper Hudson Region

Adirondack Balloon Flights
The Silo, just off I-87 Exit 19, Glens Falls • 793-6342

In truth, this lies somewhere between "extreme" and "serene" as activities go. In either case, it's a beautiful way to see the natural wonder of the Adirondack region. Anything that goes several hundred feet up in the air is going to trip off the "extreme" sensors for some people. At the same time, anything as quiet and peaceful as floating above the scenic valley between the Adirondacks to the west and the Green Mountains to the east registers pretty high on the serenity scale as well. For a special treat with your kids that they (and you) will never forget, choose an early morning or (better yet) early evening flight and enjoy the one-hour show from the sky. Flights are available daily from April through November.

Adirondack Balloon Flights is operated by Phil Jackson (not the Chicago Bulls coach), who's piloted more than 2,000 balloon flights since 1973. He recommends children be at least 10 years old to enjoy the flights. A couple of common concerns people have are:

1) What about motion sickness? Don't worry, the balloon doesn't sway, and there is hardly any sensation of motion.

2) Is it much colder up in the balloon? No, the temperature remains about the same as on the ground.

Now, before you hop in the car, keep in mind that this is a good example of "you get what you pay for." That is, it's a special treat — and costs like it. The rates for a one-hour flight work on a sliding scale from $175 for a single person to $120 per person in a group of six. Call for more specifics on special family, private and spring rates.

Garnet Hill Lodge
Naturalist Programs
Garnet Hill Lodge, 13th Lake Rd., North River • 251-2444

You and your kids can enjoy a guided nature walk here and discover the natural history of the Adirondacks. As you walk along trails used for cross-country skiing in the winter, your kids will learn tree and plant identification, interpret signs of wildlife and enjoy the simple pleasures of the Adirondack environment. The tours last about two hours and run on Tuesdays and Saturdays in July and August. The cost is $4 for adults and teens, $2.50 for children 12 and younger. The Log House Restaurant at the Garnet Hill Lodge is open for breakfast before or lunch after your tour, and it offers a beautiful view of 13th Lake.

Garnet Mine Tours
N.Y. Rt. 28, North River • 251-2706

Kids think mines are pretty neat, so they should definitely get a kick out of this open-pit mine, one of the largest in the world. Tours are available, and your kids can collect specimens along the way. The Garnet Mine tours operate daily from late June through Labor Day, then on weekends through Columbus Day. You can visit from 9:30 AM until 5 PM Monday through Friday and 11 AM until 5 PM Sundays. Tours cost $4 for adults and teens and $3 for children 12 and younger.

Natural Stone Bridge & Caves
Stone Bridge Rd., Pottersville, off I-87 Exit 26 • 494-2283

Kids love caves. Anybody want to argue with that? As the only cave attraction in the Adirondacks, this is a magnificent natural attraction to share with your kids. It's also a throwback to the kind of 1950s tourist attraction you'd expect to see the Cunningham family from *Happy Days* stopping to visit. From the series of signs that beckon and guide you along as you approach to the big wooden caveman standing at the entrance, you know you're not in EPCOT anymore. And that's just fine with us, because this is one of those underrated spots that offers fun, education, a beautiful setting and warm smiles. It's been owned and managed by the same family since (gulp!) the Revolutionary War. How's that for the ultimate in "mom and pop" operations?!

The star attraction here is the 180-foot-long stone bridge on top of which is the gift shop and main building, and under which runs a river! To see it, you take a self-guided tour that leads you along trails to caves, grottoes and other geological wonders courtesy of the glacial age 10,000 years ago. According to co-owner Jan Beckler, the Natural Stone Bridge is one of the oldest rock formations in the United States, containing marble rock that dates back nearly a billion years (give or take a hundred-million). One suggestion: The only restrooms are near the beginning of the trail, so stop there first before venturing out. The sound of rushing water won't do you any favors once you're under way.

For kids in particular, there's a gemstone mining area where they can pan for semiprecious minerals (or cool, shiny rock-stuff as they will know it). Since the troughs have been "pre-loaded" (or should we say "pre-loded"), everyone is bound to find something in his or her pan to shout about. There's also a play area for kids and a trout fishing area. A snack bar and coffee shop are available as are pleasant shaded picnic areas. Save time to browse the extensive rock and gift shops.

The Natural Stone Bridge & Caves are open daily from late May through Labor Day, 9 AM to 7 PM; and Labor Day through Columbus Day, 10 AM until 6 PM. Admission is $8.50 for adults and teens, $4.25 for children ages 6 to 12 and free for children younger than 6. One nice feature here is that your admission fee gets you in all season, so you can stop back and enjoy this peaceful setting again and again.

Picnic on Prospect Mountain
Prospect Mountain Veterans' Memorial Hwy., Lake George

From the entrance just off U.S. Highway 9 at the southern end of Lake George Village, you can drive your family transport 5 miles up, around and up some more to this 2,030-foot summit. Once you arrive at the parking area (just shy of the summit), you can either stroll up a paved walkway, hike up or take one of the continuously running "viewmobile" shuttles to the top. There you'll find picnic areas that offer what's advertised as the "100-mile view." Well, sometimes, maybe. The fact is, the view is awesome from here, looking north up the length of 32-mile-long Lake George and the mountains that surround it. To the east you can see the Green Mountains of Vermont and (sometimes) the White Mountains of New Hampshire and, to the northwest, the High Peaks area of the Adirondacks.

It can get pretty breezy up top, so you may want to do your actual picnicking at one of the tables near the parking area, which is more protected than the exposed summit. For $5 per carload (sorry, no credit cards accepted), this is a bargain of a natural show, and it lasts from late May through late October. You can access the mountain from 9 AM until 5 PM daily.

Warren County Fish Hatchery
Echo Lake Rd., Warrensburg • 623-2877

Here's another neon-free natural attraction that provides both fun and education for your kids in a parent-friendly environment. That is

to say, it's free! Begin your visit by viewing the 15-minute film, then move on to view the indoor troughs teeming with incubate fry and par-size rainbow and brook trout. Next, move outside to see the ponds where full-size yearling trout get ready for their journey to Warren County lakes and streams. There are picnic tables set up on the grounds, so bring along some lunch (anything but a fish sandwich or fish sticks are acceptable) and take your time enjoying the surroundings. The Warren County Fish Hatchery is open daily year round from 8 AM until 4 PM.

Southern Adirondack Lakes Region

The Adirondack Museum
N.Y. Rt. 30, Blue Mountain Lake • 352-7311

We describe this showplace of Adirondack culture in the Attractions chapter, but we wanted to mention it here as a good place to give your kids a feel for what the Adirondacks are all about. While your youngest might get bored here pretty quickly, children 10 and older should enjoy seeing such exhibits as "Boats and Boating in the Adirondacks, 1840-1940" with its collection of beautifully restored wooden boats. Kids might also enjoy the 50 or so horse-drawn vehicles in "The Age of Horse" in the Adirondacks building, the "Logging the Adirondacks" exhibit building and the "Mining in the Adirondacks" exhibit. If they start to get bored and hungry, take them back to the Lake View Deck, which is just outside the cafeteria and overlooks Blue Mountain Lake from a height of 220 feet.

For more information about The Adirondack Museum, including rates and hours, see the Attractions chapter.

Canoe Rentals on Peck's Lake
Peck's Lake Marina, Peck's Lake Rd., off N.Y. Rt. 29A, Gloversville • 725-3996

Few means of transportation are better suited for getting acquainted with nature than canoeing. We cover canoeing in the Other

---

FYI

Unless otherwise noted, the area code for all phone numbers listed in this guide is 518.

Summer Recreation chapter, but we wanted to mention Peck's Lake as a particularly good place to canoe with little paddlers. Peck's is a man-made lake, with lots of shallow little coves to explore, tree stumps that can be whatever your kids' imaginations allow and crystal clear water for excellent bottom viewing at depths up to 10 feet. It's a very quiet lake, with no Jet Skis or boat motors of more than 40 hp allowed, so you don't have to worry about much boat traffic. Canoe rentals are only $6 per adult per day and $3 for children 10 and younger. Life jackets and paddles come with the rentals. Besides the fun your kids will have gliding along the surface of the water, you'll likely find an afternoon of canoeing on Peck's Lake a "mental hot tub" for you as well.

Lakeview Orchards
Mountain Rd., Mayfield • 661-5017

Off N.Y. Rt. 30 near the southern end of Great Sacandaga Lake, here's a place you can take your kids for a classic fall outing. You can pick your own apples and choose from lots of homemade, fresh-baked goodies like doughnuts and pies plus cider to wash it all down. There's also a good selection of jams, jellies and maple products to choose from. There is no admission charge at Lakeview Orchards, and you can visit daily from September to January.

Timberlane Blueberry Farm
Mussey Rd., off N.Y. Rt. 10, Caroga Lake • 835-6335

From mid-July through the end of August, you and yours can pick plump, juicy organically grown blueberries here, then rush home and make up a batch of pancakes (who cares if it's 4 PM?). More than 250 new bushes were planted in 1997, so the crop should be big and blue by summer 1998. You can also choose from a variety of fruit sauces, maple syrup, pottery and other crafts in the rustic barn that serves as "Berry Central." Visit Timberlane from 9 AM until 5 PM daily during berry season.

Old Forge/ Raquette Lake Region

McCauley Mountain Chairlift Rides
McCauley Mountain Rd., off Bisby Rd., Old Forge • (315) 369-3225

Unlike the Lake George region, there are no hot-air balloon flights available in this region to soar you above the magnificent landscape, but this is the next best thing. For $4, you can take each of the kids up the 2,200-foot-long double chairlift that ascends more than 600 vertical feet up the side of McCauley Mountain. A beautiful view of the central Adirondacks and Fulton Chain of Lakes awaits you at the summit. Some white-tailed deer make their home here and are used to being photographed, so bring your camera. The free parking and picnic area make McCauley a good spot to take your time and enjoy the surroundings with the whole gang.

The McCauley chairlift operates 10 AM until 5:30 PM weekends from Memorial Day until mid-June and 9 AM until 4:45 PM weekdays. From mid-June through Labor Day, you can ride Thursday through Monday. Fall foliage rides operate weekends from Labor Day through Columbus Day.

INSIDERS' TIP

You can go broke paying individual admission fees to the various Olympic Authority (ORDA) venues, but a single-site tour package offers one-time admission to the Whiteface Memorial Highway, the Whiteface chairlifts, the ski-jumping complex, the bobsled-and luge-run trolley and discounted admission to the Olympic museum. Kids also can earn a Lake Placid Gold Medal in a "Go for the Gold" game. The site package can be purchased between June and October at all ORDA sites and many hotels, motels and campgrounds. For information call ORDA at 523-1655 or (800) 462-6236.

Bird's Seaplane Service Inc.
N.Y. Rt. 28, Inlet • (315) 357-3631

Here's a way to combine the beauty of the Adirondacks' natural setting with the exhilaration of an airplane ride. And not just an airplane — a seaplane! Any kid will tell you that's "way more cool" than just a regular old airplane. Well, folks, here is your chance to be heroes. You and your kids are sure to love the scenic 15-minute rides offered by Bird's. In fact, just the takeoff and landing on the water make the trip worthwhile. Bird's has 35 years of flying experience and operates seven days a week from mid-April through mid-November. The cost is $40 for one or two adults, then $20 per additional passenger 11 and older up to a total of five passengers. The cost is $10 for children ages 6 through 10 and $5 for kids 5 and younger (easy on the wallet, easy to remember). So, for $60 your family of four can have an experience everyone will remember for years.

Mailboat Rides
Old Forge Lake Cruises, N.Y. Rt. 28, Old Forge • (315) 369-6473

Rounding out our trio of unusual modes of transportation for viewing the natural scene in the Old Forge/Raquette Lake Region is a ride on a real, live mailboat delivering real, live mail to summer homes and camps along four of the Fulton Chain of Lakes. Your kids will get a kick out of tagging along in the unique boat that's designed after an original mailboat of the early 1900s. The mailboat operates daily (if there's mail delivery, so no Sundays or holidays) from June 1 until September 15 and leaves each morning at 9:15 AM for the three-hour trip. The cost is $13 per adult or teenager and half-price for children 12 and younger.

Big Fun for Little Ones

Lake Placid/ Tri-Lakes Region

Project Playground
Old Military Rd., Lake Placid

The construction of playgrounds has become the modern version of a barn-raising, where the entire community pitches in to get the task done.

Kids told the designer what they wanted in a playground, the ideas were put into the plan, and the community rallied together to construct what is known as "Project Playground" behind the Lake Placid Elementary School.

There's everything a kid could want: slides; things to climb over and under; swings that move forward and backward, and others, in circles; and great hiding spots.

Playgrounds are one of the things visitors often forget to ask about at information centers, and they don't appear in brochures.

Santa's Workshop
Whiteface Mountain Memorial Hwy. (N.Y. Rt. 431), North Pole (west of Wilmington) • 946-2212

In an era of the super theme park, Santa's Workshop, one of the country's original theme parks, has a long-lost charm that delights particularly young children and families who keep the Santa tradition alive. This re-creation of the North Pole offers families a chance to see Santa and his helpers busy at work making Christmas magic.

The park is decidedly low-key and personable. Depending on the length of the lines (they are generally short), Santa and his helpers will actually converse with your children. The artisans practicing their crafts in shops around the park will also spend time answering your questions. While the rides — slow-moving trains, a merry-go-round and other simple rides — and shows are low-tech, they will delight the youngsters for whom the park is designed. Santa's Workshop often is the highlight of a vacation for any child who believes in the magic of Santa.

The park is large enough to amuse a youngster for a good part of the day, but you may want to consider letting any cynics in your group find another activity — it's all Santa here. All shows in the park are weather-dependent.

You'll find Santa's Workshop just before the toll gate on Whiteface Memorial Highway (N.Y. 431). Admission is $11.95 for adults, $7.95 for children. It is open every day 9:30 AM to 4:30 PM in July and August, then weekends only from September through early October.

The Visitor Interpretive Centers in Paul Smiths and Newcomb provide insights into the delicate environment of the Adirondack wilderness.

Lake George/ Upper Hudson Region

Aqua Adventure Water Slides/ Skateland Family Fun Center
U.S. Hwy. 9, Queensbury • 792-8989

We cover this complex in the previous "Non-serene & Extreme" section, but we want you to know that you can bring your youngest along for fun here as well. Specifically, they can enjoy the kiddie water play area, with its wading pools and fountains, in the water park. For dry fun (never a guarantee with toddlers) there's a kiddie track at the LeMans Go-Kart area where you can ride along with them at a Mini-Mach speed. See the previous listing for rates and hours of operation.

The Great Escape/ Splashwater Kingdom
U.S. Hwy. 9, Lake George • 792-3500

With more than 125 rides, shows and attractions, The Great Escape and Splashwater Kingdom offer lots for everyone in the family, including your littlest tourists. We give an overview of the park in the Attractions chapter and previously highlight the "Non-serene & Extreme" elements of the 140-acre theme park earlier in this chapter.

Specifically for your little ones, The Great Escape and Splashwater Kingdom offer a variety of kiddie rides, attractions and shows. Some favorites include the U-drive Turnpike Cars, Swan Boats and a beautiful classic carousel. There are several themed areas that will pique the imagination of any child, including Storytown, the original section of the park, themed after nursery rhymes; Ghost Town, an 1880s-style mining town; and Arto's Small World, featuring a village constructed at quarter-scale. At Splashwater Kingdom, little water tykes will enjoy Noah's Sprayground with its five pools, play fountains and miniature slides.

Shows that entertain children of all ages include the Super Circus, High Divers, Marshal Wild Windy Bill McKay and the Ghost Town Stunt Show. The Great Escape is big — but not so big that you can't let the older kids wander while you hang out with their little brother or sister. For more specific information, refer to the Attractions chapter and this chapter's previous listing in the "Non-Serene & Extreme" section.

Magic Forest
U.S. Hwy. 9, Lake George • 668-2448

If you only have children younger than 10 or so, you may want to skip The Great Escape altogether and visit the Magic Forest instead. It is more intimate and manageable for parents, less than half the cost and, in the eyes of a 5-year-old, just as much fun. You'll find about 25 rides and attractions here — all presented in a nostalgic, low-tech atmosphere that may seem outdated to some, but to us, a refreshing throwback to simpler times. A couple of rides will get the blood pumping — the Scrambler and the Parasails in particular — but for the most part the emphasis is on little thrills for little folks.

Highlights for our little ones include the giant twisting slide and the Ferris wheel, which spins you smoothly between the protection of a couple big trees that seem close enough to touch. There also are some deer and goats on display along a wooded walking trail plus a tram ride that is the low-budget distant cousin to the Jungle Cruise at Disney World (but again, little kids don't care how many moving parts the fake giraffe has!). Santa (looking somewhat underpaid and overdressed for midsummer), the Macaw Show and the Diving Horse are all part of the entertainment here throughout the day.

One nice feature about Magic Forest is that most of the park is densely wooded with pines, so you are in the shade most of the time, even on the hottest summer days. Admission is $11.95 for adults and kids 11 and older and $9.95 for children 10 and younger. The park is open 9:30 AM until 6 PM weekends between Memorial Day and the end of June, and daily in July and August before closing after Labor Day.

Spanky's Fun Place
U.S. Hwy. 9, Queensbury • 761-0449

Locally owned and operated since 1994, Spanky's is a "Discovery Zone" type of indoor playground and entertainment center for kids. It is intended for children from 12 months to 12 years old, any of whom would enjoy the variety of fun games, ball pits, tunnels and slides available here. There's also a miniature train ride that runs every half-hour or so and takes kids on a somehow fascinating 100-foot loop inside a little area surrounded by a white picket fence. Oh well, kids love train rides of any size. A snack bar with hot dogs, popcorn, soda and other typical concession fare is available, as are private "party rooms" for birthday celebrations. The cost for an hour or a whole day of fun is $4.82 (including tax) per child. Spanky's is open year round, with hours that vary from 9 AM until 6 PM during winter weekends to more limited hours during midweek summer days. The hours change almost weekly, so we suggest you call ahead. On a rainy (or snowy) day, Spanky's could be just what your kids are looking for.

Water Slide World
U.S. Hwy. 9, Lake George • 668-4407

We cover this place fully in this chapter's previous "Non-serene & Extreme" section and include it here for its toddler-friendly features. We recommend the Pirate Ship Cove Toddler Lagoon with its wading pool, fountains and minislides — all surrounding or coming out of a cute replica of a pirate ship. Our 5-year-old spent all afternoon at this one spot last summer. There's also the Amazon River to float lazily along in tubes, with only the occasional waterfall to avoid or paddle under, depending on your mood. As much fun as water parks can be on a hot day, the combination of crowded pools and hard surfaces can result in occasional stumbles, cuts and bruises, so keep a close eye on your young ones as you enjoy the surroundings. For more specifics on

INSIDERS' TIP

During the summer months, the Adirondacks are a prime breeding ground for orange-and-black Monarch butterflies, which flutter in abundance during August before embarking in September on a spectacular winter migration to Mexico.

hours and rates, see the listing earlier in this chapter.

Wild West Ranch & Western Town
Bloody Pond Rd., off U.S. Hwy. 9, Lake George • 668-2121

This brand-new attraction opened in summer 1997 and is geared to kids and their parents. You'll find a big slate of "Old West" themed activities and attractions, including pony, horse, mule and stagecoach rides plus a Wild West Show & Rodeo, Wild West Saloon Steakhouse, Ice Cream Parlor, Old-Fashioned Bakery and Country Shops. Admission is free, then you'll need to pick and choose which of the pay attractions you'd like to try.

The Wild West Show and Rodeo costs $5 for adults and teens and $3 for children 12 and younger. The show includes comedy, rope tricks, trick riding, stunts and Foxfire, the trained movie horse. Other costs range from $4 for pony rides to $15 per hour for trail rides. You can take the whole family on a narrated horse-drawn wagon trail ride past real buffaloes, longhorn cattle and elk for only $3 per person. Wagon rides depart every half-hour between 10 AM and 5 PM. Your kids will also enjoy the Petting Corral with its baby ranch animals, and the Frontier Playground.

All this western cowboy stuff is bound to make the whole gang hungry, so check out the Wild Horse Saloon & Eatery for steaks, chili, barbecued ribs and homemade baked goods. If your kids have hit the "cowboys are cool" phase of their lives, and if their favorite toy is Woody from *Toy Story*, be a hero and bring 'em here.

Southern Adirondack Lakes Region

Adirondack Animal Land
N.Y. Rt. 30, Mayfield • 883-5748

The Adirondack region is known for its wildlife, but not the tigers, lions, zebras, monkeys and even the giraffe you'll find here. As the only designated wildlife park in the region, Adirondack Animal Land is well worth a visit. It is set on 75 acres and provides natural settings for its hundreds of exotic birds and animals. Your kids will also enjoy the petting zoo, the Western Town and Shetland pony rides while visiting. The park is open daily from late May through Labor Day. Hours are normally 10 AM until 5 PM. Admission is reasonable: $6.75 for adults and $4.75 for children 12 months to 12 years old. If you think $4.75 is steep for a 1-year-old, just watch how their eyes light up throughout the day.

Sherman's Park
N.Y. Rt. 10, Caroga Lake • 835-4110

Trust us on this one. Few summer-evening, family experiences are more of a simple pleasure than a visit to Sherman's Park. A small lakeside amusement park that enjoyed its heyday in the 1950s and 1960s, Sherman's is enjoying a rediscovery of sorts from Adirondack-area families of the 1990s. You'll find a century-old carousel in a beautifully restored pavilion, with nice long rides for $1.50. While you're watching the kids enjoy themselves, check out the old photos of the park from decades past displayed around the inside of the pavilion.

Recently reintroduced to the park is the Ferris wheel, which did not operate due to insurance costs for many years. As you round the top of the wheel, you feel as if you are going to descend directly into Caroga Lake, just a hundred feet in front of you. The Ferris wheel is mellow enough for all but the youngest members of your family to enjoy, and it costs only $1.50 for a generous spin.

The surrounding park is nicely landscaped, and the former bumper-car pavilion is now a pavilion for everything from simple family picnics to elaborate weddings. Just a few steps away is Sherman's restaurant and dance hall, which features casual eats and live entertainment on summer weekends (see the Nightlife chapter). Plan on not leaving until you buy some of the famous soft ice cream at the separate kiosk outside — and why not take one more spin on that Ferris wheel?

Sherman's Park is open noon until 9 PM Saturday and Sunday from Memorial Day weekend until Fourth of July weekend; then the same hours Tuesday through Sunday until Labor Day. There is no admission fee; you just pay as you go (around and around).

Old Forge/
Raquette Lake Region

Adirondack Scenic Railroad
Thendara Railroad Station, N.Y. Rt. 28, Thendara • (315) 369-6290

You and your family can relive the golden age of railroading on the line that played host to the rich and famous en route to their summer camps and grand old resort hotels at the turn of the century. Departing from the Thendara Railroad Station, you can ride in vintage open-window coaches through the forest and past lakes and rivers as you experience magnificent scenery. Of course, your little conductors won't care where you're going, they'll just think it is "pretty neat" to ride on an old-fashioned train.

For specific information on rates, routes, operating hours and other amenities, see the Adirondack Scenic Railroad entry in our Attractions chapter.

Enchanted Forest/Water Safari
N.Y. Rt. 28, Old Forge • (315) 369-6145

This combination theme park/water park features plenty of fun for toddlers and younger children alike. One parent-friendly feature: Strollers are available at no charge. That's a good start. Themed areas specifically for your smallest thrill-seekers include Animal Lane, with it's kiddie rides and Mother Goose's menagerie; Storybook Lane; and the Wild West-themed Yukon Village. At Water Safari, the Pygmy Pond includes a kiddie-size river tube ride, shipwreck slide and activity wading pool with fountains. Next door at Calypso's Cove, little racers can enjoy the miniature go-cart track.

For more information on Enchanted Forest/Water Safari, see our Attractions chapter.

A Baker's Dozen
Great Hikes With Kids

What do kids want when it comes to mountain climbing? Well, it seems that the words conjure an image of climbing on and over things, like huge boulders, or climbing across or through things, like streams. Kids don't climb mountains — they climb things *on* the mountain. Then, there must be a host of interesting things to do or see along the way. Although you may think the goal is to get to the top of the mountain, most kids couldn't care less. Don't adults know that you can't do anything with that beautiful vista? You can't eat it, you can't crawl over it, you can't play with it. But if you can throw rocks off it or get close enough to the edge to make parents scream their bloody heads off . . . well then, that's a kid's mountain.

The following hikes require less than a few serious hours of walking. Since hiking with kids is far from serious, add some additional time for necessary diversions such as picking blueberries, playing in streams, finding hiding spots, collecting pine cones and leaves, climbing rocks and, most importantly, eating snacks with soiled hands (kids always find a way to get filthy on a hike knowing full well that there is no way to wash their hands before eating). For information about additional hikes, see the Hiking chapter.

Lake Placid/
Tri-Lakes Region

Owl's Head
N.Y. Rt. 73, north of Keene

It's likely that Owl's Head — great for beginners — has had more first-time climbers than any other mountain. It's a little gem with great views and short sections of challenges

---

for youngsters (and adults) followed by easy trail. As you sit on the summit in August, expect your kids to begin feeding you wild blueberries. The berries are rarely big and juicy, but your kids will tell you that they are the best ever, as they discovered them along the way.

Owl's Head is 2,120 feet high, with .55-mile trail. The trailhead is off N.Y. 73, approximately 3 miles north of Keene. If approaching from the Lake Placid side, the mountain is halfway down the big hill after Cascade Lakes. Note the sign on the right reading "Owl's Head Estates." Please follow directions and park your car in designated spots because access to the trailhead is through private property. On warm days bring extra water; much of the top portion is exposed and gets hot.

Mount Jo
Adirondack Loj Rd., Lake Placid

This is one of those mountains that kids attack, and by the time they get to the summit — a mere 1.2-mile, 710-foot climb that's great for beginners — they have spent enough energy to have climbed Mount Everest. There are two approaches to Mount Jo — one boring, one not so. The "boring" trail works itself around the back of the mountain and is relatively unencumbered by obstacles. The frontal approach is open warfare with boulders of every imaginable size and shape. Kids (and some parents) love to climb over, around and under them as well as rest on them. Then you proceed upward through some narrow crevices and beneath some cliffs dripping with water. This water is particularly important because it allows for mud to collect on bodies and in snacks. (Ah, no wonder the trail mix tastes so good.)

Once you get to the top, you have a beautiful view of the high peaks and Heart Lake below, and here's where you might tell kids the story of how Mount Jo got its name. In 1877 Henry Van Hoevenberg visited the Adirondacks with his fiancée, Josephine Scofield. The two climbed Mount Marcy to get a view of the area and select a site for their future home. They selected the area near the heart-shaped lake, just below the mountain on which you and the kids are sitting and which would be named Jo after Josephine. Alas, the story turns

sad as Miss Josephine died the following year. The bereaved Henry, however, returned and built a home on the site where Adirondack Loj sits today.

After relating such a dramatic tale, the kids should be slightly tired (the climb also might have something to do with their fatigue), so take the "boring" (backside) way down. The kids might even thank you for this.

Access to Mount Jo is through the Adirondack Loj. To get to the Loj, take N.Y. 73 from Lake Placid. About a half-mile beyond the ski jumps, turn right on the Adirondack Loj Road and follow it to the end. Park in designated spaces. A parking fee may be imposed. Follow the signs to Mount Jo and Heart Lake.

Mount Baker
E. Pine St., Saranac Lake

Mount Baker is in the running for the mountain hike with the best view with the least effort. The ascent is only a short and moderate 900 feet but offers an unsurpassed view of both the High Peaks and the lake country surrounding Saranac Lake. The beginner trail begins on the north side of Moody Pond and is in walking distance from downtown Saranac Lake. Simply take Main Street to Pine Street and Moody Pond. Follow the old road for 100 yards, pass the stone quarry, then turn left through the evergreen forest to the summit. The hike is 1.8 miles round trip.

Cobble Hill
off Cobble Hill Rd., Lake Placid

Mount Jo (see previous entry) and Cobble Mountain are two perfect places to let kids explore the thrill of rock climbing since the ascent involves discovering ways over and around some very immovable erratics. To reach Cobble Hill, take N.Y. 86 east. About 1 mile past the traffic light at the junction with N.Y. 73, turn left onto Cobble Hill Road. Turn right onto the narrow road and proceed about a quarter-mile. Park in the small space a few feet down the road. The trailhead begins past the house on the left and is marked with red paint. For a few feet, you travel over private property, so be respectful. You will pass a few paths in the next hundred yards or so that are blocked on your left; always move right.

Ampersand Mountain
N.Y. Rt. 3, Saranac Lake

This is one of those sneaky intermediate climbs that starts off easy but quickly becomes difficult. It is, however, worth the effort — the view is spectacular once you reach the summit. Curiously, the summit was once dense with trees, but the trees were cut down by Verplanck Colvin, the man who first surveyed the Adirondacks for the State of New York. Colvin cut the trees so he could use the mountain as a triangulation point. More than 100 years after Colvin's tree-cutting, the summit remains bare; all the topsoil, which took thousands of years to accumulate, washed away, preventing any new tree growth. The trail begins on the south side of N.Y. 3, halfway (about 8 miles) between Saranac Lake and the junction with N.Y. 30 near Wawbeek. A DEC sign marks the trailhead; the trail is easy to follow. (Note: To the right is the trail to Middle Saranac Lake.) The ascent is 1,800 feet, and the round-trip hike is about 6 miles.

Copperas, Owen and Winch Ponds
N.Y. Rt. 86, Lake Placid

About 6.4 miles from the traffic light at N.Y. routes 73 and 86 in Lake Placid is the trailhead to a perfect day hike offering a perfect reward — a cool swimming hole in a mountain pond. The trails make a loop bringing you to the ponds and back to N.Y. 86. Although a second trailhead is a mile beyond the first one, try to begin your hike at the first trailhead — it's easier, and a brook follows the trail up to the pond. About 15 minutes into the trail, a section of the brook nears the hiking path and offers an opportunity to see what is going on in a mountain stream. Although there are no fish, there's plenty of insects, among which you should find a few water striders — big daddy-longleg–type insects that walk on water. Check out their locomotion as they scoot across the surface. Also, since this brook is at the base of a minigorge, water in the atmosphere makes for an ideal habitat for a variety of mosses.

Return to the trail and begin your ascent, but look for what David Letterman might call a "stupid tree trick." You can't miss the healthy hardwood tree — a good 75 feet tall — growing atop a rather large boulder. The roots cover the rock like some giant claw. Since the kids probably are wet from the stream at this point, why not let them get dirty climbing the rock on which every kid has to have their picture taken?

While the tree trick is a particularly dramatic example, you also will find plenty of seedlings growing in and on not only rocks, but also rotting logs in the forest. Fallen logs often make for prime nurseries. Check out some logs and note what grows on and around them.

About a half-mile from the road, you will reach Owen Pond. Note the diversity of trees along the shore — beech, birch, hemlock, pine, spruce and cedar. Continue along the clearly marked path, which follows the shore. Within a short distance, the trail will go left. Consider taking a short diversion by bushwhacking the section straight ahead and along the shore. The cedar forest is quite different than most forests in the Adirondacks.

The next pond is Copperas. As you walk around the pond, you will see a lean-to on the opposite side. When you come to a foot bridge, note the shallow water and sandy bottom — perfect for some water explorations with youngsters. A few hundred yards down the path, DEC signs direct you to a return route back to N.Y. 73; but for the moment, continue along the path. The swimming hole is a few feet ahead, off the rocks. The water is clear, deep and cool. And a million pollywogs in every stage of development will bump into your toes. A few hundred feet past the swimming hole is a DEC lean-to.

Winch Pond has a very different look to it than Owens and Copperas and makes for an interesting diversion. A sign will direct you to the pond along the return route. Please be aware that the route to N.Y. 73 is steep in sections.

It's hard to top the fun to be had at a local swimmin' hole.

Middle Saranac Lake Beach
N.Y. Rt. 3, Saranac Lake

Why is the parking lot at this trailhead always packed to the gills on weekends? The
answer is at the end of this .6-mile walk. There's
a long sandy beach and shallow water with a
sandy bottom that's perfect for wading with
little ones. The trail is about 6 miles from
Saranac Lake on the north side of N.Y. 3. Just
look for the cars.

Bloomingdale Bog
CR 55, Bloomingdale

Every kid deserves a good bog to explore,
as they'll find meat-eating plants, mysterious
bubbles and a great selection of bugs and
frogs. The Bloomingdale bog is one of the
largest in New York, but it's an easy walk, as it
traverses an old railroad right-of-way. A good
hand lens or pocket microscope is appropriate on this trail; there are many funky things

growing on the trees, on the ground and in muck that are worth looking at in detail. Read up on bogs — particularly their lichens, mosses and carnivorous plants — before the hike, and go on a hunt to find as many as possible. The bog's varied habitat provides wildlife with shelter and food, so birding and butterfly watching are great options here.

There are two routes to the bog. Option 1: Take N.Y. 86 from Saranac Lake to Asplin Tree Farm, then turn right just after the farm. The entrance to the bog is about 3 miles down the road and is marked with a DEC sign. There is a pull-off onto a dirt road blocked by a gate. Option 2: Take N.Y. 3 from Saranac Lake. Once you come to the stop sign in Bloomingdale (it's the first and only one for miles), continue straight and bear slightly left. The first pull-off is private property; the one you want is about 1 mile farther.

Panther Mountain
N.Y. Rt. 3, Tupper Lake

Panther rivals Mount Jo and Owl's Head (see previous entries) for great first hikes. The trail — 1.5 miles east of the confluence of N.Y. routes 3 and 30 between Tupper and Saranac lakes — is found on the north side of N.Y. 3. Parking, however, is across the road from the trailhead. The trail to the summit is .8 miles and follows the markers.

Plattsburgh/Western Lake Champlain Region

Snow Mountain
N.Y. Rt. 73, Keene Valley

Whatever kids want in a hike, this relatively easy 3.4-mile (round trip) hike probably has it. There's a stream with waterfall; a narrow passage way, or secret passage way, depending upon how you look at it; a good view; and blueberries in-season.

Silver Lake Mountain
Silver Lake Rd., Silver Lake

If you find yourself in the Silver Lake area, but the conditions sour for a river ride (see the previous Tubing on the Saranac River entry), don't fret too loudly: There is a decent hike 2.9 miles down Silver Lake Road, just south of where the power lines cross the road. A yellow-on-brown sign marks the trailhead, and red discs mark the 1.8-mile (round trip) trail up Silver Lake Mountain. The hike is easy and offers views of Alder Brook, Catamount Mountain, Silver Lake and Union Falls.

Coon Mountain Preserve
Halds Rd., Wadhams

According to legend, the Coon Mountain panther (cougar or mountain lion; they are the same creatures), would lure local men ever-deeper into the woods with a cry like a damsel in distress. Then the giant cat would spring on its victims. During one hunt, the panther was shot in mid-leap and, as it crashed down a cliff, sunk into one of the mysterious tarns that dot the summit's ridge. The animal's body was never recovered, leaving the legend that the Coon Mountain panther remains. If it still lives, it has a great view of Lake Champlain and the High Peaks.

The trail to the summit of Coon Mountain is about a mile long, with an ascent of 500 feet. Although the entire trip takes approximately one hour, it is steep and rocky in sections, and is considered difficult by many. Kids, however, should find the trail challenging and interesting. To avoid getting lost or wandering onto adjoining private lands, hikers should stay on the marked trail. As you enter the site, the young successional woods indicates that the forest was logged in the distant past. The skid roads used to haul out logs are still visible. The trail quickly leaves the wood road, and you enter a hardwood forest of mature beech, maple and oak trees. Barbed wire may be seen grown in the trunks of some trees, indicating

---

INSIDERS' TIP

The Ferris wheel at Sherman's Park in Caroga Lake is a great value at $1.50 a ride. It's scenic (overlooking the lake shore) and provides a ride that is exciting enough for the teens but not too scary for your little ones.

that years ago the property was used as pasture. While walking through this section, look for claw marks on the smooth gray bark of the beech trees; bears love beech nuts.

At the base of the ravine, the forest begins to change as the soil grows increasingly moist and rich. During the early spring, this is a good place to look for wildflowers — just avoid the stinging nettles. As you climb through the ravine, stay on the rocks to reduce soil erosion caused by your boots. Take a breather and enjoy the first view of Lake Champlain. If you hike the trail in the spring, you might notice small pools of water along the trail. These vernal pools serve as breeding grounds for frogs and salamanders.

The trail winds to the "first" summit. Continue in a northwesterly direction, then due west, down a dip, then back up to a rocky outcrop, where you will have a 240 degree vantage. In the spring, hawks may be seen migrating up the Champlain Valley. The 246-acre Coon Mountain Preserve helps in protecting the area's working farms, timber-producing forest and open spaces.

From N.Y. Route 9N in the village of Westport, take N.Y. 22N toward Essex. In .4 miles turn right onto Lakeshore Road. Keep right at the junction with Beekman Road (1 mile) and continue 3 miles to Halds Road on the left (no sign). Take Halds Road about .75 miles to the trailhead on the right.

Boreas River Trail
N.Y. Rt. 28N, Newcomb

The Boreas River is the allure of this loop trail in the central part of the Adirondack Park in Newcomb. The trailhead is on the west side of N.Y. 28N, south of the Boreas River bridge. After 1.2 miles on the trail, you arrive at Hewitt Eddy, where the river broadens. You can continue for another .8 miles and find yourself back on N.Y. 28N, where you need to walk .8 miles back to your car.

In Hamilton County alone — the least populous of all counties in New York State — the tourism office lists a whopping 214 festivals and activities on its events calendar from May through October!

Annual Events

"There's nothing to do in the Adirondacks but hike and fish." Is that right?

"It's just a bunch of mountains and remote lakes." Oh really?

Well, consider that in Hamilton County alone — the least populous of all counties in New York State — the tourism office lists a whopping 214 festivals and activities on its events calendar from May through October! Believe us, a lack of population doesn't mean a lack of activity in the Adirondacks.

There are literally hundreds of events, festivals, fairs and exhibits to see and experience in this vast region throughout the entire year. Granted, there is more going on midsummer than mid-November, but you can search out enjoyable activities for you and your family in any season. July and August are the busiest months in the Adirondacks, and towns and villages throughout the region put on their Sunday best, so to speak, to attract visitors. Almost every town has something going on, with many of the larger villages offering weekly lectures, music or some other amusements. For information about these weekly events, see the "July" and "August" sections.

In this chapter, we provide you with a sampling of general-interest, wide-appeal events that take place throughout the year and throughout the five regions of the Adirondacks. By no means is this a complete listing, but it will give you a pretty good idea of the kind of happenings you can engage in and enjoy — or just sit back and watch.

With few exceptions, we don't include the somewhat generic events and activities that tend to take place just about everywhere — Fourth of July celebrations, Christmas holiday celebrations, garage sales and chicken barbecues. (See this chapter's related Insiders' Tip for hints on finding these.) The chapter is set up with listings in each region on a month-by-month basis, in chronological order as the events take place. You will notice that in some months there are no events listed for some regions. Does that mean there isn't anything happening there? Absolutely not! However, the type of activities taking place are probably either arts-related or recreation-related, in which case they may be included in other chapters such as Skiing, Other Winter Recreation, Other Summer Recreation or Arts and Culture.

There are certain hotbeds of activity that are always worth checking with throughout the year, as they are likely to offer a wide variety of events and programming within their own operations. Some examples are the regional arts centers such as the Adirondack Lakes Center for the Arts in Blue Mountain Lake and the Arts Center/Old Forge (see our Arts and Culture chapter); major recreation centers such as Gore Mountain, Whiteface Mountain and the ORDA facilities in Lake Placid (see the Skiing chapter); civic centers and arenas such as the Lake Placid Arena and the Glens Falls Civic Center (see the Attractions chapter); and major museums such as the Adirondack Museum in Blue Mountain Lake and The Hyde Collection in Glens Falls (see the Attractions chapter). Unless otherwise noted, all events listed offer free admission. In some cases, admission is free for the event in general, and specific activities such as meals or attractions have separate costs. You'll need to call the phone number listed with the event to get the specific breakdown on what is free and what isn't.

Happy hunting!

January

Lake Placid/ Tri-Lakes Region

Skating and Skiing Competitions
Olympic Center, Main St., Lake Placid • 523-1655

The entire month of January is booked with skating and skiing competitions at the various Olympic venues in Lake Placid. The events include regional long-track speed skating, international figure-skating events and world-cup competition at Whiteface Mountain. Admission fees range from free to $10 or so, depending upon the level of competition. Access to downhill skiing events at Whiteface often require the purchase of a lift ticket. Call the Olympic Authority at the listed number for details.

Demo Days at Big Tupper
Big Tupper Ski Area, Country Club Rd., Big Tupper • 359-9481

Snowboarders and contour (curved skis) skiers get a chance to sample the latest equipment during what seems like monthly demo days at Big Tupper Ski Area. The first demo day generally takes place in December, and others are scheduled regularly throughout the ski season. Skiers can demo the equipment for free, but to do so you must have a lift ticket for Big Tupper (see Skiing). Some of the equipment is not yet in full production, so the demo days are a good way to stay ahead of the radical trends. World Cup Ski and Bike shop (see Shopping) generally sponsors the demo days; call the shop at the listed number for details.

FYI

Unless otherwise noted, the area code for all phone numbers listed in this guide is 518.

Lake George/ Upper Hudson Region

New Year's Day Polar Bear Club Swim
Shepard Park Beach, Canada St., Lake George • 668-5755

If you really need something to wake you up after an overindulgent New Year's Eve, this should do it! Members of the Lake George Polar Bear Club actually take a dip in the icy waters of Lake George, presumably for just long enough so the local TV news cameras can record it for their annual New Year's Day human-interest story. So, if you're bored or hungover at 1 PM, come on down to the beach and watch — or feel free to join in. The event is free, but they probably couldn't pay you enough to participate!

Snowboard Festival
Gore Mountain, off N.Y. Rt. 28, North Creek • 251-2411

On a Sunday in late January, Gore gets crazy with snowboard contests, races and tricks by enthusiasts from across New York State. This event is at least as much fun to watch as it is to try, particularly if your an advanced skier but virgin 'boarder. There's lots of music, food, whoops and hollers to go along with the loops and jumps on the mountain. You can either watch from the lodge for free (doable but distant) or buy a lift ticket for $39 (adult) and ski or 'board right down to the snowboard park for a close-up view of the action and fun.

Southern Adirondack Lakes Region

Caroga Lake Outhouse Races
N.Y. Rts. 29A and 10, Caroga Lake • 725-1070

What's a Saturday in mid-January without a good, old-fashioned American outhouse race? If you've always wondered what design of commode would be the fastest on ice, this is your

Photo: Dave Paczak

Plattsburgh's annual Mayor's Cup Race is the largest sailing event on Lake Champlain.

chance to find out. Obviously, this "just for fun" event is designed primarily to get people out and about from midwinter hibernation for some laughs with neighbors and friends.

Fulton County Winter Festival
throughout Fulton County • 725-0641, (800) 676-3858

Lasting from mid-January until mid-February, this series of events includes such activities as snowmobile races, car racing on frozen lakes, ice fishing, cross-country skiing and other recreational fun. The events take place on and around Great Sacandaga Lake, Gloversville and Caroga Lake. Most of the activities are free, but some require a fee, so call ahead for the schedule and details.

February

Lake Placid/ Tri-Lakes Region

Saranac Lake Winter Carnival
throughout Saranac Lake • 891-1990

The oldest winter carnival in the country is now into its second century — and it shows no signs of age. Every year the carnival grows, with more and more events added to the week-long schedule of festivities. Once the king and queen are crowned, the events continue nonstop. The games range from highly competitive hockey, basketball and logging-skills tournaments, to the humorous challenges of volleyball played in knee-deep snow, broom ball and controlling an inner tube as it races downhill.

The carnival also hosts two parades, the Gala and Kiddie Parade. The Gala involves the entire community in a distinctly North Country display of antics and clowning around.

The famed Ice Palace, which appears in almost all tourist publications depicting winter in the North Country, began as an outgrowth of the village's ice industry, which harvested ice from local lakes for use in early 20th-century ice boxes. The elaborate structure continues to evolve every year, and it's a sight to behold on the first and last days of the carnival when fireworks serve as a backdrop.

The carnival is held during the first week of February. Most events are free.

Empire State Winter Games
Olympic Center, Main St., Lake Placid • 523-1655

These citizen games, held in late February and early March, offer competition in figure and speed skating, luge, bobsled, cross-country and downhill skiing, and other winter sports. Fireworks, special events and an atmosphere of fun prevail during the games. Spectators pay fees to attend certain events, but many are free. Athletes compete at various skill levels.

Plattsburgh/Western Lake Champlain Region

Rouses Point Winter Carnival
throughout Rouses Point • 297-3040

Oh, what we will do to keep ourselves amused during the winter? Want to play shuffleboard or compete in a foot race? Traditionally held in late February, this carnival offers antiques, games, races and music. For a hearty meal, attend the Perch and Prime Rib dinner for $11.95. For the most part, admission to events is free for spectators, but small fees (less than $5) apply to compete in many events. All proceeds benefit a local charity.

Lake George/ Upper Hudson Region

Lake Luzerne Winter Extravaganza
N.Y. Rt. 9N, Lake Luzerne • 696-2713

For one day in early February (usually on the first weekend), you can enjoy watching or participating in that most American of winter traditions — the outhouse race. If you'd prefer another option, you can choose from sleigh rides, snow sculpting and snowshoe races. Too cold for that stuff? Then enjoy the craft fair. This is as fun as February gets.

Hague Winter Carnival
Town of Hague • 543-6161

If you're on a roll after enjoying the Lake Luzerne Winter Extravaganza on the first weekend in February (see previous entry), you can keep your activity momentum going on the second weekend with this event. Held in Hague, at the northern end of Lake George, this festival starts out with a torchlight parade Friday night and "peaks" with the National Ice Auger competition on Saturday. Want to see how fast somebody can drill through the frozen surface of Lake George? This is the place to find out. You'll also find plenty of food and other activities throughout town.

Lake George Regional Winter Festival
throughout Lake George • 668-2233

Who said there's nothing to do in February around here? This "event" is really a series of events over the course of four consecutive weekends that helps take the "dead" out of "dead of winter." You can witness or participate in lots of fun races and activities, beginning with the "Coronation Ball" that kicks off the event. From that point, all kinds of stuff starts happening all over the place: International Dog Sled Weight Pulls (pretty much what it sounds like), a "Polar Bear Swim," (nothing at all what it sounds like — humans do the ice-cold lake dipping!), ice sculpting, fireworks, snowmobile races, Olympic-style games for the kids and on and on. In all, more than 50 festival-related activities take place during the month, so your bound to find something to get you out and about.

Southern Adirondack Lakes Region

Indian Lake Winter Festival
throughout the Town of Indian Lake • 648-5112

Usually held over President's Weekend, this festival celebrates midwinter with a variety of outdoor and indoor activities. You can choose from "snow golf," a snowshoe softball game, ice fishing and snowmobile runs for outdoor fun. Indoors, you can enjoy the craft show, book sale or one of the community suppers and breakfasts taking place throughout town this weekend.

FebFest
throughout the Town of Speculator
• 548-4521

Expanded from one weekend to four in 1997, this series of events includes a familiar combination of outdoor and indoor fun. Most activities are geared for the whole family, so if the kids are feeling as house-bound as you are, this could be your solution. Outdoors, you can enjoy dog-sled races, ice-fishing contest, cross-country ski races and even a (brrr!) parachute jump near the beach on Lake Pleasant. Indoors, there's storytelling, films and games for the kids.

Old Forge/
Raquette Lake Region

Raquette Lake Winter Carnival
various locations around Raquette Lake
• 624-3077

Mid-February means big fun around Raquette Lake, as the Winter Carnival brings folks out from in front of the wood stove and onto the frozen lake and its surroundings. There's lots of games, races, food, hot chocolate and fun for everyone involved.

March

Lake Placid/
Tri-Lakes Region

Ice Breaker Canoe Race
Saranac River, downtown Saranac Lake
• 891-1990

The first canoe race of the season — in late March — is wet, wild, cold and not taken very seriously. In fact, the 5-mile race down the Saranac River is as much about staying warm as winning. There are various categories to enter ($12 entry fee).

Approximately 20 major canoe races take place in the North Country throughout the year, beginning with the Ice Breaker and ending with the Fall Foliage race in Tupper Lake. The races take place on lakes in the Saranac Lake, Tupper,

Blue Mountain and Newcomb areas, and on rivers such as the Hudson, Ausable, Bog, Oswegatchie, Erie Canal and Grasse. For additional information, contact the Saranac Lake Chamber of Commerce at the listed number.

Lake George/
Upper Hudson Region

New York State High School Basketball Championships
Glens Falls Civic Center, Glen St., Glens Falls • 798-0202

For two weekends in mid-March, the southern Adirondacks is the center of the high school basketball universe for New York State. Teams representing schools from throughout the state and from every size classification vie for their respective state titles in the 4,800-seat Civic Center. You can't help but get caught up in the excitement (kind of like a miniature Final Four), even if you don't know any of the teams. These are the best players, teams and coaches in the state, so sit back and watch future college and maybe even pro stars battle it out.

Southern Adirondack
Lakes Region

St. Urho's Festival
Lapland Lake Cross-Country Ski Center, 139 Lapland Lake Rd., Benson
• 863-4974

A Finnish spoof on St. Patrick's Day, St. Urho was "invented" by Finnish-Americans so they could have a reason to celebrate mid-March too!

St. Urho apparently protects the Finns from losing their crops of grapes to grasshoppers (all part of the illusion since neither exists in Finland!), so all of the activities are themed to "give thanks" for this. The Finns have a good sense of humor, and it's exhibited through the variety of fun and funny events that take place this day. Your choices include the "Lusikka Viesti" (grape-on-a-spoon ski race), the "Grasshopper Hoppett Loppett" (three-legged ski race) and the Jiminy Cricket Purple and Green Costume Contest for the kids. There are also horse-drawn sleigh rides, snowcat rides and an outdoor barbecue to keep your insides warm and full.

April

Lake Placid/
Tri-Lakes Region

Pedal, Paddle, Pole Race
Cascade Ski Touring Center, N.Y. Rt. 73, Lake Placid • 523-9605

We try to say goodbye to winter and hello to spring in early April as teams of four bike, paddle down the Ausable River and cross-country ski. This event marks the beginning of a host of bicycle, canoe and footraces held throughout the region. While many events are for the more serious athlete, at some point an event is offered for virtually any skill level; a few are even designed for children.

There are simply too many races to list, so it is best to ask for information at Chamber of Commerce offices or other information centers. Many of these events are co-sponsored by local sporting good stores — also good places to get the lowdown about upcoming events.

Typically, High Peak Cyclery, 523-3764; Mountain Run, 523-9443; or World Cup Ski and Bike, 359-9481, is involved in your event of interest; if they are not, the staff will direct you to a good source.

Ausable River Whitewater Derby
Ausable River, along N.Y. Rt. 9N, Keene to Jay • 946-7200

The late April challenge: Stay upright for 6 miles in the fast-flowing whitewater of the east branch of the Ausable River. Don't necessarily expect to win the first time out; but you will pick up a few pointers from some very good racers. The race begins at the intersection of N.Y. routes 9N and 73 in Keene and ends in Jay, the next town downriver. The entry fee is less than $10.

May

Plattsburgh/Western
Lake Champlain Region

Rotary International
Fishing Classic
Snug Harbor Marina, N.Y. Rt. 9N, Plattsburgh • 564-2035

The water is still a wee bit cold in late May, but since the derby is held soon after ice out, the fishing is generally better than average as is the grand prize money for the largest fish — approximately $17,000! About 1,200 anglers from across the country, including many professionals, compete in this event. Some $30,000 of prize money from the entry pool ($30 per person) is awarded in various categories. Since some serious money is involved, competitors use boats of every kind, especially those with fish-finder gadgets. This is not exactly a spectator sport because the fishing takes place all over Lake Champlain.

Essex Organ Concert Series
Essex Community Church, Main St., Essex • 963-7766

This concert series is hosted by the Essex Community Church. Organists from around the world perform on a restored tracker organ. The series generally begins in late May and runs into August. The schedule varies. Admission is $5 per person per performance; the concerts begin at 7:30 PM.

INSIDERS' TIP

The Saranac Lake Chamber of Commerce, 891-1990 or 891-1991, compiles a listing of all the canoe and kayak races in the region and publishes a complete guide to North Country Canoe Races. Call for a copy.

Lake George/ Upper Hudson Region

Annual Whitewater Derby
off N.Y. Rt. 28, North Creek • 251-2612, (800) 896-5428

With the chilly waters of the upper Hudson River running fast and high, this event in early May celebrates the end of winter with a variety of "just for fun" and "serious" canoe and kayak races. There's a Street Fair with rides and game booths along Main Street and the Derby Music Festival at Ski Bowl Park. You don't have to be an expert to participate in the Crazy Canoe Race, but you probably want to be in decent shape to try the "40-Mile Paddle." It's fun just to watch, too, so grab something to eat from one of the nearby vendors, try to find a spot that's not muddy, and enjoy!

The Queen's Great Boat Race
Bolton Landing, Lake George • 668-5771

Here's a once-a-year opportunity to see cruise boats usually reserved for calmly plying the waters for diners or "leaf-peepers" battle each other for the speed title of Lake George. Of course, "speed" is a relative term here; the primary term is "fun." Lake George Steamboat Company's *Mohican*, Shoreline Cruise's *MV Horican* and *Defiance*, and The Sagamore's *Morgan* are the participating vessels in this 10-mile race (actually, it's more of a processional) from Bolton Landing south to Lake George village. The race is really just a good excuse for the first festival of the spring, and after the long winter, not much excuse is needed. The slate of activities over the weekend includes live bands, a boat show, tethered hot-air balloon flights and a big fireworks display on Saturday evening.

Southern Adirondack Lakes Region

Indian Lake Town-wide Flea Market
Indian Lake • 648-5112, (800) 328-LAKE

Pretty much what it sounds like, this event is usually held over the third weekend in May.

It's as informal as the town, with no big entertainment or fancy food displays. However, if you are itching to get out, here's your chance to walk around and do some browsing with the "locals" after a long, cold winter. Depending on the weather, you'll find at least a couple dozen neighbors and vendors set up along the street. You might even find some great bargains and new friends.

Old Forge/ Raquette Lake Region

Giant Garage Sale
various locations from Old Forge to Inlet • (315) 369-6983

Over Memorial Day weekend, this informal area-wide flea market/garage sale stretches from Main Street in Old Forge all the way to Inlet, some 10 miles away. Along the way, friends and neighbors have set up everything from the simple to the elaborate displays of merchandise they no longer find essential. Good bargains on everything from kids' clothing to books to garden tools are everywhere, so take your time and browse all day.

June

Lake Placid/ Tri-Lakes Region

The Great Adirondack Outdoor Rendezvous
N.Y. Rt. 73, Lake Placid • 523-3961

The Rendezvous is a family-oriented, interactive three-day "campfire" filled with hands-on demonstrations, seminars, equipment displays and more — all related to the outdoors. If you want to learn about rafting, fly-fishing, mountain biking and such, bring along your tent or RV and join in the campfest. The camping fee plus admission ranges from $20 to $60. Single-day admission is also available for approximately $4. If you are not sure whther or not you would like a particular sport, or if you want to find out more about a sport that you know nothing about, the Rendezvous is a good place to consult vendors, suppliers and knowledgeable people about the activity. Although there is a great deal of knowledge (and some used tents) exchanged, there are also a few tall tales told and a bit of singing by some local professionals.

Whiteface Mountain Footrace
N.Y. Rt. 431, Wilmington • 946-2255

The footrace is all uphill — all 8.3 miles — to the top of Whiteface Mountain via the Veterans Memorial Highway (N.Y. 431). This early June event is one tough race as the climb is constant and steep. The entry fee for competitors is $15, which generally includes a buffet following the race. The 1998 race marks the 20th anniversary of this event.

Lake Colby Fishing Derby for Kids
Lake Colby, N.Y. Rt. 73, Saranac Lake • 891-4309

If you don't know a thing about fishing, you can quickly learn from a member of the Saranac Lake Fish and Game Club, which sponsors this event. Everyone comes out a winner at this mid-June derby, which has become a traditional way for families to celebrate Father's Day. The derby begins at 8 AM and ends at noon, with prizes awarded (generally fishing gear) for the biggest fish, the most fish and whatever else can be imagined to make as many kids as possible winners. The admission fee is less than $5 per family.

I Love New York Horse Show
Horse Show Grounds, N.Y. Rt. 73, Lake Placid • 523-9625

Many of the world's top riders and mounts compete in this Grand Prix equestrian event. Purses are in the $50,000 range, so this is a major competition. The event begins in late June and runs into July. Admission costs around $5, but many local businesses often have a few day passes available for the asking.

Lake George/ Upper Hudson Region

Americade
throughout Lake George • 656-3696

Depending on how you want to look at it, this is either one of the biggest and best events of the whole year, or one of the biggest and best weekends to head out of town. Going on now for more than 15 years, this annual reunion brings an estimated 35,000 motorcycle enthusiasts into the Lake George area for a long weekend in early June. The activities are as "all over the map," as are the participants, with everything from charity golf events to guided bike tours throughout the area to an exposition with 200 vendors. The highlight of the week is the huge motorcycle parade, which starts at the Million Dollar Beach on Lake George, rolls through Lake George village, then winds its way up the Prospect Mountain Veteran's Memorial Highway to the 2,000-foot summit. These are serious cycle enthusiasts, but fun-loving, friendly folks, so don't hesitate to join in the fun.

LARAC Arts & Crafts Festival
Glens Falls City Park, off Glen St., Glens Falls • 798-1144

One of the biggest and most popular arts festivals in the Adirondacks, this event draws thousands of arts enthusiasts, craft groupies and families in search of free fun. It is usually held the second weekend in June and features more than 200 art and craft exhibitors set up in the park. Live music and lively food are spread throughout the park.

This is a great way to stroll away spring and welcome the coming of summer. The LARAC Arts & Crafts Festival takes place both Saturday and Sunday from 10 AM until 5 PM.

Adirondack Air Show
Warren County Airport, County Line Rd., Glens Falls • 798-2082

Held for the first time in 1997, this early

Photo: Warren County Tourism Department

The Adirondack Balloon Festival attracts thousands of spectators to Glens Falls.

June event is the only one of its kind in the Adirondack region. You can get up-close and personal with a variety of vintage and military aircraft, then sit back and watch performers such as the Black Hawk Aerobatic Team and the Misty Blues Skydiving Show. The Adirondack Air Show is held on both Saturday and Sunday, and costs $10 for adults, $5 for students (K through 12); children younger than 5 get in free.

Summerfest
Shepard's Park, Canada St., Lake George • 668-5755

This late June event celebrates the long-awaited arrival of summer after the long winter and two or three days of spring. Live music, children's activities, food vendors, more than 100 arts and crafts displays and the beautiful setting of the Lake George waterfront make this a fun, free and free-spirited weekend for all.

Southern Adirondack Lakes Region

No-Octane Regatta Weekend
Adirondack Museum and various other locations, Blue Mountain Lake
• 352-7311

Held on a weekend in mid-June (late spring by Adirondack standards), this is a fun event for both children and adults, with the only prerequisite being that you need to like boats (at least a little). It was conceived in 1991 as a celebration of the history of boats and boating in the Adirondacks. Events during the weekend take place at the Adirondack Museum, the town beach and the Adirondack Lakes Center for the Arts (ALCA) as well as other community locations.

Kids enjoy watching the Toy Boat Regatta on the reflecting pool at the museum, along with other children's activities such as puppet shows. Adults appreciate the Grand Parade of wooden boats on Blue Mountain Lake (a couple miles from the museum), arts and crafts exhibits at the ALCA, and the variety of fun and funny regattas and races featuring Adirondack guide boats, sailing canoes and wood-canvas canoes. During the three-day event, you can also participate in a variety of workshops, see demonstrations on boat construction and take a behind-the-scenes tour of this renowned museum's boat collection. There's plenty of food options at the sprawling museum as well as in the village of Blue Mountain Lake. Some of the activities charge admission, others are free, so call ahead to get details before planning your visit.

Old Forge/ Raquette Lake Region

Neighbor Day
Arts Center, Main St., Old Forge • (315) 369-6411

Usually held in early June, this event features an open house at the Arts Center/Old Forge, a chicken barbecue, live music and educational lectures on Adirondack history and culture. As much as anything, it's a chance for folks around here to finally say goodbye to winter, wonder what happened to spring, and say hello to summer and each other all in one event.

July

Lake Placid/ Tri-Lakes Region

The Adirondack Festival of American Music
P.O. Box 562, Saranac Lake 12983 • 891-1990

For 25 years, this month-long festival, centered in Saranac Lake, has featured a variety of world-class performances of choral, chamber and classical music. The schedule of events varies depending upon location as does the admission fee, which is generally in the $5 range. Contact series musical director Gregg Smith at the listed address and phone number for up-to-date information about performers.

Saturday Night Ice Show
Olympic Center, Main St., Lake Placid • 523-1655

Most Saturday nights at 7:30 PM in July and August, Lake Placid's Olympic Center hosts a figure-skating show. The talent varies from skaters trying out their programs for the first time, to well-rehearsed skaters, even some world-class skaters. Admission is in the $5 range, and the show lasts for about two hours. Don't arrive late as these shows often sell out.

Lake Placid Sinfonietta Concert in the Park
Main St., Lake Placid • 523-2445

The famed Lake Placid Sinfonietta has attracted some of the world's finest concert musicians. Performances are scheduled every Wednesday evening at 7 PM, July through August, and take place in the band shell on Main Street. Bring a blanket or a lawn chair and get there early for a prime location.

Friday Night Concerts
Riverside Park, Broadway Ave., Saranac Lake • 891-1990

The entire town comes out for these Friday evening (7 PM) shows in July and August. The free shows covering a range of musical genres, from pop to classical to rockin' blues, are performed by some very talented groups from all over the country. Once in a while, some other antics — jugglers, clowns, storytellers and magic shows — are tossed into the mix.

Adirondack Almanac Lecture Series
Adirondack Park Visitor Center, N.Y. Rt. 30, Paul Smiths • 327-3000

Every Wednesday evening during July and August at 7:30 PM, a free lecture on some aspect of the natural history of the Adirondacks is presented. Stargazing with the Tri-

Lakes Astronomy Club generally follows the lecture.

Willard Hanmer Guideboat and Canoe Race
Lake Flower, River St., Saranac Lake
• 891-1990

The Adirondack guideboat was a local invention, created in the late 1800s as a means to transport guides and clients in and around the wilderness. Many of these classic handcrafted boats are on display, along with modern versions. The race features solo, tandem and eight-person war canoes. The race is held in early July, and the entry fee is $12 per person.

The Saranac Lake Chamber of Commerce schedules a host of canoe races, water-ski challenges and other events during the summer. If you are going to be in the area, give the chamber a call at the listed number to find out what's going on.

Jay Summer Concert Series
Jay Village Green, N.Y. Rt. 9N, Jay
• 946-7301

Throughout July and August, summer concerts are held every Saturday at 6:30 PM on the Jay Village Green. Jay is a small town, so don't expect any big-name national acts. Bring a lawn chair, sit back and relax with the folk, pop or country performers in this easy-going little town. Don't forget your fishing rod — the Ausable River and its trout beckon just below the village green.

Old Time Folkcraft Fair
N.Y. Rt. 22, Willsboro • 963-4478

Traditionally held on the final Saturday of July, the fair celebrates "things done well by hand." There are plenty of fine crafts on sale from approximately 100 artisans who create all their pieces by hand. During the past 15 years, the fair has developed a loyal following of both artisans and buyers because of the high quality of the crafts.

Many artisans offer demonstrations of their craft during the fair. Like most craft fairs in the region, there's something to be found here in every price range. Items include baskets, stenciled items, pottery, paintings and knitted products. Admission is free.

Woodsmen's Field Days
Municipal Park, N.Y. Rt. 3, Tupper Lake
• 359-3328

Logging and lumberjacks have played a significant role in the history of Tupper Lake, and the village celebrates its heritage with old-time lumberjack skill competitions, such as ax-throwing, log rolling, speed chopping, skidding, etc. There are parades, equipment displays and games for kids. The event is traditionally held the second weekend in July, and there is a $4 admission fee.

Craftfest
The Lodge, N.Y. Rt. 30, Lake Clear
• 891-1990

This is one of the few juried shows of authentic Adirondack crafts. It's held mid-July, and there are some 100 craft vendors of the highest quality. Food is available. Musical entertainment, generally of the folk or bluegrass variety, helps keep the shoppers in an upbeat mood. There is a $2 admission fee.

Tinman Triathlon
60 Park St., Tupper Lake • 359-3328

This mid-July event is not for the faint of heart. The three legs consist of a 1.2-mile swim in cool 65 degree waters, a 56-mile bike race on a rolling course and a 13.1-mile run through the wilderness and ending in downtown Tupper Lake. The fees for competitors — anyone ages 15 to 70 can take the challenge — begin at $75 with teams at $125. There is no fee to watch the events, which are held in downtown Tupper Lake.

Plattsburgh/Western Lake Champlain Region

Concert on the Bluff
Clinton Community College, N.Y. Rt. 22, Plattsburgh • 562-4160

A series of 6:30 PM concerts, ranging from classical to pop, is presented in July and August on the bluff at the community college overlooking Lake Champlain. The view of the lake is great. Bring your own lawn chair or blanket.

Meadowmount School of Music
Lewis-Wadhams Rd., Westport
• 873-2063

This summer school for accomplished young violinists, violists and cellists offers a series of free concerts throughout July and August, generally starting at 7:30 PM Sunday, Monday and Wednesday. Call for information on special concerts.

Ticonderoga Festival Guild
Village Green, Montcalm St.,
Ticonderoga • 585-6716

Every Friday evening in July and August at 8 PM, artists and ensembles from the region and beyond perform under the tent in downtown Ti. The programs are generally classical. Admission is $8 per adult, with special prices for tickets to all events.

The guild presents storytelling, clowning, music and more during its award-winning children's program series every Wednesday morning. All children's events are free.

Antiques Show and Vintage Car Meet Festival
Old Plattsburgh Air Force Base,
Plattsburgh • 561-0340

The Clinton County Historical Association sponsors this mid-July event. If antique cars — many from before most of us were born — are your thing, this festival has plenty, with some for just show and others for sale. You'll also find a vintage auto exhibition and judging contest, horse-drawn carriage rides, fife and drum corps providing musical entertainment and other activities. Admission is $4 for adults, and kids younger than 15 get in free. The hours are 10 AM to 4 PM.

Clinton County Fair
N.Y. Rt. 3, Plattsburgh • 565-3300

This week-long, mid-July event is the largest county fair in the region. You'll find plenty of rides of the swirling, spinning and rolling kinds plus games of chance in which the odds are generally not in your favor, but the big stuffed animal prize is too enticing not to try your luck. You also will find farm-type exhibits, stunt shows and music performed by some nationally known acts, generally of the country variety. And the food is the typical fair fare that has ruined many a diet. Admission costs approximately $7 per person.

Mayor's Cup Sailing Race and Landlubber Festival
throughout downtown Plattsburgh
• 563-7709

The Mayor's Cup is the largest event in Plattsburgh and attracts thousands of visitors each year in mid-July. The race itself has various divisions for sailboats. When spectators tire of viewing the race from the many vantage points in the downtown area, they can head to the Landlubber's Festival, starting at 10 AM near the Farmers' Market. Three entertainment stages host different acts: jazz and other instrumental music on one stage; acrobats and such on another; and entertainment just for kids on the third. Street entertainers also cruise about the area an provide many pleasant surprises. Many area restaurants offer food in street cafes, and some even provide entertainment. Admission to the festival is free. Various fees apply to the racers, however. A word of advice for spectators: Begin your quest for parking as soon as you near the downtown area.

FYI

Unless otherwise noted, the area code for all phone numbers listed in this guide is 518.

Press-Republican Sand Sculpture Competition
Cumberland Bay State Park, 152
Cumberland Bay Rd., Plattsburgh
• 288-7323 newspaper, 563-5240 park

Folks of all ages can enjoy a day of sun and fun at this mid-July competition sponsored by the *Press-Republican*. Participants vie to build the biggest, best and most creative sand castles on the biggest beach on Lake Champlain, and spectators enjoy the sculptors' creations. The event gets underway mid-morning. Winners in different categories receive modest cash prizes. There is no entry fee for either participants or spectators.

Photo: Dave Paczak

The Saranac Lake Winter Carnival and its famous ice castle are festive highlights of winter.

Lake George/ Upper Hudson Region

Summer Jam
West Mountain Ski Area, West Mountain Rd., Glens Falls • 761-9890

Vintage rock 'n' roll music for the adults, activities like the Bouncy Bounce and face painting for the kids, lots of food for the hungry at the food court, and a big fireworks display for everyone sum up Summer Jam. Usually held the evening of July 3 on the grounds of the West Mountain Ski Area, this event is free (parking costs $1 per vehicle). The gates open a 5 PM, the show starts at 7:30 PM, and fireworks close out the evening at 10 PM.

Smoke-eaters Jamboree
Recreation Field, off Library Ave., Warrensburg • 623-9598

Here's your chance to (safely) watch expert fire fighters in action as they compete in a variety of skill contests. The late July weekend also includes a carnival with games, live music and plenty of food and drink.

Southern Adirondack Lakes Region

Bleecker Black Fly Festival
Town Hall, CR 112, Bleecker • 725-6897

Here's something you won't find anywhere else. A celebration (somewhat tongue-in-cheek) of that early summer pest, the black-fly, this event is small but unique. How many other festivals crown a Black Fly Queen (talk about a resume-builder!). You can also enjoy the parade, craft exhibitors, music and community pancake breakfast during the course of the weekend. The Black Fly Festival is usually held the third weekend of July. Don't expect too much and you'll be pleasantly surprised by the simple fun you'll have here.

Caroga Historical Association Annual Art Show & Sale
London Bridge Rd., Caroga Lake
• 835-4400

This mid-July event, held on a Saturday, features a mix of art for sale and entertainment of the acoustic or choral variety for free. Combine it with a visit to Sherman's Park (see our Kidstuff chapter) for soft ice cream and a spin on the Ferris wheel for a full day of browsing and fun.

Piseco Craft Fair
Piseco Community Hall, Piseco Lake Rd., Piseco • 548-8732

This one-day event, sponsored by the Piseco Women's Club, celebrated its 20th anniversary in 1997. Usually held the last Saturday in July, it features more than 50 craft exhibitors plus food and refreshments. You'll find handmade quilts, woodwork, cross-stitching, pottery and more on display here.

Old Forge/ Raquette Lake Region

Adirondack Discovery
P.O. Box 545, Inlet 13360
• (315) 357-3598

Adirondack Discovery coordinates a parkwide lecture program beginning in July and continuing throughout summer in dozens of locations. The free evening lectures and daytime outings cover virtually every topic on Adirondack history, lore and ecology. Wherever you stay in the Adirondack region, Adirondack Discovery is likely to offer a program. The schedule is variable, so call for up-to-date information.

Annual Craft Fair
North Street Pavilion, North St., Old Forge • (315) 369-6411

One of dozens of events sponsored and organized by the Arts Center/Old Forge, this three-day event usually takes place over the first weekend in July. You can browse among the more than 75 craft exhibitors in attendance. Admission costs $2 per person.

Annual Arts in the Park Craft Fair
Arrowhead Park, N.Y. Rt. 28, Inlet
• (315) 357-5501

Celebrating its 21st anniversary in 1997, this longtime event features two days of outdoor craft displays, food and music — all in the scenic setting of Inlet's Arrowhead Park. A free shuttle bus will take you from nearby Fern Park to the fair if you don't want the hassle of finding a parking spot.

August

Lake Placid/ Tri-Lakes Region

Can-Am Rugby Tournament
throughout Saranac Lake and Lake Placid • 891-1990

This is America's largest rugby tournament with more than 100 teams from Canada and the United States participating. The event is held at various locations in Saranac Lake and Lake Placid. Make sure you have hotel reservations if you plan on visiting the area during Rugby week, the first weekend in August. Admission for spectators is free. A few fans along the sidelines may even be able to explain the rules of this game to you.

Adirondack Wildlife Festival
Visitor Interpretive Center, N.Y. Rt. 30, Paul Smiths • 327-3000

This one-day festival in early August celebrates the flora and fauna of the Adirondacks through crafts, music, special trail walks and presentations. There are lots of fun activities — craft demonstrations, nature trail explorations and live animal demonstrations with raptors and perhaps a wild wolf — in which kids, in particular, can experience hands-on learning.

Civil War Encampment & Re-enactment
John Brown's Farm, John Brown Rd., Lake Placid • 523-3900

In the early part of the month, Civil War buffs from far and wide set up camp in the fields on John Brown's farm and relive what it was like during the 1860s. Everything is authentic. A similar encampment is held in Fort Ticonderoga in early fall.

Whiteface Mountain Native American Festival
Whiteface Mountain, N.Y. Rt. 73, Wilmington • 946-2223

This early August festival features native dancers, storytellers, cultural presentations and art and crafts, including a kids craft tent. The admission fee is $7 for adults, $5 for children. Food is available.

Plattsburgh/Western Lake Champlain Region

Lake Champlain Antique Boat Show
Essex Marina, off N.Y. Rt. 22, Essex • 963-7222

This boat show, held in early August, celebrates the nearly 200-year maritime history of Essex by presenting wooden power boats and antique sailboats. The oldest boat in the 1996 show was a 35-foot, six-cylinder gas-powered motor boat built in 1902; another antique classic measured 65 feet. Many of the boats are hand-crafted and come from all over Lake Champlain. Special daytrips are provided on a classic 42-foot Chris Craft to anyone fighting cancer. This is an event to learn about old — oops, antique — boats. Ask questions — you will find plenty of boaters willing to provide detailed answers. Admission is free.

Essex County Fair
Westport Fairgrounds, N.Y. Rt. 9N, Westport • 962-4810

This is an old-fashioned country fair with a 150-year tradition. It offers fairgoers an unusual mix of new and old with plenty of spinning, rotating and swinging rides for the younger generation as well as more sedate entertainment such as jugglers and clowns. Vendors, crafters and hobbyists of all types set up their wares for sale and display under tents. Watercolor and oil paintings are exhibited and judged for rib-

bons, while groups such as the state police provide informational booths. There's also a petting zoo, livestock and agricultural displays, plenty of 4-H exhibits by the Cooperative Extension Service and food for every taste.

The five-day event is held mid-August. Admission costs $5 for adults, and children 16 and younger get in free. Hours are generally 9 AM to 10 PM.

Pondstock
Twin Ponds Resort Campsite, 224 Fuller St., Peru • 643-9305

In the middle of the month, eight blues, rock, country and reggae bands perform throughout the day and evening at the popular Twin Ponds campground. The $20 per person fee includes all music and two nights' camping. A portion of the proceeds is donated to charity.

Heritage Day
Penfield Museum, off N.Y. Rt. 22, Crown Point • 597-3804

This is one of three fund-raising events for the Penfield Museum, the birthplace of the electrical age (see Arts and Culture). Heritage Day is held in early to mid-August and features a craft fair of contemporary arts. There is music (often bluegrass) during the day, oxen and pony rides and demonstrations by the various crafters. To us the best deal here is the chicken barbecue for $7 per person. Admission to the fair is free.

Lake George/ Upper Hudson Region

Warren County Country Fair
County Fairground, Horicon Ave., Warrensburg • 623-3291

A great old-fashioned family country fair, this early August event combines four days of fun and food for all ages. There's a carnival midway, animal and agricultural exhibits, performances by local bands, even a talent show featuring local youth. If you look real close, you might see the ghost of Norman Rockwell sitting somewhere with a sketch pad — this is as Americana as it gets. Admission is free for children 11 and younger, $2 for youth ages 12 to 18 and $3 for adults.

Adirondack Folk Music Festival
Dock St., Schroon Lake • 532-9259

This two-day mid-August music festival is an Adirondack classic. But music is only part of the action, as there are demonstrations and workshops by Adirondack artisans and plenty of good food. Bring your own instrument and take part in the never-ending jams. Admission costs $10 for adults and teens 15 and older; children younger than 15 get in free. Call the Schroon Lake Arts Council at the listed number for details about other planned events.

Southern Adirondack Lakes Region

Adirondack Opry
Caroga Lake Historical Association and Museum, London Bridge Rd., Caroga Lake • 835-4400

Usually on a Thursday evening in mid-August, this performance event presents a mix of musical styles and forms reflective of the Adirondacks. Past events have featured fiddlers, folk singers and storytellers. Admission is free to this sponsored event.

Old Forge/ Raquette Lake Region

Fulton Chain House Tour Benefit
on Fulton Chain of Lakes, Old Forge to Inlet • (315) 369-6411

As they used to say on *Monty Python's Flying Circus*, "And now for something completely different." Here's your chance to visit beautiful homes — some contemporary, some historic — along the Fulton Chain of Lakes via "party barge" — that is, pontoon boat. It's a great way to see the sights, both inside and out, and enjoy some refreshments along the way. As you might expect, this benefit for the Arts Center/Old Forge is a popular event, and reservations are required.

The cost is $20 for Arts Center members and $25 for nonmembers and guests.

September

Lake Placid/ Tri-Lakes Region

Olympic Classic Car Show
Main St., Lake Placid • 523-2633

The speed-skating oval in Lake Placid is filled with classic cars, motorcycles and street rods of all makes and models for this annual swap meet and competition. The cars may include classics from the Model A and T era to more recent vintages, such as classic Chevys and Ford Mustangs. The cost to exhibit a car is $15. Admission for spectators costs $3 per person. In previous years some 100 cars were exhibited at the event, and hundreds more lined the streets.

Plattsburgh/Western Lake Champlain Region

Field, Forest and Stream Festival
Adirondack Center Museum, N.Y. Rt. 9N, Elizabethtown • 873-6466

This celebration of the harvest, hunt and traditional North Country recreation is filled with activities such as guideboat-, basket- and furniture-making demonstrations, fly tying and maple sugaring. Music, storytelling and other antics of local talent, along with contests and activities for kids, provide additional amusements.

The festival usually is held the last Saturday of September. Admission is $4 for adults and $2 for kids.

Lake George/ Upper Hudson Region

Lake George Jazz Festival
Shepard Park, Canada St., Lake George • 686-2616

You can wrap up the summer season the weekend after Labor Day by swinging to the sounds of jazz groups from across New York State along the shore of Lake George. The free music and fun is continuous Saturday and Sunday afternoon, and Shepard Park is a beautiful setting in which to enjoy it.

Most of the summer tourist crowd is long gone, so you're likely to enjoy a little more "elbow room" as well.

Oktoberfest
The Great Escape, U.S. Hwy. 9, Lake George • 792-3500

Who says all the fun ends on Labor Day? The third weekend in September at The Great Escape (see our Kidstuff chapter) would prove them wrong, for sure. The recipe for fun? Take a genuine German feast with plenty of bratwurst and beer; add continuous performances by German bands and folk dancers; toss in more than 20 available thrill rides (including the renowned Comet roller coaster — *not* a good bratwurst follow-up); and sprinkle in a craft show with a few dozen exhibitors. . . . You've got one hoppin' time. Oh, did we mention you'll be surrounded by a sea of colorful autumn leaves? You can enjoy all of this for $11.95, or just $6.95 for general admission (without access to the rides, but what fun is that?!).

Oktoberfest at Gore Mountain
Gore Mountain, off N.Y. Rt. 28, North Creek • 251-2612

If you just didn't get enough tuba music at The Great Escape's Oktoberfest, you can enjoy this festive follow-up the very next weekend (the last weekend in September). Take all the fun stuff we described in the previous entry, delete the amusement rides, add in the awesome fall scenery you can experience while riding New York's only gondola to the top of the mountain, and you've got Oktoberfest at Gore. Admission is $6 for adults and teens and $4 for children 12 and younger.

Adirondack Balloon Festival
Warren County Airport, County Line Rd., Glens Falls • 761-6366

A regional fall tradition for more than 25 years, this late September event, usually held the third weekend of the month, is one of the biggest hot-air balloon festivals in the East.

As many as 100 hot-air balloons fill the sky near Glens Falls and Lake George from Friday evening through Sunday afternoon. The big "ascensions" take place (very) early on Saturday and Sunday morning — around 6:30 AM! That's when the winds are calmest, which is essential if you're trying to ride a 75-foot-tall dinosaur balloon around safely. You'll also see flying polar bear balloons, a giant newspaper balloon and lots of other crazy shapes that your kids will get a real charge out of (enough to justify the early wake up). There is a also variety of activities — music, crafts and food — going on at the airport while the balloons are earthbound. If you'd prefer the evening activities, check out the Moon Glow in the Lake George Battlefield Park, where 20 balloons are lit up like giant party lamps just as darkness falls. It's quite a sight — and impressive enough to make you forget about the inevitable traffic you'll have to deal with to see it.

Southern Adirondack Lakes Region

Eagle Mills Cider Company Annual Arts & Crafts Show
Eagle Mills Rd., off N.Y. Rt. 29, Broadalbin • 883-8700

Just a teensy bit south of the Adirondack Park border, this event is worth crossing the boundary for. It combines a big craft show with more than 150 exhibitors, along with gemstone mining, fresh-baked pies, cider doughnuts and a real waterwheel-powered cider mill. The covered bridge, waterfall and mill pond all add to the classic fall ambiance.

This event is repeated over two consecutive weekends — usually the last weekend in September and the first weekend in October. The pies and doughnuts are so good, we recommend you visit both events.

Rustic Mountain Furniture Maker's Fair
Adirondack Museum, N.Y. Rt. 30, Blue Mountain Lake • 352-7311

"Unique" accurately describes what you will see at this event since everything is "one-of-a-kind" and made from natural materials. Some of it is beautiful, some functional, and some just downright different-looking. In all, some 35 rustic furniture makers from all corners of America descend on Blue Mountain Lake for this early September event. The $10 museum admission price covers the fair as well as a variety of workshops, demonstrations and activities.

Old Forge/
Raquette Lake Region

Raquette Lake Clambake
Raquette Lake Fire Hall, N.Y. Rt. 28, Raquette Lake • (315) 354-4223

We include this early September event because it celebrated its 50th anniversary in 1997, so you know it's got to be good times and good eats! In fact, it's all you can eat at this traditional event featuring live music, steamed clams and full tummies.

Inlet Fall Festival
Fern Park, off N.Y. Rt. 28, Inlet • (315) 357-3281

Celebrate the changing seasons at this late September event, which kicks off with a parade from Woods Hotel to Fern Park. At the park, there's music, crafts and antiques for the adults, animals on display for the kids plus games, demonstrations and lots of food!

October

Lake Placid/
Tri-Lakes Region

Octoberfest
Whiteface Mountain, N.Y. Rt. 73, Wilmington • 523-1655

Ump-pa-ba. Omp-pa-ba. You'll find plenty of German music, food and drink, crafters selling their wares and activities for kids at Whiteface Mountain in early October at the first Octoberfest of the season. We don't think they are celebrating their harvest, but rather the

potential for snow. Admission is $7 for adults and teens, $4 for kids ages 6 to 12 and free for kids 5 and younger. An additional $3 will get you a ride on the chairlift.

Octoberfest
Big Tupper Ski Area, Country Club Rd., Tupper Lake • 359-7902

How is Octoberfest at Big Tupper different from the one at Whiteface (see previous entry)? For those who like to comparison shop, Big Tupper's happens the week after the one at Whiteface — generally on Columbus Day weekend — and costs $3 per person or $10 per carload, which makes this one plenty affordable for a family. Included in the admission fee is a ride up the chairlift for a look at the fall foliage. There's music, craft vendors selling their wares, wagon rides and plenty of German food.

90 Meter Ski Jump International
Ski Jump Complex, N.Y. Rt. 73, Lake Placid • 523-1655

The event marks the beginning of the winter sport's season in the Olympic village as ski jumpers from all over the world compete in 90-meter ski jumping. (The 90-meter jump is the larger of the two ski jumps in the complex.) The viewing area is very close to the action, so spectators get a real feel for the nature of this sport — gliding down the jump, taking off, soaring through the air and landing (hopefully) without a big thump. Admission is $7. Ask around town for discount tickets.

Call the Olympic Regional Development Authority (ORDA) at the listed number for a schedule of national and international athletic events held in the Lake Placid area throughout winter.

Lake George/
Upper Hudson Region

World's Largest Garage Sale
throughout Warrensburg • 623-2161

Playfully billed as the "world's largest," it's definitely a big garage sale, with nearly 1,000 (you read that right) sites all over town displaying and selling goods and not-so-goods. Hey, it's a garage sale, so you've got to look around and bargain for your bargains. This is more than just a big town-wide flea market, though. Food courts dot the scene, and there's a "Las Vegas" gambling night at the firehouse on Saturday. This event usually is held the first weekend in October. It's so big, organizers arrange shuttle buses to move you around town.

November

Lake Placid/ Tri-Lakes Region

Discover Stars on Ice
Olympic Arena, Main St., Lake Placid • 523-1655

Traditionally, the first ice show of the Discover Stars on Ice tour, which includes Scott Hamilton, Paul Wylie and Kristi Yamaguchi, has opened in the Olympic facilities in late November. The event is often a sellout and includes single and group programs by many former Olympic and current world champions. Almost every seat in the small 1980 Olympic Arena is a good one, and the event is as good as figure skating gets. Admission costs approximately $30 per person, and the best seats go fast.

Plattsburgh/Western Lake Champlain Region

Art and Craft Fair
State University of New York campus, Rugar St., Plattsburgh • 564-3824

This two-day arts and crafts fair, held in the Field House on the SUNY-Plattsburgh campus in mid-November, is one of the largest in the region. Some 150 vendors, representing the finest artisans and crafters in the region, offer a

stunning array of items for sale. Admission to the event is $2 per person, which benefits student activities at the college. This craft fair is generally packed with shoppers getting a jump on the holiday shopping season, so if you plan to go, get there early to get the best selection of products.

December

Lake Placid/ Tri-Lakes Region

Sparkle Village and Craft Fair
downtown Saranac Lake • 891-1990

The holiday spirit comes alive with thousands of sparkling tiny white lights and a variety of special holiday events including the arrival of Santa Claus, a fashion show, craft show, community Christmas caroling and much more. The craft fair is one of the last before the holiday season and generally has some 60 vendors selling everything from holiday cookies to balsam wreaths and pillows to non-holiday craft items.

Southern Adirondack Lakes Region

Northville Old-fashioned Christmas Weekend
throughout Northville • 863-4026

In early December you can enjoy a celebration of the coming holiday season along the northern shore of the Great Sacandaga Lake. Enjoy simple pleasures of traditional activities such as a tree lighting, horse-drawn sleigh rides, a Christmas craft fair, caroling and the Community Christmas Concert (at the Methodist Church on Sunday evening).

Museums in the region showcase everything from former Presidential residences to Native American life to the "Old Masters" of European art.

Arts and Culture

You may think that a geographic area so heavily populated with lakes, pines and mountains and so sparsely populated with humans would be a cultural wasteland, but the Adirondack region is proof that a rich arts landscape can thrive along with a beautiful natural landscape. As you'll see in the coming pages, the Adirondacks enjoy a surprising diversity of artistic and cultural offerings on a year-round basis. Granted, your chances of finding a renowned art exhibit, concert or festival are considerably better on a summer weekend than a Tuesday night in February. Even so, you'll probably be surprised to see that museums in the region showcase everything from former Presidential residences to Native American life to the "Old Masters" of European art. In performing arts, you can find everything from bluegrass festivals to opera festivals; and from experimental theater to dinner theater.

History is everywhere you look, and in virtually every community you'll find a historical society museum that tells the story of their heritage. While we haven't been able to list each and every one here, we encourage you to check with the local chambers of commerce for complete listings. In most cases, all you have to do is look for a former church, courthouse or one-room schoolhouse in the middle of whatever two-block town you're in, and that's your historical society.

The line between arts and crafts often is blurred in the Adirondacks. You'll find many art centers that display regional crafts as "art" as well as retail galleries that sell regional art alongside crafts and gift items. For our purposes here, we leave any retail outlets for art and crafts to the Shopping chapter, and restrict our listings here to art exhibits.

We have broken this chapter into sections on "Museums and Historical Organizations," "Performing Arts/Music and Theater" and "Arts Organizations." We have included our "must-sees" along with some interesting finds, but

admit that we only touch on a sampling of all that's offered throughout our five Adirondack regions.

We encourage you to explore further as your own time and interest allow. In particular, the listings in the "Arts Organizations" section can help you in your quest for crafts. We consider some notable museums — Fort Ticonderoga, Crown Point, Fort William Henry and The Adirondack Museum — more broad-appeal attractions that incorporate museums as part of their offerings; thus you'll find their primary listings in the Attractions chapter. Wherever possible, we include operating schedules, admission fees and a sampling of the arts programs you can find at each venue. However, these things can be as fickle as the Adirondack weather, so please save yourself some trouble and call ahead.

Like a homemade patchwork quilt, the arts and culture of the Adirondacks have many colors and textures, so enjoy them all for the richness they can bring to your time here.

Museums and Historical Organizations

Lake Placid/ Tri-Lakes Region

John Brown's Farm
John Brown Rd., Lake Placid • 523-3900

John Brown, the famous abolitionist of the Civil War era, came to the Lake Placid area in 1849. Brown acquired 244 acres of land from Gerrit Smith, who had been offering homesteads to free blacks. Brown himself did not stay in the area long, as he soon joined his sons to carry on his fight. Brown did return a few times to his wife before he made his ill-fated raid on the Federal Arsenal at Harper's Ferry, West Virginia. After his trial and execution in 1859, Brown's remains were returned to Lake Placid, his final resting place.

For a man known for a violent act, John Brown's Farm is a remarkably peaceful place. The historic site is simple, including Brown's grave and his small house, preserved along with many original artifacts. In addition to his home, there are illustrated displays detailing Brown's emergence as one of the country's most passionate opponents of slavery, a short nature walk past a pond (with a zillion polliwogs to delight the kids) and a few outbuildings. Although the house is open throughout the summer — 10 AM to 5 PM Wednesday through Saturday and 1 to 5 PM Sunday — the site can be visited at any time. It is just off N.Y. Route 73, near the Olympic ski jumps. It is a great place to sit, read a book and enjoy the view.

Traditionally, a Civil War encampment is re-enacted at the site in mid-August (see Annual Events). Various events such as concerts, historic reenactments and demonstrations are held throughout the summer months, so call for details.

Charles Dickert Memorial Wildlife Museum
100 Main St., Saranac Lake • 891-4190

This small museum downstairs from the Saranac Lake Library displays stuffed mammals, birds and fish of the Adirondacks. It is open daily from 1 to 4 PM in July and August. Admission is free.

Lake Placid-North Elba Historical Society Museum
Averyville Rd., Lake Placid • 523-1608

Within a restored Penn Central Railroad station, the museum presents a collection of artifacts and memorabilia depicting the history of Lake Placid, including the 1932 Olympics. The museum is open Tuesday through Sunday 1 to 5 PM from July through September. There is no admission fee.

Winter Olympic Museum
Olympic Center, Main St., Lake Placid • 523-1655 Ext. 263

One of only three towns in the world to have hosted two winter Olympic games — an honor shared with St. Moritz, Switzerland, and Innsbruck, Austria — Lake Placid's place in Olympic history is recalled in exhibits of the 1932 and 1980 Olympic games, along with many other Winter Games memories in this small museum near the box offices in the Olympic complex. The exhibit features highlights of the "Miracle on Ice," when the 1980 U.S. hockey team upset the favored Soviets; speed-skater Jack Shea's bid to become the first winter Olympian to win two gold medals; and the record-setting accomplishments of figure skater Sonja Henie and speed-skater Eric Heiden.

The museum is open daily 10 AM to 5 PM from late May through early October, when variable winter hours go into effect. Admission is $3 for adults and teens, $1 for children 12 and younger.

Six Nations Indian Museum
CR 30, Onchiota • 891-2299

In a world of high technology, museums like this have become rare. There are no videos, no slick presentations, no fancy graphics — just an eye-catching collection of Native American crafts and artifacts from floor to the ceiling in no logical order. Wherever the eye moves, however, there's something to grab your attention.

The museum is dedicated to the preservation of the culture of the Six Nation Confed-

FYI

Unless otherwise noted, the area code for all phone numbers listed in this guide is 518.

INSIDERS' TIP

Many of the historical and arts organizations are also the most active organizers and promoters of special events throughout the year. Whenever visiting a museum or arts center, ask about an events list to take with you for future leisure-time reference.

Photo: LPCA

The Lake Placid Center for the Arts hosts theater and dance productions throughout the year.

eracy, consisting of the Mohawk, Oneida, Onondaga, Cayuga, Seneca and Tuscarora tribes. (The U.S. Constitution owes a great deal to the philosophy behind this confederacy.) The museum is also a testament to the dedication of the Fadden family, who runs the museum and has collected the myriad artifacts, ranging from pre-Columbian to contemporary and including canoes, baskets, tools, beadwork and other objects. The longest beaded record belt in the world — 75 feet — is part of the collection.

Various examples of Native American campfires and other camp-related items are on display outside the building.

The museum is open 10 AM to 6 PM Tuesday through Sunday from July 1 through Labor Day. Admission costs $2 for adults and $1 for children. Although the hours are posted, we recommended you call to ensure they have not changed for the day.

Robert Louis Stevenson Cottage
Stevenson Ln., Saranac Lake • 891-1462

Famed author Robert Louis Stevenson spent part of 1887 in Saranac Lake — or as he called it, "The Little Switzerland in the Adirondacks." Stevenson's quaint farmhouse, originally named Baker Cottage (the "hatbox on the hill"), is preserved in its origi-

nal state and holds the largest collection of Stevenson mementos in America, including his writing desk and velvet smoking jacket.

Stevenson came to the area to be treated for tuberculosis, but Dr. Edward L. Trudeau never actually found definitive signs of the disease in Stevenson. The clear, dry mountain air and Trudeau's treatments, however, provided relief from Stevenson's chronic lung problems, which possibly stemmed from his chain smoking.

Stevenson, best known for *Dr. Jekyll and Mr. Hyde*, was rather productive during his stay in Saranac (not yet called Saranac Lake at that time), where he wrote most of *The Master of Ballantrae* and numerous articles for *Scribner's* magazine.

The cottage is open 9:30 AM to 4:30 PM Tuesday through Sunday from July through mid-September; it's closed briefly at midday for lunch. Admission is $2 for adults, $1 for kids.

Historic Saranac Lake
132 River St., Saranac Lake • 891-0971

This organization works towards preserving historic buildings and educating residents about the unique architecture in the village, including the famous "cure cottages" (see the discussion of Saranac Lake in Area Overview for details). The group also has produced various publications on cure cottages of Saranac Lake.

Beth Joseph Synagogue
Lake St., Tupper Lake • 359-9594

In the early 1900s Jewish peddlers, carrying packs of needles, pins, fabrics and other small goods, began arriving in the Adirondack region. Many settled in Tupper Lake, where they constructed the Beth Joseph Synagogue in 1905. The synagogue, known as the "peddler's synagogue," is registered as a National Historic Building. Restored by the community, the building now houses art exhibits and hosts concerts and other events. It is open Monday through Friday from 11 AM to 3 PM during July and August. Admission is free.

www.insiders.com

See this and many other **Insiders' Guide®** destinations online — in their entirety.

Visit us today!

Plattsburgh/Western Lake Champlain Region

Adirondack Architectural Heritage
1759 Main St., Keesville • 834-9328

This regional historic preservation organization serves to encourage better understanding, appreciation and stewardship of the Adirondack region's unique architectural heritage. The group plays an advocate's role in historic-preservation issues and is active in the restoration of Camp Santanoni and fire towers in the region.

Essex Community Historical Organization (ECHO)
N.Y. Rt. 22, Essex • 963-7088

In the early 1800s, the small town of Essex was a thriving community on the shore of Lake Champlain. When the railroad bypassed the town in the middle part of the century, the town's fortunes built in part from iron mining, shipbuilding and trade on the lake began to decline. Today, Essex attracts visitors because of its historic charm, thanks in part to the efforts of this historical organization. If you want to know what you are looking at in Essex, ECHO produces a booklet describing the sites in the village and conducts various tours of the historic buildings in the community.

Town of Moriah Historical Society
Town Hall, Park St., Port Henry • 546-7524

This small grassroots organization collects, preserves, interprets and displays historical information relating to Moriah and Port Henry, generally in the Town Hall. Monthly meetings are held the third Monday of each month, and the public is welcome. The group is working on establishing a permanent facility in which to house its artifacts relating to the iron industry.

Adirondack Center Museum
U.S. Hwy. 9, Elizabethtown • 873-6466

Do you know what a lice comb is? In the 18th century in Adirondacks, you likely needed one for, well . . . combing away lice. Ten exhibit areas on three floors of this former schoolhouse contains an eclectic collection chronicling two centuries of life in pioneer settlements in the area, particularly those in Essex County. The extensive collection of antique dolls is a favorite.

During the summer, a formal colonial garden features modern varieties of old-fashioned plants. A short nature trail extends from the gardens. An appointment is required to visit the Brewster Library, which houses a solid collection of resource materials relating to Essex County and the central Adirondacks. Admission costs $4.50 per adult or teen and $2 per child 12 and younger.

The facility also houses the Essex County Historical Society.

Almanzo Wilder Homestead
Burke Rd., Malone • 483-1207

The boyhood home of Almanzo Wilder, husband of Laura Ingalls Wilder and hero of her book *Farmer Boy*, provides a glimpse into 19th-century life with displays and exhibits in the historic farmhouse. The homestead is open Memorial Day through Labor Day — 10 AM to

4 PM Tuesday through Saturday and 1 to 4 PM Sunday. Admission is $3 per adult and $1.50 per child.

Clinton County Historical Museum
48 Court St., Plattsburgh • 561-0340

The Battle of Plattsburgh was the culminating event in 1814 in a century of warfare on Lake Champlain. In this small museum, in the heart of Plattsburgh, the area's history — from the earliest settlers in 1600 to the present — is recorded in paintings, maps, furniture, decorative arts and artifacts. Many archeological discoveries recovered from Lake Champlain highlight the many naval battles on its waters.

The museum is open year round from noon to 4 PM Tuesday through Friday and 1 to 4 PM Saturday. Admission costs $2 per adult, $1 per child.

1812 Homestead
N.Y. Rt. 22, Willsboro • 963-4071

This museum and "hands-on" working farm recreates life in the 19th century. Unlike other museums in which exhibits are for viewing only, the implements at the Homestead are meant to be handled. Visitors may try candle-making or hearth cooking or watch demonstrations in blacksmithing, spinning, quilting or other crafts. The museum includes a farmhouse, barn and schoolhouse.

Children may help tend to the chickens, sheep, pigs and oxen on the farm. There is a self-guided nature trail along the shore of Long Lake.

The museum offers some unique seasonal activities, including cider-making, maple sugaring, a pioneer Thanksgiving and caroling party, its world-famous "pig walk" and various craft workshops.

The 1812 Homestead is open noon to 4 PM daily in summer. Admission costs $2.50 per adult and $1 per child.

Kent-Delord House Museum
17 Cumberland Ave., Plattsburgh • 561-1035

Built in 1797, the Kent-Delord house is one of the oldest residences in the region. The Delord's, owners of the house between 1810 and 1913, traveled extensively and brought back souvenirs from wherever they went; thus, the museum serves as both the history of the family and of the changing eras. The museum houses an extensive collection of furniture from the mid-18th through the 19th century, a unique collection of porcelain and glass objects and everyday objects used by the family in daily life. Admission costs $3 for adults, $1 for children. The museum is open noon to 4 PM Tuesday through Saturday from March through December.

Alice T. Miner Museum
U.S. Hwy. 9, Chazy • 846-7336

About 12 miles north of Plattsburgh, the Miner Museum was created by Alice Miner, the wife of railroad industrialist William Miner, in 1924. The 15 rooms in the museum are filled with period and miniature furniture, a vast collection of china, porcelain and glass, and a superb collection of textiles. The focus is on 18th- and 19th-century materials.

The museum is open Tuesday through Saturday from 10 AM to 4 PM. It's closed late December through late January. Admission is $3 for adults, $1 for children.

Penfield Homestead Museum
off N.Y. Rt. 22, Crown Point • 597-3804

What is significant about Allen Penfield switching on an electromagnet to help him in his process of iron ore separation in 1831? And who, you ask, is Allen Penfield anyway? His name may be lost to many history books, but his action was the world's first industrial application of electricity. (Will the answer ever appear on *Jeopardy*?)

The museum preserves his legacy, along with an extensive collection of Civil War artifacts and equipment used in the iron industry. Its 550-acre site includes ruins of iron works.

The museum is open 10 AM to 4 PM Wednesday through Sunday from mid-May through mid-October and seven days a week from July through Labor Day. Donations are welcome. Ask about festivities at its Heritage Day in mid-August (see our Annual Events chapter).

State University of New York at Plattsburgh Art Museum
SUNY Plattsburgh campus, Rugar St., Plattsburgh • 564-2474

The SUNY Plattsburgh Art Museum, with a collection of more than 4,500 works, is one

Photo: Plattsburgh State University of N.Y.

The Winkle Gallery Art Museum and the Rockwell Kent Gallery
are both on the Plattsburgh State University campus.

of those hidden gems that often is missed by locals and visitors alike. The museum facilities are spread throughout the campus. The primary galleries are in the Myers Fine Arts Building and in the Feinberg Library, which houses an extensive collection of paintings, drawings, prints, books and ephemera of the late American artist Rockwell Kent and much of the college's permanent art collection. Asian, 19th- and 20th-century prints, sculptures, and paintings, and a photography collection also are housed in various sections of the library.

More than 50 works by Nina Winkel are displayed in the Winkel Sculpture Court, the largest space in the United States dedicated to the art of a woman. A Student Sculpture Park also continues to grow, showcasing the college's many talented and artistic students.

The SUNY Plattsburgh Art Museum is open daily year round, except on public holidays.

Ticonderoga Historical Society
Moses Cir., Ticonderoga • 585-7868

Housed in the Hancock House, a replica of John Hancock's house in Boston, this historical society maintains a museum and research library. Various period furnishings and exhibits on the area's social and civil history from its first settlers in the 1700s to the present are displayed in the museum.

The reference library focuses on Lake Champlain, Lake George and, to a limited extent, the Adirondacks. It is a good source for genealogical information.

The museum is open Wednesday through Saturday 10 AM to 4 PM. Admission is free.

Ticonderoga Heritage Museum
Montcalm St., Ticonderoga • 585-2696

The building that houses this museum was constructed in 1888 and is listed on the National Register of Historic Places. It is one of the few examples of High Victorian architecture in the region. The museum focuses upon the industrial history of "Ti," including its role in papermaking, water power and other forest-related products.

The Ticonderoga Heritage Museum is open 10 AM to 4 PM daily from late June through Labor Day, then weekends only through mid-October. Admission is free. Call for information on special exhibits or activities.

Lake George/ Upper Hudson Region

Chapman Historical Museum
348 Glen St., Glens Falls • 793-2826

While just outside the southern Adirondack Park border, the Chapman is one of the best places to rediscover the history of the southern Adirondack region. It is housed in the Second Empire-style DeLong House, which dates back to 1865. The home is authentically restored to give you a glimpse at what life was like for two generations of the DeLongs who lived here from 1860 to 1910. Visitors will also see changing exhibits on the history of the southern Adirondack region, along with an ever-evolving exhibit from the museum's highly regarded collection of late 19th-century photographs of the region by Seneca Ray Stoddard. The museum shop features a good variety of Adirondack-related history books and is worth some browsing time.

You can visit the Chapman Historical Museum Tuesday through Saturday from 10 AM until 5 PM. Admission is $2 for adults, $1 for seniors (55 and older) and students (12 and older), and free for children younger than 12.

Fort William Henry
Canada St., Lake George • 668-5471

A modern restoration of a log fortress originally built in 1755 during the French and Indian War, Fort William Henry is set at the southern end of Lake George. It provides an entertaining and educational look at a crucial period in American history and the region's role in the birth of our nation. For complete information, see the Attractions chapter.

Ulysses S. Grant Cottage State Historic Site
Mt. McGregor Rd., off U.S. Hwy. 9, Wilton • 587-8277

As you speed north on Interstate 87 just beyond Saratoga Springs and just a few miles shy of the Adirondack Park, you'll notice a ridge of foothills to your west. Nestled at the top of the ridge is a historic site of which many people are unaware and, in their hurry to reach the mountains, pay little attention to. We suggest you take a few extra minutes to veer off the six lanes of superhighway and head up the windy road off Exit 16. There you'll find the scenic spot where Ulysses S. Grant, the nation's 18th President, spent six weeks rushing to complete his memoirs before throat cancer would claim his life. Nearly broke from bad postwar investments, he knew the publication of these memoirs could help provide security for his family after he was gone. Family friend Mark Twain had agreed to publish the book, and Grant accomplished his goal with just a few days to spare. He died at the cottage on July 23, 1885.

Grant Cottage provides an interesting look at the fascinating life of Civil War Union Gen. U.S. Grant. It remains much as it was during Grant's residency. The Friends of Grant Cottage, a nonprofit group that manages the facility, hold special events throughout the sum-

---

INSIDERS' TIP

Arts organizations are not only a great source of entertainment, but also a great resource for learning. Ask about workshops and classes, roll up your sleeves and get your hands dirty with something other than yardwork for a change. You'll learn about Adirondack culture, meet new friends and develop a new skill. That's much more fun than worrying about the fickle Adirondack weather!

mer months such as a Grant remembrance day in July and a Victorian picnic in August. There is also a cottage shop featuring various items related to Grant's life and the Victorian era.

A visit to Grant Cottage will also treat you to a magnificent view of the Hudson River valley and the Green Mountains of Vermont on the eastern horizon some 30 miles distant. The cottage shares the mountain top with the Mt. McGregor Correctional Facility. In order to access the cottage, you need to stop at the check point first. Don't be nervous, they're much more concerned about their people leaving the area than you and yours visiting.

Grant Cottage is open Wednesday through Sunday, 10 AM to 4 PM, Memorial Day weekend through Labor Day weekend, and the same hours weekends only from Labor Day to Columbus Day. Admission is $2.50 for adults, $2 for seniors, $1 for children ages 5 through 16, and free for children younger than 5.

The Hyde Collection
161 Warren St., Glens Falls • 792-1761

Founded by Charlotte Pruyn Hyde in 1952, this expansive complex has evolved into what is recognized as one of the finest art museums in the northeastern United States. The centerpiece of the museum is the Hyde home, which is an Italian Renaissance-style villa. In it you will find a collection of European "Old Master" works from such artists as Rembrandt, da Vinci and El Greco as well as more modern works of art by Van Gogh, Renoir and Picasso. American artists are also well represented, including works by Winslow Homer, Childe Hassam and Whistler. This impressive collection is displayed among a selection of Italian Renaissance and French 18th-century antiques and furniture, providing a most regal ambiance.

In addition to the permanent collection, temporary exhibitions are shown in the three galleries of the museum's Education Wing. Lectures, fine-art classes, concerts and school programs are scheduled throughout the year at The Hyde Collection. Save time to visit the museum shop during your visit.

The Hyde Collection is open on Tuesday through Sunday year round — noon until 5 PM from January through April and 10 AM until 5 PM from May through December. You can take a guided tour of the collection between 1 and 3 PM.

Admission to the collection is $3.50 for adults, $2.50 for seniors and students, and free for children younger than 5. Your clan can also take advantage of the family rate ($10), or better yet, visit between 10 AM and 2 PM Sundays for free.

Lake George Historical Association
Canada St., Lake George • 668-5044

Of the several small historical society museums scattered in towns throughout the region, this is perhaps your best bet for revisiting the past of the best-known and most popular southern Adirondack destination. It is set right along Lake George's "main street," a stately Greek-Revival departure from the neon-lit T-shirt shops a couple blocks away. Inside you'll find photo exhibits of the area, archaeological artifacts, an Adirondack cabin kitchen display, an Indian dugout canoe and even a lighthearted display about the lake's mythical monster, George. There's also a museum shop with a number of photographs and prints for sale, along with historic books, maps and other gift items.

You can visit year round, Monday through Friday from 10 AM until 4 PM. The museum is also open Saturday and Sunday in summer from 1 until 5 PM. Admission is $3 for adults and $1 for children younger than 10.

North Creek Railway Depot Preservation Association
off N.Y. Rt. 28, North Creek • 251-5811

The North Creek Train Depot played an important role in U.S. history. In 1901, it was to this depot that Vice President Theodore Roosevelt traveled from Mount Marcy on "Teddy's Wild Ride" after he learned that President McKinley had died from his gunshot wounds, and it was from here that Roosevelt took a train to Buffalo to be sworn in as U.S. President. The depot was built in 1874, and operated for many years as the northern terminal for the Adirondack Railroad.

This nonprofit organization was formed in 1993 to "acquire, stabilize and restore" the depot for use as a museum and a excursion train stop. The organization hopes to completely restore the depot inside and out by the end of 1997, after which an interpretive museum is scheduled to be established on the site.

Southern Adirondack Lakes Region

The Adirondack Museum
N.Y. Rt. 30, Blue Mountain Lake • 352-7311

While this is a museum, technically speaking, it is so much more than that; so we include its primary listing in the Attractions chapter. There is simply no better place in the Adirondacks to be exposed to so much of what the region and its people represent. With 23 indoor and outdoor exhibit areas that showcase how people lived, worked and played throughout the region's history, this place merits an all-day visit. So extensive and well done is The Adirondack Museum that *The New York Times* called it "the best of its kind in the world." More than 100,000 people visit each year during its season from Memorial Day weekend through mid-October.

For more information about The Adirondack Museum, including rates, hours and exhibits, see the Attractions chapter.

Fulton County Historical Society Museum
237 Kingsboro Ave., Gloversville • 725-2203

At the southern end of this region, the museum contains the only complete glove-making exhibit in the United States, along with a leather tannery of the early 1900s. While a few miles outside of the Adirondack Park border, it's an easy trip for visitors to the Caroga, Canada, Peck's and Great Sacandaga lakes area looking for a rainy-day activity. Also on display is an authentic Indian Long House and a variety of industrial and farm-related exhibits. You can visit April through November — Tuesday through Saturday from 10 AM to 4 PM and Sundays from noon to 4 PM. Admission is free, but donations are gladly accepted.

Old Forge/ Raquette Lake Region

Forest Industries Exhibit Hall
N.Y. Rt. 28, Old Forge • (315) 369-3078

Forestry was the key industry in the early development of the Adirondacks, and this museum illustrates the values of managed forestry to the ecology. It contains a variety of dioramas of forest management, recreational activities and wildlife management, along with models of a sawmill and a plywood mill. You can also see a display of typical products made from the northern forest, such as paper products, toys, novelties and sporting goods.

While nowhere near as elaborate as The Adirondack Museum in Blue Mountain Lake, this warrants a visit if you're staying in the Old Forge area and are curious about the region's industrial past. You can visit Memorial Day through the third week of June on weekends only, noon to 5 PM; then, through Labor Day, the museum is open daily (except Tuesday) from 10 AM to 5 PM on weekdays, and noon to 5 PM on weekends. The schedule reverts back to weekends-only, noon to 5 PM from Labor Day until Columbus Day weekend. Best of all, admission is free.

Great Camp Sagamore
Sagamore Rd., off N.Y. Rt. 28, Raquette Lake • (315) 354-5311

The creation of the great Adirondack entrepreneur William West Durant, this huge lodge was built in 1897 and became the home of the Alfred Vanderbilt family in 1901. The lodge was designed to look like a Swiss chalet and is the centerpiece of an elaborate complex that includes 27 buildings and (what else?) an open-air bowling alley. There is also a dining hall, guest cottages, artisan's barn, blacksmith shop and boathouse. Besides now serving as a museum and attraction for visitors to enjoy, the Great Camp Sagamore also hosts attendees of workshops and small conferences throughout the summer.

If you're within a tank of gas, we strongly recommend you save a day during your Adirondack visit to experience this gem of rustic elegance (it sounds like a contradiction, but in this case it applies). Guided tours of the compound last about two hours and begin each day at 10 AM and 1:30 PM from the Fourth of July weekend to Labor Day and then weekends only until Columbus Day. The cost is $7 for adults, and $3 for children. After the tour, the gift shop is worth a stop, and a coffee shop is available as well if you need to personally "refuel" before your departure (if you can convince yourself to leave!).

Performing Arts/ Music & Theater

Lake Placid/ Tri-Lakes Region

Lake Placid Sinfonietta
P.O. Box 1303, Lake Placid 12946 • 523-2051

Founded in 1917 by members of the Lake Placid Club, the 18-member Sinfonietta performs free concerts every Wednesday evening at the Bandshell Park overlooking Mirror Lake, and at weekly concerts at the Lake Placid Center for the Arts. Weekly performances feature selected guest artists; tickets generally cost $8 to $10.

Pendragon Theater
148 River St., Saranac Lake • 891-1854

Pendragon is one of those small-town professional theater organizations that consistently produces quality performances and has been doing so for 15 years. The organization also serves the region as a source for educational programs and workshops and helps

other organizations develop theatrical productions.

Regular repertory performances are held throughout the year; tickets cost $14 for adults and $12 for students. Past productions include *The Importance of Being Earnest* and *Six Degrees of Separation*.

Plattsburgh/Western Lake Champlain Region

Boquet River Theater Festival
Whallonsburg Church, N.Y. Rt. 22, Willsboro • 963-8414

This nonprofit theater company conducts classes and produces original children's theater performances in the Whallonsburg Church theater. Children 8 and older — both year-round and summer residents of the Champlain Valley — are encouraged to participate. An all-kid cast performance generally is held in late August. Admission is $7 per adult and $4 per child.

Depot Theater
N.Y. Rt. 9N, Westport • 962-4449

Depot Theater has earned its well-deserved reputation for its quality professional summer theater presentations. The musicals, comedies and dramas take on special flavor in the restored 19th-century freight room of the Delaware & Hudson train station. A gallery of regional crafts is open year round; special gallery exhibits are held during the summer.

Theater performances are held daily from June to September. Tickets cost $15 per person.

> ## FYI
> Unless otherwise noted, the area code for all phone numbers listed in this guide is 518.

INSIDERS' TIP

Can you name five famous novels written in or with an Adirondack setting? Robert Louis Stevenson wrote *The Master of Ballantrae* while living in Saranac Lake. Theodore Dreiser turned an Adirondack tragedy into *An American Tragedy*. E.L. Doctorow's *Loon Lake* speaks of a lake of the same name in the northern Adirondacks. Ian Fleming obviously knew about the region's sleazy hotels, as depicted in *The Spy Who Loved Me*. And James Fenimore Cooper's *Last of the Mohicans* is set here.

The Saratoga Performing Arts Center regularly brings world-class performers to the region.

Essex Theater Company
Masonic Lodge, Main St., Essex
• 963-4025

This community theater group creates and performs dramas and musicals in its summer home at the Masonic Lodge. Past performances include *Trial By Jury*, *Arsenic and Old Lace* and *A Funny Thing Happened on the Way to the Forum*. Tickets are $5 for adults and teens; children 12 and younger are admitted free.

Meadowmount School of Music
Lewis-Wadhams Rd., Westport • 873-2063

This summer school for accomplished young violinists, violists and cellists boasts alumni including such legendary musicians as Michael Rabin, Itzhak Perlman, Kyung-Wha Chung and Pinchas Zukerman. The school presents free classical concerts — Bach, Brahms, Beethoven et al. — Wednesdays and Sundays from July through mid-August.

Pleasant Valley Chorale
Elizabethtown Social Center, Maple St., Elizabethtown • 873-6408

Some 40 members form this community chorale, which performs winter holiday music in December and various choral arrangements in May for the public. Admission to concerts is free.

The group invites newcomers to its rehearsals, which generally are held Tuesday evenings at 7 PM beginning in September.

Ticonderoga Festival Guild
P.O. Box 125, Ticonderoga 12883
• 585-6716

This guild provides diverse performing arts programming throughout the region. Programs include music, theater and other performing arts. The guild sponsors many events during summer, including musical performances by Adirondack musicians and the Lake Placid Sinfonietta (see previous listing in this chapter) as well as theater performances, many designed especially for children. Admission to events for children generally is free, while other performances cost around $10. If you plan to be in the Ti area, call for a schedule of events.

Lake George/
Upper Hudson Region

Adirondack Theater Festival
N.Y. Rt. 149, Lake George • 798-7470

Relatively new to the region, the Adirondack Theater Festival (ATF) had its inaugural season in 1995. It is based at the French Mountain Playhouse on the grounds of the Lake George RV Park. While that may not seem as prestigious an address as Lincoln Center, ATF is a professional equity theater group offering a wide variety of challenging theater during its relatively short season. The Festival produces two main-stage productions — usually one play and one musical. In addition, the troupe offers cabaret, readings and children's workshops. The ATF season lasts from mid-June to early July. If you're looking for something other than your basic Neil Simon summer-stock production, call to find out what ATF has lined up. In 1997 the schedule featured the original play *The Deal* by ATF founding member Ron Burch. Ticket prices range from $9 to $15.

Lake George Dinner Theatre
Holiday Inn-Turf, U.S. Hwy. 9, Lake George • 668-5781

Now *this* is where you want to go to see the proven standards that populate summer-stock theaters around the country. If you'd rather just sit, eat and be entertained, and not worry about the deep meanings the playwright may or may not have intended, this is a great place to spend an enjoyable night out. Produced and performed by a professional equity company, Lake George Dinner Theatre offers one show per summer season, and runs it nightly, except Sunday. You can also pick a Wednesday luncheon matinee, but be prepared to battle the bus-tour crowds that frequent the midday shows. The food and setting at the Holiday Inn are just fine, given the nature of this type of theater (in other words, it ain't Broadway; then again, it doesn't profess to be). See the entry in our Nightlife chapter for specifics on ticket prices and shows.

Lake George Opera Festival
Queensbury High School Auditorium, Aviation Rd., Queensbury • 793-3859

Before you turn your nose up and your car around because this is "opera," consider a few things. This festival celebrated its 35th-anniversary season in 1997, so it must be doing something right. Plus the cast sing everything in English, so you've got a fighting chance to follow the stories as they unfold. Finally, you're on vacation! Try something different, won't you?!

Seriously, we think the Lake George Opera Festival is well worth checking out, particularly if you've never been to an opera before. The 1997 season, which ran from July 20 to August 13, included productions of *Othello* and *A Midsummer Night's Dream*, the latter with a special guest performance by the Harlem Boys Choir. One particularly nice touch for opera novices is that Artistic Director Joseph Illick gives a little "Opera Insights" orientation one hour prior to each production. It's a fun and informative way to learn enough about this art form to really enjoy the performance.

All performances take place at the Queensbury High School auditorium, which is just off Exit 19 of the Adirondack Northway (I-87). Each production is performed about three times during the season, usually on a Tuesday, Wednesday or Saturday. Showtime is 8 PM, with the exception of Wednesday matinee performances at 2 PM. Opera is "up there" on the ticket-price scale, but the value is fair for the production you will experience. Ticket prices range from $19 to $45 for adults and $15 to $39 for seniors and students. There's also a Family Special, in which one child younger than 12 may attend free when accompanying a paying adult. It's a good deal if you can convince the kids to go!

Luzerne Chamber Music Festival
Lake Tour Rd., Lake Luzerne • 696-2771

World-class musicians from the Philadelphia Orchestra (it takes up residence during August at the Saratoga Performing Arts Center, about 20 miles south of here) present a chamber music concert series Monday nights during late July and August. The concerts are at 8 PM and cost $10. If you love classical music in a more intimate form and setting, you'll love an evening at the Luzerne Chamber Music Festival.

Seagle Colony for Singers
Charley Hill Rd., Schroon Lake • 532-7875, 532-9059

It's amazing what you can discover, when you start looking. Did you know that the oldest summer training program for singers in the United States is in the Adirondacks? The Seagle Colony, established in 1915 by the famed tenor Oscar Seagle, is a rural retreat for aspiring singers. The colony also entertains the public with show tunes, opera and religious music in a series of concerts, beginning in late June and running throughout the summer. Please call for ticket prices, which were unavailable at press time.

Southern Adirondack Lakes Region

Adirondack Lakes Center for the Arts
N.Y. Rt. 28, Blue Mountain Lake
· 352-7715

Check out the schedule here to find out which of the many offerings of music, art, crafts and theater are being presented throughout the summer. The 1997 schedule included the Adirondack Ensemble (a chamber music group), acoustic folk music and Irish music, all presented in a coffeehouse setting. Most events cost $9 for nonmembers and $7 for members. A membership donation of $25 entitles you to one free admission.

Old Forge/ Raquette Lake Region

Mountain Theatre Co.
Main St., Old Forge · (315) 369-2484

The Water's Edge Inn & Conference Center serve as the home of this professional dinner-theater group. Now in its 10th year, Mountain Theatre Co. presents performances two nights a week in July and August. Productions in 1997 included the Broadway-musical revue *Street of Dreams* and the comedy *A View From Here*. Tickets, including dinner and the show, cost $20 to $25 per person — pretty darn reasonable, if you ask us.

Arts Organizations

Lake Placid/ Tri-Lakes Region

High Peak Artists
P.O. Box 64, Keene Valley 12943
· 576-4457

This group of artists from Keene and Keene Valley produces an annual art exhibit of its members in the Keene Valley Fire Department. The art exhibition and sale generally is held in August. Admission is free.

Lake Placid Center for the Arts (LPCA)
91 Saranac Ave., Lake Placid · 523-2512

The LPCA is the largest arts organization in the Tri-Lakes region and one of the few in the entire Adirondacks region that is open year round and has its own facilities. The organization produces local community theater and hosts professional dance troupes, such as Rebecca Kelly Dance, classical concerts and theater presentations. Special events range from zydeco, Latin and Celtic bands to unusual dance troupes from Asia and elsewhere. The center also is one of the few places in the region where art films a shown on a regular basis — generally Fridays at 7:30 PM. Admission to the film showing is $5 per person. The cost for other events ranges from $10 for community theater to around $20 for professional theater, concerts and shows.

LPCA offers a series of programs for youngsters and school groups throughout the year. While many of these youth programs fill up quickly, it is always worth a call to inquire about space.

The center also hosts exhibits in the Fine Arts Gallery throughout the year.

INSIDERS' TIP

The Lake Placid Library offers a great view of Mirror Lake from its reading room and the small shoreline section down the steps on the outside. And the Paul Smith's College library, only a few towns and 20 miles away, overlooks the pristine Lower St. Regis Lake.

Lake Placid Institute for the Arts and Humanities
P.O. Box 988, Lake Placid 12946
• 576-2063

This institute develops cultural and educational programs for the Tri-Lakes region. Its efforts include hosting leadership seminars, co-hosting the Festival of the Lakes and conducting cooperative marketing studies for the region.

Mountain Artists of New York (MANY)
P.O. Box 429, Wilmington 12997
• 946-7152

MANY is a group of Adirondack artists and crafters who work cooperatively to exhibit their work. The group showcases its artists every Memorial Day and Thanksgiving weekend in Wilmington's Town Hall, off N.Y. Route 3. Admission is free.

Paint and Palette
P.O. Box 965, Saranac Lake 12983
• 523-3837

This group of artists, primarily painters and illustrators from Saranac Lake and Lake Placid area, arranges group and individual exhibits for its members. A summer exhibit and sale is generally held in the Town Hall in Saranac Lake in early August. Admission is free.

Plattsburgh/Western Lake Champlain Region

Adirondack Art Association
N.Y. Rt. 22, Essex • 963-7270

The association is comprised of professional and amateur artists from Essex County. It produces group exhibits that feature artists from the Adirondack region. Exhibits are housed in a restored schoolhouse and generally open in June. Admission is free.

Arts Council for the Northern Adirondacks (ACNA)
N.Y. Rt. 22, Westport • 962-8778

ACNA is the place to call for information on the arts in Clinton, Essex, St. Lawrence and Franklin County areas of upstate New York. In addition to being the source of information, the council produces juried exhibits, performance series and festivals and provides funding to organizations in portions of the region.

Council of the Arts for Clinton County
60 Bridge St., Plattsburgh • 563-5222

Founded in 1962, the council supports the arts in Clinton County through programs for the public as well as support for arts organizations and individual artists. The council provides artist referrals, sponsors professional workshops, and organizes exhibits and community outreach.

Lake George/ Upper Hudson Region

Lake George Arts Project
Old County Courthouse, Canada St., Lake George • 686-2616

This organization both operates a gallery and promotes musical and literature events within the Village of Lake George. The gallery is open on Tuesday through Friday from noon to 5 PM, or can be open by request other times. Admission to the gallery is free, and you will see a wide variety of art forms displayed there throughout the year. The Lake George Arts Project (LGAP) is perhaps best known as the promoter of the Lake George Jazz Weekend (see Annual Events), which usually takes place on the weekend after Labor Day in Shepard Park. LGAP also conducts a summer concert series on Wednesday nights in July and August, featuring a variety of musical styles performed by bands from around the region and beyond. Admission to all events is free, so if you're walking the town and hear the music down by the lakefront, check it out.

Lower Adirondack Regional Arts Council
10 Ridge St., Glens Falls • 798-1144

Founded in 1972, the Lower Adirondack Regional Arts Council (LARAC) is a nonprofit organization that serves artists and cultural organizations in Warren, Washington and northern Saratoga counties. It focuses on serving as a clearinghouse for area arts information, providing education to artists on the business of art and promoting special community events that showcase the arts. Its signature event is the June Arts & Crafts Festival, which takes place at City Park in Glens Falls during the second full weekend in June. More than 200 juried arts and crafts exhibitors displaying their wares, live music and plenty of food all make for a great time and a great arts event (see the Annual Events chapter).

Schroon Lake Arts Council
Main St., Schroon Lake • 532-7675

This active council brings music, dance, storytelling, theater and good times to the Schroon Lake area. If you plan on being in Schroon Lake, contact the arts council for information about scheduled programs.

The Writer's Voice of The Silver Bay Association
N.Y. Rt. 9N, Silver Bay • 543-8833

The goal of The Writer's Voice is to create a permanent literary-arts center in the Adirondack region. The Silver Bay Association is the northern end of Lake George, along the western shore — a magnificent setting — and is a YMCA conference center complete with lodges and recreational facilities. The organization offers a series of workshops and readings by highly regarded nationally known writers and poets that appeal to both adults and children. (This book's co-author, Michael Mendrick, had the pleasure of performing in 1992 as part of their "Readings by the Bay" series.)

While the general public is invited to some events such as the "Readings by the Bay" for a small admission fee ($3 to $5), only members of the Silver Bay Association may participate in workshops. The annual membership cost is $50 for an individual and $100 for a family. Program fees for any and all activities and workshops then work as follows: daily, $8 for an individual and $25 for a family; weekly, $50 for an individual and $100 for a family; and annually, $300 for an individual and $550 for a family.

Southern Adirondack Lakes Region

Adirondack Lakes Center for the Arts
N.Y. Rt. 28, Blue Mountain Lake • 352-7715

In addition to scheduling musical performances (see listing in this chapter's "Performing Arts" section), this facility also is the site of a wide variety of classes and workshops on such topics as woodcarving, basketry, photography and painting. It is open year round, so call to see what new skill you can learn while the snow mounts outside. Workshop costs for members range from $20 for soap making to $300 for guide boat making; most workshops cost between $25 to $50.

Old Forge/ Raquette Lake Region

The Arts Center/Old Forge
N.Y. Rt. 28, Old Forge • (315) 369-6411

This multifaceted arts center offers year-round classes, performances and exhibits with a wide variety of art forms. Pottery, folk arts, quilting and photography are a few things you can learn and enjoy at The Arts Center. When you're not learning, you can enjoy the gallery exhibits or the sponsored special events such as the Neighbor Day in June, the Craft Fair in July, the Regional Art Exhibit in August, the National Watercolor Exhibit in September and the Quilt Exhibit in October (see Annual Events).

Skiing has been a big part of the Adirondack winter scene ever since the 1930s, when "ski trains" brought hundreds of enthusiasts from New York City to the North Creek Ski Bowl.

Skiing

The Adirondacks are truly a skier's and snowboarder's paradise, offering everything from the same trails that tested 1980 Olympians at Whiteface to the more knee-joint friendly slopes of smaller, family-run and family-oriented areas like Big Tupper and West Mountain.

With nighttime temperatures that consistently drop below freezing from November into April, snowmaking guns fire up to supplement the 10 feet of natural snow that falls throughout the region's winter. The result is a long, fun-filled ski season that for many areas exceeds 150 days of operation. Even with a very liberal vacation and comp-time policy, it's hard to imagine that you could get away for much more than that!

Skiing has been a big part of the Adirondack winter scene ever since the 1930s, when "ski trains" brought hundreds of enthusiasts from New York City to the North Creek Ski Bowl. In those days, skiers were just hoping to escape the "Great White Way" (a.k.a. Broadway) for a great white way *down*. Much has changed since those early days of winter fun, but what hasn't changed are the views of pristine wilderness that stretch out in all directions as you make your way down an Adirondack slope. You can thank the State of New York for the view. It remains unspoiled due to the strict regulations and development restrictions within the Adirondack Park boundaries. It is what sets Adirondack skiing apart from its more commercial New England neighbors.

While you can't see ribbons of slopeside hotels and condos dotting the landscape, your après ski options for lodging, food and entertainment are plentiful and convenient at many of the major Adirondack ski centers. In fact, Whiteface Mountain's neighboring community of Lake Placid is consistently ranked as one of the best ski resort towns in America for lodging, dining and events (see our Accommodations, Restaurants and Annual Events chapters for details).

The Adirondacks may feel isolated, but somehow the locals found out about snowboarding because you can see them in abundance just about everywhere now. Most ski areas welcome them with open arms, open minds and designated "snowboard parks." The grooming wizards manipulate the slopes into "half-pipes" (think of a rain gutter, only made out of snow) and other contortions of snow that snowboarders love and the rest of us just don't get.

So take your pick. Two boards or one — the Adirondacks offer up a full plate of options for slip-slidin' your way down and around some of the most beautiful territory in America.

This chapter provides you with listings of downhill skiing and snowboard areas by region, followed by cross-country ski centers and trail systems. For more information on skiing in the Adirondacks, request a *New York State Winter Travel and Ski Guide* from the I Love New York tourism information office at (800) I LOVE NY. Another good resource is the Ski Areas of New York association, which provides a daily ski report and other useful information at (315) 696-6550.

Downhill Skiing and Snowboarding

The downhill ski and snowboard centers of the Adirondacks will give you all the speed, thrills, bumps and cruising you can handle. Unless otherwise noted, all downhill ski areas offer food service and have available rental equipment such as skis, poles, boots and snowboards. All downhill ski centers also are open to snowboarders and offer lessons for both you and your two-boarded friends on skis.

Keep in mind that while it may seem appropriate to keep your wardrobe as rustic as the surroundings when skiing in the Adirondacks, wearing jeans and a bomber jacket is more likely to get you frozen extremities than admiring looks. The Adirondacks can kick up some serious weather and dangerously low wind-chill factors, so dressing for the elements is essential for a safe and enjoyable experience. As a rule, you should dress in layers of synthetics and wool blends that help trap body heat and repel moisture. The less skin exposed to the elements, the better, and it's always a good idea to have extra socks or gloves along. Check with the ski shop at the mountain for other useful ideas and accessories that can help keep you warm. Also, make sure to read the Climate and Outdoor Safety chapter for other helpful guidelines.

Of the eight downhill ski areas listed here, only Whiteface and Gore are considered "destination" mountains that draw skiers for overnight stays on a regular basis. We mention the types of accommodations found at those two areas in their respective entries, but we suggest you check out the Accommodations chapter for details about specific lodgings.

Lake Placid/ Tri-Lakes Region

Big Tupper Ski Area
Big Tupper Rd., Tupper Lake • 359-7902, (800) 824-4754

What would you say about a ski area where they let kids 8 and younger ski for free, accept Canadian money at par and offer two-for-one lift tickets on Mondays? Well, if you are a Canadian with at least one other friend, little kids and can get off work on Mondays, you should check out the skiing at Big Tupper. That goes for the rest of you skiers too. In fact, the only prerequisite that owner Peter Day has for visitors to his area is a desire to have fun.

With 28 slopes and trails rising 1,152 vertical feet to the summit elevation of 3,136 feet, there is plenty of space at Big Tupper for having fun. Five lifts will get you up the slopes, including three double chairs, one T-bar and one handle tow. Big Tupper's 100 percent snowmaking coverage, meticulous grooming and northern exposure practically guarantee good conditions on the downward journey.

Snowboarders and "little boarders" are both taken care of at Big Tupper. The snowboard park offers all the "air" essentials such as jumps and half-pipes. The Children's Center offers both child care and a "snow play" program to kids 1 and older for $5 an hour (parent's money is accepted).

A variety of lift-ticket plans and packages are available. In 1996-97 adult lift tickets cost $23 midweek, $28 weekends and holidays. Big Tupper is open daily.

FYI

Unless otherwise noted, the area code for all phone numbers listed in this guide is 518.

Mount Pisgah
Mount Pisgah Rd., Saranac Lake • 891-0970

Not as intimidating as you might expect of a place with the same geographic prefix as "Everest," Mount Pisgah is a small, community-oriented ski center geared to families. Owned by the Village of Saranac Lake, its origins date back to 1921.

Mount Pisgah offers one main slope that drops 300 vertical feet, a T-bar to get you back up and snowmaking to keep you sliding along. If you bruise your ego and other extremities after a day at nearby Whiteface, you might want to try Mount Pisgah so you can live (and ski) with yourself again.

Adult lift prices at Mount Pisgah range from $10 to $15, which is about what a large soda and a cup of chowder will cost you at big-time resorts. You can ski at the center on Tuesday through Sunday, including evenings on Tuesday through Friday.

Titus Mountain
Johnson Rd., Malone • 483-3740, (800) 848-8766

Though not formally within the boundaries of the Adirondack Park, Titus is considered an Adirondack ski center. With a 1,200 foot vertical served by 26 trails and a network of seven double and triple chairs, Titus is also one of the largest "Adirondack" ski centers. You'll find both broad smiles and friendly slopes at Titus, which make it an excellent mountain for nov-

Gore Mountain ski area is ideal for family ski outings.

ices and children. As those children become more confident and want to trade in the bunny slope for the race course, Titus offers a variety of racing programs for kids ages 6 to 15. The Titus team puts an emphasis on grooming and snowmaking, which can cover 95 percent of the terrain. Although this northernmost of the Adirondack ski centers can produce some cold and blustery days, Titus' atmosphere is always warm.

Titus is open daily throughout the season, with night skiing available on Wednesday through Saturday. In 1996-97 adult lift tickets cost $25.50 on weekends and only $21 on weekdays — a real bargain by today's standards.

Whiteface Mountain
N.Y. Rt. 86, Wilmington • 946-2223, (800) 462-6236

This is it — the "Adonis" of all Adirondack ski areas. Host of the 1980 Winter Olympic downhill skiing events, Whiteface is huge and muscular, with 66 slopes and trails dropping out of the sky some 3,216 vertical feet. Owned by the State of New York, Whiteface is operated by the Olympic Regional Development Authority (ORDA).

When the skies are clear, which admittedly is not a sure bet, the view from the top of the summit triple chair is simply awesome. You can see for nearly 100 miles, including views of Lake Placid to the west and Mount Marcy to the south. To the east the long ribbon of white outlines Lake Champlain, with the silhouettes of Vermont's Green Mountains beyond.

But wait, there's more! You don't even have to be an expert to enjoy this view and survive the descent. Whiteface offers intermediate routes down from the summit, such as Ridge Runner, Paron's Run, and the newest addition, The Follies.

Of course, if you're a geometry nut and believe in that whole "shortest distance between two points is a straight line" mumbo jumbo, then you can point them down (and I mean straight down) Upper Cloudspin and Upper Skyward. Bump skiers will love Upper Wilderness, and for the rest of you who want to try out an occasional bump or two on gentler terrain, there's Lower Valley.

While Whiteface will challenge even the most serious skiers, it takes great pride in being kid-friendly and family-oriented too. You'll find that more than a third of the mountain terrain appeals to novice and beginner skiers. Kids Kampus is a separate section with a lodge, nursery, chairlift, and network of eight "green circle" runs that will keep your tots entertained all day.

Another convenient feature at Whiteface is the Mid Mountain Lodge and Boule's Bistro, located at the base of Little Whiteface and its collection of advanced and intermediate trails. Now you won't have to visit the base lodge until the end of the day, which means more skiing and less time waiting in cafeteria lines! Of course, if you would rather eat off-mountain, a variety of restaurants and nightspots awaits just down the road in the village of Lake Placid (see our Area Overview chapter).

Snowboarders are not only welcome at Whiteface, but also make up close to a third of all visitors to the mountain. The combination of air-inspiring terrain along with a variety of instructional programs makes Whiteface a premier destination for boarders.

While Whiteface offers usually dependable skiing conditions, it can be a very cold and windy place. Bring a variety of clothing and accessories to handle the variable weather. Natural snowfall is usually plentiful, with more than 120 inches in a typical season. Even in a poor snow year, the Whiteface team can cover 93 percent of their terrain with snowmaking. Don't let the brown muck at home keep you from throwing the skis on the rack!

For the 1997-98 season, you can expect trail enhancements, more snowmaking and possibly the opportunity to ski "out of bounds" in the natural slide area. This assumes you become bored with the "in bounds" skiing at Whiteface, which isn't likely.

You have dozens of choices for nearby accommodations, ranging from full-service conference hotels to luxurious country inns and small family-owned motels. Most are clustered in and around the village of Lake Placid, with some additional options in nearby Wilmington. See the Accommodations chapter for more details.

No visit to the Adirondacks during the winter is complete without a day at Whiteface, so block out your calendar, block out your apprehensions that it's too tough and go have some fun!

Whiteface Mountain is open daily. Adult lift tickets for 1996-97 cost $34 during the week

and $39 on weekends and holidays — arguably one of the best bargains in big-time skiing.

Lake George/ Upper Hudson Region

Gore Mountain
Peaceful Valley Rd., off N.Y. Rt. 28, North Creek • 251-2411, (800) 342-1234

Gore is the "sister" mountain to Whiteface and is also state-owned and ORDA-operated. Big plans and big changes are underway at Gore that are helping it escape the shadow of Whiteface and carve out its place in the upper echelon of eastern U.S. ski areas.

Already, Gore has a lot going for it that eastern New York skiers have known for years. For example, Gore has 46 trails and a 2,100-foot vertical drop from its summit. That gives it more vertical skiing than some of the "big-name resorts." It offers some of the longest cruising terrain in the East, with runs stretching more than a mile. A detachable high-speed triple chair makes it all possible again in just 6 minutes! (Detachable chairlifts are great because they "come off" the lift cable at the loading station, slow to a crawl until you are safely seated, then "re-attach" to the fast-moving cable for your ascent.) Advanced skiers have a quad chairlift on the upper mountain that serves the bumps and steeps. Snowboarders enjoy the jumps, bumps and half-pipe of Terrain Park.

Gore's location in the southern Adirondacks makes it one of the most accessible big mountains in the East. Even so, Gore's reputation throughout its 33-year history is that of a "daytrip" mountain, not a "destination" mountain.

That reputation is about to change . . . big time. More than $30 million in major projects will dramatically change Gore over a six-year period leading up to the new century. Some of the highlights include the development of an entire new section of the mountain, with more

than a dozen new trails, new lifts, a brand-new summit lodge and complete renovation of the existing base lodge. Also scheduled for replacement is Gore's signature gondola. In its place you will be able to take a state-of-the-art high-speed gondola to the top of the new summit in less than half the time of the old relic.

More immediate improvements that you can enjoy in 1997-98 include a greatly expanded snowmaking capacity, thanks to the completion of a 2-mile pipeline from the Hudson River. The $4.4 million project brings Gore's snowmaking capacity to nearly 100 percent of its terrain. It has already paid off, as Gore opened its 1996-97 season on the weekend before Thanksgiving and did not close until mid-April when skiers ran out before the snow did. In addition, a new quad lift will replace the north-side double chair, and a new intermediate cruiser will join the options off the popular Sunway trail. For experts, a new super-steep trail will open next to current thrillchamp, The Rumor. To expand the variety of skiing experiences available at Gore, plans are underway for the addition of glade skiing and lift-served backcountry skiing.

Mountain Manager Michael Pratt, who has been at Gore for more than 11 years, takes great pride in working to provide skiing families a quality recreational experience and a safe, friendly environment. With an extensive variety of teaching programs, a new beginners' area with its own lift, and the Bear Cub Den for tiny skiers-to-be, Pratt seems well on the way to achieving and maintaining this goal.

The list of available accommodations convenient to Gore keeps growing, with townhouses, country inns and full-service lodging available in nearby North Creek and (relatively nearby) Lake George. See the Accommodations chapter for details on your lodging options.

Gore is open daily, with a variety of ticket plans and discounts. Regular full-day adult tickets in 1996-97 cost $29 weekdays and $39 on weekends and holiday periods.

West Mountain
West Mountain Rd., Queensbury
• 793-6606

Just off Exit 18 of the Adirondack Northway (Interstate 87), West is probably the only ski area in (well, very near) the Adirondacks that can safely say, "You can't miss us." The white fingers of snow that snake 1,010 vertical feet down the face of West Mountain serve as a sentinel to northbound travelers, welcoming all at the gateway to the Adirondack region.

West is primarily a day area for families from adjacent Glens Falls and nearby Saratoga Springs. It features extensive night skiing on all but a few of its 22 slopes and trails. The views at night of the lights below make Glens Falls seem quite romantic and cosmopolitan, an illusion not fully realized in the daylight.

West can cover 70 percent of its terrain with snowguns. Two double chairs, a triple and three surface lifts easily handle the skier traffic at West, making long lines a rarity.

One convenient feature at West is the four- and eight-hour "start anytime" lift ticket — particularly handy for skiers with small children who haven't been anywhere "on time" in the last five years! For adults, the four-hour ticket costs $20, and the eight-hour ticket is only $25. West Mountain is open daily throughout the season.

Southern Adirondacks
Lakes Region

Oak Mountain
Elm Lake Rd., off N.Y. Rt. 30, Speculator
• 548-7311

Oak did not operate during the 1996-97 season. It is one of the few ski mountains that, to date, has not added snowmaking capabilities

Photo: Plattsburgh/North Country Chamber of Commerce

Spectacular winter scenery is a constant companion of the cross-country skier.

to its arsenal. The Germaine family, which owns the center, hopes to change that in time for the 1997-98 season and re-open. That would be good news for everyone because Oak is a great-looking ski mountain in the heart of some of the prettiest land in the Adirondacks.

Oak Mountain features a vertical drop of 650 feet on 13 slopes and trails. Three T-bars provide the uphill transport. Here's hoping that when you call Oak Mountain in 1998 you'll hear, "We're open and the skiing is great, so come see us!"

Royal Mountain
N.Y. Rt. 10, Caroga Lake • 835-6445

If you measure a ski area by the dedication and involvement of its owner, then Royal definitely warrants an A-plus. Jim Blaise has been the owner and operator of Royal since 1971, and the pride he has in the mountain is reflected in the happy faces of its skiers.

Just outside the southern boundary of the Adirondack Park, Royal is a classic family ski center serving visitors and residents of the Great Sacandaga Lake, Gloversville, Johnstown and throughout the Southern Adirondack Lakes area. It offers a modest but challenging vertical drop of 550 feet, 11 slopes and trails, one double chair and two surface lifts.

The recent addition of snowmaking has improved the consistency of conditions dramatically at Royal as well as lengthened its season (into April in 1996-97). You can enjoy Royal Mountain on weekends and holidays during the season. In 1996-97 adult lift tickets cost $18.

Old Forge/ Raquette Lake Region

McCauley Mountain
McCauley Mountain Rd., off Bisby Rd., Old Forge • (315) 369-3225

If you are a fan of skiing on natural snow, McCauley might just be the place for you. The westernmost of the Adirondack downhill ski centers, McCauley is close enough to Lake Ontario to benefit from its generous dumpings of "lake effect" snow that can produce upward of 200 inches in a season.

As the "snow-dome" of New York State, the Old Forge area is very popular with snowmobilers. You're likely to make several dozen "sightings" of such on your way to this ski area. Once at McCauley, however, you are more likely to see lift attendants feeding deer than snowmobilers feeding gas tanks.

As for the skiing, you'll enjoy some of the most challenging terrain in the Adirondacks, in spite of its deceptively mild vertical drop of 633 feet. You can take your pick of 14 slopes and trails, but choose carefully or you will find yourself on the steep and bumpy instead of the smooth and groomed. Don't worry, there is plenty of both here. In those rare Old Forge winters when Mother Nature needs some help, McCauley can carpet 60 percent of its terrain with the machine-made stuff.

One double chair, two T-bars, a poma (with a disc for a seat instead of a T-shaped bar) and a rope tow provide the uphill transport, while back at the bottom you'll find a bag of McDonald's fries awaiting you. That's right, McDonald's has set up shop in the base lodge. You can decide if that's a clever convenience or a decidedly non-rustic distraction.

McCauley is open daily throughout the season. In 1996-97 adult lift tickets cost $12 during the week and $22 on weekends and holidays.

Cross-country Skiing

Perhaps the winter activity closest in spirit to what the Adirondacks is all about is cross-country skiing. How better to enjoy and appreciate the beauty of winter than gliding across a meadow under the watchful eye of the wooded peaks standing sentinel above? Cross-country skiing allows you to become enveloped in the environment, rather than rush through it on the way to catch the next lift. You can feel your blood pumping and your body warming up much easier on cross-country skis than sitting high up in a chairlift as it ascends, unprotected from the cold Adirondack winds of winter. Don't get us wrong — we love both — it's just that there is something undeniably serene and special about cross-country skiing in the Adirondacks. And while it might not look so pretty at the end of your driveway, the sight of untouched snow blanketing a wooded trail as you stride and slide along might just make you change your mind about winter.

You will find more than 800 kilometers of designated cross-country ski trails in the Adirondacks, including municipal parks, upscale Nordic ski resorts and backcountry wilderness. A good workout for just about anybody, don't you think? And don't forget to bring the kids along. Many of the ski centers feature programs for kids, a full line of rental equipment, and for skinny-skiers-to-be, pulks (small sleds) that mom and dad (mostly dad) get to pull them along.

The following are descriptions of some of the most popular cross-country ski centers in the Adirondacks, along with a listing of the primary trail systems available for skiing. As a rule, trail fees range from free at some of the publicly owned ski areas to $10 at a few of the full-service, upscale Nordic resorts.

While most ski centers offer access to their trails from 8:30 AM until 4 PM, some also feature night skiing on limited terrain. We note those areas that offer night skiing. Unless otherwise noted, all ski centers offer lessons — a good idea because it's not as easy as pictures of skiers gliding across flat terrain make it look. Even so, with just one lesson a novice can get out, explore and enjoy miles of trails.

Some of the most popular cross-country ski centers offer inns and restaurants on site, which you'll find an attractive (and much appreciated by your weary bones) option. We let you know in their respective descriptions which areas offer such amenities.

As with downhill skiing, clothing yourself with layers of synthetic, wool blend and moisture-resistant fabrics is important to staying warm and dry. Cotton, though comfy, is not a good choice for winter recreation because it retains moisture but not heat. Once again, we suggest you read, re-read, then read again the chapter on Climate and Outdoor Safety.

In any case, cross-country skiing gives you an impressive scenic and exercise value for your dollar. You should call ahead for the latest trail fee rates and packages.

For more information, contact the New York State Cross-Country Ski Areas Association at 283-5509. The *New York State Winter Travel and Ski Guide* has a comprehensive listing of cross-country ski centers and trail systems. Call the New York Division of Tourism office at (800) I LOVE NY to request a copy.

Lake Placid/ Tri-Lakes Region

Adirondack Visitor Interpretive Center at Paul Smiths
N.Y. Rt. 30, Paul Smiths • 327-3000

This is probably the only place in the Adirondacks where you can get both an education and exercise for free. The Visitor Interpretive Center (VIC) has 17 kilometers of trails available for skiing, along with a number of programs on the natural history of the Adirondack Park. There is no better way to appreciate the scenery than to learn how it got to be that way. Unlike some of the full-service Nordic ski resorts, the VIC does not offer lessons, a ski shop or rental equipment. If you are an experienced skier with your own equipment, this can be a perfect place to spend an Adirondack afternoon.

There is also a VIC with a trail system in Newcomb, 582-2000, some 25 miles south of Paul Smiths. Though rough conditions make snowshoeing the trails at Newcomb the recommended mode of transportation, you might want to try skiing the Santanoni loop that leads to the great camp of the same name.

Adirondack Loj
Adirondack Loj Rd., Lake Placid
• 523-3441

This ski center is unique in that it is owned by the Adirondack Mountain Club (see the related Close-up in Other Summer Recreation), the education-, conservation- and recreation-focused organization that celebrated its 75th birthday in 1997. Therefore, the emphasis here is on instruction and guided tours throughout 20 kilometers of backcountry trails. Though the trails are not machine-groomed, they are usually track-set by skier traffic.

The "lodge" itself is more than 70 years old but retains its charm and ability to provide a comfortable setting for both the serious enthusiast and casual recreational skier. If you'd like to stay as a guest at the Loj, you'll find both private and dorm-style accommodations with semi-private (that is, down the hall and shared) baths as well as family-style meals. For those of you who feel the Loj is much too cosmopolitan, ADK maintains five cabins available on nearby Heart Lake and along some of their backcountry trails.

The Bark Eater Cross-Country Ski Center
Alstead Hill Rd., Keene • 576-2221

In the Keene Valley meadows beneath an impressive collection of the High Peaks, the Bark Eater Inn offers the comforts of a true country inn with a wide variety of skiing options. Besides its 20 kilometers of groomed,

track-set trails, the Bark Eater provides easy access to the eastern end of the renowned Jackrabbit Trail (see the subsequent "Cross-country Ski Trails System" section).

Joe-Pete Wilson, a former U.S. Olympic Cross-country team member and teammate of Olavi Hirvonen (see the subsequent Lapland Lake entry) at the 1960 Squaw Valley games, is the owner of the Bark Eater (see our Accommodations chapter for more information). The inn offers one of the best combinations of comfortable lodging, fine dining and great skiing in the Adirondacks. A rental shop is available, as are lessons for guests of the inn.

Cascade Cross-Country Ski Center
Cascade Rd., Lake Placid • 523-9605

Cascade is a full-service, designed-for-Nordic ski center that opened in 1978. While it has 20 kilometers of groomed trails of its own to enjoy, you can access more than 100 kilometers of skiing from Cascade's strategic location along the Jackrabbit Trail between Lake Placid and Keene. It is also convenient to the Olympic ski trails at the Mount Van Hoevenberg complex, just a mile or so away. If you're feeling particularly adventurous, you can join up with one of Cascade's guided overnight backcountry ski tours. If you're not quite that adventurous but still want a taste of the wild, try one of the center's full-moon parties. You will join other enthusiasts in celebrating your trek deep into the moonlit woods with bonfires and refreshments upon arrival in the exact middle of nowhere. And you thought there was nothing going on there!

Cascade offers all the amenities you could need, including a ski shop, rentals, lessons, a restaurant and bar.

Lake Placid Resort
One Olympic Dr., Lake Placid • 523-2556

On the grounds of the famous (former) Lake Placid Club resort, this ski center offers 25 kilometers of groomed and track-set cross-country skiing along two golf course layouts.

INSIDERS' TIP

Whiteface Mountain often hosts World Cup racing and freestyle events. Check the event schedule at the Olympic Regional Development Authority, (518) 523-1655.

Much of the skiing is out in the open of the golf course fairways, and the views of the surrounding mountains are spectacular. You can find rental equipment, take a lesson and warm up at the clubhouse. Being so close to the shops, lodging and restaurants of Lake Placid make this one of the most convenient places to "get away from it all" in the Adirondacks.

Dewey Mountain
N.Y. Rt. 3, Saranac Lake • 891-2697

More a community-oriented recreation area than a Nordic ski resort, Dewey Mountain is unpretentious and diverse in its offerings. Here you can find a good variety of terrain for both beginners and experts on 20 kilometers of groomed trails. Some trails scale the sides of 2,100-foot Dewey Mountain and reward you with outstanding views of Lower Saranac Lake. After a hard day in the office (Is there such a thing in the Adirondacks?), you can reward yourself with a relaxing evening of skiing on the 5 kilometers of lighted trails. Check out the calendar of events at Dewey and you'll find snowshoeing contests, orienteering outings, an annual chili cook-off and more. Lessons, rental equipment and the warmth of a wood stove are available in the base lodge.

Jackrabbit Trail
Paul Smiths to Keene • 523-1365

The Jackrabbit Trail deserves special mention. It is a unique system linking backcountry trails with a number of ski centers and their trail systems, including Mount Van Hoevenberg, Cascade, Lake Placid Resort and the Lake Placid Nordic Center. Also nearby and accessible to the system are the Adirondack Loj, Dewey Mountain and the Bark Eater Inn. (See the previous sections for details about these centers.)

The Jackrabbit resulted from the combined efforts of a group of skiing enthusiasts who formed the Adirondack Ski Touring Council with the mission of combining the area's many trail networks into a continuous system. You can ski the resulting network all the way from Paul Smiths to Keene, some 55 kilometers (33 miles) away. The trail is named for Herman "Jackrabbit" Johannsen, a Norwegian who made a tremendous impact on the skiing scene in Lake Placid in the (this is not a typo)

111 years he lived on this earth. "Jackrabbit" lived in Lake Placid from 1916 to 1928, during which time he taught skiing and guided groups across the terrain that would one day be named for him.

Lake Placid Lodge Cross-Country Ski Center
Whiteface Inn Rd., Lake Placid • 523-2700

You will find one of the most luxurious skiing, lodging and dining experiences in the Adirondacks along the shores of Lake Placid at this magnificent facility. Owned since 1993 by the same family that operates the ultra-upscale The Point on Upper Saranac Lake, this is truly a place where every occasion is special. Not surprisingly, it is also one of the most expensive resorts in the region, but if you're ready to splurge, do it here. The skiing combines existing trails at the lodge with terrain at the Whiteface Inn golf course, providing a total of 20 kilometers of meticulously groomed, track-set trails. In particular, don't miss the views of Whiteface Mountain as you ski across the frozen surface of Lake Placid.

A variety of skiing itineraries is available, including natural history tours and skiing under the full moon. If you would rather just browse than ski, the beautiful ski shop will hold your interest a lot more easily than you'll be able to hold on to your money! There is nothing that you could need or want in a cross-country getaway weekend that you won't find here. The toughest part will be persuading yourself to go back home. (See Accommodations for more information about Lake Placid Lodge.)

Lake Placid Nordic Center
N.Y. Rt. 86, Lake Placid • 523-2551, (800) 422-6757

Another popular option in the Lake Placid area, this center offers 30 kilometers of groomed trails around the grounds of the Whiteface Inn, about half of which are track-set. You'll catch glimpses of Whiteface Mountain and the frozen surface of Lake Placid along the way. High Peaks Cyclery manages the operation, offering a full line of rental equipment and lessons. Rustic cabin lodging as well as modern condos are available here at the Whiteface Inn.

Mount Van Hoevenberg Olympic Sports Complex

N.Y. Rt. 73, Lake Placid
• 523-2811, (800) 462-6236

As big as it sounds, this multisport center is home to a myriad of activities and events. This is where the 1980 Olympic bobsled and luge runs took place as well as the cross-country skiing competition. Have no fear — there's plenty of fun and friendly terrain here for non-Olympians as well. In fact, with 50 kilometers of groomed and track-set trails, Mount Van Hoevenberg offers as much skiing as any area in the Adirondacks, and no place can rival its history. The wide trails here set up well for both classical- and skating-style skiing and are ideal for the strong instruction available here.

Operated by the Olympic Regional Development Authority, this is also the site of many national and world-class racing events. Make sure you call ahead to get a schedule of events for the complex. You may be able to get some scenic exercise in the morning and witness an exciting (and humbling) event in the afternoon. If you have one day in the Lake Placid area, you should definitely make time for Mount Van Hoevenberg.

Plattsburgh/Western Lake Champlain Region

Ausable Chasm Cross-Country Ski Center

U.S. Hwy. 9, Ausable Chasm • 834-9990

The deep gorge at Ausable Chasm is one of the natural wonders of the Adirondack region and provides this ski center with a unique backdrop. You will find 26 kilometers of groomed trails here, along with rental equipment, warming huts and lessons by appointment. Limited night skiing also is available.

Lake George/Upper Hudson Region

Cunningham's Ski Barn – North Creek

1 Main St., North Creek • 251-3215

For a change in both pace and scenery, try cross-country skiing along the vigorous headwaters of the Hudson River (yes, the same Hudson that flows under the George Washington Bridge connecting upper Manhattan and Fort Lee, New Jersey — it has to begin somewhere!). Cunningham's offers both 30 kilometers of groomed trails along the Hudson and through stands of Adirondack hardwood, along with backcountry skiing in its new Beaver Meadows trail system. You'll find everything you need here, including a terrific ski shop, full line of rentals (including the fun and easy "short skis"), snack bar and lessons.

Friends Lake Inn Nordic Ski Center

Friends Lake Rd., Chestertown • 494-4751

If R&R (romance and relaxation) are as big a priority to you as skiing, then this is the place for you. At Friends Lake, you'll find 32 kilometers of groomed cross-country and wilderness backcountry skiing ranging from gentle glades along the Murphy's Romance trail to the pulse-quickening challenge of Cardiac Hill. All this great skiing will only help to build up your appetite for what is truly one of the finest restaurants in the Adirondacks . . . which just so happens to be in one of the most romantic country inns anywhere in the East. As much as we love kids — leave them at home with their grandparents for this one! You may want to time your getaway to coincide with one of Friends Lake's special "ccc" (cross-country culinary) events, such as the Wilderness Ski and Fondue Party (usually in February) and the Gourmet Ski Fest (early

---

INSIDERS' TIP

You can enjoy the views and convenience of Amtrak's "ski train" service, called *The Adirondack*, on its run between New York City and Montreal. The train makes several stops within the Adirondack region and is equipped to carry skis, so leave the car at home! Call (800) USA-RAIL for details.

Photo: Plattsburgh/North Country Chamber of Commerce

The High Peaks of the Adirondacks cast a jagged silhouette against the winter sky.

March). Stopping for a break at gourmet food displays set up along the scenic trails — now that's our idea of leading a balanced lifestyle.

For more information on the Friends Lake Inn and Restaurant, check out the Accommodations and Restaurants chapters.

Garnet Hill Cross-Country Ski Center
13th Lake Rd., North River • 251-2444

Owner George Heim is obviously proud as he stands on the balcony of this resort's main lodge and points out Thirteenth Lake some 1,300 feet below. Beyond that lies the Siamese Ponds Wilderness, a seemingly endless vista of rounded mountains and hills that surrounds this full-service resort. Along with wife Mary, George has owned Garnet Hill since 1977 and has seen it grow and evolve into a four-season resort featuring first-class lodging, fine dining and a wide variety of winter and summer recreation. The focus remains on cross-country skiing, for which Garnet Hill earned the plaudits of *Snow Country* magazine as "one of the ten best cross-country ski resorts in North America."

At an elevation of 2,000 feet, Garnet Hill averages more than 120 inches of snow each winter. On March 28, 1997, there was still a base of 18 inches around the main lodge,

called the Log House. Not only can you enjoy skiing here into early April, you also can enjoy skiing "downhill" here as well. One of the special features at Garnet Hill is the option to ski a 4-mile route down a gradual drop of 500 vertical feet to a shuttle bus that will take you back to the top. Now that's our kind of cross-country! Also fun and different is skiing to the working Sugarhouse when the sap is flowing in springtime.

Garnet Hill Cross-Country Ski Center features 55 kilometers of groomed trails with both set-track and skating lanes. Night skiing is offered on limited terrain. Lessons, rental equipment and a large ski shop are available. You can choose from accommodations in three lodges and enjoy full-service dining in the Log House. See the Accommodations and Restaurants chapters for more information.

Gore Mountain Cross-Country Ski Center
Peaceful Valley Rd., North Creek • 251-2411

While downhill skiing is definitely the big (and getting bigger) focus here, cross-country skiing is getting a share of the spotlight here as well. Presently, there are 11 kilometers of groomed trails that conveniently originate at the base lodge of the downhill area.

This opens you up for another bumps-and-jumps (for the kids)/slide-and-glide (for the parents) combo, if that's what will preserve the family peace and the family knee joints. While alpine skiing remains the emphasis at Gore, plans call for lift-served backcountry and cross-country skiing by 1998, which will definitely set Gore apart from the pack. With such a strong and varied collection of cross-country ski centers nearby (Garnet Hill, Friends Lake, Cunningham's; see previous entries), it might take such a development to entice you to try out Gore for more than just the steeps, bumps and cruising under the lifts. Gore offers a full slate of lessons, rentals, food service and an extensive ski shop. (See Accommodations for details about lodging options in nearby North Creek.)

Southern Adirondack Lakes Region

Lapland Lake Cross Country Ski and Vacation Center
139 Lapland Lake Rd., Northville • 863-4974

The summer of 1998 will mark 20 years since Lapland Lake owner and former U.S. Olympian Olavi Hirvonen bought the property that would become, according to *Snow Country* magazine, one of the top-10 cross-country ski resorts in the East. He and his wife, Ann, have much to be proud of. Lapland Lake is truly a special place that feels familiar and foreign at the same time: familiar from the warmth of the visitors and the employees; foreign because of the distinctively Finnish flavor to just about everything here, from the tupas (housekeeping cottages) to the trail names.

Lapland, in the southern Adirondacks, is just an hour or so drive from Albany. Once here, you'll find 38 kilometers of meticulously groomed trails, with both track-set and skating lanes, along with another 10 kilometers of wilderness trail on adjacent state land. You will find a couple of real reindeer waiting to greet you along the Lake Trail that leads out to Woods Lake (which is also skiable). A good mix of beginner, intermediate and expert terrain awaits you at Lapland Lake, along with

lessons in both classical and skating technique so you can handle it all. The ski shop features rental equipment if you're just starting out and retail equipment if you're hooked and want your own stuff.

When you need a rest, the lodge has a pleasant sitting area, complete with wood-burning stove and Finnish folk music to help you relax (which, we assure you, won't be difficult to do). And if you simply can't get enough exercise during the day, night skiing is available on 3.5 kilometers of trails both Friday and Saturday evenings. After a day on the trails, you might want to stay put awhile and enjoy The Tuulen Tupa Restaurant featuring (you guessed it) hearty Finnish cuisine as well as more familiar items. Even better, stay overnight at one of the 10 tupas (housekeeping cottages) so you can get up tomorrow and do it all over again.

Old Forge/Raquette Lake Region

Adirondack Woodcraft Ski Touring Center
Rondaxe Rd., Old Forge • (315) 369-6031

This family-run ski center benefits from good late-season snows (thanks to the lake-effect dumps from Lake Ontario) and skier-friendly terrain that is particularly pleasant for beginners and novices. You can ski on 12 kilometers of groomed trails that in summer serve as camp roads. Rental equipment is available, but not lessons or food. Night skiing is available Friday and Saturday evenings.

Fern Park Recreation Area
Loomis Rd., Inlet • (315) 357-5501

Considered by locals to be the "best kept secret of the Adirondacks" (although we suspect there are quite a few well-kept secrets in these parts!), the 20 kilometers of groomed trails at Fern Park are, at the very least, a terrific bargain. That is to say, they're free. While you won't find resort-like amenities such as a ski shop, lodge or restaurant (there are several options nearby), you will find a fun variety of scenic terrain.

Photo: ORDA

The view from atop Whiteface Mountain ski area is breathtaking.

McCauley Mountain
McCauley Mountain Rd., Old Forge
• (315) 369-3225

You can have your snow and ski it too at McCauley, where you can enjoy both the steeps of the alpine ski center and the 20 kilometers of groomed, track-set cross-country trails as well. Here's an idea: Let the kids catch a bunch of air on the mountain while you enjoy the serenity of the woods that surround it. McCauley offers the best of both worlds, almost always good snow and a range of amenities including rentals, lessons, a ski shop and food service.

Cross-country Ski Trail Systems

Along with the wide variety of dedicated ski centers and resorts throughout the Adirondack region, you also will find dozens of marked trail systems awaiting your exploration. Be aware that conditions on these trail systems will vary, and much of the terrain is ungroomed. The following is an alphabetical listing (by region) of some of the most popular trail systems.

Lake Placid/Tri-Lakes Region

Black Bear Mountain, Eagle Bay, 10 km • (315) 357-4403
Cold River Horse Trail, Tupper Lake, 17 km • 359-7559
Covewood Lodge, Eagle Bay, 50 km • (315) 357-3041
Cranberry Lake Ski Trail, Cranberry Lake, 16 km • (315) 386-4000

Lake George/
Upper Hudson Region

Caroline Fish Memorial Trail, Chestertown, 11 km • 494-2722
Glens Falls International, Glens Falls, 7 km • 761-3813
Keith DeLarm Bikeway, Lake George, 13.5 km • 623-2877
Pharaoh Lake Wilderness Area, Schroon Lake, 50 km • 532-7675

— continued on next page

Rogers Rock Campground, Hague, 10 km • 543-6161
Warren County Trails, Warrensburg, 25 km • 623-2877

Southern Adirondack
Lakes Region

Abanakee Loop, Indian Lake, 6 km • 648-5112
Kunjamuk Loop, Speculator, 10 km • 548-4521
Piseco Airport Loop, Speculator, 10 km • 548-4521

A Few Words About Backcountry Skiing

Just when you thought you had exhausted both your legs and all your options for cross-country skiing in the Adirondacks, someone leans over and whispers into your ear, "backcountry." Backcountry skiing is, in effect, making your way through the wilderness at your own pace, in your own chosen direction. Or at least that's the plan. The Adirondacks present almost limitless possibilities for this type of activity, provided you have developed your skills, studied your maps and prepared for your journey. We strongly suggest you read the Climate and Outdoor Safety chapter to help you prepare for backcountry skiing. The Adirondacks can be as severe a region in its climate and environment as it is serene in its beauty.

For more information on planning a backcountry ski trip, contact the Adirondack Mountain Club at 523-3441, or the Adirondack Ski Touring Council at 523-1365. The Discover Series of 11 regional recreational guides published by Lake View Press provide detailed reviews of backcountry ski trails.

With all the dozens of downhill and cross-country skiing options available to you in the Adirondacks, you'll almost be thankful for the springtime "mud season" as a chance to rest those weary muscles. Almost.

Options for winter recreation are as varied as the weather, with virtually every form of sliding, skating and otherwise propelling yourself over and through "the white stuff" available here in the Adirondacks.

Other Winter Recreation

For those of you who plan to limit your Adirondack recreational experiences to an occasional round of golf and, for the sheer adventure of it, maybe sticking your big toe in the lake on the Fourth of July, wake up and smell the snowflakes! You're missing half the fun of the Adirondacks — the winter half, that is! Just because it is cold, snowy and iced-over for nearly half the year doesn't mean you can't have fun with it. In fact, you should learn to enjoy it, because there isn't much meteorological data indicating any big changes in future Adirondack winter weather patterns.

Fortunately, your options for winter recreation are as varied as the weather, with virtually every form of sliding, skating and otherwise propelling yourself over and through "the white stuff" available here in the Adirondacks. As you could see if you tried to make it through the Skiing chapter in one sitting, folks take their winter recreation pretty seriously in the Adirondacks. In this chapter, we'll take a "big picture" look at three of the most popular and accessible activities (above and beyond skiing and snowboarding): ice fishing, ice skating and snowmobiling. We'll also mention some other activities you might want to try, depending on your energy level and your nerve.

Keep in mind the importance of good common sense, awareness of your surroundings and the climate, the proper clothing and equipment — in short, preparation is the key to enjoying the Adirondack outdoors during the wintertime. We strongly suggest you read and memorize (well, at least be familiar with) the Climate and Outdoor Safety chapter before heading out, at any time of the year, to enjoy the Adirondacks.

Ice Fishing

For those anglers who don't have their fill of fishing during the warm-weather season, the sport of ice fishing awaits, where the challenge is not only to catch some fish, but also to stay warm. Although fish become somewhat lethargic during the cold weather, most species have little choice but to remain active and seek out their daily meal. Using different techniques than those employed during the warmer months, anglers actually might discover ice fishing offers better action and catches than summer fishing.

Ice fishing requires no fishing pole. A tip-up is used — fishing line attached to a foot-tall, seesaw-like device that tips up a little flag when a fish is hooked. (The name and address of the operator must be on all tip-ups, and he or she must be present when the lines are in the water.) The angler then pulls up the line by hand and attempts to maneuver the fish through an approximately 8-inch-diameter hole in the ice. If the fish is larger than 8 inches, which is entirely possible on Lake Champlain and other large lakes in the region, the angler encounters the perplexing problem of getting a large, wiggling albeit slightly sluggish fish through the smaller hole.

This challenge is compounded by the fact that ice fishing is not a solitary sport like fly fishing. Anglers tend to congregate in shacks or shanties at the better fishing spots on the lake. In these heated shanties, which feature many of the comforts of home — stoves, beds and portable TVs — a group of friends talk, play cards or whatever to pass the time until the flag signals an event. The group then meanders out of the shanty to watch the contest between angler and fish unfold. Since the shanties are near each other, and everyone watches the others' tip-ups, the little group can become a large crowd. Everyone in the crowd offers suggestions on how to get the potentially large fish through the small hole.

Will the fish or the angler win? The answer may not be as important as how the angler can retell the tale of the momentous struggle, given all those witnesses.

Ice fishing can be fun in itself if you enjoy angling, but being with friends makes the sport even more fun.

For the uninitiated, it's easy to learn. The easiest way is buy a few tip-ups — generally less than $10 — and some bait and go find a hole in the ice left by a previous angler. With a little chiseling, the day-old ice will open up. Since ice anglers tend to sit around waiting for something to happen, you can generally find a kindly type who will gladly give you tips, if you ask. You don't need a shanty, although it does make the experience far more comfortable than sitting out in the cold. Shanties rent for about $15 per person per day with heat and tip-ups often included. Towns along Lake Champlain such as Moriah, the self-proclaimed fishing capital of the region, or Crown Point offer plenty of rentals. Shanty owners often will show you the basics of setting the tip-ups and suggest the best bait. The trick, however, is finding the owners. As a rule, rentals are far

easier to find on larger lakes than on smaller ones. Local sporting good stores, bait shops and the chamber of commerce are good starting points.

Anglers need New York State fishing licenses and must follow ice-fishing regulations and restrictions. Call or write the Department of Environmental Conservation (DEC) for details at the Region 5 office, N.Y. Route 86, P.O. Box 296, Ray Brook, New York 12977. The telephone number is 897-1200. People can also contact the Sub Office, Hudson Street, P.O. Box 220, Warrensburg, New York 12885. The telephone number is 623-3671.

FYI

Unless otherwise noted, the area code for all phone numbers listed in this guide is 518.

Where to Fish

Knowing where to ice fish is the first requirement for a successful trip. Generally, ice fishing is allowed in all non-trout waters, but check with the DEC if you are unsure. A selected list of public lakes, with fish species in parenthesis, follows. Please note that special restrictions may apply to the lakes mentioned.

Fish-code Key
BC — black crappie
BT— brown trout
LLS — landlocked salmon
LMB — largemouth bass
LT— lake trout
NP — northern pike
PKL— pickerel
PKS — pumpkinseed
RB — rock bass
RT — rainbow trout
SMB — smallmouth bass
SPK — splake
WAE — walleye
WF — whitefish
YP — yellow perch

Lake Placid/Tri-Lakes Region
Buck Pond (NP,YP)
Fish Creek Ponds (NP, YP, PKS)
Franklin Falls Flow (NP, YP, WAE, RB, PKS)
Indian Lake (BT, YP, PKS)
Lake Clear (BT, NP, SPK, YP, LLS)
Lake Colby (BT, RT, LLS, YP, PKS)

Ice fishermen are a hardy lot.

Lower, Middle and Upper Saranac Lakes (NP, YP, PKS)

Meacham Lake (SPK, NP, YP, PKS)

Tupper Lake (LLS, LT, NP, WAE, WF, YP, PKS)

Plattsburgh/Western Lake Champlain Region

Lower Chateaugay Lake (LT, LLS, RT, YP, PKS, NP)

Chazy Lake (LT, RT, LLS, YP, PKS)

Eagle Lake (BT, WF, YP, PKS)

Indian River (LT, LLS, BT, SMB, LMB, NP)

Lake Champlain (varies by location)

Lake George/ Upper Hudson Region

Hudson River (WAE, NP, YP)

Lake George (LT, LLS, RT, BT, NP, PKL, BC, YP)

Paradox Lake (LT, RT, YP, PKS)

Schroon Lake (LT, LLS, YP, PKL, BC)

Southern Adirondacks Lakes Region

Great Sacandaga Lake (WAE, NP, YP, BC, BT, RT)

Piseco Lake (LT, YP, WF)

Old Forge/ Raquette Lake Region

Raquette Lake (LT, ST, YP, WF, LLS)

Sacandaga Lake (PKS, YP, WAE, BT, RT)

Seventh Lake (RT, LT, YP, LLS, ST)

Sound Lake (BC, PKL, YP, PKS)

Ice Skating

In the history of winter sports in Lake Placid, discussion usually focuses upon the 1932 and 1980 Winter Olympics, but there is far more sports history found in this little town, especially as it relates to the world of figure skating.

The modern world of figure skating, with its triple and quadruple jumps, flying sit spins and choreographed programs set to music, can trace its roots to Lake Placid where Gustave Lussi, one of the most influential and innovative coaches in the history of the sport, taught.

From 1932, when Lussi introduced the sport's first summer skating school in Lake Placid, through today, Lussi's ideas and innovations continue to influence the sport. The flying sit spin; the flying or "Button" camel, popularized by the Olympic Champion, Dick

Button; the "Hamill" camel of Dorothy Hamill fame; the double axle; the first triple jumps . . . all originated with Lussi. While spectators today continue to marvel at the jumps and maneuvers invented by Lussi, his influence also is felt in the methodology used to teach the sport. Lussi was the first to study the physics of skating and use physics laws in the development of a figure skating maneuver. For example, he understood what steps to follow and how the body should be positioned to accomplish a particular jump. He also was one of the first coaches in any sport to extend his teaching beyond technique and consider the whole athlete. Perhaps without ever realizing it, coaches throughout the world use many of Lussi's techniques and methodology in instructing future champions.

The list of Lussi students who became world and Olympic champions remains arguably the most impressive in all of sports. Students of Lussi who trained with him in Lake Placid include: Dick Button, a two-time Olympic champion and the first skater to land a double axle in competition; Olympic champions Tenley Albright, Dorothy Hamill and John Curry; and world champions Hayes Jenkins, David Jenkins, Otto and Maria Jelinek, Emmerich Danzer, Aja Zanova and John Petkevich.

Today, skating programs for virtually every level of skater, from world-class competitors to beginning students, are available year round at the Olympic Center, Main Street, Lake Placid, 523-1655 (see Kidstuff for more information). Students can learn from a host of former Olympic competitors, including U.S. National Men's Champion and Ice Capades star Tommy Litz, Lorna Wighton-Aldridge and Karen Courtland Kelly. For students interested in the techniques of Gus Lussi, who died in 1993, Cecily Morrow carries on his tradition.

www.insiders.com

See this and many other **Insiders' Guide®** destinations online — in their entirety.

Visit us today!

In summer 1992, the International School of Ice Dancing, under the direction of the former Soviet Union Olympic coach Natalia Dubova, considered the world's foremost ice-dancing coach, relocated to Lake Placid. Dubova's students include numerous Olympic gold, silver and bronze medalists.

The Olympic Center hosts various skating programs throughout the year. A 12-week summer program attracts skaters of all levels from throughout the world, who train with coaches of their choice in free style, dance and pairs. Students can try out their newly learned techniques to an enthusiastic audience during the Saturday evening ice shows featuring local, national and international skaters. The summer ice-skating program has recently expanded its offerings to include off-ice training.

Of special interest to summer visitors is a newly established program that allows adults and children visiting the area to take a group or individual lesson from one of the professionals. Group lessons cost approximately $15 per person (skate rental not included), with special rates for a family. Reservations should be made by noon; lessons generally are held in the late afternoon or during public skating sessions in the evening.

Throughout the year, visitors are welcome to watch skaters of all levels in action. While many students are beginners, many national and international competitors train in the facility regularly. Session schedules generally are posted in the arena. There is no fee to watch practice sessions.

Indoor Facilities

Although the Olympic Center in Lake Placid offers the only year-round skating program in the Adirondacks, many excellent programs exist during the winter months throughout the region. Most programs, however, are designed for local residents or members of the local skating club and thus offer no services for visitors.

Most rinks in the region offer a few public skating sessions during the week. These sessions change regularly to accommodate the schedules of ice hockey and figure skating programs.

With the exception of the Olympic Arena, few rinks offer skate rentals so if you wish to skate, bring your own blades. Rinks generally do not offer private lockers or dressing rooms. Most rinks have concession stands, but do not count on them being open or providing more than a hot cup of coffee.

Skating programs as well as public skating sessions can be found at the following indoor rinks:

Lake Placid/Tri-Lakes Region

Olympic Arena
Main St., Lake Placid • 523-1655

The Olympic Arena is by far the most consistent of all the rinks in the region as far as scheduling public skating sessions — generally 1 to 3 PM Monday, Wednesday and Thursday from mid-November through March. Additional hours often are added during busy holiday seasons. However, these hours are by no means a hard and fast rule; they will vary depending upon what is going on in the arena, so it is best to check in advance. Rentals are available here for approximately $3 per session or across the street in the Cobbler Shop, 223 Main Street, 523-3679 (see Shopping for specifics). The 1932 facility is heated, and viewing takes place from the stands.

Saranac Lake Civic Center
Ampersand Ave., Saranac Lake • 891-3800

The hours of public skating sessions vary here; hockey is a priority on the schedule. Generally, an afternoon public skating session will be offered on Saturday and Sunday, and special sessions often are scheduled during holiday weeks. Be sure to dress warmly because the rink is not heated; it is open during the winter months, generally November through March. A heated viewing area overlooks the rink. There are no skate rentals or dressing rooms available here, but a concession stand is open during public skating sessions.

Tupper Lake Civic Center
McLaughlin Ave., Tupper Lake • 359-2531

The hours of public skating vary weekly with a session generally offered on a week-

Frozen ponds and rinks offer youngsters an early start on sharpening their hockey skills.

end afternoon. The rink is open November through late March. A small heated area with a concession stand overlooks the rink here. No rentals are available.

Plattsburgh/Western Lake Champlain Region

Crete Memorial Civic Center
U.S. Hwy. 9, Plattsburgh • 563-4431

Public skating sessions generally are scheduled on weekend afternoons but may vary, especially during holiday seasons. The rink is open November through late March. This heated rink does not offer skate rentals, but a concession stand is available.

Lake George/ Upper Hudson Region

Glens Falls Recreation Center
Fire Rd., Glens Falls • 761-3813

This busy facility offers public skating on weekends only, and hours vary from week to week. At this time, it won't cost you anything to skate here, but that may change according to staff. The center is open from November 1 until March 31. With refrigerated ice, you can count on good skating conditions. There is a concession stand available with snacks and hot dogs, and you can rent skates if needed. Skate rentals cost $4 for adults and $2 for anyone 17 and younger.

Old Forge/ Raquette Lake Region

Fern Park Pavilion
Loomis Rd., Inlet • (315) 357-5771

This rink, operated by the Town of Inlet, used to be more of an outdoor facility, but the recent addition of side panels and improved lighting have made this a much more comfortable place to enjoy ice skating. While protected from the snow, rain and wind, the outside air still gets in — and keeps the non-refrigerated ice frozen. You can skate for free here, but you'll have to bring your own equipment and food. The facility does have a warming room and restrooms, and it's open daily from approximately 10 AM until 9 PM. The Town Clerk

informed us that hours and days of operation are subject to change in 1998, so please call ahead.

North Street Park Pavilion
North St., Old Forge • (315) 369-6983

The rink at the North Street Pavilion is owned by the Town of Webb and operated by the Old Forge Youth Advisory Board. The metal building is unheated, and the ice is not refrigerated, but in these climes with consistent sub-freezing winter temperatures, that's usually not a problem. Public skating is typically offered from mid-December until mid-March. While Tuesday evenings are reserved for youth hockey, the general public can skate every other day. Hours are normally 3 until 8 PM on Monday, Wednesday and Thursday; 3 until 10 PM on Friday; 9 AM until 10 PM on Saturday; and noon until 5 PM on Sunday. Neither concessions nor rental equipment is available at North Street Pavilion, but there are restrooms and a heated warming room.

Outdoor Facilities

Various Adirondack towns maintain outdoor rinks. With few exceptions, however, many outdoor rinks are simply a snow-cleared section of a pond or lake or a small oval in a town park. Facilities at these rinks are limited. Local chambers of commerce can provide the most up-to-date information. Some outdoor skating options to check out include the following:

Lake Placid/Tri-Lakes Region

Olympic Speed Skating Oval
Main St., Lake Placid • 523-1655

Speed-skating competitions for the 1932 and 1980 Olympic Winter Games were held on this track. A warming hut is available for skaters. Rentals are offered in the facility for approximately $3 per session or across the street in the Cobbler Shop, 233 Main Street, 523-3679 (see Shopping for details). Public skating sessions are held most evenings between 7 and 9 PM. Admission costs $5 per adult or teen and $3 per child 12 or younger.

Recreational snowmobiling is one way to enjoy vast areas of the Adirondacks during the winter.

Lake George/ Upper Hudson Region

Crandall Park Ice Rink
Glen St., Glens Falls • 761-3813

Weather permitting, you can enjoy free skating at this lighted rink weekdays from 3 until 9 PM and weekends from 10 AM until 9 PM. There are restrooms and a warming hut but no rentals or concessions available here.

Southern Adirondack Lakes Region

Speculator Pavilion
N.Y. Rts. 8 and 30, Speculator • 548-4521

This rink, operated by the Village of Speculator, offers free public skating from December until March, depending on the weather. It is a covered rink with open sides, so skaters are somewhat protected from the outside elements. The rink also is lighted, so you can enjoy evening skating (usually until 10 PM). There are no concessions or rental equipment available here, but there are restrooms.

Snowmobiling

Many Americans think of snowmobiling as a fun little diversion that people "up North" do to keep from being bored to death in the wintertime. The "fun" part is true enough, but there is nothing "little" about snowmobiling in the Adirondacks, and it's much more than just a boredom-fighting diversion. Snowmobiling is as much about comradery and friendship as it is sport. It is a very social activity, with talk of conditions, performance, weather and where to get a great lunch all weaving in and out of the dialogue. For thousands of enthusiasts and residents, snowmobiling is not just a way to have fun, it's a way of life — and a practical way to get around.

Consider that in 1996 the New York State

Office of Parks, Recreation and Historic Preservation reported 91,620 snowmobile registrations in New York, including 3,000 for out-of-state snowmobiles. Consider that in Hamilton County alone, there are more than 750 miles of groomed snowmobile trails, dozens of races and events, and six membership clubs dedicated to the sport. Sounds like there's nothing "little" about it.

You can stick a pin anywhere in a map of the Adirondacks and either land on or very near excellent snowmobile territory. It is truly a land of great snowsled opportunity, and nowhere is the opportunity greater or more fun than the Old Forge and Inlet areas. This is the rarely disputed "snowmobiling capital of the East," with hundreds of miles of scenic, groomed and patrolled trails. Old Forge and the southwestern Adirondacks also offer consistently good snow cover (thanks to the average 15 feet of yearly snow it receives courtesy of Lake Ontario) and amenities such as sled dealers, lodging and restaurants all geared towards snowmobilers.

There are trail fees required for the popular trail systems of Old Forge and Inlet. The fee is $75 per season or $40 per week. Still, compared to downhill skiing, it's a real bargain.

Some of the most popular trail systems in the region connect Old Forge and Inlet to the Sargent Ponds area (between Raquette Lake and Long Lake), the Moose River Recreation Area (near Indian Lake) and the Jessup River Wild Forest (west of Speculator). The areas surrounding the towns of Speculator, Piseco and Wells are also popular with snowmobilers. Farther to the north, the Lake Placid/Tri-Lakes region also has much to offer snowsledders, including more than 450 miles of trails.

Before you saddle up your snow buggy, keep in mind that New York State requires you to register and insure all snowmobiles. The registration fee is $15 for state residents and $25 for nonresidents, and registration can be obtained from any county clerk's office or the N.Y.S. Department of Motor Vehicles.

For more information on snowmobiling in the Adirondacks, contact the Adirondack Snowmobiling Association, P.O. Box 771, Indian Lake, New York 12842, (800) 648-5239; New York Snowmobile Coordinating Group, P.O. Box 62, Whitesboro, New York 13492,

(315) 736-7905; or the N.Y.S. Department of Environmental Conservation, 50 Wolf Road, Albany, New York, 457-3521.

For trail maps, permit requirements and other information related to specific areas, call the following: Inlet Information Office, (315) 357-5501; Old Forge Visitor Information Center, (315) 369-6983; Warren County Parks and Recreation, 623-5576; Fulton County Publicity Office, 762-0700; Hamilton County Tourism, 648-5239; Speculator Office of Tourism, 548-4521; Franklin County Tourism, 483-6788; Lake Placid/Essex County Visitors Bureau, (800) 44-PLACID.

Now before you let the fact you don't own a snowmobile dissuade you from trying out this stuff, there are plenty of dealers available to suit you up, equip you and, in some cases, even guide you around. For information on snowmobile dealers, see the "Fun Stuff" sections of the Shopping chapter.

Other Options (from Mellow to Macho)

If you are *still* looking for adventure and excitement beyond the slopes, rinks and trails, you do have a few more options.

Horse-drawn Sleigh Rides

If you prefer to slide on a more horizontal plane, you can take a horse-drawn sleigh ride at either of the following places.

Lake Placid/Tri-Lakes Region

XTC Ranch
Forest Home Rd., Saranac Lake
• 891-5684

The XTC offers a combination of snowmobiling and sleigh rides in winter and horseback riding and hiking in summer. See the XTC entry in Attractions for details.

Lake George/ Upper Hudson Region

Circle B Ranch
Friends Lake Rd., Chestertown • 494-4074
You can go two ways with this: Take an

intimate ride on Circle B's small sleigh built for two; or grab a bunch of your friends for a group ride on the large "cutter" sleigh that holds as many as 16 partying people. Rides last about a half-hour and take you through the surrounding meadows. The cost is approximately $8 per person and includes hot cider, hot chocolate and doughnuts upon your return. You must call ahead to enjoy this, as rides are scheduled by appointment only.

Wild West Ranch & Stables
Bloody Pond Rd., Lake George • 668-2121

You can enjoy half-hour horse-drawn sleigh rides here for about $5 apiece, or take a winter trail ride atop a horse for $15. Either way, this is a fun and relaxing way to enjoy the winter scenery at a slower pace. Call ahead for specific hours and to make a reservation.

Ice Climbing

One activity you definitely won't find boring is ice climbing — the winter cousin to rock climbing with a few more degrees of difficulty and, often, many fewer degrees of temperature. There are hundreds of places throughout the "High Peaks" area and the mountains of the central Adirondacks where you will find good climbing. As one of the most dangerous recreational activities you can attempt, you should educate yourself and rely on the guidance of experts before taking this on. The best source for information on ice climbing is the Adirondack Mountain Club (ADK), N.Y. Route 9N, Lake George, 668-4447. These folks offer everything from books on the subject to maps, workshops, suggestions on gear and recommended suppliers. See the ADK Close-up in the Other Summer Recreation chapter for more information.

Sledding and Tobogganing

For just good old-fashioned slide-down-the-hill fun, you can't do much better than the Adirondacks. Your options for sledding and tobogganing are limitless. Your best bet is to contact the local chamber or tourism office and ask where the good (public) hills are.

Snowshoeing

Snowshoeing has enjoyed a resurgence in popularity over the past few years, and for good reason. As one cross-country ski area operator described it, snowshoeing is a great entry-level winter activity similar to a pleasant nature hike in the summertime. For people who want to get outdoors and enjoy the surroundings during the winter but don't necessarily want the risks associated with skiing or snowmobiling, snowshoeing can be a great alternative. It is easy to get the hang of it quickly, and many who start out snowshoeing trails eventually graduate to cross-country or backcountry skiing.

You can snowshoe just about anywhere there is snow, and most cross-country ski centers now offer rentals. While snowshoeing may seem timid, it can be as demanding as you want it to be, so give it a try before you dismiss it as boring. A good spot to start out is either of the two Visitor Interpretive Centers, where you can borrow some snowshoes and try it out for free. Contact the VIC at Paul Smiths, 327-3000, or the Newcomb VIC at 528-2000. The N.Y.S. Department of Environmental Conservation office, Hudson Street, Warrensburg, 623-3671, has a collection of useful hiking and snowshoeing brochures.

There is no doubt that
Adirondack golf affords
some of the most
spectacular views and
picturesque landscapes
you could ever
find and enjoy.

Golf

The golfing experience in the Adirondacks is best summarized by referring to the five B's: beauty, bumps, bugs, bogies and birdies. While you're cleaning your clubs, let's look at these one at a time.

Beauty: There is no doubt that Adirondack golf affords some of the most spectacular views and picturesque landscapes you could ever find and enjoy. In fact, you'll find yourself surrounded by so much natural beauty that you may even be able to shake off that last double-bogey a little more quickly than back on your home course. Most courses in this region have been around for awhile, and some date back to the last century. Many of them are virtually unchanged since then, providing you with a taste of the game back when hickory was the high-tech shaft of the day, not titanium. What that means to you is a different type of golf than you may be used to back home in Metroplex, U.S.A., or the kind of waterlogged bunker-infested resort courses you find down in Florida. That's no knock on Florida — it's definitely the preferable place to golf in February — it's just to say that in Florida, golf architects had to "create" character (since the landscape was lacking much) by adding hazards such as alligator-laden ponds and sand traps the size of mall parking lots.

In the Adirondacks, the character of the courses is everywhere you look. The renowned course designers of the early 20th century such as Donald Ross, Alex Findlay, Seymour Dunn and Alister MacKenzie (all of Scotland, golf's "Fatherland") simply needed to find general paths from a teeing ground to the green. The region's restless topography and abundant water took care of providing all the character and challenge a golfer could want. That's not to shortchange their efforts in creating such masterpieces as The Sagamore course and the Lake Placid Club Resort course — it's just that the magnificence of these layouts is in their surroundings.

While the variety of settings you'll find here is diverse, for the most part Adirondack courses will offer you a variety of wide-open and "thread-the-needle" holes. Love to hit the ball a mile without repercussion from the ball's chosen direction? Then try out such courses as Ticonderoga Golf Club or the Westport Country Club. Prefer to hit 4-irons off the tee to keep it in play and out of the woods? (You do? What fun is that?!) The Whiteface Inn Golf Club is for you.

The one characteristic you're unlikely to find very often is a level lie, which leads to the second "B". . . .

Bumps: Count on plenty of sidehill, uphill and downhill lies, along with some shots that defy description, when playing a round of Adirondack golf. The terrain is often bumpy, rolling and "natural-looking." That is to say, don't expect the typical course here to have the smooth, manicured and buffed look and feel of a Scottsdale desert resort. This is golf "without any makeup," and you might as well try to enjoy the variable conditions that result from the combination of rugged terrain and sometimes ragged maintenance budgets at courses here. There are some luxurious exceptions — the Sagamore, Hiland, Kingswood and Malone — but for the most part, you're bound to get as many tough breaks as lucky ones, so don't let it ruin your day. Your swing will probably compete for those honors, and if you play here in May or June, so will the third "B". . . .

Bugs: The black flies and deer flies that recreate on you while you try to recreate on the golf course will make the mosquitoes you have back home seem like "girlie-bugs" (to quote Hans and Franz of *Saturday Night Live* fame). Not to mention the Adirondack variety of mosquitoes that seem to be on a steady dietary supplement of steroids to go along with the daily staple of humanoids.

Before venturing out to play a springtime round of golf here, you'll want to master the following move, along with grooving your driver swing and putting stroke. Raise your right hand just above shoulder height, reach back behind your neck (making sure to feel a good stretch of the deltoids and lats in the process), open hand fully, then bring down hand with great force upon back of your neck, making a loud slapping sound in the process. Remove your hand from the neck, bring in front of you, and open to inspect for evidence of a close encounter of the "ouch" kind. (Optional: Practice various combinations of verbal outbursts to go along with this move.)

Do you have any recourse to stay on the course during the spring and early summer without getting eaten alive? After all, some of the courses here will do a good job of that, without any help from bugs! You have only two real choices: 1) wait until July 4 to get the clubs out, but that will seriously shorten an already short season of swinging; or, 2) get up-close and personal with some Off Skintastic®. We can report this as our greatest defense in warding off biting bugs, although we also report no known defense to the fourth "B". . . .

Bogies: Adirondack golf can be tough, no question about it. While not known for sheer length, almost every course here has at least a couple of real "testers" on the card. More than likely, they won't give you as much trouble as the seemingly short-and-innocent par 4s that look like "cake" on the card until you end up shooting some big number because you "didn't know those trees stuck out around the corner."

Local knowledge is a big plus around here on these quirky layouts, so don't be surprised (or too frustrated) by an occasional bogey or dreaded "others" your first time around these tracks. Now the second and third times, you'll have to come up with some new excuses. Some believable ones to try in the Adirondacks: 1) "It's too cold, I can't loosen up"; 2) "The scenery distracted me"; and, 3) "I lost my ball in the snow." Don't worry, you'll come up with plenty of others. And if you're lucky and a little bit skilled, you may even come up with a few of the final "B". . . .

Birdies: Adirondack golf can also, on oc-

casion, be an ego-gratifying exercise that includes almost driving the green a short par 4 (of which there are many), or being "on the dance floor" in two shots on a short par 5 (of which there are many as well). Finding yourself in such strong strategic locations can often result in very makeable birdie putts, which can be a lot of fun when you make them and a "head shaker" when you don't. In any event, if you can keep you ball in play on the tight holes (the predominant species), you can shoot a good score here — or at least good enough to make you want to come back for more. If worse comes to worse, you can always lift your head, look around and soak up that magnificent scenery.

There are nearly 50 places you can tee it up and play in the Adirondack region. About half those courses are nine-hole tracks, while the other half are regulation 18-holers. We have limited our listings here to 18-hole courses only, as they remain the most popular format of play. By no means is this intended to discount the nine-hole courses as a fun and challenging golfing experience, and we encourage you to explore those available in your region by checking with the local chamber of commerce. In fact, for some of you trying to juggle golf with mountain biking, swimming, hiking and the like, spending two hours on the golf course to play a "quick nine" might be a more attractive option. Unless otherwise noted, all courses listed here offer some type of pro shop, ranging from those that offer a few sleeves of balls under the glass counter to large golf emporiums featuring $60 shirts. You can also get a lesson before playing (or after playing when you *really* need it) at any of these courses, hit a bag of practice balls at a driving range and rent clubs if you've forgotten yours (or thrown them in a lake). At most courses here, you'll be able to replay every highlight and "lowlight" with your playing partner while enjoying a beverage and burger in anything from snack bars to full dining rooms. Golf carts (both powered and pull-carts) can be found at all courses as well, unless we indicate otherwise.

The course yardage indicated is for the back tees, or "blue" tees in most cases. As

FYI

Unless otherwise noted, the area code for all phone numbers listed in this guide is 518.

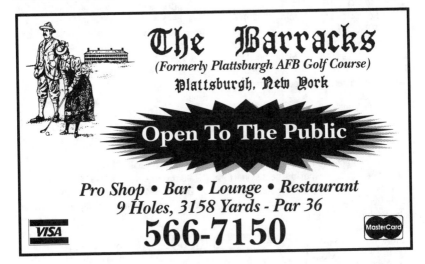

you might expect, the yardage from the women's or regular men's tees (the "whites") is shorter (sometimes a lot, sometimes just a couple of paces ahead of the "blues"), and the championship "back" tees create a longer, more challenging test. We have quoted the most recent rates available for 18-hole greens fees and power-cart rentals (full cost for one or two golfers) here, based on the 1997 golfing season. Speaking of "season," for the most part you can expect the golfing season in the Adirondacks to last from early May through October. Consider anything before or after those dates to be the minigolf equivalent of getting your last putt in the clown's mouth and winning a free game.

Lake Placid/ Tri-Lakes Region

Craig Wood Golf Club
N.Y. Rt. 73, Lake Placid • 523-9811, (800) 421-9811

You're thinking, "Why does that name sound familiar?" Perhaps you recognize Craig Wood as one of the greats of golf history, winning both The Masters and the U.S. Open in 1941. Craig Wood was tall, handsome, charming and could hit the ball a "country mile" more than 50 years before Tiger Woods came on

the scene. He grew up caddying and learning the game here, and the course was renamed from the Lake Placid Golf and Country Club to honor him in 1954.

Craig Wood was built in 1925 as a nine-hole course, and then lengthened to 18 holes in 1932. The par 72, 6554-yard course is owned and operated by the Town of North Elba, which is good (it keeps the greens fees down to a reasonable $20 to play all day, any day) and not so good (the conditioning can fall a tad below privately owned resort courses). Trust us, you won't care that your lie is occasionally imperfect — you'll be too busy closing your mouth over and over from the spectacular mountain views that envelope you here. The Seymour Dunn design is open and inviting for the front nine and then takes you on a journey through the woods for most of the back nine. This is a fun course with good length and enough room that you can swing away for most of the day.

The signature hole is likely the par 3 13th, a beautiful but demanding test. Your elevated tee shot must clear the ravine in front but not fly over the green into the gaping bunkers behind. The course is hilly enough that you may want to take a cart, which you can rent for $24 per twosome. After your round, enjoy the Craig Wood Cocktail Lounge and Restaurant and its large second-floor outside deck, which is open daily during the season for lunch and dinner.

Lake Placid Club Resort
Mirror Lake Dr., Lake Placid • 523-4460, (800) LPR-GOLF

These two grand old courses — the Links (Lower) Course and the Mountain (Upper) Course — both built in the late 1890s, offer distinctively different yet equally rewarding golfing experiences.

Noted Scottish designer Alex Findlay built the Mountain Course (par 70, 5852 yards), which features breathtaking views from its many open fairways and elevated tees. You'll get plenty of practice on your hillside lies here, so don't be surprised when the occasional (or in our case, predominant) shot seems to veer off from your intended destination. Stand-out holes include the 1st, a 368-yard par 4 from an elevated tee that offers a great view of Mount Marcy, and a 156-yard par 3 nicknamed "Mae West" for reasons you'll just have to see for yourself.

The Links Course (par 70, 6235 yards) was designed by another noted Scotsman, Seymour Dunn (see previous Craig Wood Golf Course entry). It is longer and has a more traditional Scottish-links look to it, with flatter fairways but large undulating greens to make up for it. Both courses are more fun than severely difficult, which make them a real treat to play.

There is also a nine-hole par 3 "executive course" here as well, bring the total available golfing holes here to 45. That should keep you busy until lunch. Greens fees for either the Mountain or Links courses will cost you $20, and a cart will cost another $24 for your twosome. If you can wait until 2:30 PM (just about the time it starts to warm up around here!) the greens fee drops to $13 per person

— a great value. Another good deal is the "Two Fees & a Cart" special for $60, which will save you and your partner a couple of bucks apiece. Try that out, then rent *Four Weddings and a Funeral* that evening, and you've created an entire "themed" day.

Before or after your round, you can enjoy breakfast, lunch or drown your swing-thought sorrows in a beer on the restaurant's shaded veranda that overlooks the surrounding mountains.

Loon Lake Golf Club
CR 99, Loon Lake • 891-3249

Built in 1894, this is one of the oldest courses in the Adirondacks. It apparently was built when length was not the omnipresent obsession it is in today's golf, as most of the holes are quite short (300-yard par 4s, for example). That doesn't mean this par 70, 5400-yard track is easy, though. The greens are as small as the holes seem short, so accuracy is at a premium here. You'll find yourself having to chip and pitch a lot of "birdie attempts" from off the green instead of trying to lag 40-foot putts.

www.insiders.com

See this and many other **Insiders' Guide®** destinations online — in their entirety.

Visit us today!

Loon Lake is fun to play, if only for the nostalgic look at the early days of American golf. You can play all day at Loon Lake for only $15, or just $8 after 4 PM (18 holes is entirely possible from late May to late July when darkness doesn't close in until 8:30 PM or later). You can rent a cart for your first 18 holes for $16 and then pay another $8 for the next nine if you choose to continue. So, to summarize, you and your partner could play 36 holes of golf here, with a cart, for $31 apiece. If you ask us, it's a pretty good deal when you can play all day with a cart for less than a buck a hole.

INSIDERS' TIP

Want a pleasant golfing experience with your family, but don't want to make a whole day of it? The Adirondacks have more than 20 scenic and fun nine-hole golf courses that could be your ideal solution for an enjoyable family outing. They are generally short, easy and only take a couple of hours to play. Check with the chamber of commerce in your area to see what's available nearby.

Photo: Plattsburgh/North Country Chamber of Commerce

The Adirondack golf season may be shorter than in many areas
of the country, but the scenery is well above par.

Malone Golf Club
Country Club Rd., Malone • 483-2926

While technically outside of the Adirondack Park by a dozen or so miles, this complex of two Robert Trent Jones golf courses is well worth the drive. It probably wins the award for "Best Courses That You're Least Likely To Expect Finding Here," as there's not much around Malone to indicate the quality golfing experience that awaits.

The par 72, 6545-yard East Course has the distinction of being played by Babe Ruth at its official opening in July 1939 (the Sultan of Swat shot 37 on the par 35 nine-hole course). In 1956 a second nine was added, and in 1984 the par 71, 6592-yard West Course opened. Both courses have become very popular, and the mix of members and daily-fee guests add up to more than 50,000 rounds each season. In fact, Malone Golf Club is considerably more popular with "road-tripping" golfers playing hooky from their offices in Montreal and Ottawa, Canada, than it is with Adirondack golfers. Don't let that dissuade you, though. This is a gem you won't want to miss.

Both courses are very well maintained and offer an attractive combination of rolling hills, white sand bunkers and abundant natural water throughout. As one of the few golf complexes in the Adirondack region with tee-to-green irrigation, you'll find lush fairways here even in the driest of summers (admittedly not normally a problem). The beautiful greens are a pleasure to putt, depending on how your playing, of course.

Greens fees to play Malone cost $26 — more expensive than many Adirondack courses, but a great value for the variety and quality offered here. You and your partner can rent a cart for $22, but there is no restriction placed on walking (as is the case with some upscale resort courses). A full-service bar and restaurant await your triumphant march from the 18th.

Saranac Inn Golf & Country Club
off N.Y. Rt. 30, Saranac Inn • 891-1402

Yet another Seymour Dunn creation, this course is among the longest in the Adirondacks. Nearly a century old, this par 72, 6631-yard impressive course has stood the test of time — and it still will give you all the test of your golfing skills you could want.

Though carved from the surrounding forest, the fairways are generously wide. With an automated irrigation system, the fairways, tees and greens all remain lush and smooth. This course is a little bit out of the way, but by now you should be used to the miniature road trips required to enjoy the Adirondacks, so give it a try.

Greens fees at the Saranac Inn Golf & Country Club cost $50, including a cart, any day of the week.

Tupper Lake Country Club
Country Club Rd., Tupper Lake
• 359-3701

Another famous Scottish-designer creation, this course was crafted by Donald Ross in 1932. It is one of the "hilly" variety of Adirondack layouts, and you're sure to be playing plenty of downhill and sidehill lies throughout the day. Of course, "hilly" also means "scenic" in these parts, and you'll be treated to postcard views throughout your round. The combination of rolling terrain, good length and small greens make this par 71, 6254-yard layout one of the more challenging courses in the Adirondacks.

Tupper Lake Country Club will cost you $20 to play any day of the week, and if you choose to ride in a power cart (a serious consideration at this course), you and your partner will need to come up with another $22 between you.

Whiteface Club Golf Course
Whiteface Inn Rd., Lake Placid
• 523-2551, (800) 422-6757

This classic resort course (par 72, 6490 yards) celebrates its centennial in 1998, and it's aging with much more grace than many of its visiting golfers swing! What hasn't changed in the hundred years it has been open is the setting — and the views. Few golf courses in America can claim better: numerous vistas of the majestic Whiteface Mountain and glimpses of the adjacent Lake Placid.

From the time you check in at the log cabin pro shop, you realize that you're in for a rustic, classic golfing experience. Whiteface doesn't disappoint and plays very similar to how it did

decades ago — very tight and unforgiving in some places, open and generous in others. Pick your spots well to take chances here, or you'll be scratching some big numbers on your score card in a hurry. In particular, you'll enjoy the par 5, dogleg-left 6th hole with it's backdrop of Whiteface Mountain welcoming you to the green, and the 218-yard par 3 14th hole, considered one of the toughest par 3s in the Adirondacks.

Greens fees at Whiteface range from $30 down to $20 after 3 PM, and a power cart costs an additional $12 apiece for you and your partner. The adjacent Whiteface Club resort offers both a restaurant and lounge to enjoy (or recover in) after your round.

Plattsburgh/Western Lake Champlain Region

Adirondack Golf & Country Club
88 Golf Rd., Peru • 643-8403

This is one of the newest (opened in 1990), longest (nearly 7000 yards from the "tips") and toughest courses in the Adirondack region.

Just outside the Park border between Ausable Chasm and Plattsburgh, this par 72, 6851-yard course has received good reviews from *Vermont Golf*, *Adirondack Life* and readers of *Golf Digest*. Designed by Geoffrey Cornish, one of today's top golf course architects, Adirondack was nominated in 1990 for best new design by the American Society of Golf Course Architects. If it weren't for the cooler climate, you'd think you were playing at one of the Pinehurst (N.C.) area courses here, with tall pines and hardwoods shaping and lining many of the holes. (See *The Insiders' Guide® to Golf in the Carolinas* for the lowdown on Pinehurst's courses.) This is a challenging course — fun for low and mid-handicappers, but perhaps a little too tough to really enjoy if you're just starting out.

INSIDERS' TIP

Many golf courses in the Adirondacks offer reduced greens fees after 3 PM or so. From late May until early August, daylight hangs tough until past 8:30 PM, so you can get 18 in for fewer dollars and hours out of the middle of your precious vacation day.

Greens fees to play at Adirondack range from $24 (walking) during the week to $28 on weekends. If you take a cart, it will only cost you an extra $6 during the week ($30 total) and $7 on weekends ($35 total). It's a pretty good deal for the level of golf. While there is no full-service restaurant here, there is a small lounge serving catered muffins and Danish in the morning and sandwiches in the afternoon.

Bluff Point Golf & Country Club
75 Bluff Point Rd., Plattsburgh
• 563-3420, (800) 438-0985

Bluff Point is a semiprivate golf club that is open to the public. Club management is proud to claim Bluff Point, which opened in 1890, as the third-oldest course in the United States. With its open layout and setting overlooking the spectacular Lake Champlain, this par 72, 6309-yard track is one of the most scenic golfing experiences you can enjoy. You'll also enjoy the hospitality of the friendly, professional staff here that makes guests feel like longtime members.

Whether you choose to walk or ride, Bluff Point will cost you the same to play: $29.90 Monday through Thursday and $34.90 Friday through Sunday. For an old club, it offers a decidedly modern convenience — "club runners," which essentially are electric pull carts that give your clubs a ride while you walk alongside. Again, the same rates apply if you choose this option. After your round, you can enjoy the full-service restaurant and lounge for breakfast, lunch or a beverage.

Ticonderoga Country Club
Hague Rd., Ticonderoga • 585-2801

While somewhat isolated from the heart of the Adirondacks, this history-laden site is well worth the road trip. What you'll find here is a golfing experience unique in the Adirondacks. For one thing, no other course in the region (or perhaps in the whole country) was once the site of a major battle between British troops and their French and Indian counterparts nearly 250 years ago. As you walk the course, try to remember that for our ancestors, life could get a lot more challenging and dangerous than the downhill lie you've got for your approach into the green. If you can keep that perspective, you'll love playing here.

This par 71, 6287-yard course started out as a nine-holer forged from farmland in 1929 and then enlarged to its present 18-hole configuration by the omnipresent Seymour Dunn in 1932. It is set in a beautiful valley, and it's wide-open, rolling terrain encourages free swinging with "the big dog."

You'll find an interesting layout here, with the front nine playing par 37 and the back nine, par 34. There's quite a mix of long and short holes here, and the stand-out is probably the 495-yard, par 5 No. 4, a beautiful hole that requires some local knowledge to play properly. That is, you can hit it into Trout Brook on your second shot if you're not conservative enough. In fact, you can hit into Trout Brook all over the place here, as it comes into play on almost a third of the holes. Two 430-yard plus par 4s at the 10th and 16th plus the uphill 370-yard, par 4 18th all give you plenty of challenge to go along with the fun and scenery.

Ticonderoga has an all-day greens fee of $27, and an after-5 PM fee of $13.50 for "all you can squeeze in." A cart rental will cost you and your partner a total of $24 for 18 holes. You'll find it tough to leave after only 18, so stick around — you've got another nine holes to think of an excuse for why you are so late! (Note: We recommend staying away from the "stuck in traffic" excuse. It usually doesn't fly in this part of the world. Try something more realistic like, "Cows were blocking the road.")

Westport Country Club
Liberty St., Westport • 962-4470

This is another old, classic Adirondack course that has stood the test of time. The par 72, 6600-yard layout is pretty wide open, which makes it easy for "Army golfers" (those who hit it right, left, right, left), but also means it can get windy here, adding a new element to the challenge. It's a scenic course near one of the few Adirondack towns that is more "quaint" than "rustic" (Westport) and one of the most beautiful lakes in America (Lake Champlain).

To play at Westport, greens fees will cost you $20 during the week and $25 on weekends. During the 1997 season, the course ran a special that encouraged the use of "spikeless" golf shoes by offering a $5 discount to players using them. (Spikeless, or "soft spiked," shoes are less damaging to greens, and many private and upscale courses are converting over to them from the traditional clickety-clack metal spikes.) Before 2 PM, you must rent a cart ($10 apiece) and then walking becomes an option.

Westport has been much written about and has a lot of character, and we think you'll enjoy a visit here regardless of how you play.

Lake George/ Upper Hudson Region

As you might imagine, the Lake George area, along with being a hotbed of just about every recreational activity available in the Adirondacks, is also one of the region's most popular golfing destinations. We have selected a sampling of the courses available here for your information.

Cronin's Golf Resort
Golf Course Rd.,
Warrensburg • 623-9336

Using the analogy of golfing attire, if The Sagamore resort course in nearby Bolton Landing is Ashworth, then Cronin's Golf Resort would be Dockers. Hey, that's not a negative! Dockers are comfy, casual and friendly — so is Cronin's. As a family-run operation for more than a half-century, the Cronins don't have much choice but to keep things as friendly and welcoming as possible. After all, this is both their life and their livelihood. They certainly can't afford unhappy golfers, so they work hard year after year to continually improve and enhance their par 70, 6121-yard course.

Two generations ago, Glens Falls Country Club superintendent Patrick Cronin designed the first nine holes here in 1930. His son Bob, who became a golf professional, bought the place in 1945 and added the second nine along the banks of the upper Hudson River in 1969. The current generation, Bob's sons Jim and John Cronin, continue the family commitment today. It hasn't always been easy. In the spring of 1980 the moody Hudson lost its thick ice cover in one massive thaw that destroyed

the adjacent 10th, 11th and 12th holes. The Cronins repaired and reconfigured their course, "river-proofing" it as much as possible without losing the attraction of a riverside setting. What you'll find now is an interesting mix of holes through the pines and along the river that reminded us somewhat of Nick Stoner Golf Course in Caroga Lake (see the subsequent "Southern Adirondack Lakes Region" section). You won't need overwhelming length here, but you will need to pay attention to club selection and "distance control" in order to score well here. It's a course where local knowledge comes in handy, and fortunately it's readily available as you're likely to be paired up with some "regulars" that can fill you in on all the dos and don'ts.

Cronin's is a good value — only $16 to play during the week and $18 on weekends. You can take a cart yourself for $11, or it will cost you and your partner $12 apiece. There's a restaurant and bar here plus a bunch to choose from in nearby Warrensburg.

Hiland Golf Club
195 Haviland Ave.,
Queensbury • 761-4653

Hiland is one of the newest, most luxurious and challenging golf destinations in the Adirondack region. Built in 1988 to be the centerpiece of a luxury housing development that never came to be, Hiland the course has had much more success than Hiland the development. Bought in 1995 by Family Golf Centers Inc., the par 72, 6785-yard course is meticulously maintained, providing teeing areas as good as many Adirondack course greens, lush fairways and excellent (large!) greens.

When it first opened, Hiland was named one of the "Best New Courses You Can Play" by *Golf Digest*. It since has hosted the 1992 New York State Open, proof of its acceptance as a tournament-caliber test of golf.

Set just outside of the "blue line" of the Adirondack Park border, Hiland serves up vistas of both the mountains that frame nearby Lake George and the Green Mountains of Vermont to the east. The first thing you'll see upon arriving is the sprawling clubhouse that looks like it would be more at home in Palm

FYI

Unless otherwise noted, the area code for all phone numbers listed in this guide is 518.

Photo: Plattsburgh/North County Chamber of Commerce

On your next visit to the North Country, bring your clubs
and take a swing and enjoy the scenic beauty.

Springs than the foothills of the Adirondacks. The facilities, from the locker rooms to the grill room to the pro shop, are all beautifully designed and make you feel like the pampered member at some exclusive club rather than just a visitor teeing it up while on vacation.

As for the golf, we think you'll love some of the holes and shrug your shoulders with indifference to others. There are some great holes here, such as the par 5s at Nos. 7, 9 and 18, plus some short par 4s that seem like they were squeezed into the available tract of land. Probably the toughest hole of all is No. 17, a 440-yard par 4 into an almost constant breeze that will require two great shots to reach in regulation. Even on the short holes, there are more than a dozen ponds and streams lurking around the course to keep things interesting and tricky.

A round of golf at Hiland is relatively expensive (for the Adirondacks) — greens fees are $30 during the week and $35 on the weekend — but still not bad compared to golf destination resorts in Arizona, Florida and North Carolina. Cart rentals are $13 apiece during the week and $15 weekends. Regardless of how you play, enjoying a frosted mug of ice cold beer in the grill room as you overlook the 18th green and mountains beyond is a simple pleasure worth pursuing.

Kingswood Golf Club
Notre Dame St. Ext., Hudson Falls
• 747-8888

You are in for a real surprise if you venture out of the Park a few extra miles to this gem of a public course. About a 20-minute drive from Lake George, Kingswood is definitely worth the trip. The course was the brainchild of Michael Woodbury (whose family owned the Woodbury Lumber chain of stores in the Northeast) who designed and had Kingswood built to be ready for play in June 1992. Since then, it has been drawing a growing legion of play-ers who appreciate the meticulous grooming of the bentgrass fairways and greens, the interesting variety of holes that require both finesse and power, and the terrific views of both the southeastern Adirondacks and the Green Mountains of Vermont.

Kingswood has achieved an impressive balance of fun and challenge, along with the rewards of playing a well-conditioned golf course. Right out of the blocks, your tee shot on the 501-yard par 5 No. 1 tempts you to cut the corner of a pond in order to reach the green in two. Your first tee shot of the day could very well determine how the day is going to go here. The 518-yard par 5 No. 5 is a real beauty, with solid woods along the right, a gully to clear off the tee, stands of trees along the left, and a sprinkling of bunkers surrounding the green.

One thing that makes Kingswood so much fun is you can hit your driver most of the day, with generous fairways encouraging you to swing away. There's quite a bit of length here, too, with a third of the course made up of par 4s that exceed 400 yards from the "blues." Certainly the prettiest, if not the toughest hole, is the 17th. It is a relatively short but tight par 4 of 374 yards, beautifully framed by tall pines, with a few left out near the fairway to stand sentry for approaching shots. You get to finish your round with a dogleg-left par 5 of 506 yards, providing you with an ego-boosting chance at birdie or a (relatively) easy par.

Afterward, enjoy the view from the second-level deck as you recount your strokes and your pleasant memories of the day. A round of golf at Kingswood will cost you $22 during the week ($18 after 2 PM), and $30 on weekends ($22 after 2 PM). You and your playing partner can rent a power cart for $12 apiece for 18 holes.

Kingswood has become quite a popular course, so make sure to call ahead to reserve a tee time.

INSIDERS' TIP

We love to walk when we play golf, but some Adirondack courses can border on a hiking experience with their rolling terrain. You should inquire at the pro shop about the terrain, then decide whether it's best to walk or take a power cart.

The Sagamore
Federal Hill Rd., Bolton Landing
• 644-9400

Playing The Sagamore course is a special experience, and at $99 to play, including cart, it had better be. Is it worth it? Hmmm. Yes, if you're on an expense account; yes, if you just painted the whole house and want to reward yourself for a job well done; probably not, if you're just a casual golfer looking for a fun day of golf. That's not to say playing The Sagamore isn't a lot of fun; it's just that there are far better values in the region that you'll probably enjoy just as much. However, if you are a real golf enthusiast and a real student of the game and its history, you shouldn't miss it (if you can afford it).

The Sagamore has quite a storied history, and has had its share of both good times and hard times. Completed in 1929, the course is the work of one of the world's most famous designers, the Scotsman Donald Ross. His trademark of using the natural terrain to lend character and challenge to his courses is evident here. The course is separate physically — a couple of miles and a couple of hundred vertical feet up the hillsides that climb from Lake George — from the Sagamore Resort Hotel that operates it. The course and resort hit upon bad times in the 1970s, and both closed in 1979, not reopening until 1984. By that time the course was virtually unrecognizable and more resembled a wheat field than a championship-caliber golf course. It took a tremendous effort and commitment to bring the course back, and now it is recognized as one of the "Top 40 Golf Resorts" in America by *Golf* magazine. It's quite a comeback story, one that makes the playing experience here that much more appreciated. Now, on to the golf.

While every picture you will see of The Sagamore shows Lake George below, you can actually only see the lake from the 1st tee. No matter, there's plenty of other beauty and scenery around this par 70, 6890-yard golf course to keep your eyes occupied. The 1st hole is not only magnificent in its setting, but also a real challenge at 415 yards. Your tee shot is hit from the elevated tee to a narrow gully between woods on both sides, followed by a severely uphill approach shot to the large sloping green. Relax, they're not all this tough! Virtually every hole has a character of its own, though, and you're not likely to be bored at anytime throughout your round.

Your most rewarding par of the day, if you can achieve it, will be the 427 yard par 4 13th. With its elevated tee, two ponds that come into play, tight fairway and slick green — this hole has everything! Don't feel bad if you end up with an "X" on your card here; you won't be the first or last to suffer the same fate.

Everything about The Sagamore is first-class, so enjoy your day here, revel in the luxury of it all, and don't worry about your score or your credit card for a few hours.

Southern Adirondack Lakes Region

Nick Stoner Golf Course
N.Y. Rts. 10 and 29A, Caroga Lake
• 835-4220

Hey, any course that's only 5380 yards and gives you 70 strokes to shoot par is easy pickin's, right? Wrong! Throw in lots of sloping fairways, small greens, trees as ominous as those scary ones in *The Wizard of Oz*, and you've got a nice test of golf regardless of what the score card might indicate. And like we said in this chapter's introduction, Adirondack golf is not about length, anyway; it's about character — the course's, and yours.

At Nick Stoner, you'll find a fun variety of holes, and you'll end up using a lot more of your clubs than you might first think. On some holes, like the wide-open par 4 365-yard 10th and the 475-yard par 5 15th, you can swing away with the big stick and hardly any fear of an errant shot. Two par 4s on the front, the 4th and 5th, also provide driving-range–size fairways. Get them while you can, because there also are plenty of testers out here that will challenge your ability to "keep it in play." The 380-yard par 4 12th, with its sloping fairway, trees on both sides and small green, immediately comes to mind.

Nick Stoner also has the distinction of having the shortest par 5 — the 385-yard 7th — we have ever played. It's very tight and plays from an elevated tee to a gully, then back up

Photo: Plattsburgh/North Country Chamber of Commerce

No mere water hazards, beautiful lakeside settings add to the challenge of this and many other Adirondack golf courses.

to an elevated green. If it were a par 4, it would probably rank as one of the best in the Adirondacks. The 8th is a beautiful 320-yard par 4 framed by tall pines, and looks like something you'd see at Pinehurst in North Carolina (see *The Insiders' Guide® to Golf in the Carolinas* for details). The greens are in nice shape, the fairways are here-and-there in good shape, but play "winter rules," roll the ball over, and you'll find a good lie.

Oh yeah, and that name. While some courses might pay homage to Nick Price or Nick Faldo, this one is named for a hunter and trapper from these parts who lived from 1761 to 1853 and fought in both the Revolutionary War and the War of 1812. There's a statue of Nick at the course's highest point, just behind the 2nd tee. Stop and tip your cap.

Greens fees at Nick Stoner Golf Course will cost you $12 during the week and $15 on weekends, and power carts cost $20 per round

for one or two people. After your round, you can enjoy lunch or dinner at The 19th Hole in the Nick Stoner Inn, just across the road from the pro shop.

Old Forge/ Raquette Lake Region

Inlet Golf Course
N.Y. Rt. 28, Inlet • (315) 357-3503

Inlet Golf Course is one of two renowned golfing tracks in these parts (the other one being Thendara Golf Course; see next entry), and it is a pleasure to play. It has all the hallmarks of a good mountain resort course: fairways lined by hardwoods and pines, white sand bunkers and an occasional pond to negotiate, all in the scenic setting of the picturesque Inlet area. You'll find a new log cabin

---

INSIDERS' TIP

Remember, changes in Adirondack weather can be as quick as your herky-jerky backswing, so be prepared. Bring a golf umbrella, windbreaker and hat — even if it seems sunny and warm. You never know when a sneaky little rain shower awaits on the other side of that mountain over there.

clubhouse, pro shop, restaurant and bar here as well, with an outdoor patio overlooking the par 70, 6130-yard course for post-round refreshments.

You can play all day at Inlet for $20, or wait until 3 PM and play the rest of the day for $10. Cart fees are assessed at $5 per golfer for every nine holes you play.

Thendara Golf Course
off N.Y. Rt. 28, Thendara
• (315) 369-3136

Thendara opened in 1921 with its original nine holes designed by the renowned Donald Ross; it became an 18-hole layout in 1959. Since then, such golfing greats as Sam Snead, Arnold Palmer and Jack Nicklaus have played here for various events and exhibitions. The par 72, 6435-yard Thendara is really two different nine-hole courses from different eras joined together for one golfing experience that is never short on variety.

The front nine is relatively flat and open, but the real challenge is putting the slick, undulating greens. The 9th green is particularly severe and once was accused by the visiting Lee Trevino as having an elephant buried underneath it due to its large hump in the middle of the putting surface. The second nine reverses the challenge with mellower (read flatter) greens and tight, tree-lined fairways that put a higher premium on accuracy off the tee. Holes 11 through 14 run along the Moose River — a peaceful if somewhat buggy stretch. Enjoy the variety, for this is the best golf within 50 miles in any direction.

You can play 18 holes at Thendara for $20, or wait until 4 PM and play it for $10 (but risk being carried off by 7 PM mosquitoes). Carts cost $10 per golfer. Drop in Thendara's a full-service restaurant and bar after your round.

Campers in the Adirondack region can set up camp at state campgrounds, private campgrounds and in the backwoods.

Camping

Since the inception of the Adirondack Forest Preserve in the late 1800s, New York State's Department of Environmental Conservation (DEC) has been responsible for developing policies designed to comply with the state's Constitution to protect portions of the preserve as "forever wild" and, at the same time, ensure the Park offers the greatest benefit for the people. So, simply put, DEC has always found itself in the unenviable position between the proverbial rock and the hard place. No matter what it does, critics of the policy abound — some contending that the department is not doing enough to protect the wilderness, and others asserting that more accommodations are needed for the ever-increasing number of people wishing to explore the great outdoors.

Fortunately, those camping in the Adirondacks are never caught in such behind-the-scenes discussions and benefit from a camping-management program that works not only most of the time, but also for the greatest number of people. And that in itself is a major accomplishment!

Campers in the Adirondack region can set up camp at state campgrounds, private campgrounds and in the backwoods. All three options have pluses and minuses.

State campgrounds in the Adirondacks generally provide no electrical or sewer hookups. While a few sites provide scheduled recreational programs for children, most do not. Playground-type recreation opportunities also are limited, but the sites often offer plenty of natural recreation, such as hiking, boating and swimming.

Private campgrounds are well-suited for high-tech, RV campers — most sites allow hookup to the grid — as well as "primitive" campers who still prefer pitching tents. Many private campgrounds offer the same natural wonders as state facilities, with hiking and water-access options. They also offer other essentials (for some) such as game rooms, heated swimming pools, basketball courts and fax services from their main lodges.

While public campgrounds typically cost less than $15 per night, private campsites may run $20 to $25 for full-service accommodations. If basic, low-tech services will suffice, fees at private campgrounds are competitive with those at state facilities.

Most campgrounds in the region are open May through October. Specific opening and closing dates vary, however, so it is best to check if traveling at the beginning or end of the season.

Unless otherwise noted, both state and private facilities provide the same basic services, including showers, flush toilets and dumping stations.

Then, there is backpacking. With few exceptions, you can pitch a tent in the backwoods of the Adirondack Park for free. You do, however, pay for the privilege by packing everything you need to survive and still can carry comfortably on your back — trotting it to a site that may be miles away. In some instances, the site may be just a short hike, but then it is likely that someone else already will be there. At popular backpack destinations, such as Marcy Dam, primitive privies may be available.

About the DEC . . .

The Department of Environmental Conservation (DEC) operates all state campgrounds in the Adirondack Park, and tries to make it easy to obtain accurate information and make reservations. Of course, it helps to call the right telephone numbers:

•Campground reservations only: (800) 456-CAMP. Operators provide only general information regarding available sites; they can't help you select which campground is best for you.

•Campground information only: (518) 457-2500. These people know the campgrounds and can give you information on them.

•General information: (518) 457-3521. This is the number to call for information about fishing, hunting, boating or camping regulations.

All telephone numbers listed for state campgrounds will connect you to the campground itself, but someone will answer only during the camping season. They can't make reservations for you. You can call for information on available spaces for that day, but campground personnel can't hold spaces for you. It is first come, first served. Surprisingly, many state campgrounds can accommodate the last-minute camper, except on busy weekends.

All state facilities are listed as "State Campgrounds," even if not part of the official title. Also, the phone number we list with each state campground is the on-site phone, not the reservations phone. That number again is (800) 456-CAMP. Another source of information on camping in the Adirondacks is the Adirondack Campground Association, 1053 U.S. Highway 9, Queensbury, 798-6218.

As readers you are in the enviable position of having a great variety of camping options in the Adirondacks — nearly 50 DEC campgrounds and dozens more privately owned campgrounds. As writers, however, we are in the less enviable position of having to pick and choose a relative sampling for your reference. We have tried to give you a good variety here, but keep in mind that this is not an all-inclusive list. In fact, if you have a terrific experience at a campground we haven't included, please let us know so we can include it in the next edition.

FYI

Unless otherwise noted, the area code for all phone numbers listed in this guide is 518.

Campgrounds

Lake Placid/Tri-Lakes Area

High Peaks Base Camp
Springfield Rd., Upper Jay • 946-2133

High Peaks is one of the few rustic, undeveloped campsites left in the region. There are facilities for water, but not much else. You will find 200 sites on which to pitch a tent in either a forest or meadow setting. Each site includes a table and a fire ring. The fee is only $3 per night — the best bargain in the region. The camp is near Whiteface Mountain and Lake Placid.

Lake Placid KOA & Log Cabins
Fox Farm Rd., Wilmington • 946-2171

This is a great family vacation campground with 165 sites. Campers can choose from heated log cabins, rustic tent sites and complete RV hookups. The Ausable River, with its famed fishing holes and deep pools for swimming, borders the campground. Heated pools, playgrounds, a basketball court, minigolf course, game rooms and planned activities provide the kids with plenty of options. During the summer months, special events for kids give parents a few moments to themselves.

Skiers take note. This KOA is open year round, and Whiteface Mountain is only minutes away. Even if you don't have an RV, the cabins, cottages and ski dorm offer economical choices for relaxing amid a pine, maple and birch forest.

Meadowbrook State Campground
N.Y. Rt. 86, Ray Brook • 891-4351

There is no swimming, boating or canoeing here, but Meadowbrook is attractive because it is only minutes away from Lake Placid

---

INSIDERS' TIP

If you spot moose in the North Country, report the sighting to researchers at the Adirondack Wildlife Program, 582-4551, who keep track of the animals.

Photo: Warren County Tourism Department

Camping and spending time in the great outdoors can build a grown-up appetite.

and Saranac Lake, making it an ideal base campground for touring the area. While the on-site attractions are few, this campground offers some very quiet, isolated and private sites in a forest setting.

Meadowbrook is open May through Labor Day.

North Pole Campground & Motor Inn
N.Y. Rt. 86, Wilmington • 946-7733, (800) 245-0228

This full-service campground with 78 tent, RV and cabin sites on the Ausable River at Whiteface Mountain consistently receives high ratings in RV travel magazines. There are plenty of on-site activities for individuals and groups alike, including swimming, fishing and playing in the game rooms. Although Wilmington is much quieter than nearby Lake Placid, the town bustles with activity, especially during the summer. Ask around for the hot fishing holes or information on back-road bike trails.

The campground is open all year.

Wilmington Notch State Campground
N.Y. Rt. 86, Lake Placid • 946-7172

At the base of Whiteface Mountain, amid a birch and pine grove, this small 54-site camp-

ground is convenient for folks who wish to explore Lake Placid and the High Peaks region. It is also on one of the best trout-fishing brooks in the East, so if fly-fishing is your passion, this is your place. And you can't beat the location if you are planning to mountain bike on Whiteface.

Buck Pond State Campground
Franklin County Rt. 30, Onchiota • 891-3449

Great boating, fishing, canoeing, swimming and hiking can be found at the Buck Pond campground and in the near vicinity, yet only rarely is this 116-site facility filled to capacity. Although it is slightly off the beaten path, it is still within a 30-minute drive to destination areas such as Saranac Lake and Lake Placid. Plattsburgh and Lake Champlain are also less than an hour's drive.

Buck Pond is open May through Labor Day.

Cranberry Lake State Campground
off N.Y. Rt. 3, Cranberry Lake • (315) 848-2315

Cranberry Lake, in the western part of the Adirondacks, is the third-largest lake within the Park and is adjacent to some of its least traveled wilderness areas. The site makes a good base camp for exploring some serious wilderness areas by foot or canoe. The hamlet of Cranberry Lake is the spot for basic supplies, but the campsite is miles away from what would be considered a large town (such as Tupper Lake).

The 173-site facility is open May through October.

Deer River Campsite
Red Tavern Rd., Duane • 483-0060

In the north-central portion of the Adirondack Park, near Malone, Deer River is on a remote lake. The campground offers electrical hookups on most of its 84 sites, but only a few sites have sewer hookups. Although relatively small, the campsite has a good range of on-site activities, including canoeing and boating (rentals are available), fishing, swimming at a sandy beach and hiking. A playground and recreation hall also are available.

The campground is open May through mid-October.

Fish Creek
State Campground
N.Y. Rt. 30, Tupper Lake • 891-4560

During the busy summer season, Fish Creek, with 355 campsites, fills to the brim with campers of all ages. It is not a quiet place, but if you have kids looking for activities, there are plenty of playmates and programs to be found. Although the campground bustles with activity — it's not recommended for campers seeking solitude — the peaceful natural world of the St. Regis Canoe Wilderness Area is easily accessed via canoe or motor boat.

With many campsites directly on the lake, Fish Creek offers endless possibilities for the

www.insiders.com

See this and many other **Insiders' Guide®** destinations online — in their entirety.

Visit us today!

avid canoeist. Good hiking trails and fishing in dozens of ponds and lakes, many just a stone's throw from each other, also are within the area.

This state campground operates from mid-April through mid-November and accommodates all equipment from tents to RVs. Hot showers, canoe rentals and recreation programs are available during the summer. Make your reservations early.

Little Wolf Beach and Campground
N.Y. Rt. 3, Tupper Lake • 359-3000

Little Wolf Beach, on Little Wolf Lake in Tupper Lake, is one of the more popular beaches in the region. The campground has 52 trailer and tent sites, 28 with electricity. Many sites are directly on the water, and there is a public boat launch on site.

Meacham Lake State Campground
N.Y. Rt. 30, Paul Smiths • 483-5116

Meacham Lake, with its 200-plus sites, is another popular campground for families. This site has everything, including hiking, canoeing, swimming and a daily activities program for the kids. Meacham Lake is a great lake for exploring. Saranac Lake and Malone, the nearest villages, are about 30 minutes away.

Rollins Pond
N.Y. Rt. 30, Tupper Lake • 891-3239

Adjacent to Fish Creek, Rollins Pond is the quiet alternative, but with the same great access to area lakes. Rollins's 290 campsites, however, are open only mid-May through Labor Day.

Fishing within this area is fantastic, and even though plenty of people may be visiting the campsites, many of the small ponds are devoid of crowds.

INSIDERS' TIP

Early regulations adopted by the State's Conservation Commissioners in 1913 made all Adirondack lean-tos state property for use by all hikers and campers, no matter who constructed them. Some 10 years later, the Commission established the first public campsite in the region on the Sacandaga River below the town of Wells.

Backpack Camping

Almost every wilderness trail offers some designated site for camping. Whatever you need, however, you backpack in and backpack out. Surprisingly, there are relatively few restrictions on camping in the wilderness.

One reason for the lack of restrictions is simple: Most campers leave their camping site in better condition than when they arrived.

As more and more people begin to enjoy a true wilderness camping experience, the pressure to impose restrictions increases, especially when abuses to the present system are noted. Every year thousands upon thousands of hikers camp in the backwoods and respect the rules. All of these positive experiences can be quickly undermined by the careless camper who abuses the privileges shared by all. We all share a responsibility in preserving and protecting the wilderness. It is a privilege — it isn't a right which is guaranteed.

Respect the rules, and we all will continue to enjoy unencumbered access to the wilderness.

Abuse the rules, and stricter rules will follow.

General Backcountry Camping Guidelines

•Camp at designated campsites with yellow and black markers that read "Department of Environmental Conservation: Camp Here" whenever possible. Avoid setting up camp within 150 feet of any body of water or trail, when possible. No person or group can stay more than three consecutive nights at a primitive campsite.

•No camping is permitted above 4,000 feet, except from December 1 to April 30. Since the ground is frozen and most likely snow-covered during this time, no damage to plant life can occur.

•Don't wash dishes or yourself with soap in any lake, pond or stream. No soap, including biodegradable soap, should ever get into a source of water. Wash your dishes in a pot of water and dispose of the waste water at least 150 feet from the source of water.

•Bury all human waste at least 150 feet away from any water source and beneath at least 4 inches of soil. Bury or burn all toilet paper. If a privy is available, use it.

•Build campfires only in established fire rings where available, or on rocks or sand. Burn only dead and down timber in campfires. At popular campsites, dead wood is often scarce, so remember to take along a backpacking stove. Use common sense when building a fire — never leave a fire unattended and make sure it's completely out before leaving.

•If you carry it in, carry it out. All trash must be either completely burned or carried out. Do not bury trash, especially metal cans or aluminum foil, as they will not biodegrade.

•Leave only your footprint as the trace that you were ever there.

Adirondack Lean-tos

Adirondack lean-tos are unique to this part of the country. About 250 of these three-sided structures are located throughout the Park along trails, ponds, lakes and rivers. Their design is simple: three walls, a sloped roof with an overhang and a dirt floor. Providing more shelter than a tent, but less than a cabin, lean-tos are a curious combination that have hosted generations of the down-and-dirty to the up-and-coming (as in President-to-be Teddy Roosevelt in the 1870s).

Adirondack lean-tos can be found along many backcountry trails and even are

— continued on next page

designated on some maps, but don't always trust the maps or count on availability. Lean-tos are not permitted in designated "forever wild" wilderness areas, thus many have been removed. In high-traffic areas, lean-tos are often occupied, but if space is available, occupants are required to share it with anyone else who wishes to use it (up to capacity, of course). A lean-to may not be occupied for more than three consecutive nights. No nails or other fasteners may be used to secure tarps or ropes to the lean-to, and no tents may be set up inside the structure.

Group Camping

No camping permits are required for groups of fewer than 10. Any group of 10 or more people needs to obtain a permit from the Department of Environmental Conservation. No groups of 10 or more people are allowed to camp in the High Peaks region.

Photo: Nancie Battaglia

The low hum of activity in front of the Adirondack Loj near Lake Placid . . .

Saranac Lake Islands State Campground
N.Y. Rt. 3, Saranac Lake • 891-4590

On islands in Lower and Middle Saranac Lake, these public camping sites are accessible by boat or canoe only, but they are well worth the effort to access, as campers often have an island all to themselves. Islands often come with their own sandy beaches and spectacular views. Although islands offer limited hiking opportunities, the canoeing and fishing options are endless. All 87 sites are primitive — an outhouse is the only facility offered. The campgrounds has no running water, no showers and generally no neigh-

bors. Whatever you need, you must boat it in and boat it out!

Plattsburgh/Western Lake Champlain Area

Ausable Chasm Campgrounds
U.S. Hwy. 9, Ausable Chasm • 834-9990, (800) 562-9105

This is one of the highest-rated KOA campgrounds in North America, so it must be doing a lot of things right. Among its notable qualities is its location, on the grounds of the famed

Ausable Chasm. The campground offers 135 sites — 68 have electric hookups — and a complete range of services. There are free movies every night, along with a swimming pool, tennis and volleyball courts and walking trails. Special rates for exploring the chasm are available for guests. If you want to enjoy mountain and lake on your vacation, the campground is a convenient carhop to both.

Ausable Point State Campground
U.S. Hwy. 9, Plattsburgh • 561-7080

Ausable Point, with its location on Lake Champlain, offers 123 sites, 43 with electric hookups. The site offers a sandy beach of its own, and the campground is a popular family destination. It's open May through mid-October.

Bulwagga Bay Campsite
14 Park Pl. (N.Y. Rts. 9N and 22), Port Henry • 546-7500

More sightings of the legendary Lake Champlain sea monster have occurred in Bulwagga Bay than anywhere else, so if you hope to see Champ, park your RV at this 175-site, full-service campground and rent a boat or launch your own.

Brookwood Park
N.Y. Rt. 9N, Ticonderoga • 585-7113

This full-service campground with 65 sites is near Fort Ticonderoga and Lake Champlain. It is open from May through mid-October.

Cumberland Bay State Park
152 Cumberland Bay Rd., Plattsburgh • 563-5240

This park has the greatest beach on which to build the perfect sandcastle! In fact, in early July, the beach is littered (so to speak) with castles for every lord and lady during the annual competition. On the northwest shore of Lake Champlain, this park is both a popular day-use and camping area, mainly because of the 2,700-foot sandy beach. There are more than 200 campsites plus playgrounds, playing fields, volleyball nets, horseshoe pits and picnic areas. It's a great place for a family reunion.

Crown Point State Campground
4 miles east of N.Y. Rt. 22, Crown Point • 597-3603

There are only 64 sites, but most have a view of Lake Champlain. This campground is an ideal base for exploring Vermont, as well as the Adirondacks. A five-minute drive across the Crown Point Bridge puts you in Vermont farm country, and a one-hour drive in the opposite direction will put you in the High Peaks. The site, near historic Crown Point, offers plenty of open areas, good shore fishing, a spot to launch a boat and basic services, including showers. The site is open April to October.

Lincoln Pond State Campground
N.Y. Rt. 7, Elizabethtown • 942-5292

This small campground — only 35 sites — offers good fishing, swimming and boating on site. The High Peaks are nearby, making Lincoln Pond a good base camp for exploring the region.

High Falls Campground
N.Y. Rt. 11, Chateaugay • 497-3156

Chateaugay is off the beaten path, but this campsite near the Canadian border has plenty going for it. It is only an hour from the great

---

INSIDERS' TIP

Bear-proof your food by storing it in a pack or a sack hung from a branch 15 feet from the tree trunk and away from your tent. If you do experience a bear in your tent camp, try to scare it off by banging together pots and pans. If that fails, bid farewell to your belongings, and retreat quietly until out of danger. Generally, bears won't be the creatures that attack your food. A mouse will more likely be the one to chew through your pack to get at goodies, but the bear-proofing technique also will keep your food relatively mouse-proof.

city of Montreal, about a half-hour from Lake Champlain and less than an hour's drive to the mountains. There are also spacious wooded pull-through sites, hiking trails, a full range of hookups, all the usual amenities of a popular creature-comfort campground — hot showers, a recreation room and camp store — and a 120-foot waterfall on site.

Iroquois RV Park & Campground
270 Bear Swamp Rd., Peru • 643-9057

With 190 sites — all with electric hookups, 185 with sewer hookups — 20- to 30-amp service, a pool, recreation room, fishing . . . sounds like a typical campground with all the expected amenities. There is, however, one special perk: a nine-hole par 3 golf course within walking distance of your campsite. Lake Champlain is just minutes away.

Lake Harris State Campground
N.Y. Rt. 28N, Newcomb • 582-2503

Not many people can tell where to find Lake Harris. It deserves a better reputation — a spectacular lake amid a great wilderness hiking area. The campground offers 57 sites, almost all of which are on the lake or within a stone's throw. The Newcomb area is one of the less traveled in the Park, but offers exceptional opportunities for boating, canoeing, fishing and hiking. It's an hour's drive to Tupper Lake or Lake George, the nearest major towns. Nearby villages of Long Lake and Blue Mountain Lake provide basic conveniences and plenty of personality.

Macomb Reservation State Park
201 Campsite Rd., Schuyler Falls
• 643-9952

This state park with 175 sites is a few miles outside Plattsburgh on man-made Davis Pond. The main activities in the park are fishing in the pond and in the nearby Salmon River plus swimming and hiking. There are showers, picnic and ball-playing areas, nature trails, playgrounds and, in winter, cross-country ski and snowmobile trails.

Paradise Pines Campground
Blue Ridge Rd., North Hudson • 532-7493

This family-oriented campground has miniature golf, a pool and planned activities including movies and hay rides. A hundred wooded and riverside sites are available, and the majority of them have electric and sewage hookups. Pop-up rentals are available on site. The campground is within walking distance to Frontier Town (see our Attractions chapter).

Putnam Pond State Campground
N.Y. Rt. 74, Ticonderoga • 585-7280

Known locally as "Putt's Pond," after famous American Revolutionary general Israel Putnam, this campground offers one of the finest and sunniest beaches around. You'll find good hiking, fishing and boating on site. The roads throughout the campground are great for biking. This is an ideal site for exploring both the central Adirondacks and Vermont, as both are less than an hour's drive away.

Lake George/
Upper Hudson Region

Alpine Lake Camping Resort
78 Heath Rd., Corinth • 654-6260

Just within the southeastern fringe of the Adirondack Park, about 15 miles from Lake George, this huge camping resort offers 500 sites with full hookups (water, electric and sewer) set between two private spring-fed lakes. Both lakefront and wooded sites are available. One of the real advantages to Alpine Lake is its location, approximately midway between the family-oriented attractions of the Lake George area and the more adult-oriented attractions of Saratoga Springs (see our Daytrips chapter). Both are within a 15-minute drive, yet the serene setting of this camping resort is a stark contrast to the kinetic summer action in those destinations. In other words, it's nice to be near the action without being swallowed up in the middle of it.

In addition to the great location, Alpine Lake offers a tremendous variety of recreational amenities and activities that may make you wonder why you'd even need to go to Lake George or Saratoga Springs. You can swim in either the two swimming pools or the private lakes, one with a sandy beach. If you choose lake fun, you can also rent rowboats, canoes and paddleboats, or even do some fishing. Back on land, there are two lighted tennis courts, basketball and volleyball courts, a softball field, playgrounds and an indoor play room with video games and pool tables. If you run out of your own ideas, the activities director is sure to have plenty of suggestions. For example, you can take the kids to visit "Alpie" and "Woody," the two resident (sculpted) dinosaurs.

For those of you who want to "try before you buy," there are RV rentals available so you can ease into the camping lifestyle. If you are driving or pulling your own, there are 300 pull-through sites to choose from.

Alpine Lake Camping Resort is open from May through September.

Evergreen Camping Resort
E. Schroon River Rd., Lake George • 623-3207, (800) 327-3188

Another big camping resort, but this time set on a river instead of a lake, Evergreen offers 260 sites, of which 110 offer water and electric hookups. Evergreen is tucked away just a few miles from the hustle of Lake George village, but it's in a world of its own along the banks of the Schroon River. Its setting allows for plenty of water-related recreation options including fishing, beach-hanging (yes, the river has a beach!), canoeing, tubing, boating and swimming in either the river or the two swimming pools. Other outdoor activities you can try include a nine-hole pitch-and-putt golf course, minigolf, tennis, basketball, volleyball, horseshoes, hiking and lots more.

For rainy days (an inevitable occurrence), you can enjoy the game room, the country store and movies and even get cable TV hooked up to your camper for a small fee. And the shops of Lake George are just a few minutes away.

Novices can choose from 24 on-site RV rentals.

Evergreen Camping Resort is open from late May to mid-October.

Lake George Islands State Campsites
Glen Island • 644-9696
Long Island • 656-9426
Narrow Island • 499-1288

For a unique Adirondack camping experience that emphasizes natural beauty over modern conveniences, you may want to try camping out on one of the Lake George Islands State Campsites. These campsites are accessible by boat only, which is either half the fun or most of the hassle, depending on how you look at it. If your attitude is the latter, you probably won't enjoy this setting too much, because this is for "real" campers, not the cable-ready variety that populate the big camping resorts.

All three islands offer the basics only: tent sites, picnic tables and fire pits. Glen Island has 213 sites and is reachable by boat from Bolton Landing. To get to Long Island, launch your boat from Cleverdale. Once there, you will find 90 tent sites. For Narrow Island and its 86 sites, you should depart by boat from Hulett's Landing on the east side of Lake George.

As you might imagine, these sites are very popular for the entire time they are open (mid-May through early September), so you must call ahead to reserve a site.

Lake George RV Park
74 N.Y. Rt. 149, Lake George • 792-3775

In business for more than 30 years, this is one of the premier camping resorts in the region, offering 350 sites with full hookups. Of those, 250 sites offer pull-through convenience for RVers. You can also rent one of seven RVs on site.

This park offers some special amenities

INSIDERS' TIP

Following a steady decrease in their population since the 1960s, moose, the largest mammals in the Adirondacks, are once again beginning to take up permanent residency in the Park. The best estimate is that 25 to 50 reside here year round. Populations initially declined due to over-hunting and destruction of habitat from logging and fire.

that set it apart from many others. For example, included in the nightly rate (which admittedly is $5 to $10 higher than at other parks) is a free trolley service that will shuttle you into Lake George village a little more than 3 miles away. Other special features for no extra charge include an indoor pool (in addition to the two outdoor pools), live entertainment, three indoor movie theaters, cable TV and a stocked fishing pond. You'll also find eight tennis courts, paddleboats, hiking trails and basketball and volleyball courts.

If you want to preview your experience at the Lake George RV Park, we suggest you call and ask them for their video brochure. For a fun family vacation or even a nostalgic getaway with a loved one in a natural setting with first-class facilities, it's hard to do better than this.

You can enjoy the park from the beginning of May until mid-October.

Ledgeview Village RV Park
321 N.Y. Rt. 149, Lake George • 798-6621

The Lake George area's newest RV park, Ledgeview offers clean, modern facilities in a beautifully wooded setting about 4 miles from Lake George village. All 104 sites offer full hookups, and 17 sites offer pull-through convenience. The sites are level and the driveways paved, making getting around and parking a breeze (well, relatively speaking) for large RVs.

Ledgeview offers the typical recreational amenities such as a pool, rec hall and playground. We think it's a good value.

Ledgeview is open from May until mid-October.

Mohawk Campground on Lake George
3144 Lakeshore Dr., Lake George • 668-2760

Billed as the only private campground right on Lake George, this is the place to stay if your kids insist on running from the campsite down to the water four or five times a day. There's a small private beach as well as rental canoes and rowboats. Of the 75 terraced sites, 17 offer full hookups, and 58 provide water and electric service. Basic recreational amenities such as video games and a playground are available, but the real attraction here is camping on the shore of one of America's most beautiful lakes.

Mohawk Campground is open from late May until early September.

Rogers Rock State Campground
N.Y. Rt. 9N, Hague • 585-6746

Rogers Rock is another lakeside option; however, as a state campground, this one offers just the basics: tent sites, flush toilets, showers, fireplaces and picnic tables. It's a big area, with a total of 331 sites, and it does offer some real positives, such as a boat launch and the uncrowded waters of northern Lake George. As with most state campgrounds, this one is for veteran campers.

You can camp at Rogers from early May until mid-October.

Lake George/Schroon Valley Resort
Schroon River Rd., Warrensburg • 494-2451, (800) 958-CAMP

Set along the Schroon River, this resort features 140 grassy, open and shaded campsites. It combines a scenic, peaceful setting with convenience to the action and attractions of nearby Lake George. Thirty-seven sites have full hookups, and 103 provide water and electric service. Twenty-six of the sites offer pull-through convenience. You can also choose to rent an on-site RV if you don't own one.

Recreational options range from fishing and river tubing on the Schroon to lounging by the heated pool or playing video games in the recreation hall. The usual combo of playgrounds, basketball courts, horseshoe pits and the like are also available.

Lake George/Schroon Valley Resort is open from mid-May until mid-October.

Eagle Point State Campground
U.S. Hwy. 9, Pottersville • 494-2220

The primary attraction of Eagle Point is nearby Schroon Lake, a 4,230-acre and 9-mile-long gem. Swimming, boating, canoeing and hiking are available on site. Schroon Lake,

---

FYI

Unless otherwise noted, the area code for all phone numbers listed in this guide is 518.

Photo: Warren County Tourism Department

Family camping combines Adirondack adventure with moments of quiet relaxation.

just off of I-87, attracts boaters of every kind. Sailing, water-skiing and Jet Skiing are all popular activities. Free public boat launches are available in the village of Schroon Lake and in Horican at the southern tip of the lake. Lake George and Lake Champlain are less than one hour away. Lake Placid is slightly more than an hour's drive.

Wakonda Family Campground
3901 E. Schroon River Rd., Pottersville • 494-2610

About 20 miles north of Lake George village and just a mile from Schroon Lake, Wakonda is nestled between Lake Wakonda, Blueberry Pond and the Schroon River. In fact, you can access Schroon Lake (less than a mile away) via the campground's frontage on the Schroon River. Of the 140 wooded sites, 128 offer electric and water hookups, while 12 offer full hookups including sewer. Twenty-four of the sites are pull-through.

You have lots of recreational options here: two sandy beaches for swimming or lounging, three clay tennis courts, a basketball court, softball field, volleyball court and children's playground. If you're looking for a truly natural setting for your camping vacation, Wakonda is worth considering.

You can visit Wakonda from Memorial Day weekend until mid-October.

Southern Adirondack Lakes Region

Caroga Lake State Campgrounds
N.Y. Rt. 29A, Caroga Lake • 835-4241

The first state campground you come to when entering the Adirondack Park from the south is Caroga Lake. It is about a half-hour's drive north of New York State Thruway Exit 29 (Canojoharie) and is set along the shore of East Caroga Lake. The elevation is 1,460 feet — high enough to cause a temperature differential 5 or so degrees lower than you might expect. Of course, if you're escaping the heat of large Northeastern or Mid-Atlantic cities during the height of the summer, the relatively cooler temps will come as a welcome relief.

You will find 161 campsites here, none of which have electric, water or sewer (as is typical with state campgrounds). Some basic amenities are available, such as hot showers, flush toilets and a trailer dump station. In addition, boat owners will be happy to know there is a boat launch available. For those of you who would rather watch the boats than ride in them, you can enjoy the vantage point from the sandy beach. Finally, if you can actually feel your muscles starting to atrophy from a little too much hanging out under the party lamps, you can tackle the exercise course/jogging path and its 18 activity stations. There's also a playground for the kids to enjoy.

Caroga Lake State Campground is open from mid-May until Labor Day.

Indian Lake Islands State Campsites
N.Y. Rt. 30, Indian Lake • 648-5300

This is one of four state camping areas in the Adirondacks that offers island camping via boat access. The others are at Lake George, Saranac Lake and Alger Island near Old Forge. At Indian Lake, 55 campsites are available on various islands that dot the long narrow lake. They are tent sites only, and other than showers, there are no other amenities. It's camping at its most basic (and some would say, most beautiful).

Lake Durant State Campground
N.Y. Rt. 28, Blue Mountain Lake • 352-7797

About 3 miles east of Blue Mountain Lake, this state campground offers 61 sites, none of which have hookups. There are showers, picnic tables, fire rings and sewage disposal available (both the trailer-dump variety and the flush-toilet variety). Recreationally, you can launch a boat at the ramp on Lake Durant and then fish or swim all you want in the uncrowded, refreshing waters. Camping at Lake Durant is convenient to the outstanding

Adirondack Museum (the unofficial heart of the Adirondacks) and the Adirondack Lakes Center for the Arts, both of which you'll want to remember for rainy days. You can camp at Lake Durant from mid-May through early October.

Piseco Lake State Campgrounds
Little Sand Point Campground, Old Piseco Rd., off N.Y. Rt. 8, Piseco Lake • 548-7585
Point Comfort Campground, Old Piseco Rd., off N.Y. Rt. 8, Piseco Lake • 548-7586
Poplar Point Campground, Old Piseco Rd., off N.Y. Rt. 8, Piseco Lake • 548-8031

While these three are separate state campgrounds, we have listed them together because they're strung one after the other along the northern shore of Piseco Lake. Poplar Point is the oldest, opening in August 1927, followed by Point Comfort (1929) and then Little Sand Point (1953). The campgrounds sit at about 1,600 feet elevation, so hot and muggy days are rare. Poplar Point has 21 campsites, Point Comfort has 76 campsites, and Little Sand Point offers 78 sites. None of the sites offer hookups. All three campgrounds have a boat launch, sand beach and recreational activities including canoeing, fishing and lifeguard-staffed swimming. There are no showers at these campgrounds, but there are bathhouses for changing at Point Comfort and Poplar Point. A couple of notable natural attractions worth checking out nearby are the Panther Mountain Echo Cliffs, which reach heights of 700 feet. The .75-mile trail begins near the Little Sand Point Campground. Also, the T Lake trail begins its 5-mile trek from Poplar Point Campground to T Lake at an elevation of 2,460 feet.

Poplar Point and Little Sand Point are open from mid-May until Labor Day; Point Comfort's season extends until mid-October.

Moffitt Beach State Campground
N.Y. Rt. 8, Speculator • 548-7102

This large campground set along the eastern shore of Sacandaga Lake (not the Great Sacandaga Lake some 30 miles to the southeast) dates back to 1932. It offers 261 campsites, about a third of which hug the shoreline of the lake. At an elevation of 1,724 feet, the air rarely gets steamy — and the water rarely gets warm — so a visit here certainly should leave you refreshed.

While you're definitely in the middle of nowhere at Moffitt Beach, it's nice to know there's a "somewhere" fairly nearby. In his case, you are only a few miles in either direction along N.Y. 8 to the villages of Speculator and Lake Pleasant, both of which offer ample supplies and even some nice restaurants (take a break from the campfire scene). Moffitt also offers some amenities — showers, for one — not found at the nearby Piseco Lake campgrounds. There's also a picnic pavilion, two boat launches, lifeguard-staffed swimming and even a general store in a private section of the park.

Moffitt Beach is open from mid-May until mid-October.

Northampton Beach State Campground
N.Y. Rt. 30, between Mayfield and Northville • 863-6000

This is the one state campground on the shore of the Great Sacandaga Lake — and with 224 sites, it's a big one. The big advantage to Northampton is accessibility, in two ways. First, it's only about an hour north of the New York State Thruway Exit 28 (Johnstown). Second, it is along one of the biggest lakes in the entire state, making it a terrific spot for campers with boats (or who like to boat and don't mind renting).

All the basic state-style amenities are here, including fire rings, picnic tables, hot showers, flush toilets, a trailer dumping station and boat launch. You can stroll nearby Northville on a rainy day (check out the Adirondack Country Store, listed in the Shopping chapter), or shop the leather outlets in and around Gloversville. For the most part, you'll probably want to stick around and enjoy this beautiful and busy lake.

Northampton is open from early May through mid-October.

Pine Lake Park & Campground
N.Y. Rts. 10 and 29A, Pine Lake • 835-4930

In a region dominated by the state campgrounds (the opposite of Lake George, where private camping resorts are the rage), this is a fun little find. Everything about the place makes it look like it was built on a one-third scale. The lake is a cute little circle, with cute hills surrounding it, and a cute sandy beach at one end.

Don't take us wrong, we *like* cute little campgrounds. And just because it's cute doesn't mean it's not fun! The canoe rentals, minigolf and arcade games make sure of that. It also has a perfect family beach, with firm sand, plenty of room and (because the lake is so small) relatively warm water. As for the camping, you'll find 81 sites here with electric and water hookups. If you're looking for family fun without the neon of Lake George or Old Forge, Pine Lake is worth considering.

You can visit from early May to early September.

Old Forge/ Raquette Lake Region

Brown Tract Pond State Campground
off N.Y. Rt. 28, Raquette Lake • (315) 354-4412

Open from mid-May until Labor Day, this state campground offers 90 tent and trailer sites spread around the eastern perimeter of Lower Brown Tract Pond. This isolated campground sits at an elevation of 1,768 feet and offers the ultimate in peaceful, basic camping. There are picnic tables and fireplaces, vault toilets (one baby-step above a latrine on the luxury scale) and a trailer dump station for garbage. No hookups for water, electric or sewer are provided, nor are there any shower facilities. The best you can do is a bathhouse along the sandy beach.

For recreation, you can swim, canoe, fish and hike. Small non-motorized boats can be launched at the boat ramp.

Eighth Lake State Campground
N.Y. Rt. 28, 6 miles east of Inlet • (315) 354-4120

Set between the waters of Seventh Lake and Eighth Lake in the Fulton Chain of Lakes, this campground offers 126 tent and trailer sites. While no hookups are available, you will

A sugar shack boils up the region's world-famous maple sugar.

find hot showers, flush toilets (a luxury this deep in the woods), plenty of picnic areas with fireplaces and a swimming beach with lifeguards on Eighth Lake. This area offers a beautiful, isolated setting, yet it is convenient to the attractions and amenities of Old Forge, Inlet and Raquette Lake. You can enjoy Eighth Lake State Campground for a couple of months longer than many other state campgrounds, as it opens in mid-April and doesn't close until mid-November.

Limekiln Lake State Campground
off N.Y. Rt. 28, Inlet • (315) 357-4401

With 271 campsites, Limekiln Lake is one of the largest state campgrounds in the Adirondacks. It is also one of the most complete in amenities, with showers, flush toilets and a trailer dumping station available as conveniences. For recreation, a beach with lifeguards, boat and canoe rentals, a boat launch

for your own vessel, fishing and hiking are all options for you to enjoy.

Nicks Lake State Campground
off N.Y. Rt. 28, Old Forge • (315) 369-3314

Just a couple of miles from Old Forge, Nicks Lake is a good alternative if you want to be close (but not in the middle of) the action and attractions. You will find 112 campsites (again with no hookups), but there are showers and flush toilets. No motor boats are allowed on the lake, but you can canoe or row to whatever fishing hot spot they're talking about around the campfires. A sandy beach with lifeguards is the alternative spot for watching all the water "action."

Old Forge KOA
N.Y. Rt. 28, Old Forge • (315) 369-6011

Now this is the place to camp if you want

to slide and ride your way around the adjacent Enchanted Forest/Water Safari theme parks without getting in the car. You can either walk or ride on the complimentary shuttle to enjoy the parks. A total of 210 sites are available, both in a wooded setting or along KOA's private lake. Fifty-seven sites offer full hookups, and another 50 provide water and electric (but no sewer). A notable feature at KOA: the 46 heated Kamping Kabins available on a year-round basis (popular with fall hunters and spring fishing enthusiasts).

In addition to the action next door at the theme parks, a wide variety of on-site recreational options are available: canoe, boat and bike rentals; a game arcade; nightly movies; a playground; and courts for basketball, volleyball and horseshoes. If you love camping but the rest of the family isn't so sure, this could be just the ticket to win them over.

Singing Waters Campground
off N.Y. Rt. 28, 6 miles south of Old Forge • (315) 369-6618

Another rare year-rounder, this privately owned campground is along the Moose River. It offers 142 sites in both wooded and open settings. Sixty-four of the sites offer full hookups, and another 53 provide water and electric service. There is also a one-bedroom cabin with loft — available for those who prefer walls to canvas. For amenities, you'll find heated showers and restrooms, picnic tables, a trailer dumping station, fireplaces and a small grocery store.

Recreational options include fishing, swimming and canoeing on the Moose (River, that is), two tennis courts, a rec room with games, a softball field, horseshoe pits, badminton courts and a playground. While technically open year round, keep in mind that Singing Waters Campground is fully operational only from mid-May until mid-November.

In the High Peaks region, Mount Marcy attracts an estimated 100,000 hikers every year.

Hiking

Approximately 2,000 miles of trails traverse the Adirondack region — greater than the distance from New York to Orlando or Dallas to Los Angeles.

Where do we begin to describe these trails? Which ones are the best? The most difficult? The easiest or the most scenic? One trail, the Northville to Lake Placid trail, traverses 132 miles of wilderness. It might be the best trail, the most difficult, the easiest and the most scenic all wrapped into one. In the High Peaks region, Mount Marcy attracts an estimated 100,000 hikers every year. The number of hikers makes it one of the most popular trails, but is it the best? Is it one that you should hike or avoid?

The problem of being in a hiker's paradise is that the options are endless. Do you want a 20-minute hike ending at a beautiful waterfall? There's a hike for you. Do you want to bushwhack to a remote pond where almost no one goes? There's a hike for you. How about climbing a mountain with a great view, or ending up at a great backwoods swimming hole? Do you want to explore a cave, a marsh, a bog or look for eagles, hawks, woodpeckers or moose? You'll find hikes to meet each of these goals.

The Adirondack Mountain Club (ADK) publishes a variety of very useful and interesting hiking guides to the Adirondack region. In addition to "Sampler" books, which give a good overview of your options, there are also detailed guidebooks for seven distinctive regions within the Adirondacks as well as a series of trail guides. We suggest you contact the ADK and take advantage of these wonderful resources — your hiking enjoyment and safety could depend on it. You can call the ADK, (518) 668-4447, or visit their information office just off I-87 Exit 21 on N.Y. Route 9N in Lake George. These guides lead you from trailhead to destination and back. In a few cases, they describe the trailhead, then mention that there is no trail to the top of a particular peak. In such instances, hikers must bushwhack through some of the wildest country east of the Mississippi River to reach the summits.

Maybe someday in the future Insiders' Publishing Inc. will have a series devoted solely to hiking in the Adirondacks; in the meantime we'll get you started. So, here are some basics.

Hiking References

There are a number of good guidebooks available on hiking in the Adirondack region. Those from the ADK provide the best detail on the trails, but do not give you a good feel for the scenery or the ecology. The Discover the Adirondack series by Barbara McMartin, published by Backcountry Publications, provides basic overviews of what to look for and expect on some great hikes, but falls short of the trail details in the ADK publications. In various issues of *Adirondack Life* magazine, articles describe some worthwhile hikes and provide full-color photographs, but you have to collect the magazines. *Adirondac*, published by ADK, is also an excellent source.

DEC Brochures

The Department of Environmental Conservation (DEC) offers free hiking and canoeing brochures for various sections of the Adirondack region that provide basic information on most of the popular trails and routes. To obtain copies, visit, write or call DEC Headquarters, 50 Wolf Road, Albany, New York 12233, 457-7433, or DEC Region 5, Route 86, Box 296, Ray Brook, New York 12977, 897-1200. Offices are open Monday through Friday, 8:30 AM to 4:45 PM.

(Save a tree and ask only for those brochures you'll need.)

Trail maps are available for:
• "Big Moose Region"
• "Bog River Flow"
• "Brewster Peninsula Trail"
• "Cranberry Lake Region"
• "Lake Lila Primitive Area"
• "McKeever-North Lake Region"
• "Trails in the High Peaks"
• "Lake George Region"
• "Blue Mountain Lake Region"
• "Northville-Lake Placid Trail"
• "Moose River Region"
• "Nordic Skiing Trails"
• "Old Forge-Brantingham Lake"
• "Otter Creek Horse Trails"
• "Saranac Lake Area"
• "Camping Middle Saranac"
• "Camping Upper Saranac"
• "Schroon Lake Region"
• "Siamese Ponds Wilderness"
• "Stillwater Reservoir"

Other brochures of interest include:
• "Adirondack Canoe Routes"
• "5 Rules for Survival"
• "Use of NYS Public Forest Lands"
• "Adirondack Mountain Reserve"
• "Horse Trails in NYS"
• "Snowmobiling in NYS"

Oft-asked Questions

Do I need trail maps? Yes, no and maybe. (How's that for clarity?) The majority of trails in the region are marked with Department of Environmental Conservation (DEC) trail markers. On many of the more heavily traveled trails during the height of hiking season, the trails are well worn and traveled, making the hike as easy as playing follow-the-leader. If you are taking a day hike along one of these popular routes, a trail map is good to have, but not mandatory as long as you stay on the marked trail. If you are planning an overnight hike, or are hiking off the beaten path, a trail map becomes increasingly important as it provides trail details, campsite options and distances.

As a general rule, always follow the DEC markers. If you don't see the markers on a trail, you probably should return to the last trail junction; you might have taken the wrong route.

Is there any dangerous wildlife in the woods? Most of the wildlife in the region is relatively harmless as long as it is left alone; any animal can be dangerous if threatened. There are, however, no poisonous snakes* or mammals in the Park, and only a few poisonous-to-the-touch plants. (*One isolated and protected habitat in the Lake George area is inhabited by rattlesnakes, though the area is virtually inaccessible to hikers.) Poison ivy is found in only a few lowland areas, but is not a threat on any hiking trails. There is also little danger of encountering wood ticks. Some diagnosed cases of Lyme disease have been recorded in the Adirondack region. But the tick that causes Lyme disease is found more in meadows or grasslands than in the woods. Although the incidence of Lyme disease is regarded as low in this region, it is always a good idea to check for ticks after a day of outdoor activity.

What will I see on a hike? The Adirondacks boast of the largest old-growth forest east of the Mississippi River plus 82 different types of natural communities (12 of which are considered among the finest examples of their kind in the world) and more than 240 rare plant and animal species.

While species such as the wolf and mountain lion disappeared in the late 1800s due to over-hunting, there is still plenty of wildlife to see. An estimated 25 to 50 moose inhabit the region, and although elusive, they can be spotted, especially in the spring as the males seek out one of the too few females. White-tailed deer and black bears are prevalent in the area, but it is most likely that you will see much smaller mammals, such as chipmunks, squirrels, red foxes or porcupines.

Then again, it is possible that you won't see any animals. Just because you want to see them, doesn't mean they'll reveal themselves to you. To increase your chances, learn a little about the natural history of the region; it'll give you an idea of what to look for and where to look. (See this chapter's Close-up, "A Brief Natural History of the Adirondacks," for a primer.)

Photo: Adirondack Nature Conservancy/Gary Randorf

A staff member of Adirondack Nature Conservancy explains about endangered plants atop Mount Marcy.

A Selection of Hikes

The following sample of hikes will provides a good overview of the natural diversity found in the region. In some cases, the trail was selected because it is simply a good walk.

Lake Placid/ Tri-Lakes Region

Brewster Peninsula Nature Trails
off Saranac Ave., Lake Placid

A great after-dinner walk, a great walk with kids, or an easy walk with a great view of Lake Placid . . . pick one. The Peninsula Trails, situated on a 133-acre site, is a favorite short walk for locals as well as tourists — once the tourists discover it, that is. And it is even within walking distance of all the major hotels on Main Street.

It is also easy to find. Simply look for the Howard Johnson's Hotel on Saranac Avenue, then follow the signs to the motor lodge on top of the hill. Don't go into the parking lot, but rather proceed straight. The paved road quickly turns into a dirt road with plenty of pot holes and ruts, so drive slowly. After a sharp

turn you will see an iron gate blocking another dirt road. Park in the pull-off area, which is the trailhead.

As you walk down the road, look toward the wetlands on your right. You're likely to spot wildlife, especially woodpeckers pounding the many dead and dying trees in the marsh in search of a meal. This wet area generally offers many examples of fungi, especially shelf-fungi or artist's fungi, growing on the dead trees; the fungi help decompose the trees.

A few hundred feet past the marsh, another trail crosses the road. Take the trail to the left; it will lead you along a brook, then to Lake Placid. The trail to the right leads to a new-growth forest. This section, cut over in the 1940s, is more open and yields better food sources than an older forest. Consequently, more wildlife (i.e. muskrats, moles, shrews and rabbits) is likely to be seen on this trail. Ignore the storm drains, but notice how quickly the forest changes along the path, especially the variety of trees, shrubs, flowers, mosses and ferns.

As you near the brook and lake, notice the differences between the plants near the water and those only a few feet away.

At the dam, stay on the trail to the right; it

weaves along the shore and takes you through a hardwood forest typical of the Adirondacks. Eventually, you will end up on an old road, the same one on which you began your trek.

Cascade Mountain
N.Y. Rt. 73, Lake Placid

If the goal is to simply break the 4,000-foot mountain barrier, then Cascade Mountain, 6 or so miles east of Lake Placid on N.Y. 73, meets the criteria — 4,098 feet. The round trip is slightly less than 5 miles and requires an easy to moderate climb.

Cascade Mountain, once known as Long Pond Mountain, rises high above the Cascade lakes, the two long lakes along N.Y. Route 73. (At the turn of the century, a major resort hotel once sat between the lakes, which is now a small picnic area.) The trail crosses a number of small brooks and traverses a white birch forest.

There are a number of false summits along the way, with the first spot offering a nice view of the Cascades. This, however, is not the summit. The climb continues a steep grade, then begins to moderate — just when you need it — to the top of the mountain, with a view of 30 of the highest peaks in the Adirondacks. There is great view through Avalanche Pass.

Northville-Placid Trail
Washburn Rd., Northville to Averyville Rd., Lake Placid

One-hundred-thirty-two miles in 40 hours — that's the record high school runner Richard Denker set for traversing the Northville-Placid Trail, the longest continuous trail in the Park. You may take a bit longer, as this "trunk trail" introduces hikers to a cross-section of the Adirondacks, from the southern lowlands to the High Peaks region.

The trail is more of a lowland or valley-type trail than a high-peak one. It rarely exceeds 3,000 feet, which makes it ideal for backpacking excursions; it's more of a steady walk than a climb. The entire trail takes about 12 to 19 days to hike, but you can just as easily hike one of the five trunks or just take a day hike along one of its sections.

Although it's cut by roads in only four places, feeder trails divide this trail into five sections. Section A brings hikers from Northville to Piseco; section B, from Piseco to Wakely Dam; section C, to routes 28, 30 and 28N in the Newcomb area; Section D, from Long Lake to Shattuck Clearing; and section E connects Shattuck Clearing with Lake Placid.

A map of the trail is essential, as it describes access points, camping locations, water sources and good places off the trail to replenish supplies or grab a shower.

The trail begins (or ends, depending on your point of view) at the Trailhead Lodge at 206 Washburn Road in Northville and ends on Averyville Road in Lake Placid.

Mount Marcy
off N.Y. Rt. 73, Lake Placid

Mount Marcy, named after former New York Gov. Marcy, is the highest peak in the state — 5,344 feet above sea level. A professor named Emmons bushwhacked his way through virgin forests without trails or guides to complete the first recorded ascent of the mountain in 1837. Marcy, known to the Native Americans as Tahawus or Cloud Splitter, splits more than the clouds; it divides the Hudson and St. Lawrence watersheds and is the home to Lake Tear-of-the-Clouds, the source of the Hudson River.

FYI

Unless otherwise noted, the area code for all phone numbers listed in this guide is 518.

INSIDERS' TIP

As you hike high peaks areas, you might notice that some stands of balsam fir seem to grow shorter as altitude increases. At the tree line, these trees form a ragged line of shrubs, twisted and stunted from their battles against wind and cold. These dwarf forests are known as *krummholz*, a German word meaning "crooked wood."

While Emmons struggled to find his way to the top more than 150 years ago, today's hikers struggle only with the steep grade. Clearly marked and clearly visible trails approach the peak from the Mt. Van Hoevenberg trail from the north, the John's Brook trail in Keene Valley from the east, Tahawus from the south, and from an approach known as Corey's, more than 30 miles to the west, near Tupper Lake.

Along the approach from the north, hikers get to enjoy the sights of Marcy Dam; lakes Avalanche, Colden and Tear-of-the-Clouds; Avalanche and Indian passes; and numerous brooks, including Calamity, Opalescent and Feldspar. Be forewarned: This approach is absolutely, positively the one with the greatest crowds!

The approach from Keene Valley begins with a spectacular view of the destination from the valley. The trail follows the John's Brook route for nearly 10 miles, past John's Brook and Bushnell Falls. The Hopkins trail, the most difficult, is more than 10 miles long. Another option is the Range trail, the most scenic, which travels over the summits of Saddleback and Basin mountains.

The 12-mile-long southern approach is found in Newcomb. There are three approaches: one via Lake Sally, East River and Hanging Spear Falls; the second via Calamity Brook and Lake Colden; and the third from Elk Lake.

The western approach is accessed about 9 miles east of Tupper Lake on the Ampersand Road and takes a 33.4-mile route through what is known as Cold River country.

The routes provide some truly great hiking experiences for an estimated 100,000 hikers per year. During peak summer weekends, some trails are so crowded that follow-the-leader is the hike of the day, and the sound of the wind rustling through the trees can not be heard over the din of hikers.

Herein lies a dilemma. Mount Marcy is a great hike; therefore, people want to hike it. Atop Marcy, however, is a rare and protected alpine meadow habitat. In New York State there are only 80 acres of such habitat — all within the High Peaks region of the Adirondacks. While many of the plants in these rare habitats also grow in the region's wetlands, the alpine habitat itself is threatened by hikers — even more specifically, by their feet.

Odd as it seems, the sole of a single hiking boot can destroy a habitat that took Mother Nature many hundreds and even thousands of years to create. The soil atop Mount Marcy is a precious commodity as it serves as a habitat for the few plants capable of surviving the harsh alpine conditions. In a single instant, a single misplaced step can carry off this soil, thus destroying thousands of years of nature's handiwork.

When walking atop alpine summits, it is important to walk only on marked trails. Many people argue that the safest or best solution in protecting these endangered habitats — and all habitats in the region, for that matter — is to simply eliminate the problem by banning hiking entirely, or at least limit the number of hikers on a particular mountain or trail. Hikers can be part of the solution by following two simple rules when atop the summit: Stay on designated paths; and treat the wilderness as if it was your prized possession — which it is.

Before hiking Mount Marcy in the peak summer and fall hiking seasons, consider your options carefully. Marcy is without a doubt a great hike, but there are equally good or better hikes with better views.

Red Dot Trail
N.Y. Rt. 30, Paul Smiths

This 2.5-mile loop would make many a top-10 list — if more people knew about it. The trail, originally developed by students at Paul Smiths College, traverses an esker and flows along ponds formed by glaciers. Along the trail is one of the most majestic groves of towering white pines in the Park, forming a place locals called The Cathedral — this aptly named spot has an almost sacred feel. Bring along a swimsuit; there is a natural beach along the trail. The trailhead is in the parking lot opposite the college, at the intersection of N.Y. routes 30 and 86.

Everton Falls Preserve
N.Y. Rt. 99, Malone

Logging plays an important role in the history of the Adirondacks (see our History chapter), with much of the entire region having been logged at one time or another. In the late

1800s, the little logging hamlet of Everton thrived. One-hundred years later, little evidence of the town remains; nature has reclaimed the area.

The site, however, was logged as recently as 1960 and today serves as an example of what happens to a forest after logging has taken place. Contrary to a popular belief, logging isn't always bad for an area's ecology. In many instances, logging actually improves the conditions of a habitat by allowing new growth to occur in the understory — a process known as succession — which, in turn, serves as a food source for wildlife. The particular sequence of succession depends upon prevailing environmental conditions such as soil moisture, length of growing season and the severity of the ecological disturbance. The site offers numerous examples of different stages of succession, from open meadows to young- and old-growth forests.

A short, one-hour walk along an interpretive trail through the preserve illustrates the phases of forest succession. Along the trail you will find plenty of shining clubmoss and tree clubmoss (*Lycopodium obscurum*), a distinctive miniature evergreen that millions of years ago grew as large as towering trees. Tree clubmoss also was an essential ingredient in the flash powder used in photography in the 1800s and serves as an anti-chafing agent. Clubmoss received its popular name because it produces spores upon a "club." Shining clubmoss (*Huperzia lucidulum*) is also known as "staghorn moss."

The preserve is accessed off N.Y. Route 30, between Paul Smiths and Malone. Look

www.insiders.com

See this and many other **Insiders' Guide®** destinations online — in their entirety.

Visit us today!

for N.Y. Route 99 on the east side of N.Y. 30 at Duane Center, near Malone. Opposite N.Y. 99 is County Route 14 (a.k.a. Red Tavern Road). The trailhead is about 7 miles west on Red Tavern Road.

Plattsburgh/Western Lake Champlain Region

Clintonville Pine Barrens Preserve
Buck Hill Rd., Ausable Forks (Clintonville)

Twelve-thousand years ago, water flowing from a melting glacier deposited the sandy soil in which this pitch pine-heath barren grows. (The Adirondack Nature Conservancy owns 232 acres of the estimated 900 acres in this natural community.) The barren is one of the state's best examples of this type of natural community, and is the home to two rare plants — prairie redroot (*Ceanothus herbaceus*) and Houghton's umbrella sedge (*Cyperus houghtonii*) — and two rare moths — *Xylena thoracica* and *Lithophane lepida lepida*.

A pitch-pine–heath barren is characterized by a fairly open canopy of pitch pine (*Pinus rigida*) with a concentration of low-growing heath shrubs in the understory, such as bearberry, sheep laurel, wintergreen, pipsissiwa, huckleberry, sweet fern and blueberries. Blueberries are found throughout the preserve. (Feel free to sample a handful if they are ripe, but save some for the animals.)

Pitch pine is identified by its clusters of three needles, 2 to 5 inches long, and a trunk

---

INSIDERS' TIP

A young Teddy Roosevelt spent the summer of 1871 at the Paul Smith's Hotel on Lower St. Regis Lake in Paul Smiths. Roosevelt took extensive notes on the wildlife in the area and six years later, at age 18, published his first book, *The Summer Birds of the Adirondacks in Franklin County, N.Y.* A fictionalized version of his notebooks is recreated in the interpretive signs on the Barnum Brook trail at the Adirondack Park Visitor Interpretive Center in Paul Smiths.

A Brief Natural History of the Adirondacks

The natural history of an area is very much like a good detective story. Most of the facts are visible, and the clues are easy to find. The challenge is to know an important clue when you see one and then figure out what it is telling you. This is not too difficult once you know a few basic facts.

Figuring out what is going on in the Adirondack forest begins with two questions: Why? and How? Why are the forests in the region the way they are? And how did the forests get that way?

One of the more prevalent clues can be found throughout the region, but is most obvious atop mountains where huge boulders often are strewn. The boulders typically are bigger than a small house, and they could not have fallen from a nearby mountain as there are none higher. It is also obvious that no ancient cult could have moved the boulders in some mysterious ceremony; the monoliths are all about, not just atop mountains.

So how did the boulders get there? A quick game of 20 Questions might suggest an answer. Did a flood move the boulders? Possibly, but unlikely — a collection of boulders in one location would be more likely. How about the wind? Impossible — the boulders are too big. What force in nature is capable of moving tons of debris and depositing it everywhere and anywhere?

There appears to be only one logical answer. Anyone who has ever seen pictures of an avalanche knows that the force of moving ice and snow is capable of moving massive quantities of materials. Since the boulders are atop the mountain, an avalanche is out of the realm of possibility — but the force of ice isn't.

A glacier is the likely culprit. So where is the glacier now and what does it have to do with the forests?

A Lasting Impression

About 14,000 years ago (give or take a few years), the last of the continental glaciers finally disappeared from the Adirondacks. As the glacial ice melted, a number of things happened that still influence the region's ecology.

As the ice sheet moved across the land, it collected most everything in its path, including rocks, soil and huge boulders. Then, when the sheet began melting, it deposited its collection of debris along the way. Many of these deposits can be easily recognized. Erratics, for instance, are huge boulders that have been deposited virtually anywhere, including mountain tops.

In addition to the highly visible erratics, the glacier also deposited till and outwash. Till is essentially a jumble of angular rocks, stones and other debris of all shapes and sizes. Outwash is a mixture of rounded stones, clay, soils and sand, deposited or "washed out" in a layered fashion by the glacier. As melting water flowed over these deposits, the materials were sorted out — the heavier materials being deposited first, and the lighter materials, mostly sand, deposited farther downstream.

Since till tends to be heavier than outwash, it was deposited first and therefore is thickest in the valleys, with the layers becoming thinner moving up the slopes of mountains. Till is generally a deeper and richer mix of soil than outwash. Life on the glacial outwash is more harsh than on till, as nutrients and water quickly seep through the sandy soil.

Every gardener knows that each plant species prefers its own specific condi-
— continued on next page

tions; generally, the most important condition is the soil. In the forest, soil composition dictates which trees will grow. Plants with deep root systems, including northern hardwood species such as aspen, birch and sugar maple, need deep, rich soils like those in till. Evergreens have a shallow root system and are less demanding of soil nutrients; thus, they are better suited to outwash conditions. Generally, till and outwash can be identified simply by looking at what is growing in an area.

Other Signs of the Glacier

The north-central portion of the Adirondacks in particular is dotted with eskers, kames and kettles — all land formations created by the glacier.

An esker looks like a long, huge mound formed by a giant mole ransacking the landscape. Eskers were formed as meltwater flowed beneath the glacier, creating tunnels or valleys. Sand and other materials were deposited along the walls of these rivers. Once the ice melted, these deposits formed long, mounds of sand primarily.

When large blocks of ice occasionally broke from the glacier, sand and debris from the outwash would cover the blocks; but as the ice melted, the debris would settle, creating hollow craters of a few to thousands of feet wide. Eventually, water filled these craters, creating kettles.

Kames are the circular mounds of outwash formed when a hole atop the glacier was filled, then deposited.

Glacial Influence on Plant Life

As the glacier receded, huge rivers formed from the melting ice and further shifted the debris, resulting in some subtle blends of till and outwash soils. Plant species have a remarkable ability of "filling in the blanks." Wherever some type of void exists, some type of plant will adapt to the conditions. As these soil conditions change — sometimes the conditions change within a few feet — the plants growing in the soil also change.

In the Adirondacks, there are many types of forests. And there are many clues as to why these different forest types survive.

Forests of the Adirondack Region

Northern Hardwood Forests

The northern hardwood (leaf-producing trees) forest is the dominant forest type in the Adirondacks and typically occupies the region's best glacial till soils. Barring a catastrophe, such as fire or blowdown, this forest type can maintain itself indefinitely once established.

Why and how? Again, look to the ground for clues.

Each year an estimated 2 tons of organic material falls on a single acre of forest. This layer of debris is particularly noticeable in a stand of hardwoods during the fall as millions upon millions of leaves fall to the ground. The leaf-covered humus provides a habitat rich in nutrients. While this is ideal soil for many species, the hardwoods in the forest also produce a deep shade during summer that prevents sun-loving seeds from germinating. Tiny seedlings simply can't penetrate the duff, so pioneer species (the first species to settle a disturbed area) with tiny seeds, such as aspen and paper birch, die away and are replaced by beech, yellow birch and sugar maple — all trees with larger seeds.

A number of woodland wildflowers flourish in these rich soil conditions. However, unlike the majority of wildflowers that bloom in the summer months, virtually all woodland

— continued on next page

flowers — trailing arbutus, trout lily, trillium, bloodroot, clintonia and Lady's slipper — flower during the early days of spring (May and June in the Adirondacks). Why? Once the leaves on the trees emerge and the forest floor is cast in shadow, the plants can no longer take advantage of the sun's energy, as too little sunlight reaches the forest floor. Since most plants need sunlight to flower, woodland plants need to flower before the hardwoods' leaves open and block the sunlight. By early summer the flowers of most woodland plants are long gone and have begun to produce large seeds needed to penetrate the duff to become established. The constant shade of northern hardwoods is also home for an understory of striped maple, witch hobble, mosses and ferns.

Mixed-wood Forests

Mixed-wood forests grow on soil derived from outwash. Mixed woods are characterized by a mixture of conifers and certain hardwoods. Very subtle changes in soil fertility and the water table determine which species grow where. A high water table is generally indicated by trees that like "wet feet" or wet roots, such as red spruce, hemlock, red maple, black cherry and yellow birch. Since water percolates quickly through sandy outwash, species that tolerate dry conditions, such as white and red pine, dominate.

A carpet of greenery composed of ferns, mosses, wood sorrel and Canada mayflower flows beneath the trees, contrasting with the bed of leaves that covers the hardwood forest floor.

Softwood Forests

Needles and spongy organic materials blanket the floor in evergreen forests, creating an entirely different scenario than in hardwood forests. The lack of nutrients in the outwash soils and the generally acidic soil conditions — partially the result of the acids released by decaying pine needles — preclude hardwoods from entering. Blueberries, wood sorrel, wood ferns, sheep laurel and other acidic-loving plants grow here, along with what appears to be a continuous blanket of mosses and liverworts.

Boreal Forests

Dramatic changes in plant and animal life occur on mountains because conditions there are harsher than in the valleys and flats below. Above approximately 2,500 feet, the northern hardwood community gives way to stands of red spruce and balsam fir, which are better adapted to life on high mountain slopes. Yellow birch generally dominate the transition zone between the two forest types.

From about 2,800 feet to 4,000 feet, spruce and fir hold sway. This is the boreal forest, named for Boreas, the Greek god of the north wind. (The influence of Boreas can be seen in much of the Adirondack high country, as catastrophic winds swept through the region in 1950 and 1995, causing massive blowdowns. On these disturbed sites, young coniferous forests now grow beneath an overstory of hardwoods, especially paper birch, that originally clothed the scarred landscape.)

Sub-alpine and Alpine Forests

Red spruce can't tolerate conditions above 4,000 feet, leaving the higher sub-alpine slopes to the domination of balsam firs.

Rare arctic-alpine communities thrive on about a dozen of the highest Adirondack peaks. Curiously, the conditions on these high mountain summits are surprisingly similar to those found in lowland bogs. Sphagnum moss, Labrador tea and leatherleaf are common to both environments. Unlike the bog, however, where wet conditions

— continued on next page

Photo: Adirondack Nature Conservancy/Gary Randorf

The boardwalk at the Silver Lake Nature Preserve provides a peaceful pathway through a vibrant Adirondack ecosystem.

prevail, cold, wind and ice control life on summits. In places exposed to the full force of the wind, only mosses and lichens survive. In tiny crevices in the bedrock, where clumps of organic debris collect, diapensia and mountain sandwort might grow. Alpine bilberry, the most common member of the community, invades clumps of sphagnum. A few softwoods may survive in sites protected from desiccation. Mountain alder, bunchberry, false hellebore, mountain ash and mountain paper birch also are common here.

Of all the communities in the Adirondacks, the arctic-alpine is most threatened by humans. Amazing as it seems, the misplaced foot of a hiker can remove in the ribbing of the sole of the boot a clump of soil that took nature a thousand years to generate. Without the nutrients from this precious soil, a rare plant may not survive. When walking on alpine summits, take care in where you step, and stay on the bedrock.

Pine Barrens

In the rolling sand plains along the eastern edge of the Adirondack Park, especially in the Plattsburgh region, a number of unique pine barrens exist. Fire plays an important role in these drought-prone communities; it not only kills most young hardwoods that continually sprout, but also releases the seeds of the pitch pine. The cones of this tree open with heat, releasing many seeds to grow in the openings left by fire.

— continued on next page

Other Adirondack Habitats

Wetlands

Although soil is the prime ingredient in determining the type of forest, ground water also plays a crucial role. Fifteen percent, or nearly 1 million acres, of the Adirondacks are wetlands. Whenever water is stopped, allowed to accumulate or made to move slowly, a wetland forms, and it will influence which trees grow where.

The role of wetlands in the balance of nature is crucial: They assist in modulating the flow of water, thereby reducing flooding and erosion; filter out sediments and other impurities and, therefore, help purify drinking water; and provide desirable habitat for fish and wildlife.

Although there are different types of wetlands — marshes, bogs, swamps or wet meadows — all can be identified by the aquatic and semiaquatic plants characteristic of wetlands. It is also important to remember that nature doesn't distinguish habitats the way we do. Within each wetland there might be conditions of every type of wetland. Heron Marsh, at the Adirondack Park Visitor Center in Paul Smiths, is a good example of a wetland with swamp, marsh and bog conditions.

Swamps

Looking at the plant life is the simplest way to identify a swamp. This is especially helpful when the soil conditions are dry and the wetland looks anything but wet. In many swamps, water may be visible only during the spring and after a heavy rain, but because the ground generally remains saturated, the land is still classified as a wetland since only water-tolerant plants grow in these moist soils.

Typical swamp trees include red maple, black ash, balsam fir, tamarack and black spruce. Buttonbush, willow, dogwood, speckled alder, winterberry, wild raisin, sweet gale and mountain holly are common shrubs. Even if you don't know the trees, you can generally tell that you are in a swamp if trees are uprooted. Because trees cannot root deeply in wet soils, trees are easily uprooted during a wind storm.

One of the lesser known swamp communities to look for is a conifer swamp, which is distinguished by a luxuriant green carpet of sphagnum moss.

Marsh

Marshes are the wettest of Adirondack wetlands. A marsh looks like a wet meadow, grassland or prairie, and is covered by grasses, sedges, reeds and other plants. Few trees or shrubs survive in the depths of the marsh since the soil is too wet. Marshes are most common along the edges of ponds and lakes.

The abundance of sunlight and water combine to make marshes favorable places for muskrats and beavers (within the marsh) as well as coyotes, foxes, deer and minks (along marsh edges). (See this Close-up's subsequent "Animal Life in Adirondack Habitats" section for related information.)

Bogs

Bogs resemble other types of wetlands, but because the flow of water is restricted here, bogs make life for plants and animals difficult. Sphagnum moss is the dominant plant in bogs and often forms a living mat across the water of a bog. The mat not only blocks out light and oxygen, but also withdraws precious nutrients and adds to the acidity of the water, making it difficult for decomposer organisms to function. All of this combines to inhibit not only growth, but also decay.

Sphagnum moss helps create the very conditions that allow it to thrive.

Since bogs are nutrient "deserts," only a few plants can survive. Leatherleaf, bog laurel, cranberry, Labrador tea and a few other bog species grow on the floating

— continued on next page

sphagnum mat. Pitcher plants and sundews have adapted uniquely in order to obtain the necessary nitrogen for their survival — they eat meat by capturing insects. The pitcher plant has a special funnel leaf that traps rainwater. Insects, attracted to the water, can climb into the leaf but, because of the hundreds of downward-pointing hairs growing in the funnel, can't climb out. Bacteria and enzymes help digest the victim. Sundews capture prey with sticky, jewel-like tentacles that attract and then curl around their victims.

Wooded Swamps

Wooded swamp communities vary with general climatic and topographic conditions. In high elevation areas, conifers such as balsam fir, black spruce, tamarack, and white cedar tend to dominate. In lower-elevation sections, such as those in the valley, deciduous species such as red maple, black ash and elm are more common. These broad-leaved trees provide critical habitat for tree-nesting birds and migratory waterfowl during spring and fall flooding.

Animal Life in
Adirondack Habitats

Most animals, like plants, prefer specific conditions where food and water is readily available and where they can raise their young successfully. Obviously, if you are looking for a loon or other waterfowl, you wouldn't look deep in a hardwood forest since there's is no appropriate food, water or acceptable nesting site.

Transition habitats (zones or edges), where two or more habitats meet, generally attract a variety of both insect- and plant-eating birds and other mammals. (Areas where meadow and forest, or wetland and forest, meet are prime transition zones.) Here is a short list of habitats and some birds and mammals that might be found in each.

Meadows: Open fields and meadows are prime habitats for meadowlarks, song sparrows, bluebirds, thrashers and robins. Deer also feed in meadows.

Softwood forests: Pine siskins, golden-crowned kinglets, evening grosbeaks, red-breasted nuthatches, crossbills, warblers, owls and chickadees are commonly found in the conifer or evergreen forest.

Hardwood forests: Scarlet tanagers, woodpeckers, wood thrushes, red-eyed vireo, broad-winged hawks and ovenbirds prefer hardwood forests, as do black bears and chipmunks, which love beechnuts. Snowshoe hares and deer also venture here, eating tender shoots.

Wetlands: Waterfowl, such as Canada geese, mallards and herons, prefer the open waters of marshes, but because wetlands generally are a source of clean water, many other animals can be found there.

Tree-lined roadways: Birds of prey (a.k.a. raptors), such as hawks, cover considerable territory in search of food. Look for hawks in trees along the edges of roads as you drive. Many will perch, looking for small animals in the open spaces along highways. If you spot a raptor while driving, pull over, but don't get out of your car. Most birds accept cars as natural objects, making vehicles excellent observation blinds for bird watching.

---

full of knots. During pioneer days, the abundant resin in the knots was used to light torches.

Pitch-pine barrens depend upon fire for continued survival. Fire not only burns the fallen needles, thereby releasing nutrients into the soil, but also provides the heat necessary to open the cones and release the seeds. With-

out a periodic fire, the pitch pine would soon be replaced by other species, such as the birch and quaking aspen now growing in sections along the path, and the ecology of the barrens would change forever. The Nature Conservancy conducts prescribed burns to preserve this community.

To reach the preserve, take N.Y. 9N to

Ausable Forks. At the blinking light, go northeast on N. Main Street to the stop sign. Go straight on Golf Course Road about 2 miles to Palmer Hill Road. Turn right and go a quarter-mile. Make a left turn on Buck Hill Road. The trailhead is a half-mile up the road on the left.

Baxter Mountain
N.Y. Rt. 9N, Keene Valley

On N.Y. 9N, between Keene and Elizabethtown, the 2.2-mile round-trip trail to Baxter offers great views of the High Peaks, plenty of good blueberry picking during the summer season and a relatively moderate climb. Hurricane Mountain, a 5-mile round trip and a difficult climb, and Owl Head Lookout, another 5-mile round trip with a moderate climb, also are on this stretch of road. Hikers are treated to great views from all mountains.

Cathedral Rocks/Pyramid Falls/Bear Run
N.Y. Rt. 73, just east Keene Valley

The St. Huberts region, a few miles east of Keene Valley on N.Y. 73, offers many fine hiking trails. Many of the trails are accessed via the Ausable Club, a half-mile off N.Y. 73 on a road known as Lake Road. Since the club is private property, hikers should observe all the restrictions posted by the club regarding the use of its property.

The West River Trail follows the Ausable River to Lower Ausable Lake. From here the trail traverses some old-growth, perhaps virgin, forest. Along the way, there are some waterfalls and hemlock forests and what seems like a never-ending series of small streams cascading down some rather rocky terrain. (The never-ending streams are best noticed after a rain or before the dry season in summer.)

There are numerous places to go off the trail systems, with one fun diversion to Cathedral Rock and a splendid waterfall. This short route is off the West River trail on the Pyramid Brook trail. The reward is views of Giant, Noonmark and Round mountains, with the sound of the waterfall thrown into the mix.

Gadway Sandstone Pavement Barrens Preserve
Cannon Corners Rd., Mooers

On the global scale, this sandstone pavement barren represents one of only 20 such known communities in the world. It becomes obvious almost immediately upon entering the site why it is called a "sandstone pavement" barren — the site looks as if it has been paved in sandstone by some mythical creature. Although you may consider creating some tall tale on how this was accomplished, the best guess is that it formed as a result of a massive flood.

The sandstone on the site is exposed bedrock, which is often completely covered with lichens and mosses. Jack pines, relatively uncommon trees in New York, have adapted to the harsh conditions on the site. Many of the small jack pines are some 100 years old, but have grown in their distinct gnarled and twisted fashion to only 4 to 6 feet in height. (A bonsai gardener likely would be envious of such natural masterpieces of survival.)

To reach the barrens, take N.Y. Route 11 toward Ellenburg. A few miles east of Ellenburg, turn left on Cannon Corners Road. Proceed 2.5 miles, then look for unmarked Gadway Road on the left. Follow this road about a quarter-mile until you reach the barrens, where you can park.

Giant Mountain
Chapel Pond, off N.Y. Rt. 73, Keene Valley

Peaking out at 4,627 feet, the 6-mile round-trip hike up and down Giant — technically, Giant of the Valley — is a worthwhile "High Peaks" alternative to the crowded trek at Mount Marcy. Get going early for a rewarding day hike, even with kids.

There are two trails up Giant, both accessed off N.Y. 73 at Chapel Pond, east of

---

INSIDERS' TIP

For a directory of licensed guides, write to the New York State Outdoor Guides Association, P.O. Box 916, Saranac Lake, New York 12983.

Keene Valley. The longer trail is via Roaring Brook, with many excellent views of the valley, including the Ausable Club, Round Pond and, on a clear day, the Green Mountains of Vermont. The other trail is via a rocky ridge above what is called Giant's Washbowl. Sections of this trail are quite steep and include a number of bare, open spots near the summit.

Silver Lake Bog Preserve
off Union Falls Rd., Black Brook

In the 1960s, two farmers uncovered a perfectly preserved body in a bog in Great Britain. Scotland Yard was called in to investigate, as all signs of decay pointed to a fairly recent homicide. Scotland Yard, however, wasn't going to "get their man." It turned out that the victim was killed some 2,000 years ago. The natural conditions in the bog preserved the body in such a state that investigators could still determine the victims last meal — burnt toast. The Bog Man remains one of the oldest murder investigations on record.

Bogs act in much the same way that a pickle jar preserves a pickle. The low oxygen content and acidic nature of the bog preserves whatever falls into its midst, leaving scientists an accurate record of life in the distant past to compare with the present conditions.

The Silver Lake Camp Preserve provides a variety of habitats in close proximity of each other. A half-mile boardwalk trail in the bog and a .75-mile trail overlooking the bog allow visitors the opportunity to see how plants and animals respond to different ecological conditions within the bog itself as well as in surrounding habitats.

The green "lawn" of the bog is sphagnum (or "peat") moss. This plant holds water like a sponge, thereby restricting the flow of water through the bog. More than any other plant, sphagnum makes the bog what it is. As you

walk along, your challenge is to identify the 15 different species of sphagnum found along the trail. You'd better bring along an excellent plant guide, because even scientists have a tough time distinguishing these species.

Throughout the entire walk, note how the slightest change in environmental conditions, such as increases in elevation or the water table, cause a dramatic change in the vegetation. For example, species such as paper birch, balsam fir and red maple survive in well-drained soils only. If the soil remains too wet, these trees will be replaced by trees that are more tolerant of wet soils, such as tamaracks (eastern larch) or black spruce. (The tamarack, with short, soft needles clumped together along its branches, is the only northern conifer that sheds its needles each fall.)

As you walk along the boardwalk, look at the different species of trees growing and try to decipher the existing conditions that have allowed them to grow. Also look for the "old man's beard lichen," a pale beard-like mat growing on branches (this should be easy to spot), and the "witch's broom." The broom is a little harder to find. It is a parasitic mistletoe that grows on the branches of the black spruce. The mistletoe attacks the stem tips and distorts the growth, forming broom-like distortion on the tree. The broom almost looks like a new tree growing up the old tree.

Lake George/ Upper Hudson Region

Black Mountain
off N.Y. Rt. 22, near Whitehall

Black Mountain is the tallest mountain to rise from the eastern shores of Lake George, topping out at 2,646 feet. That may not sound

---

INSIDERS' TIP

How can you tell what kind of woodpecker made that hole in a tree? The pileated woodpecker prefers dead trees or snags; it makes a big rectangular hole in dead wood. The hairy woodpecker prefers pecking on live trees. To distinguish woodpeckers by sound: the pileated delivers an average of 12 strokes, with the loudest in the middle of the sequence; the downy drums in a more rapid and longer, but less pronounced, sequence.

Photo: Plattsburgh/North Country Chamber of Commerce

Though seemingly rugged and enduring, mountain peaks provide a delicate environment for many plants and lichens.

all that high (compared to the Rockies), but when you look down at the waters of the lake more than 2,000 feet below you, it will seem as though you're on top of the world. Which is also how you'll probably feel after your successful 1,200-foot ascent from the trailhead, some 2.5 miles back. The hike is considered moderate in difficulty, with only occasional steep sections. From the summit, you will see "The Narrows" below — a beautiful section of Lake George dotted with dozens of islands. Across the lake to the west are the peaks of the Tongue Mountain Range (also with many outstanding hiking trails), and glimpses of Mount Marcy and other "High Peaks" are farther in the distance. Looking to the east, you'll see the southern tip of Lake Champlain and the Green Mountains of Vermont beyond.

From the summit, you can either return the same way you came (a 5-mile round trip) or take the "loop trail," which provides several good vantage points of the lake on your descent. The loop trail makes the total round trip 6.7 miles.

To get to the trailhead for Black Mountain, follow N.Y. 22 about 4.5 miles north of Whitehall, then turn left at the sign for Hulett's Landing. Proceed 2.7 miles to Pike Brook Road. Turn left on Pike Brook Road, proceed

another .8 miles, and you'll see a large N.Y.S. DEC (Department of Environmental Conservation) sign and parking area on the right.

Blue Ledge
off N.Y. Rt. 28N, near Minerva

Not all hikes have to lead to the top of a mountain to be enjoyable. Some, like this one, can lead along a path lined with spring wildflowers to an overlook of an impressive river. In this case, that river is the turbulent waters of the upper Hudson. The trail leads to a spot near a horseshoe bend in the river opposite a 300-foot cliff that drops straight down to an (uncharacteristically) calm section of water. This is a relatively easy 5-mile round-trip walk from the trailhead. To find it, travel about 6 miles to the end of North Woods Club Road, which in turn is off N.Y. 28, just north of Minerva.

Buck Mountain
off N.Y. Rt. 9L, eastern shore of Lake George

A few miles south and a few hundred feet below Black Mountain is Buck Mountain. The moderately difficult hike rises 1,990 feet from the trailhead to the 2,334-foot summit. Moderate grades with occasional steep sections alternate along the way. The effort is well worth it, as you'll be treated to a magnificent view of the southern portion of Lake George. In the summertime, you'll also be in for the "bonus round" view — dozens of sailboats fluttering like tiny butterflies a couple thousand feet below you in what is generally the most popular sailing area of the lake.

The round trip to the summit of Buck Mountain is 6.6 miles. To reach the trailhead, follow N.Y. Rt. 9L from Lake George village up the eastern shore of the lake until you see a sign for Pilot Knob (a right-hand turn onto Pilot Knob Road). Then follow this road for 3 miles until you see the DEC sign and parking area on the right for Buck Mountain.

Hadley Mountain
off N.Y. Rt. 9N, 8.5 miles northwest of Hadley

This is one of those hikes that will get you and even the least enthusiastic members of your family (we might still be referring to you here) hooked on hiking. Why? It's easy to get to, it's pretty easy to get to the top of, it's an easy afternoon round-trip hike of three or so hours, and the view from the top will make you think you climbed Mount Everest (well, Marcy anyway!). The 2-mile hike to the summit of 2,675-foot Hadley Mountain rises 1,526 feet from the trailhead, and most of that is along the steady (but moderate) uphill grade of an old jeep trail. There is nothing here that your 10-year-old child or 50-year-old friend, spouse or uncle couldn't handle. You'll feel a sense of accomplishment without paying for it (too much) the next day when you try to get out of bed.

The real benefit of hiking Hadley Mountain is that its strategic location in the southeastern Adirondacks and open summit terrain allow you to enjoy sweeping views of recogniz-

able landmarks in all directions. To the south, you'll see the long finger of the Great Sacandaga Lake pointing at you; and on a perfect low-humidity day, the Catskill Mountains on the horizon. To the north, far in the distance, you can make out some of the High Peaks when the visibility is good. The northeastern horizon reveals the lower section of Lake Champlain, with the Green Mountains of Vermont stringing along farther to the south. You'll find it hard to believe that the neon glow of Lake George arcades is only a half-hour or so away by car.

To find the trailhead to Hadley Mountain, take Stony Creek Road north out of Hadley 3 miles until you see the sign for Hadley Hill Road (a left turn). Follow Hadley Hill Road 4 miles until you come to Tower Road. Turn right and proceed 1.5 miles to the Hadley Mountain trailhead on the left. It is marked by a sign, and parking is available.

Southern Adirondack Lakes Region

Blue Mountain
off N.Y. Rt. 30, Blue Mountain Lake

Blue Mountain is one of the best known and most popular hiking destinations in the Adirondacks — and for good reason. It is centrally located at the geographic "heart" of the park, and at 3,759 feet, it is one of the highest peaks in the central Adirondacks. Blue Mountain also happens to play sentry to one of the prettiest lakes in the region, Blue Mountain Lake. The 2-mile hike to the top climbs 1,569 vertical feet and can be covered by hikers with some experience in about two hours. The trail is moderately difficult,

---

INSIDERS' TIP

Hikers shouldn't expect to see any mountain lions (a.k.a. pumas, cougars, panthers, painters, catamounts) during their treks through the region. The mountain lion (*Felis concolor*) is listed as "extinct" in the Adirondacks, and it remains on both New York State's and the federal government's endangered species list. (Although unconfirmed sightings suggest a few mountain lions may have returned to the Adirondacks, it is likely that they are former pets that have been released into the wild.)

The Nature Conservancy

Often called "Mother Nature's real estate agent," The Nature Conservancy is an international organization whose mission is to preserve the diversity of life on earth by protecting plants and animals in their natural communities. The Conservancy has operated in the United States for nearly a half-century and has protected an estimated 7.5 million acres of ecologically important land. The nonprofit organization owns and manages more than 1,300 nature preserves throughout the world, making it the largest operator of private nature preserves.

The Conservancy is unique among environmental organizations in that it is apolitical and does not advocate any environmental position. Because of the organization's quiet nature, the general public rarely hears much about its work in protecting ecologically sensitive areas. It is likely that the Conservancy operates a preserve within your community, no matter where you live in this country.

The Adirondack Nature Conservancy operates a number of preserves within the Adirondack region and invites you to visit them. Each of these preserves is special for its own reason, and hopefully, you will discover for yourself why these are special places.

To ensure the continued protection of these preserves, the Conservancy's staff asks that you respect the following guidelines when visiting one of their preserves:

• No camping, motorized vehicles or littering;
• No removal or destruction of plants;
• No hunting or fishing;
• Take out what you take in;
• Obey all trail signage and stay on marked trails.

At most Conservancy sites, trails are maintained for hiking only. Adirondack Nature Conservancy Preserves are noted with the word "Preserve." For additional information, contact the Adirondack Nature Conservancy, P.O. Box 65, Keene Valley, N.Y. 12943, 576-4203.

---

with a steep middle section. Your reward at the top from the fire tower above the trees is one of the great Adirondack panoramas. Blue Mountain Lake and its dozens of islands are nearly 2,000 feet below you to the west. To the southwest, farther out, you can see the jagged outline of Raquette Lake. The High Peaks string out before you on the northern horizon. To the south is Snowy Mountain, another "big" mountain in this part of the Adirondacks.

If you are planning to hike the Blue Mountain trail, we suggest you pick up a copy of the *Blue Mountain Trail Guide* produced by the Blue Mountain Fire Tower Committee (c/o Cornell Cooperative Extension of Hamilton County, 548-6191). The illustrated guide highlights 14 stops along the trail of geological interest and provides horizon views

from the summit that tell you what you're looking at.

The trailhead for Blue Mountain is easy to find. Simply take N.Y. Route 30 1.3 miles north from the intersection of N.Y. 30 and N.Y. 28 at the village of Blue Mountain Lake, and look for the large parking area off to the right (east) side.

Cascade Pond
off N.Y. Rt. 30, near Blue Mountain Lake

For a hiking experience that is an enjoyable and relaxing alternative to scaling mountain summits, and with views perhaps less exhilarating but just as rewarding, this hike is well worth the time. It is an easy 5.6-mile round trip over mostly flat terrain in a beautiful setting. Toward the beginning of the trail, you'll cross a 200-foot boardwalk bridge over Rock

Pond, a serene setting you won't want to rush through. Beyond that, you'll traverse a narrow valley between two high ridges and finally come upon the still waters of the unspoiled Cascade Pond. Don't make any plans for later in the afternoon; you'll want to stop time during your visit to Cascade Pond.

To access the trailhead, travel .9 miles east of the intersection of N.Y. 30 and N.Y. 28, and turn right onto Durant Road. The trailhead is just .2 miles down Durant Road on the left side.

Cathead Mountain
off N.Y. Rt. 30, near Benson

For one of the best views you can find of the expansive Great Sacandaga Lake, it's hard to beat this hike. With an estimated round-trip time of three hours to reach the 2,427-foot summit, and a vertical rise of 1,273 feet over sometimes steep and rocky terrain, this is probably not a good beginners trail. If you're in decent shape from water-skiing all summer on the lake, you shouldn't have any problem. In fact, it could be kind of fun to look down at all the spots you've been in your boat while visiting the Great Sacandaga Lake area. You'll find a fire tower at the top, but it is no longer open for climbing. No matter, as the bare rock of the summit provides plenty of vantage points.

Cathead is relatively easy to access, just a few miles off N.Y. Rt. 30, one of the primary roads serving the southern Adirondack region. To reach the trailhead, turn left off N.Y. 30 at the sign for Benson and the Northville-Lake Placid Trail. You'll climb a long hill 2.8 miles, then turn right onto North Road. Follow North Road 1.2 miles until it dead-ends at the trailhead.

Echo Cliffs at Panther Mountain
off N.Y. Rt. 8, Piseco Lake

The location of this hiking destination—overlooking Piseco Lake and adjacent to three popular state campgrounds (Point Comfort, Little Sand Point and Poplar Point; see the Camping chapter) — makes this a popular and well-worn route. The vertical rise is only 725 feet, but the view from the 2,425-foot summit is spectacular. Below you shimmer the waters of Piseco Lake and the Silver Lake Wilderness area beyond. About two-thirds of the .8-mile ascent is fairly easy, with the last couple of tenths heading up some fairly steep (but manageable) terrain to Echo Cliffs. The total round-trip hike should take no more than a couple of hours, with generous provisions for standing and gawking.

To hike up to Echo Cliffs, from N.Y. Rt. 8 take West Shore Road along Piseco Lake 2.6 miles until you see the DEC sign marking the trailhead. You can park on the opposite side of the road. It's easy in, pretty easy up and hard to leave once you get there!

Old Forge/ Raquette Lake Region

Bald Mountain (Rondaxe Mountain)
off N.Y. Rt. 28, between Old Forge and Eagle Bay

First, about that name. Informally, most everyone calls this peak Bald Mountain, while state officials in the Conservation Department call it Rondaxe Mountain (to avoid confusion with another, less popular Bald Mountain in the Park). In any event, this is one of the most popular mountains in the Adirondacks

---

INSIDERS' TIP

The green spots often seen on rocks are lichens, which are actually two symbiotic life forms — algae and fungi. Algae needs water to survive, but has no roots to get water. So it relies on fungi, which also has no roots, but draws water from the air. In return the algae (by way of chlorophyll) supplies food to the fungi, which can't make their own food. Lichens are important contributors to soil because they produce an acid that eventually crumbles rocks, adding to the soil mix. They are also good indicators of clean air; they can't survive in polluted air.

to hike, and it's easy to see why. Its location just north of the Fulton Chain Lakes makes it accessible to thousands of summer and fall visitors to this area. It's a relatively easy, short hike of 2 miles round trip and can be enjoyed in an hour and a half. The trail rises only 400 vertical feet to the 2,350-foot summit and has only one short, steep section before following along the spine of a ridge to the top. From the summit, you are treated to lake views stretched out before you from right to left. You can see several of the Fulton Chain Lakes, including Fourth Lake (the largest) directly below. Off to the left, approximately 30 miles distant, you can see Blue Mountain. Beyond and farther left, you can spot Mount Marcy nearly 60 miles away on a good visibility day.

The trailhead for Bald Mountain is easy to access. Just look for Rondaxe Road about halfway between Old Forge and Eagle Bay on N.Y. 28. (It's about 6 miles east of Old Forge.) Turn onto Rondaxe Road and follow just .2 miles to the parking area on the left. You'll see a large wooden map of the area at the entrance to the trailhead.

Black Bear Mountain
off N.Y. Rt. 28, near Eagle Bay

Black Bear is another relatively short and easy hike that nonetheless produces some tremendous views of the Fulton Chain Lakes for the effort. The 4.4-mile round trip can be covered in about three hours. The vertical rise of the trail is only 542 feet, ascending to the summit elevation of 2,448 feet. There is only one steep section of the trail; the rest is moderate or easy hiking. The summit provides excellent views in all directions as well as some interesting vegetation such as wild blueberries and mountain ash. You'll see Seventh Lake below as well as Fourth Lake from a westward vantage point a short walk away.

Access to the trailhead is reached from Uncas Road, which is off N.Y. 28 just east of Eagle Bay. Follow the DEC sign for the Browns Tract Ponds Campground. Travel 2.9 miles on Uncas Road until you see the trailhead sign and parking on the right side of the road.

Moss Lake Circuit Trail
off N.Y. Rt. 28 and Big Moose Rd., near Eagle Bay

For a non-mountain hike that's peaceful, scenic and relaxing, the Moss Lake Circuit Trail is a good option. With a total loop distance of 2.5 miles over easy terrain that circles the lake, this is an easy hike to complete within a couple of hours — and a good alternative for families. The trail follows the route of what was an old bridle trail for a girls camp that used to exist here. The lake and beach are only 135 yards from the trailhead. To reach the trailhead, follow Big Moose Road north from N.Y. 28 for 2.1 miles. You'll see the trailhead and parking on the left side of the road.

Within the region's
2,300 lakes and ponds
and 20,000 miles of
rivers and streams,
plenty of monster fish
await battle with anglers
of every age.

Fishing and Hunting

This wilderness is often called the "Sportsman's Paradise"; and so I hold it to be, when all its advantages are taken into account. If any one goes to the North Woods, expecting to see droves of deer, he will return disappointed . . . Or if one expects to find trout averaging three or four pounds, eager to break surface, no matter where or when he casts his fly, he will come back from his trip a "sadder and wiser man." If this is his idea of what constitutes a "sportsman's paradise," I advise him not to got the Adirondacks. Deer and trout do not abound there in any such numbers; and yet there are enough of both to satisfy any reasonable expectation. . . .

In beauty of scenery, in health-giving qualities, in the ease and romantic manner of its sporting, it is a paradise, and so will it continue to be while a deer leaves his track upon the shores of a lake, or a trout shows himself above the surface of its waters. . . . —from William H.H. Murray's Adventures in the Wilderness (Fields, Osgood & Company: Boston: 1869)

William "Adirondack" Murray's *Adventures in the Wilderness* was the first tour guide written about the Adirondacks. Even though Murray often was accused of exaggerating, we feel compelled to echo his sentiments more than 125 years later in order to describe hunting and fishing in the Adirondacks today.

Murray also suggested that mere presence of game does not ensure good sporting: "A poor shot, and a green hand at the rod, will have poor success anywhere, no matter how good the sporting is . . ." Skill and knowledge play an important role.

In Murray's time, there was little guidance in the form of books, web pages and magazines. Today, information on what to use, how to use it, when and where to go is available from many sources. So, we suggest that you do a little homework to best take advantage of the many hunting and fishing possibilities in this Adirondacks. The Department of Environmental Conservation (DEC) is a good place to start, as its staff regulates hunting and fishing in the region. DEC also publishes *The CONSERVATIONIST*, a magazine filled with useful tips and articles on hunting and fishing in New York State. To subscribe, call (800) 678-6399. Six issues cost $10 — a real bargain in our opinion.

Exactly where do you hunt or fish in the Adirondacks? It's a tough question to answer, primarily because of this region's size. We hate to belabor the point, but there are more than 6 million acres up here, nearly 3 million acres of which are public lands. That leaves a heckuva lot of options — and leaves plenty of room for hunters and anglers to discover their own secret spots.

In this chapter, we provide separate fishing — including a few details on lakes Champlain and George and two "typical" Adirondack rivers, the famed Ausable and the Saranac — and hunting sketches followed by a broad overview of the fishing and hunting opportunities in some of the designated wilderness areas in each region. Since hunters and anglers in the wilderness areas essentially cover the same territory, we discuss both activities together for those areas. The wilderness areas (see Area Overview for details about the physical characteristics of each) are unique in that they are forever protected; no man-made features will ever change their natural conditions. These preserves within the Adirondack Park provide truly unique possibilities for hunting and fishing that would make even Adirondack Murray comfortable.

Fishing and Hunting Seasons

Actual dates for fishing and hunting in the Adirondacks are subject to change, but here are the dates that were observed in 1997.

Fishing

State inland waters, including the Adirondacks

Trout and landlocked Atlantic salmon — April 1 through October 15.

Largemouth and smallmouth bass — third Saturday in June through March 15.

Northern pike — first Saturday in May through March 15.

All other species — open year round.

Hunting

General

Deer and bear — next to last Saturday in October through the first Sunday in December.

Bowhunting

All species — September 27 through the Friday immediately preceding the next to last Saturday in October.

Muzzleloading

Seven-day period ending the day before the regular season begins.

Small game

Seasons vary depending upon the species and where you hunt. Turkey season, for example, is closed entirely in some sections of the Adirondack Park, but is open October 1 through 17 in other areas. There are simply too many variables to give the reader accurate information for every area of this region. Hunters need be aware of the specifics governing the species being hunted and the area in which it is being sought; this information is best found in the hunting guide booklet provided by Department of Environmental Conservation (see the "Fishing Licenses" section for DEC contact information).

Photo: Plattsburgh/North Country Chamber of Commerce

Lakes, ponds and streams throughout the Adirondacks offer anglers plenty of challenges.

Fishing

The Adirondack region is regarded by many anglers to be among the East's best freshwater fisheries. Fishing here means secluded ponds teeming with native brook trout, picturesque rivers and streams abounding with rainbow and brown trout, wilderness lakes with thriving populations of lake trout, bass and northern pike and the famed lakes Champlain and George with more fish than it seems possible to count.

No matter what type of freshwater angling you desire, it can be found in the Adirondacks — and it is consistently good. Many professional guides can lead you to waters with some of the best trophy fishing in the region, but it is also possible to succeed on your own.

Old-timers will regale you with tales of the great fishing "way back when." The fish will always be bigger, easier to catch and in greater quantity than those caught today. The tall tales may well be true — it is likely that a few are — but the fishing today in the Adirondacks is arguably (and the arguments only add to the lore) some of the finest in the world. Within the region's 2,300 lakes and ponds and 20,000 miles of rivers and streams, plenty of monster fish await battle with anglers of every age.

Be warned, however: The fish have allies. The Adirondacks contain some of the most prolific hatches of mayflies, caddisflies, stoneflies and notorious blackflies in the country. The fish don't appear bothered by these insects, but during the blackfly season — primarily May and June — you will have plenty to itch about. Blackflies hatch in the early spring from the very streams in which the trout await. When the blackflies disappear, mosquitoes begin to sample your blood. So, be prepared with whatever bug spray or lotion works for you.

Fishing Licenses

Local lore has it that Adirondack fish are smarter than most and bite only if you have a New York State fishing license. While this may not be legally true, state law requires all anglers 16 and older to have a valid New York State license in their possession while fishing. A fishing license can be purchased statewide in most town and county clerk offices and authorized sporting good stores. Licenses also can be obtained via mail by calling DEC in Albany, 457-8862; you'll need a credit card for this option as well as proof of a hunting/trapping license if not currently registered as a hunting license holder in New York State.

Anglers are also responsible for knowing the various fishing regulations in effect at a particular location or during a particular time. For example, when fishing the trophy section of the Ausable River, anglers should know the opening and closing dates for trout season (see "General Fishing Seasons" gray box) and that only artificial lures may be used.

For specific fishing rules and regulations, creel limits, bait restrictions, maps and stocking lists for the Adirondack Park, visit or write any of the following New York State Department of Environmental Conservation offices: N.Y. Route 86, Ray Brook 12977, 897-1200; Box 220, Hudson Street Ext., Warrensburg 12885, 623-3671; Main Street Ext., Northville 12134, 863-4545 or 863-8216; State Office Building, 317 Washington Street, Watertown 13601, (315) 785-3326; 30 Court Street, Canton 13617, (315) 386-4546 or (315) 386-4547; 225 N. Main Street, Herkimer 13350, (315) 866-6330 or (315) 793-2566.

Fishing License Options and Fees

All anglers 16 and older need New York licenses to try their luck in state inland waters. Sporting license applications are available through the New York State Department of Environmental Conservation's Albany office, 457-8862; town and county clerk offices; and authorized sporting goods stores. While fees are subject to change, here are some examples from 1997:

Resident

Annual	(ages 16 through 64)	$14
Annual	(65 and older, military disability)	$5
Annual	Sportsman (big/small game and fishing)	$31
Lifetime	Sportsman (4 and younger)	$250
Lifetime	(ages 5 through 11)	$350
Lifetime	(ages 12 through 64)	$500
Lifetime	(65 and older)	$50
Three-day	(16 and older)	$6

Nonresident

Annual (16 and older)	$35
Five-day (16 and older)	$20

Note: Other special stamps are available. Please contact the DEC for details.

Health Advisory

New York State officials have issued the following health advisory: "Generally, no one should eat more than one meal of fish per week from any of the state's freshwaters." Although many of the waters in the Adirondack region are remarkably clean, chemical contaminants do exist in even some remote mountain streams and ponds. How do you know if the fish you caught is safe to eat? Your fishing guide, obtained when you purchase you license, provides general guidelines.

Additional information can be obtained from the Department of Health, (800) 458-1158 Ext. 409, or through the local DEC office (see previous section).

Catch and Release

Anglers who love to fish but want to lessen the potential risks associated with eating contaminated sport fish, should consider practicing catch and release. Try to follow these guidelines:

• Release the fish quickly. If possible, release it while the fish is still in the water. A pair of needle-nose pliers makes releasing the hook easier on you and the fish.

• When a fish is deeply hooked, do not tear out the hook, but rather cut the leader or the hook. This increases the survival rate fourfold.

• Avoid playing with the fish when reeling it in.

A Fishing-hole Sampler

Where do we begin to tell you where to go?

This question could turn into a good joke, but we won't go that route. It's tough enough to figure out how to tell a visitor where to fish or how best to fish one of the ponds or lakes that comprise more than 240,000 acres of water (and that excludes the region's two largest lakes — Champlain and George) or the thousands of miles of streams. Since the options are infinite and space limited (and we don't want you to question our degree of expertise), the following discussion offers only a sampling designed to give you a sense of the possibilities.

Lakes

While many of the higher-elevation lakes in the region are devoid of fish, the vast majority have healthy populations. (The lack of fish in higher elevation lakes is due to a number of factors, including acid rain, normal acidic conditions and overfishing.) For the most part, the best fishing in the region's lakes and ponds is done by boat or canoe.

Canoe fishing is ideal. A canoe easily fits atop almost any car and allows anglers to pond or lake hop. In the Fish Creek or the St. Regis area of the High Peaks, for example, dozens of ponds and lakes are connected via water or short portages (land carries). When the fishing is slow in one lake, carrying a canoe — far easier than carrying a boat — to the next pond may be the answer. Pond hoppers should carry

an array of fishing tackle since different species of fish lurk in different ponds.

The biggest dilemma anglers face on major lakes like Champlain and George is deciding where to begin!

Lake Champlain

Often called the "sixth Great Lake," Lake Champlain is one of the largest freshwater lakes in the United States. It flows from Whitehall, New York, northward about 120 miles to its outlet along the Quebec border. Lake Champlain has 587 miles of shoreline, 70 islands, more water to explore than most anglers can fish in a lifetime and more species of fish — 83 to be exact — than most anglers know. What's more, it can be fished in spring, summer, fall and winter.

Because Champlain's depth varies widely, the lake provides a productive warm-water fishery — northern pike, pickerel, walleye and largemouth and smallmouth bass — and also is home to cold-water quarry, including landlocked Atlantic salmon as well as lake, brown and rainbow/steelhead trout. Champlain also holds innumerable panfish species — crappie, perch and smelt, to name a few — as well as large numbers of such unusual, hard-fighting species as bowfin, whitefish, burbot, cisco, sheepshead, longnose gar and channel catfish. There's even a chance you'll catch what many anglers consider North America's most elusive game fish, the mighty muskellunge.

Champlain has produced more than a dozen New York and Vermont state-record catches, including a record salmon caught from the Vermont shore. While Lake Champlain is a boat-angler's paradise, some great fishing also can be found in the lake's many tributaries, particularly during the spring and fall when salmon ascend Champlain's feeder streams and rivers to spawn and feed.

The sheer size of the lake creates only part of an angler's dilemma. Most of the west-

---

INSIDERS' TIP

Hunters should treat every gun as if it were loaded, keep it pointed in a safe direction, be sure of their targets and areas beyond, and always wear blaze orange. Studies show that wearing orange hunting gear is seven times safer than donning other colors

ern shoreline of Lake Champlain is privately owned, making shore access difficult. Fishing from the shore is possible in state parks as well as from land owned by various towns and villages. Public access is available at Point Au Roche State Park, in Port Kent near the ferry docks; in Willsboro, just below the dam and at the public-access site on the privately owned Willsboro Point; and at Essex Town Park.

Interested anglers can obtain a free copy of the *Lake Champlain Fishing Guide* from the Vermont Fish & Wildlife Department, 103 S. Main Street, Waterbury, Vermont 05676, (802) 241-3700. It includes information on when, where and how to catch Lake Champlain's most popular fish, and it breaks the lake down to 16 maps that detail where you are most likely to catch certain species, along with depths, access points and other valuable information.

Lake George

Lake George, also known as the Queen of American Lakes, is a glacier-formed lake measuring 32 miles long and 2 to 3 miles wide. The shoreline ranges from beautiful sandy beaches to rocky crags, cliffs and marshes. There are still miles of undeveloped shoreline on the northeast side of the lake, but much of this is inaccessible to anglers on foot.

Lake George's depth ranges from rocky shoals to holes up to 195 feet deep, which helps support a two-tier (cold- and warm-water) fishery. Notable cold-water game fish include trout (primarily lakers) and landlocked salmon, and catches of 10-pound fish are not uncommon. The warm-water fishery includes some of the best bass action in the Northeast, with smallmouths reigning supreme in the north and south basins. Smallmouth catches average 2 to 3 pounds per fish, with a number of "five-spots" (5 pounders) taken every year. Largemouth bass and northern pike like the shallower big bays filled with weeds and other forms of cover. The "Grand Slam Fishing Warren County, NY," available at many regional tourism offices, including Warren County's (of course), states the northerns range from small 4- to 6-pound "ax-handles" to 20 pound-plus "barracudas." Panfishing also is consistently good.

FYI

Unless otherwise noted, the area code for all phone numbers listed in this guide is 518.

The lake is best fished by boat, although anglers can try their luck from the shore on public property, primarily at the public beach and park near the downtown areas in Lake George and in public areas in Bolton Landing and Hague.

Rivers and Streams

The Adirondack region's rivers and streams are heaven for fly-fishermen and spin-casters. While no one will reveal their favorite spot (we each have our own), there are plenty that are common knowledge and will get you into the swing of things.

The best advice is rather simple: Whenever you see a little brook, a beautiful stretch of river, a peaceful pond or lake, try fishing it — just be respectful and stay off posted or private land. Sooner or later, you will find one that will become your secret place. If you have kids, don't dismiss this advice quickly, especially when it comes to little streams. Many of the small streams you'll happen upon harbor plenty of small fish — and a few large ones. Streams are good training grounds for youngsters in honing the art of stream fishing (it's very different from lake fishing).

The Ausable and Saranac are good examples of the different types of river fishing available in the Adirondacks. Other major fishing rivers and streams in the region include: Fish Creek, Osgood River, Raquette River, Chateaugay River, Hudson River, St. Regis River, Great Chazy River (north branch), Bouquet River and Little Ausable River.

Ausable River

Arguably the East's No. 1 trout stream, the west branch of the Ausable River consists of more than 25 miles of prime trout-fishing water. The best fishing in this cold-water river is during the mayfly, stonefly and caddisfly hatches in spring. The west branch also offers a special Trophy Trout section, where special artificial lure-only restrictions apply — but where the largest fish also lurk. The "trophy" section begins only a few miles outside Lake Placid on N.Y. Route 86. While this section is

Fishing With Kids

No matter what anyone says about the art or Zen of angling, there is only one goal when fishing with kids — to catch some fish. It doesn't matter how big or how many fish you catch, but kids want action. So, the first thing to do is to call the DEC hotline and get the inside scoop on the hot spots. The number is 891-5413 in the northern sections of the park, 623-3682 in the southern part. Staff at a few of the fishing supply stores listed in this section also can offer some good hints.

Thinking Like a Fish

Seriously consider making it a game by telling the kids that to catch a fish, you must begin to think like a fish. If you don't catch any fish, the reason why can be easily explained: "We must not have thought like a fish." Curiously, trying to think like a fish is more than a game. The idea actually helps you catch fish, especially when fishing unfamiliar waters. Consider the following:

• Fish need to eat, so look for places where the favorite food of a particular fish might be. Bluegills and trout, for example, like insects, so look for hatches of insects on calm waters. Bass eat smaller fish, frogs and crayfish, so look for plants where frogs hang out or for areas where crayfish might hide, like under logs or near rocks. Instead of just going fishing for whatever bites, consider the lifestyle of the fish you wish to make famous.

• Fish have enemies that like to eat fish. If you were a fish and didn't want to get eaten, where would you hide to avoid your predators? Fish like to stay near fallen trees, stumps, weeds, deep water or anything else that provides shelter and helps them avoid becoming a meal. But, while they want to avoid predators, they also want to eat (see previous bullet).

• Big fish eat little fish. If you are catching a lot of little ones, a big one may be lurking near, so consider enlarging your casting area.

• What did Dr. Seuss tell us in the fishing classic *One Fish, Two Fish, Red Fish, Blue Fish*? No two fish are alike, which makes it necessary to go even beyond these general rules and think about specific fish.

Getting Started

If you are 16 or older, you need a valid New York State fishing license to fish in state waters. Licenses are available at many bait and tackle shops, sporting good stores, some state campgrounds and by mail through DEC's Albany office, 457-8862. (See this chapter's "Fishing Licenses" section for information on contacting one of the various regional DEC offices.)

General all-purpose equipment should include some of the following:

• A medium-action spinning, spin-casting or bait-casting rod and reel, with 6- to 8-pound test line; or

• A 6- to 9-foot fly-rod and reel setup with a #6-7 double taper (thicker in the middle than at either end) of weight-forward floating line.

• A few #10 hooks, swivels, sand weights, a few half- to 1-inch bobbers, a few hook hangers, spoons, spinners and jigs.

Speaking in Specifics

• **Lake trout.** The best time to fish for lake trout is in early spring (as soon as the ice melts) and in late fall. Try trolling or casting in deep waters where streams enter lakes. Lakers tend to be very deep in lake during summer months. During these times they are

— continued on next page

slow to feed, so jigging or spoon-dunking may entice one to strike. The best baits: a live shiner or worm rigged to trail a spoon.

•**Smallmouth bass.** Smallmouth action is best from around the third Saturday in June (opening day of bass season) into mid-July, then from September to November 30 (closing day). Early to mid-morning and late-afternoon fishing seem to produce the best results. Since smallmouth like to chase bait, try casting along rocky drop-offs or the edge of weed beds. If you catch one, fish the spot again; smallmouth travel in small schools, so others should be lurking near. The best baits: crawfish, shiners or night crawlers.

•**Largemouth bass.** Fish for largemouth the same as you would smallmouth, but expect the best catches during evening hours. Bass like to lurk around fallen logs and in lily pads. Surface lures work well. Bass like shade (but slow, warm water) in deep summer, so fish weedy shallows. On bright days fish in slightly deeper water than on shady days. The best baits: crawfish, shiners and night crawlers.

•**Northern pike.** Pike season opens the first Saturday in May and closes March 15, the following year. Pike fishing is best midday. Pike go deep during the warmer months of summer, so either fish early in the season (when they may be near the surface) or in deep water in summer. Pike are aggressive and territorial, so whatever passes their way gets chased or eaten. Use big, active lures in and around weed beds and vary the retrieval rate. Don't forget to add a wire leader as pike can bite through other types of line. Handle these fish with extreme care when unhooking them; they can (and will) bite your hands. Northern pike and largemouth bass often share habitat. The best bait: *big* shiners.

•**Brown trout.** The best times to fish for "browns" are early and late in the season, which ranges from April 1 through October 15. Browns don't like the sun, so fish near the bottom of deep pools, under overhangs and at stream junctions during the summer months. Browns are more skittish than brookies or rainbows, so cast quietly and don't

— continued on next page

Photo: Warren County Tourism Department

In the Adirondacks, you'll always find a nearby stream in which to wet a line.

let your shadow fall on the pool in which you are casting. The best bait: worms, spinners with a worm trailer, grasshoppers and crickets.

•**Brook trout.** New York's state fish, brookies are a native species that have been in all the region's watersheds since the last ice age. Their longevity may have something to do with the fact that even the best anglers have trouble catching them in the summer, so try your luck during cooler times. In streams, cast up and across streams, letting the lure or bait drift to the bottom and bounce. In ponds, use weighted nymphs during summer months. The best bait: worms, either alone or trailing a spinner. (Note that many streams and ponds have special regulations regarding brook trout that are posted on site.)

•**Rainbow trout.** Like other trout, rainbows are most active during early morning and late evening in the spring and fall. In streams, use lures that glitter and flash (silver and gold spinners and spoons). In ponds, look for dead insects on the surface; a rainbow may be near. Where there is one, there may be others. The best bait: worms.

•**Landlocked salmon.** Landlockeds, like brookies, are another native species, but much of their original habitat has been lost due to industrialization. Unlike most other fish in lakes, landlocked salmon don't hang out near shoals or logs. Instead they are often found suspended in the water column, just hanging about. During the summer, fish in the upper depths of the lake by trolling with a down rigger. When you catch one, fish at the same depth again.

•**Panfish** (a.k.a. "fun fish"). Perch, crappies, sunfish, rock bass and bullheads don't usually make it onto the trophy list, but they are fun and challenging to catch, especially for kids. Just put a worm on the hook and snap on a bobber about 12 to 18 inches up the line, then let the kids have at it.

---

considered prime, good fishing can be found all along the river.

Generally, the waters during the first days of spring are still frozen over in many spots, making fishing difficult if not impossible. Fishing picks up once the high waters of the spring thaw begin to retreat, with the best fishing beginning in May and lasting through June.

Saranac River

The Saranac River is rather unusual in that both warm- and cold-water fishes can be had, depending upon where you fish. Although sections of the river have been dammed for hydroelectric projects, the river also remains one of the few that can be fished extensively by canoe throughout most of the year.

The river flows from Lake Flower in Saranac Lake, along N.Y. Highway 3 to Plattsburgh, some 65 miles away. Since the initial flow from Saranac Lake is deep and slow, this section is best fished by boat. (There are a few good foot-access spots just below the Lake Flower dam.) The bass and northern pike can be quite large here. As the river picks up speed in Bloomingdale and flows to Franklin Falls,

brown and rainbow trout can be had in the faster sections, and pike, bass, panfish and other species in the slower pools.

While the waters of Lake Flower are classified as cold, the Department of Environmental Conservation classifies the waters in Franklin and Union Falls as warm. In both Franklin and Union ponds, walleye and smallmouth bass are sought-after game fish, with Franklin considered the better pond for walleye. An occasional brown trout can be had, along with some perch, bullhead and other panfish. Either pond is a good choice for kids.

River Road (just past the town) in Bloomingdale, Cold Brook Road in Vermontville (the next town), and the Alder Brook Road at its junction with County Road 26, all provide access to Franklin and Union Falls.

In fact, fishing is good all along the river, and there are simply too many choices to list.

As the Saranac nears Lake Champlain, you'll find plenty of fishing holes filled with trout and salmon right in downtown Plattsburgh. The salmon fishing is best in early spring and late fall.

Hunting

The varied terrain in the Adirondacks, from its rolling hills and valleys to its high mountain peaks, forests and lakes, provides hunters in pursuit of big and small game a challenging and potentially rewarding experience.

Big-game hunters will find abundant white-tail deer and black bear in the area. In the Adirondacks, the bear-hunting season begins in mid-September and continues through early December. The largest bear taken in New York State was shot in the town of Altamont near Tupper Lake in the High Peaks section of the Park. The bear tipped the scale at an estimated 750 pounds.

Trophy deer in excess of 200 pounds with racks in the 10-point range are also common, especially in mountain regions where light hunting pressure and the terrain itself tend to produce an older deer population. More hunters work the lower elevations, in the Champlain and St. Lawrence valleys or the southern portion of the Park, where the deer population tends to be larger as more food sources are available. The harsh conditions in the High Peaks region tend to keep the population in check.

The largest canoe wilderness area in the East is in the western part of the Adirondack Park. Some hunters travel by canoe to remote areas for a unique experience.

Small-game hunters can pursue snowshoe hare, cottontail rabbit, ruffed grouse, partridge, woodcock, ring-necked pheasant, wild turkey, coyote and red fox as well as waterfowl. Again, the harsh conditions in areas of higher elevation result in fewer animals. Consider the wild turkey to illustrate this difference. Although many attempts have been made to introduce the wild turkey to northern and High Peaks sections of the region, few (if any) permanent populations exist. An hour away, however, in the valley regions, the bird is a common sight.

Hunters can add to the challenge of the sport by participating in special archery (September 27 to October 20 in 1997) or muzzleloader (October 15 to November 19 in 1997) seasons.

Since more than 50 percent of the Adi-rondack Park is privately owned, hunters need to be aware of the strict trespassing laws and obtain permission from the land-owner to hunt on or pass through private land. Land that is posted with No Trespassing signs should be respected and not encroached upon.

One of most popular forms of hunting in the region is at a private hunting club. In many cases, these clubs lease large tracts of land from lumber and paper companies. In some cases, the clubs construct primitive camps (no electricity, no running water) on the land for its members. The industrial owner generally retains the right to manage the forests on these lands, which works to the advantage of the club. Managed forest lands produce not only a greater crop of wood, but also increase wildlife populations.

Unfortunately, these clubs are private, so there is no public listing for them or information on them. Since membership in these clubs often involves a process as well as yearly fees, it is not something that a casual visitor can access. However, where there is a will to gain information, there also is a way. You might begin by inquiring at local sporting good stores or local rod and rifle clubs in various towns.

Hunting Hotline

For up-to-date information on current hunting conditions, deer-check stations, season and regulation changes and information, the Department of Environmental Conservation (DEC) operates a hotline 24 hours a day from September through December; call 891-5413.

Hunting Licenses

The New York State hunting license year is October 1 through September 30. For specific hunting rules and regulations, bag limits and maps for the Adirondack Park, visit or write any of the New York State Department of Environmental Conservation offices. Licenses can be obtained in the same locations as fishing licenses (see the previous "Fishing Licenses" section). Special regulations may apply in obtaining a license, so it is best to contact DEC.

Hunting License Options and Fees

All hunters are required to carry a New York state hunting license. Rates are subject to change, but 1997 fees were as follows:

Resident

Annual (ages 12 through 15, 65 and older)	$5
Annual (small game)	$11
Annual (big game, trapping)	$13
Annual (bowhunting or muzzleloading)	$11
Annual (junior trapping; ages 16 and younger)	$6
Annual Sportsman (big/small game and fishing)	$31
Turkey permit	$2

Nonresident

Annual	(small game)	$50
Annual	(deer only or bowhunting)	$100
Annual	(muzzleloading)	$75
Annual combination (hunting, fishing, deer hunting, bowhunting and muzzleloading)		$225
Bear tag or turkey permit		$25

Note: Other special stamps are available. Please contact the DEC for details.

Wilderness Areas

Many portions of the following wilderness areas are remote and difficult to access and negotiate — even for trained emergency rescue personnel. Please do not attempt to explore any of these regions without a good map and practiced orienteering skills!

Lake Placid/ Tri-Lakes Region

While many higher-elevation lakes in the region are devoid of fish — due to acid rain, normally acidic conditions and overfishing — the vast majority has healthy populations. For the most part, the region's lakes and ponds are best fished from a boat or canoe.

Canoe fishing is ideal. Canoes are easily transported atop a vehicle, and they allow anglers to pond- or lake-hop. In the Fish Creek or St. Regis areas of the High Peaks, for example, dozens of ponds and lakes are connected via water or short land carries. When the fishing is slow in one lake, carrying the canoe — far easier than carrying a boat — to the next pond may be the answer. Pond hoppers should carry an array of fishing tackle, as different species of fish will lurk in different ponds.

Anglers have ample opportunities, especially for trout fishing in the Opalescent River, Johns Brook, Klondike Brook, Marcy Brook, Cold River, Moose River and the famed Ausable River (see "Rivers and Streams" in the previous "Fishing" section for details about the Ausable).

Two of the more unusual game fish in the region are Kokanee salmon and splake. In this region, Little Green Pond and Lake Colby have Kokanee salmon. Splake are found in Lake Colby, near Saranac Lake and Upper St. Regis, in the St. Regis Canoe Area (see subsequent section).

High Peaks Wilderness Area

High Peaks, the largest wilderness area in the Park, encompasses 193,000 acres, including almost all the mountainous region between

Lake Placid and Keene in the north and ranging west to Long Lake, south to Newcomb and east to North Hudson.

The topography ranges from small wetland areas, mostly along the rivers, to high-mountain country. Although many hunters search for big game in the High Peaks themselves, these highly mountainous areas are not prime big-game territories as this region's winters are too harsh for even large animals.

A section of the High Peaks Wilderness area called Cold River, near Tupper Lake, has become increasingly popular to hunters in search of a remote wilderness experience. After hiking or canoeing a few miles into the forest, they discover just how rugged and challenging this section of truly is. The Raquette River (see "Canoeing" in Other Summer Recreation) provides canoe access to many remote camping spots.

www.insiders.com

See this and many other Insiders' Guide® destinations online — in their entirety.

Visit us today!

St. Regis Canoe Area

St. Regis Canoe Area encompasses 20,000 acres west of Paul Smiths and includes 58 lakes and ponds. This area, along with Five Ponds (see the subsequent "Old Forge/Raquette Lake Region" section), may be heaven on earth as far as canoeists and anglers are concerned. In some sections, canoeists can travel for some 30 to 40 miles among dozens of lakes with only short carries of the canoe overland. The lake fishing in this area is among the finest anywhere. (Technically, St. Regis Canoe Area is not an official wilderness area. It is a designated "Canoe Area," but it is managed as a wilderness area, so we include it here but not in the official wilderness-area count. Officially, there are 16 Wilderness Areas plus the St. Regis Canoe Area.)

Plattsburgh/Western Lake Champlain Region

The Plattsburgh region is known more for its fishing in Lake Champlain (see "Lakes" in the previous "Fishing" section for details), than for its hunting. Much of the land in this region is privately owned, therefore it often is posted "No Hunting." If you wish to hunt in this region and are uncertain about which land you may legally access, check with the New York Department of Environmental Conservation for details. (Check the previous "Fishing Licenses" section for the regional DEC offices' addresses and telephone numbers.)

Lake George/ Upper Hudson Region

Siamese Pond Wilderness Area/ Thirteenth Lake

The Siamese Pond Wilderness Area, near the towns of Lake Pleasant, Wells, Johnsburg and Thurman, covers more than 112,000 acres. The area includes some 36 ponds and lakes, including Siamese Pond, Thirteenth Lake and portions of Indian Lake, all of which are good fishing spots. Brook and lake trout and panfish can be found in both lakes, and brown and tiger trout, splake and landlocked salmon have been stocked in Thirteenth Lake in recent years.

The area includes relatively low rolling hills with only a few mountains at elevations higher than 3,000 feet, including Bullhead, Eleventh,

INSIDERS' TIP

Can't catch a fish? If you are desperate, or just want to catch a nice rainbow trout, you'll find the fishing easy in the privately stocked pond at Cold Brook Fish Farm, Cold Brook Road, Vermontville, 891-3585. The catch will cost you $4 per pound, but you don't need a fishing license, and the farm will even supply a rod and reel for free. The farm is off N.Y. Route 3; look for the signs.

Puffer and South Pond mountains. Numerous beaver meadows and wetlands and a mixture of hardwood and softwood forests make this a popular big- and small-game hunting area for white-tailed deer, black bears, coyotes, an occasional bobcat, beavers, minks and otters. Special hunting and fishing regulations apply in some sections of this wilderness area, so check the DEC hunting and fishing guides before venturing out. Sections of the Kunjamuk River and the East Branch of the Sacandaga River, both of which originate here, are designated as "wild rivers" and offer good fishing opportunities.

Most major ponds in the area have designated primitive tent sites along their shores. Accessing these sites takes some work, particularly at the Twin Siamese Ponds near Johnsburg, but the outstanding hunting and fishing possibilities make the effort well worth it. For example, trophy-size lake trout in the 15-pound range are not uncommon catches at the Twin Siamese Ponds. Both ponds offer good brook trout fishing, and in the lower pond, anglers can hook up with a whitefish, a hard fighter that, undeservedly perhaps, is not reputed as a sought-after game fish.

The Schroon River offers consistently good, sometimes excellent, fishing. Some of the best holes can be found below the Starbuckville Dam, near Brant Lake. When the water level is high early season, the Schroon River provides some good canoe fishing. If action is slow in the river, anglers can try Brant Lake for bass and brown trout.

Schroon Lake should not be overlooked. Although much smaller than Lake George — it's only 9 miles long — it offers good two-tier fishing. Trout and salmon in cold, deeper waters, and bass, northern pike, pickerel and panfish can be found in warmer shallows.

and Glens Falls areas, the Silver Lake Wilderness is a popular spot for hunters, particularly those seeking big game. Lake Pleasant, Silver Lake, Mud Lake, Rock Lake and Loomis Pond are popular trout-fishing spots, as is Big Eddy on the west branch of the Sacandaga River. An upper stretch on the east branch of the Sacandaga River in the towns of Thurman and Johnsburg offers good brook trout fishing.

Because the entire area was heavily logged in the earlier parts of this century, it offers diverse hardwood and softwood forests at different maturity levels. Large portions of these forests are now relatively mature, but there is still enough diversity to attract big game — and big-game hunters, especially since much of the region is readily accessible from the perimeter roads. Some sections, however, are private posted lands.

West Canada Lake Wilderness Area

West Canada Lake includes more than 160 lakes and ponds within its 157,000 acres. Numerous ponds, lakes and streams support a healthy trout population, with the most popular being West Canada Lake, Spruce Lake and Cedar Lake. These three lakes' elevations are among the highest in the region. The Indian River, from its source to the south branch of the Moose River, is a designated wild river and offers some fine fishing, but anglers have to work (hike) a bit to fish it.

A trail from Piseco to West Canada Lake covers more than 30 miles without any signs of civilization and is considered one of the wildest trails in the entire Adirondack region.

Public campsites at Piseco Lake and Lewey Lake make for convenient base camps for hunters and anglers.

Southern Adirondack Lakes Region

Silver Lake Wilderness Area

On a map, the 105,000 acres of the Silver Lake Wilderness Area are near the towns of Lake Pleasant, Benson, Wells, Arietta and Piseco. Because of its proximity to the Albany

Old Forge/ Raquette Lake Region

Stillwater Reservoir/Pepperbox and Five Ponds Wilderness Areas

Stillwater Reservoir, consisting of 6,700 acres, is one of the largest man-made structures within the Park, and over the years it has

Photo: Ken Brown

A fly-fisherman plies the waters of the Ausable River.

become an increasingly popular site for anglers because it allows motor boats. Access to Stillwater is via N.Y. Route 28 in Eagle Bay and N.Y. Route 12 in Lowville. The once-remote atmosphere, however, has been somewhat lost due to the area's ever-increasing popularity. If you don't mind sharing the reservoir with the other anglers cruising about, try Stillwater year round for splake, bass, perch and bullheads.

Pepperbox and Five Ponds, with a combined 130-plus ponds and 106,000 acres, border Stillwater and provide less crowded conditions for both anglers and hunters.

Five Ponds, near Cranberry Lake at its northern border and Stillwater Reservoir at its southern end, may be the most remote and least used Adirondack wilderness area. Its 101,000 acres include 95 bodies of water, and elevations here range from 1,486 feet to 2,460 feet. This is one of the few in the northeastern United States where you can find stands of virgin timber. The old-growth pine and red spruce stand on the esker between Big Five, Little Five and Big Shallow, Little Shallow and Washbowl ponds. Hunting and fishing in these areas gives one a true sense of what it was like more than 100 years ago, when settlers where just beginning to explore the region. Only a few lean-tos still exist in the area, so camping is primitive but at its wild best.

There are also numerous clear, spring-fed ponds in the Five Ponds area, most of which support healthy trout populations. The Oswegatchie River, once considered the top brook trout river in New York State, is now filled with perch, which virtually has eliminated most of the trout from the river.

Five Ponds is an area where anglers, hunters and experienced campers can travel miles deep into the backwoods to rid themselves of any scent of the civilized world. Although not as rugged as the High Peaks area, Five Ponds is as remote and wild as wilderness gets, so use caution and common sense when exploring here.

If it involves physical activity, if it is legal, if a specialized piece of footwear is needed to conduct the athletic activity, or if ESPN ever mentioned it in one of its sportscasts, then that activity likely can be found somewhere in the Adirondacks.

Other Summer Recreation

No matter where you are in the Adirondack region, you are not far from great hiking, mountain and road biking, walking, whitewater rafting, horseback riding, water skiing, sailing, canoeing, kayaking, in-line skating, wind surfing, swimming, fishing, rock climbing, scuba diving . . . the list goes on.

Is there any recreational activity you can't find in the Adirondacks? Well, there's no bungee jumping, as far as we know, and no parasailing off cliffs. But who needs a sail when you can slide off a ski jump, do a couple of midair flips and land in — what else? — a pool of water? Oh, you don't want to land in water? Would you rather just ski off a 90-meter ski jump in midsummer and land on terra firma? Don't worry about the lack of snow on the ski jumps — plastic snow works just as well and doesn't melt. We're not kidding — ski jumping in summer is possible here. You must be a member of a ski jumping federation, but if it's your heart's desire, it is possible. In fact, if it involves physical activity, if it is legal, if a specialized piece of footwear is needed to conduct the athletic activity, or if ESPN ever mentioned it in one of its sportscasts, then that activity likely can be found somewhere in the Adirondacks. Yes, the region has hosted two Olympic Winter Games and is renowned for its cold-weather activities (see our Skiing and Other Winter Recreation chapters), but summer-recreation pursuits reign supreme in sheer abundance.

This chapter includes highlights of what to do, where to go and who to see. Be sure to check out the "Fun Stuff" section of our Shopping chapter, as many of the outfitters and ski and bike shops listed there are prime sources for information and rental equipment. If one shop doesn't have what you need, ask; the outfitters with the best reputations will refer you elsewhere when they can't serve you.

In this chapter, we include separate sections for the following summer recreational activities: horseback riding; canoeing; boating, water skiing and personal watercraft (a formal name for the very informal Jet Skiing); whitewater rafting and river tubing; mountain biking and cycling; in-line and ski skating; rock climbing; swimming; and summer camps. Note that some activities are heavily concentrated in certain geographic regions, such as horseback riding in the "Dude Ranch Trail" portion of the Lake George/Upper Hudson Region, rock climbing in the Lake Placid/Tri-Lakes Region, and power boating in the Great Sacandaga Lake and Lake George areas.

In some cases we provide an overview of the areas in which you can enjoy a particular activity, such as with canoeing and mountain biking, and then refer you to sources for more information and assistance in planning your excursions. Other times, such as with horseback riding, whitewater rafting or boating, we list specific operators that provide such a service.

We do not cover golf, hiking, hunting or fishing here as they have been promoted and receive their own chapters. (Congratulations to them all!) Also, you'll notice we do not cover swimming and beaches extensively. With 2,800 lakes and ponds in the Adirondack region, do you really *want* us to cover swimming? Seriously, there are numerous great spots to swim in the Adirondacks, from town beaches to state campgrounds to old-fashioned swimmin' holes. All of them share one thing in common — *brrrrrr*. Well, not all the time, but let's just say you can count on your Adirondack swimming experience to be "refreshing," even on the hottest late July days. Your best bet for finding a great beach is simply asking the locals, whether at the chamber of commerce or the town general store. We also include five beaches to "dig" for (if not to die for) in the "Swimming" section toward the end of this chapter.

Horseback Riding

There are miles of scenic wilderness trails in the Adirondacks, many of which are specifically designed for horses. Unfortunately, in many instances you need your own horse, so we only include stables at which you can rent horses and receive basic riding instruction. Rides at these stables range from an hour-long loop to a daytrip.

Lake Placid/ Tri-Lakes Region

Cold River Ranch
N.Y. Rt. 3, Tupper Lake • 359-7559

Cold River offers half-day, full-day and overnight trail rides. Rates are approximately $25 per hour, but special packages are available for guests staying at the ranch. The Cold River area, between Saranac Lake and Tupper Lake,

offers access to the Saranac Lakes and Raquette River. Horse trails traverse pristine forests and flank the shorelines of many area lakes. (See the Saranac Lakes entry in the subsequent "Canoeing" section as well as the Bed & Breakfasts and Country Inns chapter for related information.)

Sentinel View Stables
Harrietstown Rd. (N.Y. Rt. 86), Saranac Lake • 891-3008

These stables offer miles of bridle paths, riding instruction, half- and whole-day picnic rides and horse rentals with English or Western saddles. The rates are $22 per hour, including a trail guide.

FYI

Unless otherwise noted, the area code for all phone numbers listed in this guide is 518.

XTC Ranch
Forest Home Rd., Saranac Lake • 891-5684

XTC Ranch is on a 150-acre site and offers miles of great trails. Rentals are $85 for a full day (including lunch), or $25 per hour. The ranch offers a combination lesson and trail ride for youngsters who never have ridden before at $25. (See our Attractions chapter for additional information.)

Wilson Livery and Stable
Alstead Hill Rd. Keene • 576-2221

This stable, adjacent to the Bark Eater Inn (see Accommodations), offers miles of trails through a woodland setting. The rates are $25 per hour, including a trail guide.

Lake George/ Upper Hudson Region

In the 1940s and 1950s, there were so many dude ranches offering horseback riding, square dancing and rodeos in this part of the Adirondacks that it became known as the "Dude Ranch Capital of the East." While many of the ranches of those days are gone, there are still a few big dude ranch resorts left, along with a number of riding stables. Many of these are strung along a portion of N.Y. Route 9N that has been designated the "Dude Ranch Trail" by the Adirondack North Country Association. We cover the major dude ranch resorts in the

This Lake George beach scene debunks the myth about the lack of summertime sunning and swimming opportunities in the North Country.

Accommodations chapter, and therefore include only riding stables here. Do yourself a favor (particularly on summer weekends) and call ahead to make a reservation to avoid being disappointed by a long wait upon your arrival.

Bailey's Horses
N.Y. Rt. 9N, Lake Luzerne • 696-4541

Bailey's offers a variety of guided trail rides, ranging from one-hour rides for $15, 1½-hour rides for $20 and a two-hour ride, which includes some stream crossings and climbs to a lookout point, for $30. Your kids can get a pony ride for just $5, which includes a souvenir cowboy hat they can treasure forever (or at least until you unpack the car back home). Bailey's Horses is open daily from mid-May until Columbus Day, and in the winter by appointment.

Bennett's Riding Stables
N.Y. Rt. 9N, Lake Luzerne • 696-4444

About 5 miles south of Lake George along the "Dude Ranch Trail," Bennett's has been open as a family-run operation since 1942. Don't worry, they've bought new horses since then! Bennett's offers a variety of guided trail rides throughout a mix of terrain. The rides are all suited to skill level of the riders, so you can relax and enjoy the surroundings. If you're just starting out and are a little apprehensive about the whole thing, don't be a hero — request a helmet. One 2½-hour excursion takes you all the way to the top of Beech Mountain for a spectacular view. Pony rides for the kids are also available, which consist of a pony led around a small corral by a cowboy who looks like he'd rather be "on the trail." With the beautiful scenery around here, it's tough to blame him.

You can enjoy a visit to Bennett's year round, daily in the summer and on weekends in the spring and fall. Other times are by appointment. Trail rides cost from $5 for a kid's pony ride to $17 per hour for guided trail rides. You can enjoy the popular 2½-hour ride to the summit of Beech Mountain for $35 per person.

Circle B Ranch
**Friends Lake Rd., Chestertown
• 494-4074**

The owners of the Circle B Ranch, just about a 20-minute drive from Lake George, describe it as a "small, homey atmosphere" versus some of the much larger operations on the "Dude Ranch Trail." They normally have between 13 and 15 horses available, compared with 30 or more at some of the Lake George area stables. This just means that if you're looking for a little less commercial place with fewer cars in the lot and fewer people on the trails, the Circle B might be a good alternative for you. They operate a nicely maintained trail network and offer anything from a one-hour jaunt to an all-day trail ride. Most folks opt for something between one and three hours. Your cost is $17 per hour, but coupons for a couple of bucks off can be found at local sport shops, according to management. For only $2, your little "pardners" can enjoy a pony ride. Helmets are available for riders of any age if requested. You can also take riding lessons here for $17 per person for a half-hour.

Circle B Ranch is open year-round, and also offers sleigh rides in the winter time (see Other Winter Recreation).

Saddle-Up Stables
Lake Shore Dr. (N.Y. Rt. 9N), Diamond Point • 668-4801

For a trail riding experience that adds the bonus of views of Lake George along the way, Saddle-Up Stables is worth checking out. Just 3 miles north of Lake George village, Saddle-Up offers a variety of guided trail rides, horses for hire to ride on your own, horses for children, and pony rides for your youngest. One nice safety feature here is the availability of helmets, perhaps not as traditional as cowboy hats, but from 7 feet up (the height of an average horse), safety probably prevails over fashion (at least for beginners).

Saddle-Up Stables is open daily during the summer, and costs range from around $5 for a pony ride to $15 per hour for trail rides.

Wild West Ranch & Western Town
Bloody Pond Rd., off U.S. Hwy. 9, Lake George • 668-2121

This is a brand-new attraction geared to kids and their parents, offering a big slate of pony, horse, mule and stagecoach rides, along with a Wild West Show & Rodeo, Wild West Saloon & Steakhouse, Ice Cream Parlor, Old-Fashioned Bakery and Country Shops. Costs range from $4 for pony rides to $15 per hour for trail rides. They offer a 2½-hour trail ride to a scenic Lake George overlook for $30 per person. See the listing in the Kidstuff chapter for more details.

Southern Adirondack Lakes Region

Airdwood Dressage Center
N.Y. Rt. 8, 6 miles west of Speculator • 548-5454

Airdwood is both a dressage training center as well as a trail riding center. Management explained that "dressage" is sometimes mistakenly perceived as teaching horses to "dance and prance," when in fact it refers to basic horse and rider skills training. So, at Airdwood you can both learn how to ride, drive a horse-drawn carriage, or simply hire a horse and guide for some recreational trail riding. Trail rides range from a one-hour loop for $20 to an all-day excursion with lunch included for about $100 per person. If you want to take a lesson, it will cost you $30 per hour (for riding) and $40 per hour (for driving). Airdwood also offers pony rides in a slightly different format than many other stables. Pony rides cost $15 for a half-hour, but you can toss on how ever many kids you have to take turns throughout the time — one at a time, please.

The operation is open year round, but they strongly encourage people to call first before coming out to ensure availability of both horses and staff.

www.insiders.com

See this and many other **Insiders' Guide®** destinations online — in their entirety.

Visit us today!

Canoeing

During the summer months, a canoe remains a fixture atop many a car, as locals and visitors alike travel throughout the region to take advantage of the many miles of great canoeing waters. For some, canoes serve as the vehicle for fishing excursions into a backwoods pond; for others, canoeing simply relieves the pressure of a hectic lifestyle. In either case, the lakes, ponds and navigable rivers in the Adirondacks are very relaxing places that afford visitors ample opportunity to experience the region's diverse nature.

Canoe rentals are available in most major towns in the region for single- and multi-day trips. Many outfitters also provide pickup services, meaning that they will meet you and your party up at a specific location and transport you back to your car. Rental outfitters are detailed in the "Fun Stuff" section of our Shopping chapter. Many provide trip planning, instruction and equipment. Sometimes these services cost a little extra, but in the long run they will save you time and energy.

Although you don't need to register or hold a license to operate a canoe, as you do for most boats, you should know how to safely operate one. If you don't, rent from a outfitter that offers basic instruction. New York State law requires a life jacket or personal flotation device (PFD) for all paddlers. The Department of Environmental Conservation (DEC) publishes a number of maps and guides outlining popular canoe routes (see our Hiking chapter for a rundown of DEC office addresses).

Another good resource, providing dozens of thumbnail overviews of canoe routes, is *Adirondack Waterways: A Guide to Paddling "The Northeast's Last Great Wilderness."* It is free, published and distributed by the Adirondack Regional Tourism Council, P.O. Box 2149, Plattsburgh, N.Y. 12901, 846-8016.

In this section we offer an overview of a few of the many canoeing areas. For specific routes, either consult an outfitter or one of the following references: *Adirondack Canoe Waters: North Flow* by Paul Jamieson and Donald Morris (Adirondack Mountain Club, 1991) or *Adirondack Canoe Waters: South and West* by Alec Proskine (Adirondack Mountain Club, 1989). A detailed map, "Adirondack Canoe Waters," published by Adirondack Maps in Keene Valley, can be found in many book or sport shops in the region.

We assume that most of you are interested in canoeing of the kinder, gentler variety, and therefore have limited our descriptions to those

canoe routes including only Class I and II waters. Those of you itching for some real whitewater may want to jump to the subsequent "Whitewater Rafting and River Tubing" section of this chapter.

Warning: Be aware of the weather forecasts in the area, especially the wind conditions, *before* you depart on a canoeing excursion. The weather conditions when you start out in the morning may be ideal for a canoe trip across a large lake, but they may change dramatically once an evening breeze picks up. Many a paddler has become stranded on the far side of a large lake, unable to paddle against the wind to return to the starting point. If the forecast predicts changes in the weather, change your plans accordingly, such as canoeing a smaller and more manageable expanse of water.

Lake Placid/ Tri-Lakes Region

The Saranac Lakes

The Upper, Middle and Lower Saranac lakes offer nearly 30 miles of waterways and ample opportunities for full- and half-day trips. Upper Saranac, the largest of the Saranacs, offers 37 miles of shoreline and 20 primitive campsites, available on a first-come, first-served basis. The numerous ponds west of the lake are ideal for short paddles or as starting points for longer trips into the Saranacs. Middle Saranac features numerous islands, some of the finest natural beaches in the area and 20 campsites on islands and on the shore. The lake also provides access to the secluded Weller Pond and its five campsites. Lower Saranac Lake, the closest to the village of Saranac Lake and its boat and canoe outfitters, provides a variety of popular daytrips. A favorite begins in Lower Saranac and continues down the Saranac River through Oseetah

---

INSIDERS' TIP

Overlook Management Group organizes mountain and road biking package tours suitable for beginners to experts and lasting from one full day to a three-day weekend. You can get details from them at 743-1735.

Lake and Lake Flower. More than 55 campsites dot the islands and the shore.

All campsites on the Saranac lakes are maintained by the Department of Environmental Conservation and fees apply for their use. Call (800) 456-CAMP for the New York State campsite reservation system.

St. Regis Canoe Area (Paul Smiths)

The St. Regis Canoe Area, 15 miles northwest of Saranac Lake in the Paul Smiths/Lake Clear area, is the largest wilderness canoe area in the Northeast United States. While there are many lakes here, continuous excursions of nearly 40 miles often require extensive portages.

St. Regis is easily accessed at various sites, including Paul Smith's College, Little Clear Pond and Upper St. Regis Lake. One of the more popular routes is the famed 9-mile "Seven Carries," beginning at Little Clear Pond and ending at Upper St. Regis Lake, with eight other ponds and lakes in between. The longer "Nine Carries" places great physical demands on your back. Both trips can be shorter or longer as desired.

Although the area is known for its wilderness, a number of Great Camps — notably Camp Topridge, White Pine Camp and Northbrook Lodge — can be seen from the lakes. Camp Topridge, built by the Post family, is at the northwest end of the Upper St. Regis Lake near North Bay. White Pine and Northbrook are on Osgood Pond.

Numerous primitive campsites throughout the area are available on a first-come, first-served basis. No motor boats are permitted on many of the waters in the area, making canoe trips rather serene.

Tupper Lake and Raquette River

Raquette River can be accessed at Axton Landing, 3 miles south of Upper Saranac Lake on N.Y. Route 3, or via a state-maintained launch site 16 miles west of Saranac Lake on N.Y. routes 3 and 30. Downstream is Tupper Lake; upstream are Raquette Falls and Long Lake.

You'll find a number of primitive campsites along the gentle Raquette. A shallow delta and marsh connect Tupper Lake and Simon and Raquette ponds. State land on the western shore of Tupper Lake has several campsites, including lean-tos at Black Bay and Sorting Gab, and a short trail leads to Bridge Brook Pond.

Another interesting excursion is across the shallow waters of Piercefield Flow at the extreme northwest end of Tupper Lake.

Raquette River, the second-longest river in New York State, begins in Blue Mountain Lake. The mostly flatwater river traverses lakes and river channels. Long Lake to Axton Landing covers 23-miles and includes a 1.3-mile carry at Raquette Falls. The Axton to Tupper Lake route is 16.5 miles. Start on Long Lake, and you'll travel with the current. Campsites and lean-tos are available all along the route. If you want an even longer trip, exit the Raquette River near Axton Landing, put in at the Stony Creek Ponds, then take the Indian Carry to connect to the Saranac Lakes Chain. The total distance traveled with this option is nearly 75 miles!

Cranberry Lake

Amid a large wilderness area, Cranberry Lake invites exploration in its many flows and bays as well as along the many hiking trails that start from the shores and lead to remote ponds and mountains. There are 46 designated campsites on the lake. Its outlet offers a brief section of Class I and II rapids; the rest of the nearly 7-mile-long river is flatwater as it winds through Chaumont Swamp on its way to the Newton Falls reservoir. For the adventuresome canoeist, there's a 40-mile round-trip paddle that takes a minimum of three days to complete — two days up and one day down the Upper Oswegatchie River, starting at Inlet. There are many hikes along the trail into the

Adirondack Mountain Club

A very important organization celebrated a very big birthday in 1997. The Adirondack Mountain Club, more commonly referred to around these parts as ADK, turned 75! While most things that are 75 years old begin to show some signs of age, perhaps even slow down a little, ADK continues to grow stronger and more vibrant with each passing year. So what is ADK, why does it go by those initials that don't seem to fit, and what is its secret to long life and prosperity?

According to its mission statement, the Adirondack Mountain Club is "dedicated to the protection and responsible recreational use of New York State's Forest Preserve, parks, and other wild lands and waters." ADK is a member-directed nonprofit organization that brings together people who are interested in recreation, conservation and environmental education. The organization helps to protect the interests and environment of the Adirondack Park, its smaller downstate sister, the Catskill Park, and other public lands throughout the state.

Basically, the folks at ADK want you to not only explore and enjoy the Adirondacks, but also respect and help protect the fragile environment of this immense wilderness. The club is called ADK because, when incorporated in 1922, the founding members were concerned about confusion with the already existing Appalachian Mountain Club, whose initials were AMC. After haggling over various identities — Adirondack Mountain Association, Adirondack Association, Adirondack Club — they stuck with what people had been calling the club since it began meeting informally in 1916. The original abbreviation was to be ADK M.C., but that was simplified even further to ADK. There you have it.

Over the course of its 75-year history, ADK has been cutting hiking trails (the Northville-Lake Placid trail was cut in 1922), presenting workshops (Dr. Orra Phelps conducted a "school of the woods" as far back as the 1930s at Johns Brook Lodge) and

— continued on next page

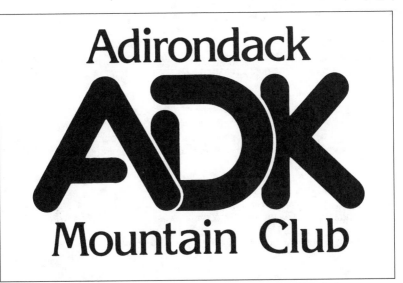

promoting conservation (the club's first conservation policy was developed in 1928). In 1932, ADK produced the Olympic Ski Map for the Winter Games in Lake Placid. Two years later ADK published the first-ever trail guide, *Guide to Adirondack Trails: Northeastern Section*. The book not only served as a useful resource for hiking enthusiasts of the day, but also inspired what is now an entire series of eight trail guides on the Forest Preserve accessed by thousands of hikers annually.

In effect, what the Adirondack Mountain Club stood for in 1922 is what is still stands for today, except that the degree of its activity, the strength of its membership and the positive results of its efforts have grown to heights rivaled by only the tallest of the "High Peaks."

Today, ADK is made up of more than 22,000 members in 26 chapters from throughout the northeastern United States and Canada. Its three primary areas of emphasis continue to be conservation, education and "responsible" recreation. Conservation efforts include lobbying against legislation that could adversely effect the New York State Forest Preserve, such as commercial expansions near threatened habitats or the resumption of commercial logging within state park land.

By teaching outdoor skills and natural-history appreciation, ADK succeeds in its mission of promoting outdoor recreation consistent with the region's character and respectful of its environment. For example, in 1996 ADK educated more than 13,000 hikers atop the highest peaks in the Adirondack Park about endangered alpine vegetation and what they can do to protect it. The club conducted a whopping 240 workshops attended by more than 4,000 people on such topics as diverse as map reading to building an Adirondack chair.

A big part of ADK's environmental education and recreation efforts is its publication of more than 30 books, booklets and pamphlets, including canoeing, climbing and hiking guidebooks, maps and natural- and cultural-history books. Titles include such specialized works as *Forest & Trees of the Adirondack High Peaks Region: A Hiker's Guide*, *Classic Adirondack Ski Tours*, *Climbing in the Adirondacks: A Guide to Rock & Ice Routes* (try to find *that* in your local drug store) and even general history books such as *Our Wilderness: How the People of New York Found, Changed, and Preserved the Adirondacks*. ADK also publishes a magazine, *Adirondac*, which comes out seven times a year. (See our Media chapter for details.)

ADK serves as a great recreational and information resource for visitors and outdoor enthusiasts. In 1996 the ADK Information Centers at ADK headquarters in Lake George and at Heart Lake in the High Peaks welcomed and assisted nearly 80,000 visitors. These facilities offer brochures, maps, ADK publications, educational displays and even some souvenir merchandise and trail snacks.

ADK works not only to inform and educate the public on how to best enjoy the Adirondacks, but also to improve visitors' recreational experience as well. For example, in 1996 trail crews completed more than 10,000 hours of trail work, including the construction of hundreds of rock steps, 1,500 feet of drainage to help keep trails dry (or less muddy, anyway) and more than 300 feet of bridging. Volunteers were organized to help maintain 131 lean-tos and 34 trails throughout the Adirondacks and New York State.

ADK is even in the accommodations business! It operates the 46-bed Adirondack Loj at Heart Lake (see Accommodations), the 16-bed Wiezel Trails Cabin, the Adirondack Loj Wilderness Campground, the Johns Brook Lodge (a hike-in backcountry facility) and three cabins for use by the public on a year-round basis.

To commemorate its 75th birthday in 1997, the Adirondack Mountain Club launched a year-long celebration that included some serious and not-so-serious events. For example, a yearlong contest called "Oh, Baby!" awarded a lifetime membership (worth

— continued on next page

$1,000!) to a child born in 1997 as a way to emphasize that "the future of our wild lands is in the hands of today's children." In September, the club organized a 75th Anniversary Commemorative Hike on the 130-mile-long Northville-Placid trail (the club's first trail) called "May the Forest Be with You." Participants hiked a section of the trail, got a T-shirt, ate barbecued chicken and had a grand old time in the woods and along the rivers.

By serving both the natural needs of the Adirondack environment as well as the desires and interests of the people who want to experience it, the Adirondack Mountain Club has established itself as a vital component of Adirondack health and prosperity, both environmentally and economically. Its place in Adirondack history is respected, and its role in the future of the Adirondacks is assured.

For more information on the Adirondack Mountain Club, its programs, facilities or publications, contact ADK, 814 Goggins Road, Lake George, N.Y. 12845, 668-4447.

wilderness for diversion, and plenty of carries over obstacles such as beaver dams.

Fish Creek Area (Saranac Lake)

The headwaters of the Saranac River begin somewhere amid the 37 lakes and ponds near the Fish Creek State Campground, a few miles outside Saranac Lake village. This area is a pond-hopper's paradise as well as a paradise for the tireless angler, as each pond has a distinct personality and, in many cases, different species of fish. Many day excursions are possible here, as are extended trips into the St. Regis Wilderness Canoe Area and the Saranac Lakes Chain (see previous entries).

Plattsburgh/Western Lake Champlain Region

Lake Champlain

Although Lake Champlain is better noted for power boating and sailing, the lake also offers miles of beautiful water for canoeing, especially in the myriad protected bays. Valcour Island, in the Adirondack Park, has several state campsites and is a popular canoeing destination for daytrippers as well as overnight canoe campers.

If you plan to paddle on Lake Champlain, pay special attention to weather conditions; the lake not only is rather large, but also generally has some "big air" (nice winds), as sailors might say — not something a canoeist will relish.

Lake George/ Upper Hudson Region

Lake George

The beauty and geography of Lake George make it not only irresistible to paddlers, but also a destination that requires you to become a well-informed enthusiast if you want to safely enjoy it. Because it is a large (32 miles in length) and very popular lake, it would be easy to get caught farther away from home base than you want to be when the weather changes for the worse, or when the afternoon power boat traffic and Jet Skis make some sections of the lake seem more like midtown Manhattan than the southern Adirondacks.

You may want to consider exploring Lake George by sea kayak, whose combination of speed, agility and room for packing gear in a

INSIDERS' TIP

Which park is the largest: Yellowstone, Grand Canyon, Yosemite, Everglades or Great Smoky Mountains national parks or the Adirondack Park?
Answer: It would take all five national parks added together to equal the size of the Adirondack Park.

protected compartment make it more suitable for handling long trips in open water. If canoeing, consider avoiding the lake in the peak boat-traffic months of July and August, or at least do your exploring early in the morning when the water is likely to be calmer, as is the boat traffic. You should also avoid the lower end of the lake near Lake George village, which is almost always busy with cruise boats, Jet Skis and power boats. There are literally dozens of access points around this lake, so just check with a local outfitter or dealer for suggestions on the best spot to put in, explore and get back out safely.

Lower Hudson River

Canoeing in the section of the Hudson River just south of its confluence with the Schroon River provides plenty of mileage (17) and variety, from the wide and calm to the quick and fun. You can put in at the Thurman Station Bridge on Warren County Route 418. The current is swift, but remains as Class I (more fun than dangerous). There are few obstacles to maneuver around, with the exception of an occasional sandbar if the water level is low.

Upper Schroon River

The 7-mile stretch of the Schroon River as it meanders south to Schroon Lake makes for a scenic and relaxing excursion, with a beautiful "pot" at the end of the rainbow — Schroon Lake. The entire length of trip is Class I, with no difficult stretches of water to negotiate. Expect your trip to last about two hours, during which time you should make plenty of wildlife sightings (don't worry — no hippos in the water or snakes hanging from tree limbs!). You can launch near the Sharp Bridge Campsite on U.S. Highway 9, which roughly parallels the Schroon River.

Southern Adirondacks Lakes Region

Indian Lake

Accessed off N.Y. Route 30 near its outlet to Lewey Lake, Indian Lake is popular with canoeists for several reasons. It is long (14 miles) and relatively narrow (less than a mile across) plus it has dozens of small islands (some with campsites; see Camping) to stop on and explore. Toward the north end of the lake, you also can stop on the eastern shore at Norman's Cove for a short (1.2 mile) hike to the top of Baldface Mountain for a spectacular view of the lake and beyond.

Peck's Lake

Accessed from Peck's Lake Road, off N.Y. Route 29A, this may be one of the best canoeing lakes in the southern Adirondacks. With no personal watercraft (i.e. Jet Skis) allowed, and no boat motors exceeding 40 hp, this is primarily a fishing lake with a smattering of pontoon boats cruising the shoreline after dinner. This is also a private lake with a privately operated campground, so unless you own property or are renting a campsite, you'll need to rent a canoe here as well. Canoe rentals cost $6 per person 11 and older per day and $3 for children 10 and younger (see Kidstuff's "Natural Selections" section). It's worth it, as the lake's clear water and many little coves and inlets, combined with the lack of boat traffic, make it ideal for an afternoon of exploring.

Peck's Lake is approximately 5 miles long, and a circuit of the lake can be made in an afternoon if you keep moving.

INSIDERS' TIP

Apolos "Paul" Smith was one shrewd backwoods guide. In addition to building the world famous Paul Smiths Hotel on Lower St. Regis Lake, the guide also created his own electric, telephone and railroad companies. Although Smith was a self-taught individual, he knew how to make money. In 1896 he sold four acres of land on Lower St. Regis Lake for $20,000— the exact amount he paid for 13,000 acres a few years earlier. Most likely the buyer had a good laugh over the deal as Smith likely sold the land while telling one of his favorite tales. Smith was one of the best story tellers of his day.

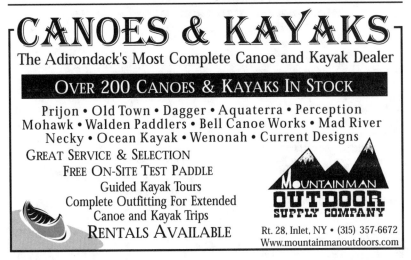
Sacandaga River and Kunjamuk Creek

This is a pleasant and interesting round trip of 7 miles, beginning with access to the main branch of the Sacandaga River at the Lake Pleasant outlet bridge (N.Y. routes 8 and 30). After paddling a couple of miles upstream (the current won't fight you much), you then head north (left) on the Kunjamuk Creek to Elm Lake (about 5 miles farther). You may need to lift out a couple of times to clear beaver dams, but that's part of the whole experience, so don't complain. Once you turn around at Elm Lake for the return trip, you can stop and make a short hike to Kunjamuk Cave (on the east side of the creek) and then choose to head east on the Sacandaga River for 4 miles of stillwater paddling.

Old Forge/ Raquette Lake Region

Blue Mountain Lake to Raquette Lake

Actually combining elements of two regions (we consider Blue Mountain Lake part of the Southern Adirondacks Lakes Region, albeit the extreme northern tip), this is a beautiful 15-mile trip that treats even novices to two of the most scenic lakes in the Adirondacks.

The put-in is at the Blue Mountain Lake public beach off N.Y. Route 28, from which you head west through the lake, proceeding through the narrow Eagle and Utowana lakes. You then need to make a half-mile carry at the end of the lakes to the Marion River, which winds its way through meadows and marshes to Raquette Lake.

Raquette Lake has 99 miles of shoreline, with dozens of bays and coves to explore. However, to the inexperienced it can be very disorienting and easy to get lost, so plan a route in advance and stick to it.

Fulton Chain of Lakes

Old Forge is the starting point for this famous chain-link fence of water that combines channels and eight lakes over the course of 16 miles. It is a very popular canoeing route, and the portion from First Lake to Fifth Lake is a continuous (no carry) waterway lined on both sides by summer cottages. The remaining lakes are connected by two carries and are much less developed. From the edge of Eighth Lake, a 1-mile carry can connect you to Brown's Tract Inlet and on to Raquette Lake. While power boats and personal watercraft are allowed on the Fulton Chain, they are strictly enforced to a speed limit of 5 mph within 200 feet of shore (which is where you should be paddling), so they shouldn't pose a nuisance or a threat.

Wilderness Guides

Wild Scenes in the Forest and Prairie, published in 1839 by Charles Hoffman, introduced to the world the exploits of John Cheney, Adirondack guide. Records indicate that Cheney killed some 600 deer, 48 bears, 19 moose, 400 martens, six wolves, a panther and possibly the last beaver in New York State during a 13-year period beginning in 1830. (Eventually the beaver would be reintroduced in the region.) His exploits were legendary, with most accounts recalling his most famous story about the time he broke his rifle over the head of a wolf.

Although Cheney was not the first guide in the region, he was the most famous — that is, until other guides began garnering more publicity for themselves. In 1869, "Adirondack Murray," a former preacher from Boston, wrote *Adventures in Wilderness*. The book  spoke highly of the parson's adventures and the healing powers of the Adirondacks. The book quickly became a bestseller and set off what became known as "Murray's Rush" into the Adirondacks. "Murray's Fools," as his followers were often called, journeyed to visit the minister, who would take his followers for a fee into the wilderness to become rejuvenated. Murray the preacher soon became Murray the famous guide.

In the latter part of the 1800s, another guide exploited his wilderness skills to become one of the most famous men in America. According to legend, the name Apolos "Paul" Smith found its way into print more than President Grover Cleveland, who on occasion visited the guide at his famed hotel on Lower St. Regis Lake. The legend of Paul Smith lives on in Paul Smith's College. (Ironically Smith disliked higher education and once proclaimed "There's no fool, like an educated fool.")

Today wilderness guides still play an important role in providing visitors a safe and rewarding backwoods experience. Unlike many legendary guides of the past, today's guides are fully licensed, insured and, in many cases, specialized in specific outdoor skills such as mountain climbing, kayaking, wilderness camping, fishing and hunting. Some are even capable storytellers, which can make a camping excursion more enjoyable, especially if they can spin a good yarn while cooking a good meal.

Whether or not you need a guide depends upon you — what

Photo: Paul Smiths College

Paul Smith was a legendary guide and founder of a famous hotel that drew thousands of tourists to the region at the turn of the century.

— continued on next page

you want and the depth of your pocketbook. A guided half-day fishing trip can cost around $100 per person, but if you know nothing about fishing, have little time and want to catch some fish, it may be a worthwhile proposition. Costs continue to rise as you add to the list of things you want to do. For instance, an overnight canoeing and camping excursion can cost from $200 to $500 per person. The fees often include all equipment, meals and guide services. You simply tell the guide what you want, then just show up; the guide can outfit the excursion entirely. Naturally, the fee begins with the guide's service, then rises with equipment fees.

Before hiring a guide, obtain a listing of licensed guides in New York State. Write the New York State Outdoor Guides Association (NYSOGA), P.O. Box 4704, Queensbury, N.Y. 12804, or call 798-1253. Many tourist information centers also carry the pamphlet "A Guide to the Licensed Guides of New York State." Although members of NYSOGA agree to adhere to a code of ethics and follow the policies of the organization, it is always a good idea to ask any guide for additional references, especially one from a hotel in the region. (Many hotels offer lists of recommend guide services.) It is also a good idea to make sure the guide is properly insured. Then, speak to your guide. Remember, if you're planning an extended trip, you will be spending a good bit of time with him or her, so try to get a sense of what he or she is like before you make final arrangements. Compatible personalities can make all the difference. During the summer months, guides can be booked way in advance. It's tough to find a guide with short notice.

Many guides also provide trip-planning services: They will plan and outfit your entire canoe or hiking trip, but won't accompany you. Once you complete your journey, the guide also might pick you up at a predetermined destination and return you to your starting point. If you are unfamiliar with what you want to do, but are comfortable with your abilities to do it, this trip-planning service may be worth considering.

Moose River – North Branch

Don't confuse this with the Lower Branch of the Moose River, notorious for its "experts only" Class V rapids. The 11-mile stretch of the North Branch above Old Forge is slow-moving, isolated and peaceful. About the only traffic you'll encounter is the deer, otter, beaver and even the occasional Great Blue heron along the shore. Put-in is at North Bridge, off N.Y. Route 28. There is one short carry required at Indian Rapids, but it is well marked.

Boating, Water Skiing and Personal Watercraft

Particularly in the southern Adirondack power-boat havens of Lake George and the Great Sacandaga Lake, boating and personal watercraft (i.e. Jet Skis) are hugely popular. On Lake George alone, there are nearly 15 places where you can rent power boats and nearly 20 marinas or dealers offering full boating services. We include a sampling here of outlets that offer boat and personal watercraft rentals as well as full-service marinas that offer services, equipment and repairs for power boats.

One publication you'll want to make sure to pick up is the *New York State Boater's Guide*, published by the NYS Office of Parks, Recreation and Historic Preservation, Bureau of Marine and Recreational Vehicles, Agency Building #1, Empire State Plaza (can you tell this is a government address?!), Albany, 474-0445. The 72-page booklet offers valuable information on boating equipment, registration, operation and aquatic safety. This office also provides the "NYS Boat Launching Sites" brochure.

Other sources of boating information, including boat launch sites, are: for Lake George and Warren County, the *Warren County Travel Guide*, Warren County Tourism Department, Municipal Center, Lake George, (800) 95-VISIT extension 2757; for the Great Sacandaga Lake and Southern Adirondack Lakes Region, the annual *Vacation Guide* published by The

Leader-Herald newspaper (see our Media chapter) in Gloversville; and for the Fulton Chain of Lakes in the Old Forge region, write to request the "Boating Information" brochure produced by the Fulton Chain of Lakes Association, P.O. Box 564, Old Forge, N.Y. 13420.

Lake Placid/
Tri-Lakes Region

Captain Marney's Boat Rentals
3 Victor Herbert Rd., Lake Placid
• 523-9746

The captain rents fishing boats at $20 per hour and power boats — some suitable for water skiing — at $40 to $90 per hour on Lake Placid. He'll even provide some basic water-skiing instruction with a boat rental.

Ampersand Bay Boat Club
12 Ampersand Bay Rd., Saranac Lake
• 891-3001

This small marina on Lower Saranac Lake rents canoes and fishing boats with motors. Canoes cost $15 to $17 per day, and the 14- to 16-foot boats rent for $55. The marina also offers lodging in log cabins and a small hotel unit.

Crescent Bay Inc.
N.Y. Rt. 3, Saranac Lake • 891-2060

On Lower Saranac Lake, this is a full-service marina, offering boat repairs, boat storage and sales. Canoe rentals are $15 per day, while small fishing boats with motors cost $50. The marina offers cabin rentals on the lake at $500 per week.

Plattsburgh/Western
Lake Champlain Region

Dozens of commercial marinas — far too many to mention — are available on protected bays of Lake Champlain, including Rouses Point, Chazy, Point au Roche, Plattsburgh, Peru, Willsboro, Essex, Westport and Ticonderoga. Most cater to season-long reservations but offer nightly rates (check in advance; they can be very expensive) as well. Most marinas provide dockside electricty and dumping stations, and many have shower facilities, dockside restaurants and bars, and marine supplies.

The following are two of the regions "biggies:"

Snug Harbor
3962 Lake Shore Rd., Plattsburgh
• 561-2134

One of the largest full-service marinas on Lake Champlain, Snug Harbor provides rentals, repairs and sales. Power boat rentals, suitable for water skiing, are available at approximately $185 per day, and fishing boats rent for $85 per day. A restaurant, serving everything from sandwiches to a steak dinner, overlooks the bay. Two marine stores furnish all your equipment needs.

Westport Marina
9 Washington St., Westport • 962-4356

This full-service marina rents 13- to 20-foot power boats — some suitable for water skiing — from $99 to $259 per day, boat repairs and service, along with a restaurant with entertainment on weekends during summer.

Lake George/
Upper Hudson Region

Note: Boat traffic at the highly commercial southern end of Lake George near Lake George village can be very heavy. For that reason, we suggest only rental facilities "up the lake" where casual boaters would be able to more safely enjoy the beautiful surroundings.

Chic's Marina
N.Y. Rt. 9N, Bolton Landing • 644-2170

Chic's is a full-service marina offering sales and service for all boats, including gas and mechanical and fiberglass repairs. Its location about 10 miles up the lake from Lake George village at Bolton Landing makes it a conve-

---

FYI

Unless otherwise noted, the area code for all phone numbers listed in this guide is 518.

nient stop for service of your own boat or rental of one of theirs. Chic's is a dealer for Boston Whaler, Celebrity, Mercury and Yamaha boats and motors.

Boat rental rates range from $35 per hour for a 10-hp fishing boat to $95 per hour for a 175- to 200-hp speedboat. You can rent a pontoon boat (a.k.a. "party barge") for a four-hour minimum at $175 (capacity of eight people), a canoe for $15 for the first hour, and Waverunners or Jet Skis for $40 per half-hour. Hourly rental rates drop as rental length of time increases. For example, that 10-hp fishing boat that cost you $35 for an hour will only cost you $45 for two hours, $85 for the day or $325 for an entire week.

Dunham's Bay Boat Co. Inc.
N.Y. Rt. 9L, 5 miles north of Lake George village • 656-9244

If you'd prefer to have your boat serviced or rent a boat on the less crowded eastern shore of Lake George, this may be a good alternative. In addition to marina services and supplies such as gas and repairs, Dunham's also has a large retail shop with boating accessories, water-skiing equipment and clothing. Five different types of power boats can be rented for $225 per day. All are 17 to 20 feet in length and powered by 135-hp motors.

Island View Marina & Dockside Boat Rentals
N.Y. Rt. 9N, Hague • 543-8888

Talk about meeting your every need on the north end of Lake George — this place can do it all. It's a marina, grocery store, restaurant, bait and tackle store, and boat rental facility all in one.

Sample rental rates are: $75 a day and $375 a week for a 14-foot aluminum 8-hp fishing boat; $200 a day and $1,000 a week for a 19-foot bowrider 140- to 210-hp speedboat;

$200 a day and $1,000 a week for a 22-foot 60-hp pontoon boat; and $50 per hour for a 500cc Waverunner personal watercraft. Ask about weekly specials. When we checked, you could rent an 18-foot ski boat for a seven days at $825. Don't get any more boat than you really need, and you can save some good dollars.

Werner's Boat Rentals
N.Y. Rt. 9N, Silver Bay • 543-8866

Werner's is in the less-congested, just-as-pretty northern end of Lake George. Their only business is boat rentals, and they've got a bunch of them (about 100 are available!). They also have a deli and grocery on site, with fast food, ice cream, ice, firewood, bait and tackle all available. You can rent a boat here from May 1 until October 15, with rental rates running 20 percent less before Memorial Day and after Labor Day. Also, their rental rates include free water skis, cushions and life preservers.

Some examples of available boats and rates are: 17-foot canoe, $22.50 for a half-day (four hours) or $30 for a full day (eight hours); 19-foot power boat with 115-hp motor, $165 for a half-day, $220 for a full day and $1,100 for a week; and a 24-foot pontoon boat with 70-hp motor, $165 for a half-day, $220 for a full day and $1,100 for the week.

Yankee Boating Center
N.Y. Rt. 9N, Diamond Point • 668-2862

In addition to providing marina services such as gas and boat repair, Yankee also rents sailboats, which are considerably tougher to find than power boats and pontoon boats. You can enjoy a day on a Capri 16-foot sailboat for $115, or a Panther 22-foot sailboat for $155. Yankee also rents power boats, such as a 19-foot speedboat with a 90-hp Honda motor for a full-day rate of $210.

INSIDERS' TIP

According to New York State law you can not ride in campers or trailers with a ball-type hitch. State police do not recommend riding in trailers with a "fifth wheel," although regulations do not prohibit it. New York State does not allow multiple trailers on its roads, meaning you can't pull a camper in tandem with another trailer carrying your boat.

Yankee Boating Center is about 4.5 miles north of Lake George village, convenient but far enough from the congestion of the lake's south end.

A Word About Parasailing

Those of you so inclined to be pulled by a power boat while you are strapped to a big parachute at the end of a 300-foot rope will be happy to know that you can do just that high above the waters of Lake George. The following services will help you make your dreams to fly come true. All use a floating platform as a launch point, and it's as safe as anything that looks so totally crazy can be.

National Water Sports
Christie Ln., Lake George • 668-4828

In Lake George village, you can score 10 to 15 minutes of sheer exhilaration here for $40. Of the places we researched, they claimed the lowest rates for the longest rides. We're guessing the first minute is the longest of your life, then the rest of the trip goes much too quickly.

Parachuting Adventures
Shoreline Cruises dock, off Canada St., Lake George • 668-4644

This is the most convenient service to those strolling and daring each other as they walk around Lake George village, and the prices reflect their dependency on the "impulse buy." It will cost you $45 for a six- to eight-minute ride.

Sun Sports Unlimited
Parasail Rides
Chic's Marina, N.Y. Rt. 9N, Bolton Landing • 644-3470

About 10 miles "up the lake" from Lake George village, Sun Sports will take you up and over probably the prettiest part of the lake, and you won't be on display for all of the Million Dollar Beach (see subsequent "Swimming" section) patrons to see (unless that's your goal). The rate is $40 for a "five to 10 minute ride." Hmmm. We wonder if they realize there's a 50 percent variance in ride time for the same number of bucks. Negotiate for the 10 minutes before they harness you in.

Southern Adirondack Lakes Region

Canada Lake Store & Marine
N.Y. Rts. 29A and 10, Canada Lake
• 835-6069

Canada Lake is a beautiful and quiet spot for boating. This combination general store (see "Milk and Light Bulbs" in Shopping) and marine supply center can set you up with a pontoon boat in which to enjoy this cottage-lined lake for just $100 a day. Compare that with full-day pontoon boat rentals of $200 or more on Lake George, and you can see why this part of the Adirondacks benefits from its "non-popularity." If you prefer to power your own canoe, you can rent one here for only $7 for two hours or $25 for one whole relaxing day.

Lake Pleasant Marine
N.Y. Rt. 8, Lake Pleasant • 548-7711

Here's another great example of how a location in the central Adirondacks can benefit you, the customer and boat renter, by providing the same kind of fun and scenery as Lake George but for quite a bit less money. In addition to being a full-service marina offering gas, repairs, a boat launch, accessories and groceries, you can also rent a variety of watercraft here. Some examples are: A 17-foot 90-hp speed boat for $100 (half-day) or $150 (full-day); a 20-foot pontoon boat with a 40-hp motor for $90 (half-day), $125 (full-day) and only $225 for three days; and Sea-Doos for $48 per hour. You can also rent a Sunfish sailboat for $25 (half-day) or $50 (full-day).

North Shore Marine
2335 North Shore Rd., Hadley
• 696-2168, (800) 818-BOAT

Toward the north end of the sprawling and busy Great Sacandaga Lake, this full-service marina and boating supplier has a variety of rental boats available. You can choose from a 16-foot ski boat with a 70-hp motor for $100 (three hours) to $180 (five days — a bargain!). Both 20- and 24-foot pontoon boats are also available, starting at $75 for three hours for the smaller boat (the 24-footer is $100) to $150

Photo: Plattsburgh/North Country Chamber of Commerce

Every journey can be a new one for bicyclists exploring Adirondack back roads.

and $200, respectively, for a full day. The Great Sacandaga may not be as glamorous and well-known as Lake George, but it's not far behind in either size or beauty, so it's worth checking out.

Old Forge/
Raquette Lake Region

Rivett's Marine
South Shore Rd., Old Forge
• (315) 369-3123

Conveniently located on the waterfront in Old Forge, at the southwest end of the Fulton Chain of Lakes, Rivett's is a great place from which to start out your explorations. You'll find a full-service marina with gas, a boat launch, repairs and storage as well as a complete marine store with boating supplies and accessories. Rivett's also carries a full line of water skis, wetsuits, knee boards, tubes and clothing.

They rent everything from 10-hp fishing boats at only $40 for a half-day up to a 150-hp ski boat for $176 per half-day. You can also rent a pontoon boat at $99 per half-day or $155 per full-day. Canoe rentals are particu-

larly popular here, since it is the beginning of a very popular canoe route through the Fulton Chain. You'll find reasonable prices beginning at $18 for a half-day, $26 for a full-day and, if you're planning a multi-day excursion, only $91 for five days.

Whitewater Rafting
and River Tubing

The Adirondack region offers some of the finest whitewater rafting in the East, with rapids ranging from Class II to Class V. Before venturing out in a canoe or kayak, however, you should make sure you understand the International Scale of River Difficulty and then judge appropriately what type of journey you can safely enjoy. Let's put it this way — if you don't already know what the class system is, you shouldn't attempt anything more than Class I for now.

•Class I indicates moving water with a few riffles and small waves, but few or no obstructions.

•Class II indicates easy rapids with waves up to 3 feet and wide, clear channels easy to see without advance scouting.

•Class III are rapids with high, irregular

waves that are capable of swamping an open canoe. It also indicates narrow passages that requires complex maneuvering.

• Class IV (are you nervous yet?) indicates long, challenging rapids with very turbulent water demanding precise and aggressive maneuvering. Class IV rapids are not generally possible with an open canoe.

• Class V rapids are extremely difficult, long and very violent with highly congested routes. Significant hazards to life exist.

• Class VI (did you happen to see *The River Wild* with Meryl Streep?) are Class V rapids on steroids and should be left to teams of experts only.

A rafting trip provides a thrill that can't be duplicated in a water theme park — and, best of all, one doesn't have to be an experienced rafter to enjoy it. Many rafting companies not only provide rafts, wetsuits, life jackets, lunches and transportation back to the base, but also guide you down the roaring rapids. Rafting is not a passive sport in which you sit back and enjoy the scenery, but rather an active one where you must paddle (to earn your lunch, perhaps?).

The 17-mile stretch of the Hudson River between Indian Lake and North Creek, which passes through the dramatic Hudson River Gorge, is by far the most famous because of its Class V whitewater and unspoiled scenery. The Hudson's greatest flow rates occur during April and May freshnets, but recent arrangements with the region's power authority — it controls water releases from hydroelectric dams — allow rafters to continue excursions throughout the summer.

The Sacandaga and Schroon rivers in the southeastern Adirondacks provide Class II and Class III rapids. Both rivers provide plenty of thrills and are good rivers on which to perfect the skills needed for the more challenging stretches of the Hudson and Moose rivers. The mighty Moose contains numerous sections of Class V rapids and is considered as one of the more challenging stretches of whitewater in the United States, especially during the spring thaws.

Saranac Lake village has established a short, 500-foot whitewater practice area along the Saranac River in the village, immediately downstream from the Lake Flower Dam. The technical difficulty of the rapids is Class I and Class II. Access to the area is available at the downstream end of the rapids in the municipal parking lot, behind the police station in the center of town. Use of the area is free.

Rafting Outfitters

All the following rafting services provide licensed and experienced guides, all the proper equipment and instruction. All also provide food on full-day excursions, but it's best to get some details about the meals provided; call ahead. Rafting typically is not an activity in which you simply call up and make a next-day reservation. You can try last-minute calls, but it is best to plan in advance for a trip. Generally speaking, the best reservations go to those who call the farthest in advance.

Note: Although rafting services maintain a home office in a particular region, they all travel down the same rivers (and, often, the same sections of river), so we do not divide this section geographically.

Adirondack Rafting Co.
7 Patch Ln., Lake Placid • 523-1635, (800) 510-RAFT

The highly experienced guides of the Adirondack Rafting Co. will take you down the Hudson River for $75 per person, or the Black River in the Watertown area for $59. This company uses self-bailing rafts. As with all other services, there is a reduced rate for groups of six or more.

Adirondack River Outfitters
N.Y. Rt. 9N, Lake Luzerne • 696-5101

ARO (as they refer to themselves) offers a variety of rafting and tubing adventures from spring through the fall at three different locations within the Adirondacks. In the spring, river guides take you on the challenging Class III and IV rapids of the 17-mile Hudson River Gorge south of Indian Lake, and the Class V whitest of water in the Lower Moose River near Old Forge. In the summertime, their attention turns to the fun and lively Sacandaga River near Lake Luzerne for family rafting and tubing adventures. Then in the fall, the Hudson River Gorge (slightly tamer this time of the year) is again the focus of Adirondack operations.

All trips include shuttle service and professional-grade river equipment, including top-notch rafts, paddles, life jackets and helmets. On the spring trips, high-energy snacks and warm beverages are provided, with cold beverages available for the summer and fall trips. Hot meals are served following all Hudson and Moose River excursions. Costs increase from a minimum of $14 to rent a tube for one trip down the Sacandaga River to $75 or more for longer rafting excursions on the Hudson and Moose Rivers.

Adventure Sports Rafting Co. Inc.
Main St., Indian Lake • 648-5812, (800) 441-RAFT

This outfitter provides trips for serious whitewater enthusiasts in the Hudson River Gorge and on the Moose River. Staff schedule river runs daily for the first weekend in April through the third weekend in June, then again on weekends only between Labor Day and Columbus Day. Provisions include transportation, Avon self-bailing rafts, maximum-protection life jackets and helmets for your safety. You will also be served a riverside snack during your trip and a steak cookout at the end of the long day. Each raft is assigned a licensed, experienced and friendly professional guide to ensure your safety (the rivers will ensure the fun!).

The per person costs are $75 for the Hudson River trip and $85 for the Moose River excursion. You'll get a break of five bucks apiece if you bring along a group of 10 or more. You can also rent wetsuits for $15 apiece ($10 for groups of 10). It's an excellent investment, particularly in the spring when the water is so cold you won't believe it's not still frozen.

Beaver Brook Outfitters
N.Y. Rts. 28 and 8, Wevertown • (888) 454-8433

Beaver Brook Outfitters is both an extensive outdoor adventure retail outlet (see our "Fun Stuff" section in Shopping) and a guide service for river trips. They run exclusively on the nearby Hudson River Gorge. Trips are available daily from April through June; Tuesdays, Thursdays and weekends during July and Au-

gust; and weekends only from Labor Day through Columbus Day. Excursions include all the standards — self-bailing raft, wetsuit and booties, helmet, lunch and a hot dinner for $90 per person weekends and $80 per person during the week.

If you're really hooked by the whole experience, Beaver Brook invites you to try a two-day overnight trip that includes "two great days of whitewater and one heckuva relaxing evening," according to staff. Ready to go? Just come up with the $200, and you're there!

Hudson River Rafting Company
1 Main St., North Creek • 251-3215, (800) 888-RAFT

In the rafting business since 1976, this company operates raft trips on the Hudson, Sacandaga, Black, Ausable and Moose rivers. A full-day excursion down the Hudson costs $75 per person, while a two-hour — and much gentler — trip down the Sacandaga cost $15. This company also operates the 15-minute rafting excursions that are part of the Ausable Chasm tour on the Ausable River (see Attractions).

Middle Earth Expeditions
N.Y. Rt. 73, Lake Placid • 523-9572

Middle Earth has been guiding rafting excursions for more than 15 years. A daytrip down the Hudson costs $85 per person, with reduced rates for a group of eight or more. One-, two- and three-day raft trips are also available, with rates for an individual beginning at $475. The guide service will develop a multi-day trip to suit a customer's needs.

Syd & Dusty's Outfitters
U.S. Hwy. 9 and N.Y. Rt. 149, Lake George • 792-0260

This outfitter runs all-day river rafting trips in the springtime on the Hudson River that include breakfast, lunch and dinner upon return to the store at the adjacent — and very good — Log Jam Restaurant (see Restaurants). The price is $125 per person and includes the only available "dry suits" for rafters, which essentially are Gore-tex bodysuits with gaskets at the wrists and ankles to keep you dry and (relatively) warm throughout the day.

Whitewater Challenges
P.O. Box 8, White Haven, PA 18661
• (800) 443-RAFT

Established in 1974, this company operates three rafting excursions in New York: in North River, Watertown and Old Forge. The rates depend upon which river you choose to raft, the time of year and the number of people in the group. Costs range from $32 to $150 per person.

Wild Waters Outdoor Center
N.Y. Rt. 28, near Warrensburg
• 494-4984, (888) 945-3420

WWOC (their self-imposed acronym) has been providing river-rafting adventures on the Hudson River Gorge and Moose River for more than 15 years. They offer spring and fall trips in the Hudson Gorge and on the Moose as well as mellower trips for first-timers, school and church groups on the Middle Hudson River Gorge (a 7-mile stretch out of the 16-mile gorge). In the summertime, the slower and higher waters of the Sacandaga River are available for your enjoyment on one of four trips daily.

All the standard equipment and amenities as provided pretty much across the board are also included in the prices here. Costs range from $15 per person for summer rafting on the Sacandaga River to $45 per person for the Middle Hudson trips to between $80 and $100 per person for springtime Hudson River Gorge and Moose River trips.

In-line and Ski Skating

In-line skating is the modern version of roller skating. But ski skating? Well, it's skiing on roller skis — miniature skis with wheels. Because ski skating uses many of the same muscles as those used in skiing, it is a great way for skiers to stay in shape off-season and practice skiing strokes at the same time.

Now that you know what it is, you might try ski or in-line skating on one of the many backroads in the region. During the summer months, the Olympic Speed Skating Oval on Main Street in Lake Placid is one place to begin practicing either version of skating, as there are no cars to avoid as you learn to master starting and stopping with wheels on your feet.

Access to the oval during summer is free, but you must bring your own skates; no rentals are available here.

Many of the same shops that rent bikes or skis also sell or rent in-line skates (see our Shopping chapter). No shops rent ski skates.

Mountain Biking and Cycling

In 1993, a number of people who long knew the benefits and reputation of bicycling in the Lake Champlain region — an area which encompasses sections of New York, Vermont and Quebec, Canada — decided that a little organization and cooperation would make bicycling in this area even better. Their first project identified a 350-mile route using existing roads and facilities. Naturally, bikers didn't have to travel the entire loop, but rather could pick and choose shorter routes. Well, this group of cooperators, which included staff from the New York State Office of Parks and Recreation, the Vermont Department of Forests, Parks and Recreation, the U.S. Park Service, officials from Quebec, and plenty of other organizations and individuals, had so much fun identifying the initial route, they also identified an additional 1,200 miles.

Today the grand total distance of identified bike routes in the Lake Champlain region alone is 1,550 miles. And that does not include miles of trails in other regions within the Adirondack Park itself.

Within the Park, for instance, the High Peaks section gives cyclists stiffer competition with steep mountain grades. But once you travel beyond the High Peaks into the Southern Adirondack Lakes region of the Park, the lowland areas make for less-strenuous climbs.

A new and very comprehensive resource for mountain bikers is the "Adirondack Park Mountain Bike Preliminary Trail & Route Listing," produced by the Adirondack North Country Association and the Adirondack Mountain Club (ADK). It is the only listing of trails in the Park, covering 98 tours in 11 counties. You can purchase a copy for $14.95 from ADK by calling 668-4447.

For informational brochures on bike trails in Franklin County, including the Malone, Paul

Thrill-seekers will find whitewater rafting on the Hudson River provides all the adventure they could ask for.

Smiths, Tupper Lake and Saranac Lake areas, contact Franklin County Tourism, P.O. Box 6, Malone, N.Y. 12953, 483-6788. In Essex County, including the Lake Placid, Keene, Westport and Schroon Lake areas, contact the Lake Placid/Essex Visitor Bureau, Olympic Center, Main Street, Lake Placid, N.Y. 12946, 523-2445. Ask specifically for the Bike Trail Guides.

We identify only a few basic routes here; there's plenty more to choose from. For more information, we suggest you contact a cycle shop listed in the Shopping chapter.

We offer special thanks to the folks at High Peaks Cyclery and Placid Planet Bicycles, both in Lake Placid, and Viking Ski and Bike Shop, in Plattsburgh, for their suggestions on mountain and road biking trails.

A few final words about road rules and safety before we hit the trails:

If you are riding a bike, in-line skating or using any skating device on any road in New York State, you are required to follow all traffic codes, as if you were driving a car. Always:

• Ride or skate on the right side of the road.

• Stop at all Stop signs and follow appropriate rules for all traffic signals.

• Follow the speed limit.

• BE CAUTIOUS.

Please be aware that no children younger than 1 are permitted on bicycles. All children between ages 1 and 5 must be seated in an approved seat. All children younger than must wear an approved safety helmet when riding a bike or using skating devices on roadways.

Mountain Bike Trail Etiquette

•**Be Courteous.** Mountain bikers share trails in the Adirondacks with many hikers. Leave others with a good impression of mountain bikers to ensure continued harmonious use of the trail.

•**Use Only Designated Trails.** Officially designated Wilderness Areas are off-limits. Use only designated trails, or face the consequences of arrest.

•**Use Control.** Hikers and horseback riders have the right of way. Bikers should yield, but to do this you need to be in control of your bike.

•**Leave No Trace.** Minimize the impact on trails and pack out what you pack in.

Lake Placid/ Tri-Lakes Region

Road Bike Trails

The Tri-Lakes region is mountainous, so if you are not in shape, it is best to chose your routes wisely, or you may find yourself not only sore all over, but also stuck in the middle of nowhere too tired to bike back to your starting point. The following trails are not necessarily the best trails in the region, but rather are among the "flatter" ones. We provide specific directions for these routes for good reason — they let you ride the steeper sections going downhill.

The Ausable/River Road Loop
N.Y. Rt. 86 to River Rd. to N.Y. Rt. 73, Lake Placid

From Lake Placid, head east on N.Y. Route 86 towards Whiteface Mountain. You'll pass the Lake Placid Resort golf course. Then the road will begin a winding, fairly steep grade downhill with just a few shorter uphill sections, so be careful. When the road begins to open up, you will cross a small bridge. Just after the bridge, turn right on River Road (this is actually your first right after the golf course). This is another winding road with many blind curves, so don't surprise a car driver by cycling in the middle of the road. The road follows the Ausable River for about 3 miles. Eventually you will see the ski jumps. Turn right on N.Y. Route 73. About a mile past the Horse Show grounds, you will be back where you began.

Bear Cub Road Route
Bear Cub Rd., off Military Rd., Lake Placid

Bear Cub Road is a winding country road off Old Military Road, near the Olympic Training facility in Lake Placid. The road eventually dead-ends, so you return the same route. This 5-mile round trip is a decent practice ride to see if you and the kids are in shape.

Paul Smiths Loops
N.Y. Rts. 86 and 30, Paul Smiths

The Paul Smiths area is relatively flat compared to Lake Placid — approximately 22 miles to the east — and offers some of the best biking in the Tri-Lakes neighborhood. Paul Smith's College, on N.Y. 30, is a good beginning point for a variety of possible excursions.

Paul Smiths/Lake Clear Loop. Head south along N.Y. 30. At the first intersection (some 6 or 7 miles), turn left. After 4 or 5 miles, you will come to another intersection with a blinking traffic light. (The famed Donnelly's Ice Cream stand, serving the richest soft ice cream available, is on your right.) Turn left onto N.Y. 86 and head west back to Paul Smith's College, some 8 miles away.

Paul Smiths/Rainbow Lake Loop. From the college, head east on N.Y. 86 for about a mile. Turn left onto Rainbow Lake road, the second road on your left; it winds along Rainbow Lake. At the first intersection, about 3 miles down the road, turn right and proceed to your first left. You will eventually arrive at the intersection of N.Y. 86, where you turn right to head back to the College.

Check out a map for other possibilities in this area.

Mountain Bike Trails

Brewster Peninsula Nature Trails
off Saranac Ave., Lake Placid

This is a popular hiking and biking trail; no wonder, as it is almost downtown in Lake Placid. (See Hiking for related information.)

Flume Falls Trails
N.Y. Rt. 86, Wilmington

Just past the Hungry Trout Motor Lodge in Wilmington (see Accommodations) and a mile or so past Whiteface Mountain Ski area, there's a parking area on the left. The old ski trail and roads are good routes for riders of all levels of ability, beginner to advanced. As you travel toward Whiteface Ski area, please note that these trails become part of the Whiteface Mountain Ski trails and are private property. Although mountain biking is allowed on these trails, access requires a fee. The cost for trail access and use of the chairlift is $15 for adults and teens and $10 for kids 12 and younger.

Mount Van Hoevenberg Mountain Bike Center
N.Y. Rt. 73, Lake Placid

The former site of the 1980 Winter Olympic cross-country ski trails is converted into a mountain bike center during the summer months. Bike rentals are available on site. (See Kidstuff for more information.)

Pine Pond Trail
end of Averyville Rd., Lake Placid

The popular 14-mile Pine Pond trail is at the very end of Averyville Road in Lake Placid. Averyville Road is off N.Y. 73, just past the IGA supermarket. The trail begins at the very end of Averyville. (There's no legal parking space at the end, so park at the trailhead to the Northville-Placid trail, about a few miles prior to the end of the road.)

The trail is easy to follow and well traveled by hikers, four-wheelers, horses and bears, so be courteous to others (or you will be fed to the bears).

The trail is easy to intermediate and ends up at a popular swimming hole.

Whiteface Mountain Bike Center
N.Y. Rt. 86, Wilmington

Whiteface Mountain Ski Center is converted into a mountain bike center during the summer. (See Kidstuff for details.)

Bloomingdale Bog
CR 55, off N.Y. Rt. 86, Bloomingdale

The bike trail is easy as it follows an old railroad grade. (See Kidstuff for more information.)

Fish Creek/Rollins Pond State Campgrounds
N.Y. Rt. 30, Saranac Inn

Intermediate and advanced bikers may find the 15 miles of trails at the Fish Creek/Rollins Pond state campgrounds challenging. For those not camping on the site, a nominal day-use fee applies. Information about trail access can be obtained at the campground.

Jackrabbit and Railroad Track Ride
Saranac/Placid Hwy., Saranac Lake

As you drive from Lake Placid to Saranac Lake, you will come to a short, straight stretch of road a few miles past Ray Brook. The forest on the left was devastated by a storm, so it is hard to miss. Just after this stretch, you

---

INSIDERS' TIP

The spring freshnet is the best time to go whitewater rafting in the Adirondacks as the water is high and fast. It was also the best time to drive logs down the rivers to saw and paper mills which dot the region. Although the last log or river drive occurred in 1949, many an old time logger remembers the challenging job of a "rider," men who would ride the fat part of a log down river, poking and prodding logs stuck in the river or on land back into the flow. When the riders had nothing to do, they challenged another rider to a game of burling or trying to run the other rider off his log into the water.

will see a pull-off parking area, which is usually filled during summer with vendors selling produce. The path along the train tracks makes for good biking, with the route behind the parking area a little flatter and easier than the track route across the road. No trains travel this route, so if you discover one along the way, immediately seek medical attention — you likely are dehydrated and thus hallucinating.

Keese Mills-Blue Mountain Road
junction of N.Y. Rts. 30 and 86, Paul Smiths

This trip is 20 miles one way. It is relatively flat and follows a dirt road for much of the journey, making it a great trail to challenge the endurance of a beginner. The trail begins at the junction of N.Y. Routes 30 and 86, at the parking area opposite Paul Smiths College. Keese Mill Road is opposite the lot.

Keese Mill Road begins as a paved road, but eventually gives way to a packed dirt surface. Follow the road as long as you wish, but remember that you have to return the way that you rode.

Meacham Lake State Campground
N.Y. Rt. 30, Paul Smiths

Some 20 miles of good beginner and intermediate trails can be accessed from the Meacham Lake State Campground (see Camping), 8 miles north of Paul Smiths. For those not camping on the site, a day-use fee applies. Additional information about the trail can be obtained at the campground.

Trombley Landing
N.Y. Rt. 3, Tupper Lake

The trailhead is at the junction of N.Y. Routes 3 and 30, east of Tupper Lake. The 3.2-mile round-trip trail begins at the state gate, just south of the junction, and follows an old truck trail, ending at a sandy beach on the Raquette River.

Plattsburgh/Western Lake Champlain Region

Road Bike Trails

Lake Champlain Biking Routes

The Western Lake Champlain region is a road cyclist's paradise. There are plenty of scenic routes along the shores of Lake Champlain, with great view of the Adirondack Mountains to the west and the Green Mountains of Vermont to the east. Simply pick a road — with the exception of the Northway — and begin pedaling. When you find a road that looks interesting, take it. The back roads are safe, quiet and roll easily past apple orchards and small farms and through various historic and quaint villages. Along the way, there's a good supply of services, including classic bed and breakfast inns, campgrounds, restaurants and shops.

If you get bored with the roads in New York, just continue along the shore of Lake Champlain. The Haut Richelieu region of Quebec, Canada, is less than an hour's ride from Plattsburgh, or you can hop aboard the ferry and arrive in Grand Isle or Burlington, Vermont — that is if you don't wish enter Vermont by bridge.

You can bike to historic sites by traveling N.Y. Route 9N from Fort Saint Fredric, built in 1734 at Crown Point, to Fort Ticonderoga. Or travel N.Y. Route 22 through the charming, quaint towns of Westport, Essex and

---

INSIDERS' TIP

In the May 1883 issue of *Forest and Stream* magazine, a writer named Piseco wrote a good guide "selected camping grounds, felled trees and peeled bark for our shanties, fitted up balsam beds, shelves and racks, kept the campfires and smudges going at night and day, prepared and cooked the meals, washed dishes and, nights or early morning, left me sleeping to slip away and return with venison or fish."

Willsboro. This route is easily accessed by city dwellers in New York City and every other city served by Amtrak. Hop aboard one of Amtrak's special trains for bikers and get off in Westport. Daytrippers can have breakfast in Willsboro, lunch in Essex and dinner in Westport.

In the Plattsburgh area, U.S. Highway 9 affords stunning views of the lake and traverses some countryside with farm stands every few miles where you can sample the pick of the day. A few farm stands even offer homemade pies, pastries and calorie-laden candies, which you can burn off by biking to the next stand.

A series of free publications on Lake Champlain bike routes is available by writing or calling Lake Champlain Bikeways, RR 1, Box 220 Bridge Road, Crown Point, N.Y. 12928, 597-4646.

Jay Loops
N.Y. Rt. 9N, Jay and Upper Jay

It's a side of Jay that few tourists ever see. In fact, few locals even see it, but the biking and in-line skating on the relatively flat back roads of Jay is quiet and peaceful.

One loop begins on N.Y. Route 9N at the town park in the center of the village. Travel west along the Ausable River toward Ausable Forks. Three or 4 miles down the road, make a left at the first bridge. Bear right and follow the winding country road to the first bridge on your right, just below the famed Flume waterfalls (see previous section's Flume Falls Trails entry), where you might consider taking a dip.

Another loop in the opposite direction also is possible. Simply reverse directions. At the town of Upper Jay, 3 or 4 miles east of Jay on N.Y. 9N, make the first left and follow that winding country road back toward the Flume.

Mountain Bike Trails

Point au Roche State Park
19 Camp Red Cloud Rd., Plattsburgh • 563-0369

This state park offers an ideal family mountain biking setting. The trails are relatively easy and lead to great views and swimming spots on Lake Champlain. (See Attractions for more about Point au Roche State Park.)

Lake George/ Upper Hudson Region

Warren County Bikeway

This well-maintained and scenic 9-mile paved bikeway is suitable for both road bikes and mountain bikes — and all members of your family. It begins in Queensbury at Country Club Road (just off Quaker Road) and ends with a downhill descent that opens to a beautiful view of Lake George. The trail was opened in 1978 and partially follows former railroad and trolley lines. There are a couple of hills along the way that will get your attention, but the last one rewards you with the beginning of the long downhill ride to the shore of Lake George. To obtain a detailed map of the Warren County Bikeway, call the Warren County Parks and Recreation Department in Warrensburg at 623-2877.

Glens Falls Feeder Canal Trail

This 9-mile hard-packed gravel bikeway offers a flatter, easier ride than the Warren County Bikeway. It follows the route logging companies used to move their logs around Hudson River rapids and falls. There are a few "at grade" road crossings along the route that need to be handled with caution. One of the highlights along the route is The Five Combines, which are five locks lined up one after another, just as they have been since 1845. To receive a map and details on this trail, call the Feeder Canal Alliance in Glens Falls at 792-5363.

Mountain Bike Trails

Garnet Hill Lodge Mountain Biking
13th Lake Rd., North River • 251-2444

This popular cross-country skiing area becomes an excellent mountain biking destination in summer, with more than 30 miles of trails for bikers of all skill levels. Rental bikes are available for $15 per four hours, or $25 for a full day. Bike rentals include trail-use fees and helmets. If you have your own equipment, the trail fee is just $3. There is a great variety of terrain here to explore, from fun and scenic to tough and steep. One nice feature is the option to just bike the "easy way" — that is, downhill. Since Garnet Hill Lodge is at the top of a 2,000-foot mountain, you can bike your way down the trail system, get picked up by the lodge's shuttle 10 miles distant, then return to the top for more fun.

Gore Mountain
Peaceful Valley Rd., off N.Y. Rt. 28, North Creek • 251-2411

Summer 1997 marked the beginning of what is hoped to be a long tradition at this major ski mountain — lift served mountain biking. It's the only place in this part of the Adirondacks where you can ride a chairlift up 1,500 vertical feet and then pick your trail to descend. Trails range from gravel work roads to challenging single-track trails that keep your attention the whole way down. Mountain biking is available daily here from July 4 through Columbus Day and costs $7 per adult or teen and $5 per child 12 or younger.

Southern Adirondack Lakes Region

Blue Mountain Lake, Speculator, Indian Lake Biking Routes

These towns are all great starting points for a variety of both road and mountain bike excursions. The extremely rural nature of Hamilton County minimizes the traffic concern here, even on major highways such as N.Y. 28 and N.Y. 30. To find the right route or mountain bike trail for you in this area, contact the individual chambers of commerce: Hamilton County Tourism, 648-5239; Indian Lake Chamber of Commerce, 648-5112; Speculator-Lake Pleasant-Piseco-Morehouse Chamber of Commerce, 548-4521.

Road Bike Trails

Great Sacandaga Lake Loop

This 45-mile route for road bikes begins northbound on N.Y. Route 30A toward Mayfield at the southeastern end of the lake, and proceeds north on N.Y. Route 30 along the western shore of the lake to Northville. After crossing the bridge into the village of Northville,

follow Main Street north to Water Street, then on to Ridge Road. From there, Fulton County routes 113 and 4 lead to Edinburgh, where you cross the lake via bridge to the eastern shore. The southbound journey follows County Route 7 to County Route 110, leading to Broadalbin. From there, Main Street in Broadalbin leads to N.Y. 30, and you are back at your starting point.

Old Forge/ Raquette Lake Region

Road Bike Trails

South Shore Road

Stretching along the southern shoreline of the Fulton Chain of Lakes from Old Forge to the end of Fourth Lake, this public highway is a good road biking alternative to the more heavily traveled N.Y. 28, which follows the northern shorelines.

Mountain Bike Trails

Old Forge/Town of Webb Mountain Bike Trail System

The Town of Webb (Old Forge is part of it) maintains a trail system for hiking and mountain biking that provides diverse terrain for all levels of mountain biking enthusiasts. There are nine designated trails concentrated in the wilderness areas north of Old Forge and northwest of the Fulton Chain of Lakes, including a trail that leads to the network from the village of Old Forge, and another that originates in nearby Thendara. To obtain a map and guide to the trail system, call the Old Forge Tourist Information Center at (315) 369-6983.

Rock Climbing

If you are afraid of heights, this may not be the recreational activity for you. Then again, it may be exactly what the doctor ordered to help you overcome your fear. Rock climbing (and in winter, ice climbing) in the 'Dacks (a named coined by Canadian climbers for Adirondacks) presents plenty of challenge for novices and seasoned professionals alike. Contrary to popular opinion, the rock climbing here is exceptional, not because the mountains are very old and craggy, but rather because the glacier of thousands of years past and ice from every passing winter have left their marks on the rocks and cliffs. The best rock climbing is in the High Peaks region, where you'll find a climb for every degree of difficulty. All primary suppliers and guides also are in this area.

Lake Placid/ Tri-Lakes Region

Adirondack Mountain Club (ADK)
Adirondack Loj Rd., Lake Placid • 523-3441

ADK offers educational workshops on rock climbing and mountaineering at its lodge near Lake Placid (see our Accommodations chapter). These programs are a good way to learn about the sport without spending a bundle. A two-day workshop costs around $100 for ADK members and $115 for nonmembers. One day is spent climbing at ADK's facilities in Lake Placid, and the second day's climb usually takes place in Keene.

Adirondack Rock and River Guides
Alstead Hill, Keene • 576-2041

This full-service, accredited school offers professional rock- and ice-climbing instruction and guiding year round — and at all levels. Group, family and individual sessions are available. The guide service also operates two lodges, serving as a base for its operations (see Accommodations). A two-day novice course, including instruction in basic climbing techniques followed by an actual climb, costs $160 per person.

Eastern Mountain Sports (EMS)
51 Main St., Lake Placid • 523-2505

EMS stocks a full line of mountaineering equipment and supplies (see our Shopping chapter) and offers various clinics on mountaineering and other mountain sports throughout the year. Call for the schedule of free and fee-based clinics.

High Peaks Cyclery and Mountain Adventures
331 Main St., Lake Placid • 523-3764

High Peaks offers mountaineering equipment (see our Shopping chapter) and provides one of the few rock-climbing walls in the region for practice. A two-hour session costs just $5 per person. The center offers basic instructional programs, including some designed for children.

The Mountaineer
N.Y. Rt. 73, Keene Valley • 576-2281

Mountaineers of every skill level eventually find their way to this store (see our Shopping chapter), which has long catered to mountain climbers via equipment sales. In January 1997, The Mountaineer and Adirondack Rock and River Guides (see previous entry) sponsored the first Adirondack International Mountaineering Festival, a two-day series of clinics on subjects for novice and experienced mountaineers alike. Plans are in the works for a 1998 event. The cost of each clinic is $100 per person. Some clinic sessions were limited to eight or fewer people, enabling all registrants personalized attention.

Swimming

With the thousands of lakes and ponds in the Adirondack region, a public beach is never far away; most villages within the Adirondack Park have one. Beaches also can be found in many state parks, state campgrounds and private campgrounds. Day-use fees (generally a parking fee) in $3 to $5 range may apply.

Generally speaking, facilities at public beaches include nothing more than restrooms, which may double as changing facilities. That's about it. Few, if any, beaches offer concessions of any kind; we mention some that do. An ice cream truck may drive into the parking lot, but don't count on it. Most public or municipal beaches provide lifeguards between 9 AM and 5 PM during July and August. "No Swimming" notices generally are posted and enforced on municipal beaches when lifeguards are not on duty.

There are dozens and dozens of great spots to swim in the Adirondacks, provided you have a wetsuit (just kidding). We're not here to rank beaches, but we want to provide you with at

Come sail away on the windswept waters of Lake Champlain.

least one suggestion for each region that you may want to check out. While these beaches may not be "to die for," they definitely are worth a plastic pail, shovel and some serious digging.

That said, the following are five beaches to "dig" for.

Lake Placid/ Tri-Lakes Region

Lake Placid Municipal Beach
Park St., Lake Placid

This small public beach has everything — fine sand for play, a number of docks for swimming to and diving from, a small rest and changing room and a swimming area designated for little kids. The water often stays cool (refreshing?) throughout the season. The municipal tennis and basketball courts and a small playground are adjacent to the beach. No concessions are available.

Plattsburgh/Western Lake Champlain Region

Cumberland Bay State Park
152 Cumberland Bay Rd., Plattsburgh • 563-5240

This state park and the adjoining City of Plattsburgh Beach provide public access to the longest stretch of beach on Lake Champlain. The beach is a favorite of locals and visitors alike. There are changing rooms, playgrounds, picnic tables and food concessions in addition to the fine sandy beach and clean water of Lake Champlain. And for those who don't want to be in the sun all day, there are even some shady groves.

Lake George/ Upper Hudson Region

Million Dollar Beach
Beach Rd., Lake George • 668-3352

Named for the amount of money it supposedly cost to create by the State of New York, this beach has one of the most beautiful views in the Adirondacks — straight up the length of Lake George and its mountain framing. While it can get very crowded here, it is both long and wide enough to handle even busy July weekends without starting to resemble the Jersey shore. In addition to swimming, there are picnic tables, volleyball nets, a bathhouse and concession stand. Admission cost is $2 to park and another $2 per person.

Southern Adirondack Lakes Region

Pine Lake Park
N.Y. Rts. 10 and 29A, Pine Lake • 835-4930

This is Lake George's Million Dollar Beach in miniature — smaller lake, smaller mountains around the lake, smaller beach and a lot fewer people. However, it is every bit as attractive, and the smaller lake provides an extra bonus — warmer water! No rocks, no weeds — just nice, firm sand all the way out to the "end of the ropes" in the large designated swimming area. There's a small playground, volleyball nets, picnic area (both in a pavilion and open), minigolf, a game room and a concession stand. Parking is free, and admission is $2 per person.

Old Forge/ Raquette Lake Region

Arrowhead Park
N.Y. Rt. 28, Inlet • (315) 357-5501

From your vantage point here on the eastern end of Fourth Lake, you can look across the water and witness some of the best sunsets in the Adirondacks. Plus, this beach gives you the sunbathing advantage of "facing the sun," so you can lie there all afternoon with minimum manipulation to achieve maximum tanning (of course, we advise caution and sunscreen, even with the relatively weak Adirondack sun). The public beach at Arrowhead Park is free, has free parking and a lifeguard on duty. Other amenities in the park include a picnic area, public tennis courts, public restrooms and free public docks if you come by boat. Arrowhead Park is also adjacent to the many interesting little shops of Inlet, which will come in handy if you get a little too much sun or sand.

Summer Camps

The history of summer camps begins in the Adirondacks. Camp Dudley, the first summer camp in the United States, opened in 1885 along the shores of Lake Champlain. Camp Dudley is still around and offers many of the same recreational opportunities as it did more than 100 years ago plus some modern forms of entertainment.

As you might imagine, there are dozens upon dozens of summer camps in the Adirondack region that host children and teens from all over the country (and often beyond) for anywhere from a day at a time to eight weeks at a time. Some are sports-related, some are arts-related, some have a little of both and much more, some are affiliated with religious organizations, and some are non-denominational.

We provide just a sampling here of what's available to you and your family in Adirondack summer camps. For more information, a good resource is the NYS Camp Directors Association in New York City, (212) 928-8060. A search of the World Wide Web will provide a listing of many camps in the region. Adirondack Life magazine is also a source of camp advertisements. Or, request a listing from the Chamber of Commerce when you ask for your vacation planner.

Camp fees vary considerably depending upon services provided and length of time one stays. The base fee for all camps ranges from $600 to $1,000 per week.

Lake Placid/
Tri-Lakes Region

Can/Am Summer Hockey Camps
P.O. Box 160, Williams Bay, Wis. 53191 • (800) 678-0908

She shoots! She scores!

Hockey is no longer a sport just for boys, and there is plenty of evidence of this at the Can/Am (Canadian/American) Camps in Lake Placid. No matter the level of hockey player or position, Can/Am offers week-long sessions for boys and girls, beginning in late June and continuing into August. Camps combine instruction in shooting, scoring and skating, on-ice competition and off-ice training.

Can/Am also offers adult camps and international hockey tournaments throughout the year. The camp uses various facilities throughout Lake Placid. Campers are generally housed in one of the area motels.

Mountain View Soccer Camp
P.O. Box 847, Lake Placid, N.Y. 12946 • 523-4395, (800) 845-9959

This soccer camp does not have the feel of a traditional summer camp. It's . . . well, soccer, some free time and more soccer. If soccer is your thing, though, the long list of world-class coaches will surely improve your skills and approach to the game. The camp offers programs from beginners through advanced students and uses the Coever Method, which focuses upon fundamentals as well as teaching students moves and tactics.

The camp offers five weekly sessions, with four in Lake Placid at the private, residential Northwood School and one at St. Lawrence University in Canton, New York.

Mountain View continues to earn accolades from both camp and sporting organizations as well as from coaches who appreciate the marked improvement in their players. If you're at all interested in attending, don't hesitate to inquire about enrollment; the camp fills early with returning campers and newcomers.

Camp Treetops
North Country School, N.Y. Rt. 73, Lake Placid • 523-9329

Camp Treetops, founded in 1921 and forerunner of North Country School, is the legacy of Helen and Doug Haskell, who purchased the camp in 1928. The camp is run much like the school, emphasizing a tradition of physically and mentally challenging its students in a non-competitive learning environment. This approach is reflected in its program offerings, such as swimming, canoeing, sailing, horseback riding, music, creative arts, camp craft, athletics, nature study and farm work on an operating farm, complete with animals and organic gardens. (The gardens are a beautiful sight!)

Campers plan their own activities — beyond the required swimming and riding classes — including camping excursions into the High Peaks wilderness area, and all participate in a work program for the good of the camp community. Camp Treetops offers two camp communities — a junior division for about 60 children ages 7 through 10, and a senior division for about 90 children ages 11 through 13.

Regis – Apple Jack
N.Y. Rt. 30, Paul Smiths • 327-3117

With a capacity of 300 boys and girls ages 6 to 16, Regis remains the largest camp in the region. Its large enrollment speaks of its popularity. This is one of those classic camps you see in movies, with a pristine location on a lake — in this case, Lower St. Regis — and counselors telling campers stories about their "good old days" as campers.

With its location on the lake, campers can stay wet with a full array of watersports, including swimming, water skiing, canoeing and sailing.

Like many other camps in the region, Regis works with each camper to build individual confidence, skills and sense of individuality, while recognizing the fact that camp is also about the community. A few daily chores are thrown into the day's mix of fun to build a team sense.

Plattsburgh/Western Lake Champlain Region

Camp Chateaugay
Gadway Rd., Merrill • 425-6888

Camp Chateaugay is a co-ed, fully accredited American Camping Association (ACA) camp for children ages 7 through 16. On Lake Chateaugay, not far from the Canadian border, Camp Chateaugay attempts to build lasting relationships with its campers. The camp offers a full slate of traditional activities plus some special ones, such as martial arts and drama, so campers can select many of their weekly activities. Counselors fill out the schedule to ensure a complete experience. The approach gives campers the opportunity to actively explore specific interests while building confidence and skills in a particular area. Chateaugay programs encourage participation on an individual basis as well as in a competition-free group setting.

Camp Dudley
Camp Dudley Rd., Westport • 962-4720

Camp Dudley, established in 1885, is the oldest summer camp in the United States. It offers a complete range of activities for 10- to 15-year-old boys. Its location on Lake Champlain makes water activities a logical focus of daily camp life. Strong arts, crafts and drama programs round out the day.

The camp is affiliated with the YMCA, but operates independently. Its heritage is Christian, and devotions are observed daily; campers, however, come from various denominations.

North Country Camps
Auger Lake, Keeseville • 834-5527

North Country Camps operates separate camps for boys (Lincoln) and girls (Whippoorwill). Both camps occupy 150 acres of forest and meadow and enroll fewer than 80 boys and 70 girls ages 9 and 15 in each camp. As many as 80 percent of eligible campers return each season, which speaks well of the family-like atmosphere and activities.

Like most other camps, this one offers activities that take advantage of its setting in the Adirondack Mountains: boating programs, including sailing and wind surfing on the lake, and outdoor activities including hiking, horseback riding and mountain climbing. This camp also conducts special overnight camping trips, some via bicycle, others by foot.

North Country Camps prefers accepting students for the entire season, so weekly sessions are limited.

Pok-O-MacCready Camp (Girls)
Pok-O-Moonshine Camp (Boys)
100 Mountain Rd., Willsboro • 963-8366

These brother and sister camps, which opened in 1905, have a unique 300-acre location on the site of a living museum, the 1812 Homestead, on rustic, 2.5-mile-long Long Lake. A complete range of watersports is available, including sailing, wind surfing and canoeing. The camp offers strong programs in the arts and sports, especially horse riding. Art programs include ceramics, pottery, writing, drawing, music and weaving. Other camp activities include backpacking, camping, canoeing, science trips, rock climbing, survival programs and other traditional activities. Because of its location on a working farm, campers may tend the animals as well as participate in stable management with the horses. Campers also may return home with some unusual skills discovered on the homestead, such as blacksmithing, splitting shingles and rails, spinning, weaving, soap making and knowing what and how to feed sheep, pigs and oxen.

During the school year the Homestead serves as an environmental education center.

Lake George/ Upper Hudson Region

Camp Baco
Camp Che-Na-Wah
on Lake Balfour, Minerva • 251-2919 (Baco), 251-3129 (Che-Na-Wah)

These two sister camps operate as individual campuses for boys (Baco) and girls (Che-Na-Wah) about a half-mile apart. Both are on private Lake Balfour, and each has its own staff, facilities and programs. Che-Na-Wah was established in 1923, and Baco opened in 1953. Campers can experience the best of both "camping" worlds here, with separate activities and programs to encourage leadership development and self-confidence, along with many opportunities for co-ed socialization as well. Both camps offer such activities as water skiing, canoeing, fishing, softball and horseback riding. There are a couple of differences — Baco has roller hockey for the boys, while Che-Na-Wah offers field hockey for the girls — but for the most part, the programs are similar. Both take campers ages 6 to 16 for eight-week sessions.

Camp Chingachgook on Lake George
Pilot Knob Rd., Kattskill Bay • 656-9642

This is a perfect example of one of those camps that requires the entire first week just to learn how to spell its name! Affiliated with the YMCA and established back in 1913 along the picturesque east side of Lake George, Chingachgook is a co-ed camp. Backpacking, canoeing, biking, sailing and water skiing are all on the physical-activities menu here. Arts, drama and environmental education are available to stimulate the mind as well. Campers range in age from 7 years to adult, and sessions last from one to two weeks.

Camp Echo Lake
Hudson St., Warrensburg • 623-9635

This beautiful camp, situated on a 35-acre spring-fed lake and surrounded by mountains, is within minutes of Interstate 87. Camp Echo Lake was founded in 1946 and has maintained the goal of "building confidence and self-esteem by reinforcing positive human values." The camp has been owned and directed by the same family (the Steins) since its inception, and now has the third generation (Amy Medine Stein, Tony Stein and George Stein) in charge. About 250 children ages 7 to 12 spend eight weeks at Echo Lake's Main Village, and another 200 or so kids ages 13 to 17 camp in Echo Lake's Senior Village (the summer campers' equivalent of a retirement home, we guess). More than 200 staff members are on hand during the summer to guide and assist the children and keep things running smoothly. In fact, the Echo Lake staff is split into two specialty areas: activity specialists, who teach skills in specific sports or crafts; and cabin specialists, who help the children adjust to camp life and enjoy their stay.

Echo Lake also has a 24-hour health center staffed by an on-site physician and a team of five nurses. In addition, the Warrensburg Health Center is only a mile from the camp. While at Echo Lake, campers will enjoy a wide variety of watersports, mountain adventures such as hiking, and creative arts programs.

Camp Walden
Coolidge Hill Rd., Diamond Point • 587-7301

This co-ed summer camp, established in 1935 on Trout Lake is secluded but conveniently within 5 miles of both the excitement of Lake George and the accessibility of the Adirondack Northway (I-87). Camp Walden offers both four- and eight-week sessions for campers ages 7 to 16, and about 220 campers enroll each year. They not only enjoy the usual variety of sports and craft-related activities, but also benefit from the camp's convenient location. Daytrips are planned to such spots as Waterslide World in Lake George, the Saratoga Performing Arts Center in Saratoga Springs, and The Great Escape Amusement park just south of Lake George village. Camp Walden prides itself on a superior watersports program that includes kayaking, water skiing, wind surfing, sailing, swimming and canoeing. One unique feature here is the 75-by-100-foot dock-enclosed lake. There is also an indoor gym with facilities for full-court basketball, seven outdoor tennis courts, even an on-site golf driving range. Music, theater, dance and crafts round out the great diversity of offerings.

Southern Adirondack Lakes Region

4-H Camp Sacandaga
Page St., Speculator • 548-7993

Campers need not be current members of a 4-H club to participate in this co-ed camp for children ages 8 to 19. The camp was established in 1945 and offers one-week sessions that include environmental education, watersports, horseback riding and creative arts.

Deerfoot Lodge
Whitaker Lake, Speculator • 548-5277

This is a non-denominational Christian camp for boys ages 8 to 16. Two-week sessions include wildlife study, overnight camping and canoeing trips, and the usual assortment of watersports and other recreational activities.

Fowler Camp
Sacandaga Lake, Speculator • 548-6524

Another in the cluster of Speculator-area summer camps, this co-ed camp is affiliated with the Reformed Church in America. It was established in 1954 and serves campers ages 9 to 18. Keep in mind that this camp is on the smaller, more northern cousin to the Great Sacandaga Lake. The one-week sessions offer all the basics, including watersports, hiking, nature study, overnight camping and canoeing.

Old Forge/
Raquette Lake Region

Adirondack Woodcraft Camp
Rondaxe Rd., Old Forge • (315) 369-6031

This camp has a great tradition in the Old Forge area — generations of families have enjoyed it since it was established in 1925. Grandfather through grandson have all eaten their meals in the huge 3,000-square-foot dining hall with its trademark massive pine logs supporting the roof and symbolizing the traditional and rustic Adirondack style.

AWC considers "wilderness tripping" to be the cornerstone of its program, and campers have several opportunities during their stay to camp out in the Adirondack wilderness. Outdoor Living Skills is one of the most important and popular programs here. AWC also boasts a strong watersports program and offers four separate waterfronts and 3 miles of shoreline along Lake Kan-ac-to and Lake Ta-jee-na. Campers also get an opportunity to canoe the nearby Moose River. In addition, the arts and crafts programs here go well beyond the typical and include such activities as black and white photography, printing, pottery making, metalworking and woodworking.

Adirondack Woodcraft Camps serves boys and girls ages 6 to 16, broken down into six individual age groups. See the "Cross-country Skiing" section of the Skiing chapter for more information about this destination.

Raquette Lake Camps
Raquette Lake • (315) 354-4544

The Raquette Lake Camps have been around since 1916 and serve both boys and girls ages 6 to 16. The eight-week sessions here offer a wide variety of recreational and educational opportunities, all set along the waters of the Adirondacks' largest natural lake.

The Adirondacks are surrounded by three very sophisticated cities, from small to extra-large, that await your daytrip.

Daytrips

For all the natural wonders you can enjoy visiting the Adirondacks, after awhile you may very well feel the need to sit in a place called a "bistro" instead of a "tavern" and shop at a "boutique" instead of a "general store." Or, if you're "citified" enough, you may simply miss the sight of vehicular traffic. Well, you're in luck, because the Adirondacks are surrounded by three very sophisticated cities, from small to extra-large, that await your daytrip. To the north is Montreal, Quebec, a Canadian city famous for its beauty and European atmosphere. To the east, just across Lake Champlain, is scenic Burlington, Vermont. To the south is the cosmopolitan resort community and horse-racing mecca of Saratoga Springs, New York.

In this chapter, we take you on a quick visit to all three and give you some ideas on how you can enjoy a day's visit. (Hint: There's so much to do in each, you're toughest challenge will be staying for just a day!) All three destinations are an easy trip: Montreal, just an hour or so drive from the northern reaches of the Park; Saratoga Springs, less than a half-hour's drive from Lake George; and Burlington, just a short ferry ride across Lake Champlain. All are chock-full of major attractions, fine restaurants and diverse shopping opportunities. In fact, all three could probably warrant their own Insiders' Guides! Our point is simply that they're great spots to visit, and you should definitely check them out for a day if you have the time.

Happy exploring!

Burlington, Vermont

Without question, Burlington is one of the most scenic and attractive cities in the entire country. In some respects, its setting is like a much smaller version of Seattle. The Adirondacks loom on the western horizon (instead of the Olympics) above the waters of Lake Champlain (vs. Puget Sound), and Mount Mansfield of Vermont's Green Mountains stands sentry to the east, just as Mount Rainier of the Cascades does in Seattle. In fact, the area's promotional slogan is "Vermont's Lake Champlain Region: The West Coast of New England." While everyone seems to know about Seattle now, a lot of folks (and businesses) are just discovering the charms of this upscale, vibrant city of nearly 40,000 people. With *Reader's Digest*, *Money* and *Outside* magazines recently touting Burlington as a desirable place to live, visit and do business, that discovery is bound to continue.

Burlington is extremely easy to get to from the Adirondack region — that is, if you're not afraid of ferry boats. A ferry ride is the most direct means of reaching the eastern shore of Lake Champlain from points west (see the Getting Here, Getting Around chapter for details). Depending on where you start out, you also can reach Burlington by car by driving around the south end of the lake via N.Y. Route 22, or around the north end via U.S. Highway 2 at Rouses Point.

Upon arrival, your first stop should be the Tourism Center at the Lake Champlain Regional Chamber of Commerce, 60 Main Street, (802) 863-3489. The staff will be thrilled that you left the confines of the wide-open Adirondack spaces for a visit and more than happy to suggest dozens of ways and places for you to spend your time and money.

From there, you might as well explore downtown Burlington (since you're surrounded by it). Careful though — there are so many interesting shops and restaurants in this very walkable downtown that it may be all you get to in one day. And that's OK — hey, it's your daytrip! One area you won't want to miss (and probably couldn't if you tried) is Burlington's famous historic Church Street Marketplace, (802) 863-1648, a four-block pedestrian mall featuring more than 150 shops, restaurants and street vendors. You'll find such big-name retailers as Ann Taylor, Laura Ashley, Banana Republic and The Nature Company among the offerings here. There's a variety of locally owned and regionally focused shops to explore as well, including Vermont Pasta, Apple Mountain Vermont Gifts and the Vermont State Craft Center/Frog Hollow on the Marketplace. Church Street Marketplace is the vibrant heart of this lively city, and you're likely to happen upon some festival or special event — or at very least, a guy making balloon animals — while you wander.

Just in case the weather turns nasty as you're wandering the Church Street Marketplace, you can always duck into the Burlington Square Mall, off Church Street, (802) 658-2545. Here you'll find Porteous, one of New England's finest department stores, along with a combination of about 60 other national chain specialty stores such as The Gap, The Limited and American Eagle Outfitters. There's also an enclosed parking garage and food court for your shopping convenience.

If you didn't get enough of Lake Champlain during the ferry ride, you can enjoy a somewhat more luxurious and educational cruising experience aboard the *Spirit of Ethan Allen II*. Several daily sightseeing cruises depart from the Burlington Boathouse, College Street, (802) 862-8300, and travel the shoreline of "America's Sixth Great Lake" for a 1½-hour narrated tour. You can also choose from a variety of brunch, dinner and sunset cruises as well. Cruise fares range from $7.95 for the Scenic Cruise to $24.95 for the Captain's Buffet Dinner Cruise to $34.95 for the Murder Mystery Dinner Cruise. Children ages 3 to 11 can enjoy the Scenic Cruise for $3.95, and it is free for little sailors younger than 3.

While we're on the Ethan Allen theme here,

you can travel back in history by visiting the Ethan Allen Homestead, off Vt. Highway 127, (802) 865-4556, the residence of the famous Revolutionary War hero and furniture store inspiration. You'll learn about native Americans, French colonists and British settlers and their attempts to live and control their destiny here in the Champlain region through exhibits in the modern Orientation Center. In the restored 1787 farmhouse, you can learn about the life of Ethan Allen who, in addition to being a war hero, was also the founder of Vermont. Busy guy. . . . The museum is open daily mid-May to mid-October. Admission will cost you $3.50 if you're an adult, $2.50 if you are a senior citizen or a student age 5 through 17, and if you're younger than 5 — well, you might need someone to read this for you (and admission is free).

FYI

Unless otherwise noted, the area code for all phone numbers listed in this guide is 518.

If you have visited The Adirondack Museum and loved it (and how could you not?), you must include time during your visit here to see the Shelburne Museum, U.S. Highway 7, Shelburne, (802) 985-3346. Seven miles south of Burlington, the Shelburne is described as "New England's Smithsonian" and is recognized as one of the world's great museums of American folk art, artifacts and architecture. When you see all that's here, you might wonder why they don't refer to The Smithsonian as "Washington's Shelburne!" You can explore 37 exhibit buildings (just writing that makes us want to find a bench!) featuring more than 80,000 artifacts spread out on 45 scenic acres near the shores of Lake Champlain. Included are three galleries of American paintings and decorative arts, seven furnished historic homes ranging from a rural cabin to a lighthouse, and an entire restored "community" with a one-room school, general store, meeting house and covered bridge (yes, you're in New England now). Cer-

INSIDERS' TIP

Resist the temptation to pull the old *If This is Belgium, It Must Be Tuesday* routine of squeezing too many good times into one day. Minimize your stress and maximize your fun and relaxation (isn't that why you're visiting?) by picking out a couple of things you really want to see, then leisurely visit them.

Just a short drive north of the Adirondacks, Old Montreal
offers a genuine European cultural experience.

tainly one of the most recognizable and impossible-to-miss features here is the original steamboat *Ticonderoga*, a National Historic Landmark that sits in its entirety on the museum grounds like a newly discovered Noah's Ark.

As you might expect with an attraction of this magnitude, the Shelburne Museum has a full slate of amenities and services including a cafe, snack bar, free transportation shuttle around grounds and wheelchair and stroller rentals. As you also might expect, the admission charge here is sizable: $17.50 for folks 15 and older, $7 for students ages 6 to 14 and senior citizens and free for children 5 and younger. One nice feature is that your paid admission gets you into the museum on a second consecutive day for free. Of course, then you've just stretched your "daytrip" into a "getaway," so that's a decision you'll have to make. In any event, the Shelburne Museum is well worth the time and money to visit. Just don't leave it for a quick stop at 4 PM before catching a late-afternoon ferry back to New York.

The Shelburne Museum is open daily from late May until late October, with a tour of selected building available at 1 PM daily during the rest of the year.

From the historical to the whimsical, another fun stop worth considering is The Vermont Teddy Bear Company, U.S. Highway 7, Shelburne, (802) 985-3001. If you have kids, this could be your "bargaining chip" stop, as in "If you kids go with us to the Shelburne Museum, we'll take you to the Vermont Teddy Bear Company." Actually, you'll all have fun here. Who doesn't love teddy bears? Here, you can take a tour and watch how they "bring teddy bears to life," then visit the Bear Shop filled with (you guessed it) hundreds of irresistible teddy bears. You can even create your own teddy bear in the "Make a Friend For Life" workshop. Visit and take a tour any day for only $1 if you're an adult and for free if you're younger than 17. You can try to convince the folks here that you'll always be a kid at heart and see if you can skate on the tour charge.

Speaking of fun companies to visit with fun products to watch being made and take home for yourself, how do we get out of this chapter alive without mentioning the Ben & Jerry's Ice Cream Factory Tours, Vt. Highway 100, Waterbury, (802) 244-5641. This is about a half-hour's drive from Burlington, but it's relatively risk-free on the "Is It Worth It?" scale. What it isn't is fat-free.

Ben & Jerry's is famous for its super-premium chock-full-of-ingredients ice cream recipes, and here you get to see the magical place where all this yummy stuff is made. You'll start your visit with an eight-minute "mooovie" (their dairy-inspired spelling, not ours!) called *The Ben & Jerry Story*. Then you'll be herded (sorry) to the mezzanine overlooking the Production Room to see how they make this stuff, and finally (what you really came here for) visit the Flavor Room for some free ice cream samples. Tours are available daily year round, although there is no ice cream production on Sundays, holidays and "company celebration" days. The tour is free for children 12 and younger and only $1.50 (less than the cost of a small ice cream cone) for adults and teens.

www.insiders.com

See this and many other **Insiders' Guide®** destinations online — in their entirety.

Visit us today!

Make sure to save some room in your tummy for Burlington's restaurants. There are dozens and dozens to choose from, and we suggest you browse the listings in the Lake Champlain Regional Chamber of Commerce's *Area Guide* for details and descriptions. One of our favorite moves is to wander about downtown and read some menus, adding a sense of discovery to the dining process. Of course, don't get too hungry before you start out your culinary quest.

If you are downtown, you may want to visit one of the following for anything from a quick drink and bite to eat to a leisurely dinner. For New Orleans-style Cajun and grilled cuisine (not to mention a "killer" Caesar salad), try the Bourbon Street Grill, 213 College Street, (802) 865-2800.

Carbur's Restaurant & Lounge, 115 St. Paul Street, (802) 862-4106, is a downtown landmark known for its eclectic "Vermontabilia" decor and 16-page menu. You can choose from more than 100 "Grandwiches" plus one

of the most extensive beer lists in Burlington. Sounds like the perfect lunch spot to us!

The Daily Planet may not be a real newspaper, but it is a real restaurant at 15 Center Street, (802) 862-9647. It's known for its use of regional products and its interesting, innovative menu.

Nowadays, you've got to have a brewpub in town, and Burlington's offering is the Vermont Pub & Brewery, 144 College Street, (802) 865-0500. In addition to the expected varieties of ales, lagers and stouts, it also serves its own root beer, so bring the kids.

It's tough to be in such a beautiful lakeside setting and not want to eat at the waterfront. Fortunately, you have lots of attractive options to choose from here, including the Dockside, 209 Battery Street, (802) 864-5266, with its fresh seafood and "off-menu" chef's specials; Isabel's on the Waterfront, 112 Lake Street, (802) 865-2522, featuring outdoor dining and daily pasta specials; Shanty on the Shore, 181 Battery Street, (802) 864-0238, one of Burlington's most popular seafood restaurants and the only raw bar in town; and Whitecaps at the Boathouse, at the foot of College Street, (802) 862-1240, with some of the best lake views and burgers in Burlington.

If you don't mind hopping in the car for a short drive, you'll find a variety of terrific restaurants within just a few minutes and miles.

South Burlington has a cluster of good spots: Perry's Fish House, U.S. Highway 7, (802) 862-1300, for a big selection of steak and seafood in a big setting; the Sirloin Saloon, U.S. Highway 7, (802) 985-2200, voted "Overall Favorite Restaurant" in a local newspaper poll for its hand-cut steaks, fresh seafood, wood-grilled entrees and lively atmo-

INSIDERS' TIP

One good way to keep everybody in the family happy on a daytrip to Saratoga Springs, New York, is drop off the kids at the new Children's Museum for an hour or two, then check out the many shops, boutiques, festival-style markets and cafes in the surrounding area known as "The Gut." You can explore for two hours and stay within two blocks of the kids at all times!

sphere; and The Windjammer Restaurant, 1076 Williston Road, (802) 862-6585, popular for its prime rib and 40-item salad bar.

As you can probably tell by now, probably the toughest thing about a daytrip to Burlington is limiting it to one day. Oh well, there's another ferry tomorrow, so you can always come back again if you need another "Vermont fix."

Saratoga Springs, New York

Saratoga Springs is a small yet surprisingly cosmopolitan resort city of about 26,000 that has lured visitors for three centuries.

People have been daytripping here ever since the Iroquois brought British Indian agent Sir William Johnson here in 1771 for a couple of drinks. Well, let's rephrase that. He was brought here to sample the mineral waters at what would later be called High Rock Spring. The Indians believed the "healing waters" of this area would help Johnson ease the pain of an old wound. Sir Johnson must have felt better, because he told buddies Gen. Philip Schuyler and Gen. George Washington, who soon made visits of their own. Saratoga was off and running! (Actually, that came later with horse racing. Hey, we'll get to all of it here, so don't worry.)

The fact is, Saratoga Springs has grown and evolved over the course of three centuries — from a place people visited for its mineral waters, to a world-class thoroughbred-racing center, to a performing-arts mecca and, nowadays, a combination of all three (not to mention hoppin' nightlife, restaurant and shopping scenes).

Saratoga Springs, or just "Saratoga" as locals lazily abbreviate it, is an easy daytrip from just about anywhere in the southern, central or southeastern Adirondacks. It's location directly off exits 13 through 15 of Interstate 87 (The Northway) brings it within a half-hour's drive of Lake George and only two hours from Lake Placid. Saratoga Springs is also less than an hour's drive via N.Y. Route 29 from the Great Sacandaga Lake area.

As you make your way into town southbound on U.S. Highway 9 from I-87, you'll find yourself suddenly surrounded by beautifully restored three- and four-story Victorian-era buildings that signal your arrival on Broadway, Saratoga's "Main Street." At first it may look like just another main drag in Small Town, U.S.A., until you notice the colorful awnings, trendy shops, outdoor cafes and sidewalks filled with strolling visitors. Granted, you may not notice all those things on a Tuesday in February, but most any day from April until October, it's a typical scene.

Like Burlington, Vermont, you can either make a whole daytrip to Saratoga Springs by parking once and walking around town, or by driving from spot to spot throughout the compact area. In any event, just about anything you would or could enjoy in a day is within a 3-mile radius of downtown.

Your best bet (there's that racing lingo again) is to drive through downtown (about six blocks) and make your first stop at the Saratoga Springs Urban Cultural Park Visitors Center, 297 Broadway, 587-3241. The visitors center is open daily 9 AM until 4 PM and offers educational exhibits about Saratoga's rich history, walking tours of the city and a variety of visitor brochures and maps provided by the Saratoga County Chamber of Commerce. It's location at the south end of downtown makes it a good place to begin your exploration of the shops, galleries and restaurants of Broadway and the adjacent "Gut" area just a block off Broadway.

Just across Broadway from the visitors center is historic Congress Park. This beautiful and intimate park (you can see the whole length of it from Broadway) is a great spot to stroll, find a bench and check out all the stuff you picked up at the visitors center. While in the park, you may to get a refreshing drink from Congress Spring, one of more than a dozen active springs around town. "Refreshing" may not be the way you'd describe the spring water to a friend, as some seem to emphasize "mineral" over "water." Hey, it's supposed to be good for you, so you can't expect it to taste good too, right?

Also in Congress Park, smack in the middle and holding court over the whole place, is the historic Canfield Casino. Once an actual gambling casino at the turn of the last century, the Canfield Casino now hosts many a gala reception and wedding in its grand ballroom.

Upstairs you'll find the Historical Society of Saratoga Springs, 584-6920, worth a quick visit if you're more interested in Saratoga's history than its shops.

From Congress Park, you can stroll up the length of Broadway and browse among the dozens of shops. You'll find funky little boutiques, upscale clothing stores and more than 20 restaurants, cafes, bars and coffeehouses along the way. Saratoga Springs prides itself on its vibrant downtown retail and restaurant community. One of the simple pleasures of visiting here is wandering around, discovering and exploring these little emporiums of all things discretionary. You may not be able to buy a crescent wrench downtown, but you're sure to find the perfect little hand-crafted walnut-and-cherry–inlay box to put one in.

While the retail offerings here are too numerous and diverse to cover, a few of the stand-out shops include: Impressions of Saratoga, 368 Broadway, 587-0666, an upscale gift, souvenir and clothing store specializing in Saratoga-related items; Crafters Gallery Fine Arts & Fine Crafts, 429 Broadway, 583-2435, a collection of displays from local and regional artisans and craftspeople; Nostalgia, 436 Broadway, 584-4665, featuring distinctive gifts and accessories for the home; and Designers Studio, 492 Broadway, 584-

1977, for fine-quality woodwork gift items. In addition, there are many quality clothing boutiques and shops to visit along both sides of Broadway. Rather than name a few at random, we'll simply say it's worth an "up and back" to see for yourself all that's available and browse at will.

If all this strolling and shopping makes you hungry, you're in luck, as about every third door along this street seems to open to a restaurant or cafe. Just about all of the restaurants in downtown Saratoga Springs now feature some form of outdoor dining from April until October, ranging from a couple of plastic tables out front to large wooden decks adorned with flower boxes. Some of those we have enjoyed and recommend are: Scallions, 404 Broadway, 584-0192, for gourmet lunches featuring healthy fare balanced by the world's most dangerous (and delicious) carrot cake, all set in a bright and airy atmosphere; Lillian's, 408 Broadway, 587-7766, for fresh fish and terrific steaks; The Wheat Fields, 440 Broadway, 587-0534, featuring an eclectic and innovative variety of dishes made with the fresh homemade pasta you see the kitchen staff working on in the window; and Professor Moriarty's, 430 Broadway, 587-5981, with its Sherlock Holmes theme, friendly tavern at-

Photo: Carolyn Bates

The Church Street Marketplace in Burlington, Vermont, shines with storybook quality at Christmastime.

mosphere and consistently good food, from sandwiches to steak and seafood.

Now if you've mastered Broadway and are feeling just a little adventurous, go for the gut — the neighborhood called "The Gut," that is. Just one block east of Broadway and down a little hill along such streets as Caroline, Phila and Spring, is a fun and funky section of town. The 1995 opening of the Putnam Street Market, 63 Putnam Street, 587-3663, once a beer warehouse and now a festival market and gourmet grocery, reflects the transformation of this neighborhood from a paunchy warehouse district to Saratoga's sleek "where-to-go" district.

Where pallets once stood stacked with cases of beer, you now will find everything from oven-fresh farm bread from the nearby Rock Hill Bakery to Lake Champlain Chocolates to other regionally made sauces, syrups and jams.

After visiting the Putnam Street Marketplace, spend some more time fighting off temptation at Palmetto's Market, 42 Phila Street, 581-0168, which is less glitzy than Putnam Street Marketplace and more like an old-fashioned farmers' market (albeit with some upscale touches). After an overstuffed deli sandwich, specialty coffee and still warm baked goodie, stroll next door to Chapter XIV, 44 Phila Street, 580-1516. A self-proclaimed bookstore and boutique, it's quaint and efficient layout is like shopping in Martha Stewart's den (we mean that in a nice way). Another interesting shopping stop in The Gut is the Lyrical Ballad Bookstore, 7 Phila Street, 583-8779, featuring a maze of books and crannies — the former in both new and "pre-read" varieties.

If you're toting kids along, you may want to turn them loose in the new Children's Museum of Saratoga, 36 Phila Street, 584-5540. It was created in 1995 from a (surprise!) old fruit and vegetable warehouse, and it's a fun and educational interactive museum for children ages 2 to 12. The Children's Museum is open year round, and admission costs $3. One particularly nice feature of The Children's Museum for both kids and parents is its location right next door to Ben & Jerry's Ice Cream, on the corner of Phila and Putnam streets, 584-3740. Open year round, this was one of the first franchises in the company's history.

"The Gut" has lots of non-ice cream–related dining options as well, and because it is so compact and walkable, you may want to just wander about Phila Street and Caroline Street and do a little menu R&D. One Caroline Street Jazz & Blues Bistro, 1 Caroline Street, 587-2026, is a popular new spot that features both hot and spicy Cajun dishes along with cool blues and jazz several nights a week. Sperry's, 30½ Caroline Street, 584-9618, is known for its soft-shell crab and eclectic cooking, and was a popular "kick back and relax" spot for Robert Redford during the spring 1997 shooting of his *The Horse Whisperer*, filmed in the Saratoga area.

Gaffney's, 16 Caroline Street, 587-7359, offers casual dining and the city's biggest and most popular outdoor patio. The Original Saratoga Springs Brew Pub, 14 Phila Street, 580-2739, is this town's entry in the "every town's got to have one" craze of homemade beer emporiums, and good, casual pub food supplements its ales and lagers. If real southern cookin' is what you're after (a tough find in upstate New York), Hattie's, 45 Phila Street, 584-4790, is a must. For decades, locals and adventurous tourists have flocked here for southern fried chicken, catfish and homemade fruit cobbler.

Assuming that at some point you will tire of shopping, there are plenty of attractions in Saratoga Springs that, this visit or next, you should check out. First on the list is the beautiful and sprawling Saratoga Spa State Park, set on 2,000 acres just a couple miles south of downtown on U.S. Highway 9. Within the park, you'll find the magnificent Saratoga Performing Arts Center, 584-9330, a 5,100-seat indoor/outdoor amphitheater that serves as the summer home of the New York City Ballet, Philadelphia Orchestra and Newport-Saratoga Jazz Festival, along with hosting a couple dozen rock and pop concerts. Also within the park are miles of walking trails; picnic grounds; an 18-hole championship golf course and nine-hole "executive" course; and two mineral bathhouses, the Roosevelt and the Lincoln. The Lincoln Baths are open daily in July and August for your complete, therapeutic massage and mineral bath pleasure, and the Roosevelt Bathhouse is open year round and just underwent a major renovation.

Just outside the entrance to the Spa State

Park, in the former Washington Bathhouse, is the National Museum of Dance, 99 S. Broadway, 584-2225. It is the only museum in America completely devoted to dance, and it features photos, costumes and memorabilia during its operating season of Memorial Day through early December. Adults can visit for $3.50 admission, students older than 12 can enjoy the museum for $2.50, and aspiring ballerinas 12 and younger can learn about their heroes for only $1.

No daytrip to Saratoga Springs is complete without a visit to the National Museum of Racing & Thoroughbred Hall of Fame, 191 Union Avenue, 584-0400. Featuring interactive displays, art, silks and other memorabilia from the "sport of kings," this world-class museum is interesting to even the most casual horse lover. You may visit year round and enjoy the museum for just $3 admission for adults, $2 for students and free for children younger than 5.

Of course, it's even more fun to see the races in action, and Saratoga has two different tracks for two different types of horse racing.

The Saratoga Equine Sports Center, off Crescent Avenue, 584-2110, is locally known as the "harness track." It features live harness racing several nights each week from April until November, along with afternoon simulcasts of other racing action from around the country. Call ahead for the specific racing schedule.

The reason 23,000 people a day come to visit this community in late July and August is the historic Saratoga Race Course, 584-6200. On Union Avenue just off I-87 Exit 14, this is one of the most beautiful and elegant race courses in all of horse racing. Built in 1865, it is also the oldest, and a trip here is like a trip back in time a slower and more refined era. In fact, many people visit the "flat track" (as it's

known locally) as much to people-watch and soak in the festive atmosphere as to bet on the ponies.

And if you like horse racing, you'll find none better than right here in Saratoga during the six-week meet. General admission is only $2 for adults and teens and free for children 12 and younger, but good luck getting out of here for less than $50. Besides the betting, there are discretionary-dollar temptations everywhere you look, from upscale dining to snacks, racing programs to T-shirts. A fun and relaxing tradition is "breakfast at the track," where you can watch the horses train in the early morning (as in 7-ish) as you either munch on your own bagels at the rail, or enjoy a full-service breakfast in the clubhouse.

One last bit of Saratoga lore with which to leave you: It was here, at Moon's Lake House in 1853, that the potato chip reputedly was invented. Ever since, people have been finding it impossible to eat "just one."

Experience the magic of Saratoga Springs, and you will find it impossible to visit "just once."

Montreal, Quebec

Montreal is one of the world's great cities. Although it is the second-largest French-speaking city in the world, being the cosmopolitan city that it is, English also is prevalent, reflecting the British influence that has colored Montreal's history. The city is only an hour's drive from Plattsburgh and less than two hours from the Tri-Lakes region of the Adirondacks, making it a popular daytrip for residents and visitors here, alike.

Americans traveling to Montreal do not need passports, but all visitors should carry proper identification.

Interstate 87 is the most direct route to Montreal, and just a few miles past the border

INSIDERS' TIP

When heading off to visit Burlington, Vermont, consider tossing a windbreaker in your tote. The ferry ride is windy, and once there, it still can be pretty breezy and cool, even in midsummer. Burlington's northern clime and location on the eastern shore of Lake Champlain (the wind has about 12 miles of open water to gather momentum) contributes to the cause.

The Burlington Boathouse is symbolic of the city's
efforts to open its waterfront to the public.

at Champlain, New York, you'll find a large tourist information center, which has brochures for every possible exploration. The facility also includes a bank where you can exchange currency. If you wish to exchange some currency before entering Canada, an exchange is available at Champlain Center North, N.Y. Route 3, off I-87 Exit 37, Plattsburgh (see Shopping). Otherwise, if you have a major credit card, you can simply charge everything, and your credit card company will handle the exchange and bill your account at the prevailing exchange rate.

Montreal offers hospitality with a definite French flavor. Monuments, museums and world-class sports arenas hosting national and international events dot the city. Its streets, theaters and other centers for the performing arts are alive with an endless stream of festivals and artistic events attracting the world's best.

Of course, with so many possibilities in this city, we can offer only a glimpse at what you can see and do in an exhausting day.

If it's food you're after, Montreal is the gastronomic capital of Canada and can hold its own against any city for its culinary delights. Sidewalk cafes, quaint bistros, chic dining rooms and restaurants — there are some 4,000 of them — offer a smorgasbord of the most tantalizing local and ethnic specialties in a range of prices to suit virtually every budget.

Among the most popular culinary neighborhoods is Chinatown, just minutes away from Old Montreal. Chinatown comprises only a few blocks, so you can explore it and Old Montreal as an easy daytrip. De La Gauchetière is Chinatown's main street. It is also a pedestrian walkway between Saint-Laurent and Jeanne-Mance and is generally filled with people and vendors. On weekends the area buzzes with visitors searching for a perfect meal in one the many excellent restaurants, or shopping for items found only in Chinatown.

Pavillon Nanpic, 75A de La Gauchetière Street W., (514) 395-8106, is among the many fine restaurants in the area and one of the oldest restaurants in the neighborhood. It specializes in Szechuan and Cantonese food.

Montreal is the Smoked Meat Capital of the World — a tradition dating back to the 1600s. For a taste of some of Montreal's best, the Restaurant Briskets Beaver Hall, 1073 Côte du Beaver Hall, (514) 878-3641, serves (surprise!) award-winning briskets.

Naturally, a number of restaurants specialize in French cuisine, but the Beaver Club (The Queen Elizabeth), 900 René-Lévesque Boulevard W., (514) 861-3511, is one of only two restaurants in all of Canada that has earned the highest critical acclaim. The Beaver Club serves continental and regional cuisine in an elegant setting.

Chez Frédéric, 1175-A Crescent Street, (514) 395-8730, and Chez la Mère Michel, 1209 Guy Street, (514) 932-1630, continue to receive plenty of rave reviews by local and international publications. Both serve authentic French cuisine in a cozy and romantic setting.

At this writing, the exchange rate is favorable for American tourists, making shopping in Montreal even more exciting. Numerous bargains and distinctly Canadian fashions await your discovery. Montreal is a shopping mecca, so much so that the above-ground shopping is only the tip of the iceberg. There's a 29-kilometer network of boutiques, restaurants and theaters underground. In winter, this underground city makes it possible to live, work, play and shop in Montreal without ever setting foot outside! Just hop on the famed Metro and travel from shopping center to shopping center.

The city's main shopping artery runs along Sainte-Catherine Street. Eaton, 677 Sainte-Catherine Street W., (514) 284-8844, one of the city's more chic department stores, offers top fashions as well as plenty of souvenirs. Ogilvy, 1307 Sainte-Catherine Street W., (514) 842-7711, houses several of the city's most elegant boutiques. The complex is hard to miss — the founder's Scottish origins are celebrated daily by a bagpiper. Another shopping tradition is The Bay, 585 Sainte-Catherine Street W., (514) 281-4614, which has a retail history dating back to 1670. A number of new and highly fashionable boutique complexes, such as Cours Mont-Royal, Place Montreal Trust and Les Promenades de la Cathédrale also can be found in the area.

Visiting shoppers should note the hefty tax — some 15 percent — on all retail purchases. While sticker shock is a definite possibility, tourists can save receipts and file for a rebate with Customs at the international border. Filing is relatively easy and takes only a few minutes. You also can obtain a rebate by mail; information about this method is available at Customs.

When it comes to the performing arts, the city again has something for everyone. It is home to such world-renowned groups as the Montreal Symphony Orchestra, the Grands Ballets Canadiens and the Cirque du Soleil, not to mention I Musici, the Orchestre Métropolitain and the Opéra de Montreal. In fact, Montreal boasts more than 100 theater troupes, 50 dance companies and more than 150 concert venues.

The Montreal Symphony Orchestra, 260 de Maisonneuve Boulevard W., (514) 842-3402, is one of the world's most prestigious orchestras. It performs approximately 130 concerts each year, including the popular summer Festival Mozart Plus, which takes place in Notre-Dame Basilica, the majestic masterpiece of neo-Gothic architecture in the heart of Old Montreal.

L'Opéra de Montreal, 260 de Maisonneuve Boulevard W., (514) 985-2222, is considered one of the eight most important opera companies in North America. It presents both tradi-

INSIDERS' TIP

Drivers hesitant to take on Montreal's downtown traffic can park in the large lot at the Longueuil Metro Station and ride the clean, safe subway system throughout the city.

tional and lesser-known works — six each season. Recent performances include *Suor Angelica* (Puccini)/*I Pagliacci* (Leoncavallo), *Rigoletto* (Verdi) and *Turandot* (Puccini).

While Montreal is a bilingual city, the majority of the theater companies perform in French only. The Centaur Theater Company, 453 Saint-François-Xavier Street, (514) 288-1229, is an exception and remains Quebec's premier English-language theater. Centaur presents a seven-play lineup each year ranging from contemporary Canadian dramas to Broadway hits, all performed by international talent.

The new Molson Centre, 1250 de La Gauchetière Street W., (514) 932-CLUB, is the home of the National Hockey League's Montreal Canadiens, 24-time winners of the Stanley Cup and the main venue for rock concerts, classical music performances and family entertainment. The hockey season runs from October through April, and seats generally are available on relatively short notice. Canadiens tickets range from $15 to $112.

Museums are also very much a part of the Montreal landscape. The Montreal Museum of Fine Arts, 1379-1380 Sherbrooke Street W., (514) 285-2000, offers various exhibits of paintings, sculptures, drawings, photographs and decorative *objets d'art*. Summer 1997 exhibits featured the work of famed French photographer Henri Cartier-Bresson as well as 120 European artists who fled that continent before the rise of Hitler. The museum is open Tuesday through Sunday from 11 AM to 6 PM.

Adjacent to the Museum of Fine Arts is Musée d'Art Contemporain (Museum of Contemporary Art), 185 Sainte-Catherine Street W., (514) 847-6212. This museum is the only gallery in Canada devoted solely to contemporary art.

The Canadian Centre for Architecture, 1920 Baile Street, (514) 939-7026, is a world-renowned museum and study center devoted to international architecture. The museum is in the Shaughnessy House, a greystone mansion dating back to 1874. A summer 1997 exhibit explored the creation of Disney's theme parks via more than 300 objects from the Walt Disney Imagineering archives, including plans, drawings, posters, advertisements and historical photographs.

The McCord Museum of Canadian History, 690 Sherbrooke Street W., (514) 398-7100, serves as a way for both U.S. and Canadian citizens to discover Canada's history, including such essential facts as when and where the first hockey game on record took place. The museum is open Tuesday through Friday from 10 AM to 6 PM, and Saturday and Sunday until 5 PM. Admission is free on Saturday until noon.

While Atlantic City and Las Vegas attract the majority of gamblers in the United States, Montreal deals its cards and rolls its dice in the former French Pavilion and Quebec Pavilion from Expo '67, which now serve as home to the Montreal Casino, one of the 10 largest casinos in the world. Casino de Montreal, Notre-Dame Island, (514) 392-2746, offers 112 gaming tables, more than 2,700 slot machines, complete restaurant services and a brand-new theater. Guests must be 18 or older, and a dress code applies. The casino is open 9 AM to 5 AM daily.

So, in this city with so much going for it, what do we do when we visit Montreal? That's simple. When we travel with the kids, we wing it. When we travel alone, we consider one of the many entertainment options and plan ahead — to a degree.

The old section of Montreal, along its waterfront, bustles with activity, making it a great place to explore. There are hundreds of shops and restaurants for every taste, along with street musicians, magicians and other performers. During the summer, the piers in Old Montreal are a jumping-off point for a variety

Photo: Carolyn Bates

The Church Street Marketplace is the heart of downtown Burlington, Vermont.

of short (one-hour to one-day) cruises and river tours, exploring old sailing boats and more. If you feel like losing yourself (literally) in Old Montreal, try finding your way through a 2-kilometer maze of corridors filled with jokes and pranks, fog and dead-ends; call (514) 496-7678 for details. If being lost in a maze is not enough for you, try navigating the Internet for $5 per half-hour at Café Electronique, 405 Saint-Sulpice Street at the corner of Saint-Paul Street W., (514) 849-1612. After wandering about for a time in cyberspace, let a street artists illustrate a special portrait of you. Kids and adults alike can be entertained all day in Old Montreal.

The Montreal Tower supporting the roof over the Olympic Stadium dominates the city's skyline. The Olympic Stadium is home to Major League Baseball's Montreal Expos. An Expos game (the season runs April through September) is one of the best bargains in professional sports; general admission ($5) is generally less than the cost of parking your car ($7). The Expos have been among the most consistent winners in baseball for the past few years. If you don't want to wait in long lines, get reserved tickets; call (514) 790-1245, (800) 678-5440 (in the United States) or (800) 361-4595 (in Canada).

At the heart of the Olympic Park, the world's tallest inclined tower is next door to the Biodôme, 4777 Pierre-De Coubertin Avenue, (514) 868-3000, a unique environmental museum recreating the four ecosystems of the Americas: a tropical forest, the Laurentian forest, the Saint-Lawrence marine environment and the polar world. The climate-controlled environments, complete with vegetation and wildlife, are open 9 AM to 5 PM daily.

Directly opposite the Biodôme is Montreal's Botanical Garden, the second largest of its kind in the world after London's Kew Gardens. Open daily year round, from 9 AM to 5 PM, the Botanical Garden features 10 exhibition greenhouses, more than 30 outdoor gardens and extensive Chinese and Japanese gardens. The Insectarium, with one of the largest collections of insects in the world, also is on site; kids seem particularly fascinated by this attraction.

A special package deal includes a day visit to the Biodôme, the Botanical Gardens and the Insectarium. Although you could spend an entire day at each site, visiting all three in a day is a viable option — and not as hectic as you might think.

Montreal serves up an exciting nightlife, with live entertainment for every taste — from comedy clubs and piano bars to rhythm 'n' blues clubs, jazz bars and salsa and lambada clubs. The Divine Comedia, 1037 de Bleury

Street, (514) 392-9268, offers a dramatic meal — servers sing, joke, dance and do whatever for a laugh. If the combination of frivolity and food is not your thing, consider a frighteningly good La Maison Hantée (The Haunted House), 1037 Bleury Street, (514) 392-9268. If frivolity and fright aren't your style, try a taste of the blues at Medley, 1170 Saint-Denis Street, (514) 842-6557, a short walk from Old Montreal.

The bars and clubs usually come alive around 10 PM — and pulsate until closing time (3 AM). Bars, nightclubs and discotheques abound from Bishop to Peel streets near Sainte-Catherine, with the trendiest nightspots dotting Saint-Laurent Boulevard from south to north open until the wee hours. Many bistros and cafés on and near Saint-Denis offer a more relaxed atmosphere. Like any club scene in a major city, the hot spots in Montreal change with the seasons, and the "in" place today may not be by the time you read this. That said, we'll leave you on your own to find your nightstalking nirvana — just remember, it's a two-hour drive back to the Adirondack wilderness and your favorite tent.

If you are thinking about building a dream cabin on some remote lake, it may be possible; but you will be limited as to what you can do and how you can do it.

Real Estate/ Vacation Rentals

So, do you want a piece of the Park?

Joseph Totten and Stephen Crossfield were the first land speculators in the Adirondack region. In 1771, these two Manhattan shipwrights acted as middle men for two brothers, Edward and Ebenezer Jessup, and purchased 800,000 acres — or so they thought. They lucked out in the deal as later surveys found that the Totten and Crossfield purchase contained 1.1 million acres of land. The extra 300,000 acres of land, however, were not a sure path to wealth. The majority of the land had to be sold for pennies per acre.

Some 100 years later, New York State would also discover the value of Adirondack land, as speculators found that the timber on the land was more valuable than the land itself. After the timber was cut, landowners simply abandoned the land, as it wasn't worth the tax burden. Initially, the state even tried to give these abandoned lands away, but without any marketable timber, no one wanted it. The land that no one wanted would serve as the foundation of the Adirondack Park.

Today, land speculation in the Adirondack Park remains a risky business, as this publicly and privately owned park is regulated by the Adirondack Park Agency (APA). The APA attempts to channel much of the future growth in the Park around existing communities, where roads, utilities and other services exist, while limiting the extent and type of development in remote areas. To accomplish this, all private lands are classified into six categories: (1) hamlet or the growth and service centers; (2) moderate-intensity use; (3) low-intensity use; (4) rural use; (5) industrial use; and, (6) resource management. More than 50 percent of the land

in the Park is classified as resource-management, meaning that special restrictions apply to prevent development while preserving the natural spaces of the land. Resource-management land requires 42.7 acres for every principal building, as well as approval of any construction plans by the APA.

So, while it is possible to own a piece of the Park, ownership comes at a price beyond the purchase price of the property. A backcountry parcel may be inexpensive, but its land-classification status determines what you can do with the parcel today and well into the future. If you are thinking about building a dream cabin on some remote lake, it may be possible; but you will be limited as to what you can do and how you can do it.

Today the vast majority of private lands in the Park are owned by pulp and paper companies such as Finch, Pruyn and Company, St. Regis Paper and International Paper. Rarely are large tracts of these lands offered for purchase, as the paper companies either log the properties or lease them to hunting and fishing clubs for private use.

The majority of the real estate transactions in the region occur within the hamlet zones or within the town limits. For the most part, this market is comprised of second or vacation homes and permanent homes.

The vacation market is built upon the famed real estate cliché: location, location and location. In the Adirondack region, the prime location is on a lake — especially a prime lake such as Lake Placid, Lake George or Lake Champlain. The existing-home market is far stronger than the market for vacant land on lakes, as building regulations not only limit what can be done with lakefront property, but also add to the overall expense of building a new structure. As there is only so much lakefront property available, especially with existing housing, this property seems to hold its market value in both hot and cold times.

When the prime lakefront location is beyond the means of the pocketbook, the rule for vacation homebuyers is to purchase a view. Again, great care is necessary to ensure the land classification is appropriate for the intended use.

Speculation, however, is not the primary reason for purchasing land in the region. Second-home ownership continues to grow because people fall in love with the mountains and lakes and want to enjoy the endless recreational opportunities. The desire for winter or summer activities determines the "neighborhood" in which the second home is purchased.

If, for example, Alpine skiing is part of the picture, the prime locations are Lake Placid and the Tri-Lakes region in the northern Adirondacks and Gore Mountain in the southern part.

Residential Homes

Lake Placid/ Tri-Lakes Region

For the most part, tourism remains the primary focus of most towns in this region. The prime hub for winter recreation in this region is Lake Placid. The fame of this resort town, along with its world-class athletic facilities, gives it a distinct market edge over nearby Saranac and Tupper lakes. If winter activities are not part of the vacation-home formula, and the focus is upon summer activities, then a great many more options are available, especially in many of the smaller towns and villages in the region.

The second home, whether it be a condominium or house on a resort-town lake such as Lake Placid, often will sell for $200,000 or more, while a cabin on a pristine lake miles away from the nearest town may be had for

less than $30,000. Both offer similar opportunities for enjoying the great outdoors, but obviously, one has a better mailing address and will prove easier to sell in the future.

The resort towns are prime locations, but the best buys are in the outlying villages and towns. Prices drop dramatically once the name address is left behind. For example, the village of Saranac Lake was recognized as the No. 1 small town in America in Norman Crampton's *The 100 Best Small Towns in America*. The village, less that 15 minutes away from Lake Placid, bustles with year-round activities and charm. More house can be purchased for the same money in Saranac Lake than in Lake Placid; but again, the town does not have the prestigious name of Lake Placid, even though it earned the status of the best small town in America.

For the most part, second homes in this region are houses rather than townhouses or condos. Condominium units are generally limited to resort towns, such as Lake Placid, with few, if any, units available in the smaller villages. Condo units in resort towns generally begin around the $100,000 figure, although a few basic units may be had for less.

Outside the major resort villages, prices on second homes are relatively consistent with prices of similar houses throughout the region. Second homes can be found in virtually every price range, beginning at the $30,000 level for a small cabin on a woodland lot and skyrocketing to the multi-million dollar level for a plush "camp" or modern home on a lake. As with residential homes, the prime location is on lake front. Demand for vacation homes in this region is fueled in part by buyers from nearby cities, such as Albany, Syracuse, Rochester and Buffalo, which are all less than a few hours' drive from this region.

You don't have to own a great amount of land in this part of the Adirondacks to reap the region's recreational benefits. Public wilderness is only minutes away from any location, and while you may not own the trout stream or the lake shore, access to everything the Park has to offer is always nearby.

Plattsburgh/Western Lake Champlain Region

The overall economic nature of this region, with few job "booms" or "busts," is reflected in its general residential housing market conditions. Home values are generally stable throughout the region. A major influence on home values, however, is proximity to Lake Champlain. This is especially true with higher-value properties. Interestingly, though not surprisingly, the region's property values are linked with Canada and the Canadian economy as well.

With its close proximity to Montreal, much of the area's industrial growth is coming from Canadian companies doing business in the United States. These companies often bring Canadians with them who buy homes locally. A substantial portion of the second-home market is made up of Canadian residents as well.

A unique result of this U.S./Canadian in-teraction is the influence upon the local economy of the relative values of the U.S. and Canadian dollars. Simply stated, when the U.S. dollar is strong against the Canadian dollar, Canadians buy less in Clinton County; less from store shelves and less from property listings. Of course, when the relative dollar situation is reversed, Canadians buy more. Ultimately, property values in the region reflect these fluctuations.

Though not a major "bust," the closure of Plattsburgh Air Force Base in 1995 dealt a blow to the area's economy, including the housing market. Many homes up for sale over a short period of time put a downward pressure on selling prices. Since that time, a slow but steady influx of companies into Clinton County has returned the market to slow but steady growth.

Newcomers want their homes to fulfill certain desires, which influence where they will settle. Obviously, distance to place of employment is one influence. But many also want to escape from their prior urban experience and choose to settle in sparsely populated rural towns.

The northern half of the Plattsburgh/Western Lake Champlain region consists of Clinton County, which has the City and Town of Plattsburgh at its center. Homebuyers who prefer an urban setting but by no stretch of the imagination a "big city" gravitate to this area. In popular neighborhoods here, well-maintained three-bedroom homes range from $100,000 to $200,000, while luxury homes in preferred locations within the city sell for $175,000 to $350,000.

Though the City of Plattsburgh and much of the town flank Lake Champlain, very few homes have actual lake frontage. Buyers seeking this prime property need only talk with a Realtor to find out exactly what is on the market. Be forewarned, however, that lake frontage comes with higher property assessments, which are measured by the foot and converted into additional taxes.

www.insiders.com

See this and many other **Insiders' Guide®** destinations online — in their entirety.

Visit us today!

Some condo living is available in Plattsburgh and priced along the lines of residential properties.

Outside Plattsburgh in Clinton County, homes are generally more moderately priced. Three-bedroom homes are more likely to be found in the $60,000 to $100,000 range with many both above and below those figures.

The Northern Tier of the county, which borders Canada, includes several small communities that serve both as bedroom communities for Plattsburgh as well as small social and economic centers for the local population.

The same can be said for areas west and south of Plattsburgh, particularly in the communities of Morrisonville and Peru.

Once again, along the shore of Lake Champlain both north and south of Plattsburgh, property values increase dramatically. The length and nature of the shoreline, along with the size and condition of the home, will greatly influence property value, but little can be found along the lake for less than $150,000, and most shoreline property sells for a great deal more.

Property on or near Lake Champlain is where many second homes and vacation homes can be found. Throughout the Western Lake Champlain region, most of these homes tend to be in the sub-$200,000 bracket. Of course, many higher-priced second homes exist throughout the region.

While Clinton County enjoys easy access to the Adirondack Park (and portions of it fall within its boundary), it shares very little of its mountainous geography or forever wild forests. But to the south, the Essex County portion of the Western Lake Champlain region blends wild Adirondack forest with the grandeur of Lake Champlain. Communities such as Port Kent, Willsboro, Essex and Westport are popular for retirees and second-home owners who appreciate both environments. The sub-$200,000 price range for second homes remains consistent.

Little industry exists in this region until you reach Ticonderoga, home of International Paper, so the housing market does not have to cope with industry-based turnover. Three-bedroom homes generally range in price from $50,000 to $110,000, with lakefront homes generally selling for between $120,000 and $225,000.

Lake George/ Upper Hudson Region

As is the case throughout the Adirondacks, there is a tremendous diversity of residential properties and prices in this region, depending heavily on location, accessibility and the surrounding environment. Residential environments include small city neighborhoods in Glens Falls, suburban housing developments in Queensbury, luxurious lakefront homes and estates on Lake George, the Victorian-style homes of Warrensburg and good old-fashioned rural living throughout most of the region's northern and western areas.

The general mood of Realtors serving this region has been pretty positive in recent years. In fact, the Warren County Association of Realtors reported that both 1995 and 1996 were record years in terms of the number of housing units sold throughout the county. Granted, much of that growth can be attributed to the most heavily developed areas of Queensbury and Glens Falls, and the "boom" doesn't necessarily reach all corners of the county.

You can find a small three-bedroom home in a city neighborhood such as Glens Falls for $89,000 and up. Three-bedroom homes in neighboring Queensbury are likely to run between $110,000 and $140,000, with four-bedroom homes beginning at about $125,000 and climbing to $200,000 and beyond.

What you pay for a waterfront home depends a lot on what water it is we're talking about here. A three-bedroom year-round home on small but convenient Glen Lake can be had for $129,998, whereas a similar home on world-renowned Lake George (only 4 miles away) would likely go for triple that amount. In fact, if you want to live year round or have a second home on Lake George, be prepared to spend a minimum of $500,000 for anything new, big or in good shape.

There are a number of townhouse and condominium developments along the western shore of Lake George. They can make great second homes with their contemporary construction style and terrific waterside locations, but even a two-bedroom condo will cost upward of $200,000. Even if you just want to buy some lakefront land and build your own dream house, you could still have to come up with $300,000 or more just for a decent size (1 acre or more) building lot.

As you get farther "up county" and away from Lake George and into the communities of Warrensburg, North Creek, Chestertown

and the like, prices once again drop to a more palatable range for most folks. You'll find three-bedroom properties available for $65,000 and more, depending on their location and condition.

The Preserve at Gore Mountain is one of the newer attempts at developing an upscale year-round development in the northern part of Warren County, near North Creek. It will include 55 homesites of $40,000 and more and homes from $140,000, all in a 675-acre mountainside setting. Almost 600 of those acres will remain forever wild. Also in the Gore Mountain/North Creek area for your second-home consideration are a number of townhouse developments, all of which have units available beginning in the low to mid-$100,000s.

Relative to Lake George, Schroon Lake offers a good value, with lakeside building lots for less than $100,000. Two-bedroom townhouses here start at $169,900, which is about $40,000 less than Lake George prices for a similar set-up.

Southern Adirondack Lakes Region

If there's a "bargain region" for real estate in the Adirondacks, this probably is it (for now). The southern Adirondacks around Great Sacandaga Lake, Caroga Lake, Canada Lake and up to Lake Pleasant, Speculator and beyond to Indian Lake offer a big selection of relatively affordable housing, including both year-round permanent residences and seasonal second homes. Some of the same rules apply here as in the Lake George region, just on a different scale. For example, a nice three-bedroom home on the Great Sacandaga Lake or Peck's Lake may cost $250,000 or more, but that's still a bargain compared to Lake George prices. In fact, if it's not crucial to be "on the water," you can buy pretty cheaply around these parts. For example, "lake access" versus "lakefront" can cut prices on properties by $50,000 or more. There are still a lot of seasonal cottages and camps lining the Great Sacandaga, Caroga Lake and Canada Lake that are not winterized and pretty basic, but they're also pretty cheap (less than

$60,000) for a second home if all you need is a location convenient to the water.

Just outside the Park boundary, the small cities of Gloversville and Johnstown, while hurt to varying degrees by downturns in the upstate New York economy over the past two decades, offer some great real estate buys as a result. For example, three-bedroom "in-town neighborhood" homes can be found for as little as $55,000. According the Fulton County Board of Realtors, the average selling price for the 229 homes sold in the county in 1996 was only $66,000. With the southern gateway to the Adirondacks at your doorstep, it's an area worth considering.

Old Forge/
Raquette Lake Region

The real estate scene has improved considerably here since the 1970s, according to local professionals. What once was almost exclusively a summer seasonal home market has seen big growth in permanent year-round home construction. The booming winter-recreation business that developed here thanks to the snowmobile gave this region a (well, almost) year-round economy and encouraged more people to put down some roots here in the sometimes frozen soil.

While the Old Forge area remains a popular second-home market, the second homes are considerably enhanced and improved over the uninsulated cottages of the past. Many times, what were $40,000 seasonal lakefront cottages are bought, torn down and replaced with $200,000 to $300,000 year-round homes.

As a rule, you can expect to pay about $1,000 per frontage foot for a waterfront building lot on a navigable lake, such as the Fulton Chain of Lakes. So, a lot with 100 feet of waterfront would cost a cool $100,000. Access is another big factor in prices here, as some waterfront lots on such places as Raquette Lake use the waterfront as a driveway too. That is, some homesites in this region are only accessible by boat or seaplane, which make them great for seclusion and privacy but not so convenient the next time you need a gallon of one-percent. Obviously, prices for this type of lot are more flexible since they are less accessible.

Vacation Rentals

A great number of private homes, cabins and camps throughout the region are available as vacation rentals on a daily, weekly and monthly basis. The prices vary depending upon the facility and location, i.e. a cabin on Lake Placid or Lake George during the peak summer months may rent between $400 and $900 per week, while a similar cabin on a less popular lake may be had for less.

Since the region's economy greatly depends on tourism, vacation rentals are big business. You can find virtually any accommodation to suit your needs and pocketbook — from a plush estate to host a corporate retreat, to a cabin with a room full of bunk beds to sleep all your kids and their friends. If you are thinking about a rental unit, think about it long before you hope to visit, as the prime units are booked early.

We also recommended that you use as many services as possible to find a suitable rental. In other words, don't place all your hopes on one source.

Most Realtors in the region offer rental units. Naturally, those in more popular area offer the most rentals, so if you want a rental in a remote section of Cranberry Lake area or in the wilds of Hamilton County, you may have to search pretty hard to find the right accommodations. Any of the agencies listed in the subsequent "Real Estate Agencies" section are good places to start, but you should also consult other agents and regional chambers of commerce, which maintain lists — not listings — of units available for rent. These lists often include every possibility from the family with an extra cabin on their property to commercial services renting everything from condos to Great Camps. You can work from the lists and call to learn about available accommodations as well as the provisions in the rental agreement (linens, dishes, utensils are provided, but you must bring your own towels; or, the agreement is for six people, and additional guests require an additional fee). Although chambers simply provide a list of accommodations, a listing with a chamber usually suggests a basic degree of reliability about the facility (that is, it actually exists and is habitable). When a facility's accommodations are

The Adirondack Dream

[**Ed. note:** In adition to co-writing this book, Michael Mendrick is a humor columnist. We thought you'd enjoy his humorous take on the dream of owning an Adirondack camp.]

Have you ever dreamed of owning a camp on an Adirondack lake, where you would end each day sitting on the dock with a fishing pole in one hand, a cold one in the other, and a setting sun dropping at your feet into the glassy waters? You're convinced you would love it. You're convinced you would use it for lazy summer weeks, crisp fall weekends and crackling fires on romantic winter getaways. You're convinced it would be a great investment.

Well, then let me make a suggestion backed with considerable personal research. Wake up and smell the Off Skintastic®! Save yourself from this cursed dream while there's still time!

I know, I know — the pages of *Adirondack Life* are overflowing with scenic vistas, cable-ready log cabins and serene waters plied by the solitary paddle of a forest green canoe. What those magazine pages *don't* show you is what it takes to get to the moment when you can actually enjoy the above-mentioned.

Let me explain my point of reference. I am blessed with a wife who, along with her two brothers, own a family "camp" on Peck's Lake in the southern Adirondacks. As such, I am extended "brother-in-law" ownership status, which means I continually feel like I should be re-shingling the roof or making some positive contribution to the place to help overcome the guilt I feel about using it via my marital status. Her brothers in particular seem to enjoy this arrangement. My wife and her brothers split up the summer three ways, so everyone gets to enjoy approximately three weeks, four days and six hours of packing up cars in the stretch between the end of one school year and the beginning of the next.

Now I know you *think* you want to own such a camp, but I'm here to help you regain

— continued on next page

This "camp" at Peck's Lake is the Smith family's Adirondack dream.

some sense of perspective. You see, renting versus owning an Adirondack camp will provide you with two entirely different experiences from two distinctly different perspectives.

When you rent a camp, you see it as a combination of R & R & R. That is, rest and relaxation and recreation. Just some of the plethora of soul-enriching activities you can enjoy include:

A) Boating.

B) Hiking.

C) Fishing.

D) Lazing about on the dock with some type of lemon peel-laden beverage.

E) Browsing among the local antique shops.

F) Engaging in lively discussions with the locals about life in the Adirondacks.

G) Enjoying nature.

H) Commemorating your perfect Adirondack vacation by buying a gift of a local craft to take home.

When you own a camp, you see it as a combination of C & P & R — cleaning and preparing and repairing, followed closely with E & R — entertaining and running errands. If you're not careful, this combination can result in you being given CPR in the ER from the stress. Such stress-inducing scenarios include:

A) The *boat* needs to be emptied of rain water because *somebody* forgot to put the cover on last night — *after* you couldn't get it to start.

B) Since the dryer is broken and it has rained the last three days, you can't go *hiking* because your gear is still damp from the wash. Doesn't matter . . . it's *still* raining.

C) The *fishing* pole is hopelessly tangled with a life jacket, garden hose and the front tire of your mountain bike out in the shed.

D) Any thoughts of *lazing about on the dock* are eliminated by the realization that somebody (after a couple of weeks it really doesn't matter who) will be stopping by to visit for a "casual supper" that you will spend the next three hours preparing for and cleaning up from.

E) You desperately drive from one local *antiquated* grocery market to the next, with a minimum of 7 miles between each, in search of one small $3 container of sour cream for the dip that will be served to your guest(s) (see D).

F) Your *lively discussions with locals* are limited to the reprimands from the marina owner for forgetting to mix in oil with the gas in the boat motor, which is why it is broken. (See A.)

G) If you feel the discarding of last night's "mouse trap lottery winner" is enjoyable, and if dodging mosquitoes big enough to carry advertising banners behind them that read "Visit the Adirondacks — Wear Your Tank Tops!" is hours of fun for your whole family — then yes, you can *enjoy nature*.

H) You receive a *gift* each year celebrating your proprietary status — a local property tax bill.

Perhaps the most maddening aspect of owning a camp in the Adirondacks is simply this: The rare moments when you actually experience the scenes out of *Adirondack Life* make the decades between worthwhile. So, if you happen to own a place on a lake — enjoy the moments. If you don't own but still dream of doing so, let me suggest a slight alteration as you drift off to sleep and find yourself (imagine dreamlike waves in your vision and cascading harp music right now, like they do on TV) . . . driving down a long gravel road, glimpses of blue water up ahead, a perfect A-frame with floor-to-ceiling windows appearing around the next corner, the front door opens as you approach and you recognize — *your best friends* who own the beautiful camp o' the woods. Ah, *now* you have the perfect Adirondack dream.

poor, the chambers are the first to hear the complaints and may exclude that facility's listing in the future. Of course, a listing with a chamber of commerce is not an endorsement.

Many rental agencies take credit cards — a practice that serves as a buffer for any disputes about the services provided. Dissatisfied individuals can always register a complaint with their credit card company, which in most cases will suspend payment until the issue is resolved to the satisfaction of both parties.

Adirondack Life magazine is a reasonable source for rental listings, as are local newspapers (see Media). Folks with Internet access can search of the World Wide Web for information on vacation rentals via links to real estate agency and, in some cases, chamber of commerce web pages. But the telephone typically is the most effective means of getting information; many real estate agencies and chambers have both local and toll-free numbers, and personal contact with an agent ensures that he or she is "on the case." (Remember, if booking through an agency, your rental fee includes the services of a rental agent). The better agents will work for you to earn that fee and ensure that your vacation — and renting experience — is well remembered; they certainly would like your business again.

Read your rental agreement carefully and ask questions about which services are and are not provided. Many times, you can arrange for additional services not included in the basic agreement, such as an extra bed or catered meals.

See our Accommodations chapter for information about some cabins and cottages. Towns such as Schroon Lake, Tupper Lake, Blue Mountain Lake and Long Lake long have been known for their cabin "colonies" or commercial hotel units offering one-, two- and three-bedroom cabins on lakes or in wilderness settings. And many motels throughout the region offer motel accommodations as well

as cabins. While they may not afford the privacy of a single cabin on a lake, they often provide acceptable and reasonably priced family accommodations. The price range of a one-room cabin begins around $300 per week, with slightly higher rates (approximately $400 per week) during peak season. Many of these cabins rent in summer only.

Lake Placid/ Tri-Lakes Region

The most popular vacation rental properties in the Tri-Lakes region are found in Lake Placid — but these are definitely *not* for the budget-minded.

Supply and demand definitely drive this market with high demand for a limited number of units. Add to this formula prime accommodations in sought-after locations during popular periods of the year, and you rapidly move into four-digit numbers for a one-week stay.

A few Realtors seem to handle most of the prime rental properties, and they begin taking reservations a year or more in advance. Their favorite customers are those who rent a property and reserve it for the following year as well. Needless to say, this keeps demand high and prices up.

Weekly rentals for automobile-accessible multi-bedroom residences during the most popular summer months (July through September) as well as winter holiday weeks (Christmas, Presidents Week) range from $800 to as much as $5,000 on Lake Placid (the lake, not the village). If you don't mind a little more isolation and adventure, you'll also find rental properties on Lake Placid that are only accessible by boat, and these can be had for about half the previously mentioned rate — generally around $1,000 per week. However, there are few listings — probably fewer than 50 — of this sort.

Some condos available in the Lake Placid vicinity average from $1,200 per week to between $1,500 and $3,000 for larger units (three or more bedrooms).

Another popular spot for vacation rentals is along the chain of lakes in Saranac Lake (Lake Flower, Lower Saranac, Middle Saranac, Upper Saranac, Kiwassa, St. Regis). These units are accessible by car and range from $1,000 to $3,000 per week during the summer months.

Once you begin to look into summer rentals outside these prime vacation centers, level of comfort and availability vary greatly, but the cost will be less — considerably less in most cases.

Condos in the Lake Placid vicinity are also popular for winter rentals where nightly rates of around $200 to $400 are available. Remember, however, popular winter ski weeks work on the same rule of supply and demand.

Call the Lake Placid/Essex County Visitors Bureau, (800) 44PLACID, to request a "Vacation Planner," which lists several rental properties as well as the names of some rental-property management firms.

Plattsburgh/Western Lake Champlain Region

The supply and demand for summer vacation rentals in the Clinton County portion of this region are much less intense than in the Lake Placid/Tri-Lakes Region, and no property management firms here specialize in this business. Several public and private campsites as well as RV parks are on or near Lake Champlain, and these attract a large portion of the summer vacationers. It is best to contact several Realtors and ask what might be available.

Summer rentals are more popular in the Essex County portion of the region but, again, it is best to contact individual Realtors for listings. The communities of Port Kent, Willsboro, Essex and Westport are popular summer-vacation destinations.

While Lake Champlain is, by far, the most popular body of water in the region, there are several smaller lakes and ponds that offer their own charm and rental accommodations. Talk to a Realtor to learn more about the specifics.

Lake George/ Upper Hudson Region

In this region, the vacation rental market primarily is focused on Lake George, the Lake Luzerne area, Schroon Lake and the North Creek/Gore Mountain area (particularly during ski season). Of these four areas, clearly the most popular — and therefore most expensive — is Lake George.

According the area real estate professionals, anything other than a Lake George waterfront setting is "tough to rent." Not surprisingly, if people are going to renting something in Lake George for a week, month or the whole summer season, *on* Lake George is where they want to be.

As pricey as it is to buy a home in this market, it's also very expensive to rent in Lake George in summer — and few renters look here any other time. A basic, no-frills small cottage in "passable" condition will cost you in the neighborhood of $750 a week, or $2,750 to $3,000 a month. An average two- or three-bedroom home on the lake and in good condition will cost approximately $2,000 per week, although owners would prefer to rent by the month and usually are willing to give a break of a few hundred a week if you do so. For a

FYI

Unless otherwise noted, the area code for all phone numbers listed in this guide is 518.

real spread that can host the entire family re-union, with upward of five bedrooms and all the trappings, you can expect a bill upward of $10,000 per month or $30,000 for the summer season. Are you still coming?

There are alternatives. The Lake Luzerne area, only about 10 miles from Lake George, has some small and simple cottage-types that you can find for $500 to $700 per week. To the north, Schroon Lake falls somewhere between Lake Luzerne and Lake George on the sliding scale of rental prices for vacation homes and cottages. The North Creek area near Gore Mountain has several townhouse complexes and a number of vacation homes available for rent. The range of prices varies considerably, with the best bargains in summer (say, $500 to $1,000 per week for a two-bedroom place) versus winter, when ski-weekend getaways can drive the prices to between $500 and $700 just for a two-night weekend.

Southern Adirondack Lakes Region

This region provides perhaps the best deals for vacation rentals in the Adirondacks. Case in point, a nice three-bedroom camp (i.e., home) on one of the lakes here can be found for less than $3,000 per month, or about $700 per week. Compare that to Lake George! And if you're willing to downgrade to a seasonal, no-frills cottage such as you might find on Caroga Lake, you may get away with spending less than $2,000 per month.

The Great Sacandaga Lake, with its 29-mile length are fairly heavy development, usually has a big selection of vacation rentals available, again at relatively attractive prices. A three-bedroom home with a private dock can be found for $600 to $700 per week during the summer months.

In the northern end of the region at Blue Mountain Lake, prices are somewhat more expensive for rental properties. There is a little more "name" here, a little more prestige that goes with being the home of The Adirondack Museum and being in the geographic heart of the Adirondacks. Two- to three-bedroom camps and cottages can be as much as $1,000 per week in July and August but drop as much as 50 percent in the spring and fall months.

Old Forge/ Raquette Lake Region

According to area real estate professionals, the primary vacation rental time period here is a 10-week slice of the summer from the end of June until Labor Day. The most requested rentals are weekly, and the most requested housing type is the waterfront home. Prices here vary considerably based on the dwelling's location, accessibility (can you get there by road or will you also have to rent a seaplane? — a significant added expense, if you ask us), size and condition. Even the type of waterfront makes a difference. There's a lot of water around here in the form of swampy wetlands, ponds and unnavigable streams that technically may be considered waterfront, but there's not much you can do with it or on it. As with any real estate transactions anywhere in the free world, the key is to ask around, ask some more, then ask again.

To give you an idea of what to expect in rental prices: A small basic two-bedroom cottage on a navigable lake will run you around $500 per week; a two-bedroom year-round home in good condition on that same lake would be $750 to $1,000 per week; and a three-bedroom place would be more in the $1,000-and-more category. There are some townhouse-style complexes available here, such as Rocky Point on Fourth Lake. Rentals at Rocky Point for a three-bedroom, three-bath unit with access to a private beach and indoor pool cost $1,300 per week. While that gets you great amenities and modern facilities, it also gets you neighbors on the opposite side of either wall. So, with vacation rentals as with most things in life, you have to choose your priorities.

Vacation-rental Specialists

Note: Because of the large number of rental units in the Lake Placid/Tri-Lakes region, many specialized rental services exist. In other Adirondack regions, Realtors handle rental units.

Lake Placid/
Tri-Lakes Region

Adirondack Elegance On The Lake
Whiteface Inn Rd., Lake Placid • 523-4724, (800) 220-1940

This service offers two- to five-bedroom condominium units on the Whiteface Inn property. Tennis, boating and golf all are available on the premises. The rates range from $175 to $550 per day.

Brookhill & Lakeside Residences
Whiteface Inn Rd., Lake Placid • 523-9861, (800) 982-3747

This service rents fully furnished two- and three-bedroom units on Lake Placid. A golf course and tennis courts are adjacent to the properties. Many units include whirlpools, Jacuzzis and fireplaces. Rates range from $150 to $400 per day.

Lake and Mountain Properties of Lake Placid
P.O. Box 406, Lake Placid 12946 • 523-4724, (800) 220-1940

The rental agency offers condominium, townhouse and private-home rentals with one to eight bedrooms, all totally furnished. Many units feature fireplaces and Jacuzzis as well as lake or golf course frontage. Rates range from $125 to $700 per day.

Lakefront Condominium
Whiteface Inn Rd., Lake Placid • (803) 856-3848, (914) 452-0392

This service rents two-bedroom waterfront condominiums at the Whiteface Club, in Lake Placid. There is golf, tennis, a beach and a marina on site. The rates range from $85 to $275 per day.

Lake Placid Condo Rental Management
13 Main St., Lake Placid • 523-9861, (800) 982-3747

This rental agency offers one- to five-bedroom condos, townhouses, chalets and exclusive residences. Most rentals are luxuriously furnished and may include Jacuzzis, swimming pools or private beach access. Rates range from $100 to $400 per day.

Lake Placid Village Lakefront Condominiums
Mirror Lake Dr., Lake Placid • 523-9861, (800) 982-3747

This service rents fully furnished one- to three-bedroom units, some with lofts and all walking distance to the village of Lake Placid. Rates range from $100 to $300 per day.

Water's Edge Condominiums
Victor Herbert Rd., Lake Placid • 523-9861, (800) 982-3747

These condo units near the Main Street district overlook Lake Placid. The multilevel units are fully furnished, and many include a fireplace and whirlpool or Jacuzzi baths. There is a beach, boat dockage and a pool on the premises. Rates range from $175 to $250 per day.

Whiteface Club Condominiums
Whiteface Inn Rd., Lake Placid • 523-2551, (800) 422-6757

This service rents condominiums and townhouses at the Whiteface Club. Many units overlook Lake Placid and include whirlpools and Jacuzzis. Rates range from $250 to $550 per day.

Real Estate Agencies

What follows is a representative listing of real estate companies that serve the five regions of the Adirondacks. By no means is this meant to be all-inclusive, as there are hundreds of Realtors that represent property in this vast geographic area. Nor is it intended as an endorsement of the Realtors listed. If you receive outstanding service from an realty agency not listed here, please let us know, and we'll be sure to include it in future editions.

Finally, keep in mind that many Realtors now offer listings on the Internet (particularly those affiliated with national companies such as Century 21 and Coldwell Banker). Be sure to call and ask if you're equipped to go online.

Lake Placid/ Tri-Lakes Region

Century 21 Wilkins Agency
63 Saranac Ave., Lake Placid • 523-2547
42 River St., Saranac Lake • 891-0001
With offices in both Lake Placid and Saranac Lake, this agency's 10 Realtors handle residential and commercial listings as well as vacation rentals, including fully furnished camps, homes, ski chalets and condominiums.

Lake Placid Real Estate
159 Main St., Lake Placid • 523-4404, (800) 724-8778
This four-agent, full-service brokerage specializes in land development and sales of existing residential and commercial properties in the Lake Placid area. The agency, established in 1976, also provides rental services.

Merrill Thomas Agency
65 Main St., Lake Placid • 946-2458, (800) 244-7023
The Merrill Thomas Agency, with some eight to 10 agents, has been a fixture on Main Street for more than 20 years. Its brokers handle listings of residential, commercial and rental properties in the Lake Placid area, including fully furnished Adirondack-style condominiums, townhouses and private residences.

Prudential Terry Horrocks Real Estate
13 Main St., Lake Placid • 523-4162, (800) 252-7492
This full-service agency offers a range of lake and mountain resort properties throughout Lake Placid and the northern Adirondacks for sale and rent. The agency staffs approximately 10 agents. Rental listings range from $900-per-week two-bedroom units to a seven-bedroom Adirondack-style camp on Lake Placid for $3,300 a week.

Rob Grant and Associates
52 Broadway, Saranac Lake • 891-3745
One of the larger full-service brokers in the area, this realty covers the Lake Placid, Saranac Lake, Loon Lake and Paul Smiths areas. Grant's staff of 10 provides full sales and rental services. One agent specializes in vacation rentals and handles listings from $600 to $3,000 per week.

Cherri Williams Real Estate
54 State Rd., Saranac Lake • 891-7070, (800) 368-7070
This full-service broker staffs three full-time agents who handle residential sales and services and rental units throughout the Tri-Lakes region.

La Valley Real Estate
N.Y. Rt. 3, Tupper Lake • 359-9440
This full-service agency staffs three full-time agents. It offers home and business sales and rentals, including many waterfront units in the Tupper, Cranberry and Upper Saranac Lake region.

Plattsburgh/Western Lake Champlain Region

Bradamant
32 S. Main St., Westport • 962-8313
This five-person agency, celebrating its 20th year in business, offers commercial and residential properties, real estate management and rentals on the shores of Lake Champlain, especially in the Westport and Essex areas. The agency began booking summer rentals

in 1997 and booked 98 percent rentals before the summer season started.

Duley and Associates
132 Cornelia St., Plattsburgh • 563-3500, (800) 639-0090

Established in 1988, this full-service brokerage with 12 agents offers relocation services, land sales and commercial and residential properties.

Friedman Realty
Main St., Schroon Lake • 532-7400, (800) 284-LAKE

In business since 1949, Friedman specializes in the home and land sales and vacation rentals in the Schroon Lake and southeastern Adirondack areas. With more than five agents plus additional offices in Pottersville and Elizabethtown, Friedman covers a good bit of territory.

Anne Porter and Associates
1694 Front St., Keeseville • 834-7608

Porter and her four agents specialize in residential property, including lakefront lots and homes south of Plattsburgh, in Keeseville and Willsboro. The 6-year-old agency also offers rental units on Lake Champlain.

Whitbeck Associates
49 Clinton St., Plattsburgh • 562-9999
103 Lake St., Rouses Point • 297-9999

Rouses Point is on the border of Canada, making it an ideal location for import and export businesses. Whitbeck specializes in commercial and investment properties as well as residential services in both Rouses Point and the Plattsburgh area.

Lake George/ Upper Hudson Region

Coldwell Banker King George Realty
Lakeshore Dr. at Grist Mill Rd., Bolton Landing • 644-2243
73 Main St., Queensbury • 793-7700

With two offices and the resources of the Coldwell Banker national realty company to draw from, King George Realty can offer you

a wide variety of properties and services. Call for a free brochure featuring more than 150 homes and vacation properties in the Lake George area and southeastern Adirondacks.

Grandma's Realty
613 N.Y. Rt. 9N, Lake Luzerne • 696-5499

This agency with the easy-to-remember name has been helping visitors and residents find property and homes for more than 25 years. Agents represent year-round homes, seasonal cottages, vacation rentals and lots from the Great Sacandaga Lake to Lake George, along with the Lake Luzerne area in between.

Charles W. Jefts Real Estate
67 Canada St., Lake George • 668-5731

Charles W. Jefts brings more than four decades of experience in the Lake George market and represents a wide variety of lakefront homes, seasonal cottages, town houses and vacation rentals throughout the area. The office is in the heart of Lake George village, just across from the Fort William Henry Motor Inn.

Robert W. Leavitt Inc. Realtors
U.S. Hwy. 9, Lake George • 668-3333

Established in 1928, this is one of the oldest agencies to serve the southeastern Adirondacks. A staff of four full-time brokers is available to help you find anything from lakefront homes to condominiums to vacant shorefront property on which to build your dream home.

Najer Realty
Theriot Ave., Chestertown • 494-2012

Najer Realty specializes in sales and vacation rentals of Adirondack properties on Lake George, Brant Lake, Loon Lake, Friends Lake and Schroon Lake. Najer is a member of the Multiple Listing Service and is now in its second generation of providing real estate services in the southeastern Adirondacks.

Ulrichs Realty of Bolton Landing
Sagamore Rd., Bolton Landing • 644-3800

A member of the Warren County Multiple Listing Service, Ulrichs can show you listings on choice lakefront and other vacation homes and rentals from 55 area brokers.

Southern Adirondack Lakes Region

Coldwell Banker Arlene M. Sitterly Inc.
363 N. Comrie Ave., Johnstown • 762-9885

In 1997, this agency and its still-active founder celebrated their 41st year in business serving Fulton County and the southern Adirondacks.

It ranked an impressive ninth in residential sales volume for the entire Capital Region (including the much larger areas of Albany, Schenectady and Troy), and has ranked as high as 28th among 2,400 Coldwell Banker agencies worldwide in number of listings. The firm includes 23 licensed brokers who represent widespread properties, including those in the Great Sacandaga Lake, Caroga Lake and Peck's Lake areas.

Glove City Realty
22 Cayadutta St., Gloversville • 725-3405

Enjoying a 30 percent increase in properties listed and sold during 1996, this agency continues to grow, recently adding two more agents for a total of eight. They represent properties in Broadalbin, Northville, Mayfield and Caroga Lake within the Adirondack Park. Two features offered by Glove City Realty are optional lighted "For Sale" signs and live radio broadcasts of open houses on local stations.

Illustrated Properties Better Homes and Gardens
N.Y. Rt. 30, Mayfield • 661-5992

Seven staff people, backed by the resources and marketing tools of the Better Homes and Gardens national real estate network, combine to make this a good choice in the Fulton County and Great Sacandaga Lake areas. Some of the resources available include the *Home Buyer's Action Guide* and the *New Home Planning Guide*, both of which help potential owners feel more comfortable with the home-buying or building process.

Mountain Lakes Real Estate
N.Y. Rt. 30, Speculator • 548-7862

Mountain Lakes Real Estate, an independent agency, has been in the business since 1992. Its principal has more than 20 years of experience and is joined by three other agents. Properties in the south-central Adirondacks, including Lake Pleasant, Speculator, Indian Lake, Piseco Lake and Wells, are represented by this firm.

Old Forge/ Raquette Lake Region

Century 21 Herron Realty
Main St., Old Forge • (315) 369-6910

Herron Realty offers lakefront homes, year-round properties, seasonal cottages and camps, and buildable lots in the Old Forge, Inlet and Fulton Chain of Lakes areas. Weekly, monthly and summer rental properties are available for you to review. Herron has been in the business for more than 20 years. Its staff includes seven agents and brokers.

Coldwell Banker Timm Associates
Main St., Old Forge • (315) 369-3951, (800) 582-2312
N.Y. Rt. 28, Blue Mountain Lake • 352-7395

With two offices this agency represents homes and vacation properties throughout the central Adirondacks including those in Old Forge, Inlet, Long Lake, Blue Mountain Lake and Raquette Lake, along with many other towns and lakes. Owner Greg Timm and wife Dawn bring more than 30 years of real estate experience to the firm. Their efforts are supported by more than a dozen year-round agents. Services offered include appraisals, Home Warranty Plans and Seller Security Plans, along with nationwide referral and relocation service.

Healthcare

The Adirondack region, unlike many similar rural communities, attracts doctors and other medical professionals. While the financial rewards of practicing in the region might not be as good as in a more urban setting, the lifestyle makes up for it. Many doctors who practice here are avid skiers, hikers, nature-lovers, anglers, artists — and highly skilled healthcare professionals.

One of the greater challenges in the region for both patients and doctors is the great distances one may have to travel to obtain emergency and specialized medical care. For the most part, no matter which Adirondack town you are in, an emergency room is less than an hour's drive away. While this may not sound comforting, especially when you or a loved one are in need of care, it is not as bad as it seems. Remember, this is the wilderness, so you shouldn't expect a doctor's office behind every other tree.

Because of the distance and time factors with respect to emergency facilities, the region depends heavily on cooperative services among hospitals as well as emergency air flights with helicopters and ambulance services. Emergency patients often initially are stabilized in local facilities, then transported to larger hospitals in cities such as Burlington, Vermont, and Albany, New York, for more specialized care. In addition, many of the region's park rangers, police officers and volunteer rescue personnel are trained in specialized wilderness-rescue skills; unfortunately, those skills are put to the test regularly.

Again, we must stress the need for visitors to take proper safety precautions in whatever they plan to do. Don't boat without safety equipment. Don't begin a hike without proper preparation, and *always* let someone else know your plans. Of course, don't drink and drive.

If you do need medical care, the following hospitals and medical centers will provide the proper care or make the proper physician referrals for you. For the most part, local doctors are affiliated with one or more hospitals in the region. Folks who have a chronic condition should gain a referral from their local family doctor for a doctor in the Adirondack region before traveling here.

Emergency Assistance

For emergency service in the Adirondack region, dial 911. In some locations a telephone operator — not an emergency services operator — will pick up your call and forward it to the New York State Police or the nearest emergency-service unit.

Although many small towns provide their own police and emergency services, visitors may not know which department serves which area. When in doubt, call the New York State Police at 897-2000.

For ambulance services in the Old Forge/Raquette Lake region, call Town of Inlet Police Department at (315) 357-5091, or the Town of Webb (including Old Forge) Police Department at (315) 369-6515.

INSIDERS' TIP

Brush up on your first-aid skills and double-check your emergency kits before you set out for the Adirondacks. Properly treating a small cut or bruise might help you avoid a visit to the emergency room.

Lake Placid/ Tri-Lakes Region

Plattsburgh/Western Lake Champlain Region

Adirondack Medical Center
Lake Colby Dr., Saranac Lake • 891-4141
Church St., Lake Placid • 523-3311

The Adirondack Medical Center was established in 1991 when Placid Memorial Hospital in Lake Placid and the General Hospital of Saranac Lake consolidated. This 100-bed, acute-care general hospital with two sites — Saranac Lake (the larger facility) and Lake Placid — is the largest in the Adirondack Park. Its two sites offer 24-hour emergency care and are your first, best and only choices in the Tri-Lakes region for such services.

The center offers a broad range of medical services, including full surgical and obstetrical services, intensive care and ambulatory (outpatient) surgery units as well as complete laboratory facilities. Hospital-based primary healthcare clinics, staffed by Board Certified Family Physicians, are available at the Lake Placid site and at offices in Tupper Lake, Keene and Keesville.

The 40 members on the medical center's active staff represent a range of medical specialties and are capable of treating patients from infancy through adulthood.

Clifton-Fine Hospital
N.Y. Rt. 3, Star Lake • (315) 848-3351

This 22-bed municipal hospital is the smallest hospital in New York State. It provides basic medical services (X-rays, minor surgical services, etc.), acute care and 24-hour emergency care to folks in the Star Lake and Cranberry Lake areas.

FYI

Unless otherwise noted, the area code for all phone numbers listed in this guide is 518.

Alice Hyde Hospital
115 Park St., Malone • 483-3000

Alice Hyde Hospital is an acute-care facility that serves Malone and surrounding communities in the northern Adirondack region with a broad range of inpatient and outpatient services. Operating since 1913, this hospital offers 24-hour emergency care, comprehensive diagnostic and therapeutic services and a wide range of laboratory services.

The Alice Hyde Hospital Association also has an affiliated cancer treatment center and renal dialysis unit on its Malone campus.

Champlain Valley Physicians Hospital
75 Beekman St., Plattsburgh • 561-2000

Champlain Valley Physicians Hospital (CVPH) is a 410-bed, acute-care hospital whose 135-member medical staff offers a broad range of inpatient and outpatient services. A nonprofit facility, CVPH provides care regardless of one's ability to pay.

The CVPH Emergency Care Unit serves as a regional trauma center that provides 24-hour physician coverage and a walk-in fast-track service for minor problems. CVPH is also the regional inpatient mental-healthcare provider.

The hospital offers comprehensive diagnostic and therapeutic services, including MRI and CT scan, and a wide range of lab and cardiology testing, including a cardiac catheterization laboratory. Dialysis patients are treated at CVPH's 22-station renal center, while oncology patients are cared for through the

INSIDERS' TIP

The Adirondack mountain air might be free of human-made pollutants, but natural pollutants are another story. Many over-the-counter allergy medications may provide you some relief. Check with your doctor.

We treat you like family...

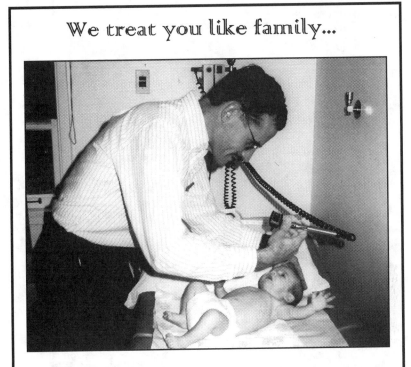

 ADIRONDACK MEDICAL CENTER

"Excellent Health Care Close to Home"

SARANAC LAKE / LAKE PLACID

Lake Colby Drive   Church Street

(518) 891-4141   (518) 523-3311

A full service hospital to meet all your health care needs
including

★ Emergency Centers at Two Locations

★ Primary Health Centers at Convenient Locations

Renal Center ★ Cancer Care Center ★ Sports Medicine

43 Active Staff Physicians

Board Certified in 16 Specialties

The Life Flight helicopter, operated by the New York State Police, is a vital link in the emergency services network for the vast wilderness region.

comprehensive programs provided at the FitzPatrick Cancer Center.

Elizabethtown Community Hospital
Park St., Elizabethtown • 873-6377

This small, 25-bed community hospital provides basic family-care services, acute and extended care and 24-hour emergency services. It is affiliated with the Champlain Valley Physicians Hospital in Plattsburgh (see previous entry).

Moses-Ludington Hospital
Wicker St., Ticonderoga • 585-2831

This 39-bed acute-care hospital provides 24-hour emergency room, X-ray, surgical and maternity services. More than 20 doctors are affiliated with this hospital, which in turn is affiliated with the Glens Falls Hospital in Glens Falls

(see subsequent entry) and the Fletcher Allen Hospital in Burlington, Vermont, two of the largest and best equipped hospitals in the region.

Lake George/ Upper Hudson Region

Glens Falls Hospital
100 Park St., Glens Falls • 792-3151

This 442-bed, nonprofit, acute-care community hospital was founded in 1897 and is the largest healthcare facility between Albany and Plattsburgh. It is the primary hospital for all of the southeastern and much of the central Adirondacks. Its 2,000 employees work to care for folks in a 2,500-square-mile cover-

Alice Hyde Hospital Association Services

Web site: www.northnet.org.ahha
Park Street, Malone, NY 12953 • (518) 483-3000; Fax (518) 483-0860

Emergency Medical Services

24 hours a day, everyday of the year • Close to home • Ready to serve with
Physician Assistants and on call Physicians • Efficient • Professional • Prompt

Full Service Hospital

Offering services in General Surgery • Family Practice • Internal Medicine •
Orthopedics • Opthalmology • Obstetrics • Gynecology • Radiology •
Anesthesiology • Pathology • Urology • Pediatrics • Dermatology •
Gastroenterology • Cardiology • Hematology • E.N.T.

Other Outpatient Services Include:

C.T. Scanning • Nuclear Medicine • Cardio/Vascular Testing (EKG, Stress Testing,
Echocardiography) Pulmonary Functioning Testing • Laparoscopic Surgery •
Lasers • M.R.I. • Hemodialysis • Brushton/Moira Health Center • Reddy Cancer
Center • Chateaugay Health Center • Bone Densitometry

Programs Offered at Alice Hyde Hospital:

Breast Cancer Awareness Project, Ongoing • Prenatal/Postpartum Education
Classes, Every Monday • Safe Sitters' Course (Safe Baby Sitters), Twice A Year •
Bystander CPR Awareness Project, Ongoing • Auxiliary offers Poison Prevention
Program • Teddy Bear Clinic • Free Monthly Health Care Screening, Ongoing

For Information Call:

Public Relations at 483-3000 ext. 248 or Educations at 483-3000 ext. 247

---

age area. Inpatient services include medicine/surgery, intensive care, coronary care, ob/gyn, pediatrics and psychiatric care. Outpatient services include ambulatory surgery, emergency care, cancer treatment, dialysis and substance abuse rehabilitation. One of its best known features is The Snuggery, a unique family-oriented approach to maternity care that was the first of its type in New York and New England.

The staff of Glens Falls Hospital consists of more than 225 affiliated physicians, ranging from primary-care practitioners to surgical subspecialists. Staff physicians are board-certified in more than 25 disciplines.

Warrensburg Health Center
Health Center Plaza, U.S. Hwy. 9,
Warrensburg • 623-2844
Bolton Health Center
Cross St., Bolton Landing • 644-9471
Chester Health Center
Main St. (U.S. Hwy. 9), Chestertown
• 494-2761

North Creek Health Center
Ski Bowl Rd., off N.Y. Rt. 28, North Creek
• 251-2541
Schroon Lake Health Center
North Ave., off U.S. Hwy. 9, Schroon
Lake • 532-7120

These five health centers are part of the Hudson Headwaters Health Network, a private, nonprofit healthcare system serving several communities in the southeastern and central Adirondacks. Its coverage area is more than 2,000 square miles. The family health centers in each of the communities offer appointments for ongoing care as well as walk-in hours for urgent care. Primary-care services at each of the health centers include family medicine, internal medicine, pediatric medicine, treatment of acute and chronic illness, and minor surgery. Preventive care such as cancer screening, PAP tests, mammography and immunizations also are offered. Specialty services include women's healthcare, podiatry, nutrition and dental care (at the Warrensburg Health Center). X-ray services are also available at the headquarters center in Warrensburg.

For off-hour healthcare needs, there is a 24-hour medical call system in place. You may always reach a healthcare provider by calling the health center nearest you. The call is transferred to the provider "on call." In addition, a Hudson Headwaters physician is on call at the Glens Falls Hospital at all times.

More than 130 staff members work for the network, including physicians, specialists, registered nurses, technologists and support staff. You can rest assured that even though the landscape may be rural in nature, the healthcare available in this region is first-class.

Southern Adirondack Lakes Region

Indian Lake Health Center
N.Y. Rts. 28 and 30, Indian Lake
• 648-5707

This health center is part of the Hudson Headwaters Health Network that serves much of the Lake George/Upper Hudson Region. See the previous listing for details about services.

Nathan Littauer Hospital and Nursing Home
99 E. State St., Gloversville • 725-8621
Nathan Littauer Primary Care Centers
99 E. State St., Gloversville • 773-5690
23 S. Perry St., Johnstown • 736-1500
2497 N.Y. Rt. 30, Mayfield • 661-5493
N.Y. Rt. 8, Speculator • 548-8155
N.Y. Rt. 30, Wells • 924-4521

Nathan Littauer Hospital and Nursing Home, along with five primary-care centers,

serve as the largest healthcare provider network for the Southern Adirondack Lakes region. The hospital is a 124-bed facility, and its adjacent nursing home is an 84-bed skilled-nursing facility. The hospital is one busy place — in 1996 they admitted 4,448 patients, delivered 353 babies and had 23,062 emergency-room visits. Among the comprehensive medical services provided by the hospital are maternity (with new family-centered birthing rooms), pediatrics, a diagnostic laboratory, diagnostic imaging, critical care, surgery and a 24-hour emergency room. Outpatient services include ambulatory surgery, The Heart Center (for heart-related rehabilitation), oncology, a pharmacy and, in late 1997, a Sleep Disorder Center. Nathan Littauer Hospital and Nursing Home has 49 active, 44 courtesy and 20 consulting physicians and employs a total staff of 815.

The primary-care centers offer comprehensive healthcare as well, including family practice and specialists in adult medicine, geriatrics, pediatrics and obstetrics/gynecology. Lab services and immunizations are also available, and anything that's not available is referred to the hospital. The Nathan Littauer Hospital has been caring for folks in the region since 1894.

Old Forge/ Raquette Lake Region

Central Adirondack Family Practice
Town of Webb Professional Office, 1 S. Shore Rd., Old Forge • (315) 369-6619

This is the one healthcare option in the Old Forge area, and it's basically a doctor's office staffed by a rotating team of four general-practice physicians. A physician is on-call seven days a week, 24 hours a day, so medical attention is always available if needed. The office normally is open Monday to Friday from 8:30 AM until 4:30 PM, but those hours vary throughout the year. According to staffers, you should call the listed phone number first, and it will either be answered by someone on site, or you will be given instructions and another phone number to call for further assistance.

Beyond that, staffers say that other healthcare options are a judgment call if you're in the Raquette Lake area, which is about equi-distant (around 20 miles) between Old Forge and Indian Lake. There you will find the Indian Lake Health Center (listed in our Southern Adirondack Lakes Region section), which is part of the Hudson Headwaters Health Network.

While the one-room schoolhouse is long gone, the one-building school with grades K through 12 remains in many smaller Adirondack-region districts.

Education

When it comes to an education, students in North Country schools get plenty of attention. Classes are generally small, and everyone in the school knows everyone else. The teacher, the principal and the school superintendent also most likely will know every parent, and many will go out of their way to chase that parent down the supermarket aisle to tell them about any lapses in homework assignments or poor grades on a recent test.

While the one-room schoolhouse is long gone, the one-building school with grades K through 12 remains in many smaller Adirondack-region districts. In some districts, such as Keene and even the famed resort town of Lake Placid, the graduating class could fit in a single school bus. In districts like Newcomb, graduates could ride in a mini van. In larger villages or small cities — in Plattsburgh, for instance — the numbers don't increase dramatically. Classes remain small, and the details of a child's education rarely get lost by teachers or parents.

Almost every village in the Adirondack region operates as its own school district. Students in a few of the smaller villages with only a few hundred people are incorporated into the district of a nearby town, but no matter how small the town, a member of the community always sits on the school board, ensuring local concerns are represented. Enrollments range from fewer than 100 students in Newcomb, one of the smallest districts in the state, to 1,825 students in Saranac Lake, the largest district within the boundaries of the Adirondack Park.

Each district has its own unique way of dealing with the educational needs of students and the logistics of operating a school system that may cover a large geographic area. School districts in larger villages, such as Saranac Lake and Plattsburgh, operate a number of community schools for the elementary grades, so as to keep travel times for youngsters at a minimum, while maintaining a larger school setting for middle and high school students. In this fashion, the district can offer more educational options to students in the higher grades, while keeping small class sizes.

The number of students and the geographic size of the district also affect the availability of some of the programs, especially those that take place after school. For instance, the majority of districts in the region do not have enough interested students to field a football team. Many schools, however, offer hockey programs, because of the availability of ice rinks in the region, and other winter sports teams, including downhill and cross-country skiing. Away games can be hectic for student-athletes — travel may take a few hours; then, upon returning to school, another long bus ride may await.

Small classes of 25 or fewer students per class for all grades is the rule in most North Country schools. In many instances these numbers are even lower. In smaller districts, like Keene, some elementary grades have fewer than 10 students. In some elective high school classes, such as business education or journalism, the student-to-teacher ratio may be as low as 3-to-1.

INSIDERS' TIP

In 1813, Keene Valley became the first public school district in the Adirondacks. Seven years later, the district constructed its first schoolhouse in one week at a cost of $168. More recently, Keene Valley was among the first districts in the region to have its own Web page.

Of course, for visitors to the region, the educational philosophy or personality of schools hardly makes a difference. If you plan on settling in the region, however, you might want to visit the school and discuss in detail the school's approach to education. The philosophy in one district may be highly traditional, with very structured classes and book- and lecture-based instruction, while the neighboring district takes a more hands-on, progressive approach. Additionally, you should consider the pros and cons of a small-town education. While students do receive plenty of individual attention, their options in alternative or even specialized classes may be limited.

These limitations quickly become apparent when alternative choices are sought for elementary or secondary grade students. The choices are only three private, secular schools. College offerings are also limited. Yet, while the number of schools is small, public and private schools and colleges have earned good marks and references for their offerings.

Private Schools

Lake Placid/ Tri-Lakes Region

National Sports Academy
12 Lake Placid Club Rd., Lake Placid • 523-3460

Founded in 1979, the name of the school accurately describes what the school is — a sports academy for high school students in pursuit of athletic dreams. National Sports Academy, which is only a short distance from the Olympic Arena's world-class facilities, has students involved in ice hockey, figure skating, Alpine skiing, luge, ski jumping and other winter sports. In 1996, the school boasted National Junior Champions in luge, ski jumping and Alpine skiing.

Because of the various schedules of the student-athletes, the academic programs offer flexible arrangements, combining traditional classes and individual instruction. Approximately 70 students attend the school, which is accredited by New York State Association of Independent Schools.

North Country School
Cascade Rd., Box 187, Lake Placid • 523-9329

Founded in 1938, this small coeducational, boarding and day school offers a general academic program in a non-competitive learning environment for grades 4 through 8. Hands-on learning is emphasized. The school, situated on a 160-acre campus, takes full advantage of its setting in the High Peaks by offering an extensive array of outdoor activities, such as overnight camping and hiking excursions. Students live in houses, not dorms, with house parents (who also may be teachers). They share in housekeeping chores and help manage the school's working farm.

Approximately 50 students, both day and boarding, attend North Country School, which is accredited by New York State Association of Independent Schools.

Northwood School
Northwood Rd., Lake Placid • 523-3357

This coeducational, college-preparatory boarding and day school is the oldest in the region — it was founded in 1905 — and offers traditional academic programs for grades 9 through 12. Of the 150 students, approximately one-third are day students, with the remainder living in two dorms on campus. The school takes full advantage of its proximity to Whiteface Mountain and the Olympic Arena and offers strong programs for students in ice hockey, skiing and figure skating. Classes are small. As most instructors and coaches live on-campus, students receive individual attention for both their academic and athletic pursuits.

Colleges and Universities

The State University of New York (SUNY) system is comprised of four-year universities and colleges as well as two-year community colleges.

FYI
Unless otherwise noted, the area code for all phone numbers listed in this guide is 518.

Photo: Plattsburgh State University of N.Y.

Plattsburgh State University has the largest college enrollment in the region.

Two-year Colleges

Lake Placid/Tri-Lakes Region

North Country Community College
20 Winona Ave., Saranac Lake • 891-2915, (800) 541-1021, (888) TRY-NCCC

North Country Community College (NCCC), 10 miles from Lake Placid in the High Peaks area of the Adirondack Mountains, is a community college of the State University of New York (SUNY) system. Approximately 1,400 students are enrolled either full- or part-time in this two-year school. The programs lead to Associate of Arts, Associate of Science and Associate of Applied Science degrees.

NCCC takes full advantage of its proximity to the world-famous Lake Placid Olympic venues and the United States Olympic Training Center by offering a Recreational Facilities Management Program, combining business and recreational courses with valuable practical experience at sites such as Whiteface Ski Center, Mount Van Hoevenberg, the Olympic Arena and the newly established Olympic Training Center, or at various smaller, privately owned facilities. The program prepares students for transfer to a four-year program or employment upon completion of the two-year program.

With an open admissions policy, NCCC accepts all students with a high school diploma, although some restrictions apply for admission to certain programs. The college offers programs in business administration, criminal justice, wilderness recreation leadership, pre-environmental science, radiological technology, office technology, nursing, secretarial science and recreation management. Radiologic technology (X-ray) is the most competitive program, with a limited number of candidates per year accepted.

Although NCCC is primarily a commuter campus, many out-of-town students are attracted to the college because of its proximity to the athletic venues in Lake Placid. It remains the only college in the region where future Olympians can take a few college courses and still maintain their training schedules. NCCC also operates satellite campuses, with limited course offerings, in Malone and Ticonderoga. Plans are being considered for dormitory space on the Saranac Lake campus; presently, however, students must find their own off-campus housing.

The college is fully accredited by the Middle States Association of Colleges and Secondary Schools. Because it is part of the SUNY system, it offers excellent transfer services to four-year schools.

Paul Smith's College
N.Y. Hwy. 30, Paul Smiths • 327-6000, (800) 421-2605

Paul Smiths College, which boasts of being the "College of the Adirondacks," is the only private college within the boundaries of the Adirondack Park. At one time, this two-year school had the largest campus in the world — some 50,000 acres. Today the college owns 13,000 acres. Few college campuses in the world can compete with the natural beauty of the setting of Paul Smith's in the foothills of the Adirondacks and overlooking the pristine Lower St. Regis Lake.

Paul Smith's, named after legendary Adirondack pioneer, guide and hotelier Appolos Paul Smith, offers 12 associate's degree programs, including ecology and environmental technology, environmental studies, forest technology and recreation, surveying, hospitality, culinary arts and liberal arts. In all academic programs, hands-on practice is united with theory learned in the classroom. In its forestry and environmental studies related programs, the Adirondacks itself serves as a lab for students, with students involved in actual research on lakes or managing their own forestry plots. Students also may find themselves operating a sawmill, sugar bush or constructing buildings in its recreational management program. Hospitality students apply their skills in the college-owned Hotel Saranac in nearby Saranac Lake, or operate food concessions at major special events such as the Kentucky Derby or the U.S. Open tennis tournament. Many programs also involve students in off-campus internships.

More than 80 percent of the 700-plus students receive financial aid. Nearly every one of the college's graduates either finds a job upon graduation or transfers to a four-year program. The combination of classroom and hands-on learning has earned the college a solid reputation in the business community, with many major companies hiring students because of the college's emphasis on practical education. Paul Smith's is in the process of developing a limited number of bachelor's degree programs as part of its changeover to a four-year program.

A few footnotes, the spelling of the college is "Paul Smith's," while the town's name has no apostrophe. Access to Lower St. Regis Lake

— great for canoeing and fishing — is gained through the college. Also, campus visitors can view a historic stagecoach from the 1800s. During maple syrup season, in early April, the college runs special programs for the public at its well-equipped sugar bush.

Plattsburgh/Western Lake Champlain Region

Clinton Community College
Lake Shore Rd., Plattsburgh • 562-4200

Clinton Community College, a member unit of the State University of New York, is approximately 4 miles south of Plattsburgh on a forested site overlooking Lake Champlain. The main campus building, atop Bluff Point, offers a spectacular view.

Like other community colleges in the SUNY system, the two-year college is well-equipped to meet students' needs, offering a low student-to-faculty ratio (approximately 12-to-1) to ensure plenty of personal attention and maintaining one of the most affordable tuition rates in the SUNY system. The college also is beefing up its facilities. A brand-new physical education building recently was completed, and construction is underway on a technical/sciences building.

The college provides offerings similar to those of other community colleges in the SUNY system, including liberal arts, business accounting, administration and office technology, criminal justice, nursing, medical laboratory technology and social services.

Although on-campus housing is not available, private dorm-style housing is adjacent to the campus. Additional housing is available nearby.

Lake George/Upper Hudson Region

Adirondack Community College
640 Bay Rd., Queensbury • 743-2200

Adirondack Community College (ACC) is a member of the State University of New York (SUNY) system. It is just outside Glens Falls in the foothills of the Adirondacks and serves students from Warren, Washington and Saratoga counties..

Approximately 3,500 students attend the college, with about an equal number of part-

and full-time students. Like many other SUNY community colleges, the student body tends to be older (the average age is 27). Although the campus is 141 acres, most activity takes place in 10 or fewer academic buildings. On-campus student housing is not available.

Two-year programs are offered in accounting, business administration, computer science, criminal justice, engineering science, food service, forestry, health information technology, liberal arts, math/science, mechanical technology, nursing, pre-environmental science and forestry, radio-television broadcasting, secretarial science and travel and tourism. Like other community colleges in the SUNY system, ACC maintains an open admissions policy for most high school graduates. Fewer than 1 percent of students come from out-of-state. With a student-to-faculty ratio of 19-to-1, everyone has the opportunity to get to know each other.

Four-year Colleges

Plattsburgh/Western Lake Champlain Region

State University of New York at Plattsburgh
101 Broad St., Plattsburgh • 564-2000

SUNY Plattsburgh (don't dare call it Plattsburgh State!) is the northernmost college in the SUNY system — situated in the scenic Champlain Valley region in a small city of approximately 25,000 people. The campus of this medium-size college (enrollment is approximately 5,000 full-time students) is designed for efficiency. Buildings are clustered together, making it easy to get around campus. Although the clusters create a somewhat "boxy" feel, the overall atmosphere is comfortable and the students and faculty friendly.

Originally a normal school (teachers college), SUNY Plattsburgh currently offers more than 50 baccalaureate programs in the liberal arts and

sciences, professional studies and business. The college is widely recognized for its outstanding natural sciences programs (many take full advantage of the Adirondacks and Lake Champlain as outdoor labs) as well as its many offerings in the social sciences. Degree programs in accounting, business, criminal justice, education, environmental science, hotel/restaurant management, psychology, nursing and mass media (radio and TV) are among the strongest and fastest growing academic programs at SUNY Plattsburgh. Distinct academic offerings include degree programs in the following: environmental science, which features a one-semester residential program at the Miner Institute in nearby Chazy; Canadian studies, with opportunities to study in residence at one of several universities in Montreal; in-vitro cell biology and biotechnology, providing exceptional opportunities for study in cell biology; and the individualized-study major, which allows students to design their own program in close cooperation with a faculty advisor.

More than 90 clubs and organizations (30 are related to academic interests) flourish on campus, and the university's Museum Without Walls program makes its permanent art collection available to the campus community in various university buildings. SUNY Plattsburgh is among the few universities nationwide to receive federal funds for its Cooperative Education Placement Program, in which students are placed with business, government and health agencies and are paid for their services while they gain practical experience — and, often, academic credit. In the athletic arena, the hockey team is a perennial powerhouse.

Generally, students with a high school average of 83, class rank in the top 50 percent and combined SAT scores of 1000 or an ACT composite score of 22 meet the minimum requirements for admission. SUNY Plattsburgh has been recognized numerous times in national publications as a "best buy" among the nation's colleges.

The print media produced by communities within the Adirondacks focus on the community, not on world events. In many cases, these publications are more likely to include news about the local pancake breakfast or a sale on fishing equipment than an impending world catastrophe.

Media

For many who visit here, the Adirondacks region is the perfect place to get away from their daily barrage of radio, television, and big-city newspapers back home. It is a good thing they feel that way, because the truth is, they don't have much choice. Media is not a strong point of the Adirondacks, or is it? Depending on why you are here, you either love the feeling of isolation from 24-hour news or find it very frustrating.

The media situation is primarily a product of the region's geography. Most visitor destinations have a central hub of activity, services and media. The Adirondack region instead relies on its perimeter communities for much of its access to news and information services. The deeper into the Adirondacks you venture, the less access to media you have. Around the fringes of the region is where you will find the majority of daily newspapers, television and radio signals. That is because perimeter communities such as Plattsburgh, Glens Falls, Albany, Utica and Watertown have the majority of media outlets.

The print media produced by communities within the Adirondacks focus on the community, not on world events. In many cases, these publications are more likely to include news about the local pancake breakfast or a sale on fishing equipment than an impending world catastrophe.

Much of the perception of isolation is just that—perception. These days, the reality is that you can pick up a *USA Today* at just about any convenience store, many communities have cable TV, and if you have a computer and a modem you can go anywhere!

Newspapers

Lake Placid/Tri-Lakes Region

Adirondack Daily Enterprise
61 Broadway, Saranac Lake • 891-2600

Adirondack Daily Enterprise, the oldest daily newspaper operating in the Adirondacks at 101 years old, focuses its local coverage on Saranac Lake, Tupper Lake and Lake Placid. Events within these communities receive good coverage, especially local sports. Major news of national and world events is briefly covered, along with box scores of major league sports. The Friday edition includes the "Weekender," one of the best means to find out what is going on in the Tri-Lakes area for the upcoming week; local hotels in the Tri-Lakes area often offer free copies. The paper is not published on Sundays. Daily circulation is approximately 6,000. Weekender distribution reaches 20,000.

Lake Placid News
Main St., Lake Placid • 523-4401

Established in 1905, *Lake Placid News* is published every Friday and covers what's happening in the Lake Placid, Jay, Wilmington and Keene areas. A variety of columns by local residents keeps readers informed about family and community events. The paper provides good coverage of upcoming events and reviews of past ones. Circulation is approximately 4,000.

Tupper Lake Free Press
136 Park St., Tupper Lake • 359-2166

This weekly paper provides all the local information for Tupper Lake, Long Lake and Cranberry Lake. The *Free Press* is a classic hometown paper with a circulation of approximately 4,000 and a small staff that manages to do a thorough job of reporting the local news.

Watertown Daily Times
260 Washington St., Watertown
• (315) 782-1000

The *Times*, from the St. Lawrence Valley, is one of the larger daily newspapers in the region; it's daily circulation is 35,695. Because of the Adirondacks region's vast geography, no paper reaches the entire region. The Times tends to focus its coverage on the northwestern portions of the park, especially in the villages bordering the region, such as Potsdam and Canton. Published seven days a week, it has limited distribution beyond the High Peaks area.

Plattsburgh/Western Lake Champlain Region

Denton Publishing
1 High St., Elizabethtown • 873-6368

Denton Publishing produces weekly papers for various communities in the North Country. All the papers provide essentially the same regional coverage, but vary the local coverage for different towns. The *Essex County Republican* and *Times of Ti*, for example, might offer the same regional stories, such as an article on the county fair, but vary the local stories, with *Essex County Republican* covering towns such as Keeseville in the northern part of the county and *Times of Ti* covering local events in Ticonderoga and southwestern Lake Champlain towns. *The Valley News*

FYI

Unless otherwise noted, the area code for all phone numbers listed in this guide is 518.

serves as the weekly paper for Elizabethtown, Keene and Westport areas, and *North Countryman* serves as the weekly paper for northeastern Clinton County.

Denton does an exceptional job in providing local news coverage for small towns in the region, especially when it comes to letting locals know about upcoming events. Articles often go beyond simply reissuing press releases of community activities and give readers the lowdown on exactly what to expect at a local event, such as a fundraising barbecue for the community fire department.

The weekly circulation for each newspaper is approximately 4,000.

Press-Republican
170 Margaret St.,
Plattsburgh • 561-2300

With a weekday circulation of nearly 23,000 and a Sunday circulation of 24,500, the *Press-Republican* is the primary newspaper in the Clinton/Essex/Franklin County portion of the Adirondack region.

Its main office in Plattsburgh and bureaus in Malone, Lake Placid and Ticonderoga provide in-depth local coverage of community news regionwide in government, business, education, human interest and local sports. New York State issues also are covered by a bureau in Albany as well as by Associated Press. National and international news and sports coverage is provided by Associated Press, Dow Jones (*Wall Street Journal*) and Scripps-Howard News Service.

A weekly TV guide in each Saturday edition outlines programming for the 10 different cable systems within the *Press-Republican's* circulation area. "Letters to the Editor" keep tabs on controversial local issues, and local entertainment, shopping news and extensive advertising information are regular staples of *"The Press,"* as it's popularly known by locals.

The *Press-Republican* came into being in

INSIDERS' TIP

WGY 810 AM is a 50,000-watt, clear-channel radio station, making it a particularly strong nighttime signal to help keep you company on those windy Adirondack roads.

This Warren County vista becomes all the more captivating
when the hardwoods don their finest fall colors.

1942 with the merger of the *Plattsburgh Daily Republican* and the *Plattsburgh Daily Press*, two newspapers with rich histories dating back to the early 19th century. Today, the *Press-Republican* is part of Ottaway Newspapers Inc., itself a subsidiary of Dow Jones and Company, publishers of the *Wall Street Journal* and *Barron's*.

Lake George/
Upper Hudson Region

Adirondack Journal
**P.O. Box 410, Warrensburg 12885
• 873-6368**

Adirondack Journal is a weekly paper serving Warrensburg and northern Warren County. The *Journal* does a good job of mixing community news with locally based columns and features. You can find everything from a new friend to a new snowblower in the extensive classified section. *Adirondack Journal* is free and readily available at stores and restaurants around town.

The Chronicle
15 Ridge St., Glens Falls • 792-1126

The Chronicle is a well-respected free weekly serving Glens Falls, Lake George and southern Warren County. It is easy to find at retail and food outlets throughout the area. "The Inside Scoop" provides the editor's musings, while "Talk of the North Country" reviews the "week that was" in bulleted, short-and-sweet paragraphs. *The Chronicle* has a strong base of advertisers, which makes for entertaining browsing. It also features a community bulletin board, arts calendar and locally written features.

Glens Falls Business Journal
55 Bay St., Glens Falls • 798-5045

You may be surprised to find a business-oriented newspaper serving such a small market as Glens Falls. As a monthly paper devoted to the commerce of Glens Falls and Lake George, the *Business Journal* does a good job providing in-depth coverage of the business scene. The editorial is strong, and the features are much more extensive than you will find in most small dailies. The "Spotlight on New Business" profiles are valuable if you are prospecting for a new job or new money generated at your current job. Each month a special section called "Spotlight on . . ." features a topic of local business interest such as tourism. *Glens Falls Business Journal* is not all business, however. It also features a well-written dining guide, which will come in handy when business wraps for the day.

The North Creek News-Enterprise
P.O. Box 85, North Creek 12853
• **251-3012**

This weekly dozen-or-so pager covers the community news and events of northern Warren County, southern Essex County and the easternmost sections of Hamilton County. Most of the coverage focuses on the Gore Mountain area and the town of North Creek. You will find the usual collection of event listings, a church service directory and a small classified section included here. The *News-Enterprise* costs 40¢ and is worth it for the quick local fix it provides.

The Post-Star
Lawrence and Cooper Sts., Glens Falls
• **792-3131**

Billing itself as "Home Newspaper of the Adirondack Region," *The Post-Star* is one of the few daily, full-coverage newspapers that actually looks like a real newspaper. It even has different sections, including "Sports," "Living" and "Local" sections. With a circulation of more than 35,000, *The Post-Star* is the major newspaper for the southeastern Adirondack region. It provides a good mix of local, regional, national and world news, along with both local and syndicated features. The reporting is dependable, the editorials well-written, and the paper attractively laid out. Reading through the Sunday *Post-Star* will even last you a couple of house blends! The paper is widely available throughout the southern Adirondacks at Stewart's shops and other convenience-type stores. The newsstand price of 50¢ is a bargain, particularly if you are suffering from World Event Withdrawal Syndrome.

Southern Adirondacks Lakes Region

The Edinburg Newsletter
819 North Shore Rd., Hadley • 863-2075

More an advertising booklet than a newspaper, this free monthly serves the northern reaches of the Great Sacandaga Lake area. Still, if you are renting a camp, boating or fishing on the lake, this is a worthwhile paper to pick up and give a "once through." One note-

www.insiders.com

See this and many other **Insiders' Guide®** destinations online — in their entirety.

Visit us today!

worthy feature of *The Edinburg Newsletter* is the inclusion of news updates from the various service clubs in the area.

Hamilton County News
P.O. Box 166, Speculator 12164
• **548-6898**

This is your best source for weekly news coverage of happenings in Indian Lake, Blue Mountain Lake, Raquette Lake and Speculator. The *News* is owned by Kline & Son Inc., which also publishes the *The Recorder* daily in Amsterdam, New York. The news sections of the paper divide geographically, a nice feature if you want to zero in quickly on a specific town. For those interested in keeping an eye on the state's political scene, you can review the "Empire State Roll Call Report" to see how your legislators are representing you. A listing of coming attractions, church services and a healthy section of classifieds round out the offerings in this 50¢ weekly.

The Leader-Herald
8-10 E. Fulton St., Gloversville
• **725-8616**

With a circulation of more than 12,000, *The Leader-Herald* is the biggest daily paper serving the central-southern Adirondacks. While based in Gloversville, just south of the Adirondack Park, the paper does cover news and events in northern Fulton County and parts of Hamilton County. It is the primary paper for those living in the Great Sacandaga Lake area as well as Caroga Lake and Pine Lake to the west. You will find enough national and world news to keep you connected, but the emphasis is on community and regional news and activities. Keep an eye out for the valuable "Summer Guide" that focuses on the southern Adirondack lakes region. The single-copy price for *The Leader-Herald* is 50¢.

Sacandaga Times
P.O. Box 129, Northville 12134
• **863-6926**

Another free monthly newsletter-type paper, *Sacandaga Times* covers the communities surrounding the Great Sacandaga Lake as well as points north and south. The emphasis is on community events and activities, not hard news.

Old Forge/ Raquette Lake Region

The Adirondack Echo
P.O. Box 188, Old Forge 13420
• (315) 369-2213

Ranging from eight to 12 pages, this weekly newspaper bills itself as the "Official Publication of the Central Adirondacks." The focus is on the Town of Webb and Old Forge. Such local news delicacies as board of education meeting minutes and school sports schedules are available here, as are church listings and classifieds. The *Echo* has been around for more than 40 years, and the price is just 30¢.

Adirondack Express
P.O. Box 659, Old Forge 13420
• (315) 369-2237

A younger, somewhat beefier rival to The Adirondack Echo, the *Express* is a free weekly with a "Dining Guide," "Express Newsmakers" feature, local sports news and an active letters-to-the-editor page. You can also catch up on some syndicated treats such as Dave Barry and Andy Rooney. A comics page and crossword puzzle are ready and waiting for those inevitable rainy Adirondack days.

Other Available Newspapers

You can find a number of large daily newspapers from non-Adirondack communities in grocery and convenience stores throughout the region. These include the *Times-Union* (Albany), *The Gazette* (Schenectady), *The Observer-Dispatch* (Utica), *The New York Times* and *USA Today*.

Magazines

Adirondac
814 Goggins Rd., Lake George
• 668-4447

This magazine of the Adirondack Mountain Club (a.k.a. ADK; see the related Close-

up in Other Summer Recreation) is published six times yearly with the goal "to encourage people to become both involved in ADK and supportive of its mission of promoting responsible enjoyment and protection of the New York State Forest Preserve." It is available both as a ADK membership benefit and as a subscription magazine to nonmembers. It also can be found at regional newsstands. Adirondac offers an interesting combination of stories and features pertaining to recreational activities and conservation efforts in the Adirondack region.

If you are a serious outdoor enthusiast, Adirondac is well worth the $20 annual subscription fee.

Adirondack Life
N.Y. Rt. 9N, Jay • 946-2191

This award-winning, bimonthly magazine offers great color photography, essays and articles about the region's natural history, culture and people. Back issues are excellent sources to give a feel for the diversity of the entire region. Its selection of ads serve as a useful shopping guide for the Adirondacks.

Radio

The mountains play havoc with radio stations in the region, making it impossible to listen to one single station throughout the entire region. As you travel from one area to another, you will have to search for something new, particularly in the central portions of the Adirondacks, as the stations have a tendency to fade in and out. Only North Country Public Radio can be heard throughout the entire region. But even with this popular station, you will have to change your dial as you travel since frequencies change from region to region.

Depending upon your location, you can tune in stations from Vermont and Canada for a little variety. If you love a particular type of music, though, you might consider bringing along some extra selections from your tape or CD collection for the ride.

News coverage, especially national and world events, on most local radio stations is limited. The one primary source is National Public Radio's "All Things Considered," aired on local public radio stations in early morning and evening.

Some of the primary radio stations that broadcast out of perimeter communities reach the southern Adirondacks, and we include them as well.

Lake Placid/Tri-Lakes Region

Adult Contemporary
WLPW 105.5 FM, Lake Placid
WNBZ 1240 AM, Saranac Lake

Country
WVNV 96.5 FM, Malone (hot country)
WSLK 103.6 FM, Saranac Lake (kick'n country)

Public Radio (including classical, jazz, news and talk)
WSLU 90.5 and 91.7 FM, Canton

Top 40
WICY 1490 AM, Malone

Various Talk and Music
WIRD 920 AM, Lake Placid

Plattsburgh/Western Lake Champlain Region

Christian
WCHP 760 AM, Champlain

Country
WIPS 1250 AM, Ticonderoga
WOKO 98.9 FM, Burlington, Vt.

Easy Listening
WEZF 92.9 FM, Colchester, Vt.

Middle of the Road
WIRY 1340 AM, Plattsburgh

News and Talk
WKDR 1390 AM, Burlington, Vt.
WZBZ 1070 AM, Burlington, Vt.

Public Radio (including classical, jazz, news and talk)
WANC 103.9 FM, Albany
WCEL 91.9 FM, Albany
WXLU 88.3 FM, Canton

Rock
WBTZ 99.9 FM, Burlington, Vt. (alternative rock)

Lake George/Upper Hudson and Southern Adirondack Lakes Regions

Adult Contemporary
WINK 105.7 FM, Glens Falls
WKBE 100.3 FM, Glens Falls

Country
WGNA 107.7 FM, Albany (hot new country)
WZZM 93.5 FM, Glens Falls

News and Talk
WGY 810 AM, Schenectady
WROW 590 AM, Albany

Public Radio (including classical, jazz, news and talk)
WAMC 90.3 FM, Albany

Old Forge/ Raquette Lake Region

Adult Contemporary
WARM 93.5 FM, Rome
WLZW 98.7 FM, Utica

Country
WFRG 104.3 FM, Whitesboro (modern country)

Public Radio (including classical, jazz, news and talk)
WXLH 91.3 FM, Canton

INSIDERS' TIP

Hey, southern Adirondack sports fans! Check out The Fabulous Sports Babe show on WROW 590 AM from 10 AM to 1 PM weekdays. If the winds are right, you can hear it all the way up to Indian Lake.

Rock

WOUR 96.9 FM, Utica (classic rock)

Television

Cable or satellite television is an absolute necessity in almost the entire Adirondacks region, as the mountains disrupt reception. Depending on your location within the Adirondack region, the following stations are either clear, barely recognizable or nonexistent. Some Adirondack communities have cable TV service, and a number of satellite-dish outlets are available as well. The local chamber of commerce should be able to help you find television service companies in the area.

With cable the options are endless and include local stations from Vermont and Canada. Again, without cable, reception truly is poor to nonexistent, especially in the central portions of the region, so don't expect to watch the ball games on your portable television at your favorite campsite.

Two stations are based in the Adirondacks region (in Plattsburgh).

Plattsburgh/Western Lake Champlain Region

WPTZ-TV Channel 5
5 Television Dr., Plattsburgh • 561-5555

This NBC affiliate provides some of the best local news coverage for the Adirondacks and the northern Vermont area. Local news and weather programs are offered early morning and at noon weekdays and at 6 and 11 PM Monday through Saturday.

The weather reports by meteorologists Tom Messner and Gib Brown are the most comprehensive available on the Adirondack region, especially the northern sections. Forecasts are rarely off the mark. Many local weather reports issued by area radio stations are borrowed from WPTZ.

Mountain Lakes Public Broadcasting, Channel 57
1 Sesame Dr., Plattsburgh • 563-9770

Our public television station offers strong educational programming during the day, including *Barney and Friends* and *Mr. Rogers*. At night, you'll find a traditional mix of public broadcasting fare, including movie classics and music and art programming.

Network Affiliates

Broadcast television stations that reach portions of the southern Adirondacks over the air and via cable include:

ABC Affiliates
WTEN News 10, Albany
WUTR Channel 20, Utica
WVNY Channel 22, Burlington, Vt.

CBS Affiliate
WCAX Channel 3, Burlington, Vt.
WRGB NewsCenter 6, Schenectady

Fox Affiliate
WXXA Fox 23, Albany

NBC Affiliates
WNYT NewsChannel 13, Albany
WKTV Channel 2, Utica

For many retirees, the Adirondack region is a four-season playground of recreation and culture that keeps them as busy as their longest of work weeks past.

Retirement

"Old Rocking Chair's Got Me . . ."

If you think retirement in the Adirondacks is about sitting on a porch in an Adirondack-style chair and watching the loons paddle by — well, you're correct about the relaxing-and-sitting-in-a-chair part. However, for many retirees, the Adirondack region is a four-season playground of recreation and culture that keeps them as busy as their longest of work weeks past. Case in point: Barb and Harold Remington of Peck's Lake in the southern Adirondacks. These friends of co-author Michael Mendrick's family keep so busy that it took three phone calls to catch them at home long enough for Michael to *ask* them about retirement. Thankfully, he didn't try to contact them in the summertime!

Barb and Harold are typical of the active retirees who choose to make the Adirondacks their year-round home and environs. Peck's Lake residents for many years, they enjoy the combination of the Adirondack Park's natural surroundings and recreational offerings with the conveniences and services provided in the nearby Gloversville area (just 10 minutes away by car). As Barb describes it, just living within the frame of a scene landscape artists (such as husband Harold) continually try to capture and enjoying the beauty of the hills, lakes and woods is reason enough to love it here. The changing seasons provide a new mosaic outside the window virtually every morning — one that leaves you either too fulfilled or too full of energy to get out and enjoy it to possibly be bored by it. Of course, much of the splendor of the Adirondacks is raw and unrefined and needs to be massaged by the positive outlook of your mind's eye to see and truly appreciate the beauty here. So, you *can* love it here — but sometimes you have to *work* at loving it here.

Barb and Harold work at it by being a part

of it. Summertime finds them swimming, boating, golfing, attending festivals, visiting friends and family or simply taking their German shepherd, Molly, for walks on the "lake road." Wintertime is colder but hardly less active as cross-country skiing, attending concerts and plays, and participating in community events and organizations keeps the calendar full. They even find ways to enjoy the decidedly dismal months of April and November. (Hey, there's always a good book and the warm flicker of light from the fireplace to pass the dampest of days.)

Theirs is perhaps the ideal setup for a retired couple: a year-round home on a lake that many from Metroplex U.S.A. would pay dearly to rent (if they could) for a week in this setting, along with the security and comfort of knowing that the things they need day to day (groceries, household goods and services) and the things they might need someday (medical care) are all within close proximity. This is why the fringe communities such as Glens Falls, Gloversville and Plattsburgh are all good alternative locations to consider for retirees versus the much smaller (with fewer services) communities in the interior reaches of the Park.

What's Barb's biggest complaint about living year round in the Adirondacks? Just hope you're not invited to too many weddings because finding a good dress in these parts can require a hour-long excursion to Albany that can make you feel like Lewis and Clark in search of Lord & Taylor. Oh well, there is no Utopia (and if there is, the property taxes are probably out of sight!).

"Retire in the Adirondacks?"

So, why would anyone want to retire in the largest park in the continental United States? The answer is found in every chapter of this book. The outdoor activities are plentiful, the culture is diverse, and the lifestyle is far from hectic.

But there are other reasons as well. Traffic jams are unheard of. The crime rate is negligible. During the non-tourist seasons, everyone in an Adirondack town knows pretty much everyone else and keeps an eye out for their neighbors. Although property taxes exist, they are relatively low compared with most urban tax rates.

Then there is the peace and quiet. . . .

People retiring to the Adirondack region have a number of options to consider. The primary concern is whether to reside here part or full time — which raises a significant caveat. The winter months are harsh; there's no other way to say it. That said, though, many retirees (a.k.a. snowbirds) travel south for the cold months and return in early spring. If this sounds like a good plan, a vacation (or non-winterized) home is an option. In the North Country, we call these "humble" abodes "camps," some of which can cost seven figures, as a camp may be an isle unto itself or consist of multiple dwellings. Other camps truly are humble, and they too may be on an isle, but could be single-room cottages on some backwoods lot.

The other options are to build your dream house or purchase a home from the existing market (see Real Estate). When constructing a home in the Park itself, special restrictions often apply, and permits must be obtained from the Adirondack Park Agency, N.Y. Route 73, Ray Brook, 891-4050, if construction is outside town limits.

Retirement communities, like those in popular retirement states such as Florida and Arizona, are virtually nonexistent within the Adirondack Park itself. We did come across one such development that positions itself as a retirement community — ParkView at Ticonderoga, Ticonderoga, (800) 795-PARK. ParkView is essentially a townhouse development targeting "today's active retiree." Its scenic location across from a town park in the valley setting of Ticonderoga, its proximity to Lake George and Lake Champlain and the nearby Ticonderoga Golf Club, and its single-level floor plans are selling points. However, there are no dedicated on-site medical facilities or staff, so the "retirement community" is more of a marketing identity than a fully realized concept.

Retirees also need to carefully consider the limits of the medical facilities in region (see Healthcare). Some towns offer no medical services at all. Specialized services also may not be available, even in towns with hospitals, such as in Lake Placid or Saranac Lake. People seeking specialized medical treatment may find themselves traveling hours to hospitals in Glens Falls, Gloversville or Plattsburgh, or even farther to Burlington, Vermont, or Albany, New York.

Generally, people who retire in the Adirondacks are familiar with the region or have visited it in the past; consequently, they have a good idea of what they want in a retirement setting or community. A good place to start in your search is by reading (or re-reading) our Area Overview chapter. As the region is not considered a prime retirement setting, few services exist, even in the form of information clearinghouses on retirement options. Local chambers of commerce can provide some basic information, but this is generally geared to relocation services rather than retirement specifically.

As illustrated in the chapter's opening example, the contingent of retirees in the region is small but vibrant. Throughout the region, especially in larger communities, retirees play an active and essential role in the area's quality of life. They are active volunteers in schools as well as religious, social and political organizations, and because of the small population base within the region, their involvement often makes a huge difference. Retirees are seen and heard in the North Country and in many cases serve as the prime "movers and shakers" in getting important if thankless jobs done.

For example, many retirees volunteer with organizations such as the Adirondack Mountain Club (ADK), 814 Goggins Road, Lake George, N.Y. 12845, 668-4447 (see the related Close-up in Other Summer Recreation), to help maintain trails in the region. The ADK also sponsors such programs for seniors as "Senior Getaway" weekends. One such excursion in October 1997 included itinerary stops at Robert Louis Stevenson's cottage in Saranac Lake, John Brown's farm in Lake Placid and a boat tour of Lake Placid.

Another Adirondack-related volunteer option to check out is the Adirondack Park Visitor

Photo: Plattsburgh/North Country Chamber of Commerce

The unspoiled quiet of an Adirondack wilderness pond is a canoeist's favorite domain.

Interpretive Centers, N.Y. Route 30, Paul Smiths, 327-3000, and N.Y. Route 28N, Newcomb, 582-2000, where seniors can help provide educational programs on environmental subjects for school children in the region and the thousands of visitors who visit the facilities every year.

For information on other volunteer options for seniors, contact the Retired and Senior Volunteer Program (a.k.a. R.S.V.P.) at 546-3565, (Port Henry); 793-3817 (Glens Falls); or 483-6767 (Malone).

A number of social-service programs specifically geared to seniors in the region include nutrition programs and home healthcare services. Most of these are coordinated by local county agencies. Information on these programs can be obtained through the county of-

fices or by calling the New York State Office of the Aging senior citizen hotline at (800) 342-9871. This hotline provides information on Medicare and Medicaid, Social Security and other services for seniors.

Each county in New York directs its own senior services programs for people 60 and older. Services vary slightly, depending upon the needs of individuals within the region. The Office for the Aging is the first place to call for information on services such as meals-on-wheels, employment training and opportunities, counseling services, in-home healthcare services, outreach programs and clubs and organizations for seniors. These offices also will provide information on local nutrition programs, which can be found throughout the region.

Offices for the Aging

Local offices for the aging within the Adirondack region are listed as follows:

Lake Placid/Tri-Lakes Region

Essex County, Essex County Complex, U.S. Highway 9, Elizabethtown, 873-3690
Franklin County, 63 Main Street, Malone, 481-1526

Plattsburgh/Western Lake Champlain Region

Clinton County, 135 Margaret Street, Plattsburgh, 565-4620

Lake George/ Upper Hudson Region

Warren County/Hamilton County, Municipal Center, U.S. Highway 9, Lake George, 761-6347

Southern Adirondack Lakes Region

Fulton County, 19 N. William Street, Johnstown, 762-0650

Old Forge/ Raquette Lake Region

Herkimer County, County Office Building, Mary Street, Herkimer, (315) 867-1121

Offices for the Aging also support the efforts of various community centers found throughout the region. These centers — many are only a few rooms in the village hall or other municipal building — are found in the more populated towns and villages, such as Lake Placid, Saranac Lake, Plattsburgh, and Keeseville, but not in towns like Black Brook, Paul Smiths and Cranberry Lake. Generally, these community centers have limited hours of operation; most are open from 9 AM to 2 PM Monday through Thursday (in the smaller towns) or Monday through Friday (in larger communities). The centers provide limited recreational activities, such as bingo and card games, art and craft activities, shopping, daytrips and a lunch program. The lunches cost approximately $2. Most, but not all, will provide transportation services to the center for certain activities. These offices can also direct you to other independent senior service and activity centers within your area.

Also worth checking into are the local chapters of such national retirement-related organizations as SCORE (the Service Corps of Retired Executives) and AARP (American Association of Retired Persons). What follows are brief descriptions and regional contacts for each.

American Association of Retired Persons

New York State Office, One Commerce Plaza, 99 Washington Ave., Albany
• 434-4194

AARP is an organization you're likely already familiar with if you're 50 or older and have undoubtedly received an invitation to join. AARP is a nonprofit, nonpartisan association dedicated to helping older Americans achieve lives of independence, dignity and purpose. Founded in 1958 and now boasting more than 33 million members, AARP is the oldest, largest and most influential organization of older Americans.

Through its network of regional and state

offices, along with local chapters, AARP is committed to expanding opportunities for volunteer recruitment, training and support. In addition, these locations provide information and assistance to members and the public on issues of concern to the association.

AARP offers a myriad of programs and services to members, including: the Purchase Privilege Program, offering discounts on travel-related products and services such as hotels, cruises and car rentals; the AARP Motoring Plan, which offers both travel planning and emergency roadside assistance through an affiliation with the Amoco Motor Club; AARP Investment Programs, offered through Scudder, Stevens and Clark; the AARP credit card, offered through Bank One; AARP Pharmacy Service, offering shop-at-home convenience on both generic and name-brand drugs; and a full line of insurance programs for protection of auto, home and life. Call the state office to get acquainted, then ask for information on the nearest local chapter.

Service Corps of Retired Executives

Champlain Valley SCORE, Chapter 0284, 11 Lincoln St., Rm. 106, Winston Prouty Federal Bldg., Essex Junction, Vt.
• (802) 951-6762
Northeast SCORE, Chapter 0127, Albany County Chamber of Commerce, 1 Computer Dr. S., Albany • 458-9851
Utica SCORE, Chapter 0198, SUNY Institute of Technology, N.Y. Rt. 12, Utica • (315) 792-7553

The SCORE association is a nonprofit organization comprised of 12,400 volunteer business counselors throughout the United States. There are 389 SCORE chapters across the country.

SCORE members are trained to serve as counselors, advisors and mentors to aspiring entrepreneurs and business owners. These services are offered at no fee as a community service. More than 3.5 million Americans have utilized SCORE's services since the organization was formed in 1964. Local chapters of SCORE provide both free counseling and low-cost workshops in their respective areas.

Closing Thoughts

So, it's your choice. You can retire to the Adirondacks year round and enjoy the seasons and all the opportunities and challenges they present, or you can sneak up here for a few months of the year when turtlenecks aren't required clothing staples. You can canoe your way along the lakes and rivers, or watch others do the same from the comfort of your front porch. You can read all about the adventure and history of this wild and wonderful region, or go on out and create some of your own. Whatever choices you make, we think you'll be surprised at just how rewarding retirement in the Adirondacks can be.

As much as they are places of formal worship, most churches in the Adirondacks serve as community centers for the hamlets and villages.

Worship

History of Worship in the Adirondacks

In a way, religion gave birth to the Adirondacks we know today. Some of the earliest white men to visit this vast region were missionaries and ministers. The stories and impressions they shared of this place with the "outside" world generated intrigue and interest in people who wanted to see and experience this natural paradise.

The first white man to see Lake George was a man of religion — Father Isaac Jogues. Father Jogues was a French Jesuit missionary to the Huron Indians, who lived in regions north of the Adirondacks. The Hurons were enemies of the Iroquois, who lived south of the Adirondacks throughout much of what is now upstate New York. Unfortunately for Fr. Jogues, his experiences in the Adirondacks were anything but recreational, and to him, the Adirondacks became the opposite of a promised land.

In August 1642, while traveling by canoe up the St. Lawrence River to Jesuit missions, Jogues and his party of Huron converts were captured by Iroquois warriors of the Mohawk tribe. They were taken on a long and torturous journey to Ossernenon, a Mohawk village about 30 miles west of what is now Albany. During the trip, he and his companions were beaten and tortured repeatedly by the Mohawks. Seemingly by faith alone, Jogues barely survived the ordeal and eventually escaped about a year later. Incredibly, he journeyed back among the Iroquois on a mission in 1646. He was put to death by the Mohawks, who suspected him of sorcery. While the date of discovery is somewhat in dispute, it is clear that at some point between 1642 and 1646, Fr. Jogues first came upon what we now know as Lake George and christened it Lac du Saint Sacrement (Lake of the Blessed Sacrement).

The trials and tragedy of Fr. Isaac Jogues's life was not to go unrecognized — he was canonized in 1930.

In September 1841, a minister from western Massachusetts named John Todd came to Long Lake in the north-central Adirondacks. While Todd was visiting the area as one of its earliest "tourists," he saw a small struggling community of 18 families and urged them to set up a church with he as their minister. On his second visit, in summer 1842, Todd organized the First Congregational Church on Long Lake and baptized eight children from the settler families. After that visit he wrote, "As soon as the road is open, population shall roll in, and I may yet live to see the day when a church shall be erected on one of their beautiful islands and a hundred little boats lie moored around while they keep holy time. What a day that will be!"

While Todd had great hopes for the establishment and growth of a vibrant community of farmers and churchgoers at Long Lake, it was not to be. His efforts to send money and books to the people from his home in Massachusetts, and his yearly visits during the summer, were not enough to overcome the harsh weather that made farming impractical and unprofitable. The scores of new farming families never came, and Long Lake went on to survive because of its hunting and fishing opportunities, not its farming opportunities. Nonetheless, Todd was an enthusiastic woodsman who praised the Adirondacks in several books he wrote during his life, and he visited the Adirondacks in summer for 20 years of his life to hunt and fish.

Perhaps the best known man of worship who made an impact on the Adirondacks was William H.H. Murray, a minister for the Park Street Congregational Church in Boston for seven years during the mid-1800s. In the 1860s he camped on Raquette Lake and fell in love with the region. His book, *Adventures in the*

Wilderness was published in 1869, became very popular and was reprinted several times. In the book, which liberally mixed a travel guide with tall tales of adventure (and left it up to the reader to discern one from the other), Murray created a picture of the Adirondack wilderness as a paradise with limitless trophy hunting, fishing, adventure and beauty.

The publishing and popularity of the Rev. Murray's book, along with the opening of the Adirondack Railroad from Saratoga Springs to North Creek in 1871, led to the first boom in visitation to the region as a tourism and recreation destination. The rich, famous and adventure-seekers came by the thousands in the years that followed. So did the sick and weak, drawn here by Murray's stories a miraculous health recoveries due to the rich environment and clean, bracing air. Some visitors loved what they saw and experienced. Some patients recovered. Many did not, and the term "Murray's Fools" was created to define those led into the mountains by the exaggerated prose of the man who became known as "Adirondack" Murray.

Murray claimed that great benefits to the clergy and its followers could be gained from visiting the Adirondacks, and wrote, "It is in the ministry that you will find the very men who would be the most benefited by this trip. Whether they should go as sportsmen or tourists or in both capacities, a visit to the North Woods could not fail of giving them precisely such a change as is most desirable and needed by them. In the wilderness they would find that perfect relaxation which all jaded minds require."

Later, Murray wrote, "If every church would make up a purse and pack its worn and weary pastor off to the North Woods for a four weeks' jaunt in the hot months of July and August, it would do a very sensible as well as pleasant act. For when the good dominie [sic] came back swarth [sic] and tough as an Indian, elasticity in his step, fire in his eye, depth and clearness in his reinvigorated voice, wouldn't there be some preaching!"

For all his good intentions and good-natured storytelling, William "Adirondack" Murray can be credited with building the first large-scale awareness of the Adirondacks as a destination for visitors.

Adirondack Worship Today

You will find most of the big denominations represented in the larger of Adirondack communities, and a drive down Main Street normally will reveal at least a Presbyterian, a Catholic, an Episcopal, a Methodist and a Baptist house of worship. You are also likely to find a few independent, nondenominational places of worship in each community. However, the only active synagogue within the Adirondack Park is in Lake Placid. Other smaller religious denominations practicing in the Adirondack region include the Church of Jesus Christ of Latter Day Saints (churches in Lake Placid, Gloversville and Queensbury); Jehovah Witness (Glens Falls, Gloversville and Warrensburg); and the Christian Science Society (Glens Falls, Gloversville and Saranac Lake). As a rule, the larger the community, the more varied the options for worship, so your best bets for finding a broad scope of denominations are the large fringe communities such as Glens Falls, Gloversville, Plattsburgh and Saratoga Springs.

As much as they are places of formal worship, most churches in the Adirondacks serve as community centers for the hamlets and villages. They are often the site of craft fairs, pancake breakfasts, chicken barbecues and other gatherings of good will. Whether you're of the faith or not, you are always welcome to join in, meet neighbors and locals, and perhaps even contribute to the good cause of the day.

One of your best options for finding out the availability of worship services in your corner of the Adirondacks is the local newspaper (see Media), which in most cases will provide at least a weekly listing of services. Since many Adirondack communities are served primarily by weekly papers for their local news, you just need to stop by a convenience store (Stewart's Shops are always a good option; see Shopping) and pick up a copy. Another source is the local chamber of commerce, which either will have a listing of services or some inclusion of churches in its publications. At the very least, staffers can point you in the right direction.

Don't automatically assume that the church of your choosing is open year round. Yes, in

Photo: Plattsburgh/North Country Chamber of Commerce

Many small villages and towns in this rural region have their own houses of worship.

the Adirondacks, even some of the houses of worship in the smaller communities are seasonal. Those that do not hold services throughout the year — the Church of the Lakes in Inlet and the Raquette Lake Chapel are two examples — are typically closed after the Christmas holidays through March (or until Easter, depending on the calendar). As we do in many of our chapters, we encourage you to call ahead to make sure of schedules and services.

There is a strong connection between summer camps and religion here, as many of the camps for youth are operated by such organizations as the United Methodist Church, the YMCA or the Word of Life. The Silver Bay Association (see Arts and Culture), along the western shore at the north end of Lake George, is owned and operated by the YMCA, includes a conference center, auditorium, dozens of cottages, cabins and lodges, and supports a wide variety of both educational and recreational activities throughout the year. While not specifically a religious camp, its affiliation with the YMCA gives the programming and activities a family-oriented, values-conscious emphasis.

The Word of Life Fellowship, which is headquartered in Schroon Lake, has perhaps a larger single influence on the economy and lifestyle of its host community than any other religious organization. Within the area, the Word of Life owns and operates the Word of Life Inn, Word of Life Family Campground, Word of Life Island and Word of Life Ranch. The Fellowship emphasizes bible teaching and supplements this with a huge variety of recreational, nature-oriented and educational programs. Throughout the year, a series of guest lecturers are brought in to address guests of the facilities and camps in the 800-seat auditorium. You can learn more about the Word of Life by calling their Schroon Lake headquarters at (800) 965-7177.

Whether you consider yourself a religious person or not, you will find the Adirondacks to be a place of renewal — and a place of spiritualism in a broad sense of the word. It is a place where the beauty and solitude of the landscape encourage self-reflection, while the warmth of the people encourages you to leap outside of your own self-imposed boundaries to try new activities and learn new skills with new-found friends. Here, you can define "worship" however you choose, and know that you are welcome in doing so.

Beginning Thoughts

Wow. You made it! Long book, huh? Big place plus lots of stuff to see and do equals big book.

We hope now that you've read about the Adirondacks (OK, we realize that you probably didn't read every single page), you agree that it's not just a big place, but a special place. A place you want to visit. A place you need to experience. So while you've reached the end of this book, you are just beginning your journey. The Adirondacks are ready and waiting, some come on up (or down, if you happen to be reading this in Canada). Just remember a few things in planning your visit.

First, this isn't EPCOT. By that we simply mean that this is not a perfect place with perfect lawns and topiary trimmed to look like Mickey and soft music floating out to the walkways from discreet speakers hidden behind the landscaping. This is a wilderness first and foremost. Granted, it's one that is civilized and even landscaped in some spots, but it's a wilderness nonetheless. It's a place that can be truly enjoyed, even loved — but mostly it needs to be respected.

The Adirondacks are a fragile place with an environment that, even though protected, will always struggle to find a healthy balance between human activity and nature's cycles. The Adirondacks can be a dangerous place, where the weather can turn from friend to enemy in the time it takes to eat your backpacked sandwich; a place where a pleasant hike into the mountains can turn to disaster with the turn of an ankle and a lack or preparation. The Adirondacks are a place where knowledge is the key to safe and complete enjoyment; the more you understand about this volatile natural paradise, the more you can appreciate and respect it.

Hopefully, these pages have given you a glimpse into the beauty, history and many attractions of this region, helped you learn about it and inspired you to experience it. No doubt, your time in the Adirondacks will include frustration. It will rain; it will be cold; it will be buggy — and that's all in June! But the moments when it all works — when the sky is pink, the waters calm, the clouds friendly and sparse, the air warming and the breeze just virile enough to keep the bugs at bay; when you sit under a canopy of stars so bright, you'll think you are looking through a kaleidoscope; when your paper plate sits on your lap, summer barbecue long since swallowed, bandstand still alive with music, kids running around the park chasing their dogs, fireworks yet to come; when you look out at an endless sea of unspoiled wilderness that looks now as it did when our nation was born — it will all be worth it, and you will feel as close to this place as anywhere you have ever been. Except in April.

Index of Advertisers

Index

Going Somewhere?

Insiders' Publishing Inc. presents 48 current and upcoming titles to popular destinations all over the country (including the titles below) — and we're planning to adding many more. To order a title, go to your local bookstore or call (800) 765-2665 ext. 238 and we'll direct you to one.

Adirondacks

Atlanta, GA

Bermuda

Boca Raton and the Palm Beaches, FL

Boulder, CO, and Rocky Mountain
National Park

Bradenton/Sarasota, FL

Branson, MO, and the
Ozark Mountains

California's Wine Country

Cape Cod, Nantucket and
Martha's Vineyard, MA

Charleston, SC

Cincinnati, OH

Civil War Sites in the Eastern Theater

Colorado's Mountains

Denver, CO

Florida Keys and Key West

Florida's Great Northwest

Golf in the Carolinas

Indianapolis, IN

The Lake Superior Region

Las Vegas

Lexington, KY

Louisville, KY

Madison, WI

Maine's Mid-Coast

Minneapolis/St. Paul, MN

Mississippi

Myrtle Beach, SC

Nashville, TN

New Hampshire

North Carolina's Central Coast
and New Bern

North Carolina's Mountains

Outer Banks of North Carolina

The Pocono Mountains

Relocation

Richmond, VA

Salt Lake City

Santa Fe

Savannah

Southwestern Utah

Tampa/St. Petersburg, FL

Tuscon

Virginia's Blue Ridge

Virginia's Chesapeake Bay

Washington, D.C.

Wichita, KS

Williamsburg, VA

Wilmington, NC

Yellowstone

Insiders' Publishing Inc. • P.O. Box 2057 • Manteo, NC 27954
Phone (919) 473-6100 • Fax (919) 473-5869 • INTERNET address: *http://www.insiders.com*